P9-CDD-207

Principles of Macroeconomics

Roy J. Ruffin
University of Houston

Paul R. Gregory
University of Houston

Scott, Foresman and Company

Glenview, Illinois

Dallas, Texas   Oakland, New Jersey
Palo Alto, California   Tucker, Georgia   London, England

To Roy Ruffin, Sr., Blanche Ruffin, and Annemarie Gregory

Library of Congress Cataloging in Publication Data

Ruffin, Roy, 1938-
  Principles of macroeconomics.

  Includes index.
  1. Economics. I. Gregory, Paul R. II. Title.
HB171.5.R82 1983   330   82-16946
ISBN 0-673-15856-X

Copyright © 1983 Scott, Foresman and Company.
All Rights Reserved.
Printed in the United States of America.

  3456-RRW-86858483

Credit Lines

Figure 10 on p. 296: Copyright © 1978 by the
University of Chicago.

PAM VICKERS
299-0908

Principles
of Macroeconomics

To the Instructor

This book provides the most modern treatment of macroeconomics that is currently available. Keynesian (demand-side) economics is covered thoroughly as a prelude to the presentation of modern aggregate demand/aggregate supply analysis. The role of expectations is stressed throughout the presentation of macroeconomic theory. Although a full chapter is devoted to rational expectations, this chapter can be considered optional because the student is given the fundamentals of rational expectations theory in the chapters on inflation and stabilization policy. Empirical data and abundant real-world examples reinforce the student's learning of macroeconomics.

Organization

This book is organized into three parts. Part I (Chapters 1–4) introduces the basic concepts of economics that must be learned before proceeding to the study of macroeconomics. These four chapters contain the standard topics of economic methodology, how to read graphs, scarcity, opportunity costs, the production-possibilities frontier, the law of diminishing returns, the law of comparative advantage, the workings of the price system, and the laws of supply and demand. In addition, the student is introduced to the concepts of relative prices and marginal decision making, which are crucial topics in modern macroeconomics with its emphasis on supply-side phenomena.

The macroeconomics sequence begins in Part II with the basic macroeconomic concepts of inflation, unemployment, and the business cycle (Chapter 5), followed by national income accounting (Chapter 6). Monetary economics (in Chapters 7 and 8) is placed between national income accounting and the chapters on Keynesian economics (Chapters 9–11). Although the monetary chapters could be taught following Chapter 10 (on the multiplier), the present location allows the instructor to move directly into monetary policy and the modern model of aggregate demand and supply. We believe it is easier to recall national income accounting while touring money than to recall the Keynesian model while touring money. In addition, learning the deposit multiplier appears to make it easier for students to learn the somewhat more difficult concept of the expenditure multiplier.

The core of modern macroeconomics is found in Chapters 12–14. Chapter 12 introduces the basic tools and concepts of aggregate demand and supply and the natural-rate hypothesis. Chapters 13 and 14 give a thorough analysis of the causes of inflation and modern views on the Phillips curve. Chapters 15–17 round out the discussion of modern macroeconomics by focusing on the debates on stabilization policy (Chapter 15), the trends and causes of unemployment (Chapter 16), and rational-expectations theory (Chapter 17). Growth and development are discussed in Chapters 18 and 19. Part III is a three-chapter unit on international economics.

Suggestions for Course Planning

This book is intended for a one-semester course in macroeconomics that is traditionally taught as a first- or second-year college course. The text for the microeconomics course is also available in a softbound volume, and a hardbound volume is available that contains both microeconomics and macroeconomics chapters.

The instructor teaching a quarter course in macroeconomics can build a course around the 15 core chapters listed below, incorporating material from the remaining 7 chapters in this book as time and interest allow.

1 The Nature of Economics
2 The Economic Problem
3 The Price System
4 The Mechanics of Supply and Demand
5 Macroeconomic Concepts
6 Measuring National Income and National Product
7 Money and Prices
8 Commercial Banking and the Federal Reserve
9 Keynesian Economics
10 Output Fluctuations: The Multiplier and the Accelerator
11 Keynesian Monetary and Fiscal Policy
12 Aggregate Demand and Aggregate Supply
13 Inflation
14 Inflation and Unemployment
15 Stabilization Policy

Instructors who want a course with a focus on growth and development should incorporate Chapters 18 and 19 on Economic Growth and Problems of Population and Economic Development. Instructors who want a course with a focus on international economics should incorporate Chapters 20–22 on International Trade and Comparative Advantage, Protection and Free Trade, and the International Monetary System.

Supplements

This book has a complete package of supplements, which includes an *Instructor's Manual, Study Guide, Test Bank,* and *Transparency Masters.*

The *Instructor's Manual* was written by the authors. Each of the 41 chapters contains sections on: points to learn in the chapter, chapter organization, special approaches, optional material, teaching hints and special projects, bad habits to unlearn, additional essay questions, answers to end-of-chapter "Questions and Problems," and answers to the "Review Quiz" for that chapter in the *Study Guide.*

The *Instructor's Manual* is a valuable teaching aid because it supplies the instructor with additional numerical examples not contained in the text and additional real-world illustrations not discussed in the text. A chapter outline gives a brief overview of the material in the chapter that assists the instructor in preparing lecture outlines and in seeing the logical development of the chapter. The special-approaches section tells the instructor how this chapter is different from other textbooks and explains why a topic was treated differently in this text or why an entirely new topic not covered by other texts was introduced in the chapter. The optional-material section gives the instructor a ranking of priorities for the topics in the chapter and enables the instructor to trim the size of each chapter (if necessary).

The *Study Guide* was written by John Vahaly of the University of Louisville. Because the *Study Guide* is quite analytical, it will challenge the student and help him or her to better prepare for exams. The *Study Guide* supplements the text by providing summaries of the crucial elements. It contains multiple-choice and true/false questions, but unlike other study guides, it contains not only the answers to the multiple-choice and true/false questions but also *explanations for the answers.* Instead of just giving lists of the correct *a, b, c* responses or a list of *T*s and *F*s, the *Study Guide*'s answer sections explain *why* a particular objective answer is the correct one. In addition to objective questions, each chapter of the *Study Guide* also contains analytical problems and questions. Again, the *Study Guide* provides not only the answers to the questions, but the step-by-step process for arriving at the answer.

At the back of the *Study Guide* is a "Review Quiz" for each chapter that contains multiple-choice questions the answers for which do *not* appear in the *Study Guide* but do appear in the *Instructor's Manual.* These quizzes can be used by the instructor as homework or as chapter quizzes.

The authors have also prepared a *Test Bank* that contains nearly 1,800 multiple-choice questions—most of which have already been class tested. The answers have been checked and double checked to minimize the chances that any of the questions have more than one answer. For each chapter in the text, the *Test Bank* contains 4 different tests (coded A, B, C, or D). Whether the instructor is trying to compose a one-chapter quiz or a 23-chapter final exam, that instructor can choose from among the questions in the *Test Bank,* the questions in the "Review Quizzes" at the back of the *Study Guide,* or the additional essay questions in the *Instructor's Manual*—more than 2,300 questions in all. The *Test Bank* is available both on perforated paper in book form and on computer tape.

Transparency Masters suitable for overhead projectors are available for all key figures and tables (about 150 items).

To the Student

How to Understand Economics

Many students find economics a difficult subject because, unlike many other courses a college student takes, economics cannot be mastered through memorization. Economics relies on economic theories to explain real-world occurrences—like why people tend to buy less when prices rise or why increased government spending may reduce unemployment. An economic theory is simply a logical explanation of why the facts fit together in a particular way. If the theory were not logical, or if the theory failed to be confirmed by real-world facts, it would be readily discarded by economists.

The successful student will be the one who learns that economics is built upon a number of fairly simple and easy-to-understand propositions. These propositions and assumptions—that businesses seek to maximize profits or that consumers base their expenditure decisions on disposable income, for example—form the building blocks upon which economics is based. These propositions are typically little more than common sense and should not intimidate a student. If a major building block is missing, however, the whole structure can fall apart. To prevent the student from overlooking or forgetting a crucial building block, we frequently engage in pedagogical review. In other words, when a new proposition is added to a theoretical structure, the underlying propositions are reviewed.

Another factor that can make economics difficult for a student is that economics—like other academic disciplines—has its own specific vocabulary. Unlike the physical sciences, however, where the student may be encountering a certain term for the first time, much of the vocabulary of economics—terms like *efficiency, capital, stock, unemployment*—has a common usage that is already familiar to the student. Economists, however, use the vocabulary of economics in a very exact way, and often the common usage of a term is not the same as the economic usage. In this book, each key term appears in boldface type where it is first discussed in text. Immediately following the paragraph where the term first appears in boldface type, the formal, economic definition of the term is set off in color. At the end of each chapter is a list of all the key terms that have been boldfaced and given formal definitions in that chapter; a glossary at the end of the book contains all the definitions of key terms and gives the chapter number in which the term was defined.

The modern developments in economics are simply new attempts to explain in a logical manner how the facts bind together. Modern developments have occurred because of the realization that established theories were not doing a good job of explaining the world around us. Fortunately, the major building blocks of modern theory—that people attempt to anticipate the future, that rising prices motivate wealth holders to spend less, that people and businesses gather information and make decisions in a rational manner—rely on common-sense logic.

Economics is only valuable if it explains the real world. Economics should be able to answer very specific questions like: Why are there three major domestic producers of automobiles and hundreds or even thousands of producers of textiles? Why is there a positive association between the growth of the money supply and inflation? Why does the United States export computers and farm products to the rest of the world? Why do restaurants rope off space during less busy hours? If Iowa corn land is the best land for growing corn, why is corn also grown in Texas while some land stands idle in Iowa? Why do interest rates rise when people expect the inflation rate to increase? Why did the price of petroleum rise so rapidly in the 1970s? The successful student will be able to apply the knowledge he or she gains of real-world economic behavior to explain any number of events that have already occurred or are yet to occur.

In writing this book, we have made a conscious effort to present arguments and evidence on both sides of every economic controversy. We attempt to make a case for each distinct viewpoint, even if it would be more interesting and less complicated to come out strongly in one camp. Although we are aware of our own free-market bias, we believe it is best to allow the student to keep an open mind at this very early stage in the study of economics.

Learning Aids

This book contains a number of important learning aids.

1. The *Chapter Preview* that precedes each chapter provides a brief overview of the important points to be learned in that chapter.
2. *Definitions of Key Terms* are set off in color following the paragraphs in which the terms are introduced in context.
3. *Key Ideas,* important economic principles or conclusions, are set off in color in bold, italicized type.
4. *Boxed Examples* allow the student to appreciate how economic concepts apply in real-world settings without disrupting the flow of the text and supplement the numerous examples already found in the text discussions.
5. A *Chapter Summary* of the main points of each chapter is found at the end of each chapter.

6. *Key Terms* that were defined in color in the chapter are listed at the end of each chapter.

7. *Questions and Problems* that test the reader's understanding of the chapter follow each chapter.

8. A *Glossary,* containing all key terms defined in color in chapters and listed in chapter ''Key Terms'' sections, appears at the end of the book. Each entry contains the complete economic definition as well as the number of the chapter where the term was first defined.

9. The *Index* of all the names, concepts, terms, and topics covered in the book is one of the most thorough indexes ever compiled for an introductory economics text.

10. Statistical data on the major economic variables are found on the front and back inside covers for easy reference.

11. *Suggested Readings* are listed for each chapter at the back of the book.

Acknowledgments

We are deeply indebted to our colleagues at the University of Houston who had to bear with us in the writing of this book. Gary Smith, Richard Bean, Joel Sailors, Thomas DeGregori, James Griffin, Dean George Daly, Peter Mieszkowski, Peter Zadrozny, Art DeVany, Louis Stern, Oded Palmon, and Thomas Mayor gave their time freely on an incredible number of pedagogical points in the teaching of elementary economics.

We are also grateful for the suggestions and contributions of numerous colleagues across the country who reviewed this manuscript in various stages of its development:

David Abel   Mankato State University
Ken Alexander   Michigan Technical University
Susan Alexander   College of St. Thomas
Richard G. Anderson   Ohio State University
Richard K. Anderson   Texas A & M
Ian Bain   University of Minnesota
George Bittlingmayer   University of Michigan
Robert Borengasser   St. Mary's College
Ronald Brandolini   Valencia Community College

Wallace Broome	Rhode Island Junior College
Anthony Campolo	Columbus Technical Institute
Shirley Cassing	University of Pittsburgh
Robert E. Christiansen	Colby College
Richard Clarke	University of Wisconsin, Madison
David Denslow	University of Florida
Tim Deyak	Louisiana State University, Baton Rouge
Dan Friedman	University of California, Los Angeles (UCLA)
Janet Furman	Tulane University
Charles Gallagher	Virginia Commonwealth University
Ronald Gunderson	Northern Arizona University
Edward Howe	Siena College
James Johannes	Michigan State University
James Kahn	State University of New York, Binghamton
Chris Klisz	Wayne State University
Byung Lee	Howard University
Robert Lucas	University of Chicago
Ron Luchessi	American River College
Roger Mack	DeAnza College
Allan Mandelstamm	Virginia Polytechnic Institute
Jim McKinsey	Northeastern University
W. Douglas Morgan	University of California, Santa Barbara
Norman Obst	Michigan State University
John Pisciotta	Baylor University
John Pomery	Purdue University
Jennifer Roback	Yale University
Mark Rush	University of Florida
Robert Schmitz	Indiana University
David Spencer	Washington State University
Alan Stockman	University of Rochester
Don Tailby	University of New Mexico
Helen Tauchen	University of North Carolina
Robert Thomas	Iowa State University
Roger Trenary	Kansas State University
George Uhimchuk	Clemson University
Roberton Williams	Williams College
Gary Young	Delta State University (Mississippi)

It was a pleasure to work closely with John Vahaly who, in addition to preparing the *Study Guide,* provided valuable and insightful comments on every chapter of this book.

We wish to thank George Lobell, economics editor at Scott, Foresman, who gave us encouragement and advice throughout the writing of this book. The skillful editing of the work was in the able hands of Mary LaMont, developmental editor at Scott, Foresman, whose contributions to style and content grace every page.

Special thanks go to Janet Blackburn, Annemarie Gregory, Roselyn Kennelly, Jane Wang, and Khalil Yazdi.

Roy J. Ruffin
Paul R. Gregory

Contents in Brief

Contents in Brief

Contents

APPENDIX **1A**
Reading Graphs   14

CHAPTER **2**
The Economic Problem   23

CHAPTER **3**
The Price System   36

CHAPTER **4**
The Mechanics of Supply and Demand   55

PART II
Macroeconomics   77

CHAPTER 5
Macroeconomic Concepts   78

CHAPTER **8**
Commercial Banking and the Federal Reserve   130

CHAPTER **9**
Keynesian Economics   150

CHAPTER **10**
Output Fluctuations: The Multiplier and the Accelerator   166

CHAPTER **11**
Keynesian Monetary and Fiscal Policy   182

CHAPTER **12**
Aggregate Demand and Aggregate Supply   202

CHAPTER **15**
Stabilization Policy   253

CHAPTER **16**
Unemployment Trends   269

CHAPTER **17**
Rational Expectations:
The New Classical Macroeconomics   282

CHAPTER **18**
Economic Growth   299

CHAPTER **19**
Problems of Population and Economic Development   313

PART **III**
International Economics   329

CHAPTER **20**
International Trade and Comparative Advantage   331

CHAPTER **21**
Protection and Free Trade   346

CHAPTER **22**
The International Monetary System   365

Glossary   385

Suggested Readings   395

Index   401

Principles
of Macroeconomics

I

Basic Economic Concepts

1

The Nature
of Economics

Chapter Preview

Understanding economics is important to each person as an individual, as a producer, and as a voter in a democratic society. Economists study many questions, but the central issue of economics is: How does the economy work? An understanding of how the economy works helps society as well as each individual. In a nutshell, the goal of economics is to sort out the sense from the nonsense in everyday economic affairs. Better information aids decision making at all levels.

Economics is an evolving and changing field. Some parts of our economic knowledge are fairly certain; other parts are uncertain. Many areas of

economics are in the process of development; many are controversial. That economics is changing shows that economics is an exciting, dynamic field in search of real answers. This book will explain the rudiments of how the economy works according to our present understanding of economics.

This chapter introduces the basic concepts and tools that economists use to understand how the economy works. The chapter explains the basic principles of scarcity, choice, specialization, and exchange and shows how economists use the scientific method to study the economy. The chapter warns about the pitfalls to avoid in studying economics and explains why (and about what) economists sometimes disagree.

3

WHAT IS ECONOMICS: BASIC THEMES

People are concerned with improving their standard of living; they are worried about inflation and unemployment; they may be disturbed by the poverty of the less fortunate. People are confronted with difficult personal choices: when to buy a home, whether to change jobs, whether to attend college. People are often confused by the economic claims and counterclaims of opposing political parties. People can find help in dealing with these questions and concerns in the study of **economics.**

> *Economics is the study of how people choose to use their limited resources (land, labor, and capital goods like trucks and machinery and buildings) to produce, exchange, and consume goods and services.*

The above definition touches on several different themes of economic science. Economists agree that each theme is an essential feature of economics.

Scarcity

Scarcity is the most important fact of economics. If there were no scarcity, there would be no need to study economics. Scarcity is defined in a more formal manner in Chapter 2. For now, it is sufficient to say that scarcity occurs when a society's wants exceed the ability of the economy to meet these wants. Scarcity does not imply that people are necessarily poor or that their basic needs are not being met. It simply means that it is human nature for people to want more than they can have, which forces people to make choices.

Choice

The second theme of economics is *choice.* Choice and scarcity go together. Individuals, businesses, and societies must choose among alternatives. An individual must choose between a job and a college education, between savings and consumption, between a movie and eating out. Businesses must decide where to purchase sup-

plies, which products to offer on the market, how much labor to hire, whether to build new plants. Nations must choose between more defense or more spending for social-welfare programs; they must decide whether to grant tax reductions to business or to individuals.

Specialization

The third theme of economics is *specialization.* Economics studies how participants in the economy (people, businesses, countries) specialize in tasks to which they are particularly suited. The physician specializes in medicine, the lawyer in law, the computer scientist in data processing, Saudi Arabia in oil production, Cuba in sugar production, General Motors in automobile production, Lockheed in military hardware, the economics professor in teaching economics, the vacuum cleaner salesperson in selling vacuum cleaners. Participants in the economy specialize in those things that they do better than others. (Chapter 3 will give more exact definitions of specialization.)

The principal message of Adam Smith, the founder of modern economics, in his 1776 masterwork, *The Wealth of Nations,* was that specialization creates wealth. To use Smith's words: "The greatest improvement in the productive powers of labor . . . seems to have been the effects of the division of labor."[1] *Division of labor* was Adam Smith's term for specialization.

Exchange

The fourth theme of economics is *exchange.* Exchange complements specialization. Without exchange, specialization would be of no benefit because individuals could not trade the goods in which they specialize for those that other individuals produce. Again, using Smith's words: "[Specialization] is the necessary . . . consequence of a certain propensity in human nature: the propensity to truck, barter and exchange one thing for another."[2] How exchange is organized is a major element in the study of economics.

1. Adam Smith, *The Wealth of Nations,* ed. Edwin Cannan (New York: Modern Library, 1937), p. 3.
2. Smith, *Wealth of Nations,* p. 13.

Exchange is all around us. We exchange our specialized labor services for money and then exchange money for a huge variety of goods. A country like America exchanges its wheat for TV sets made in Japan. Entrepreneurs constantly trade their skills in marketing, advertising, or product innovation in order to put together the best total product.

MARGINAL ANALYSIS

Economics is about people going about the ordinary business of making a living. If one can remember that individuals are the main actors, much of the mystery surrounding economics evaporates. The student of economics has an enormous advantage over the physics student who cannot ask, "what would I do if I were a molecule?" because the student of economics *is* one of the "molecules" economists study. Crucial to individual behavior are the incentives (that is, the carrots and sticks) that face people in any given situation. In economics, the "carrots" are the benefits that people receive from engaging in an economic activity; the "sticks" are the costs of the activity. Individuals base their economic decisions on costs and benefits.

Scarcity forces people to make choices, and economics studies how these choices are made. The most important tool used by economists to study economic decision making is **marginal analysis.**

Marginal analysis aids decision making by examining the consequences of making relatively small changes from the current state of affairs.

For example, how would you go about deciding how much studying is "enough"? First, you would examine the benefits of a slight increase in your present amount of studying. If you study, say, 2 hours more per day, you will likely earn higher grades, the respect of your fellow students, and perhaps a better job upon graduation. All these benefits of studying 2 additional hours per day cannot be measured exactly, but you have an idea of the benefits that additional study will yield. Next, you would examine the costs of 2 more hours of studying per day. You may have to

sacrifice earnings from a part-time job; you may have to give up leisure activities that you value highly (dating, your favorite soap opera, an extra two hours of sleep).

Finally, the answer to the question of whether you are studying enough depends upon whether you feel that the benefits of the extra study outweigh the costs. If they do, then you conclude that you are not studying enough, and you study more. If the extra costs are greater than the extra benefits, you will conclude that you should not study the extra time.

How do businesses make choices? Consider the case of the selection of airline routes. How would an airline (United, Eastern, American, and so on) determine whether it is offering "enough" flights? It would do so by making decisions *at the margin*. That is, the airline would add flights so long as the expected revenues from those added flights exceed the expected costs. Let us say that United is considering adding a daily flight between Chicago and Seattle. The management of United would make an estimate of the benefits that the added flight would bring in (the additional ticket sales) and would compare these benefits with the extra costs that the new flight would create (added fuel, additional flight attendants, advertising for the new route). If the benefits of the new route are greater than the costs, then the new route would be added to United's schedule. If the costs exceed the benefits, the new route would probably be rejected.

Decisions are made at the margin when a decision maker considers what the extra (or marginal) costs and benefits of an increase or decrease in a particular activity will be. If the marginal benefits outweigh the marginal costs, the extra activity is undertaken.

MICRO AND MACRO

Microeconomics

Economics is typically divided into two main branches called *microeconomics* and *macroeconomics*. Both **microeconomics** and macroeconomics deal with economic decision making but from different vantage points.

Microeconomics studies the economic decision making of firms and individuals in a market setting; it is the study of the economy in the small.

Microeconomics focuses on the individual participants in the economy: the producers, workers, employers, and consumers. In everyday economic life, things are bought and sold, people decide where and how many hours to work. Business managers decide what to produce and how this production is to be organized. These activities result in *transactions* (business deals) that take place in markets where buyers and sellers come together. People involved in microeconomic transactions are motivated to do the best they can for themselves with the limited resources at their disposal. They use marginal analysis to determine their best course of action.

Although we could supply an endless list, here are just a few of the issues that can be addressed by microeconomic analysis: 1) how consumers behave, 2) how business firms make choices, 3) how prices are determined in markets, 4) how taxes and price controls affect consumer and producer behavior, 5) how the structure of markets affects economic performance, 6) how wages, interest rates, rent, and profits are determined, and 7) how income is distributed among families.

Macroeconomics

Instead of analyzing prices, outputs, and sales in individual markets, **macroeconomics** studies the production of the entire economy. Topics of investigation include the *general* price level (rather than individual prices), the national employment rate, government spending, and the nation's money supply.

Macroeconomics is the study of the economy in the large. Rather than dealing with individual markets and individual consumers and producers, macroeconomics deals with the economy as a whole.

Because macroeconomics studies the economy as a whole, new measures of economic activity are required. Important to macroeconomics is the definition and measurement of macroeconomic *aggregates,* such as gross national product

(GNP), the consumer price index (CPI), the unemployment rate, and the government surplus and deficit. These measures are called *aggregates* because they add together (or aggregate) individual microeconomic components.

Just as microeconomics studies the relationships between individual participants in the economy, macroeconomics studies relationships between aggregate measures. What are the determinants of inflation? What is the relationship between inflation and interest rates? Is it necessary to trade off higher employment for lower inflation? What are the consequences of government deficits? What is the relationship between the money supply and inflation?

In modern economics, there is a close relationship between microeconomics and macroeconomics. Macroeconomists have come to apply more and more microeconomic analysis to traditional macroeconomic questions such as the relationship between inflation and unemployment. The rationale behind using microeconomic tools to study macroeconomics is that the economy is made up of individuals; how these individuals behave *on the average* can explain how the economy in the large behaves.

The modern convergence of microeconomics and macroeconomics follows from the realization that macroeconomic relationships cannot be analyzed without understanding the behavior of the individuals who make up the economy.

Three areas of investigation that exemplify the modern convergence of microeconomics and macroeconomics are:

1. How do workers alter the number of hours they work in response to generally rising prices?
2. How do business output decisions respond to inflation?
3. Can unemployment be reduced by changing government policies that affect the costs of unemployment?

To answer these questions the tools of microeconomic decision making (such as marginal analysis) can be applied to what are basically macroeconomic problems.

METHODOLOGY IN ECONOMICS

Economists rely heavily on economic theories to explain how the economy works. Why don't economists just go out and collect the facts and let the facts speak for themselves? The American economy includes millions of households and firms and thousands of separate federal, state, and local governments. All of these make decisions about producing millions of goods and services using millions of resources. Gathering information about economic choices from all these various sources is an incredibly complex and unmanageable task. Logical theories explain how the economy works by showing how the facts fit together in a coherent manner.

Theories and Hypotheses

A **theory** is simply a plausible and coherent explanation of how certain facts are related. A theory typically consists of one or more *hypotheses* about how a particular set of facts is related. Normally, but not always, theories contain some hypotheses of the form, "if A, then B." Two examples of hypotheses are: "if a good's price falls, people will want to buy more of it"; "if income rises, people will consume or save more."

> A **theory** isolates those factors that may be crucial determinants of the phenomenon being explained.

For example, economists' theories of demand hold that such things as consumer eye color, height, and IQ are relatively unimportant in explaining consumer purchases compared to such things as price and income. The process of zeroing in on a limited number of factors to explain a phenomenon is called *abstraction*.

Testing Theories:
The Scientific Method

Since theories are abstractions from the real world (whatever that is!) it is necessary to test them. For example: Suppose one theorized that higher prices for coffee induce people to buy less

Table 1
Coffee Prices and Consumption

Year	Price per Pound (constant 1979 dollars)	Yearly per Capita Coffee Consumption (in pounds)
1974	$1.78	13.0
1975	1.75	12.4
1976	2.56	12.8
1977	4.22	9.4
1978	3.22	10.9
1979	2.78	11.5

Source: *Statistical Abstract of the United States* (1980), Tables 211, 802, 808.

coffee. This theory seems to make sense. But is it true? By the patient collection of data one might find the results shown in Table 1.

Clearly, as the price of coffee in *constant dollars* (dollars that have been adjusted for inflation) more than doubled between 1974 and 1977, per capita coffee consumption fell dramatically—from 13 pounds per year to less than 10 pounds per year. When the price started to fall after 1977, per capita coffee consumption rose again. Thus, the data on coffee prices and coffee consumption are consistent with our theory that higher prices for an item cause people to consume less of the item. The data *fail to refute* the theory but have not really *proved* the theory beyond any doubt. Data from another time or place may contradict the theory. When data are obtained that are *not* consistent with the theory, the theory must be reformulated or revised.

For example, Table 2 shows that egg prices fell substantially between 1974 and 1979, yet egg consumption per capita remained about the same. These data appear to contradict the theory that higher prices for an item induce people to consume less of the item. In this situation we could either say that the theory does not hold for eggs, or we could revise the theory so that it would explain why eggs were an exception to the rule. The case of eggs suggests that things other than price influence consumption. The 1970s was a period in which the egg had lost some of its popularity because of allegations that egg consumption lowers human longevity. These allegations, of course, have been debated.[3] The point is that the unfavorable publicity might have had a substantial impact on consumption. The theory can be reformulated to reflect the fact that factors other than price influence consumption. Chapter 4 will do this more precisely, but for the moment the theory could be reformulated as follows: the higher the price of an item, the less of it people will want to buy, holding other factors (like unfavorable publicity, in this case) constant. The above examples illustrate how the scientific method can be applied to a simple economic theory:

1. a theory was formulated,
2. facts were gathered (Tables 1 and 2),
3. the theory was evaluated in light of the facts and
4. when the facts failed to confirm the theory, the theory was revised.

The process of formulating theories, collecting data, testing theories, and revising theories is called **the scientific method.**

The **scientific method** is one of the truly great creations of the human mind. Hard as it is to believe, at one time people did not evaluate their beliefs in light of the facts or even formulate their beliefs in a way that could be tested by others. What makes the scientific method such a valuable tool is that it raises human thought above the level of the individual, separating the idea from the person as much as possible. Claude Bernard, a 19th century writer, once perceptively summarized the orientation of all scientific subjects in comparison to artistic ones: "Art is I; science is we."

The Uses of Economic Theories

Economic theories that use the scientific method allow us to make sense of an extremely complicated world. They enable us to understand economic relationships, to make sense of past events, and even to predict the consequences of

3. A good pro-egg discussion is found in James W. Vaupel and John D. Braham, "Egg in Your Bier?" *The Public Interest* (Winter 1980).

Table 2
Egg Prices and Consumption

Year	Price per Dozen (1979 dollars)	Yearly per Capita Consumption (number of eggs)
1974	$0.93	288
1975	0.84	279
1976	0.89	274
1977	0.75	272
1978	0.69	278
1979	0.69	283

Source: *Statistical Abstract of the United States* (1980), Tables 211, 802, 808.

actions that have yet to be taken. Economists have at their disposal well-tested theories of the relationship between product prices and the quantities purchased. For example, economists have established (largely on the basis of the experiences of other countries) that people cut back their gasoline consumption when gasoline prices rise substantially. Many government officials, consumer advocates, and politicians felt that this cutback would not happen in the United States, because Americans are so dependent on automobile transportation. The United States entered into uncharted territory when it left the age of cheap energy behind in the early 1970s, and it was comforting to have a scientifically tested theory as a guide, despite its skeptics. True enough, after the higher prices went into effect in the mid-1970s, people did indeed cut back on their gasoline purchases just as economic theory predicted. This cutback became so strong that oil-producing countries had trouble finding buyers at the higher prices in 1982.

Theory can say something about facts that have yet to be collected and about events that have yet to occur; that is, **theory can be used to make predictions.**

This discussion should lay to rest the erroneous notion that a theory can be a good one even if it does not work in practice. By the criterion of the scientific method, if a theory does not work in practice it cannot be a good theory.

COMMON FALLACIES IN ECONOMICS

False economic propositions can have substantial appeal because they may appear on the surface to be eminently reasonable. Consider the following statements drawn from various newspaper reports:

U.S. Steel today announced a 10 percent increase in the price of rolled steel products. This price increase was made necessary by the 10 percent wage increase granted the steel workers' union.

The drought of the summer of 1980 has caused a disastrous harvest of wheat and corn in the midwest and southwest. The hard-pressed farmer is being pushed closer to economic ruin.

Despite a substantial rise in home mortgage rates between 1977 and 1979, there are no signs of a slowdown in home building. This shows that rising mortgage rates have little impact on home buying.

All of these statements appear to be logical and to be based upon facts, and they will probably be accepted by the average reader without much hesitation. Yet close examination of these statements reveals that they exemplify three logical *fallacies* that plague economic thinking. These fallacies are the *false-cause fallacy,* the *fallacy of composition,* and the *ceteris paribus fallacy.*

The False-Cause Fallacy

*The **false-cause fallacy** is the assumption that because two events occur together one event has caused the other.*

The fact that Event A occurs with or precedes Event B does not mean that A has caused B. The absurdity of this proposition is illustrated by the following example: between 1970 and 1980, U.S. whiskey consumption rose by 25 percent, and the number of public-school teachers rose by 30 percent.[4] To conclude from this evidence that the in-

4. *Statistical Abstract of the United States,* 101st ed. (Washington, D.C.: U.S. Government Printing Office, 1980), pp. 211, 802,808.

crease in the number of teachers caused the increase in whiskey consumption is false.

A statistical correlation between two variables does not prove that one has caused the other or that the variables have anything whatsoever to do with one another.

How does one determine whether or not two variables that are statistically correlated are involved in a cause-and-effect relationship? Economic theory attempts to determine in a coherent manner whether a logical case of cause and effect exists. Consider this counter example: whiskey consumption increased by 25 percent between 1970 and 1980, while family take-home pay increased by 33 percent (after adjustment for inflation). In this case, a logical theory could be constructed that increases in family income will be channeled into purchases of whiskey. Thus one could argue that the rise in income is a possible cause of the rise in whiskey consumption. Economic theory supports a cause/effect relationship.

One of the most difficult problems of science is the determination of cause-and-effect relationships.

An example from medical science is the endless debate over smoking and heart disease. Does smoking "cause" heart disease? Government and the tobacco industry have spent millions of dollars trying to prove or disprove a cause-and-effect relationship. Many of the unresolved controversies of economics center on cause-and-effect relationships.

The report of the steel-price increase cited above is an example of a possible **false-cause fallacy.** Just because the wage increase preceded the price increase does not prove that the one caused the other. Whether or not the wage settlement was indeed a cause of the price increase is a matter for economic theory to settle. As later chapters will point out, the theoretical relationship between wage and price increases is not clear-cut.

The Fallacy of Composition

*The **fallacy of composition** is the assumption that what is true for each part taken* *separately is also true for the whole or that what is true for the whole is true for each part considered separately.*

To illustrate the **fallacy of composition,** consider what would happen if the government were to print money and give each person $10,000. Clearly, this action would make each individual person better off. With the $10,000 windfall, the person could buy a new car, invest in the stock market, or finance a college education. But if the government were to give everyone a windfall of $10,000, consumer spending would increase, prices would generally rise, and it is likely society as a whole would not end up any better off. This example shows that what is true for each part taken separately—namely, that receiving money makes people better off—would not necessarily be true for the whole.

The report of the 1980 summer drought cited earlier is an example of the fallacy of composition. It is true that farmers in drought-stricken areas were made worse off by the drought, but farm income actually increased for those farmers in nonstricken areas who benefited from higher farm prices. What was true for each part taken separately was not true for the whole.

The *Ceteris Paribus* Fallacy

*The **ceteris paribus fallacy** occurs when the effects of changes in one set of variables are incorrectly attributed to another set of variables.*

For example, U.S. crude-oil consumption between 1970 and 1974 rose from 14.7 million barrels per day to 16.2 million barrels. The U.S. price of crude oil, during the same period, rose from $3.18 to $6.74.[5] Does the fact that prices and consumption were both rising mean that there is a positive relationship between energy prices and energy usage?

Ceteris paribus is a Latin term meaning "other things being equal." If the relationship between

two variables is to be established, the effects of other factors that are changing as well must not be allowed to confuse the relationship. To establish the relationship between energy prices and energy usage, the effects of "other things" must somehow be understood. What other things were happening between 1970 and 1974 that would affect oil consumption in addition to rising oil prices? The prices of other commodities were rising, although not as fast as crude oil. Money incomes of American families rose 44 percent, and rising income would allow American consumers to absorb higher energy prices. The point is that the true relationship between crude oil prices and oil consumption is difficult to discern because other things that affect oil consumption did not stand still. To simply look at the graphical relationship between two variables without sorting out the effects of other factors that are also changing leads to *ceteris paribus* fallacies. Sorting out these other effects is not a simple matter. In fact, an entire branch of economics that combines economic theory and statistics, called *econometrics,* has been developed to deal with the *ceteris paribus* problem.

The mortgage rate case cited above is an example of the *ceteris paribus* fallacy. During the period in question, other things were not equal. Home prices were rising rapidly, and home buyers were opting to buy homes before the price rose out of their reach, despite high mortgage rates. The true relationship between mortgage rates and home buying was clouded by changes in other factors that affected home buying.

WHY ECONOMISTS DISAGREE

Economists have received the unfair reputation of being unable to agree on anything. The image of economists in disagreement is part of our folklore. An English commentator wrote: "If parliament were to ask six economists for an opinion, seven answers could come back—two no doubt from the volatile Mr. Keynes." The *London Times* laments the "rise in skepticism about what economists can tell us," and *Business Week* complains about "the intellectual bankruptcy of the [economics] profession."[6]

5.   James Griffin and Henry Steele, *Energy Economics and Policy* (New York Academic Press, 1980), p. 18; National Foreign Assessment Center, *Handbook of Economic Statistics 1980* (Washington, D.C.: U.S. Government Printing Office, 1980).

6.   J. R. Kearl et al., "A Confusion of Economists," *American Economic Review* 69, 2 (May 1979): 28.

The image of widespread disagreement among economists is overrated. The results of a survey of 100 professional economists, reported in Table 3, confirm that there is considerable agreement among economists about *what can be done*, especially in a microeconomic context. However, there is more disagreement over *what ought to be done*. Questions of what ought to be done (Should we equalize the distribution of income? Should we increase defense spending?) require moral and political value judgments on which individuals naturally differ. Finally, disagreement among professional economists receives more publicity than other scientific professions, which contributes to the false image of economists in discord. In Table 3, more than 60 percent of the economists agree with each other on 23 of the 30 propositions. On only 7 of the 30 issues (5 macro issues and 2 micro issues) is there less than 60 percent agreement among the economists.

Positive Economics

Economists generally agree that rising prices reduce consumption *(ceteris paribus)*, that rising income will have differential but predictable effects on different products, that wage and price controls cause shortages, that tariffs and quotas raise prices to consumers, that rent controls reduce the quantity and quality of housing, that minimum-wage laws increase unemployment among youth and unskilled workers, and so on. The easiest matters on which to achieve agreement involve the microeconomic relationships that actually prevail in an economy.

Positive economics is the study of what is *in the economy.*

The areas of disagreement in **positive economics** tend to be concentrated in the field of macroeconomics, which is, after all, a relatively young field. The points of controversy and disagreement in macroeconomics include such questions as: What are the causes of inflation and unemployment? Can we combine low unemployment and low inflation? Should activist government policy be used to achieve employment and inflation goals?

Why has economics still to resolve these vital issues? The basic answer is that the economy is an unbelievably complex organism, comprised of millions of individuals, hundreds of thousands of business firms, a myriad of local, state, and federal government offices. The economy is us, and our collective economic actions are difficult to analyze. Emotions are volatile; expectations can change overnight; relationships that held last year no longer hold today; it is costly and difficult to collect up-to-date economic facts. Unlike the physical sciences, economists are denied a laboratory setting; economists do not have the physicist's vacuum, the agronomist's experimental farm, the chemist's laboratory. In addition, many economic events are random and unpredictable. Bad weather can cause poor harvests; armed conflicts can occur without warning in different parts of the globe; oil-producing countries can form an oil price-fixing alliance; consumer spending can shift in response to changing expectations.

Normative Economics

Economists do disagree—often strongly—about **normative economics.**

Normative economics is the study of what ought to be *in the economy.*

Economists disagree on whether we should have more unemployment or more inflation (a traditional Democratic/Republican difference over the years), over whether income taxes should be lowered for the middle class, the rich, or the poor, over job programs, over government-subsidized health programs. These disagreements are not over what is; opponents in a debate may agree on what will happen if Program A is chosen over Program B, but they may disagree sharply over their personal evaluation of the desirability of those consequences.

The Visibility of Economic Disputes

While disagreements in other sciences are as strong or even stronger than in economics, these disagreements are less visible to the public eye. Theoretical physicists have disagreed about the physical nature of the universe since the foundation of physics, but this scientific controversy is understood by only a few theoretical physicists.

Table 3
Do Economists Disagree?

Propositions	Generally Agree	Agree with Provisions	Generally Disagree
1. Tariffs and import quotas reduce general economic welfare.	81	16	3
2. The government should be an employer of last resort and initiate a guaranteed job program.	26	27	47
3. The money supply is a more important target than interest rates for monetary policy.	48	23	29
4. Cash payments are superior to transfers-in-kind.	68	24	8
5. Flexible exchange rates offer an effective international monetary arrangement.	61	34	5
6. The "Corporate State," as depicted by Galbraith, accurately describes the context and structure of the U.S. economy.	18	34	48
7. A minimum wage increases unemployment among young and unskilled workers.	68	22	10
8. The government should index the income-tax rate structure for inflation.	41	27	32
9. Fiscal policy has a significant stimulative impact on a less than fully employed economy.	65	27	8
10. The distribution of income in the United States should be more equal.	40	31	29
11. National defense expenditures should be reduced from the present level.	36	30	34
12. Antitrust laws should be used vigorously to reduce monopoly power from its current level.	49	36	15
13. Inflation is primarily a monetary phenomenon.	27	30	43
14. The government should restructure the welfare system along lines of a "negative income tax."	58	34	8
15. Wage-price controls should be used to control inflation.	6	22	72
16. A ceiling on rents reduces the quantity and quality of housing available.	78	20	2
17. The Fed should be instructed to increase the money supply at a fixed rate.	14	25	61
18. Effluent taxes represent a better approach to pollution control than imposition of pollution ceilings.	50	31	19
19. The government should issue an inflation-indexed security.	33	25	42
20. The level of government spending should be reduced (disregarding expenditures for stabilization).	34	23	43
21. The Fed has the capacity to achieve a constant rate of growth of the money supply if it so desired.	35	41	34
22. Reducing the regulatory power of the ICC, CAB et al. would improve the efficiency of the U.S. ecoomy.	47	31	22
23. The federal budget should be balanced over the business cycle rather than yearly.	53	30	17
24. The fundamental cause of the rise in oil prices of the past three years is the monopoly power of the large oil companies.	11	14	75
25. The redistribution of income is a legitimate role for government in the context of the U.S. economy.	52	29	19
26. In the short run, unemployment can be reduced by increasing the rate of inflation.	31	33	36
27. The fiscal policy proposed by the Ford Administration for the coming year is too restrictive.	40	19	41
28. The ceiling on interest paid on time deposits should be removed.	76	18	6
29. "Consumer protection" laws generally reduce economic efficiency.	24	28	48
30. The economic power of labor unions should be significantly curtailed.	32	38	30

Source: J. R. Kearl et al., "A Confusion of Economists?" *American Economic Review* 69, 2 (May 1979): 30.

It does not require much disagreement to bring economic disputes to the public's attention. Everyone is interested in economic questions: Will inflation accelerate? Will I lose my job? Why is the price of gasoline rising so fast? Why are home mortgages so hard to come by? Economists do disagree, particularly on some big macroeconomic issues. But often what the public perceives as disagreements over positive economics are really disagreements over what ought to be. In general, there is more agreement than disagreement among economists.

Economics studies how people use their limited resources to produce, exchange, and consume goods and services. The next chapter will begin to use the tools of the scientific method to explain how economic choices are made in a world of scarce resources. What are the costs of making choices? What arrangements are used to resolve the problem of choice? Answering these questions requires graphical analysis. The appendix to this chapter provides a review of guidelines for reading graphs.

Summary

1. Economics is important to each person as an individual, as a voter, and as a member of society. Increased knowledge improves the quality of decision making of individuals, voters, and members of society. The four themes of economics are scarcity, choice, specialization, and exchange.
2. Marginal analysis is an important tool of the economist. It aids economic decision making by examining the extra costs and benefits of economic decisions.
3. Microeconomics studies the economic decision making of firms and individuals in a market setting; it is the study of the economy in the small. Macroeconomics studies the economy as a whole and deals with issues of inflation, unemployment, money supply, the government budget; it is the study of the economy in the large. Modern macroeconomics employs tools of microeconomics.
4. Theory allows us to make sense of the real world and to learn how the facts fit together.

There is no conflict between good theory and good practice. Economic theories are based upon the scientific method of theory formulation, collection of relevant data, and testing of theories. Economic theory makes it possible to predict the consequences of actions that have yet to be taken and about facts that are yet to be collected.
5. Three logical fallacies plague economic analysis: the false-cause fallacy (assuming that Event A has caused Event B because A is associated with B); the fallacy of composition (assuming that what is true for each part taken separately is true for the whole or, conversely, assuming that what is true for the whole is also true for each part); the *ceteris paribus* fallacy (incorrectly attributing to one variable effects that are caused by another).
6. Economists tend to agree on positive economic issues (what is) while disagreeing on normative issues (what ought to be). The major unresolved issues of positive economics tend to be concentrated in macroeconomics, an evolving field in economics. Disagreements among economists are more visible to the public eye than disagreements in other scientific professions.

Key Terms

economics
marginal analysis
microeconomics
macroeconomics
theory
scientific method
false-cause fallacy
fallacy of composition
ceteris paribus **fallacy**
positive economics
normative economics

Questions and Problems

1. Consider the following scenario: You are the manager of a movie theater considering intro-

ducing an 11 A.M. matinee. You calculate
that the matinee will increase monthly ticket
sales by $10,000 and that the additional cost
of adding the matinee would be $11,000.
What would you decide?

2. An example of how to decide whether a student is studying "enough" was given in the text. Do you feel that this is an accurate description of how students make decisions?

3. Outline how you would apply the scientific method to determine what factors cause the grade point averages of students in your class to differ.

4. "I can't stand the programs I see on television. Why can't American television produce shows that the public can enjoy?" What type

of logical fallacy does this statement illustrate?

5. From your own experience, construct an example of the false-cause fallacy.

6. "For several years after the surgeon general's report that cigarette smoking was injurious to health, the sale of cigarettes increased in the United States. Therefore, the surgeon general's report had no effect on smoking habits." Evaluate this conclusion.

7. Why would economists be more likely to disagree on a national health-insurance program than on the effect of higher oil prices on the consumption of oil?

8. Why is the distinction between positive and normative economics important?

APPENDIX

1A

Reading Graphs

Appendix Preview

Graphs are an important tool in learning economics. This appendix teaches the rudiments of working with graphs. It teaches graph construction, positive and negative relationships, dependent and independent variables, and the concept of slope for both linear and curvilinear relationships. It shows how slopes can be used to find the maximum and minimum values of a relationship. Finally, three common pitfalls of using graphs are discussed: the ambiguity of slope, the improper measurement of data, and the use of unrepresentative data.

THE USE OF GRAPHS IN ECONOMICS

Economics makes extensive use of graphs. A graph is simply a visual scheme for picturing the quantitative relationship between two different variables. This book contains graphs dealing with many different economic relationships, including the relationships between:

1. consumption and income.
2. the rate of inflation and time.
3. average costs of production and the volume of production.

4. profits and business decisions.
5. oil consumption and oil prices.
6. unemployment and inflation.

Relationships such as these can be pictured and analyzed by using graphs. Not only can a graph display a great deal of data; a graph can efficiently describe the quantitative relationship that exists between the variables. As the Chinese proverb says, "a picture is worth a thousand words." It is easier both to understand and remember a graph than the several hundred, or perhaps thousands of numbers that the graph represents. Graphs are important tools in learning economics. The reader must understand how to use graphs in order to master the basic economic concepts in this book.

Positive and Negative Relationships

The first important characteristic of a graph is whether the two variables are positively or negatively related.

*A **positive (or direct) relationship** exists between two variables if an increase in the value of one variable is associated with an increase in the value of the other variable.*

For example, an increase in the *horsepower* of a given car's engine will increase the *maximum speed* of the automobile. Panel (a) of Figure 1 depicts this relationship in a graph. The *vertical axis* measures the maximum speed of the car from the 0 point (called the *origin*); the *horizontal axis* measures the horsepower of the engine. When horsepower is zero (the engine is broken down), the maximum speed the car can attain is obviously 0; when horsepower is 300, the maximum speed is 100 miles per hour. Intermediate values of horsepower (between 0 and 300) are graphed. When a line is drawn through all these points, the resulting curved line describes the effect of horsepower on maximum speed. Since the picture is a line that goes from low to high speeds as horsepower increases, it is an example of an *upward-sloping curve*.

When two variables are positively related the graph of the relationship is an upward-sloping curve.

Figure 1
Graphing Positive and Negative Relationships

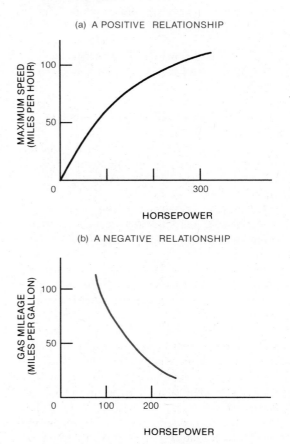

(a) A POSITIVE RELATIONSHIP

(b) A NEGATIVE RELATIONSHIP

Panel (a) shows a positive relationship. As the horizontal variable (horsepower) increases, the value of the vertical variable (maximum speed) increases. The curve rises from left to right. Panel (b) shows a negative relationship. As the horizontal variable (horsepower) increases, the vertical variable (mileage) decreases. The curve falls from left to right.

*A **negative (or inverse) relationship** exists between two variables if an increase in the value of one variable is associated with a reduction in the value of the other variable.*

For example, as the *horsepower* of the automobile increases, the *gas mileage* (for given driving conditions) will fall. In panel (b) of Figure 1, horsepower is still measured on the horizontal axis, but now gas mileage is measured on the vertical axis. Since the picture is a curve going from high to low values of gas mileage as horsepower increases, it is an example of a *downward-sloping curve.*

When two variables are negatively related the graph of the relationship is a downward-sloping curve.

Dependent and Independent Variables

In some relationships involving two variables, one variable can be the **independent variable;** the other is the **dependent variable.**

*A change in the value of an **independent variable** will cause the **dependent variable** to change in value.*

An increase in engine horsepower *causes* an increase in the maximum speed of the automobile in the first graph. A horsepower increase *causes* a reduction in gas mileage in the second graph. In both examples, horsepower is the independent variable. The other two variables are said to "depend upon" horsepower because the changes in horsepower bring about changes in speed and gas mileage. Maximum speed and gas mileage are dependent variables.

One goal of economic analysis is to find the independent variable(s) that explain certain dependent variables. What independent variables explain changes in inflation rates, unemployment, consumer spending, housing construction, and so on? In many cases, it is not possible to determine which variable is dependent and which is independent. Some variables are interdependent (they both affect each other). In some instances, there is no cause-and-effect relationship between the variables.

RULES FOR CONSTRUCTING GRAPHS

A glance is sufficient to tell whether a curve is positively or negatively sloped. More work is required to read all the information that a graph contains. To read a graph properly, one must know how a graph is constructed.

The data for our sample graph is given in Table 1. The numbers in this table describe the quantitative relationship between *minutes of typing* and *number of pages typed*. Let us assume that the quantitative relationship between minutes and pages is known: every 5 minutes of typing will produce 1 page of manuscript. Thus 5 minutes produces 1 page, 15 minutes produces 3 pages, and so on. Zero minutes will, of course, produce 0 pages.

Four steps are required to graph these data or any data. These steps have been carried out in Figure 2.

1. A vertical *axis* and a horizontal *axis* are drawn perpendicularly on graph paper, meeting at a point called the *origin*. The origin is labeled 0; the vertical axis is labeled *Y;* the horizontal axis is labeled *X*.
2. *Minutes of typing* are marked off along the horizontal *X* axis in equally spaced increments of 5 minutes, and the horizontal axis is labeled "Minutes of Typing."
3. The *number of pages typed* is marked off in equally spaced increments of 1 page along the vertical *Y* axis, and the vertical axis is labeled "Number of Pages Typed."
4. Each pair of numbers in Table 1 is plotted at the intersection of the vertical line that corresponds to that value of *X* and the horizontal line that corresponds to that value of *Y*. Point *a* shows that 5 minutes of typing produces 1 page. Point *c* shows that 15 minutes of typing produces 3 pages, and so on.

Points *a, b, c, d,* and *e* completely describe the

Table 1
The Relationship Between Minutes of Typing and Number of Pages Typed

	Minutes of Typing (X axis)	Number of Pages Typed (Y axis)
	0	0
a	5	1
b	10	2
c	15	3
d	20	4
e	25	5

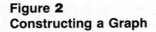

Figure 2
Constructing a Graph

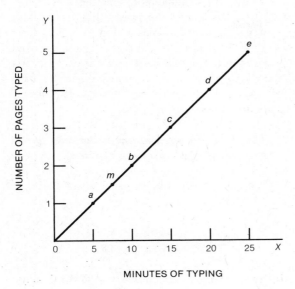

MINUTES OF TYPING

This graph reproduces the data in Table 1. Point *a* shows that 5 minutes of typing produces 1 page of typing; *b* shows that 10 minutes produces 2 pages, and so on. The upward-sloping line drawn through *a, b, c, d,* and *e* shows that the relationship between minutes of typing and number of pages typed is positive. The points between *a, b, c, d,* and *e* (such as *m*) show the number of pages typed for amounts of typing time between the 5-minute intervals.

---

data in Table 1. Indeed, a graph of the data acts as a substitute for the table from which it was constructed. This is the first advantage of graphs over tables: they provide an immediate visual understanding of the quantitative relationship between the two variables just by observing the plot of points. Since the points in this case move upward from left to right, we know that there is a *positive relationship* between the variables.

This may not seem to be a great advantage for this simple and obvious case. However, suppose the data had been arranged as in Table 2.

If one spends some time inspecting the data, it becomes clear that there is a positive relationship between *X* and *Y;* however, it is not immediately obvious. From a graph, it is easier to see the relationship between the two variables.

The first advantage of graphs over tables is that it is easier to understand the relationship that exists between two variables in a graph than in a table.

Suppose that in addition to the data in Table 1, we had data for the number of pages that could be typed at all kinds of intermediate values of typing time: 6 minutes, 13 minutes, 24 minutes and 25 seconds, etc. A large table would be required to report all these numbers. In a graph, however, all these intermediate values can be represented simply by connecting points *a, b, c, d,* and *e* with a line. Thus, a second advantage of graphs is that large quantities of data can be represented in a graph more efficiently than in a table.

The second advantage of graphs over tables is that large quantities of data can be represented efficiently in a graph.

The data in Tables 1 and 2 reveal the relationship between minutes of typing and number of pages typed. This relationship was graphed in Figure 2. The relationship can change, however, if other factors that affect typing speed change. Assume that Table 1 shows minutes and pages typed on a manual typewriter. If the typist works with an IBM Selectric, a different relationship will emerge. With the IBM Selectric, perhaps the typist can type 2 pages every 5 minutes instead of one. Both relationships are graphed in Figure 3. Thus, if factors that affect speed of typing change (for example, the quality of the typewriter), the relationship between minutes and pages can shift.

Table 2
The Relationship Between Minutes of Typing and Number of Pages Typed (data rearranged)

	Minutes of Typing (X axis)	Number of Pages Typed (Y axis)
b	10	2
a	5	1
	0	0
e	25	5
c	15	3
d	20	4

Figure 3
Shifts in Relationships

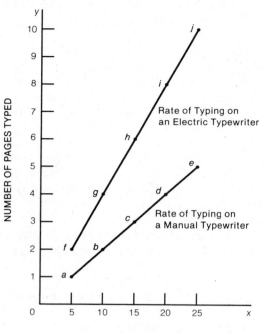

The curve *abcde* graphs the data in Table 1 that show the relationship between minutes and pages using a manual typewriter. The new (higher) curve *fghij* shows the relationship between minutes and pages with an electric typewriter. As a consequence of the change from the manual to the electric typewriter, the relationship has shifted upward.

Economists work frequently with relationships that shift, so it is important to understand shifts in graphs.

UNDERSTANDING SLOPE

The relationship between two variables is represented by a curve's **slope.** One cannot understand many central concepts of economics without understanding slope.

The slope reflects the response of one variable to changes in another. Consider the typing example. Every 5 minutes of typing on a manual typewriter produces 1 page or, equivalently, every minute of typing produces $\frac{1}{5}$ of a page. As we shall demonstrate below, the slope of the line *abcde* is $\frac{1}{5}$ of a page of typing per minute.

To understand slope more precisely consider in panel (a) of Figure 4 the straight-line relationship between the two variables X and Y. When X = 5, Y = 3; when X = 7, Y = 6. Suppose now that variable X is allowed to *run* (to change horizontally) from 5 units to 7 units. When this happens variable Y *rises* (increases vertically) from 3 units to 6 units.

The slope of a straight line is the ratio of the rise (or fall) in Y over the run in X.

The slope of the line in panel (a) of Figure 4 is:

$$\text{Slope} = \frac{\text{Rise in } Y}{\text{Run in } X} = \frac{3}{2} = 1.5$$

A *positive value of the slope signifies a positive relationship* between the two variables.

This formula works for negative relationships as well. In panel (b) of Figure 4 when X runs from 5 to 7, Y *falls* from 4 units to 1 unit. Thus the slope is:

$$\text{Slope} = \frac{\text{Fall in } Y}{\text{Run in } X} = \frac{-3}{2} = -1.5$$

A *negative* value of the slope signifies a *negative relationship* between the two variables.

Let ΔY (delta Y) stand for the change in the value of Y and ΔX (delta X) stand for the change in the value of X:

$$\text{Slope} = \frac{\Delta Y}{\Delta X}$$

This formula holds for positive or negative relationships.

Let us return to the typing example. What slope expresses the relationship between minutes of typing and number of pages? When minutes increase by 5 units (ΔX = 5), pages increase by one unit (ΔY = 1). The slope is therefore $\Delta Y/\Delta X$ = $\frac{1}{5}$.

In Figures 2, 3, and 4, the points are connected by straight lines. Such relationships are called *linear relationships*. The inquisitive reader

Figure 4
Positive and Negative Slope

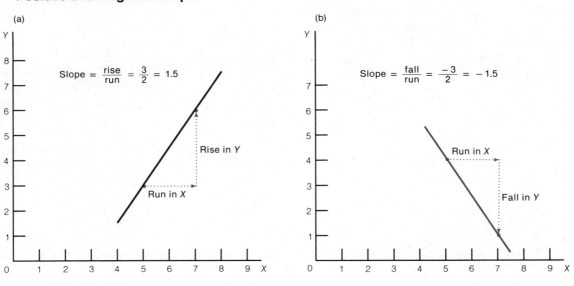

Positive slope is measured by the ratio of the rise in Y over the run in X. In panel (a), Y rises by 3 and X runs by 2, and the slope is 1.5. Negative slope is measured by the ratio of the fall in Y over the run in X. In panel (b), the fall in Y is -3, the run in X is 2, and the slope is -1.5.

will wonder how slope is measured when the relationship between X and Y is *curvilinear*.

A curvilinear example is given in Figure 5. When X runs from 2 units to 4 units ($\Delta X = 2$), Y rises by 2 units ($\Delta Y = 2$); between a and b the slope is $\frac{2}{2} = 1$. Between a and c, however, X runs from 2 to 6 ($\Delta X = 4$), Y rises by 3 units ($\Delta Y = 3$), and the slope is $\frac{3}{4}$. In the curvilinear case, the value of the slope depends on how far X is allowed to run. Between b and c, the slope is $\frac{1}{2}$. Thus, the slope changes as one moves along a curvilinear relationship. In the linear case, the value of the slope will *not* depend on how far X runs because the slope is constant and does not change as one moves from point to point.

There is no single slope of a curvilinear relationship and no single method of measuring slopes. The slope can be measured between two points (say, between a and b or between b and c) or at a particular point (say, at point a). Insofar as the measurement of the slope at a point depends upon the length of the run, a uniform standard must be adopted to avoid confusion. This standard is the use of *tangents* to determine the slope at a point on a curvilinear relationship.

Figure 5
Calculating Slopes of Curvilinear Relationships

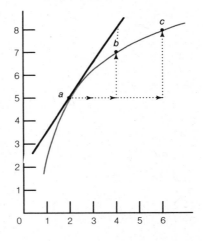

The ratio of the rise over the run yields a slope of 1 from a to b but a slope of $\frac{3}{4}$ from a to c. From b to c, the slope is $\frac{1}{2}$. To compute the slope at point a, the slope of the tangent to a is calculated. The value of the slope of the tangent is $\frac{3}{2}$.

To calculate the slope at *a*, let the run of *X* be "infinitesimally small," rather than a discrete number of units such as ½, 2, 4, or whatever. An infinitesimally small change is difficult to conceive, but the graphical result of such a change can be captured simply by drawing a **tangent** to point *a*.

*A **tangent** is a straight line that touches the curve at only one point.*

If the curve is really curved at *a*, there is only one straight line that just barely touches *a* and only *a*. Any other line (a magnifying glass may be required to verify this) will cut the curve at two points or none. The tangent to *a* is drawn in Figure 5.

The slope of a curvilinear relationship at a particular point is measured using the tangent to that point:

The slope of a curvilinear relationship at a particular point is the slope of the straight line tangent at that point.

The slope of the tangent at *a* is measured by dividing the rise by the run. Because the tangent is a straight line, the length of the run does not matter. For a run from 2 to 4 ($\Delta X = 2$), the rise (ΔY) equals 3 (from 5 to 8). Thus the slope of the tangent is 3⁄2 or 1.5.

Figure 6 shows two curvilinear relationships that have distinct high points or low points. In panel (a) the relationship between *X* and *Y* is positive for values of *X* less than 6 units and negative for values of *X* more than 6 units. The exact opposite holds for panel (b). The relationship is negative for values of *X* less than 6 and positive for *X* greater than 6. Notice that at the point where the slope changes from positive to negative (or vice versa), the slope of the curve will be exactly 0; the tangent at point $X = 6$ for both curves is a

Figure 6
Maximum and Minimum Points

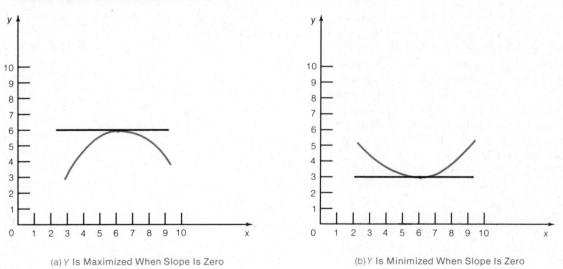

(a) *Y* Is Maximized When Slope Is Zero   (b) *Y* Is Minimized When Slope Is Zero

Some curvilinear relationships change directions. Notice that in panel (a), when the curve changes direction at $X = 6$, the corresponding value of *Y* is *maximized*. In panel (b), when $X = 6$, *Y* is *minimized*. In either case, the slope equals zero at the maximum or minimum value.

horizontal straight line that neither rises nor falls as X changes.

> *When a curvilinear relationship has a zero slope, the value of Y reaches either a high point—as in panel (a)—or a low point—as in panel (b)—at the value of X where the slope is zero.*

Economists pay considerable attention to the maximum and minimum values of relationships— as when they examine how a firm maximizes profits or minimizes costs. Suppose, for example, that X in panel (a) represents the 1982 *production* of automobiles by General Motors (in units of 1 million) and that the variable Y represents GM's *profits from automobile production* (in billions of dollars). According to this diagram, GM should settle on $X = 6$ million units of automobile production because GM's profits would be higher at $X = 6$ than at any other production level.

Suppose that in panel (b) Y measures GM's costs of producing an automobile while X still measures automobile production. Production costs per automobile are at a minimum at $X = 6$. In other words, GM will produce cars at the lowest cost per car if GM produces 6 million cars.

PITFALLS OF USING GRAPHS

When used properly, graphs illuminate the world in a convenient and efficient manner. Graphs may, however, be used to confuse or even misinform. Factions in political contests, advertisers of competing products, rivals in lawsuits can take the same set of data, apply the standard rules of graph construction, and yet offer graphs that support their own position and demonstrate the falsity of the opposition view. This is especially apparent in national political campaigns, where the incumbent party or president seeks to demonstrate how well the country's economy has been managed, while the opposition attempts to show how badly the nation's economic affairs have been bungled.

It is important to be able to form an independent judgment of what graphs say about the real world. This section warns the graph consumer about three of the many pitfalls of using graphs:

1. the ambiguity of slope,
2. the improper measurement of data, and
3. the use of unrepresentative data.

The Ambiguity of Slope

The steepness of the rise or fall of a graphed curve can be an ambiguous guide to the strength of the relationship between the two variables because the graphed slope is affected by the scale used to mark the axes and because the slope's numerical value depends upon the unit of measure.

Improper Measurement

A second pitfall in reading and evaluating graphs is *improper measurement*. Improper measurement covers a multitude of sins but does not mean simply an incorrect count of a variable (counting 20 chickens instead of 15). A variable may give the appearance of measuring one thing while in reality measuring another. Improper measurement is often subtle and difficult to detect, and the user of graphs must constantly be on the alert for this misuse.

In economics, two types of improper measurement that are encountered most often with time-series graphs are 1) inflation-distorted measures and 2) growth-distorted measures. A *time-series graph* is one in which the horizontal X axis measures time (in months, quarters, years, decades, etc.), and the vertical Y axis measures a second variable whose behavior is plotted over time.

Examples of inflation-distorted time-series graphs are not difficult to find. Consider the following misleading statement: "The American worker is better off today than three years ago; take-home pay has never been higher." Money wages alone do not measure worker living standards because inflation must be considered.

In interpreting time-series graphs, one must also be wary of *growth distortions*. An example of a growth-distorted measure is American alcohol consumption. The question is: Has alcohol abuse become a greater social problem over the past decade? The answer depends on which statistics you use. Alcohol consumption in the United States from 1965–1977 rose 38 percent, but the increase in alcohol consumption may be explained simply by the growth in population. When the figures are corrected for the increase in population, we find that alcohol expenditures *per adult* increased by only 12.5 percent.

Misinterpretations of time-series graphs can be avoided 1) by careful distinction between graphs that do and do not account for inflation and 2) by using per capita figures where appropriate or expressing graphs as percentages.

Unrepresentative Data

A final pitfall of using graphs is the problem of *unrepresentative or incomplete data*. The direction of a graphed relationship may depend upon the selection of the time period. For example, Soviet harvests have fluctuated dramatically in recent years with disastrous harvests following good harvests. If a good harvest year is chosen as the first year of a graph and a bad harvest as the last, the assessment of Soviet agricultural performance will be unfavorable. It will be more favorable if the graph starts with a bad harvest year and ends with a good one. Because the graphical relationship depends upon the choice of years covered by the graph, biased observers have the opportunity to present their version of the facts to the confusion of the user of the graph.

Summary

1. Graphs are useful for presenting positive and negative relationships between two variables.
2. A positive relationship exists between two variables if an increase in one is associated with an *increase* in the other; a negative relationship exists between two variables if an increase in one is associated with a *decrease* in the other.
3. In a graphical relationship, one variable may be an independent variable, and the other may be a dependent variable. In some relationships, it is not clear which variable is dependent and which variable is independent.

4. To construct a graph, four steps are necessary: 1) perpendicular vertical and horizontal axes are drawn on graph paper; 2) each variable is assigned to a particular axis; 3) units of measurement and scale are chosen for the X variable and for the Y variable; and 4) each related set of variables is plotted at the intersection of the appropriate grid lines on the graph. The advantages of graphs over tables are that graphs require less time to understand the relationship, and graphs can accommodate large amounts of data more efficiently.
5. For a straight line curve the slope of the curve is the ratio of the rise in Y over the run in X. The slope of the curvilinear relationship at a particular point is the slope of the straight line tangent at that point. When a curve changes slope from positive to negative as the X values increase, the value of Y reaches a *maximum* when the slope of the curve is zero; when a curve changes slope from negative to positive as the X values increase, the value of Y reaches a *minimum* when the slope of the curve is zero.
6. There are three pitfalls to avoid when using graphs: 1) choice of *units* and *scale* affects the apparent steepness or flatness of a curve; 2) the variables may be inflation-distorted or growth-distorted; and 3) omitted data or incomplete data may result in an erroneous interpretation of the relationship between two variables.

Key Terms

positive (or direct) relationship
negative (or inverse) relationship
independent variable
dependent variable
slope
tangent

2

The Economic Problem

Chapter Preview

The economic problem is how to use resources in a land of scarcity. Chapter 2 will explain how the production-possibilities frontier can show how an economy solves its economic problem and defines such crucial concepts as *resources, scarcity, scarce goods, free goods,* and *opportunity costs.* In solving its economic problem, every society must answer three questions: *What* should be produced? *How* should it be produced? *For whom* should it be produced?

UNLIMITED WANTS IN A SANTA CLAUS WORLD

We live in what John Kenneth Galbraith has called "the affluent society."[1] Although many people in our society are poor, the standard of living of most American families is comparatively high. Is it appropriate to speak of scarcity in an affluent society?

This question underscores how important it is to understand the exact meaning of economic terms. In economics, *scarcity* has a specific meaning that differs from the one in the dictionary. Scarcity is not determined by one's standard of living, not by whether one has life's basic necessities, but by comparison of wants with those things available to satisfy wants.

Suppose there really were a Santa Claus, who every Christmas tried to bring people all the

1. John Kenneth Galbraith, *The Affluent Society* (Boston: Houghton Mifflin, 1957).

things that they desired. People want different things, so everyone's Christmas list would differ. Children would want all kinds of toys; teenagers would ask for motorcycles, autos, stereos, clothes. The art enthusiast would want a house full of Rembrandts and Picassos; the wine connoisseur would want a cellar full of rare French wines. The vacation traveler would want first-class air and hotel accommodations for travel throughout the world.

Consider poor Santa Claus. He would add all the requests together to determine the wants of all his clients, but he would discover rather quickly that all requests could not be met. After all, there are only a limited number of Rembrandts and Picassos and bottles of rare French wines, and they would fall far short of the number requested. Santa Claus would find that for all these goods and services, the amounts requested would exceed the amounts available.

What would Santa Claus do in this case? He would have to make choices. He would decide to meet some requests and to deny others. His decisions could be made randomly or according to some rule, like who has been good or bad. If Santa Claus is interested in maximizing his own standard of living, he may honor the requests of those who leave the best snacks by the fireplace. On the other hand, he may deliver to those in greatest need. He may appoint a committee of trusted elves to make these decisions for him.

This Santa Claus story is a useful fable because it illustrates the most basic facts of economic life: scarcity and choice. In our fable, scarcity is present because what people want far exceeds what Santa Claus could conceivably deliver. It has little to do with whether Santa's claimants are rich or poor (although he would probably run out of Rembrandts before hot dogs). Choice is necessary because Santa must decide whose wants are to be met.

The most important fact of economics is the law of scarcity: there will never be enough resources to meet everyone's wants.

THE DEFINITION OF ECONOMICS

Chapter 1 noted that **economics** is the study of four themes: scarcity, choice, specialization, and exchange:

Economics is the study of how scarce resources *are* allocated *among* competing ends.

Four terms in this definition are emphasized because their meanings must be clear if the definition is to be properly understood. What are the exact economic meanings of *scarcity, resources, allocation,* and *competing ends?*

Scarcity

In September of 1980, Air Florida announced that any tickets that were not sold 10 minutes prior to departure on all its Houston-to-Dallas/Fort Worth flights would be given away free of charge (in fact, the ticket recipients received a kiss from an attractive Air Florida employee). This offer was valid for only one week.

While these airline seats were free of charge, they were not a **free good.** Rather the seats represent a **scarce good.**

As you might have guessed, the Air Florida tickets were indeed scarce. Crowds of people gathered at the departure gate in the hope of getting one of the few available free tickets. Many disappointed travelers had to return home, after a long wait, without a ticket and without a complimentary kiss.

An item is a scarce *good if the amount available (offered to users) is less than the amount people want if it would be given away free of charge.*

A free good *is one where the amount available is greater than the amount people want at a zero price.*

The following examples will test your ability to distinguish between free goods and scarce goods:

Tumbleweeds. Along an Idaho highway, one of the authors encountered the delightful sign: "Tumbleweeds are free, take one." Like the Air Florida ticket, tumbleweeds have a price of zero, but unlike the Air Florida ticket, tumbleweeds in Idaho are a free good. Why? Tumbleweeds may give satisfaction to the Eastern tourist, who may want to take one home as a souvenir, but the number of tumbleweeds available to takers far exceeds the number people want, even though they cost nothing. This example is limited by place and circumstances. In Alaska, tumbleweeds may be such a rarity that the number people want exceeds the number available. Exotic orchids can be freely picked in some remote Hawaiian islands, while commanding a high price in New York City.

La Guardia Airport. Landing and take-off slots at major airports are not paid for by airlines. Instead, committees comprised of government officials and airline management determine which airlines will be allotted take-off and landing slots and on which days. At busy La Guardia Airport in New York City, 522 take-off slots are available on a daily basis.[2] The airlines that serve New York City collectively want more than these 522 slots and must engage in intense negotiation over which airlines get which slots. These negotiations are particularly intense for the popular 5 P.M. to 7 P.M. landing slots. Although the airlines do not pay for landing slots, they are nevertheless a scarce commodity at La Guardia Airport. Whether landing slots are scarce or free depends upon time and place. At 10 P.M., landing slots are a free good at La Guardia. At uncongested airports (say, Champaign/Urbana, Illinois) landing slots are virtually a free good.

Los Angeles Air. The early residents of Los Angeles did not have to worry about the scarcity of clean air, for prior to the automobile age and the mass migration to southern California, clean air was not scarce according to the economic definition. Now, although no one is explicitly charged for clean (or cleaner) air, it has become a scarce good. Residents are implicitly paying for clean air by purchasing homes in distant suburbs where smog is less severe, by making lengthy commutes to work, and by purchasing air-filtration systems for their homes.

Goods may be scarce even if they are free of charge, and goods may be free goods at one

time and place and scarce goods in another time and place.

Unlike landing slots and clean air, scarce goods usually command a price. The next chapter will discuss how prices help allocate scarce resources.

Resources

Resources are the natural resources (land, mineral deposits, oxygen), the capital equipment (plants, machinery, inventories), and the human resources (workers with different skills, qualifications, ambitions, managerial talents) that are used to produce scarce goods and services. Productive resources are called **factors of production.** These resources represent the economic wealth of society because they determine how much output the society can produce. Because the factors of production are limited, society's ability to produce output is limited. The limitation of resources is the fundamental source of scarcity.

*The **factors of production** can be divided into three categories—land, labor, and capital.*

Sometimes, a fourth category—*entrepreneurship*—is considered a factor of production. The economic definitions of these factors differ somewhat from the dictionary usage.

Land is a catchall term that covers all of nature's bounty—minerals, forests, land, water resources, oxygen, and so on.

Land represents those natural resources, unimproved or unaltered by inputs of the other two factors of production, that contribute to production. Desert land that had been transformed into arable land by irrigation would not be a free gift of nature. The application of the labor and capital used to build the irrigation system makes this desert land productive.

Capital refers to the equipment, plants, buildings, and inventories that are available to society.

In 1981, the total of all U.S. **capital** was approximately $11.7 trillion. Unlike land, capital is

2. "Upstarts Crack an Airline Club," *New York Times,* September 7, 1980, section 3.

not one of nature's gifts; capital is produced by combining the factors of production. Capital is long-lived: when it is used to produce output, it is not *consumed* (used up) immediately; it is consumed gradually in the process of time. An assembly plant may have a life of 40 years, a computer a life of 5 years, and a lathe a life of 10 years before it must be replaced.

When economists speak of capital, they mean physical capital goods—buildings, computers, trucks, plants. This concept of capital is distinct from *money capital*. Physical capital and money capital are related. Money capital is needed to purchase physical capital; money capital represents the ownership's claims to physical capital. The owner of 1,000 shares of AT&T owns money capital, but these shares really represent ownership of a portion of AT&T's physical capital.

One final distinction should be made between the *stock* of capital and *additions* to the stock of capital. At one point in time, there exists a stock of capital. This stock consists of all the capital (plants, equipment, inventories, buildings) that exist *at that point in time*. Each year, this stock changes; it usually grows. New plants are built, new equipment is manufactured, new homes are constructed, additions are made to inventories. Through **investment,** society adds to its stock of capital.

Investment is additions to the stock of capital.

Labor is the physical and mental talents that human beings contribute to the production process.

The ditchdigger contributes muscles; the computer engineer contributes mental abilities, the airline pilot contributes physical coordination and mental talents. Just as a society can add to the stock of physical capital, so can it add to the stock of **human capital.**

Human capital is the accumulation of past investments in schooling, training, and health that raise the productive capacity of people.

In 1981, the stock of human capital was valued at approximately $4.4 trillion. By investing in the training and education of people, society adds to the productive capacity of labor and raises the wealth of society. Investments in physical capital and human capital accomplish the same goal: they increase the capacity of society to produce output. Certain persons, called **entrepreneurs,** possess a particular talent and perform a particular role that cannot be performed by land and capital.

An entrepreneur organizes, manages, and assumes the risks for an enterprise.

Entrepreneurs are those people who organize the factors of production to produce output, who seek out and exploit new business opportunities, who introduce new technologies. The entrepreneur is the one who takes risk and bears the responsibility if the venture fails. The entrepreneur puts inventions into business practice.

Allocation

Scarcity requires that choices be made: If there is not enough of a commodity to meet unlimited wants, decisions must be made about who will receive the commodity and who will be denied it. A system of **allocation** of scarce resources must be employed. Societies cannot function unless the allocation problem is resolved in a satisfactory manner.

Allocation is the apportionment of resources for a specific purpose or to particular persons or groups.

Consider what would happen if there were no organized allocation. People would have to fight or compete with one another for scarce resources. The timid would not compete effectively; the elderly or weak would have difficulty in obtaining goods, except through stronger, more aggressive benefactors. Such an allocation system was in effect for centuries in the dark and middle ages. Such free-for-all allocation is rare in modern societies, but it reappears in cases of breakdowns of the social order. Floods, natural disasters, and wars bring out looting and violent competition for scarce goods. Martial law must be declared to prevent free-for-all allocation. If there were a drastic reduction in gasoline supplies (say, to one tenth of the current level), there would probably be considerable free-for-all allocation. Individuals armed with guns, wrenches, and nasty dispositions would seek to intimidate other customers at service stations to gain access to the scarce resource, gasoline.

It is important to have an allocation system that is not based upon strong-arm tactics. Society must develop a system for orderly allocation.

Market Allocation. The allocation system that prevails in American society is the **market;** this book is devoted primarily to the study of market allocation.

*The **market** is the coming together of buyers and sellers for the purpose of determining the conditions for the exchange of resources.*

Market allocation works as follows: A commodity—let us say, a TV set—is scarce because the number desired at a zero price exceeds the number offered. Raising the price of TV sets encourages production and discourages consumption. Market allocation uses higher prices to restrict the number of buyers of the scarce commodity to the amount available. The market sets the price to encourage the *supply* of a resource (the amount offered for sale) to match actual *demand* for that resource (the amount buyers are prepared to purchase).

Market allocation and the price system are discussed in Chapter 3. Most goods and services are allocated by the market in our society—automobiles, hamburgers, computers, furniture, fresh fruits—the list is almost without end.

Government Allocation. A second allocation system is *government allocation.* Governmental agencies, officials, and administrative authorities decide who, among all those who want the scarce commodity, will be accommodated. In Communist societies, most allocation decisions are made by the government. In our economy, airport landing slots are assigned by government regulatory agencies. The regional distribution of gasoline supplies has at times been dictated by the federal government. Licenses for television and radio stations are granted by the federal government. In all these cases, access to the scarce resource is not determined by willingness to pay, but by some administrative authority.

In Great Britain, the government National Health Service is responsible for allocating medical care. The number of doctors, nurses, and hospital beds is not sufficient to meet wants for "free" medical care, and the National Health Service must decide who will receive medical care. Some procedures are denied to patients over 65—such as kidney dialysis or transplants. The desire for operations that are not required to save a life (elective surgery) is limited by requiring patients to wait weeks and months to see a specialist.[3] In effect, the National Health Service uses rules to allocate medical care. Of course, there is a private medical market as well that supplements the public market.

Scarce resources can be allocated by different allocation systems. There is endless controversy about which system (or combination of systems) is best. The allocation system has a substantial impact on how people live. Consider the differences between American society, which uses primarily market allocation, and Soviet society, which uses primarily government allocation. The allocation system affects personal lives, the political system, and freedom of choice.

Competing Ends

Economics is the study of competition for resources. Scarce resources must somehow be allocated among the **competing ends** of individuals, families, government agencies, and businesses according to an allocation system.

*The **competing ends** are the different purposes for which resources can be used.*

First, different individuals are in competition for resources. Which families will have a greater claim on scarce resources? Who will be rich? Who poor? How will income be distributed? There is also competition for resources between the private sector (individuals and businesses) and government. Third, there is competition for resources between current and future consumption.

3. Harry Schwartz, "What is a Life Worth?" *Wall Street Journal,* September 15, 1980, p. 22.

By investing scarce resources in physical and human capital, their current use is sacrificed to produce more goods and services in the future.

Finally, the society must choose between competing national goals when allocating resources. Is price stability, full employment, elimination of poverty, or economic growth most important? Are we prepared to achieve one goal at the expense of another?

THE ECONOMIC PROBLEM

The economic problem is how to allocate scarce resources among competing ends. Three questions must be answered: *What* products will be produced? *How* will they be produced? *For whom* will they be produced?

What?

Should society devote its limited resources to producing civilian or military goods, luxuries or necessities, goods for immediate consumption or goods that increase the wealth of society (capital goods)? Should small or large cars be produced, or should buses and subways be produced instead of cars? Should the military concentrate on strategic or conventional forces?

How?

Once the decision is made on what to produce, society must determine what combinations of the factors of production will be used. Will coal, petroleum, or nuclear power be used to produce electricity? Will bulldozers or workers with shovels dig dams? Should automobile tires be made from natural or synthetic rubber? Should Coca Cola be sweetened with sugar or corn syrup? Should tried-and-true methods of production be replaced by new technology?

For Whom?

Will society's output be divided fairly equally or will claims to society's output be unequal? Will differences in wealth be allowed to pass from one generation to the next? What role will government play in determining *for whom?* Should government intercede to change the way the economy is distributing its output?

Economic Systems

Societies must solve these economic problems of what, how, and for whom if they are to function. Different societies have different solutions. Some use private ownership and market allocation; others use public ownership and government allocation. Most use an **economic system** that is a combination of private and public ownership and a combination of market and government allocation.

*The set of organizational arrangements and institutions that are established to solve the economic problem is called an **economic system**.*

Real-world economic systems exist in almost infinite variety; the list of labels for economic systems is also long. The two major alternatives are the capitalist (market) system and the planned socialist (communist) system. How the market system solves our economic problems is discussed in Chapter 3.

OPPORTUNITY COSTS

Scarcity requires that choices be made concerning what will be produced, how it will be produced, and for whom. Choice means that some alternatives must be forgone. A sacrificed opportunity is called an **opportunity cost** by economists because the economic cost of any choice is that which must be sacrificed in order to make that choice.

*The **opportunity cost** of a particular action is the loss of the next best alternative.*

If a person buys a new car, its opportunity cost is the next best alternative that must be sacrificed. The next best alternative might have been a European trip, an investment in the stock market, or enrollment in a prestigious university. Because the person chose the car, he or she sacrificed these other things. The loss of the next best alternative is the true cost of the car. If the government increases defense spending, the opportunity cost is the best alternate government program that had to be sacrificed to make the funds available.

The notion of opportunity cost supplies a

shortcut method of differentiating between free goods and scarce goods:

> *Free goods have an opportunity cost of zero. Scarce goods have a positive opportunity cost.*

Why does the Idaho tumbleweed have no opportunity cost? If one tumbleweed is taken, the amount available is still greater than the amount wanted. The taker has not had to give up anything as a consequence of taking the tumbleweed.

The opportunity cost of an action can involve the sacrifice of time as well as the sacrifice of goods. To gather the free tumbleweed, one would need to sacrifice time. What is the opportunity cost of attending a football game? To pay the price of the ticket, the buyer has to sacrifice the purchase of other goods, and the next best purchase is the opportunity cost of buying the ticket. Even if the buyer had received the ticket free of charge, however, there would still be an opportunity cost. The two hours spent at the game could have been devoted to alternate uses. The buyer could have slept, studied, or listened to records, for example. If a major exam were scheduled for the next day, the opportunity cost of the game could be quite high. The notion of sacrificed time as an opportunity cost is an important ingredient of economics. It explains, for example, why passenger trains and ocean liners have become relics of the past or why older residential areas close to the central city are being revived.

> *Every choice involving the allocation of scarce resources involves opportunity costs.*

Table 1
Production-Possibilities Schedule

Combination	Tanks (in thousands)	Wheat (in tons)	Opportunity Cost of Tanks (in tons of wheat)
a	0	18	0
b	1	17	1
c	2	15	2
d	3	12	3
e	4	7	5
f	5	0	7

PRODUCTION POSSIBILITIES

The **production-possibilities frontier (PPF)** is a useful analytical tool for illustrating the concepts of scarcity, choice, and opportunity costs.

Suppose an economy produces only two types of goods: tanks and wheat. Of course, actual economies produce more than two goods, but a simple model aids our understanding. Table 1 gives the amounts of wheat and tanks that this hypothetical economy can produce with its limited factors of production and technical knowledge. These amounts are graphed in Figure 1. The table and the graph contain the same information.

Figure 1
The Production-Possibilities Frontier *(PPF)*

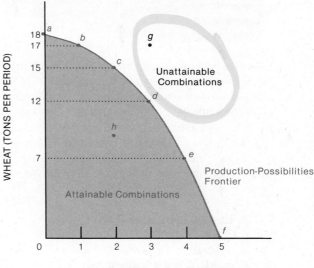

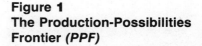

TANKS (THOUSANDS PER PERIOD)

The *PPF* shows the combinations of outputs of two goods that can be produced from society's resources when these resources are utilized to their maximum potential. Point *a* shows that if 18 tons of wheat are produced, no tank production is possible. Point *f* shows that if no wheat is produced, a maximum of 5,000 tanks can be produced. Point *d* shows that if 3,000 tanks are produced, a maximum of 12 tons of wheat can be produced. Point *g* is above society's *PPF*. With its available resources, the economy cannot produce 17 tons of wheat and 3,000 tanks. Points like *h* inside the *PPF* and, therefore, attainable represent an inefficient use of the society's resources.

What do these numbers mean? How are they to be interpreted? If our hypothetical economy chose to be at point *a,* it would be producing no tanks and the *maximum* of 18 tons of wheat from the factors of production available. At point *f* the economy would be producing no wheat and the *maximum* of 5,000 tanks. The points between *a* and *f* show the combinations of wheat and tanks that the economy is capable of producing from its available resources and technology. Point *c* shows that if 2,000 tanks are produced, the maximum number of tons of wheat that can be produced is 15. Each intermediate point on the *PPF* between *a* and *f* represents a different combination of wheat and tanks that could be produced using the same resources and technology.

> The **production-possibilities frontier (PPF)** shows the combinations of goods that can be produced when the factors of production are utilized to their full potential. The production-possibilities curve reveals the economic choices open to society.

Our hypothetical economy is capable of producing output combinations *a* through *f.* The economy is unable to produce output combination *g* (17 tons of wheat and 3,000 tanks) because *g* uses more resources than the economy has available. Point *h* is an attainable combination because it lies inside the frontier. The economy can produce any combination of outputs on or inside the *PPF.*

The Law of Increasing Cost

The production-possibilities frontier is curved like a bow; it is not a straight line. Why does it have this shape? As noted earlier, the economic cost of any action is the loss of the next best opportunity. In our example, the economy produces only two goods. The opportunity cost of increasing the production of one of those goods is the amount of the other good that must be sacrificed. In this simple case, the measurement of opportunity cost is obvious: the opportunity cost of tanks is the wheat production that must be sacrificed.

At *a,* the economy is producing 18 tons of wheat and no tanks. The opportunity cost of increasing the production of tanks from zero to

1,000 is the 1 ton of wheat that must be sacrificed in the move from *a* to *b.* The opportunity cost of 1,000 more tanks (moving from *b* to *c*) is 2 tons of wheat. The opportunity cost of the fifth thousand of tanks (moving from *e* to *f*) is a much higher 7 tons of wheat. The amounts of wheat that must be given up to increase tank production are given in the last column of Table 1. The opportunity cost per thousand of tank production rises with the production of tanks, which is consistent with the **law of increasing costs.**

> The **law of increasing costs** states that as more of a particular commodity is produced, its opportunity cost per unit will increase.

The law of increasing costs is consistent with the bowed out shape of the *PPF.* Suppose our hypothetical economy were at peace, producing only wheat, no tanks (at *a* on the *PPF*). Its archenemy declares war, and the economy must suddenly increase its production of tanks. The amount of resources available to the economy is not altered by the declaration of war, so the increased tank production must be at the expense of wheat production. The economy *must move along* its *PPF* in the direction of more tank production.

As tank production increases, will the opportunity cost of a unit of tank production remain the same? At low levels of tank production, the opportunity cost of a unit of tank production will be relatively low. Some factors of production will be suited to producing both wheat and tanks; they can be shifted from wheat to tank production without raising opportunity cost. As tank production increases further, resources suited to wheat production but ill suited to tank production (experienced farmers make inexperienced factory workers, agricultural equipment is poorly adapted to tank factories) must be diverted into tank production. Ever-increasing amounts of these resources must be shifted from wheat to keep tank production expanding at a constant rate. The opportunity cost of a unit of tank production (the amount of wheat sacrificed) will rise, as the law of increasing costs would predict.

The law of increasing costs applies across economic systems. One of the most striking movements along a *PPF* took place in the Soviet Union between 1928 and 1937. In 1928 the Soviet leadership determined to shift most resources out of agriculture and light industry into heavy industry. This reallocation was designed to make the Soviet Union economically independent and to ''build Soviet socialism.'' An unprecedented volume of resources was diverted to heavy industry. Untrained peasants entered into large industrial plants; major construction projects used people with shovels and wheelbarrows; light industry equipment was converted to use in heavy industry.

To the surprise of Soviet planners, the law of increasing costs applied to their economy. The economy fell far short of the cost targets set by planners for heavy industry.[4] Why did Soviet planners miscalculate costs so badly? To meet major targets, resources ill suited for heavy industry (untrained peasants, shovels and wheelbarrows, textile mills) had to be used in ever-increasing numbers. The opportunity costs of heavy industry rose, just as the law predicted.

The Law of Diminishing Returns

Underlying the law of increasing costs is the **law of diminishing returns.** Suppose that wheat is produced using land, labor, and tractors. The law of diminishing returns states that increasing the amount of labor in equal increments, holding land and tractors constant, eventually brings about smaller and smaller increases in wheat production.

> *In general, the **law of diminishing returns** states that increasing the amount of one input in equal increments, holding all other inputs constant, eventually brings about ever-smaller increases in output.*

Notice that the law of diminishing returns applies in our example because the input that is being increased—labor—becomes less and less effective because more and more workers are being crowded together on a fixed amount of land and physical capital. As the number of laborers increases each laborer works with a smaller plot

4. Eugene Zaleski, *Stalinist Planning for Economic Growth* (Chapel Hill, N.C.: University of North Carolina Press, 1980).

of land and fewer tractors. Suppose 10 farm workers were employed, and they each had 100 acres to farm and one tractor with which to work. Because land and capital are fixed, increasing the number of farm workers to 20 would mean each worker would have 50 acres to farm and half of a tractor with which to work (2 workers would have to share one tractor). Increasing the number of farm workers to 1,000 would result in each worker farming $\frac{1}{10}$ of an acre and 100 workers sharing each tractor. Obviously, each worker would be less productive if each had only a fraction of an acre to farm and if each worker had to wait for 99 other workers to use the tractor.

Efficiency

The *PPF* shows the combination of goods an economy is capable of producing when its limited resources are utilized to their maximum potential. Whether an economy will indeed operate on its production-possibilities frontier depends upon whether or not the economy utilizes its resources with maximum **efficiency.**

In Figure 1, if the economy produces output combinations that lie on the *PPF* the economy is said to be *efficient*. If it operates at points inside the *PPF,* such as *h,* it is said to be *inefficient* because more wheat could be produced without cutting back on the other good.

> *Efficiency results when no resources are unemployed and when no resources are misallocated.*

For example, if workers are unemployed or if productive machines stand idle, the economy is not operating on its *PPF* because resources are not being employed. Misallocated resources are resources that are used but not to their best advantage. For example, if a surgeon works as a ditchdigger, if cotton is planted on Iowa corn land, or if jumbo jets are manufactured in India, resources are misallocated.

Economic Growth

The production-possibilities frontier represents the economic choices open to society. It shows the maximum combinations of outputs the econ-

Figure 2
The Effect of Increasing the Stock of Capital on the *PPF*

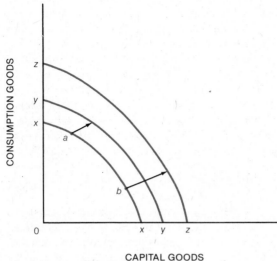

CAPITAL GOODS

Suppose the current *PPF* is curve *XX*. If the economy chooses point *a*, allocating most resources to the production of consumption goods and few to the production of new capital goods, the *PPF* in the future will shift out to curve *YY*. But if the economy chooses point *b*, with comparatively little consumption and comparatively high production of new capital goods, the future *PPF* will shift out further—to *ZZ*.

omy is capable of producing from its scarce resources. Economies that are efficient operate on their frontier; others that are inefficient operate inside their frontier. Which combination of outputs lying on the frontier is best is a matter of economic choice.

Capital Accumulation. Where to locate on the *PPF* may represent a choice between capital goods and consumer goods. Capital goods are the equipment, plants, and inventories that are added to society's stock of capital and can be used to satisfy wants in the future. Consumer goods are items like food, clothing, medicine, and transportation that satisfy consumer wants directly in the present. The capital goods/consumer goods choice is shown in Figure 2.

The economy on the *PPF* labeled *XX* must choose among those combinations of consumer

goods and capital goods located on *XX*. What are the implications for the future of selecting *a* or *b*? If *a* is chosen, more consumer wants are satisfied today, but additions to the stock of capital are smaller. If *b* is selected fewer wants are satisfied today, but additions to the stock of capital are greater. The creation of a larger stock of capital today means more production in the future. The society that selects *b* will therefore experience a greater outward shift of the *PPF* in the future and will be able to satisfy more wants in the future.

Economic growth occurs when the production-possibilities frontier expands outward and to the right. One source of economic growth is the expansion of capital.

The society that selects *a* will satisfy more wants today but will experience lower economic growth and will not be in as good a position to satisfy future wants.

These principles are illustrated in Figure 2. If society chooses *a*, then the *PPF* expands from *XX* now to *YY* in the future. If it locates at *b*, the *PPF* expands more, from *XX* now to *ZZ* in the future. At *ZZ*, the economy will be able to satisfy more wants than at *YY*.

Societies must choose between consumption today and consumption tomorrow. The society that devotes a greater share of its resources to producing capital sacrifices consumption now but enlarges its supply of capital and will thus have a higher rate of economic growth.

There are limits to the rule that less consumption today means more consumption tomorrow. If all resources are devoted to capital goods, the labor force would starve. If too large a share of resources is put into capital goods, worker incentives might be low and efficiency might be reduced.

Shifts in the Production-Possibilities Frontier. The production-possibilities frontier is based on the size and productivity of the resource base. Capital accumulation is only one reason for the *PPF* to shift. Increases in labor or land or discoveries of natural resources (coal, iron, oil) will

**Figure 3
Technical Progress in Wheat
Production**

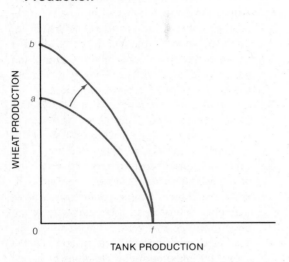

If a higher-yielding strain of wheat is discovered, a larger quantity of wheat could be produced with the same resources. Since this increase in wheat production would not influence tank production, the *PPF* would rotate from *af* to *bf*.

also shift the *PPF* outward. Technical progress occurs when the society learns how to get more outputs from the same inputs. Thus technical progress, or advances in productivity, will also shift the *PPF* outward.

Technical progress and accumulation of productive factors like land, labor, or capital have different effects on the *PPF*. Technical progress may affect only one industry or sector—whereas labor and capital and land can be used across all sectors. Figure 3 illustrates a technical advance in wheat production without a corresponding change in the productivity of the resources devoted to tank production. Accordingly, the *PPF* shifts from *af* to *bf*. Here the *PPF* shifts upward but not rightward. Figure 2 illustrates that a change in factor supply—illustrated in this case by capital accumulation—shifts the *PPF* both upward and rightward.

All societies must solve the economic problems of what, how, and for whom if they are to function. There are different methods of solving these problems. This book will concentrate on how market economies solve the economic prob-

**Figure 4
The Economic Problem: What? How?
For Whom?**

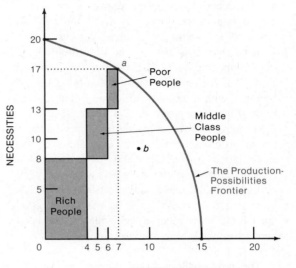

The *PPF* reveals the choices open to society. The *what* question is solved by the choice of where to locate on the *PPF*. Here society chooses *a*, or 7 units of luxuries and 17 units of necessities. The *how* question is solved when society decides how to combine resources to produce these outputs. Society can solve this problem efficiently and operate on the frontier (at *a*) or inefficiently and operate inside the frontier (at *b*). The *for whom* question is the division of society's output among the members of society. In this diagram, the rich get 4 units of luxuries and 8 units of necessities; the middle class get 2 units of luxuries and 5 units of necessities; the poor get one unit of luxuries and 4 units of necessities.

lems but will also discuss how planned economies and mixed economies deal with them as well.

In market economies, the *what* problem is solved when consumers decide what they want to buy and how much they are willing to pay and when voters cast their ballots for or against public spending programs. The *how* problem is solved when producers determine how to combine resources to their best advantage. The *for whom* decision depends on who owns the economy's land, labor, and capital.

A solution of the *what, how,* and *for whom* problems is shown in Figure 4. The *what* problem is nothing more than the choice of location on the

PPF. In this diagram, society chooses point *a*. The *how* problem is solved behind the scenes by decisions on how the factors of production are to be combined. How well the how problem is solved can be read directly from the *PPF* diagram. If the economy is operating *on its PPF*, such as at *a*, it is solving the how problem with maximum efficiency. If it is operating inside the *PPF*, at *b* for example, it is not solving the how problem with maximum efficiency. The solution to the *for whom* problem also takes place behind the scenes. We can show the outcome of the *for whom* problem on the *PPF* diagram. The consumer goods (necessities and luxury goods) are distributed among the members of society (the rich, the middle class, and the poor). In the diagram, the rich receive most of the luxury goods; the middle class receive some luxury goods; the poor receive negligible luxury goods.

The next chapter explains how the price system solves the *what, how,* and *for whom* problems, how it facilitates specialization and exchange, and how it provides for the future.

Summary

1. Wants are unlimited; there will never be enough resources to meet unlimited wants.
2. Economics is the study of how scarce resources are allocated among competing ends.
3. A good is *scarce* if the amount available is less than the amount people would want if it were given away free. A good is *free* if the amount people want is less than the amount available. Goods may be scarce even though they are given away free of charge.
4. The ultimate source of scarcity is the limited supply of resources. The resources that are factors of production are land, labor, and capital. Society can add to its stock of resources by investment in physical capital and in human beings.
5. Because scarcity exists, some system of allocating goods among those who want the goods is necessary. The two major allocation systems are market allocation and allo-

cation by government plan. These two types of allocation systems can be combined to create mixed allocation systems.
6. Allocation systems must determine what resources will be made available to which individuals, how resources are to be divided between the private and public sectors, and which resources will be devoted to current use and which to future consumption.
7. Economics is the study of how societies solve the economic problems of *what* to produce, *how* to produce, and *for whom* to produce.
8. The opportunity cost of any choice is the next best alternative that was sacrificed to make the choice. Scarce goods have a positive opportunity cost; free goods have an opportunity cost of zero.
9. The production-possibilities frontier *(PPF)* shows the maximum combinations of goods that an economy is able to produce from its limited resources when these resources are utilized to their maximum potential and for a given state of technical knowledge. If societies are efficient, they will operate on the production-possibilities frontier. If they are inefficient, they will operate inside the *PPF*.
10. The law of increasing costs says that as more of one commodity is produced at the expense of others, its opportunity cost will increase. This law applies to all economic systems.
11. According to the law of diminishing returns, increasing the amount of one input in equal increments, holding all other inputs constant, eventually brings about ever smaller increases in output.
12. The two sources of economic inefficiency are unemployed resources and misallocated resources.
13. Economic growth occurs because the factors of production expand in either quantity or quality, or because technological progress raises productivity.
14. The choice of consumer goods versus capital goods affects economic growth. Generally, the greater the share of resources devoted to capital goods, the better is the economy able to meet wants in the future. The choice of consumer goods versus capi-

tal goods is really a choice between meeting wants now and meeting them in the future.

Key Terms

economics
free good
scarce good
factors of production
land
capital
labor
human capital
entrepreneur
allocation
market
competing ends
economic system
opportunity cost
production-possibilities frontier *(PPF)*
law of increasing costs
law of diminishing returns
efficiency

Questions and Problems

1. Use the Santa Claus example to illustrate how either market allocation or allocation by government planning could be used to solve Santa's allocation problem.
2. "Desert sand will always be a free good. More is available than people could conceivably want." Evaluate this statement.
3. A local millionaire buys 1000 tickets to the Super Bowl and declares that these tickets will be given away to 1000 boy scouts. Are these tickets free goods? Why or why not?
4. In Israel, desert land has been turned into farm land by irrigation. Does this example demonstrate that nature's free gifts are not fixed in supply?

5. Do you consider your time spent in college as an investment in human capital? Is it investment or consumption? Make a brief list of the opportunity costs of attending college. Do these costs equal the dollar costs listed in the college catalog?
6. The cancer drug *interferon* has received considerable attention in the press as a promising development in the search for a cancer treatment. The amount of interferon available is quite limited, while numerous cancer patients want to try it. What alternative methods could be used to allocate interferon among users?
7. Consider the following data on a hypothetical economy's production-possibilities frontier:

Hundreds of Guns	Tons of Butter
8	0
7	4
5	10
3	14
1	16
0	16.25

   a. Graph the *PPF*.
   b. Does it have the expected shape?
   c. Calculate the opportunity cost of guns in terms of butter. Calculate the opportunity cost of butter in terms of guns. Do they illustrate the law of increasing costs?
   d. If you observed this economy producing 700 guns and 3 tons of butter, what would you conclude about how this economy is solving the *how* problem?
   e. If you observed this economy at some later date producing 700 guns and 12 tons of butter, what would you conclude?
8. "Economic inefficiency means wasted output no matter what type of economic system." Evaluate this statement.

3

The Price System

Chapter Preview

This chapter will examine how resources are allocated and how the decisions of the millions of people in the typical economy are coordinated. Market allocation of resources is achieved through the price system. The prices people pay for things are like a number of cleverly placed thermostats that balance the decisions of thousands of producers and millions of consumers. The price system achieves this balance by operating according to the principle of substitution, the law of comparative advantage, and the principles of supply and demand. This chapter will explain the difference between relative prices and money prices and will examine the role of property rights, specialization, and interest rates in the

working of the price system. The chapter will conclude by discussing some of the limitations of the price system.

RELATIVE PRICES AND MONEY PRICES

Prices in the Land of Ergs

Suppose you find yourself in a strange land—strange in every respect except that you are able to communicate with the inhabitants. The hospitable natives welcome you with a gift of local currency, which you learn is called the *erg*. Being in a hurry to eat breakfast, you do not have time to count how many ergs you have. You locate a diner and order coffee. A waitress brings you a cup of coffee and asks for 400 ergs. Is coffee cheap or expensive? Is the price high or low? You have no idea. Given the information you have at this point, the price of 400 ergs is meaningless.

How do you discover whether the price of coffee is high or low? You have to gather more information. You look at the menu and discover that a coke sells for 1,200 ergs, and you learn in conversation with another customer that the typical worker earns something like 24,000 ergs per hour. Now you decide that coffee is cheap by reasoning: "Back home I pay $0.40 for a cup of coffee and $0.40 for a coke, and I earn $10.00 an hour. At home, an hour's work will purchase 25 cokes or 25 cups of coffee. Here an hour of work will purchase 20 cokes and 60 cups of coffee." The moral of this parable is: A money price in isolation from other money prices is meaningless. What is important is how a particular money price stands relative to other money prices.

Calculating Relative Prices

A **relative price** indicates how one price stands in relation to other prices. A relative price is quite different from a **money price.** In the erg example, coffee sells for 400 ergs and cokes for 1,200 ergs. Three cups of coffee is the relative price of a coke, and one third of a coke is the relative price of coffee. If coffee and cokes had both sold for 400 ergs, then the relative price of a coke would have been one cup of coffee.

> A **money price** is a price expressed in monetary units (such as dollars, francs, etc.) A **relative price** is a price expressed in terms of other commodities.

As these examples show, relative prices can be expressed in terms of anything. The relative price of coke can be expressed in terms of cups of coffee, cups of tea, hours of work, number of T-shirts, or anything else that has a money price.

Let P_A and P_B stand for the money prices of apples (A) and bananas (B). The relative price of apples to bananas is the *ratio* of the two money prices, P_A/P_B. If the price of apples is $0.50 per pound and the price of bananas is $0.25 per pound, the relative price of one pound of apples is two pounds of bananas. Conversely, one pound of bananas costs 0.5 pound of apples. When coffee costs 400 ergs and a coke costs 1,200 ergs, the ratio of the price of coke to the price of coffee equals 3, or the relative price of cokes equals 3 coffees.

Money prices are meaningful when they are related to prices of goods that are connected in some way with the good in question. An example of a relative price is the price of U.S. cars expressed in terms of foreign cars. It makes sense to state the price of U.S. cars relative to that of foreign cars because buyers who have decided to purchase a car must choose between U.S. and foreign cars. The money prices of U.S. cars and foreign cars are graphed in panel (a) of Figure 1 (from the data in Table 1). They show that average money prices of both U.S. and foreign cars rose substantially between 1975 and 1980. However, panel (b) shows that the relative price of U.S. cars (the price of U.S. cars divided by the price of foreign cars) fell during this same period. In 1975, the relative price of a U.S. car was 1.21 foreign cars (121 foreign cars could have been purchased with the same amount of money as 100 U.S. cars). By 1980, the relative price of a U.S. car was 0.97 foreign cars (97 foreign cars could have been purchased with the same amount of money as 100 U.S. cars). The relative price of U.S. automobiles dropped even though its money price increased.

> *The money price of a commodity can rise while its relative price falls. The money price can fall while its relative price rises. Money prices and relative prices need not move together.*

Relative prices play a prominent role in answering the economic questions of *what, how,* and *for whom.* Money prices do not. Relative prices signal to buyers and sellers what goods are cheap or expensive. *Buying and selling decisions are made on the basis of relative prices.* If the relative price of one good goes sky high, buyers try to substitute other goods whose relative prices are lower.

The emphasis on relative prices does not mean that money prices are unimportant. Money prices tend to be fairly important in the context of macroeconomics. For example, *inflation* is not a

Table 1
Money Prices for U.S. and Foreign Cars

Year	Price of a U.S. Car (in dollars)	Price of a Foreign Car (in dollars)	Relative Price of a U.S. Car (in foreign cars)
1975	5200	4300	1.21
1976	5600	5000	1.12
1977	6200	5200	1.19
1978	6550	5850	1.12
1979	6700	6750	0.99
1980	7100	7300	0.97

Source: Merrill Lynch, Pierce, Fenner, and Smith, Inc.

movement in relative prices but a general increase in money prices. Elections are won or lost on the basis of inflation; the living standards of older people on fixed incomes are damaged by inflation. Rampant inflation can destroy the fabric of society. Inflation is important. But notice that even in the case of inflation, money prices are not considered in isolation. Instead, the level of money prices today is compared to the level of money prices yesterday. Ultimately, this is also a form of relative price.

Generally speaking, in microeconomics there is greater interest in relative prices than in money prices. In macroeconomics, there is greater interest in the level of money prices than in relative prices. In modern macroeconomics, relative prices have come to play a greater role in explaining macroeconomic events.

THE PRINCIPLE OF SUBSTITUTION

Relative prices are important because of the fundamental **principle of substitution.**

The **principle of substitution** states that practically no good is irreplaceable in meeting demand (the amount of a good people are prepared to buy). Users are able to substitute one product for another to satisfy demand.

Virtually no good is fully protected from the competition of substitutes. Aluminum competes

with steel, coal with oil, electricity with natural gas, labor with machines, movies with TV, one brand of toothpaste with another, and so on. The only goods impervious to substitutes are such things as certain minimal quantities of water, salt, or food and certain life-saving medications, such as insulin.

To say that there is a substitute for every good does not mean that there is an *equally good* substitute for every good. One mouthwash is a close substitute for another mouthwash; a television show is a good substitute for a movie; apartments may be good substitutes for private homes. However, carrier pigeons are a poor substitute for telephone service;[1] costly insulation may be a poor substitute for fuel oil; public transportation may be a poor substitute for the private car in sprawling cities; steel is a poor substitute for aluminum in the production of jet aircraft.

Relative prices signal consumers when substitutions are necessary. If the price of one good rises relative to its substitutes, consumers will tend to switch to the relatively cheaper substitute.

Substitutions are being made all around us. As relative energy prices rise, people substitute insulation for fuel oil and natural gas, home-entertainment equipment for driving to movies, restaurants, and parties; carpools for driving one's own car. As the relative price of crude oil rises, utilities switch from oil to coal; retailers use fewer neon lights and hire more sales personnel. When

1. In Buenos Aires telephone service at one time became so chaotic that businesses actually purchased carrier pigeons to substitute for telephone service.

Figure 1
Money Prices and Relative Prices for U.S. and Foreign Cars

(a) AVERAGE MONEY PRICES

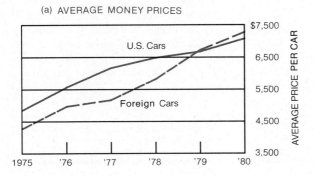

(b) RELATIVE PRICE OF U.S. CARS
IN TERMS OF FOREIGN CARS

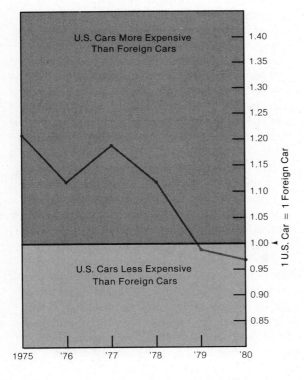

Source: Merrill Lynch, Pierce, Fenner, and Smith, Inc.

the relative price of coffee increases, people consume more tea; when beef prices rise, the consumption of poultry and fish products increases. There is no single recipe for producing a cake, a bushel of wheat, a car, comfort, recreation, or happiness. Increases in relative prices motivate consumers to search out substitutes.

PROPERTY RIGHTS

Relative prices provide information to buyers and sellers on what goods are cheap and what goods are expensive. Substitutions depend on relative prices. The manner in which buyers and sellers act on relative-price information depends on **property rights.**

Property rights are the rights of an owner to use and exchange property.

Collective Ownership

There are different forms of ownership of property. In some societies, the bulk of property (capital, land, houses, etc.) is owned by the state. In the Soviet Union, virtually all plants, equipment, inventories, apartments, homes, and land are owned by the state. The state has rights to use and exchange the property that it owns. Individuals are limited in the property they are allowed to own; they may own a few head of livestock, a private home in some circumstances, a private car, a TV, and so on. In a **socialist society,** individuals have proscribed rights to use and exchange the property they own.

A socialist society is characterized by collective ownership of property and government allocation of resources.

Private Ownership

Unlike in the Soviet Union with its extensive system of state ownership, in a **capitalist society,** the bulk of property is owned by private individuals.

A capitalist society is characterized by private ownership of property and by market allocation of resources.

⌗ **Example 1**

AT&T's Picturephone

American Telephone and Telegraph (AT&T) offers a picturephone service to customers. A picturephone is a closed-circuit system where callers in different locations can view each other on a monitor as they talk to one another. Picturephone users are charged from $150 to $395 per hour. Only two customers have their own picturephone studios, but AT&T has picturephone facilities in 13 major U.S. cities. The number of picturephone customers is quite limited despite its attractive features. Why? One reason is that picturephone substitutes primarily for business travel. Rather than traveling to meet with customers, picturephone users can substitute picturephone communication. At current rates picturephone is regarded by business as having a high price relative to travel costs. If these rates were kept constant while travel costs rose, the relative price of the picturephone would fall, and video meetings would be substituted for business travel. ⌗

Source: "Picturephone Pricing Riles AT&T Rival," *Wall Street Journal,* August 28, 1980.

These two features of capitalism are intertwined. There is no such thing as a *pure* capitalist economy in which *all* property is owned privately and in which all allocation is done through the market. In the United States, local, state, and federal governments own trillions of dollars of property.

In a society where property rights are vested in private individuals, how will they exercise their property rights to solve the what, how, and for-whom problems?

The individual owner of private property (whether it be land, a house, a horse, a truck, a wheat crop, or a can of peaches) has the legal freedom (the right) to sell that property at terms mutually agreed upon between the buyer and the seller. Normally, when property is sold, the buyer and seller agree on a dollar price. In some cases, there is an exchange of property on a barter basis; for example, a high-grade stereo may be *bartered* (traded) for a low-grade car. Instead of a dollar price, the price of the car is the stereo, and the price of the stereo is the car.

The legal system protects private-property rights. It protects private property from theft, damage, and unauthorized use and defines where property rights reside. The legal system generally places some restriction on property rights. Private owners of property may not be allowed to use their property in such a manner as to inflict damage on others. For example, the owner of farmland should not be allowed to use dangerous pesticides that may poison the community's water supply; the owner of an oil tanker should not be allowed to dump excess fuel oil near beaches (see Example 2).

Unless such restrictions apply, private property gives the owner the right to use the property to the owner's best advantage and to sell the property at the best price possible. The actions of the owners of private property will be guided by relative prices. The private owner of an oil refinery will use the relative prices of gasoline, fuel oils, and kerosene to determine how much of each petroleum product to refine and will look at the relative prices of imported and domestic crude oil to determine whether to use domestic or imported crude.

The private owner of labor (that is, the individual worker) will look at the relative wage rates in different occupations to determine where to seek employment. The private owner of farmland will look at the relative prices of agricultural products to determine what mix of crops to plant.

Private owners of property are motivated to obtain the best deal possible for themselves; they are motivated by self-interest. Legal protection of private-property rights insures that owners will reap the benefits of decisions that benefit their self-interest and will suffer the consequences of decisions that don't benefit their self-interest.

THE WORKING OF THE PRICE SYSTEM

An economy consists of millions of consumers and hundreds of thousands of enterprises, and virtually every member of society owns some labor,

Restrictions on Property Rights

Complete freedom to exercise private-property rights does not exist in any society. Complete freedom could not work. Private property cannot be used in such a way as to injure a neighbor or harm the community. The injured party has the right to petition the legal system to prevent an owner from exercising property rights in this way and to seek compensation for the damage inflicted.

In addition to this commonsense limitation on property rights, there are numerous examples of limitations on private-property rights. Most American cities have zoning laws that restrict the uses to which land can be put. The owner of land in a part of town zoned for residential use only cannot

build a factory. Automobile manufacturers are subject to limitations on the exercise of their property rights. They cannot use their plant and equipment to produce any type of car they (or the public) may want; instead, they must satisfy federal safety regulations, mileage standards, and pollution-emission standards.

There are limitations on the use of labor. In the United States, workers are prohibited from selling their labor at less than the minimum wage in covered occupations. A person cannot sell work as a plumber, electrician, pharmacist, barber, dentist, or attorney without first obtaining a license from the state. ⊠

---

land, or capital resources. Each participant makes economic decisions to promote his or her self-interest. What coordinates the decisions of all these people and businesses? What prevents the economy from collapsing when all these decisions clash? If all participants are looking out for themselves, will not the end result be chaos? Is it not necessary to have someone or something in charge?

The Invisible Hand

Adam Smith describes how the price system solves economic problems efficiently without conscious direction:

> Every individual endeavors to employ his capital so that its produce may be of greatest value. He generally neither intends to promote the public interest, nor knows how much he is promoting it. He intends only his own security, only his own gain. And he is led by an *invisible hand* to promote an end which was no part of his intention. By pursuing his own interest he frequently promotes that of society more effectively than when he really intends to promote it.[2]

The invisible hand works through the **price system.** A modern economy produces millions of commodities and services, each of which has a

2. Adam Smith, *The Wealth of Nations,* ed. Edwin Cannon (New York: Modern Library, 1937), p. 423.

money price. These millions of money prices form millions of relative prices that inform buyers and sellers what goods are cheap and what goods are expensive.

> The **price system** is the entire set of millions of relative prices that provides information to buyers and sellers.

The principal function of the price system is to provide information in an efficient fashion to participants in the economy. Each participant will specialize in price information that is personally relevant. The worker will specialize in prices of those things that affect his or her well-being: wage rates in different occupations, relative prices of various consumer goods, interest rates on home mortgages. The steel-mill manager will specialize in relative prices of inputs used in the mill and in the prices of finished steel products. The investor will specialize in the relative prices of stocks, bonds, and real estate.

No *single person need know all prices to function in daily economic life.* People and enterprises need to know only the prices of those things that are significant to them.

Equilibrium

Each participant makes buying and selling decisions on the basis of relative prices. The family decides how to spend its income; the worker decides where and how much to work; the factory manager decides what inputs to use and what outputs to produce. Insofar as all these decisions on what to buy and sell are being made individually in isolation, what is to guarantee that there will be enough steel, bananas, foreign cars, domestic help, steel workers, copper, lumber for homes? What is to insure that there will not be too much of one good and too little of another? Is Adam Smith's invisible hand powerful enough to prevent shortage and surplus?

Consider what would happen if U.S. automobile producers, acting on the price information in which they specialize, produce more cars than buyers want to buy *at the price asked by the automobile producers*. The automobile manufacturers will be made aware of this fact, not by a directive from the government, but by the simple fact that excess inventories of unsold cars will pile up. Dealers must pay their bills and cannot live from unsold inventories; therefore, they must sell the cars at lower prices. As the money price of cars falls, its relative price tends to fall, and customers begin to substitute automobiles for European vacations, home computers, or a remodeled kitchen. The decline in the relative price of automobiles signals automobile manufacturers to produce fewer cars. Eventually, a balance between the number of cars people are prepared to buy (the demand) and the number offered for sale (the supply) will be struck, and the price at which the balance is struck is called an **equilibrium price.**

> The **equilibrium price** of a good or service is that price at which the amount of the good people are prepared to buy equals the amount offered for sale.

The economy's search for equilibria through changing relative prices is not limited to a single market. The search takes place in all competitive markets simultaneously. If too much is produced, the relative price will fall; if too little is produced, the relative price will rise. As relative prices change, so do buying and selling decisions, and these changes bring markets into equilibrium. The economy is in *general equilibrium* when all markets have achieved equilibrium prices. The mechanics of equilibrium of supply and demand are discussed in Chapter 4.

Checks and Balances

The functioning of the price system is analogous to the system of checks and balances at work in an *ecological system* (the pattern of relationships between plants, animals, and their environment). These checks and balances prevent one species of plant or animal from overrunning the entire area and, in the end, extinguishing itself. Relative prices provide the checks and balances in the economic system. If one product is in oversupply, its relative price will fall; more will be purchased and less will be offered for sale. If one product is in short supply, its relative price will rise; less will be purchased and more will be offered for sale.

Just as human beings can upset nature's delicate balance, the general equilibrium of prices can be upset by interference. For example, governments can regulate and freeze prices or producer organizations may manipulate prices. When are such interventions warranted? When do they do more harm than good? Examples will be studied later in this text.

How, What, and For Whom

The price system solves the *what, how,* and *for whom* problems without conscious direction. No single participant in the economy needs to see the big picture; each participant need only know the relative prices of the goods and services of immediate interest to that person. No single person or governmental organization is required to be concerned about the economy as a whole. The millions of individual economic decisions made daily are coordinated by the price system.

Consider an economy in which all property is privately owned; property rights are vested with the owners of the property; there are no imports or exports; there is no intervention in the setting of prices. Each individual owns certain quantities of resources—land, labor, capital—that are sold or rented to business firms that produce the goods and services people want. Private-property rights are exercised; everything is sold at a price agreeable to the buyer and seller.

What is produced in the economy is determined by *dollar votes* cast by consumers for different goods and services. When consumers choose to buy a particular good or service, they are casting a dollar vote, which communicates their demand for that good or service. If many dollar votes are cast for a particular good, this means that buyers are willing to pay a high relative price for the good. Producers will exercise their property rights to produce a good with a high relative price. If few dollar votes are cast for another commodity, producers will have little incentive to produce that commodity. If consumers shift their dollar votes, producers will shift their production as well. Relative prices signal what actions to take. Relative prices signal to buyers what, where, and when to substitute and signal to producers what to produce.

The *what* problem is solved through the exercise of *consumer sovereignty* in a capitalist system. Consumers, in casting their dollar votes, determine what will be produced. If no dollar votes are cast for a particular product, it will not be produced. If enough dollar votes are cast for a product, it will be produced.

How goods are produced is determined by business firms who seek to utilize their land, labor, and capital resources as economically as possible. Business firms produce those outputs that receive high dollar votes by combining resources in the least costly way. Business firms follow the principle of substitution. If the relative price of land is increased, farmers will use less land and more tractors and labor to work the land more intensively. If the relative price of farm labor increases, farmers will use less labor and more tractors and land. If the relative price of business travel rises, businesses will travel less and use more long-distance telephoning. If the relative price of long-distance calls increases, businesses will telephone less and use more business travel. If business firms fail to reduce their costs through the use of the best available techniques and the best combination of the factors of production, the competition of other firms will drive them out of business.

For whom is determined by the dollar values the market assigns to resources owned by each separate household in the economy. The distribution of income between rich and poor reflects the prices paid for each resource and the distribution of ownership claims to scarce labor, land, and capital. People who own large quantities of land or capital will have a correspondingly large claim on the goods and services produced by the economy; those who are fortunate enough to provide high-priced labor services (doctors, lawyers, gifted athletes) will similarly receive a large share of the total output. At the other extreme, the poor are those who own few resources and furnish low-priced labor services to the market.

THE CIRCULAR FLOW OF ECONOMIC ACTIVITY

The price system, general equilibrium, the invisible hand, and market allocation are all difficult concepts to visualize. The **circular-flow diagram** is designed to illustrate how all these output and input decisions involving millions of consumers, hundreds of thousands of producers, and millions of owners of resources fit together.

*The **circular-flow diagram** summarizes the flows of goods and services from producers to households and the flows of the factors of production from households to business firms.*

Economic activity is circular. Consumers buy goods with the incomes they earn by furnishing labor, land, and capital to the business firms that produce the goods they buy. The dollars that households spend come back to them in the form of income from selling productive factors.

The circular-flow diagram in Figure 2 illustrates the circular flow of economic activity. The flows from households to firms and from firms to households are regulated by two markets: the market for goods and services and the market for the factors of production. The circular-flow diagram consists of two circles. The outer circle shows the *physical flows* of goods and services and of productive factors. The inner circle shows the *flows of money expenditures* on goods and services and on productive factors. The physical flows and the money flows go in opposite directions. When households buy goods and services, physical goods flow to the households, but the sales receipts flow to the business sector. When workers supply labor to business firms, productive factors flow to the business sector, but the wage income flows to the household sector.

For every physical flow in the economy, there is a corresponding financial transaction. To obtain consumer goods, the consumer must pay for

Figure 2
The Circular Flow of Economic Activity

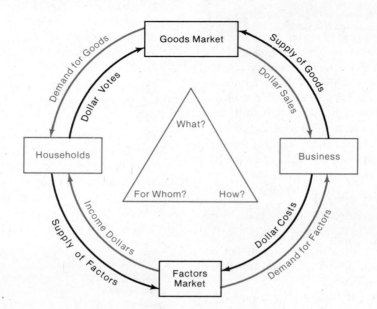

Economic activity is circular. The outside circle describes the flow of physical goods and services and productive factors through the system: business furnishes goods to households who furnish land, labor, and capital to business. The inside circle describes the flow of dollars: households provide dollar sales to business, whose costs become incomes to households. These circles flow in different directions. The triangle gives a pictoral representation of the relationship of the circular flow to the solution to the *what, how,* and *for whom* questions.

---

them. When firms deliver products, they receive sales revenues. When businesses hire labor or rent land, they must pay for them. When individuals supply labor, they receive wages.

There are two pairs of supply and demand transactions in the circular flow: 1) The supply and demand for consumer goods are mediated by the market for goods and services. 2) The supply and demand for factors of production are mediated by the market for the factors of production (see Example 3).

The price system coordinates supplies and demands and insures that they match. Shortages of goods or of factors of production cause relative prices to rise; surpluses cause relative prices to fall. The predictable responses of consumers and producers to changes in relative prices are called the *laws of supply and demand*. Chapter 4 is devoted to the explanation of these laws.

SPECIALIZATION

Suppose a sailor were stranded on a desert island with no other human beings around—a modern Robinson Crusoe. While the sailor would constantly have to make decisions about whether to make fish nets or fish hooks or whether to sleep or break coconuts, the economy of the desert island would lack many features of a modern economic system. The sailor would not be *specialized;* he would have to be a jack-of-all-trades. His consumption would have to be perfectly tailored to his production. Moreover, the sailor would not use *money*. He would still have to solve the problems of *what* and *how*. The *for whom* problem would be easy. Everything he produced would be for himself. He would have to solve *what* and *how* without explicit relative prices, property rights, or markets.

The Circular Flow as an Abstraction

The circular-flow diagram abstracts from many real-world considerations. The economy consists of more than goods, factors of production, and dollars flowing between households and businesses. The circular-flow diagram is a simplification of the real world, but it is a useful one. If you are traveling from Los Angeles to New York, you would want a road map that shows only the major interstate highways. Maps of smaller highways would not be of interest to you. The things left out of the circular flow are like the things left out of the map of the interstate highway system.

Government is left out of the circular-flow diagram. To a certain extent, government is like a business firm that provides services to the public like highways, roads, and public education in return for tax dollars. The flow of government services and tax dollars differs from other flows in several respects. There is usually no "market test" of the government service because the public typically does not have the opportunity to reject or buy the government service. Moreover, the government does not typically face competition from other business firms. The government therefore may not be forced to use the most cost-effective methods to produce its services. Government may therefore solve the how problem differently from private firms.

Markets between firms are also abstracted out of the circular-flow diagram. It is true that the ultimate purpose of the economy is to deliver goods and services to households, and the circular flow does capture these movements. There are, however, a large number of transactions among firms that take place within the business sector. The steel industry supplies steel to the auto industry; the coal industry provides coal to electric power utilities; the lumber industry provides lumber to the construction industry. The economy consists of goods and services in various stages of production or preparation. The goods that are used within the business sector are called *intermediate goods*. They are important because how these intermediate goods are used will determine whether the economy is on its production-possibilities frontier.

The circular-flow diagram assumes a matching of what businesses *as a whole* want to sell with what consumers *as a whole* want to buy. We have shown that the price system balances the supplies and demands for individual products, but can it do this in the aggregate? This is one of the most important issues in the study of macroeconomics.

✕

In the modern economy, it is somewhat unsettling to think about the degree to which people are specialized. The consumption of a typical household consists of thousands of articles; yet the principal breadwinner of the household may do nothing but align suspension components on an automobile production line. In short, everyone in our economy (except hermits) is dependent on the efforts of others. We produce one or two things; we consume many things.

Specialization obviously gives rise to exchange. Indeed, the exchange of one thing for another thing is the reverse side of the coin of specialization. If people consumed only those things that they produced, there would be no trade with anybody else and there would be no need for money. Money, trade, exchange, and specialization are all characteristics of a complicated economy.

Increased productivity was defined in Chapter 2 as the production of more output from the same amount of productive resources. We noted that Adam Smith began the *Wealth of Nations* with the observation that specialization is a basic source of productivity improvements. The reorganization of an acre of land, a tractor, and a hired hand to produce 75 bushels rather than the 50 bushels previously produced is a productivity advance. If freight transportation is organized so that trucks are utilized on return trips (rather than coming back empty), truck/driver combinations can haul more goods, and their productivity increases. In short, improving productivity is getting more from what's available. Specialization raises the productivity of the economy as well as the incomes of the individuals owning the resources themselves in two ways: first, resources are allocated to their best occupation or usage; second, the division of labor exploits economies of large-scale production.

Here are some examples:

1.   A high level of intelligence is required to become a good lawyer or a good surgeon. It is better for intelligent people with good verbal skills to become lawyers and those with quick hands to become surgeons than vice versa. It is likewise better for those people who are talkative to be disk jockeys or sales representatives while silent, introverted people are better off in occupations such as computer programming, farming, or automobile repairing that do not require outgoing personalities.

2.   Corn requires more moisture than wheat. It is better to produce wheat in Kansas's relatively dry farmland and to use Iowa's relatively wet farmland for corn. More wheat and corn can be grown if Kansas produces wheat and if Iowa produces corn than if both states produce both products.

Specialization gives rise to exchange. Lawyers must hire surgeons; surgeons must hire lawyers. Kansas and Iowa exchange wheat and corn.

Specialization means that people will produce more of particular goods than they consume and that these "surpluses" will be exchanged for the goods that they want.

The Law of Comparative Advantage

One reason for specialization is that people, land, and capital all come in different varieties. Some people are agile seven-footers, others are small and slow; some are fast-talkers, others scarcely utter a word. Some people take easily to math and computers; others are frightened by numbers and technology. Some people have quick hands; others are clumsy. Some land is moist; other land is dry. Some land is hilly; other land is flat. Some land is covered with forests; other land is populated only with mesquite bushes. Capital is different too. Some machines can move large quantities of earth; others can lift heavy loads; others can perform precision metal work; others can heat metals to high temperatures.

Because the factors of production have different characteristics and qualities, specialization offers opportunities for productivity advances.

Economists like to refer to the best employment of a resource as its *comparative advantage*. The agile seven-footer has a comparative advantage in basketball; the fast-talker can become a sales representative; the math whiz can become a computer specialist; the dextrous person might have a comparative advantage in operating a complicated machine tool. Land with high moisture content is best used in corn production; land with a relatively low moisture content is best used in wheat production. Earth-moving machinery can be used in road building: heavy-lifting equipment can be used in construction; precision tools can be used in aircraft manufacturing. Each resource has some comparative advantage.

The price system ensures that the factors of production will be used to exploit their special characteristics and skills. The Kansas farmer will make more money by growing wheat; the Iowa farmer will make more money growing corn. The agile seven-footer will make more money playing professional basketball than professional soccer. The extroverted fast-talker will earn more money as a sales representative than as a computer programmer. The person with quick hands will make more money as a surgeon than as a lawyer. The owner of the earth-moving equipment will make more money using it in roadbuilding; the owner of the heavy-lifting equipment will earn more by using it in construction. All owners of labor, land, and capital resources have to do is to use their resources in such a way as to make the most money possible, and specialization will follow naturally.

Is this an oversimplification? What about the people who have both quick minds and quick hands, the math whiz with good verbal skills, the equipment that can move large amounts of earth and lift heavy weights, or the farm land that appears suited to growing both wheat and corn? Are not some people poor at just about everything in the sense that at every task they are less efficient than other people?

In 1817, the English economist, David Ricardo, who made millions of dollars from shrewd investments, formulated the **law of comparative advantage.**

*The **law of comparative advantage** states that it is better for people to specialize in those* *activities in which their advantage over other people is greatest or in which their disadvantages compared to others are the smallest.*

The easiest way to see this principle at work is to examine two extreme cases. Suppose that you can do any and every job better than anyone else. What would you as such a superior person do? You would not want to be a jack-of-all-trades because it is likely that your *margin* of superiority will be greater in one occupation than in another. The job in which your margin of superiority over others is *the greatest* is the job you will do because it will give you the highest income.

Now examine the other extreme. Suppose there is no person in the community to whom you are superior in *any job;* you are less productive than any other person in the society in every occupation. What would you do in such an unfortunate situation? The job in which your disadvantage compared to others is the smallest would be the job that maximizes your income.

A mediocre computer programmer could possibly be the best clerk in the local supermarket. The clerks in the local supermarket may not be able to stock shelves and work a cash register as well as the computer programmer, but they have a *comparative advantage* in that occupation. An attorney may be the fastest typist in town, yet the attorney is better off preparing deeds than typing deeds. An engineering major may have verbal skills that exceed those of an English major, but his or her comparative advantage is in engineering (see Example 4).

A simple numerical example of comparative advantage will illustrate the principle in a more concrete fashion. Imagine two people, Jack and Jill, both of whom can mow lawns and type. We assume that Jack and Jill do not really care whether they type or mow lawns. Jack can type 20 pages a day or mow 2 lawns a day. Jill, on the other hand, can type 50 pages a day or mow 8 lawns a day (see Table 2). Jill is clearly more efficient in absolute terms at both tasks than Jack; she can type 250 percent ($50 \div 20$) as fast and can mow lawns 400 percent ($8 \div 2$) as fast as Jack.

Now what should Jack and Jill do? To answer this question, we must first determine the (rela-

Table 2
Computing Comparative Advantage

	Lawns per Day	Pages per Day	Opportunity Cost of Lawn Mowing (in pages)
Jack	2	20	10 pages (20 ÷ 2)
Jill	8	50	6.25 pages (50 ÷ 8)

This table illustrates the law of comparative advantage. Jill is more efficient than Jack in both typing and mowing. She can type 250 percent faster than Jack, but she can mow 400 percent faster. Jill has an absolute advantage in both lawn mowing and typing but a comparative advantage in lawn mowing. Jill will specialize in lawn mowing; Jack will specialize in typing. Note that both Jack and Jill follow the rule of specializing in that activity that has the lowest opportunity cost. Jack's opportunity cost of mowing is 10 pages; Jill's equals 6.25 pages.

tive) prices of mowing lawns and typing. Suppose typing earns $2 a page and mowing lawns pays $16 per lawn. If Jack mows lawns all day, his income would be $32 (= $16 × 2 lawns) per day; typing would earn Jack $40 (= $2 × 20 pages) per day. Thus Jack would wish to type. Jill, on the other hand, could earn $128 mowing lawns (= $16 × 8 lawns) or $100 typing ($2 × 50 pages). Thus Jill would prefer to mow lawns.

Jill has a comparative advantage in mowing lawns; Jack has a comparative advantage in typing. While Jill is better than Jack in all activities, her *greatest* advantage over Jack is in mowing lawns (she is 4 times as fast). In typing, Jill is only 2.5 times as fast. Jack's *least* disadvantage is in typing; thus Jack prefers to be a typist.

Notice that Jill will earn $128 daily mowing lawns and Jack will earn $40 a day typing. Jill's superior productivity is reflected in higher earnings. Notice that Jack in effect competes with Jill in typing by charging a lower price per unit of his time. If there are 8 hours to the work day, Jill is earning a wage of $16 per hour ($16 = $128 ÷ 8 hours) and Jack is earning only $5 an hour ($5 = $40 ÷ 8 hours). Thus Jill's hourly wage is slightly more than 3 times Jack's hourly wage. Jack's lower rate allows him to compete with Jill in typing: she is 2.5 times as efficient as a typist, but her wage is more than 3 times as high—which in the marketplace offsets her absolute advantage in typing.

Applications of the Law of Comparative Advantage

The law of comparative advantage explains patterns of specialization both within a country and among countries. It also explains why goods will not always be produced by the "best" producer. The fastest typist may be a lawyer, the best checkout clerk may be a skilled computer programmer.

The law of comparative advantage explains a wide variety of specialization patterns that would otherwise be difficult to explain. Here are three examples.

1. *GRE Exams:* The GRE (Graduate Record Exam) is an examination for students who wish to enter graduate school. It consists of two parts: a verbal exam to test verbal ability and a quantitative exam to test math ability. During the 1975–1980 period, physics majors recorded the higher scores on the verbal exam—higher than speech majors. Why would the student who appears to be better qualified for graduate study in speech choose a career in physics?

The law of comparative advantage explains this puzzling phenomenon: Although physics majors on average have an *absolute advantage* in both physics and English (they score higher on both the verbal and quantitative GREs), they have a strong *comparative advantage* in physics. On the GRE, they score 19 percent higher than speech majors on the verbal exam, but they score 55 percent higher than speech majors on the quantitative exam. The physics major is like Jill in our numerical example; both the physics major and Jill are correct in their choice of specialization.

2. *Tobacco Growing in New England:* New England is a region poorly suited to agriculture. It is hilly, rocky, heavily wooded, and cold in the winter. New England seems an unlikely place for tobacco production, which requires a warm climate and rich, well-drained soil. Yet one of the agricultural crops of Massachusetts and Connecticut is tobacco. Why is tobacco grown in New England? Is the law of comparative advantage being violated?

Even California land would be better suited to tobacco production; an acre of land in California

---

The law of comparative advantage is nothing more than the principle that people should engage in those activities where their opportunity costs are lower than others (see Table 2).

To mow one lawn, Jack must sacrifice 10 pages of typing. Jack's opportunity cost of lawns equals 10 pages of typing. To mow one lawn, Jill must sacrifice 6.25 pages (50 ÷ 8). Jill mows lawns because her opportunity cost of lawn mowing is lower than Jack's.

Economies of Large-Scale Production

If all people were the same, if all land were identical, and if all capital were the same, would there still be specialization? Even if all people in an automobile-manufacturing plant were identical, it would still be better to have one person install the engine, another bolt down the engine, and so on in an assembly line. Individuals who focus on one task can learn their jobs better and don't waste time switching from job to job. Even if all agricultural land were identical, it would still be better to plant one farm with corn, another with wheat, and so on, than to plant smaller strips of corn and wheat on single farms because of the economies of large-scale production.

Money

Money is necessary because people are specialized and do not produce everything they need without any surpluses. Money is useful in an *exchange economy*—that is, an economy where people are specialized—because it reduces the cost of transacting with others. *Barter* is a system of exchange where products are exchanged for other products rather than for money. In barter, for example, it would be necessary for barefoot bakers to meet or exchange with hungry shoemakers. In other words, a successful barter deal requires that the two traders have matching wants. In barter, successful trades require a double coincidence of wants.

would yield much more tobacco than in New England. But New England produces tobacco, while California does not. The law of comparative advantage provides the explanation. Although California has an absolute advantage in tobacco production over New England, it has a much larger absolute advantage in alternative uses of the land (growing commercial vegetables and fruits). The alternative uses of rural New England land are limited (it is difficult to grow other crops; the land is not suited to commercial development); therefore, New England has a comparative advantage in tobacco. Stated in terms of opportunity costs: tobacco is grown in rural New England because the opportunity cost is relatively low.

3. The *Manufacture of Singer Sewing Machines in Taiwan:* The Singer Company, a U.S. company established by Isaac Singer in 1851, now manufactures many of its sewing machines in Taiwan—even though American Singer employees can produce more sewing machines per hour than their Asian counterparts. Why then did Singer shift sewing-machine manufacturing to Asia? The answer is that the American worker has a much larger productivity advantage in high-technology manufacturing, such as high-speed computers and jet aircraft. The American Singer worker may be 10 percent more productive than a Taiwanese counterpart, while the American IBM employee may be, say, 50 percent more productive than the Singer employee. Because Taiwan, on the other hand, lacks the capital resources and know-how to produce high-technology computers, the productivity of a Taiwanese worker in computer manufacturing would be less than in sewing-machine manufacturing. As in the numerical example, the American worker's superior productivity would be reflected in higher earnings, and the Taiwanese worker would compete by working at lower wages, reflecting lower productivity. The opportunity cost of an American worker producing sewing machines is high; the opportunity cost of a Taiwanese worker producing sewing machines is low.

Money is useful precisely because double coincidences of wants are rare. Money enables any person to trade with anyone else in a complicated economy. The form money takes differs from society to society. Money in a simple society will be quite different from money in a complicated society. In simple societies, things like fish hooks, sharks' teeth, beads, or cows have been used as money. In modern societies, money is issued and regulated by government, and money may (gold coins) or may not (paper money) have an intrinsic value of its own.

Money is anything that is widely accepted in exchange for goods and services and that can be used for paying debts and taxes.

PROVIDING FOR THE FUTURE

Let us return to the shipwrecked sailor. Although he would not specialize, he would at least share a common problem with modern economies: how to provide for the future. In the sailor's case, he would be confronted with a clear choice of eating more today versus eating more tomorrow. If the water were clear, he could wade out and, with patient effort, catch fish with his bare hands. He may be successful in catching enough fish to survive. However, if the sailor were to devote a few days to making a fishing net from vines, he would be able to increase his catch and reduce his effort—but at the sacrifice of having less to eat for three days. Making a net to catch the fish is an example of **roundabout production** or the production of **intermediate goods.**

Roundabout Production

Roundabout production is the production of goods that do not immediately meet consumption needs. Goods that are used to produce other goods are called intermediate goods.

There can be many stages of roundabout production. The good can be used directly to produce consumer goods. It can produce a good that produces another good that assists in the production of consumer goods, and so on.

Roundabout production means that producers are dependent on things produced in the past for the things that are produced today. In modern economies, the degree of roundabout production is striking. The wheat harvested today requires a harvesting machine produced in the past; the bread produced today is baked in ovens that were produced in the past; the shirt produced today is manufactured on a sewing machine produced in the past.

The responsibility for producing the capital goods that enable society to produce more in the future is left to the price system. Households set aside some of their income in the form of savings. Households save so that they can consume more tomorrow. They accumulate funds in savings accounts and retirement programs; they buy stocks, bonds, and life-insurance policies. How do their savings find their way into productive investments? Businesses borrow from financial institutions, sell bonds, and issue stock; they use the proceeds to build plants, to buy capital equipment, and to build up their inventories.

Interest Rates

Societies must refrain from consumption today to build capital goods. Households must sacrifice consumption today to save, but by saving the household will increase its consumption in the future. The sacrifice of current consumption is the cost of saving. The benefit of saving is that **interest** will be earned on savings. The higher the interest rate, the greater the inducement to save. The rate of interest acts not only as an inducement to save; it also signals to businesses whether they should borrow for investment.

Interest is the price of credit, usually a percentage of the amount borrowed.

Like any other price, the interest rate provides a *balance*—in this case balancing the amount people are willing to save with the amount of savings businesses want to borrow for investment. If the interest rate is low, businesses will clamor for the savings of individuals because they find it

cheap to add to their capital stock. However, when the interest rate is low, few people will be willing to save. The reverse is true at high interest rates. Few businesses will want to invest, but households will be quite willing to save.

The interest rate balances the amount of savings offered by households with the amount of investment businesses wish to undertake. The price system, operating through the interest rate, solves the what problem of how to balance present and future consumption.

How interest rates are determined is much more complicated than this simplified story. Interest rate determination will be examined in later chapters.

Nominal and Real Rates of Interest

So far we have been discussing the **nominal rate of interest**.

*The **nominal rate of interest** is the rate of interest expressed in terms of today's dollars.*

At a nominal interest rate of 10 percent, $100 not spent today will yield $110 that can be spent one year from today. A nominal interest rate of 5 percent means that $100 not spent today will yield only $105 that can be spent one year from today. Because lenders and borrowers are interested in how many goods and services can be purchased with money to be received in the future, they will consider both nominal interest rates and the *general rate of change of money prices*.

Suppose that the nominal rate of interest is 10 percent and that prices are rising at 5 percent per year. The *rate of inflation* measures the rate of increase in prices in general (a more exact definition of inflation will be provided in later chapters). In this case, a person lending $100 now will have $110 in one year. But $110 in one year buys only $105 worth of tomorrow's goods (approximately) because of generally rising prices (inflation). Because the $100 loaned today in reality buys only $105 worth of tomorrow's goods, the **real rate of interest** is 5 percent.

*The **real rate of interest** equals the nominal rate of interest minus the annual rate of inflation.*

It is important to distinguish between the *actual* real interest rate that is earned over a particular year and the real interest rate that is anticipated. No one knows for sure in advance what the rate of inflation will be. Therefore, no one will know in advance what the real rate of interest will be. When people borrow or lend money, they must make their best estimate of what the real rate of interest will be.

Logic tells us the general relationship between nominal interest rates and the rate of inflation. As the rate of inflation increases, people will be less willing to save at prevailing interest rates because rising prices reduce the purchasing power of tomorrow's income. Borrowers, on the other hand, will be more anxious to borrow as inflation increases. These two forces tend to drive up nominal interest rates as the rate of inflation increases.

Decisions about providing for the future are guided by what people expect the *real* rate of interest to be in the immediate future. If the real interest rate is expected to be high, people will be more willing to refrain from consumption now; they will save for the future. If the real interest rate is expected to be low, businesses will be anxious to borrow for investment purposes. Because the future is uncertain (it is difficult to know what the inflation rate will be), lenders and borrowers may guess wrong about the real rate of interest, but it nevertheless serves as a guide to saving and investment decisions.

Throughout much of the 1970s, real interest rates were negative (see Figure 3). A negative real rate of interest means that the annual inflation rate is greater than the nominal interest rate. It would not be a good idea to put money into a savings account at 6 percent interest when the annual inflation rate is 10 percent if the purpose of saving is to consume more in the future. Saving under these circumstances actually reduces one's ability to purchase goods in the future. One would be better off buying now or borrowing. If the real interest rate is negative, one can borrow to buy homes, TV sets, computers, machinery, or automobiles at, say, 8 percent and then pay back the loan in dollars that are worth 10 percent less in

Figure 3
Nominal and Real Interest Rates, United States, 1960–1980

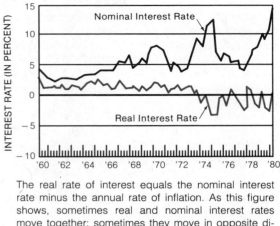

The real rate of interest equals the nominal interest rate minus the annual rate of inflation. As this figure shows, sometimes real and nominal interest rates move together; sometimes they move in opposite directions. Real interest rates can even be negative when the annual inflation rate exceeds the nominal interest rate.

Source: Mellon Bank.

one year's time, more than 20 percent less in two years' time, and so on.

LIMITS OF THE INVISIBLE HAND

This chapter has emphasized the virtues of resource allocation through the price system. The price system solves the problems of *what, how,* and *for whom* without centralized direction. It balances the actions of millions of consumers and thousands of producers, and it even solves the difficult problem of providing for the future. The price system has great strength, but it has weaknesses as well. These weaknesses must be examined to determine the costs and benefits of interfering with the workings of the price system.

Income Distribution

There is no guarantee that resource allocation through the price system will solve the *for whom* problem in such a way as to satisfy the ethical beliefs of members of society. Some people believe that income should be distributed fairly

---

The Price System at Work

This chapter has surveyed how the price system solves the what, how, and for-whom problems in a capitalistic economy. Each of the following examples illustrates the principle that through voluntary exchange, the price system can coordinate the activities of many millions of people without centralized direction.

There are 12 million people living in New York city, each of whom is concerned with an infinitesimally small part of getting that city's work done. Each person is concerned—for the most part—with making a living. Imagine the numbers of trucks, airplanes, and trains moving people and goods to the right places at the right times. The logistics of these movements that keep the city going and prevent everyone from starving are enormously complicated (think of New York's well-publicized garbage-removal problems). Yet no single person or bureaucracy is in charge of the department-for-making-sure-the-city-does-not-starve. The city works by the millions of decentralized decisions of individuals responding to their own cost-benefit calculations. The price system and supply-demand coordination works so well that no one loses any sleep over the terrifying prospect of complete breakdown—no one even gives it a thought.

This classic example also shows us how something that works smoothly often goes unnoticed. Adam Smith's term, the *invisible hand*, is an apt description.

Nobel prize-winning economist Milton Friedman relates the story called, "I, Pencil: My Family Tree as Told to Leonard E. Read," in which the pencil makes the startling announcement: *"not a single person . . . knows how to make me."* If one thinks about what it takes to make a pencil—the trees that produce the wood, the saws that fell the trees, the steel to make the saws, the engines to run the saws, the hemp to make the ropes that are necessary to tie down the logs, the training of loggers, the mining of graphite in Sri Lanka for the lead, the mining of zinc and copper for making the bit of metal holding the eraser, and the rape seed oil from the Dutch East Indies used in the eraser—it is clear that the pencil is correct. No one single person knows how to make a modern pencil. The decisions of the thousands upon thousands of people involved are coordinated through the price system; that all these activities have made it possible for you to go to the bookstore and buy a pencil for, say, a mere $0.25 boggles the mind. ✕

---

evenly; others believe that the gap between rich and poor should be large. Many believe that it is unfair for people to be rich just because they were lucky enough to inherit wealth or intelligence.

Economics can shed little light on what is a "good" or "fair" solution to the *for whom* problem, because such decisions require personal value judgments. Economics is broad enough to accommodate virtually all views on the subject of income distribution. Judgments about income distribution are in the realm of normative economics.

Nevertheless, positive economics can make a contribution to the question of income distribution. Economists can indicate what may happen to efficiency or economic growth if the income distribution is changed, but they cannot make any scientific statements about the desirability of the change in the income distribution.

The Role of Government

Another weakness of the price system is that it cannot supply certain goods—called *public goods*—that are necessary to society. Public goods include defense, the legal system, highways, and public education. In the case of private goods, there is an intimate link between costs and benefits: The one who buys a car enjoys the benefits of the car; the one who buys a loaf of bread eats that loaf. Public goods, on the other hand, are financed not by the dollar votes of consumers but by the imposition of taxes. In most cases, the benefits each individual derives from public goods will not be known. Moreover, it is difficult to prevent nonpayers from enjoying the benefits of public goods. Even if someone does not pay taxes, the national defense establishment protects that person from enemy attack just as well as it protects the payers.

The price system, therefore, breaks down in failing to provide public goods. If private individuals were left with the choice of buying and selling public goods, few public goods would be produced. Yet society must have public goods to survive.

Monopoly

The invisible hand may not function well when a single person or single group gains control over the supply of a particular commodity. What makes Adam Smith's invisible hand work so well is that individual buyers and sellers compete with one another; no single buyer or seller has control over the price. The problem with *monopoly*—a single seller with considerable control over the price—is that the monopolist can hold back the amount of goods, drive up the price, and enjoy large profits. While the monopolist would benefit from such actions, the buyer would not. Monopoly threatens the smooth functioning of the invisible hand described in this chapter.

Macroeconomic Instability

The invisible hand may solve the economic problem of scarcity but may provide a level of overall economic activity that is unstable. It is a historical fact that capitalist economies have been subject to fluctuations in output, employment, and prices—called *business cycles*—and that these fluctuations have been costly to capitalist societies.

The study of the causes of the instability of capitalism was pioneered by John Maynard Keynes during the Great Depression of the 1930s, and this theme remains a principal concern of macroeconomics.

This chapter has described in general terms how scarce resources are allocated by the price system and has explained the organization of property rights. Equilibrium prices are an invisible hand that coordinates the decisions of many different persons. The next chapter examines the detailed workings of supply and demand in an individual market and answers the questions: How is the equilibrium price set? What causes equilibrium prices to increase or decrease?

Summary

1. Relative prices guide the economic decisions of individuals and businesses. They signal to buyers and sellers what substitutions to make.

2. The principle of substitution states that no single good is irreplaceable. Users substitute one good for another in response to changes in relative prices.

3. Property can be owned by private persons, by the state, or by combinations of the two. In capitalist societies, property is owned primarily by private individuals, who are permitted to exercise property rights over the use and sale of their property subject to the restriction that such exercise does not injure other people. Socialist societies are characterized by collective ownership of property.

4. The private decisions of the millions of consumers and producers are coordinated by the price system. The "invisible hand" analogy, originated by Adam Smith in 1776, describes how a capitalist system can allow individuals to pursue their self-interest and yet provide an orderly, efficient economic system that functions without centralized direction. The price system balances supplies and demands for individual products. If too much of a product is produced, its relative price will fall. If too little of a product is produced, its relative price will rise. The balance of supply and demand is called an equilibrium. The what problem is solved by dollar votes. Consumers determine what will be produced. The how problem is solved by individual producers. Competition among producers will encourage them to combine resource inputs efficiently. The solution of the for-whom problem is determined by a) who owns productive resources and b) what the relative prices of resources are.

5. The circular-flow diagram summarizes the flows of goods and services from producers

to households and the flows of factors of production from households to producers.

6. Specialization is responsible for productivity improvements. Specialization occurs because of the differences among people, land, and capital and because of the economies of large-scale production. The law of comparative advantage states that the factors of production will specialize in those activities in which their advantage is greatest or in which their disadvantages are smallest. Money enables a person to trade with anyone else in a complicated economy. The most basic characteristic of money is that it is widely accepted in exchange.

7. The price system provides for the future by allowing people to compare costs now with benefits that will accrue in the future. The interest rate balances the amount of savings offered with the amount of investment businesses wish to undertake. Intertemporal choices are based upon real rates of interest rather than nominal rates of interest. The real interest rate equals the nominal interest rate minus the inflation rate.

8. The invisible hand can not solve the problems of income distribution, public goods, monopoly, or macroeconomic instability.

Key Terms

money price
relative price
principle of substitution
property rights
socialist society
capitalist society
price system
equilibrium price
circular-flow diagram
law of comparative advantage
money
roundabout production
intermediate goods
interest
nominal rate of interest
real rate of interest

Questions and Problems

1. Is the nominal interest rate a relative price or a money price? Is the real rate of interest a money price or a relative price? Discuss your answer.

2. "The principle of substitution states that virtually all goods have substitutes, but we all know that there are no substitutes for telephone service." Comment on this statement.

3. If you own an automobile, what property rights do you have? What restrictions are placed upon these property rights?

4. Explain why you can usually find the items you want at a grocery store without having ordered the goods in advance.

5. Assume that you have grown 50 watermelons in your backyard garden. You set up a stand alongside the highway and price them at $15 each. What do you think will happen and what will you do?

6. What determines your claim on the goods and services produced by the economy?

7. Why does your income represent someone else's costs, and why do your purchases represent someone else's sales?

8. Explain why there would be no exchange if there were no specialization, and why there would be no specialization if exchange were impossible.

9. Why is barter an inefficient means of exchange?

10. Explain why wheat is grown in Kansas while cotton is grown in Alabama.

11. Bill can prepare 50 hamburgers per hour and wait on 25 tables per hour. Mike can prepare 20 hamburgers per hour and wait on 15 tables per hour. If Bill and Mike were to open a hamburger stand, who would be the cook? Who the waiter? Would Bill do both?

12. Why would private industry find it difficult to organize national defense? How would they charge each citizen for national defense?

13. In 1974 consumer prices rose by 11 percent, and the interest rate on industrial bonds was 8.6 percent. What was the actual real interest rate?

4

The Mechanics of Supply and Demand

Chapter Preview

Chapter 3 described how capitalist economies solve the what, how, and for-whom problems by market allocation that is guided by the price system. Property is owned predominantly by private individuals who exercise private-property rights. The actions of millions of buyers and sellers are coordinated by an invisible hand. No single buyer or seller is required to know more than the prices of those things of immediate interest to that person. Each participant in the economy is motivated by self-interest. Relative prices signal to buyers and sellers what they should do. If relative prices of some goods are rising, other goods will be substituted by buyers; sellers will tend to offer more for sale. If too much of a good is produced, its

relative price will fall. If too little is produced, its relative price will rise. Through these changes in relative prices, the amounts of goods buyers are prepared to buy are brought into balance with the amounts of goods sellers are prepared to sell.

Chapter 3 provided a grand overview of how the price system works without getting into actual mechanics. This chapter will explain the workings of supply and demand and will define such terms as *demand, supply, shortage, surplus,* and *equilibrium* more exactly.

This chapter describes *how prices are determined by supply and demand*. There is a famous quip that if you teach a parrot the phrase "supply and demand," you will create a learned economist. This joke, while entertaining, does not do justice to the complexity and value of supply-and-demand analysis. An economist needs to know more than the parrot, just as the medical doctor must know more than the prescription: "Take two aspirin and call me in the morning."

The following statements (with certain details changed) were taken from two respected newspapers:

> Projections of supplies and demands reveal that there will be a large surplus of medical doctors by the end of the 1980s. The supply of M.D.s will exceed demand generally, but surpluses will be greatest in particular specialties.

> The state agriculture office reports that warm weather and sufficient moisture have produced a plentiful supply of lettuce this year. However, lettuce prices are not expected to drop because consumers usually increase their demand for lettuce when prices fall. The demand increase will offset the supply increase, so homemakers should not expect surpluses of lettuce this year.

Both of these statements may appear reasonable; they use the language of supply and demand. However, they are misleading because they confuse different supply and demand concepts; they are incorrect because they misuse the terms *supply* and *demand*.

WHAT IS A MARKET?

To develop the mechanics of supply and demand, we must narrow our vision to the study of how a *single market* works. In each **market,** buyers and sellers are guided by the price system in their buying and selling decisions.

*A **market** is an established arrangement by which buyers and sellers come together to exchange particular goods or services.*

Types of Markets

A retail store, a gas station, a farmers' market, real estate firms, the New York Stock Exchange (where stocks are bought and sold), Chicago commodity markets (where livestock, grains, and metals are traded), auctions of works of art, gold markets in London, Frankfurt, and Zurich, labor exchanges, university placement offices, and hundreds of other specialized arrangements are all markets. Markets are arrangements for bringing together buyers and sellers of a particular good or service. The New York Stock Exchange brings together by means of modern telecommunications the buyers and sellers of corporate stock. Sothebys auction in London brings together the sellers and buyers of rare works of art. The Rotterdam oil market brings together buyers and sellers of crude oil not under long-term contracts. The university placement office brings university graduates together with potential employers. The gas station brings together the buyers and sellers of gasoline. In some markets, the buyers and sellers confront each other face-to-face (roadside farm markets). In other markets, the buyer never sees the seller (the Chicago commodity markets).

Determinants of the Form of the Market

The actual form a particular market takes depends on the type of good or service being sold and on the costs of transporting the good from the point of production to the point of sale. Some markets are local (bringing together local buyers and sellers); others are national (bringing together the buyers and sellers in all parts of the nation); others are international (bringing together the buyers and sellers in all parts of the world). Real estate is traded in local markets; houses and buildings cannot be shipped from one place to another (except at great expense). College textbooks are usually exchanged in a national market. The New York Stock Exchange, the various gold exchanges, and the Chicago commodity exchanges are markets in which buyers and sellers from around the world participate.

The study of marketing arrangements is a subject area in which economics and business administration overlap. Both disciplines presume that markets develop in an orderly fashion and teach that the market form that eventually evolves will be the one that keeps the cost of delivery (or marketing cost) to a minimum.

Perfect Markets

The real world consists of an almost infinite variety of markets. This chapter deals with a very special type of market called a **perfect** (or **perfectly competitive**) **market.**

*A **perfect** (or **perfectly competitive**) **market** has the following characteristics: 1) The product's price is uniform throughout the market. 2) Buyers and sellers have perfect information about price and the product's quality. 3) There are a large number of buyers and sellers. 4) No single buyer or seller is large enough to change the price.*

The principal characteristic of a perfectly competitive market is that buyers and sellers face so much competition that no person or group has any control over the price.

The markets where most people buy and sell goods are not perfect. Buyers and sellers may not be perfectly informed about prices and qualities. Two homemakers pay different prices in adjacent grocery stores for the same national brand of cookies. Houses that are virtually identical sell at different prices. Chemically equivalent brand-name and generic drugs sell at different prices. Italy and West Germany pay different prices for the same grade of imported crude oil. Two secretaries with the same qualifications, responsibilities, and disposition in the same company earn different wages. AT&T, General Motors, and Saudi Arabia exercise some control over the prices they charge. Large buyers exercise some control over the prices they pay.

Many products, however, are exchanged in perfect markets. Stocks and bonds and commodities such as wheat, silver, copper, gold, foreign currencies, oats, pork bellies, soybeans, lumber, cotton, orange juice, cattle, cocoa, and platinum are bought and sold in perfect markets. Private investors, mutual funds, commercial banks, industrial buyers of commodities, and agricultural brokers participate in these markets. Although markets like the local grocery store, the dry cleaner, the gas station, the college placement office, or the roadside stand are not perfect, many of them function in a way that approximates perfect markets. In this respect, the behavior of perfect markets serves as a useful guide to the way many real-world markets function. The perfect market is a valuable starting point for examining economic behavior.

DEMAND

Economics is based upon the principle of *unlimited wants*. Collectively, we all want more than the economy can provide, and scarcity is the consequence of the mismatch between wants and the ability of the economy to meet these wants.

The term *wants* refers to the goods and services that consumers would claim if they were given away free. *The list of goods consumers "want" is quite different from the list of goods they **demand.*** What consumers are actually prepared to buy depends upon a variety of factors, which will be studied in this chapter.

*The **demand** for a good or service is the relationship between the amount of the good or service consumers are prepared to buy at a given price and the price of the good or service.*

The Law of Demand

A fundamental law of economics is the **law of demand.**

*The **law of demand** states that there is a negative (or inverse) relationship between the price of a good and quantity demanded, holding other factors constant.*

Thus, if prices are lowered, **quantity demanded** increases, if other factors are held constant. The importance of the *ceteris paribus* ("holding all other factors constant") restriction on the law of demand will become apparent in the course of this discussion.

*The **quantity demanded** is the amount of a good or service consumers are prepared to buy at a given price.*

The basic reason for the law of demand is that as the price of any product goes up, people will tend to find substitutes for that product. If the price of gasoline rises, drivers will cut back on less essential driving, and more people will take the bus, or walk, or ride their bicycles to work. If the price of tea rises, more people will drink coffee, or heavy tea drinkers may cut back one or two cups a day and instead buy a soft drink. The universal and natural tendency is for people who consume or use the goods to *substitute other goods or services* when the price of a good goes up. Higher prices discourage consumption.

When a price rises by enough some people may even stop consuming the good altogether. Thus as the price rises, the number of actual buyers may fall as some people *entirely* switch to other goods.

People also tend to buy less of a good as its price goes up because *they feel poorer*. If a person buys a new car every year for $5,000 (after trade-in), and the price rises to $9,000 (after trade-in), the person would need an extra $4,000 yearly income to maintain the old standard of living. The $4,000 increase in the price of the car is like a cut in income of $4,000.[1]

The law of demand shows that the everyday concept of *need* is not a very useful concept in economics. To ''need'' something implies that one cannot do without it. When the price of something changes, the law of demand says that quantity demanded will change. Since the word *need* implies an absolute necessity for something, this word is avoided whenever discussing demand.

The relationship between quantity demanded and price is called the *demand curve* or the *demand schedule*. The relationship is negative because of the law of demand. To avoid confusion, we shall henceforth talk about the *demand schedule* when the relationship is in tabular form and about the *demand curve* when the relationship is in graphical form.

The Demand Schedule

Table 1 shows a hypothetical demand schedule for corn. The buyers in the marketplace will demand 20 million bushels of corn per month at the price of $5 per bushel. Should the price of corn be lower—say, $4 per bushel—then the quantity demanded is higher. In this case, the quantity de-

---

1. It is preferable to raise the price of the car by $4000 than to reduce one's income by $4000, because the change in income cannot be avoided; the change in the price of the car can be avoided by spending money elsewhere on the next best alternative.

Table 1
Demand Schedule for Corn

	Price (dollars per bushel)	Quantity Demanded (millions of bushels per month)
a	5	20
b	4	25
c	3	30
d	2	40
e	1	50

manded at the lower price of $4 is 25 million bushels. By continuing to decrease the price, it is possible to induce or coax buyers to purchase more and more corn. Table 1 shows that at the price of $1, quantity demanded will be 50 million bushels. Notice that it is important to state the units of the measurement for both the price and the quantity. In this example, price is in dollars per bushel, and quantity is in millions of bushels per month. The time period, whether it be a minute, a day, a week, a month, or a year, must be specified before the demand schedule is meaningful.

The Demand Curve

The demand schedule of Table 1 can be portrayed graphically (Figure 1) as the demand curve. For demand curves, price is on the vertical axis and quantity demanded is on the horizontal axis. In this demand curve, prices are in dollars per bushel and the quantities are in millions of bushels per month. When price is $5, quantity demanded is 20 million bushels per month (point *a* in Figure 1). Point *b* corresponds to a price of $4 and a quantity of 25 million bushels. When price falls from $5 to $4, quantity demanded rises by 5 million bushels from 20 million to 25 million bushels. The remaining prices and quantities are graphed.

The curve drawn through the points *a* through *e*, labeled *D*, is the demand curve. The demand curve shows how quantity demanded responds to changes in price. Along the demand curve *D*, the price and the quantity are *negatively* related. This means the curve is downward-sloping.

Figure 1
The Demand Curve for Corn

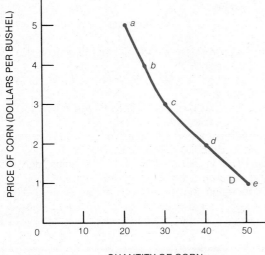

Table 1 describes how the quantity of corn demanded responds to the prices of corn, holding all other factors constant. At *a*, when the price of corn *(P)* is $5 per bushel, the quantity demanded *(Q)* is 20 million bushels per month. At *e*, when the price of corn is $1, the quantity demanded is 50 million bushels. The downward-sloping curve *(D)* drawn through these points is the demand curve for corn. Graphically, it shows the amounts of corn consumers would be willing to buy at different prices in the specified time period.

Since the relationship between price and quantity demanded is downward-sloping, the law of demand is sometimes called the **law of downward-sloping demand.**

The demand curve shows that as larger quantities of corn are put on the market, lower prices are required in order to sell that quantity. The price needed to sell 25 million bushels of corn is $4 per bushel. To sell a larger quantity of corn— say, 30 million bushels—a lower price—of $3— is required.

Figure 1 is labeled "The Demand Curve for Corn." But whose demand for corn does it represent? The units of measure are in millions of bushels, so it is definitely not the demand curve of an individual family. It could be the demand

curve of all American buyers of corn, or it could be the demand curve of Ralston Purina, a major American buyer of corn. It could even be the world demand curve for corn. The national demand curve for corn is simply the demand curve of all American buyers combined. The world demand curve for corn is the demand curves of all nations added together. Just as one must state the units of measure of prices and quantities, so one must state whose demand curve it is.

Normally, this book will use a **market demand curve.**

The **market demand curve** *is the demand curve of all persons participating in the market for that particular product.*

The *demand curve for corn* therefore refers to all buyers in the corn market. The corn market is essentially a national market or even an international market that brings together all American (or even world) buyers of corn. For example, the demand curve for Hawaiian real estate brings together all buyers of Hawaiian real estate; the demand curve for U.S. automobiles brings together the demand schedules of all private, corporate, and governmental buyers of U.S.-produced automobiles.

Factors That Cause the Demand Curve to Shift

Factors other than the price of the good can change the relationship between price and quantity demanded, causing the demand curve to shift left or right. A demand curve assumes that all these other factors are held constant and shows what would happen to the quantity demanded if *only the price* were to change. In the real world, these other conditions are constantly changing; therefore, it is crucial to understand how changes in factors other than price affect the demand for a good (see Example 1). The nonprice factors that can affect the demand for a good include: 1) the prices of related goods, 2) consumer income, 3) consumer preferences, 4) the number of potential buyers, and 5) expectations.

The Prices of Related Goods.   Goods can be related to each other in two ways: Two goods are

Example 1

Factors That Cause a Demand Curve to Shift

Factor	Example
Change in price of substitutes	Increase in price of coffee shifts demand curve for tea to right.
Change in price of complements	Increase in price of coffee shifts demand curve for sugar to left.
Change in income	Increases in income shifts demand curve for automobiles to right.
Change in preference	Judgement that cigarettes are hazardous to health shifts demand curve for cigarettes to left.
Change in number of buyers	Increase in population of City X shifts demand curve for houses in City X to right.
Change in expectations of future prices	Expectation that prices of canned goods will increase substantially over the next year shifts demand curve for canned goods to right.

---

substitutes if the demand for one rises when the price of the other rises (or when the demand falls when the price of the other falls). Examples of substitutes are: coffee and tea, two brands of soft drinks, stocks and bonds, bacon and sausage, pork and beef, oats and corn, foreign and domestic cars, natural gas and electricity. Some goods are very close substitutes (two different brands of fluoride toothpaste), and others are very distant substitutes (Toyota automobiles and DC-10 aircraft).

*Two goods are **substitutes** if the demand for one rises (falls) when the price of the other rises (falls).*

Two goods are **complements** if increasing the price of one good lowers the demand for the other. Examples of complements are: automobiles and gasoline, food and drink, white dress shirts and neckties, skirts and blouses. When goods are complements there is a tendency for the two goods to be used jointly in order to achieve something more general (for example, automobiles plus gasoline equals transportation). Thus, an increase in the price of one of the goods effectively increases the price of the joint product of the two goods together. Thus an increase in the price of one of the goods will reduce the demand for the other.

*Two goods are **complements** if the demand for one rises (falls) when the price of the other falls (rises).*

Income. It is easy to understand how income influences demand. A fact of economic life is that as incomes rise, people spend more on most—but not all—goods and services.

*The demand for an **inferior good** will fall as income rises.*

To determine what goods are **inferior goods,** a person need only ask, "What goods would I cut down on or eliminate from my budget as my income goes up?" For some people, inferior goods might be hamburger, margarine, bus rides, second-hand clothing, day-old bread, or black-and-white TV sets. But most goods are **normal goods.**

*The demand for a **normal good** increases as income rises.*

Preferences. To the economist, the word *preferences* means what people like and dislike without regard to budgetary considerations. One may prefer a 10-bedroom mansion with servants but can only afford a 3-bedroom bungalow. One may prefer a Mercedes-Benz but may drive a

Volkswagen. One may prefer T-bone steaks but may eat hamburgers! Preferences plus budgetary considerations (price and income) determine demand. As preferences change, demand will change. If people learn that walking will increase their lifespan, the demand for walking shoes will increase. Business firms spend enormous sums trying to influence preferences by advertising on television, in newspapers, and in magazines. The goal of advertising is to shift the demand curve for the advertised product to the right.

The Number of Potential Buyers. If more buyers enter a market because of population growth or movements in the population, the demand will rise. The relaxation of trade barriers between two countries may increase the number of buyers. Lowering the legal age for alcoholic-beverage purchases will increase the number of buyers of beer.

Expectations. If people learn that the price of coffee over the next year will rise substantially (for whatever reason), they may decide to stock up on coffee today. During inflationary times, when people find prices of goods going up rapidly, they often start buying up durable goods, such as cars and refrigerators. Thus, the mere expectation of a good's price going up can induce people to buy more of it. Similarly, people can postpone the purchase of things that are expected to get cheaper. For example: during the 1980s home computers grew cheaper and cheaper. Some buyers may well have postponed their purchase of home computers on the expectation that in the future the good could be purchased for an even lower price.

Changes in any of the above factors (except the price of the good itself) will *shift the entire demand curve* for the good. Figure 2 shows the demand curve for white dress shirts. This curve, *D,* is based on a $5 price for neckties (a complement), a $10 price of sport shirts (a substitute), and fixed income, preferences, and number of buyers.

An increase in the price of neckties (a complement for white shirts) from $5 to $7.50 shifts the entire demand curve for white shirts to the left from *D* to *D'* in panel (a). White dress shirts are usually worn with neckties. If neckties increase in price, consumers will buy less of them and will

Figure 2
Shifts in the Demand Curve: Changes in Demand

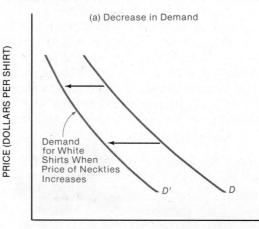

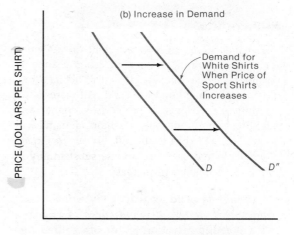

The demand for white dress shirts depends not only on the price of white dress shirts but also on the price of neckties and the price of sport shirts. When the price of neckties is $5 and the price of sport shirts is $10, the demand curve for white shirts is *D*. If the price of neckties rises to $7.50, holding the price of sport shirts at $10, then at each price for white dress shirts the demand falls. In panel (a), with a higher price of neckties the demand curve shifts to the left and depicts a decrease in demand from *D* to *D'*. In panel (b), keeping the price of neckties at $5 and raising the price of sport shirts to $15 will raise the demand for white shirts. The demand curve will shift rightward to *D"*. A rightward shift depicts an increase in demand, and a leftward shift illustrates a decrease in demand.

substitute less formal shirts for shirts that require neckties. As a result of this substitution, the demand for white dress shirts will decrease, shifting left.

An increase in the price of sports shirts (a substitute for white dress shirts) from $10 to $15 shifts the demand curve for white shirts to the right from D to D'' in panel (b). When the price of sports shirts increases, consumers substitute white dress shirts for sports shirts. As a result of this substitution, the demand for white dress shirts will increase, shifting right.

When the demand curve shifts to the left, **people wish to buy smaller quantities of the good at each price.** *A leftward shift of the demand curve indicates a* **decrease in demand.** *When the demand curve shifts to the right,* **people wish to buy larger quantities of the good at each price.** *A rightward shift of the demand curve indicates an* **increase in demand.**

Demand curves shift to the right or left when factors other than the price of the good change. If consumer income increases, and if white dress shirts are a normal good, demand will increase (D will shift to the right). If preferences change and white dress shirts fall out of fashion, demand will decrease (D will shift to the left). If buyers expect prices of white dress shirts to rise substantially in the future, demand will increase.

A change in **product price only** *will cause a movement along a demand curve. A change in a* **demand-affecting factor other than the price of the good** *(such as a related good's price, income, preferences, expectations, or the number of buyers) will cause the entire demand curve to shift.*

SUPPLY

How much corn the farmer offers for sale depends on the price of corn. Generally speaking, the higher the price, the higher the **quantity supplied.**

The **quantity supplied** *of a good or service is the amount of the good or service offered for sale at a given price.*

The relationship between quantity supplied and price is the **supply.**

The **supply** *of a good or service is the relationship between the amount of a good or service offered for sale at a given price and the price of the good or service.*

This relationship is normally—but not always—positive. A higher price for corn will induce farmers to cultivate fewer soybeans and plant more corn (this substitution occurs in production rather than consumption). A higher price for corn will make farmers more willing to put out a little extra effort to make sure that corn is not wasted during harvesting or to prevent the crop from being harmed by the weather or pests. The fundamental reason for the normally positive relationship between quantity supplied and price is the *law of diminishing returns* (see Chapter 2). The law of diminishing returns states that with other factors of production fixed, the extra output obtained by adding equal increments of a variable factor to the process of production will eventually decline. To produce more of a good under the law of diminishing returns means that as more and more obstacles are encountered, a higher price is required to overcome these obstacles. For example, farmers may find that they have to plant additional corn in areas that are rockier or that the extra harvesting requires more maintenance or more reliance on undependable labor. Whenever fixed factors are present, the productivity of the extra variable factors used to produce more output falls, and the costs of producing each additional unit of output rise.

The Supply Curve

Consider now the normal case of a positive relationship between price and quantity supplied. Table 2 shows a hypothetical supply schedule for corn that is graphed in Figure 3. When the price of corn is $5 per bushel, farmers wish to supply 40 million bushels per month (point *a*). As the price falls to $4, the quantity supplied falls to 35 million bushels (point *b*). Finally, when the price is $1 farmers wish to sell only 10 million bushels (point *e*).

The smooth curve drawn through points *a*

Table 2
Supply Schedule for Corn

	Price (dollars per bushel)	Quantity Supplied (millions of bushels per month)
a	5	40
b	4	35
c	3	30
d	2	20
e	1	10

Figure 3
The Supply Curve for Corn

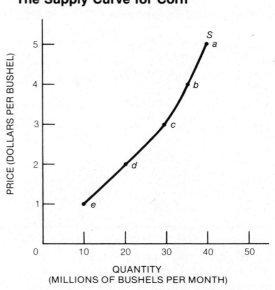

This graph depicts how the quantity of corn supplied responds to the price of corn. In situation *a*, when the price of corn is $5 per bushel, the quantity supplied by farmers is 40 million bushels per month. In the last situation, *e*, when the price is $1 per bushel, the quantity supplied is only 10 million bushels per month. The upward-sloping curve *(S)* drawn through these points is the supply curve of corn.

through *e*, labeled *S*, is the supply curve. It shows how quantity supplied responds to all price variations: *it shows how much farmers offer for sale at each price.* Along the supply curve, the price of corn and the supply of corn are positively related: in order to induce farmers to offer a larger quantity of corn on the market, a higher price is required.

Factors That Cause the Supply Curve to Shift

Just as factors other than the price of the good can change the relationship between price and quantity demanded, nonprice factors can change the relationship between price and quantity supplied, causing the supply curve to shift (see Example 2). The nonprice factors that can cause the supply curve to shift include: 1) the prices of other goods, 2) the prices of relevant resources, 3) technology, 4) the number of sellers, and 5) expectations.

The Prices of Other Goods. The resources that are used to produce any particular good can almost always be used elsewhere in the economy. Farmland can be used for corn or soybeans; engineers can work on cars or trucks; unskilled workers can pick strawberries or cotton; trains can be used to move coal or cars. As the price of a good rises, resources are naturally attracted away from other goods that use those resources. Hence, the supply of corn will fall if the price of soybeans rises; if the price of cotton rises the supply of strawberries may fall. If the price of trucks rises, the supply of cars may fall. If the price of fuel oil rises, less kerosene may be produced.

The Prices of Relevant Resources. Goods and services require certain resources that must be purchased in resource markets. As these resource prices change, the supply conditions for the goods being produced change. An increase in the price of coffee beans will increase the costs of producing coffee and decrease the amount of coffee that coffee companies wish to sell at each price; an increase in the price of corn land, tractors, harvesters, or irrigation will tend to reduce the supply of corn; an increase in the price of cotton will tend to decrease the supply of cotton dresses; an increase in the price of jet fuel will decrease the supply of commercial aviation at each price.

Technology. *Technology* is the knowledge that people have about how different things can be produced. If technology improves, more goods can be produced from the same resources. For example, if lobster farmers in Maine learn how to

---

Factors That Cause a Supply Curve to Shift

Factor	Example
Change in price of another good	Increase in price of corn shifts supply curve of wheat to left.
Change in price of resource	Decrease in wage rate of autoworkers shifts supply curve of autos to right.
Change in technology	Higher corn yields due to genetic engineering shift supply curve of corn to right.
Change in number of sellers	New sellers entering profitable field shift supply curve of product to right.
Change in expectations	Expectation of a much higher price of oil next year shifts supply curve of oil today to left. ◫

---

feed lobsters more cheaply due to a new and cheaper combination of nutritious food, the supply of lobsters at each price will tend to increase. If a firm finds that the assembly line can be speeded up by merely rearranging the order of assembly, the supply of the good will tend to increase. If new oil-recovery procedures are discovered, the supply of oil will increase.

The Number of Sellers.   If more sellers enter into the production of a particular good (perhaps because of high profits or in anticipation of high profits), the supply of the good will increase. The lowering of trade barriers may allow foreign sellers to enter the market, increasing the number of sellers.

Expectations.   It takes a long time to produce many goods and services. When a farmer plants corn or wheat or soybeans, the prices that are expected to prevail at harvest time are actually more important than the current price. A college student who reads that there are likely to be too few engineers in four years may decide to major in engineering in expectation of a high wage rate. When a business firm decides to establish a plant that may take five years to build, expectations of future business conditions in that industry are crucial to that investment decision.

Changes in each of the above factors (except for the price of the good itself) *will shift the entire supply curve.* Figure 4 shows the supply curve S for corn. The supply curve is based on a $10-per-

bushel price of soybeans and a $2,000 yearly rental on an acre of corn land. If the price of soybeans rises to, say, $15 a bushel, then the supply curve for corn will shift leftward to S′ in panel (a) because some land used for corn will be shifted to soybeans. If the rental price of an acre of corn land goes down from $2,000 a year per acre to $1,000 a year, the supply curve will shift to the right—to, say, S″ in panel (b). The reduction in the land rental price lowers the costs of producing a bushel of corn and makes the corn producer willing to supply more corn at the same price as before.

When the supply curve shifts to the left (for whatever reason), producers wish to **sell smaller quantities of the good at each price.** *A leftward shift (as from* S *to* S′ *in Figure 4) indicates a* **decrease in supply.** *When the supply curve shifts to the right,* **producers wish to sell larger quantities at each price.** *This rightward shift (as from* S *to* S″ *in Figure 4) indicates an* **increase in supply.**

EQUILIBRIUM OF SUPPLY AND DEMAND

Along a given demand curve, such as the one in Figure 1, there are lots of price/quantity combinations from which to choose. Along a given supply curve, there are similarly lots of different price/quantity combinations. Neither the demand

Figure 4
Shifts in the Supply Curve: Changes in Supply

(a) Decrease in Supply

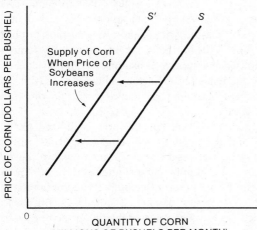

Supply of Corn When Price of Soybeans Increases

PRICE OF CORN (DOLLARS PER BUSHEL)

QUANTITY OF CORN
(MILLIONS OF BUSHELS PER MONTH)

(b) Increase in Supply

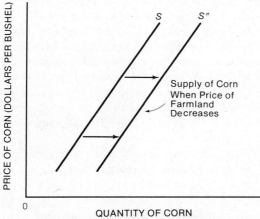

Supply of Corn When Price of Farmland Decreases

PRICE OF CORN (DOLLARS PER BUSHEL)

QUANTITY OF CORN
(MILLIONS OF BUSHELS PER MONTH)

The supply curve of corn depends not only on the price of corn but also on the price of soybeans and the price of farmland. When farmland is $2,000 an acre per year and soybeans are $10 per bushel, S might be the supply curve for corn. Panel (a) shows that if farmland stays at $2,000 per acre per year but soybeans fetch $15 instead of $10, profit-seeking farmers will switch farmland from corn to soybeans and cause the supply curve for corn to shift to the left from S to S' (a decrease in supply). On the other hand, panel (b) shows that if soybeans remain at $10 per bushel and farmland falls from $2,000 to $1,000 per acre, the supply curve for corn will shift to the right from S to S" (an increase in supply).

Figure 5
Market Equilibrium

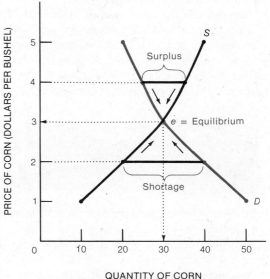

QUANTITY OF CORN
(MILLIONS OF BUSHELS PER MONTH)

This figure shows how market equilibrium is reached. On the same diagram are drawn both the demand and the supply curves for corn. The curves are the same as in Figures 1 and 3. When the price of corn is $2, the quantity demanded is 40 million bushels, but the quantity supplied is only 20 million bushels. The result is a shortage of 20 million bushels of corn. Unsatisfied buyers will bid the price up.

Raising the price will reduce the shortage. When the price of corn is raised to $4 per bushel, the quantity demanded is 25 million bushels while the quantity supplied is 35 million bushels. The result is a surplus of 10 million bushels of corn. This surplus will cause the price of corn to fall as unsatisfied sellers bid the price down to get rid of excess inventories of corn. As the price falls the surplus will diminish. The equilibrium price is $3 because the quantity demanded equals the quantity supplied at that price. The equilibrium quantity is 30 million bushels.

curve nor the supply curve is sufficient by itself to determine the *market* price/quantity combination.

Figure 5 puts the demand curve of Figure 1 and the supply curve of Figure 3 together on the same diagram. Remember that the demand curve indicates what consumers are prepared to buy at different prices; the supply curve indicates what producers are prepared to sell at different prices. These groups of economic decision makers are (for the most part) entirely different. How much will be produced? How much will be consumed? How are the decisions of consumers and producers coordinated?

Suppose that the price of corn happened to be $2 per bushel. Figure 5 tells us the same thing that Figures 1 and 3 tell us separately: at a $2 price consumers will want to buy 40 million bushels and producers will want to sell only 20 million bushels. This discrepancy means that at $2 there is a **shortage** of 20 million bushels.

> A **shortage** results if at the current price the quantity demanded exceeds the quantity supplied; the price is too low to equate the quantity demanded with the quantity supplied.

Corn-starved buyers or consumers will try to outbid each other for the available supply. With free competition, the price of corn will be bid up if there is a shortage of corn.

The increase in the price of corn in response to the shortage will have two main effects. On the one hand, the higher price will discourage consumption. On the other hand, the higher price will encourage production. Thus the increase in the price of corn, through the action of independent buyers and sellers, will lead both buyers and sellers in the marketplace to make decisions that will reduce the shortage of corn.

According to the demand and supply curves portrayed in Figure 5, when the price of corn is $3 per bushel, the shortage of corn disappears completely. At this price consumers want to buy 30 million bushels and producers want to sell 30 million bushels.

> The **equilibrium** (or **market-clearing**) **price** is the price at which the quantity demanded by consumers equals the quantity supplied by producers.

What would happen if price rose above the **equilibrium price** of $3 per bushel? At the price of $4 per bushel, consumers want to buy 25 million bushels and producers want to sell 35 million bushels. Thus at $4 there is a **surplus** of 10 million bushels on the market.

> A **surplus** results if at the current price the quantity supplied exceeds the quantity demanded; the price is too high to equate the quantity demanded with quantity supplied.

Some sellers will be disappointed as corn inventories pile up. Willing sellers of corn cannot find buyers. The competition among sellers will lead them to cut the price if there is a surplus of corn.

This fall in the price of corn will simultaneously encourage consumption and discourage production. Through the automatic fall in the price of corn, *the surplus of corn will therefore disappear*.

Again we find that the price will tend toward $3 and the quantity will tend toward 30 million bushels. This equilibrium point is where the demand and supply curves intersect. In Figure 5, there is no other price/quantity combination at which quantity demanded equals quantity supplied—any other price brings about a shortage of corn or a surplus of corn. The arrows in Figure 5 indicate the pressures on prices above or below $3 and how the amount of shortage or surplus— the size of the brackets—gets smaller.

The equilibrium of supply and demand is stationary in the sense that price will tend to remain at that price once the equilibrium price is reached. Movements away from the equilibrium price will be restored by the bidding of excess buyers or excess sellers in the marketplace. The equilibrium price is like a rocking chair in the rest position; give it a gentle push and the original position will be restored.

What the Market Accomplishes

The market coordinates the actions of a large number of independent suppliers and demanders. Their actions are brought together by the pricing of the good in a free market. The market can accomplish its actions without any participant knowing all the details. Recall the pencil example of Chapter 3: pencils get produced even though no single individual knows *all* the details for producing a pencil (from making the saw to fell the trees to making the rubber eraser).

An equilibrium price accomplishes two basic goals. First, it *rations* the scarce supply of the commodity or service among all the people who would like to have it if it were given away free. Somebody must be left out if the good is scarce.

The price, by discouraging or restraining consumption, rations the good out to the various claimants of the good.

Second, the system of equilibrium prices *economizes on the information required to match supplies and demands*. Buyers do not have to know how to *produce* the good, and sellers do not need to know why people use the good. Buyers and sellers need only be concerned with small bits of information such as price or small portions of the technological methods of production. No one person has to know everything.

Disequilibrium Prices

To understand the rationing function of equilibrium prices, let us consider what happens when prices are not allowed to reach equilibrium. For many years, the price of natural gas shipped interstate was held below equilibrium by the Federal Power Commission. During the Arab oil embargo during the summer of 1974, gasoline prices were held below market-clearing levels. In recent years, prices of consumer goods in Poland were held below equilibrium. In both cases, shortages and long lines resulted.

Rent control is an example of disequilibrium pricing. Laws are passed by municipal governments *freezing* rents (that is, preventing rents from rising).

The growing number of consumer groups demanding controls on rents is explained by a very simple fact: in the United States, the number of tenants is increasing relative to the number of homeowners.

Figure 6 shows the market for rental housing in a particular city. The supply curve is upward-sloping; the demand curve is downward-sloping. In a free market, the price of housing would settle at $500 per month for a standard rental unit. But suppose a price ceiling of $300 is established by municipal ordinance. If landlords are free to supply the number of apartments they wish, fewer units would be offered for rent: 6,000 units are supplied at a price of $300 and 8,000 units at a price of $500. The quantity demanded rises to 11,000 units as price falls. Accordingly, there will be a shortage of 5,000 units due to the rent control. If the price could rise, there would be no shortage. See Example 3 for further discussion.

Figure 6
The Effect of Rent Ceilings on the Market for Rental Housing

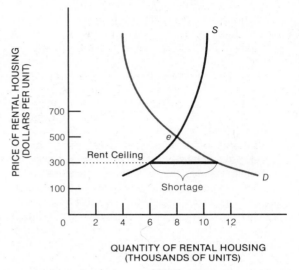

If the equilibrium price/quantity combination for the rental market is $500 per unit and 8,000 units (point e), a rent ceiling of $300 per month on a standard housing unit would lower the quantity supplied to 6,000 units and raise the quantity demanded to 11,000 units, creating a shortage of 5,000 units of rental housing.

Understanding Shortage and Surplus

The terms *shortage* and *surplus* (glut) are often misused. Earlier, the chapter quoted a newspaper report that said there will be a "glut" of doctors by 1990. One often hears reports about "shortages" of sugar or other commodities. In economics, a shortage occurs when the price is not allowed to *rise* to its equilibrium level. A surplus occurs when the price is not allowed to *fall* to its equilibrium level. If there are no impediments to these price adjustments, shortages and surpluses will disappear as prices adjust. A sugar shortage is not a shortage in the same sense as a shortage of rent-controlled apartments. By a sugar shortage writers really mean that supply and demand conditions are pushing *up* the price of sugar. By a surplus of doctors writers actually mean that supply and demand conditions push *down* the relative price of physicians' services, not that there will be doctors with no patients.

Example 3

Rent Control

The assumption that rent control breeds shortages is supported by the facts. In New York City, "temporary" rent controls were imposed in 1943. To this date, 1,250,000 apartments in that city are under rent control, and 340,000 of these remain under the controls imposed during the Second World War. New York City landlords have abandoned many thousands of buildings because they are unprofitable at controlled rental rates. To obtain a rent-controlled apartment, it is necessary to put one's name on a long waiting list or to have a friend who knows somebody. Empty units are rented immediately to whomever happens to be on the list at the right time or knows the right person or has paid a sufficient bribe. New York City is only one case of rent control. In Boston, 50,000 apartments are rent-controlled. In the District of Columbia, there are 112,000 rent-controlled units of which 5,000 have been abandoned by their owners. Rent controls are in effect in some California cities and have been proposed for Los Angeles.

Rent control offers advantages to (and is most enthusiastically supported by) people who already have a lease on a rental unit. They already have housing, and their rent cannot be raised. Unfortunately, in the long run rent controls have damaging effects on the supply of apartments and on their quality. Owners of rent-controlled apartments do not find it profitable to make necessary repairs and often decide it is better to abandon the building than to run it at a loss. Thus, a side effect of rent control is the destruction of the rental industry!

The analysis of rent control illustrates a basic fact: any effective price ceiling on a good or service will tend to cause shortages in a competitive market. Ceilings on interest rates will cause shortages of loans and mortgages. Ceilings on gasoline prices in the United States in 1974 and 1979 at times caused long gas lines in many parts of the country. In severe winters, ceilings on natural gas prices have caused shortages in northern states. In each case, the solution is the same: remove the price ceiling, and the shortage disappears!

There are both costs and benefits of shortages. When a shortage occurs, those who can get the commodity at the controlled price may be better off paying a lower price, provided they do not spend more time waiting in lines than they would in paying a comparable money price. The cost is that many who are prepared to pay the price for the controlled commodity are denied its use, even if their desire is so intense that they are willing to pay an exceptionally high price.

Source: "Reagan Leadership May Have Role in Settling Rent Control Disputes," *Christian Science Monitor*, December 19, 1980.

CHANGES IN THE EQUILIBRIUM PRICE

One important fact about the economic system is that prices always change. Sometimes prices go up, and sometimes they go down—and in relative-price terms price goes down as often as it goes up. This section will investigate the reasons why prices change. Thus far we have seen that the equilibrium price is determined by the intersection of the demand and supply curves. The only way for the price to change is for the demand or supply curves themselves to shift. The supply and demand curves can shift only if one or more of the factors besides the price of the good in question changes.

Change in Demand (or Supply) versus Change in Quantity Demanded (or Supplied)

A rise in the price of a good—as from p_1 to p_2 in panel (a) of Figure 7—induces a change in the quantity demanded but does not change the location of the demand curve. A reduction or decrease in demand occurs when a change in a factor other than the good's price shifts the entire demand curve to the left.

*A **change** (increase or decrease) **in demand** is a shift in the entire demand curve because of a change in a factor other than the good's price.*

Figure 7
Change in Demand versus Change in Quantity Demanded

(a) *Change in Quantity Demanded*

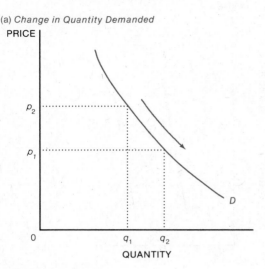

(b) *Change in Demand*

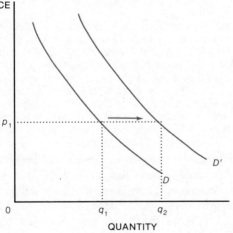

In panel (a), the increase in quantity (from q_1 to q_2) is due to the change in price (from p_2 to p_1). The change in price causes the *movement along* the demand curve (D). In panel (b), the increase in quantity (from q_1 to q_2) is due to a *shift in* the demand curve (an increase in demand) to D'. The quantity has increased due to some change that leads consumers to buy more of the product *at each price*.

A **change** *(increase or decrease)* **in quantity demanded** *is a movement along the demand curve because of a change in the good's price (see Figure 7).*

Similarly, panel (a) of Figure 8 shows that a rise in the price of a good (from p_1 to p_2) changes the quantity supplied but does not change the location of the supply curve. A reduction in supply occurs when a factor other than the good's price changes, shifting the entire supply curve to the left.

A **change** *(increase or decrease)* **in supply** *is a shift in the entire supply curve because of a change in a factor other than the good's price.*

A **change** *(increase or decrease)* **in quantity supplied** *is a movement along the supply curve because of a change in the good's price (see Figure 8).*

The Effects of a Change in Supply

Changes in supply or demand factors can influence the equilibrium price and quantity in any given market.

Consider a natural disaster, such as severe flooding, a horde of locusts, or a drought, that affects the supply of an agricultural product, such as wheat. Figure 9 illustrates the effect of a natural disaster on the wheat market. The demand curve, and the supply curve, are based on given conditions *before* the natural disaster. Suddenly, and without warning, torrential rains hit the wheat fields prior to harvest, ruining about one half of the potential wheat crop. Now at a price of $5 per bushel, instead of 50 million bushels being offered, only 25 million bushels are offered by farmers. Similarly, at all other prices smaller quantities of wheat are offered on the market. The supply curve for wheat has shifted to the left (the supply of wheat has decreased). How will this supply reduction affect the demand curve?

When the supply curve for a single good—like wheat—changes, the demand curve need not change. The factors influencing the supply of wheat *other than the price of wheat* have little or no influence on the demand for wheat. In our example, the severe rains will not shift the demand curve. Thus, in the analysis of a single market we can usually assume that the demand and supply curves are independent.

Figure 8
Change in Supply versus Change in Quantity Supplied

(a) Change in Quantity Supplied

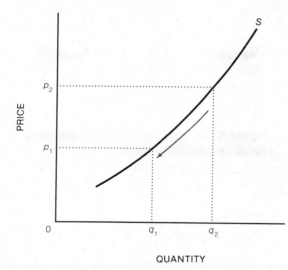

QUANTITY

(b) Change in Supply

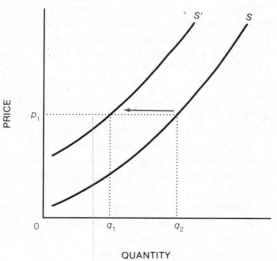

QUANTITY

In panel (a), the decrease in quantity (from q_2 to q_1) is due to a change in price (from p_2 to p_1). The change in price causes a movement along the supply curve *(S)*. In panel (b), the decrease in supply (from q_2 to q_1) is due to the shift in the supply curve (decrease in supply) from *S* to *S'*. Quantity drops without any change in price.

Figure 9
The Effects of a Natural Disaster on the Price of Wheat

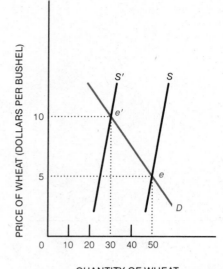

QUANTITY OF WHEAT
(MILLIONS OF BUSHELS PER YEAR)

In this graph, a natural disaster shifts the supply curve of wheat from *S* to *S'*. Where formerly $5 brought forth 50 million bushels of wheat (on *S*) now $5 brings forth only 25 million bushels of wheat (on *S'*). This decrease in supply raises the equilibrium price from $5 to $10. The movement from *e* to *e'* is a *movement along* the demand curve. Although the demand curve does not change, there is a decrease in quantity demanded from 50 million to 30 million bushels as the price rises from $5 to $10 per bushel.

The supply curve has shifted to the left (supply has decreased); the demand curve remains unchanged. What will happen to the equilibrium price? Before the flood, the price that equated quantity supplied with quantity demanded was $5. After the flood, the quantity supplied at a $5 price is 25 million bushels and the quantity demanded is 50 million bushels. At the old price, there would be a shortage of wheat. Therefore, the price of wheat will be bid up until a new equilibrium price is attained (at $10), at which quantity demanded and quantity supplied are equal at 30 million bushels. As the price rises from the old equilibrium price ($5) to the new equilibrium price ($10), there is a movement up the new supply curve *(S')*. Even with a flood, a higher price will coax out more wheat.

A decrease in supply causes the price to rise and the quantity demanded to fall. An increase in supply causes the price to fall and the quantity demanded to rise.

The Effects of a Change in Demand

A change in demand is illustrated in Figure 10. The initial situation is depicted by the demand curve *D* and the supply curve *S*. The equilibrium price is $5 and the equilibrium quantity is 50 million bushels. Hence, *D* and *S* are the same curves as in Figure 9. Now imagine a change on the demand side. Medical evidence is uncovered showing that eating bread will double one's lifespan (purely hypothetical). This event would shift the demand curve for wheat sharply to the right (from *D* to *D′*). This massive increase in demand for wheat will drive the price of wheat up to $13 per bushel (from *e* to *e′*). When the price rises, the quantity supplied rises from 50 million to 58 million bushels. *There has been no increase in supply, only an increase in quantity supplied.*

Notice again that when the demand curve shifts due to some change in demand factors other than the good's price, there is no shift in the supply curve—the supply curve remains the same. The supply curve and the demand curve should be considered to be independent of one another at this level of analysis. If a market is small enough relative to the entire economy, the link between the factors that shift demand curves and those that shift supply curves (summarized in Examples 1 and 2) is weak. In our example, the change in preferences should not affect the willingness of farmers to supply wheat at different prices.

The statement by the state agriculture office quoted at the beginning of this chapter illustrates the danger of confusing changes in quantity demanded (or supplied) with changes in demand (or supply). The bad weather reported by the agriculture office shifts the supply curve to the left and causes a movement along the demand curve. The fall in supply does not cause a fall in demand but a *fall in quantity demanded*. Another example of the widespread confusion over the difference between a change in supply (or demand) and a change in quantity supplied (or demanded) is described in Example 4.

Figure 10
The Effects of an Increased Preference for Bread on the Price of Wheat

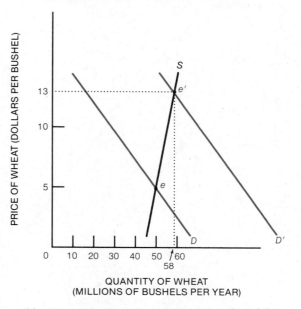

If for some reason people want to eat more bread due to a change in preferences, the demand curve for wheat will shift to the right. The shift in the demand curve from *D* to *D′* depicts an increase in demand. This increase in demand drives up the equilibrium price from $5 per bushel to $13 per bushel. As price rises from $5 to $13, there is an increase in quantity supplied from 50 million to 58 million bushels that results from the movement along the supply curve, *S*.

An increase in demand causes the price to rise and the quantity supplied to rise. A decrease in demand causes the price to fall and the quantity supplied to fall.

Simultaneous Changes in Supply and Demand

Figure 11 combines the two previous cases and illustrates what happens to price and quantity if the two events (the flood and the change in preferences) occur together. The supply curve shifts to the left from *S* to *S′* (supply falls) and the demand curve shifts to the right from *D* to *D′* (demand increases).

Prior to these changes, equilibrium price was $5, and equilibrium quantity was 50 million bush-

Figure 11
The Effects of an Increase in Demand and a Decrease in Supply on the Price of Wheat

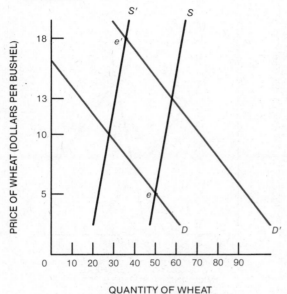

QUANTITY OF WHEAT
(MILLIONS OF BUSHELS PER YEAR)

This graph combines the supply change of Figure 9 and the demand change of Figure 10. The original equilibrium was at a price of $5 and a quantity of 50 million bushels. After the shift in supply (from S to S') and the shift in demand (from D to D'), there is a shortage at the old price (quantity supplied equals 25 million bushels and quantity demanded equals 90 million bushels). The equilibrium price rises to $18 and the equilibrium quantity falls to 37.5 million bushels.

els. The shifts in supply and demand disrupt this equilibrium. Now at a price of $5, the quantity supplied equals 25 million bushels, and the quantity demanded equals 90 million bushels—an enormous shortage. The new equilibrium occurs at a price of $18 and a quantity of 37.5 million bushels. The two shifts magnify each other's effects. As we have shown, if there had been only the supply change, price would have risen to $10. If there had been only the demand change, price would have risen to $13. The combined effects cause the price to rise to $18. In this case the causes of the changes in supply and demand are independent.

The effects of simultaneous changes in supply and demand are sometimes indeterminate. If sup-

Figure 12
The Effect of Population Growth on the Market for Rental Housing in Los Angeles

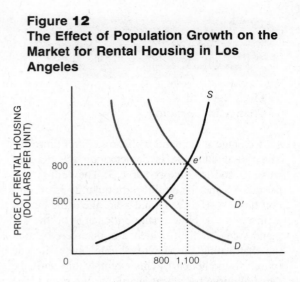

QUANTITY OF RENTAL HOUSING
(THOUSANDS OF UNITS)

When the population grows, the demand for rental housing in a city will increase, *ceteris paribus*. If the original equilibrium is point e, population growth will shift the demand curve from D to D' to a new equilibrium at e'. All those people who originally rented housing units at the lower price will find that the new population has forced up the rents they must pay.

ply increases (shifts right) and demand decreases (shifts left), the price will fall. If supply decreases and demand increases, the price will rise. If, however, both the demand and supply curves move in the same direction (if both increase or if both decrease), the price effect depends upon which movement dominates.

APPLICATIONS OF
SUPPLY-AND-DEMAND ANALYSIS

Supply-and-demand analysis is one of the most powerful tools of economics. We have already used supply-and-demand analysis to determine the effects of decreases in supply (the natural-disaster example) and increases in demand (the change-in-preferences example) on prices and quantities. What happens when prices are not allowed to rise to equilibrium levels was examined in the discussion of rent control. Supply-and-demand analysis can also help explain why rents rise and what the effects of insecticide regulation will be.

Example 4

Presidential Confusion

During his term of office, President Jimmy Carter was asked in a news conference whether or not his proposed tax on gasoline would raise the price of gasoline. The President's response was that the tax would initially push the price up, but the higher price would discourage demand and bring the price back down.

This response illustrates the common confusion of *changes in quantity demanded* with *changes in demand*. The appropriate response would be that the higher gasoline price (caused by the tax) would cause a movement up the demand curve, *reducing the quantity demanded*. It is incorrect to argue that a fall in quantity demanded can cause the price to fall.

Source: Gerald J. Lynch, "Demand or Quantity Demanded," *Collegiate Forum* (Winter 1980/81), p.5.

Why Rents Rise

One of the reasons price ceilings tend to be imposed is that many buyers perceive them to be personally beneficial; hence, any time prices rise rapidly there tends to be political pressure for price ceilings of some sort.

To the individual buyer, a high price appears to be the fault of the seller with whom he or she is dealing. There may be some cause for blaming the seller if there are not many sellers competing with one another. But in a competitive market with many buyers and sellers, the real enemy of buyers (collectively) is the existence of competing buyers. In Figure 12, the *D* and *S* curves represent the initial demand and supply curves for rental housing in a particular city—say, Los Angeles. The equilibrium is at point *e* with the average monthly rental at $500 and 800,000 units rented. If the population increases, the number of buyers increases and demand for rental housing increases. This increase in demand shifts the demand curve from *D* to *D′*. At the original price of $500 there is a shortage, so the price is bid up. As a consequence, the price goes up for the individual tenant. The individual landlords are not responsible for the increase in the price from $500 to $800 (indicated by the new equilibrium *e′*) but may get the blame from the individual tenant.

In reality, there is a larger degree of mutual interest between the buyer (tenant) and the seller (landlord) than among the individual buyers in a competitive market. Sellers gain from having many buyers to deal with and vice versa. Under a system of private property, buyers and sellers come together voluntarily because there is a presumption that both can gain from this exchange.

Unfortunately, if buyers can band together they can hurt sellers, and if sellers band together they can hurt buyers. In competitive markets, however, collusive behavior does not take place.

This example demonstrates how in those cities and parts of the country where population is rising most rapidly (the sun-belt cities and California), demand for consumer goods and housing is increasing at a faster rate than in other parts of the country. If other things are equal, we would expect prices to increase at a faster pace in these areas.

How well is this prediction of supply-and-demand analysis borne out? Los Angeles (a city that has experienced substantial population growth over the last decade) may be the next major city to institute rent control as a response to rapidly escalating rents. A more general confirmation is that consumer prices have risen much more rapidly in the sun-belt states than in those states that are declining in population.

The Effects of Insecticide Regulation

Many economic activities are regulated by government through zoning laws, occupational licensing, auto-emissions and pollution controls, safety regulations, and so on. Typically, safety,

Figure 13
The Effect of Pesticide Regulation on the Market for Raw Cotton

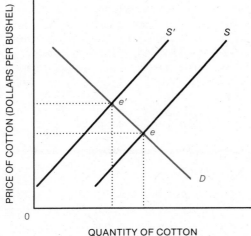

QUANTITY OF COTTON
(MILLIONS OF BUSHELS PER YEAR)

Dusting cotton crops with DDT will keep the quantity of boll weevils (a serious pest) under control. The curve S is the supply curve for cotton using DDT. The equilibrium without pesticide regulation is point e. If it is thought that DDT inflicts unacceptable ecological damage on the community, pesticide regulation (outlawing DDT) that requires a less effective insecticide will shift the supply curve to the left, raising the equilibrium price to the level indicated by point e'.

environmental, and occupational regulation affects supply and thus prices. Supply-and-demand analysis allows us to assess these effects.

Suppose a community decides to prohibit the use of DDT (Dichlorodiphenyltrichloroethane) because of its perceived ecologic damage. What would be the impact of prohibiting DDT on a single market such as cotton?

In Figure 13, the supply curve, S, shows the various quantities of cotton the market will supply at different prices when DDT can be used to control the boll weevil (a serious pest). Before DDT use is prohibited, the equilibrium price and quantity are indicated by point e. If the use of DDT (the most effective insecticide from an economic viewpoint) is prohibited, the supply curve for cotton will shift to the left: to produce cotton becomes more difficult and expensive. Prohibiting DDT has no obvious impact on the demand

curve, but is likely to raise the price of cotton and to lower the quantity of cotton produced and consumed.

Environmental and safety regulations that restrict supply (not all such regulations will limit supply) do raise prices, as supply-and-demand analysis shows. It is up to the community to decide whether the costs imposed on the community in the form of higher prices exceed the benefits imparted by a cleaner environment and by greater worker safety.

These first four chapters focused on how market economies allocate resources through the price system. The tools of supply-and-demand analysis show how equilibrium prices are established and how and why prices change. Relative prices signal to buyers what to purchase and signal to firms what and how to produce. The economic problems of *what, how,* and *for whom* are solved by the invisible hand of the market allocation system, which directs the circular flow of resources between households and businesses. The invisible hand of the market appears to work best under conditions of competition where no buyer or seller (or group thereof) can exercise control over prices.

Summary

1. A perfectly competitive market consists of many buyers and sellers in which each buyer or seller accepts the market price as given.
2. The law of demand states that as price goes up the quantity demanded falls, and vice versa; the demand curve is a graphical representation of the relationship between price and quantity demanded—other things equal. The demand curve is downward-sloping.
3. As price goes up the quantity supplied usually rises; the supply curve is a graphical representation of the relationship between price and quantity supplied. The supply curve tends to be upward-sloping because of the law of diminishing returns.
4. The equilibrium price/quantity combination occurs where the demand curve intersects the supply curve, or where quantity demanded

equals quantity supplied at the market-clearing price. Competitive pricing rations scarce economic goods and economizes on the information necessary to coordinate supply-demand decisions. A shortage results if the price is too low for equilibrium; a surplus results if the price is too high for equilibrium.

5. A change in quantity demanded means a *movement along* a given demand curve; a change in demand means the entire demand curve shifts. A change in quantity supplied means a *movement along* a given supply curve; a change in supply means the entire supply curve shifts. The demand curve will shift if a change occurs in the price of a related good (substitute or complement), income, preference, the number of buyers, or the expectation of future prices. The supply curve will shift if a change occurs in the price of another good, the price of a resource, technology, the number of sellers, or the expectation of future prices. A change in the equilibrium price/quantity combination requires a change in one of the factors held constant along the demand or supply curves.

6. Supply-and-demand analysis allows one to predict what will happen to prices and quantities when supply or demand schedules shift.

Key Terms

market
perfect (perfectly competitive) market
demand
law of demand
quantity demanded
market demand curve
substitutes
complements
inferior goods
normal goods
quantity supplied
supply
shortage
equilibrium (market-clearing) price
surplus

Questions and Problems

1. List the four characteristics of a perfectly competitive market. Explain why if any of the four conditions are not met, the principal characteristic of a perfect market (no person or group can control price) may not be met.

2. Suppose you live in a very cold climate and you pay on average 25 percent of your income for fuel. If the price of fuel rises by 15 percent, and there are no good substitutes for fuel, why would you cut back on fuel consumption?

3. Plot the supply and demand schedules in the accompanying table as supply and demand curves.

Price (dollars)	Quantity Demanded (units)	Quantity Supplied (units)
10	5	25
8	10	20
6	15	15
2	20	10
0	25	5

a. What price would this market establish?

b. If the state were to pass a law that the price could not be more than $2, what would happen to the equilibrium price? If the state were to pass a law that the price could not be more than $8, what effect would the law have on the equilibrium price?

c. If preferences changed and people wanted to buy twice as much as before at each price, what will the equilibrium price be?

d. If, in addition to the above change in preferences, there is an improvement in technology that allows firms to produce this product at lower cost than before, what will happen to the equilibrium price?

4. American baseball bats do not sell well in Japan because they do not meet the specifications of Japanese baseball officials. If the Japanese change their specifications to accommodate American-made bats, what will happen to the price of American bats?

5. "The poor are the ones who suffer from high gas and electricity bills. We should pass a law that gas and electricity rates cannot increase by more than 1 percent annually." Evaluate this statement in terms of supply-and-demand analysis.

6. Much of the automobile-rental business in the United States is done at airports. What would be the predicted effect of a reduction in air fares on automobile-rental rates?

7. If both the supply and demand for coffee increase, what would happen to coffee prices? If the supply increased and the demand fell, what would happen to coffee prices?

8. a. "The recent fare war among the major airlines has increased the demand for air travel."
   b. "The recession of 1981–82 has caused the demand for air travel to fall."
   Which of the above statements uses incorrect terminology? Explain.

P A R T

II

Macroeconomics

CHAPTER

5

Macroeconomic Concepts

Chapter Preview

Microeconomics is the study of the economy "in the small." It explains the behavior of firms and households in the marketplace. The basic analytical tool of microeconomics is supply-and-demand analysis. The most important concept of microeconomics is the notion that market equilibrium occurs when the market price equates the quantity demanded with the quantity supplied.

In contrast, *macroeconomics* is the study of the economy "in the large." Macroeconomics explains how the economy as a whole behaves: why the unemployment rate sometimes rises and sometimes falls, why inflation is high or low, why the total output of goods and services increases or decreases, and what policies could be pursued to

make the economy perform better. Macroeconomics looks at the economy at the highest possible level or aggregation. Rather than studying consumers and producers in all possible single markets, all consumers in the entire economy are lumped together in an examination of total consumption spending; all business investment is lumped together to study total investment spending; all firms are lumped together to learn about the total production of the economy. Because macroeconomics examines the entire economy, measures of prices, employment, and production for the entire economy are necessary. Macroeconomists must be able to measure total economic output, the price level, and the national unemployment rate. Chapter 6 will be devoted to the measurement of total output, or *national income accounting*. This chapter will introduce the major problems of macroeconomics: inflation, unemployment, and the business cycle. The remaining macro chapters will return to each of these problems over and over again.

Macroeconomics is in a state of flux. Economists disagree on the causes and cures of inflation and unemployment. Societies must eventually resolve the controversies over macroeconomic issues in order to make macroeconomic policy. This and following chapters will report the solutions to the major macroeconomic problems that have been offered by different economists.

MACROECONOMIC GOALS

Economic science emphasizes one message over all others: *all economic actions have opportunity costs*. The cost of taking one action is the next best alternative sacrificed. To buy a new car means giving up an expensive vacation. Attending college means time away from work. Buying bonds means passing up the opportunity to buy stocks. Macroeconomic actions can also involve opportunity costs because macroeconomic goals may conflict.

If people were asked to name the goals that they would like their national economy to achieve, the list might contain the following:

1. full employment.
2. price stability.
3. rising standards of living.
4. "fair" distribution of income amongst all citizens.
5. less fluctuation in economic activity.
6. insulation from unpredictable and adverse shocks to the economy, such as energy crises or supply disruptions.

Although many more goals could be added to this list, it is unlikely that anyone would disagree that it is desirable to achieve each of these goals. The country would be a pleasant place to live in if there were full employment, stable prices, rising standards of living, a distribution of income that society regarded as fair, and an economy that was protected from dramatic cyclical movements.

Can an economy achieve all these goals simultaneously or is the cost of achieving one macroeconomic goal the sacrifice of another?

This question divides macroeconomists into different camps. Economists disagree about whether certain trade-offs exist between unemployment and inflation, between economic growth and price stability, or between other pairs of goals.

UNEMPLOYMENT

The problems of unemployment and inflation are central issues of macroeconomics. The Federal government is committed by the Employment Act of 1946 to create and maintain "useful employment opportunities . . . for those able, willing, and seeking to work." In devising macroeconomic policy, unemployment, therefore, has played and continues to play an important role.

The Measurement of Unemployment

Every month, the Bureau of the Census surveys 65,000 households to gather information on their labor-market activities during the preceding week. The Bureau of Labor Statistics (BLS) then processes this information to estimate the number of Americans employed and unemployed in that month. A representative sample of this magnitude should yield an accurate **unemployment rate,** or estimate of total unemployment. The Bureau of Labor Statistics classifies each person 16 years or older into one of three categories: 1) *employed*,[1] 2) *unemployed*, or 3) *not in the **labor force**.*

*The **labor force** equals the number of employed plus the number unemployed.*

*The **unemployment rate** is defined as the number unemployed divided by the number in the labor force.*

A person is classified as unemployed if he or she 1) did not work at all during the previous week, 2) actively looked for work during the previous four weeks, and 3) is currently available for

---

1. One is employed if one worked at least one hour as a paid employee or in one's own business or at least 15 hours as an unpaid worker in a family business during the reference week. If a person had a job but was on vacation, ill, or absent due to poor weather or a labor dispute, that person is also counted as employed.

**Figure 1
The Unemployment Rate**

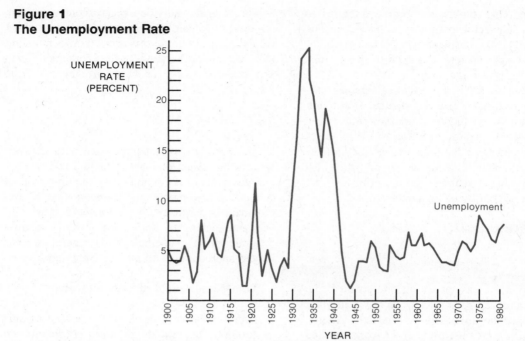

The unemployment rate has been rising in recent years, but it is far from reaching the level experienced during the Great Depression of the 1930s.

Source: *Historical Statistics of the United States,* 1970, p. 126; *Economic Report of the President,* January 1982, p. 266.

work. "Actively looking for work" means registering at an employment office, being on a union or professional job register, answering help-wanted ads, and asking friends and relatives about job openings. Persons laid off from jobs or waiting to report to a new job within 30 days are also classified as unemployed.

Persons without jobs who do not meet these three conditions are classified as *not in the labor force.* Those not in the labor force can be divided into two categories; those who choose not to work and **discouraged workers.**

Discouraged workers are those who do not actively seek work because they think no jobs are available in their line of work.

People may choose to remain outside the labor force for a variety of reasons. Examples of such people are women with young children, students, persons disabled or suffering prolonged ill health, or retired persons.

Unlike the first group, discouraged workers in an important sense do not choose to be out of the labor force. They remain out of the labor force because they have concluded that jobs are not available for them.

Government statisticians and economists have debated whether discouraged workers should be counted as unemployed or not in the labor force. The current practice is to publish separate statistics on discouraged workers but not to count them as unemployed.

**Historical Trends in
Unemployment**

Figure 1 shows long-term trends in unemployment since 1900. The unemployment rate has been subject to significant year-to-year fluctuations. It has varied from lows of near 1 percent to a high of 25 percent during the Great Depression. Between 1900 and 1947, distinct trends in the unemployment rate are not apparent, but since the 1960s, the unemployment rate has moved generally upward. During the period after World War II, the unemployment rate was generally in the range of 2.5 percent to 5.5 percent up to 1960.

After 1960, unemployment rates of 5 to 9 percent became commonplace.

Three Types of Unemployment

Economists have traditionally distinguished between three types of unemployment. People are unemployed for different reasons and with different consequences. The laid-off airline pilot or automobile worker is suffering a different type of unemployment from the contract engineer who is in the process of moving from one job to another. The 55-year-old New England textile worker who has been unemployed since the mill closed two years ago illustrates yet another type of unemployment. Economists identify three types of unemployment: **frictional unemployment, cyclical unemployment,** and **structural unemployment.**

Frictional Unemployment. Business conditions are constantly changing. Employment opportunities are being created in one business, region, or industry at the same time as they are lost in others. Employed workers are usually on the lookout for better jobs; employers are usually on the lookout for better workers. The amount of information about job opportunities that one worker possesses is incomplete. The amount of information potential employers have about prospective employees is incomplete as well.

People are constantly entering and leaving the labor force. People and firms are constantly gathering information about jobs and worker qualifications. At any point in time, some workers will be changing from one job to another. Some will be reentering the labor force; others will be leaving the labor force. The labor force is in a constant state of flux.

Frictional unemployment is the unemployment associated with the changing of jobs in a dynamic economy.

Frictional unemployment will always be with us. Its magnitude depends upon the age, sex, occupational, and racial composition of the labor force and upon how rapidly the economy itself is changing. At the individual level, frictional unemployment depends upon the costs and benefits of job searching and job changing. (Job search

will be discussed in a later chapter.) Typically, frictional unemployment is of less concern to economists and policy makers than other types of unemployment. In fact, frictional unemployment may serve to improve economic well-being. If the frictionally unemployed are moving into better jobs, then they (and society) are benefitting.

Cyclical Unemployment. Unlike frictional unemployment, cyclical unemployment will not benefit the unemployed (or society).

Cyclical unemployment is unemployment associated with general downturns in the economy.

During cyclical downturns, fewer goods and services are purchased in the aggregate, employers cut back on jobs, and people find themselves without jobs. Many workers in basic industrial employment (steel, autos, farm equipment) will be unemployed for some period of time and return to their jobs only when the economy improves. Unlike the job changes associated with frictional unemployment, the job changes associated with cyclical unemployment are largely involuntary. People become unemployed because their jobs evaporate in a generally declining economy.

Structural Unemployment. In a dynamic (changing) economy, some industries, companies, and regions experience a general increase in their economic fortunes at the same time that others experience a long-term decline. In declining industries—particularly those concentrated in specific regions of the country—employees suffer structural unemployment.

Structural unemployment is the unemployment that results from the decline of certain industries. Industries may decline because of rising costs, changes in consumer preferences, or technological advances that make the industry's product obsolete.

Structural unemployment is especially prominent when it is concentrated in a specific region of the country. An example of such structural unemployment would be the high unemployment in the Appalachian coal-mining regions associated

Table 1

The Sources of Unemployment in the United States, 1976–1981

Source of Unemployment	Percentage of Unemployed
Job losers (involuntary)	47.6
Job leavers (voluntary)	12.6
Reentrants	27.2
New entrants	12.6

Source: *Economic Report of the President,* January 1982, p. 273.

with the long-term decline in underground coal mining prior to the energy crisis of the 1970s. A primary concern about structural unemployment is that the people hit hardest by it are those who find it most difficult to relocate. Workers over fifty who have devoted a lifetime of work to underground coal mining would find it difficult to leave family and friends behind to move to areas where jobs may be available.

Sources of Unemployment

As the three types of unemployment suggest, unemployment is by no means a uniform phenomenon. Figures on national unemployment rates obscure the differences among unemployed workers because they lump all the unemployed together. For some, unemployment means a voluntary quit to take a better job in 30 days. For others, it is a traumatic firing or layoff that brings with it mental and economic distress. Different groups of people and different professions tend to have quite different unemployment rates. Teenagers suffer from chronically high unemployment; married men of prime working age tend to have low unemployment rates. Construction workers and automobile workers have more unemployment than white-collar workers and civil servants.

People become unemployed for different reasons. The President's Council of Economic Advisers reports periodically to Congress on the state of unemployment and its sources. As Table 1 shows, in the period 1976 to 1981 less than half of the unemployed (47.6 percent to be exact) actually lost their jobs. Some 12.6 percent of the unemployed left their jobs voluntarily. About 40

percent were either new entrants to the labor force or were reentering the labor force after an absence.

Full Employment

Must every able-bodied person currently have a job for full employment to exist? The answer is no because many people of working age do not wish to be employed—such as the full-time homemaker, the student, and the early retiree. Does full employment exist when everyone actively looking for work and available for work currently has a job? The answer is again no. If there were absolutely no unemployment, the economy would lack the frictional unemployment that any changing economy must have. People must have the opportunity to search out better jobs, to move from dead-end positions into more promising positions. Firms must have the opportunity to test the skills of new employees. People will naturally weigh the costs and benefits of changing jobs and of entering into the search for jobs.

Full employment is difficult to define. Is the discouraged worker unemployed? Is the worker who finds only part-time work unemployed? Is the teenager attending school but looking for a part-time job really unemployed? Is the laid-off worker who is waiting to be recalled to a former job really unemployed?

Economists' perception of what constitutes full employment has been changing over the years. In the early 1960s, the President's Council of Economic Advisers felt that full employment was reached at an unemployment rate of around 4 percent. In the late 1970s, the President's Council of Economic Advisers raised its estimate of full employment to an unemployment rate of 5 to 5.5 percent. The full-employment rate depends upon a number of conditions that will be discussed in subsequent chapters.

INFLATION

For much of our recent history (especially since 1970), **inflation** has been one of our economy's most persistent and intractable problems.

Inflation is a general increase in prices.

A general increase in prices occurs when prices in the entire economy are rising on average. During an inflation, some prices rise faster than the average increase, and some rise slower. Some prices can even fall during inflations. For example, the prices of pocket calculators, home computers, and silicon chips fell throughout the inflationary 1970s. On the other hand, crude-oil prices rose between 1972 and 1981 five times faster than the average price increase. How the average rate of change of prices (the rate of inflation) is calculated in a world of changing relative prices is discussed later in this chapter.

Whether inflation is perceived as moderate or rapid is a relative matter. In the mid-1950s, when prices were rising about 2 percent per year or less, an inflation rate of 5 percent would have been viewed with alarm. In fact the "alarming" 1966 inflation rate of 3.3 percent motivated government authorities to impose strict anti-inflationary measures. In the early 1980s, after several years of near double-digit inflation, an inflation rate of 5 percent would have been welcomed as a remarkable achievement. In countries like Israel and Brazil with prices that have more than doubled annually in recent years, the American inflation rates of the late 1970s and early 1980s would be the object of envy. The rate of inflation—just like any other measure of prices—must be evaluated in relative terms.

Types of Inflation

A general rise in prices can occur for different reasons. Over the years, economists have often differentiated between three different types of inflation: **demand-pull inflation, cost-push inflation,** and **structural inflation.** (These three types of inflation and their causes will be discussed in greater detail in later chapters but are introduced below.)

Demand-Pull Inflation.   Inflation has been described as "too many dollars chasing too few goods." Demand-pull inflation concentrates on the "too many dollars" side of the inflation equation.

Demand-pull inflation occurs when the amount of money purchasers of goods and services want to spend increases more rapidly than the supply of such goods and services, resulting in the bidding up of prices.

The increase in demand is said to pull up the general level of prices.

Cost-Push Inflation.   Cost-push inflation concentrates on the "too few goods" side of the inflation equation.

Cost-push inflation occurs when autonomous increases in the prices of the factors of production or disruptions in supplies of factors generally cause firms to reduce their offerings of goods and services to the market at prevailing prices, resulting in the bidding up of their prices.

The increase in costs is said to push up the general price level.

Structural (Bottleneck) Inflation.   As already noted, relative prices are constantly changing in a dynamic economy. Some prices are rising; others are falling. If rising prices dominate, then the general level of prices rises. Bottlenecks in the economy may cause the prices of certain critical goods—like steel or oil or precision drilling machines—to be bid up. In one part of the economy, specific bottlenecks may cause certain prices to rise while in other parts of the economy, surpluses may develop. If these surpluses cause specific prices to fall, the price rises in the bottleneck sectors are moderated by price declines elsewhere.

Structural inflation occurs when prices in some areas of the economy do not fall as readily as prices rise in a bottleneck sector, resulting in a general upward creep in prices.

Effects of Inflation

People worry about inflation out of a fear that rising prices will lower their standard of living. Alarming increases in housing prices, food prices, and so on are cited as proof that standards of economic well-being are falling. Living standards are determined by the relationship between the income people have to spend and the prices they have to pay. If income (or the wage rate) is rising faster than prices, living standards are rising; if income is rising slower than prices, living standards are falling. The relationship between changes in income and changes in prices determines the direction of change in economic well-being.

For example, between 1970 and 1973, hourly wage rates rose more rapidly than prices; in 1974 and 1975, prices rose more rapidly than hourly wage rates; from 1976 to 1978 wages rose more rapidly than prices; from 1979 to 1981, prices rose more rapidly than wages. What people actually fear is declining living standards, not simply rising prices. Basically, inflation can be a problem for three reasons:

1. Inflation can redistribute income among members of society.
2. Inflation can cause a reduction in economic efficiency.
3. Inflation can cause changes in output and employment.

Income Redistribution. Inflation tends to affect the economic well-being of members of society because it can redistribute income among families by causing the real incomes of some to rise and the real incomes of others to fall. Some people are poorly protected from inflation. In some professions, wages and earnings rise less rapidly than the rate of inflation. Examples of people who have a difficult time keeping up with inflation are persons on fixed pensions, domestic servants, some public employees (such as school teachers), and some recipients of public-welfare payments. Some workers and employees are protected or even benefit from inflation. Many union members have cost-of-living clauses in their contracts (called *COLAs* for "cost-of-living adjustments") that raise their wages at the same rate as inflation. Borrowers who obtained loans when interest rates were low benefit from inflation by being able to pay off their loans in cheaper dollars. People who have purchased property—such as real estate, investment diamonds, or rare works of art—whose values have soared with inflation benefit from inflation.

Inflation is like a tax on fixed money receipts or assets and like a subsidy on fixed money payments or liabilities. If one holds $10,000 or expects to receive $10,000 at some designated date in the future, inflation erodes its value. In this sense, inflation is like a tax on the $10,000. On the other hand, if one owes $10,000 to be repaid at some designated future date, inflation reduces the person's burden; in this sense, it is like a subsidy. During the period of time when payment obligations (rent payments, wage contracts, interest payments) are fixed, inflation redistributes real wealth from those who receive money to those who pay the money.

For example, suppose someone borrowed $40,000 in 1972 to buy a home at an annual interest rate of 7 percent to be paid over a 25-year period. In 1982, the borrower would still owe the lender about $31,500 after 10 years. But over this 10-year period, the value of money that is still owed has been eroded by inflation. In 1972 approximately $0.46 purchased what $1 purchased in 1982 (the purchasing power of money fell by about 60 percent). Hence, the borrower has purchased a home by borrowing expensive dollars but repays in dollars that are growing cheaper as inflation continues. Wealth has been redistributed just as if the lender had paid a tax to the borrower.

The distributional effect of inflation depends upon the extent to which inflation is anticipated. Creditors and debtors are, of course, aware of the effects that inflation can have on their economic well-being. Is it not reasonable to assume that they will attempt to anticipate inflation in order to protect their economic interests? In our above example, the lender did not correctly anticipate the actual inflation that occurred between 1972 and 1982.

If in one year the rate of inflation is 8 percent, the next year it is 10 percent, and the next year it is 9 percent, people will begin to *anticipate,* say, a 9 percent rate of inflation per year, since the actual rate will likely not diverge much from the average. Once an inflation becomes anticipated, individuals and firms will act to protect their interests. Fixed money contracts will be modified to take into account the erosion of money values. Creditors will realize that they are being paid in cheaper dollars and will ask for a higher interest rate to compensate them; debtors will realize that they are repaying in cheaper dollars and will be more willing to pay a higher interest rate. Landlords will ask for higher rents over the year or a shorter lease that they can renegotiate if inflation accelerates; workers will ask for a higher wage rate or a shorter contract period.

If inflation is correctly anticipated, it will not redistribute wealth from those scheduled to receive money to those scheduled to pay money. Money contracts will incorporate inflation premiums to protect recipients of payments from the effects of inflation.

Steady predictable inflation gives people the opportunity to avoid the inflation tax. If inflation is erratic and intermittent, it will be difficult for people to anticipate the actual rate of inflation. If the rate of inflation is 6 percent in one year, 18 percent the next, and 3 percent in the following year, the actual rate of inflation will be to a large extent unanticipated.

Inflation redistributes wealth from lenders to borrowers only when inflation has not been properly anticipated.

Inefficiency.   When inflation is intermittent, predicting the rate of inflation becomes a difficult business. The 1976 Nobel Laureate in economics, Milton Friedman, points out that:

> Under such circumstances, the most valuable quality on the part of a businessman becomes his ability to forecast the changes in prices and to adjust rapidly to them. This becomes more important than his ability as organizer or as a manager or as a person who can see where there are profitable opportunities. The result is that some of the most valuable and scarcest resources in the economy are diverted into activities that are socially unproductive.[2]

2. Milton Friedman, *Dollars and Deficits* (Englewood Cliffs, N.J.: Prentice-Hall, 1968), pp. 49–50. Some examples of this can be found in the classic study of German hyperinflation by Costanino Bresciani-Turroni, *The Economics of Inflation* (London: Allen & Unwin, 1937).

Inflation leads to speculative practices that would otherwise be considered somewhat frivolous. By trying to outwit everyone else, those who expect more inflation than the marketplace expects will speculate in real estate, foreign currencies, gold (in 1980 the price of gold was driven up to dizzying heights), and art objects. Such speculative investments are made *in place of* investments in plants, equipment, and inventories that would raise the productive potential of the economy. Inflation causes cash-soaked doctors and lawyers to rush to art auctions and invest in questionable schemes to avoid the inflation tax. While the poor might be just trying to make ends meet, the rich are preoccupied in a rather useless game of musical chairs.

Anticipated inflation can divert resources from productive to unproductive investments and thus reduce the economy's productive capacity.

The negative effects of inflation on economic efficiency are most pronounced during *runaway inflations*. During runaway inflations, prices may double daily or even twice daily. Workers become reluctant to accept money wages, and the money that is received will be spent immediately. Businesses refuse to enter into fixed contracts, and most transactions involve barter exchanges of goods and services. In other words, runaway inflations result in the loss of the efficiency of money transactions. Most efforts in such an economy are directed at avoiding the inflation tax rather than at productive economic activities.

Changes in Real Output and Employment.   Anticipated inflation can divert resources from productive to basically unproductive uses as people maneuver to avoid the inflation tax. But inflation can affect economic output and employment in a more direct manner by motivating firms to produce more or less than they would have otherwise and by motivating people to work more or less than they would have otherwise. Inflation and interest rates are linked, and high interest rates may affect borrowing for capital investment. Inflation pushes people into higher tax brackets; the higher the tax bracket the lower may be the incentive to work extra hours.

Some economists believe that inflation (whether anticipated or unanticipated) has a negligible effect on output and employment. Other economists say that inflation, especially when it catches people by surprise, can have a significant and positive effect on real economic variables. Inflation's impact on real economic variables such as output and employment will occupy our attention throughout the following macro chapters.

Price Indexes

If all prices rose at the same rate—say, 7 percent per year—there would be no problem measuring the general increase in prices. The inflation rate under these circumstances would obviously be 7 percent per annum. But prices do not change at the same rate; some prices rise more rapidly than others. For example, prices of food products rose 244 percent between 1967 and 1980, while housing prices rose 261 percent, apparel prices rose 177.5 percent, transportation prices rose 249 percent, and entertainment prices rose 204 percent. In other words, relative prices were changing while prices in general were rising.

A price index compares the cost of a given combination of goods in two or more different years. If a certain *market basket* (combination of goods and services consumed by a typical family) costs $200 in 1982 and $220 in 1983, the price index is 110($220/$200 times 100) for 1983 in 1982 dollars. In other words, prices were 10 percent higher in 1983 than in 1982.

A **price index** shows the current year's cost of a particular market basket as a percentage of the cost of the same market basket in some base year.

$$\text{Price index} = \frac{\text{current market basket cost}}{\text{base market basket cost}} \times 100$$

Obviously, the value of this price index is 100.0 in the base year:

$$\frac{\$200}{\$200} \times 100 = 100.0$$

To calculate the percentage change in prices, the following formula can be used:

Percentage change in prices

$$= \frac{\text{current index value} - \text{base index value}}{\text{base index value}}$$

In the above example, the percentage change in prices would be calculated:

$$\frac{110 - 100}{100} = \frac{10}{100} = 10 \text{ percent}$$

The percentage price increase could also be calculated directly: ($220 − 200)/$200 = 10 percent. The difficulties of using the index number approach to measuring price change will be illustrated in the next section.

The Consumer Price Index (CPI). The most prominent price index is the Consumer Price Index, or CPI.[3] The CPI is one of the most important statistics in the American economy. The press, radio, and television report monthly changes in the CPI. The public may form expectations concerning the future rate of inflation from past and current movements in the CPI. Presidents may be voted out of office because of public concern over soaring inflation. Moreover, the wages of many union workers and government employees are tied to the CPI: if the CPI goes up, wages are adjusted to reflect the higher cost of living. The rates of increase of many government pensions, including social security, are tied to the CPI. Government policies towards inflation tend to be based on the CPI. For these reasons, it is important that the CPI be an accurate gauge of the rate of increase in consumer prices.

---

3. The CPI is prepared by the Bureau of Labor Statistics (BLS). To compile the CPI, the BLS collects on a monthly basis prices from 85 areas across the country in about 24,000 trade and service establishments. The prices of thousands of goods and services are recorded. They are converted into a consumer price index by weighting each commodity group by its share of the average expenditures in 1972–73 of a typical urban family of four having an intermediate budget. In other words, the weights used to average the prices that enter into the CPI are taken to be the market basket of a hypothetical average American family. What does this typical market basket look like? In 1972–73, an average urban four-person family spent 24.8 percent of its budget on food, 22.5 percent on housing, 8.4 percent on transportation, and 44.5 percent on other items such as medical care, clothing, and services.

There are several conceptual difficulties in measuring general trends in consumer prices. Because the CPI is calculated by determining how much a specified market basket of goods costs in different years, critics of the CPI maintain that it exaggerates the rate of inflation. The CPI assumes that consumers do not make substitutions for products whose relative prices are increasing. In reality, if the relative price of beef rises, consumers substitute poultry, fish, or pork, often without a great loss of consumer satisfaction. Consumers respond to rising movie prices by substituting other forms of entertainment, according to the law of demand. But the CPI assumes that consumers continue to consume the same mix of goods year after year even though relative prices are changing. By making substitutions, however, families can actually reduce the rate of increase in their cost of living below the measured CPI inflation rate.

The CPI measures the rate of inflation experienced by urban consumers (and by urban wage and clerical workers). Only those families that happen to consume the same market basket of goods as the hypothetical 1972–73 average urban family will have the same personal rate of inflation. A family's personal rate of inflation can be quite different from that indicated by the CPI. For example, housing costs have been one of the most rapidly rising components of the CPI. However, if a family happens to already own their own home financed at a fixed low mortgage rate, their personal housing costs are not rising as rapidly as the CPI indicates. In this case, the CPI exaggerates the rate of inflation.[4]

The GNP Deflator. The CPI measures changes in the prices of only those goods and services that families purchase for their own consumption. It does not measure the other goods and services that the economy produces for uses other than personal consumption. In 1981, 63.5 percent of the gross national product (GNP), or the total output of the American economy, was devoted to personal consumption. The remaining 37 percent was expended on business investment, government services, and exports and imports. The CPI, therefore, is not the most general measure of the rate of inflation. A more general measure is the **GNP deflator.**

*The **GNP deflator** measures the change in the prices of all goods and services produced by the economy.*

Over the past 30 years, the GNP deflator has not behaved much differently from the CPI. The CPI and the GNP deflator show that prices have increased by a factor of 3.6 and 3.7, respectively, between 1950 and 1981, but in individual years the two indexes sometimes diverge more. Because the GNP deflator is a more general measure of inflation, many of the subsequent inflation figures subsequently cited in this book are based on the GNP deflator.

Historical Trends. Figure 2 shows the pattern of inflation since 1950. This chart shows why most of the readers of this book have come to think of rising prices as one of the constants of life along with death and taxes: the CPI has shown a price decrease in only one of the last 30 years (1955).

Trends in inflation over the past two centuries are plotted in Figure 3. This figure reveals that the sustained increases in consumer prices characteristic of the past 30 years are a fairly new phenomenon. If one excludes the last 48 years, U.S. experience shows that prices were as likely to fall as to rise. Prior to the Second World War, there were significant movements of the price level in both directions. *Deflations* (downward movements in prices) were just as common as *inflations* (upward movements in prices). The unusual feature of the last 48 years has been the notable absence of periods of deflation. Unlike earlier periods when periods of inflation tended to be balanced by subsequent periods of deflation, the postwar era has been one of continuing increases in prices, albeit at different rates.

---

4. In response to growing criticisms from economists and politicians, the Bureau of Labor Statistics has prepared a new CPI to be officially issued in 1983. The revised CPI changes the way housing costs are treated by the CPI. Instead of measuring changes in housing prices and the costs of financing housing purchases, the revised CPI will try to measure what it would hypothetically cost homeowners to rent their own homes. The revised CPI will be used to index Social Security benefits and to index individual income-tax rates starting in 1985.

Figure 2
The Consumer Price Index, 1951–1980

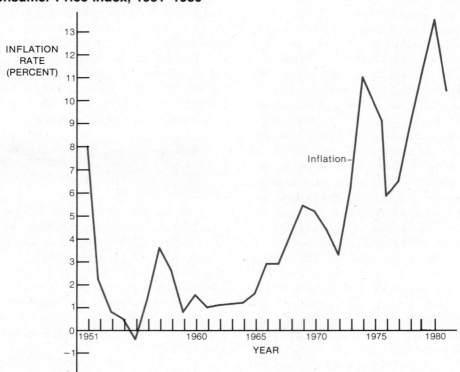

This chart shows that the rate of inflation accelerated sharply from the early 1960s to 1980.

Source: *Statistical Abstract of the United States,* 1980, p. 486; *Economic Report of the President,* January 1982, p. 236.

The facts show that inflation is not inevitable, even though it may appear so to the current generation. Later chapters will explore what is different about the postwar era.

BUSINESS CYCLES

Like prices, trends in business activity are not smooth, neat, and predictable. Countries experience episodes of sharp reductions in the volume of total output and employment, which are followed by episodes of rapid growth of output and employment. Unemployment rates rise and then fall.

Over the very long run, economies tend to increase their total output of goods and services. The labor force grows with population; capital accumulation increases the nation's capital stock; technological improvements raise productive ca-

pacity. The American economy of 1982 produces a volume of output more than 18 times that of 1890. This increase translates into an annual rate of growth of 3.3 percent.

Many distinguished economists—such as Wesley Clair Mitchell, Joseph Schumpeter, Simon Kuznets, Gottfried Haberler, N.D. Kondratieff, and Arthur Burns—have studied trends and movements in the level of business activity, or the **business cycle.**

*A **business cycle** is the pattern of upward and downward movements in the general level of real business activity.*

Economic research has discovered different types of business cycles: cycles of very short duration lasting one to two years, intermediate-term cycles lasting five years or so, long-term cycles

Figure 3
The U.S. Price Level, 1800–1981

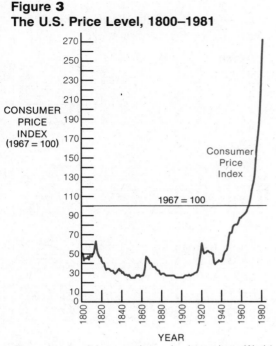

The price level has continuously risen since World War II, deviating from the pattern of the preceding 140 years.

Source: *Historical Statistics of the United States,* 1970, p. 291; *Economic Report of the President,* January 1982, p. 294.

lasting a decade or more, and *secular swings*—cycles lasting several decades or more. Some types of business cycles affect only one type of industry or business activity (such as home building or business inventory accumulation); other types of business cycles affect virtually all facets of business activity in all industries.

Recessions and Depressions

The business-cycle terms *recession* and *depression* are commonly used, but few understand their exact meanings. The U.S. Department of Commerce, which is responsible for collecting much of our economic data, provides a precise easy-to-use definition of **recession.**

According to the Commerce Department, a **recession** *is a decline in real output (GNP) that lasts for six months or more.*

A **depression** is more difficult to define precisely.

Figure 4
The Four Phases of the Business Cycle

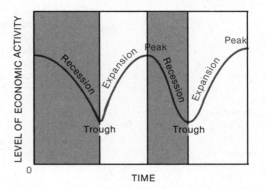

During the recession phase of a business cycle, the level of business activity is in general decline. The trough occurs when the various indicators of business activity stop falling. Output expands during the recovery phase of the business cycle, and the business cycle reaches a peak when the various indicators of production and employment stop rising.

A **depression** *is a very severe downturn in economic activity that lasts for several years. Real output declines during this period by a significant amount, and the unemployment rate rises to 15 percent or more.*

A depression is a very severe and extended recession.

The Four Phases of the Business Cycle

Business cycles are divided into four phases, irrespective of their severity and duration. As Figure 4 shows, the four classic phases of the business cycle are:

1. downturn or recession (or depression if the decline in activity is prolonged and severe),
2. trough,
3. expansion (or recovery), and
4. peak.

During the *recession* phase, the level of business activity is in general decline. The various indexes of output (described below) all indicate that the economy is producing a declining rate of output. The unemployment rate rises, and the num-

Table 2
American Business Cycles, 1924–1981

Trough	Peak	Length of Cycle, Peak to Peak (months)
July 1924	October 1926	41
November 1927	August 1929	34
March 1933	May 1937	93
June 1938	February 1945	93
October 1945	November 1948	45
October 1949	July 1953	56
May 1954	August 1957	49
April 1958	April 1960	32
February 1961	December 1969	116
November 1970	November 1973	47
March 1975	January 1980	62
March 1980	January 1981	12

Source: U.S. Bureau of Economic Analysis, *Business Conditions Digest,* June 1980; *Economic Report of the President,* January 1982, p. 234.

Figure 5
The Index of Leading Indicators and Four Major Components

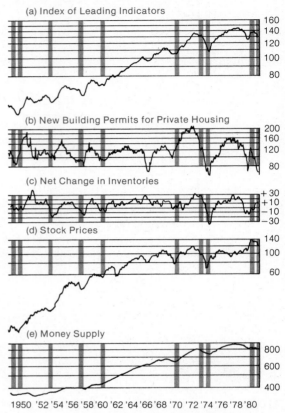

(a) Index of Leading Indicators

(b) New Building Permits for Private Housing

(c) Net Change in Inventories

(d) Stock Prices

(e) Money Supply

1950 '52 '54 '56 '58 '60 '62 '64 '66 '68 '70 '72 '74 '76 '78 '80

Prior to each of the recessions indicated by the grey areas, the composite index of leading indicators—shown in panel (a)—did indeed drop, although the amount of time between the drop and the recession varied. In addition, not all drops in the index were followed by recessions. Although the components of the index—in panels (b) through (e)—do tend to move together, the agreement is not exact.

Source: Department of Commerce.

ber employed will decline (or its rate of increase will slow down). The *trough* (or lowest point) occurs when the various indicators of business activity stop falling. The economy has reached a low point from which recovery begins.

During the *recovery* stage of the business cycle, the various output indicators point to expanding output. The final stage of the business cycle is reached at the *peak* when the various indicators of production and employment fail to yield further increases. When the next stage—recession—begins, the economy begins another business cycle. There is a big difference between small cyclical swings where the economy stays near full employment and large swings from boom to depression.

Length of Cycles

The duration of a business cycle is the length of time it takes to move through one complete business cycle. The length of the business cycle can be measured either by the amount of time (number of months) from the peak of the cycle to the next peak or by the time it takes to move from trough to trough. The duration of the cycle varies by economy and time period and by the phenomenon being studied. No two business cycles are

identical. Government studies of the American business cycle from 1924 to the present (see Table 2) show that the average duration of cycles is almost 5 years. The recession phase lasts, on the average, slightly less than one year. The expansion phase lasts, on the average, about four years.

Leading Indicators

Literally hundreds of indicators may be used to measure the rhythm of the business cycle: the length of the average work week, the layoff rate, unemployment, total output, personal income, industrial production, stock prices, the number of new private housing units started, the volume of commercial and industrial loans, and so on. Such indicators tend to move together, but they do not move in the same phase with the basic rhythm of the business cycle. Some indicators lead the basic cycle; some are coincident with the cycle; others lag behind the basic cycle. From the point of view of economists and business forecasters, the **leading indicators** are the most important because they may give information about the future.

> *Leading indicators tend to rise or fall prior to the general rise or fall in business activity.*

Figure 5 shows the composite (combined) index of leading indicators from 1948 to 1981. The shaded areas show recession phases of the business cycle; the light areas show expansion phases of the business cycle. Also shown are four of the most important components of the composite index of leading indicators: new building permits, net inventory changes, stock prices, and the supply of money.

How good a job do the leading indicators do in warning of forthcoming recessions? Prior to each of the seven recessions shown in Figure 5, the index of leading indicators indeed dropped. But sometimes the composite index begins to drop a year or more before the recession (two years before the 1957–58 recession, for example); other times it begins to drop just before the recession (4 months before the 1953–54 recession). Often drops in the index of leading indicators are not followed by recessions. For example, the 1960s was a decade of uninterrupted expansion, yet the index of leading indicators predicted three recessions during these years. Another problem is that the components of the composite index of leading indicators do not move together in exactly the same rhythm.

The role of leading indicators in predicting the future will be analyzed in more detail in later chapters. To devise sound countercyclical economic policy requires information about the timing, depth, and severity of recessions. Although the index of leading indicators is not a perfect guide to the future, it is one of the most important and widely used indicators in the economy.

The World Economy

Economies do not exist in isolation. Events in one country affect the economic fortunes of other countries. Higher interest rates in the United States raise interest rates in Europe. American restrictions on automobile imports affect jobs and incomes in Japan. The world's economies are affected by changes in energy prices, crop failures, and by political disruptions. The economic fortunes of the world's economies are strongly intertwined.

The links among economies are demonstrated by the fact that different countries tend to experience common business cycles. When the level of business activity is falling in the United States, it is likely falling as well (or soon will be falling) in Europe and Japan.

The similar timing of business cycles in the major economies is shown in Figure 6, which gives the annual rates of growth of industrial production for six Western economies plus Japan. Why business cycles of different countries are related will be discussed in a later chapter.

MACROECONOMIC TRADE-OFFS AND DISPUTES

This chapter began by listing five macroeconomic goals and by noting that some of the goals can be conflicting. This section will describe some of the trade-offs a society may have to make between pairs of conflicting goals.

Inflation versus Unemployment

In our modern economy, it often appears that as the inflation rate falls, unemployment increases. As economic activity increases and unemployed workers return to work, the inflation rate tends to rise. Why this is so (and whether or not it is always so) will be the focus of much discussion in later chapters. The inflation/unemployment trade-off is probably the most controversial and widely discussed trade-off in macroeconomics.

Discussion of the inflation/unemployment trade-off was sparked by the empirical finding of the English economist, A. W. Phillips, writing in 1958 about a stable negative relationship between the rate of wage inflation and the rate of unem-

Figure 6
Annual Rates of Growth of Industrial Production in Seven Economies

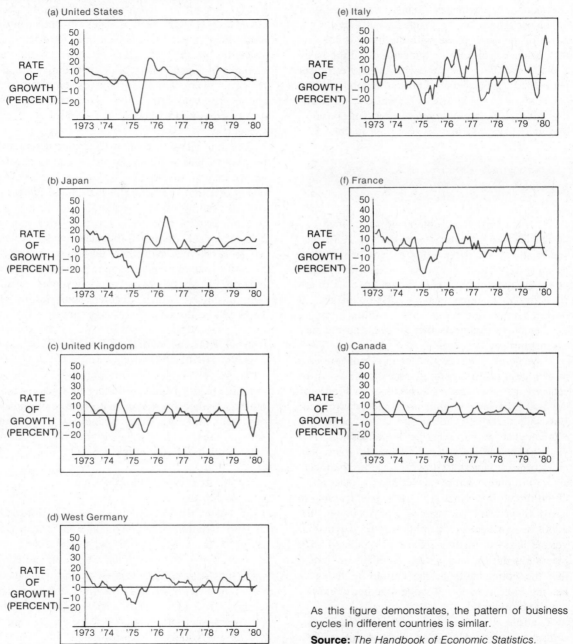

As this figure demonstrates, the pattern of business cycles in different countries is similar.

Source: *The Handbook of Economic Statistics.*

ployment for England. Phillips's study was soon followed by studies in the United States that also showed a negative relationship between U.S. inflation and unemployment. These findings suggested that societies can either have low unemployment or low inflation but that they cannot have both together. The experiences of the 1970s and the 1980s cast considerable doubt on the original Phillips relationship, sparking new macroeconomic theories.

Many of the important recent developments in modern macroeconomics deal with the inflation/ unemployment trade-off. The debate today has shifted to the role of time and of inflation expectations in shaping the inflation/unemployment trade-off. Today the consensus is that there is no long-run trade-off but that there still is a short-run trade-off under certain conditions. A full chapter will be devoted to the study of the inflation/unemployment trade-off.

Income Distribution versus Living Standards

Some economists would argue that excessive redistribution of income from the rich to the poor (through the tax system, for example) would reduce the incentives for the rich to work hard, to take risks, or to invest their money in productive ventures. If such were the case, income redistribution from the rich to the poor would slow down the rate of growth of output and of living standards. Conversely, too much emphasis on raising living standards might result in a distribution of income that is too inequitable. Thus, some economists believe there is a trade-off between the goals of an equal income distribution and the higher standard of living that results from society's greater productivity.

Economic Fluctuations versus Inflation or Unemployment

One of the most important policy disputes among economists today concerns the business cycle. Some economists feel that economic fluctuations are natural and will be merely worsened by government corrective policies. They argue that attempts to control the business cycle may only worsen inflation, unemployment, or both. Other economists feel that activist government economic policies can successfully control the business cycle. A later chapter will be devoted to the dispute over activist versus nonactivist macroeconomic policy.

Changing Public Attitudes

In addition to the disputes among economists on the opportunity costs of achieving economic goals, societies, as a whole, find it hard to agree on the appropriate rankings of the various goals and how the trade-offs should be managed. Some groups favor one goal over another and are prepared to sacrifice goals that other groups may treasure. The poor may prefer a more equal distribution of income at the cost of less economic growth. Those with secure jobs may worry more about price stability than rising unemployment. Workers protected from rising prices by cost-of-living escalators may favor rapid increases in living standards.

The conflicts over public rankings of macroeconomic goals are resolved largely in the realm of politics. Presidential, congressional, and even state and local elections are won or lost over these issues. One major party, in its electoral campaign, will emphasize that its prime concern is the spiraling inflation rate. Another major party may emphasize the plight of the unemployed. When the electorate selects among the platforms of politicians and their parties, social preferences are revealed.

Only one of the five economic goals listed at the start of the chapter is enshrined in formal legislation. The Full Employment Act of 1946 established the Council of Economic Advisers and the Joint Economic Committee of Congress and declared that it was the responsibility of government to keep employment high and to prevent undue cyclical fluctuations. According to the act, it is

> the continuing policy and responsibility of the Federal Government to use all practical means consistent with its needs and obligations and other essential considerations of national policy . . . to create and maintain . . . conditions under which there will be afforded useful employment opportunities, including self-employment, for those able, willing, and seeking to work. . . .

The other macroeconomic goals—in particular, price stability—have yet to be written into law with such specificity.[5]

Public priorities have not remained static over the years. In the 1980 presidential election, it was clear that inflation was regarded by the public as its number-one economic problem, a fact con-

---

5. The Humphrey-Hawkins Act of 1978 was the most recent effort to write macroeconomic goals into law. The Humphrey-Hawkins Act called for efforts to achieve both full employment and price stability but failed to legislate tight goals for price stability.

firmed by numerous consumer surveys. The presidential campaign of 1960 focused on the slow economic growth of the United States relative to its major military competitor, the Soviet Union. In the mid-1960s, more attention was devoted to improving the lot of the poor (the Great Society's War on Poverty) and on holding down unemployment.

Why public attitudes change over the years is a matter for political scientists or psychologists to explain. Economists have the difficult job of telling policy makers how priority goals can be achieved and outlining the opportunity costs of achieving these goals.

A PREVIEW OF AGGREGATE SUPPLY-AND-DEMAND ANALYSIS

The behavior of aggregate supply and aggregate demand is as important to macroeconomics as the laws of supply and demand are to microeconomics. Subsequent chapters will use aggregate supply-and-demand analysis to explain movements in prices, total output, and employment. This section will briefly sketch the principles of aggregate supply-and-demand analysis and will allow later chapters to fill in the details.

The Aggregate Demand Curve

The **aggregate demand** *(AD)* **curve** shows the relationship between the total demand for goods and services and the price level.

> The **aggregate demand (AD) curve** *shows the amounts of goods and services that agents in the economy (households, business firms, and government) are prepared to buy at different price levels.*

The aggregate demand curve in Figure 7 is negatively sloped. One cannot conclude that the aggregate demand curve is negatively sloping just because the demand curves of each product are negatively sloped. The law of demand is based upon relative prices and makes sense only when one price is changing relative to other prices. Aggregate demand responds to change in the *general price level*.

Figure 7
The Aggregate Demand and the Aggregate Supply Curves

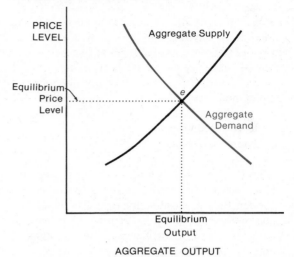

The aggregate demand curve, which shows the quantities of goods and services demanded at different price levels by all agents in the economy, will be negatively sloped. The aggregate supply curve which shows the different quantities of goods and services supplied by all agents will be positively sloped, at least in the short run. The intersection of the two curves determines the equilibrium level of aggregate output as well as the price level.

The aggregate demand curve will be negatively sloped for other reasons. As will be explained in later chapters, a higher price level reduces the real value of wealth (the amount of goods and services that the accumulated money, stocks, bonds, and so on will purchase). Households, therefore, cut back on their purchases of cars, houses, clothing, and other items. A higher price level will also tend to raise interest rates, which tends to discourage purchases of investment goods and consumer goods.

> The **aggregate demand** (AD) *curve is negatively sloped because a higher price level will cause households and businesses to cut back on their desired real expenditures.*

The Aggregate Supply Curve

Figure 7 also shows an **aggregate supply** *(AS)* **curve.**

*The **aggregate supply** (AS) curve shows the various quantities of goods and services that businesses are prepared to supply at different price levels.*

Later chapters will demonstrate that the aggregate supply curve is upward-sloping under certain conditions. In the long run, the aggregate supply curve can be vertical. Much of the discussion in modern macroeconomics today is over the shape and behavior of the aggregate supply curve.

In the short run, the aggregate supply curve can be positively sloped because a general rise in the price level will cause prices to rise more rapidly than costs, and this rate of increase will motivate profit-minded businesses to increase production and employment. Even if prices are not actually rising more rapidly than costs, businesses may perceive their prices to be rising when prices rise generally. Later chapters will show that a positive slope characterizes the aggregate supply curve more in the short run than in the long run.

Aggregate Supply-and-Demand Analysis

Aggregate supply-and-demand analysis is like microeconomic supply-and-demand analysis in the following way: The interaction of aggregate supply and aggregate demand determines the equilibrium price level and the equilibrium amount of goods and services produced. At point *e* in Figure 7, aggregate demand equals aggregate supply. As in microeconomics, changes in equilibrium will occur if the *AD* or *AS* curves shift.

Macroeconomics is the study of the effects of shifts in aggregate supply and aggregate demand on output, employment, and the price level. Two approaches to macroeconomics are **demand-side economics** and **supply-side economics.**

***Demand-side economics** focuses on the causes and effects of shifts in the aggregate demand curve.*

***Supply-side economics** focuses on the causes and effects of shifts in the aggregate supply curve.*

The following chapters will examine why these two approaches tend to view the economy in a different light and why their policy recommendations concerning the cures of unemployment or inflation are different. In order to understand macroeconomic effects on output, employment, or the price level, it is important to be able to measure them. The next chapter will examine how to define and measure aggregate economic output and its various components.

Summary

1. Macroeconomics is the study of the economy in the whole. Macroeconomists study the trade-offs among the macroeconomic goals of full employment, price stability, a fair distribution of income, and protection against the business cycle. Much of the controversy in modern macroeconomics is over the trade-off between inflation and unemployment.

2. A person is unemployed if he or she is not working, is currently available for work, and is actively seeking a job. There are three main types of unemployment: frictional unemployment (normal changing of jobs in a changing economy), cyclical unemployment (associated with general downturns in the economy), and structural unemployment (resulting from long-term economic declines concentrated in specific industries or regions).

3. Inflation is a general increase in prices measured by price indexes that determine the changing cost of buying a market basket of goods. The most important price indexes are the consumer price index (the CPI) and the GNP deflator. The three types of inflation are demand-pull, cost-push, and structural inflation. Inflation can affect income distribution, efficiency, employment, and output.

4. A business cycle is the pattern of upward and downward movements in the level of business activity. A recession is a decline in real output that lasts six months or more. A depression is a very severe recession, lasting several years or more. The four phases of the business cycle are: recession, trough, recovery, and peak. Indicators that precede the business cycle are leading indicators.

5. Because macroeconomic goals can be conflicting, a society may have to make decisions about trade-offs between inflation and unemployment, between fair income distribution and high living standards, or between economic fluctuations and inflation or unemployment.
6. The aggregate demand curve shows the quantity of goods and services demanded by all agents in the economy at different price levels. The aggregate supply curve shows the quantity of goods and services supplied at different price levels. Aggregate supply-and-demand analysis is the principal tool of modern macroeconomics.

Key Terms

labor force
unemployment rate
discouraged workers
frictional unemployment
cyclical unemployment
structural unemployment
inflation
demand-pull inflation
cost-push inflation
structural (bottleneck) inflation
price index
GNP deflator
business cycle
recession
depression
leading indicators
aggregate demand *(AD)* curve
aggregate supply *(AS)* curve
demand-side economics
supply-side economics

Questions and Problems

1. "Opportunity costs are only relevant in microeconomics where decisions are based upon marginal costs and marginal benefits." Evaluate this statement.
2. Describe the relevant criteria by which government statisticians determine whether a person is "unemployed" or "not in the labor force."
3. Suppose economic conditions are generally good but that a further increase in gasoline prices has caused a slump in the automobile industry. How would you classify unemployment in the automobile industry?
4. "The rate of inflation has meaning only in relative terms." Evaluate this statement.
5. By analogy to microeconomics, explain why "too many dollars chasing too few goods" can cause inflation.
6. Explain how inflation can redistribute wealth from lenders to borrowers.
7. Explain why, in a society where prices are doubling every week, this hyperinflation would reduce economic efficiency.
8. In Figure 7, what would happen to prices, output, and unemployment if the aggregate demand curve shifts to the right? What would happen to these if the aggregate supply curve shifts to the right?

CHAPTER

6

Measuring National Income and National Product

Chapter Preview

Because macroeconomics is the study of the economy in the large, economists must have ways of measuring the total output of the economy. **National income accounting** is a relatively old branch of economics, which dates back to Gregory King's effort to measure the total output of England in the late 17th century. Not until the postwar era, however, did economists and international organizations like the United Nations agree upon uniform methods of national income accounting. The most prominent pioneer in this field is Nobel Prize laureate, Simon Kuznets. His work in the 1930s was instrumental in developing many of the national accounting measures dis-

cussed in this chapter. This chapter will explain the relationship between an economy's total output and total income and how these are measured.

> **National income accounting** is the science of measuring the aggregate output and income of an economy.

THE CIRCULAR FLOW AND NATIONAL INCOME

National income accounting is based upon the principles of the circular flow of output and income introduced in Chapter 2. The circular-flow diagram in Figure 1 illustrates the basic principle of national income accounting: the value of total

Figure 1
The Circular Flow Revisited

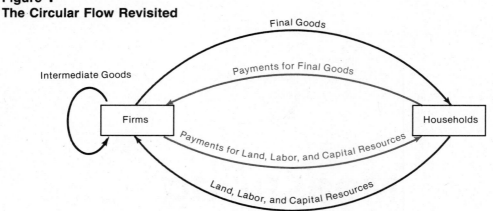

The top half of the circular-flow diagram highlights the flows of goods and services from businesses to households and the corresponding flow of money payments for these goods and services from households to businesses. The bottom half shows the flows of the factors of production from households to businesses and the reciprocal flow of factor payments (income) from the businesses to households. Intermediate goods traded within the business sector do not enter the circular flow.

　　The circular-flow diagram reveals the basic identity of national income accounting: the value of purchases of final goods and services equals the value of factor payments.

output equals the value of total income. If the economy produces a total output of, say, $500 billion, then a total income of $500 billion will automatically be created in the process. In producing output, costs are incurred. Workers must be paid, land must be rented, and capital costs must be paid. The act of producing goods and services, therefore, creates incomes for those supplying the factors of production. But what is to prevent the value of output from exceeding or falling short of the sum of factor payments? If, in our example, $500 billion worth of output is produced and sold but only $450 billion is paid to (earned by) the factors of production, the $50 billion surplus accrues to entrepreneurs as profits—and profits are income just like wages, rents, and interest. If, in our example, $500 billion worth of output is produced and sold but $550 billion is paid to the factors of production, the $50 billion deficit falls on entrepreneurs as losses—reducing their income.

Profits insure that the value of output and the value of income will be equal.

To understand the principles of national income accounting, consider a very simple hypo-

thetical economy that consists of only five industries: 1) ore and coal production, 2) steel production, 3) automobile manufacturing, 4) cotton farming, and 5) clothing manufacturing. In this simple economy, steel is made from ore and coal (in addition to land, labor, and capital), autos are made from steel, and clothing is made from cotton. The annual sales of each industry are given in Table 1.

The upper half of the circular-flow diagram in Figure 1 shows the flows of goods and services from businesses to households. In our example, only the **final goods**—cars and clothing—flow from businesses to households. Ore and coal, steel, and cotton flow from one firm to another but do not flow to households. As the cars and clothing flow to households, money payments for the clothing and automobiles flow from households to businesses.

Final goods are goods that are not used up in the production of any other goods.

To produce final goods and services, businesses must buy **intermediate** goods from other firms (automobile manufacturers must purchase steel; the clothing industry must purchase cotton).

Table 1
The Output of a Hypothetical Economy

Value of Intermediate Goods (billions of dollars of annual sales)	Value of Final Goods (billions of dollars of annual sales)	
Ore, coal 20 ⟶ steel 100 ⟶	Autos 200	
Cotton 50 ⟶	Clothing 90	
	Total 290	

In this example, ore and coal are used to produce steel, and steel is used to produce automobiles. Cotton is used to produce clothes. Goods used to produce other goods are called *intermediate goods*. Goods consumed by final consumers are *final goods*.

Intermediate goods do not enter the circular flow because they remain within the business sector. Firms must also hire factors of production—land, labor, and capital—owned by households. The bottom portion of the circular-flow diagram represents the flows of the factors of production from households to businesses and the reciprocal factor payments made by businesses to households. The dollar flow of payments for goods and services in the upper half of the diagram exactly equals the dollar flow of factor payments in the bottom half.

> *Intermediate goods are goods that are completely used up in the production of another good. The value of the intermediate products is reflected in the price of the final goods.*

GROSS NATIONAL PRODUCT

The circular-flow diagram provides a starting point for understanding the meaning of the total output of an economy. The simple circular-flow diagram includes only final goods in the flow of output from firms to households. Intermediate goods are not considered part of the total output of the industrial sector because they remain entirely within the business sector.

In our example, cotton is an intermediate good because it is used up in the production of another good—clothing. Automobiles are a final good be-

cause they are consumed by households and do not reenter the production process to produce other goods. Table 1 is divided into two parts. The left-hand side lists intermediate goods within the business sector; the right-hand side shows the final goods that are produced.

The circular-flow diagram demonstrates that intermediate goods are not important in their own right; they are simply a means to an end. Economic well-being is determined by the final goods and services that the economy produces. Because an economy may produce large quantities of intermediate goods like ores, coal, steel, and raw cotton and yet use them inefficiently to produce final goods and services, the total output of the economy must be defined in terms of the final goods and services it produces.

In our simple example, it is easy to distinguish between intermediate and final goods. In the real world, the distinctions are more difficult to make. As explained later, households are not the only ones that consume final goods.

The most comprehensive measure of the total output of the economy is **gross national product (GNP).**

> *Gross national product (GNP) is the market value of all final goods and services produced by an economy in one year's time.*

In our simple economy that produces only cars and clothing for final use, GNP equals the value of automobiles and clothing produced by the economy in one year's time. In Table 1, the value of one year's automobile production is $200 billion and the value of one year's clothing manufacture is $90 billion. GNP is, therefore, $290 billion.

GNP is not the sum of the production of both final and intermediate goods. In our example, this sum would be $460 billion ($20 + $100 + $50 + $200 + $90). If the value of the production of intermediate goods were included, some products would be counted two times or more. The value of ore and coal is already counted in the value of steel, and the value of steel is already counted in the value of autos. The value of cotton is already counted in the value of clothing. The measure of total output should not count products more than once.

Table 2
1981 GNP by Final Expenditure (billions of 1981 $)

Expenditure Category	Amount (billions of 1981 dollars)	Percentage of Total
Personal consumption expenditures	**1,858**	**63.6**
Durable goods	232	
Nondurable goods	743	
Services	883	
Gross private domestic investment	**450**	**15.4**
Nonresidential structures	125	
Equipment	202	
Residential structures	105	
Inventory investment	18	
Government purchases of goods and services	**590**	**20.2**
Federal government	229	
State and local government	361	
Net exports	**24**	**0.8**
GNP	**2,922**	**100.0**

Source: *Economic Report of the President,* January 1982, pp. 233, 248, 250.

CALCULATING GNP

The basic principle of national income accounting illustrated in the simple example in Table 1 can be applied to real-world economies. Because the total output of the economy must equal the total income of the economy, GNP can be calculated either by summing the monetary value of all final goods and services produced in one year or by summing all factor incomes earned in one year. Both approaches yield the same answer.

The Flow of Products

In Table 1, GNP is the sum of the sales of the two final products—clothing and automobiles—that were produced by the hypothetical economy. In this simplified example, only one type of final product was produced: goods for final consumption by households. In the real world, there are other types of final goods in addition to consumer goods. Table 2 lists the four major categories of final products:

1. personal-consumption expenditures,
2. federal-, state-, and local-government purchases of goods and services,
3. investment, and
4. net exports.

Personal-Consumption Expenditures *(C).* The goods and services that people buy and consume—the food, the entertainment services, the clothing, the airline tickets, the haircuts, the books, the television sets—are all final goods and services.

Personal-consumption expenditures are not used to produce other goods. They are consumed by households either immediately (such as food and entertainment) or gradually over time (TV sets, automobiles, and dishwashers). Long-lived consumer goods that are consumed over a period of time are called *consumer durables*.

Government Expenditures for Goods and Services *(G).* Local, state, and federal governments purchase final goods and services. Governments spend money to run the legal system, to provide for the national defense, and to run the schools. Although some government expenditures strongly resemble intermediate expenditures—such as government regulation of business or agricultural-extension services—by convention, almost all government expenditures for goods and services are counted as final goods and services in national income accounting.

Government produces goods and services for society by hiring civil servants and school teach-

The Internal Revenue Service and Final Goods

Whether an expenditure is intermediate or final is important for tax purposes. The dividing line between final and intermediate expenditures is often hard to draw. A sales representative may buy a car for business purposes (such as driving to sales meetings) or take his or her spouse along on a trip to Hawaii to attend a business convention. If these expenditures are intermediate (are business expenditures), the sales representative can deduct them from taxable income and thereby reduce tax payments. On the other hand, a person who uses a car for shopping, commuting, and so on or who takes a trip to Hawaii cannot deduct these expenses from taxable income.

As one might imagine, the tax courts are crowded with disputes between taxpayers and the Internal Revenue Service over whether certain expenditures were final or intermediate. ■

---

ers, by constructing public buildings and building submarines, and by employing law-enforcement officers and judges. Because these government services are typically not sold to the final consumer, there is typically no market valuation for government services. Unlike other items that enter into GNP, government services are typically valued at the cost of *supplying* them rather than at the cost of purchasing them. For example, the value of public education is taken to be the sum of public expenditures on education; the value of national defense is assumed to equal expenditures on national defense.

Only government *purchases* of goods and services enter into GNP. **Transfer payments** are not included in GNP.

Transfer payments are payments to recipients who have not supplied current goods or services in exchange for these payments.

Transfer payments, as the name implies, are simply transfers of income from one person or organization to another. Transfer payments are made by both private and governmental organizations. An industrial corporation may contribute to a worthy charity; government may transfer income from taxpayers to poverty recipients through welfare programs. The largest transfer payments are handled by the Social Security Administration, which transfers incomes from those currently working to retired or disabled workers and their dependents.

Government purchases of goods and services are quite different from government transfer payments. As explained above, transfer payments are not made in exchange for current goods or services. Moreover, transfer payments do not create factor income (such as wages, rent, or profit). Instead, transfer payments involve the transfer of income from individuals or organizations which have earned factor income to others. Because total output must equal total income, transfer payments do not belong in GNP: they produce neither income nor output.

Investment (I). Investment has already been defined as expenditures that add to (or replace) the economy's stock of *capital* (plants, equipment, structures, and inventories). Why is investment then a final good? Is not capital used to produce other goods, just like intermediate goods in our opening example?

There is a big difference between capital goods and intermediate goods. Unlike intermediate goods that are used up entirely in the process of making other goods (steel is used up to make autos, cotton is used up to make clothing), capital is only *partially* used up in the process of making other goods. A steel mill may have a useful life of 40 years. In producing steel in any one year, only a small portion (say, 1/40th) of the mill is consumed. The ore and coking coal, on the other hand, is entirely consumed in producing steel. A computer may have a useful working life of seven years (before it becomes obsolete). The bank that uses the computer to manage its accounts also uses up only a portion (say, 1/7th) of the computer in producing one year's banking services. The using up of capital is called **depreciation.**

Depreciation is the value of the existing capital stock that has been consumed or used up in the process of producing output. Depreciation includes not only the physical wear and tear on capital goods but also the loss of value due to the obsolescence of old capital.

Investment is divided into two major categories called **inventory investment** and **fixed investment.** Both types of investment increase the productive capacity of the economy.

Inventory investment is the increase (or decrease) in the value of the stocks of inventories that businesses have on hand.

If business inventories are $200 billion at the beginning of the year and $250 billion at the end, inventory investment is $50 billion. Inventory investment can be either positive or negative. Year-end inventories can be larger or smaller than inventories at the beginning of the year.

Fixed investment is the addition of new plants, equipment, commercial buildings, and residential structures.

Fixed investment is of two types: *nonresidential* and *residential* fixed investment. Nonresidential fixed investment is additions to the stocks of equipment, plants, and commercial buildings by business firms. Residential investment is additions to the stock of residential structures—apartment houses, condominiums, and private homes. The construction of private homes, cooperative housing, and private condominiums is classified as investment rather than as private consumption for two reasons: First, a home, like other types of capital, is long-lived and is consumed very slowly over the years. Second, the decision to build a private home is very much like a business investment decision. The family contrasts the housing services it expects to obtain from the home over the years with the cost of the home just as business firms compare the expected returns from investment projects with their costs. Whether or not to buy private housing is as much a business-investment decision as is the decision to build a new plant or to buy new equipment.

Net Exports of Goods and Services *(X-M)*. All the final expenditures by American households, businesses, and government added together would not equal the total output of the American economy for one simple reason: some of the items purchased are produced by other countries (imported from abroad); these goods and services would have to be subtracted from total purchases. On the other hand, some of the domestic economy's output is exported to other countries; these goods and services would have to be added to total purchases.

GNP, therefore, cannot be accurately measured without adding in the nation's exports *(X)* of goods and services and subtracting out the nation's imports *(M)* of goods and services. The value of exports minus the value of imports is called *net exports* of goods and services *(X-M)*.

The GNP formula for calculating the flow of final goods is simply the sum of 1) personal consumption expenditures **(C)**, *2) government purchases of goods and services* **(G)**, *3) investment* **(I)**, *and 4) net exports of goods and services* **(X-M)**.

Thus, Method 1 for calculating GNP is:

$$GNP = C + G + I + (X\text{-}M).$$

The Flow of Income

The value of final goods and services produced by an economy (GNP) exactly equals **gross national income (GNI).**

Gross national income (GNI) is the sum of all factor incomes. Because GNP equals GNI, GNP can also be calculated by adding together all income earned from labor, land, capital, and entrepreneurship in the course of one year's time.

GNP = GNI

GNI can be calculated in two ways; both yield the same outcome. One method adds together the incomes earned by the factors of production; the other adds the incomes paid out by producing enterprises.

Table 3
1981 Gross National Product by Type of Income

Type of Income	Amount (billions of 1981 dollars)	Percentage
Compensation of employees	1,772	60.6
Proprietors' income	134	4.6
Rental income of persons	34	1.2
Corporate profits	189	6.5
Net interest	215	7.4
Depreciation	322	11.0
Indirect business taxes and other adjustments	257	8.7
GNP = GNI	**2,922**	**100.0**

Source: *Economic Report of the President,* January 1982, pp. 254, 256, 257.

Factor Payments. GNP (or GNI) can be calculated by adding together all payments to labor, land, capital, and entrepreneurship. In national income accounting, payments to labor are called *compensation of employees;* the payments to capital and entrepreneurship are *proprietors' income, corporate profits, net interest payments,* and *depreciation;* payments to land are *rental income of persons.* Indirect business taxes are also included in gross national income, although they are not really a payment to a factor of production. The current distribution of GNP among these categories is shown in Table 3. Payments to labor dominate, with 61 percent of GNP going to labor. Rental payments represent less than 2 percent of GNP, with the remaining 19 percent going to capital and entrepreneurship.[1]

With the exception of depreciation and indirect business taxes, all these payments are actual factor payments made to owners of the factors of production. Depreciation is a payment that businesses must charge themselves to make up for the capital they have used up in the process of producing output.

1. It is difficult to separate out payments to capital, labor, and entrepreneurship. Some payments to labor are really returns to human capital. Some corporate profits are returns to capital; others are returns to entrepreneurship. Proprietors' income includes returns to labor, capital, and entrepreneurship.

Method 2 for calculating GNP is:

GNP = Compensation of Employees + Proprietors' Income + Rental Income of Persons + Corporate Profits + Net Interest + Depreciation + Indirect Business Taxes

Value Added. GNP (GNI) can also be calculated by adding together the income paid out by producing enterprises to the factors of production. In the example of a hypothetical economy in Table 1, the portion of GNP produced by any one industry—by ore and coal, by steel, by automobiles, by cotton, or by clothing—cannot be determined simply by dividing each industry's sales by total sales because of double counting. The automobile industry's share would be grossly overstated by this method because the dollar value of its sales includes the dollar value of the steel that it used to produce cars. Instead, each industry's contribution to GNP can only be determined by calculating each industry's **net output,** or **value added.**

*The **net output** or **value added** of a firm is the value of its output minus the value of its purchases from other firms. Accordingly, the **net output** or **value added** of an industry is the output of that industry minus its purchases from other industries.*

To return to the example in Table 1, the value added of the automobile industry is the output of automobiles ($200 billion) minus purchases from the steel industry ($100 billion). Its value added, therefore, is $100 billion ($200 billion − $100 billion). The value added of steel is the output of steel ($100 billion) minus its purchases from the ore and coal industries ($20 billion), or $80 billion ($100 billion − $20 billion). The value added of ore and coal equals its production ($20 billion), because in this example, ore and coal make no purchases from other industries. Several foreign nations have a *value-added tax,* or VAT, which some economists recommend for the United States as a means of raising additional tax revenue.

The value of industry output minus the purchases from other industries equals the payments to labor, capital, land, and entrepreneurship.

Table 4
GNP Calculated as the Sum of Value Added of Each Hypothetical Industry

Industry	Industry Sales (billions of dollars)	Purchases from Other Industries (billions of dollars)	Value Added or Net Output (billions of dollars)
Ore and coal	20	0	20
Steel	100	20	80
Automobiles	200	100	100
Cotton	50	0	50
Clothing	90	50	40
GNP			**290**

An industry's value added is the sum of its factor payments.

Value added will equal the sum of factor payments; profits serve to insure the equality. Anything that is left over after purchasing materials from other firms and paying for labor, capital, and land will go into profits, which is also a form of factor income.

Method 3 for calculating GNP:

GNP = the sum of the value added for all industries in the economy.

Table 4 calculates GNP for our hypothetical economy by adding up each industry's value added or by adding together the value of final products. The total GNP figure of $290 billion is the same figure yielded by Method 1 in Table 1.

Actual gross national product by industry value added is shown in Table 5. Each entry shows the net output or value added of each industry (sales minus purchases from other industries), which is the sum of factor payments made by that industry.

FROM GNP TO DISPOSABLE INCOME

Table 6 shows the step-by-step process for determining how much of gross national income households are actually free to spend.

Net National Product

Although gross national product is the broadest measure of the total output of an economy (and, therefore, of the economy's total income), it includes the value of the capital used up—depreciation—in producing output. If GNP is $2,500 billion and depreciation is $250 billion, then 10 percent of output simply replaces the capital that has been consumed. Only $2,250 billion (GNP minus depreciation) represents new goods and services available to society.

For this reason, economists often use a second, less comprehensive measure of total output,

Table 5
1980 Gross National Product by Industry

Industry	Value Added (billions of 1980 dollars)	Percentage
Agriculture, forestry, fisheries	77.2	2.9
Mining	94.1	3.6
Construction	119.7	4.5
Manufacturing	591.1	22.5
Transportation and utilities	234.5	8.9
Wholesale and retail trade	421.7	16.1
Finance, insurance, real estate	392.0	14.9
Services	343.5	13.1
Government and government enterprises	303.4	11.6
Rest of the world	49.0	1.9
GNP	**2,626**	**100.0**

Source: *Economic Report of the President,* January 1982, p. 244.

Table 6
1981 GNP, NNP, National Income, Personal Income, Disposable Income

Item	Amount (billions of dollars)
Gross national product (GNP) = GNI	2,922
minus	
Depreciation (capital consumption)	−321
equals	
1. Net national product (NNP)	2,601
minus	
Indirect business taxes*	−257
equals	
2. National income	2,344
minus	
Corporate taxes, undistributed corporate profits, social-security contributions	−273
plus	
Transfer payments	+333
equals	
3. Personal income	2,404
minus	
Personal taxes	−389
equals	
4. Personal disposable income	2,015

*plus minor items such as business transfer payments and government subsidies.

Source: *Economic Report of the President,* January 1982, pp. 254–58.

called **net national product,** to measure the total value of new goods and services available to the economy in a given year.

Net national product (NNP) equals GNP minus depreciation.

National Income

Both GNP and NNP are measured in the prices that buyers of final products pay. Included in these prices are a variety of sales taxes—called *indirect business taxes*. These indirect business taxes do not actually represent a payment to the factors of production. While adding to the revenues of government, indirect business taxes do not generate income for individuals. When indirect business taxes are subtracted from NNP, only **national income,** or the total payments to the factors of production in the economy, remain.

National income equals net national product minus indirect business taxes. National income equals the sum of all factor payments made to the factors of production in the economy.

Personal Income

Not all of earned national income is actually received by persons as income. Included in national income are three major accounts that do not enter into personal income: 1) undistributed corporate profits, 2) corporate income taxes, and 3) social-security contributions.

1. Corporations retain a portion of corporate profits for reinvestment. These earnings are not distributed to stockholders as dividend payments.
2. Corporations must pay corporate income taxes that do not enter personal income.
3. Social-security contributions are deducted from income.

Personal income can only be calculated by subtracting these three accounts. On the other hand, the transfer payments that individuals receive from government and business (which, remember, are not included in GNP) are a part of personal income. Transfer payments must, therefore, be added back in to determine **personal income.**

Personal income equals national income 1) minus retained corporate profits, corporate income taxes, and social security contributions 2) plus transfer payments.

Personal Disposable Income

Finally, individuals must pay federal, state, and local income taxes. In order to determine potential spending power, income taxes must be subtracted from personal income to yield **personal disposable income.**

Personal disposable income equals personal income minus income-tax payments.

The levels of national-income accounting categories, which are summarized in Table 6, may seem a bit bewildering. Each account gives economists a different perspective on the economy. Economists can see by comparing the different categories how income and social-security taxes can change the relationship between the amount of income earned and the amount of income available for spending; they can see that only investment in excess of depreciation adds to the economy's capital stock.

THE EQUALITY OF SAVING AND INVESTMENT

As already noted, investment is the addition to (or the replacement of) the economy's stock of capital goods. Investment expenditures are made principally by the business sector. **Saving** makes resources available for investment and is done primarily by households. Savers and investors are typically different. An important theme of macroeconomics is the relationship between saving and investment.

> *For the economy as a whole,* **saving** *is the amount of national income (total factor income) that is not spent on consumption or direct taxes.*

Individuals save by *not spending* all their disposable income. Total saving for an economy is what remains of national income after personal consumption and government expenditures for goods and services.

Consider a hypothetical economy in which there is no government and thus no government spending for goods and services ($G = \text{O}$) and in which there are no taxes ($T = \text{O}$). Assume there is no depreciation and that imports equal exports ($X - M = \text{O}$). Under these simplified conditions:

$$\text{GNP} = C + I \qquad (1)$$

because $G = \text{O}$. In this economy, income can only be spent or saved. There are no taxes; hence, saving is what remains of *GNI* after consumption:

$$S = \text{GNP} - C \qquad (2)$$

because $T = \text{O}$. Because GNP and GNI are identically equal, $C + I$ must equal $C + S$. Hence, investment must equal saving:

$$I = S \qquad (3)$$

The equality of actual saving and investment is an important cornerstone of macroeconomics. This equality does not mean that what people *want* to save will always equal what businesses *want* to invest. Instead, the amount *actually* invested will necessarily equal the amount *actually* saved. Some mechanism is required to bring the two into equality, and there has been much controversy in the economic literature over how the disparate wishes of savers and investors are coordinated. The saving/investment equality means that the amount of saving the economy undertakes in one year will always equal the amount of investment in that year.

The equality between saving and investment still holds in an economy with government spending and taxes, provided saving is properly interpreted. Under such conditions, private saving *(S)* equals the amount of income not spent on C or used for taxes *(T)*, or:

$$\text{GNI} \equiv C + S + T$$

$$S = \text{GNI} - C - T \qquad (4)$$

GNP equals the sum of final expenditures, or:

$$\text{GNP} \equiv C + I + G \qquad (5)$$

Since GNP = GNI, $(C + I + G)$ can be substituted for GNI in equation (4).

$$S = (C + I + G) - C - T \qquad (6)$$

Simplifying equation (6) and solving for I, one can see that investment equals the sum of private saving *(S)* and public saving $(T - G)$:

$$I = S + (T - G), \qquad (7)$$

where $(T - G)$ is the government surplus (or deficit, if it is a negative number), which is simply government saving. In this respect, government is like a household (although government does not have to pay taxes). The government saves if its income *(T)* exceeds its expenditures *(G)*. It increases its debt if its expenditures exceed its income.

Saving still equals investment in an economy with government spending and taxes because saving includes both private and public saving.

The previous section showed the relationships between the income categories from GNP to personal disposable income. One final relationship is that between **private saving** and disposable income.

Private saving equals personal disposable income minus personal-consumption expenditures.

Private saving is what remains of personal disposable income after personal-consumption expenditures are made (remember taxes are already subtracted from disposable income). In other words, individuals save by refraining from consumption.

Table 7 shows personal disposable income and private saving during the period 1950 to 1981. It shows that private saving tends to rise with disposable income and that the saving rate (the ratio of personal saving to disposable income) has varied from lows of near 5 percent to highs of near 8.5 percent.

REAL AND NOMINAL GNP

Since GNP is measured in dollar values, the GNP of an economy can rise for two basic reasons: First, the *quantities* of goods and services produced can increase. Second, the *prices* of these goods and services can rise. Often, of course, both occur. GNP that is measured in current market prices is **nominal GNP,** or GNP in current dollars.

Nominal GNP (or "GNP in current dollars") is the value of final goods and services for a given year in that year's prevailing market prices.

When nominal GNP rises, it is not immediately apparent whether the increase is due to rising prices or to increasing outputs of real goods and services. Presumably, the material well-being of society is improved only by the increasing output of goods and services. Society as a whole is not made better off when prices rise and the quan-

Table 7
Personal Disposable Income and Personal Saving, 1950–1981

Year	Personal Disposable Income (billions of dollars)	Personal Saving (billions of dollars)	Saving Rate (percent)
1950	206.6	11.9	5.8
1955	275.0	16.4	6.0
1960	352.0	19.7	5.6
1965	478.5	33.7	7.1
1970	695.3	55.8	8.0
1975	1,096.1	94.3	8.6
1980	1,821.7	101.3	5.6
1981	2,015.4	106.6	5.3

Source: *Economic Report of the President,* January 1982, p. 260.

tities of real goods and services remain constant or decline. For this reason, when GNP is compared over a period of time, it is typically measured in a way that eliminates the effects of rising prices. This measure of GNP is called **real GNP.**

Real GNP (or "GNP in constant dollars") measures the volume of real goods and services by removing the effects of rising prices on nominal GNP.

The GNP deflator was introduced in the previous chapter as the most general measure of the price level. The GNP deflator measures changes in the prices of consumption goods, investment goods, government goods and services, and net exports. Real GNP is calculated from nominal GNP and the GNP deflator. For example, nominal GNP in 1972 equaled $1,186 billion. Nominal GNP in 1981 equaled $2,922 billion. The GNP deflator in 1981 was 1.93 times that of 1972. Therefore, real 1982 GNP (in the prices of 1972) equaled $1,514 billion ($2,922 billion/1.93). The rates of growth of real GNP and nominal GNP can be quite different, especially during periods of rapid inflation, as Figure 2 illustrates.

OMISSIONS FROM GNP

The definition of GNP as the value of all final goods and services is not as simple as it appears.

Example 2

Housework and GNP

How nonmarketed goods are treated can have a substantial effect on the size of GNP. For example, life-insurance companies advise families to carry life insurance on homemakers because it would cost the family tens of thousands of dollars per year to replace the homemaker in the household. If services performed by homemakers were purchased—if dirty clothes were taken to the laundry or if babysitters were hired—they would definitely enter GNP. The inclusion of homemakers' services would raise GNP dramatically. There are currently more than 29 million homemakers in the United States. If each produces household services worth, say, $15,000 per year, then the total value of their services would equal $420 billion or 14 percent of 1981 GNP.

What should be done with goods that are not bought and sold in markets? Should the value of leisure be counted in GNP? How should illegal economic activities be handled? What about economic activities that may lower rather than raise economic well-being? Official measures of GNP ignore most of these questions. Illegal economic activities and household production are left out of GNP. Increases in leisure do not raise measured GNP. Methods to correct GNP for economic

Figure 2
GNP in Current and in Constant Dollars, 1960–1981

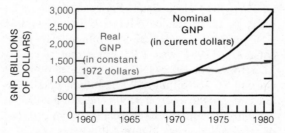

Nominal GNP has risen more rapidly than real GNP during recent decades because of inflation.

Source: *Economic Report of the President*, January 1982, pp. 233–34.

"bads" are just being developed. Although these items are not included in GNP, it is useful to consider whether they should be and, if so, what effect they would have on measured GNP.

Nonmarketed Goods

Many final goods and services are not acquired through regular market transactions. Instead of buying food at the grocery store, someone may consume the produce from a vegetable garden in the backyard. Instead of calling a plumber to repair a leaky faucet, some people may repair it themselves. A dentist may trade dental work for two weeks in a patient's vacation home.

The common feature of these transactions of **nonmarketed goods** is that they have taken place without the use of organized markets.

Nonmarketed goods are goods and services exchanged through barter arrangements or acquired through do-it-yourself activities that take the place of goods and services that would otherwise have been purchased in organized markets.

The treatment of nonmarketed goods affects comparisons of countries at different stages of development. International statistics show, for example, that the per capita GNP of the United States is 52 times that of Zaire. How could anyone survive on so little? While the differences in living standards between countries like Zaire and the United States are indeed enormous, the statistics overstate the differential in material well-being. In a country like Zaire, more goods and services are acquired outside market transactions and thus do not enter measured GNP.[2]

Illegal Activities

GNP typically does not include illegal goods and services. Such goods and services otherwise meet all the requirements for inclusion in GNP: they are final products; they are purchased in mar-

2. The nonmarketed goods that are allowed to enter into GNP are the value of agricultural products consumed on the farm and the imputed rental value of owner-occupied housing.

Example 3

The Underground Economy

The underground economy of the United States is estimated to rival the annual output of the Canadian economy. As many as 20 million Americans may engage in illegal underground activities. More than $100 billion in taxes may be lost every year, forcing honest taxpayers to ante up more.

The underground economy includes both innocuous activities—unreported income from child care and housecleaning, occasional moonlighting by professionals and craft workers, the padding of expense accounts and the charging of personal expenses to corporate accounts—and organized crime activities like casino skimming and drug and prostitution rings. Millions of workers, many of them illegal aliens, are paid in cash; there is no record of their employment on company books. No social-security deductions are withheld.

Truckers, taxi drivers, and waitresses work for cash and pocket a percentage of their earnings (which are hard to document) and report only a portion of their earnings to tax authorities. Bars and jewelers fail to report a portion of cash sales.

Organized crime likely accounts for the bulk of underground economy receipts. Arson for profit, smuggling of goods, pirated tapes, records, and films, pornography, professional assasinations, and prostitution are the lifeline of organized-crime earnings. Experts estimate that almost half of the cigarette sales in New York City are of bootlegged cigarettes because of the New York cigarette tax.

How large is the underground economy? Obviously, if tax authorities and law-enforcement agencies had firm information on such activities, they would be easy to eradicate. The information economists and government agencies have succeeded in gathering, however, points to the enormous size and scope of the underground economy. An official study of the Internal Revenue Service estimated (in 1976) that the size of the underground economy equaled 11 percent of measured GNP. But the IRS study did not even include corporate tax cheating, misuse of expense accounts, and white-collar crime. Estimates by economist Edgar Feige place the correct size of the underground economy at around 20 percent of measured GNP. The underground economy of today is likely a half-trillion-dollar business.

---

ket transactions. Yet they are goods and services—like illegal gambling, murder for hire, prostitution, illegal drugs—whose use and sale are proscribed by law. Semilegal activities—such as moonlighting, when the income is not reported to tax authorities—also belong to this category. Illegal income is not reported because of the desire to avoid paying taxes and because of restrictions on economic activities that are deemed criminal or illegal.

No one knows for sure the dollar volume of illegal market activities. The available estimates of the size of the American underground economy vary considerably. An official Internal Revenue Service study places the volume at between 6 and 8 percent of legal GNP. Estimates of the value of illegal activities made by private economists range from 4 to 33.5 percent of legal GNP. Although the American underground economy is large in absolute size, it is still likely much smaller than in other countries such as France and Italy, where it may reach 25 percent of legal GNP.[3]

Should illegal activities be included in GNP? If GNP is to be a measure of the level of economic activity, illegal economic activities would need to be included. Official GNP could show a slackening pace of production and employment when in reality, activity has simply shifted from the legal to the underground economy. Government economic policies are based upon measured GNP and measured poverty. If illegal activities are omitted, a false impression of economic activity and poverty may be obtained.

There are two basic arguments for not including illegal activities in GNP. The first is the im-

---

3. Vito Tanzi, "Underground Economy Built on Illicit Pursuits is Growing Concern of Economic Policymakers," *IMF Survey,* February 4, 1980.

possibility of obtaining reliable statistics on the underground economy. The second is that since most underground activities are illegal, legislators, at least, do not believe they raise the material well-being of society. In fact, according to prevailing legislation, such activities lower material well-being.

The Value of Leisure

The number of hours the average American works per year has declined dramatically over the past 50 years. In effect, our society has chosen to produce a smaller flow of goods and services in return for more leisure. Should this voluntary choice of leisure be reflected in GNP? After all, voluntary increases in leisure raise material well-being just like increases in goods and services.

If the value of leisure were included in GNP, GNP would be dramatically increased. In 1900, workers in manufacturing worked, on average, a 60-hour week. By 1980, this figure had fallen to 40 hours per week. If American workers worked the same number of hours now as they did in 1900, personal income would be much larger than it actually is. The fact that people have chosen leisure over higher money incomes means that they place a value on that leisure greater than the extra earnings sacrificed.

Leisure is not included in GNP because GNP is narrowly defined to encompass only tangible goods and services. It does not include intangibles such as the value individuals place on leisure, because of the difficulty of measuring intangibles.

Economic "Bads"

GNP measures the final goods and services that an economy produces. What if these goods and services are not economic goods but **economic "bads"**?

*An **economic "bad"** is a good or service that does not contribute to society's economic well-being.*

Many "bads" are already excluded because they are illegal, but what about legal "bads" such as air, water, and noise pollution? What about the prison camps that are all too common in totalitar-

ian countries or the cures offered for sale by medical quacks? Economic "bads" like pollution are particularly troublesome because economists have long recognized that polluters do not bear the full costs of their polluting activities. Insofar as firms are not charged fully for the pollution they create, society must pay some of these costs.

The existence of **economic "bads"** has caused some economists—most prominently James Tobin and William Nordhaus—to argue for a different measure of total output, called the *Measure of Economic Welfare,* or MEW. MEW subtracts the value of economic "bads" from the value of economic goods.

The art of computing MEW is in its infancy. It remains to be seen whether MEW can be effectively measured. The basic problem is how to determine what is a "bad". How does one know whether something enters MEW as a plus or a minus and what its numerical value should be?

This chapter explained how the economy's total output is measured and described its components. The next chapter will define money and examine money's impact on prices and output.

Summary

1. National income accounting is the branch of economics that measures the total output of the economy. The value of total output equals the value of total income because the act of producing output automatically creates an equivalent amount of income.

2. Gross national product, or GNP, is the broadest measure of the total output of the economy. GNP is the value of all final goods and services produced by an economy in one year's time. Only final goods and services are included to avoid the double counting of products.

3. GNP can be calculated by measuring the total value of final products or by measuring the total value of income. The total value of income can be calculated as the sum of factor payments or as the sum of the value added by all industries. Therefore, the three methods for computing GNP are:

a. GNP = personal consumption expenditures + government expenditures for goods and services + investment + net exports.

b. GNP = compensation of employees + proprietors' income + rental income + corporate profits + interest + depreciation + indirect business taxes.

c. GNP = the sum of the value added of all industries in an economy. The value added of an economic sector equals the value of output minus purchases from other sectors. Value added also equals the sum of factor payments made by the sector.

4. Net national product equals GNP minus capital consumption allowances. National income equals NNP minus indirect business taxes. Personal income equals national income *minus* factor payments not received by individuals and social-security deductions *plus* transfer payments. Personal disposable income equals personal income minus personal taxes.

5. National income accounting shows that saving and investment are equal by definition. Investment is the addition to the economy's stock of capital. Saving is that portion of income that is not spent on consumption and taxes.

6. Nominal GNP is the value of final goods and services in current market prices. Nominal GNP can rise because of either increasing output or rising prices. Real GNP measures the volume of real goods and services by removing the effects of rising prices.

7. Nonmarketed goods, illegal goods, and the value of leisure are not included in GNP, although many economists argue that they should be included. Other economists argue that the appropriate measure of total output is the *Measure of Economic Welfare,* which equals measured GNP minus the cost of economic "bads."

Key Terms

national income accounting
final goods
intermediate goods

gross national product (GNP)
transfer payments
depreciation
inventory investment
fixed investment
gross national income (GNI)
net output or value added
net national product (NNP)
national income
personal income
personal disposable income
saving
private saving
nominal GNP
real GNP
nonmarketed goods
economic "bads"

Questions and Problems

1. The economy produces final goods and services valued at $500 billion in one year's time but only sells $450 billion worth. Does this mean that the value of final output no longer equals the value of incomes?

2. Discuss the implications (in Table 1) of $5 billion worth of coal being purchased directly by households to heat their homes. How and why will this change GNP? Will it affect value added?

3. An industry spends $6 million on the factors of production that it uses (including entrepreneurship). It sells $10 million worth of output. How much value added has this industry created and how much has this industry purchased from other industries?

4. Explain why investment is regarded as a final product even though it is used as a factor of production to produce other goods.

5. A large corporation gives a grant to a classical musician to allow her to train her skills in Europe. How will this payment enter into GNP? Into personal income? Will this payment differ from one to an engineer employed by the company?

6. Which of the following investment categories can be negative: inventory investment, fixed

investment, net fixed investment (gross investment minus depreciation). Explain your answer.

7. Explain why GNP measures may tend to overstate the GNP of rich countries relative to poor countries.

8. Personal disposable income is $100 billion. Personal consumption expenditures are $80 billion. Taxes are $40 billion and government expenditures for goods and services are $50 billion. How much total saving is there in the economy? How much is private saving?

CHAPTER
7

Money and Prices

Chapter Preview

To economists the term **money** means the generally accepted commodity (or commodities) that can be exchanged for goods and services.

Money is the medium of exchange used by an economy; it is the commodity ordinarily used in transactions that transfer ownership of goods and services from one person to another.

This chapter examines the functions of money, commodities that have served as money, and the relationship between money and prices. This chapter will also show how money is related—both theoretically and empirically—to inflation and the business cycle.

THE FUNCTIONS OF MONEY

Money facilitates trade and commerce in modern economies that are characterized by specialization and exchange. In such economies, money performs four functions. Money serves as:

1. a medium of exchange,
2. a unit of value,
3. a standard of deferred payment, and
4. a store of value.

By performing these monetary functions, money allows people to specialize according to their comparative advantage and exchange goods and services with others. Thus, money allows people to earn higher incomes and, hence, to consume more goods and services than would otherwise be possible. In the language of Chapter 2, the use of money shifts the production-possibilities curve outward. The following discussion of the functions of money explains how money increases the efficiency of the economy.

Money as a Medium of Exchange

The most important function of money is that of a medium of exchange. In a modern economic system money enters almost all market transactions. A common object acceptable to all sellers eliminates the need for a *double coincidence of wants* in a barter economy. In a barter economy, for example, a seller of wheat who wants to buy some sugar must find a seller of sugar wanting to buy wheat. Since double coincidences of wants are rare, in a pure barter economy a series of transactions would be required to obtain what one wants. The seller of wheat might first have to settle for potatoes, trade the potatoes for an axe, and then finally trade the axe for some sugar.

Money eliminates the need for such costly intermediate exchanges. Because intermediate exchanges are so difficult, customs and laws designate some commodity to serve as the medium of exchange.

The object that society designates as money or the medium of exchange could be almost anything. Money is a social contrivance. The list of things that have been used as money staggers the imagination. American Indians used *wampum* (a string of shells); early American colonists used tobacco, rice, corn, cattle, and whiskey. Cigarettes have served as money in prisoner-of-war camps. Farther from home more exotic things have been used as money: whale teeth in Figi, sandalwood in Hawaii, fish hooks on the Gilbert Island, reindeer in parts of Russia, red parrot feathers on the Santa Cruz Islands (as late as 1961), silk in China, slaves in Africa, rum in Australia. Thus, we see that money can grow on trees! Money can even walk, talk, fly, be eaten, or be drunk. Our modern paper money is boring by comparison.

Money's most important function is to serve as the commodity that is generally acceptable as a means of payment (for buying things and paying debts).

Money as a Unit of Value

The value of a good or service, as Adam Smith observed, is what it can be exchanged for in the market. In a *barter (or exchange) economy,* a cow might sell for two pigs, for an acre of land, for 50 bushels of corn, for a motorcycle, or for dozens of other things. It is, of course, inconvenient to keep track of the value of a cow or anything else in terms of every other thing it would trade for. Barter is also inconvenient when the units cannot be divided, as in a case where a pig is worth half a cow. Choosing a common unit of value—money—saves much time and energy in keeping track of the relative prices or values of different things and solves the problem of converting units. When the general money prices of a number of common objects are known, it is easy to appraise the *relative* price of any item just from its money price. Money prices can also be used to add together apples and oranges. By reducing different economic entities to their dollar values, homemakers can add apples and oranges, firms can subtract expenses from revenue to obtain profit, and accountants can subtract liabilities from assets.

Money serves as the common denominator in which the values of all goods and services are expressed.

Money as a Standard of Deferred Payment

When one good is used as the medium of exchange, it is almost inevitable that the good will be used as the standard of deferred payment on contracts extending over a period of time. There are numerous contracts that extend into the future: home mortgages, car loans, all sorts of bonds and promissory notes, credit charges at the department store and on credit cards, salaries, home rents, and so forth. That which serves as money will also be that in which payments deferred into the future will be made. If in the Santa Cruz Islands red parrot feathers are money, an agreement to buy a cart one year in the future would be paid one year hence in red parrot feathers. If dollars are money, contracts to purchase some good in the future would call for payment in dollars.

Money is a standard of deferred payment on exchange agreements extending into the future.

As pointed out in Chapter 5, inflation complicates money's role as the standard of deferred payment. If the inflation is foreseen, parties entering into deferred-payment contracts can build in safeguards. The parties may agree that the deferred payment will be adjusted upward at the same rate as inflation (a cost-of-living adjustment). Interest rates, rental payments, or even salary payments may include a premium to compensate the recipient of deferred payments for the anticipated rate of inflation. When inflation is foreseen, there are ways to protect money's role as a standard of deferred payment.

Chapter 5 showed that unanticipated inflation can redistribute wealth. Unanticipated inflation will benefit debtors and harm creditors who have not had the foresight to demand a higher interest rate to compensate them for the effects of inflation. Unforeseen inflation tends to redistribute wealth from those who receive deferred payments to those who make them.

Money as a Store of Value

People, on average, do not consume all of their income, although some households do. When a family consumes less than its income, it saves, or (to say the same thing) it accumulates wealth. People can accumulate wealth in virtually any form that is not perishable—paintings, gold, silver, stocks, bonds, land, buildings, apartments—and money. A desirable characteristic of any *asset* (an object that has value) is that it should maintain or increase its value over time. During periods of rising prices, the value of money is eroded because the amount of goods and services one unit of money will purchase falls. Paper currency or coins that have a face value greater than the value of their product content are particularly vulnerable to this erosion.

Since money is the medium of exchange, it can also be used as a means of storing wealth.

THE SUPPLY OF MONEY

What is the money supply? How much money is there?

Types of Money

Money comes in three basic varieties: **commodity money, fiat money,** and **bank money.**

Commodity money is money whose value as a commodity is as great as its value as money.

For instance, when cattle, rice, or tobacco are used as money they have obvious nonmonetary uses. But the nonmonetary uses of the commodity can be slight or nonexistent. A classic example is the stone money of the island of Yap, 400 miles from Guam. Yap money consists of stone wheels, from 1 foot to 12 feet in diameter, made from stones found only on distant islands. A private citizen could produce money only by making what was often a treacherous sea journey. The cost of acquiring stones could not be much less than the value of the stones as money, otherwise enterprising residents would produce more money.[1]

Historically, the most important commodity moneys have been gold and silver. Gold and silver have nonmonetary uses in jewelry and industry; they can be easily coined, weighed, and used for large and small transactions. In early history, governments started minting gold and silver coins to avoid costly weighings each time a transaction occurred. When gold or silver serve as commodity money, private citizens can produce money simply by taking mined gold to the government mint! In a commodity-money system these can also be paper currency, but the currency can be exchanged for gold at a fixed rate at the bearer's request. Commodity money suffers from an inherent problem, known as **Gresham's Law:**

1. The story of Yap's stone money is found in William Furness III, *The Island of Stone Money* (New York: J. B. Lippincott Company, 1910), pp. 92–100. Several fascinating characteristics of the stone money are pointed out by Furness: physical possession was not necessary for ownership; on at least one occasion a family was considered wealthy because an ancestor was known to have discovered an extremely large and valuable stone that a storm sent to the bottom of the sea.

Example   1

The Dollar and "In God We Trust"

The Federal Reserve System is basically a public agency charged with regulating the money supply and serving as the bankers' bank (the central bank). The Federal Reserve issues the paper currency of the United States, called *Federal Reserve Notes*. Nothing backs Federal Reserve Notes. If you examine one of these notes you will find that it states: "This note is legal tender for all debts public and private." You will also notice along the top of the note the phrase, "In God We Trust." Not too long ago, the legal declaration contained a promise. The old declaration read: "This note is legal tender for debts public and private and is redeemable in lawful money at any Federal Reserve Bank." This, of course, was an empty promise because the Federal Reserve Notes themselves were the lawful money of the United States! In the 1950s, a Cleveland businessman tested this promise by requesting that a $20 bill be converted into lawful money. The Federal Reserve Bank sent him two $10 bills! The businessman persisted, sending in one of the $10 bills, and ended up with two $5 bills and a letter explaining that "lawful money" was not defined. Soon after this incident, the promise for redemption was dropped and the phrase "In God We Trust" was added!

Gresham's Law states that bad money drives out good. *When depreciated, mutilated, or debased currency is circulated along with money of high value, the good money will disappear from circulation; only the bad money will remain in circulation.*[2]

When people shave or mutilate gold and silver coins, the bad currency will begin to circulate along with the good currency. The lesser-valued coins will be the ones spent while the more valuable coins will be hoarded. Tobacco money in colonial Virginia illustrates Gresham's Law. Initially, tobacco of both good and poor quality circulated as money. But following Gresham's Law, people came to hoard the good tobacco and only use the worst tobacco as money. Eventually, the tobacco used as money in colonial Virginia was only the scruffiest and foulest tobacco in the entire state. This opportunism tends to raise the cost of using the commodity money as a medium of exchange as sellers of goods become suspicious of the money being used.

The basic cost to society of using commodity money is that society must devote real resources to producing the commodity money. Yap villagers had to build boats and risk their lives to produce stone money. Gold and silver mines must be discovered and operated to produce gold or silver commodity money. This gold and silver must then be set aside to circulate as money and will not find its way into use as jewelry or dental fillings.

Fiat money is money whose value or cost as a commodity is less than its value as money.

Governments have a monopoly over the issue of fiat money. If everyone were allowed to produce fiat money, so much fiat money would be issued that its value as money would fall to its production cost. The commodity value of paper money is very low.

The two basic forms of fiat currency are coins and paper currency. U.S. coins are issued by the U.S. Treasury, and the value of the metal plus the cost of minting is less than the value of the coins used as money. Sometimes such coins are called *token money*. The most important example of fiat money in the United States is paper currency, called *Federal Reserve Notes,* because they are issued by the Federal Reserve System rather than by the U.S. Treasury.

2.   Gresham's Law is named after Sir Thomas Gresham, who lived from 1519–1579. He was a successful banker and merchant, accumulated a great fortune, and endowed Gresham's College in London. Gresham's methods of making money were described as more effective than ethical. It may be that Gresham formulated his law on the basis of first-hand observation.

Bank money is money that is on deposit in checking accounts.

In a modern economy, most transactions are conducted using bank money. About 90 percent of the dollar value of all transactions in the United States are carried out by writing a **check.**

A check is a directive to the check writer's bank to pay lawful money to the bearer of the check.

Payments can be made more safely by check. Checks are a better record of transactions, and money is more secure from theft if it is in a checking account than in someone's wallet. A checkable deposit at a local bank is money, simply because it is a generally acceptable medium of exchange in the nation's marketplaces. The details on how bank money is created are described in the next chapter.

Banks offer customers the opportunity to make two types of deposits: **demand deposits** (or checking accounts) and certain types of **time deposits** (or savings accounts).

A demand deposit is a deposit of funds that can be withdrawn ("demanded") from a depository institution at any time without restrictions. The funds are usually withdrawn by writing a check.

A time deposit is a deposit of funds that cannot legally be withdrawn from a depository institution without at least 30 days' notice of withdrawal and on which the financial institution pays the depositor interest.

In recent years, the distinction between demand deposits and other types of bank deposits has become less pronounced, which has complicated the definition of bank money..

Definitions of Money Supply

The definition of **money supply (M)** incorporates all three types of money just described. A country's money supply is also known as its *stock of money*.

The money supply (M) of a country is the sum of all commodity moneys, fiat moneys, and bank moneys that are held by the nonbanking public as of a given date.

Note that the fiat money *held by banks* is not a part of the money supply. When someone cashes a check, the bank money the person holds in a checking account is converted to fiat money. Thus, the supply of fiat money in circulation has increased by the same amount as the supply of bank money has decreased. The fiat money the bank holds as cash is not counted in the money supply until it is held by someone outside the bank.

The money supply *(M)* is a stock that çan be defined as of a given moment in time—say, midnight on April 15. One's personal money supply on a given date would be the total amount of one's holdings of commodity money (which is zero in the United States), one's fiat money (currency plus coins), and the balance in one's checking account on that date. The combined money supply of all individuals and nonbanking firms on that date is the total money supply *(M)* of the country.

Most macroeconomic variables that economists study are not **stock variables** but **flow variables.**

A stock variable is a variable that can be defined for a given moment in time.

A flow variable is a variable that can be defined only over a specified period of time.

GNP, for example, is the value of output produced over a specified period of time. It makes no sense to talk of GNP at midnight of April 15. The money supply is a stock variable.

The process of determining how much money there is in the United States at any point in time has been complicated by innovations in banking that have created new types of accounts that are actually (or very nearly) demand deposits. These innovations have led to a number of changes in what bank monies are included in the nation's money supply (see Example 2).

Currency and checkable deposits are perfectly liquid: they are a medium of exchange, a store of value, and a unit of account. There is no question

Example 2

Financial Innovations of the 1970s and 1980s

The late 1970s and early 1980s saw rapid changes in the characteristics of bank monies as the amount of government regulation of the banking system decreased. These changes tended to blur the distinction between demand deposits and time deposits.

The long-standing technical distinction between **demand deposits** and **time** or **savings deposits** is that banks can legally require at least 30 days' notice before withdrawal of a time deposit. For savings deposits of households, however, banks do not usually enforce their right to 30 days' notice.

Prior to the mid-1970s, it was against banking laws to write checks on interest-paying accounts. When checks were written they had to be drawn on a commercial bank on an account that paid no explicit interest. Thrift institutions such as credit unions, mutual savings banks, or savings and loan associations were prohibited from handling checking accounts; commercial banks were prohibited from paying interest on demand deposits. The only checkable deposits from 1933 to the early 1970s were commercial bank demand deposits. Time or savings deposits were not checkable deposits.

In the late 1970s, the banking system began to experiment with ways around the legal ban on banks' paying interest on demand deposits—a ban that remains in effect today. Clever lawyers and bankers figured a way around this prohibition: they called the checkable deposit by another name—a NOW (negotiable order of withdrawal) account—or allowed automatic transfers out of savings into checking accounts whenever a check is written—called ATS (automatic transfer services) accounts.

In addition to NOW and ATS accounts, innovative brokerage firms created money-market funds on which checks could be written. These are basically *investment clubs* in various high-interest paying assets that are not accessible to small savers. These *money-market mutual funds* allow their investors to write checks over a prescribed amount. Money-market mutual funds have grown rapidly, since they have tended to pay higher interest rates than those offered by conventional savings accounts or NOW accounts.

NOW and ATS accounts have experienced phenomenal growth since 1975. In 1975, they amounted to $1.6 billion. In December of 1981, they amounted to $77.9 billion. In 1975, money-market mutual funds amounted to $3.6 billion. By December 1981, they had risen to $184.5 billion.

---

that they should be included in the money supply. But other types of money can be converted to cash with varying degrees of ease. *Money-market funds* and saving deposits on which checks may be written can be converted into cash quickly, but not on weekends or if one is out of town. Time deposits with a fixed maturity date can be converted to cash but with some penalty. Government and corporate bonds can also be converted into cash quickly but only when the banks are open or the bond market is open. Also, when these bonds fall in value, they have to be sold at a loss. Even assets such as land or old paintings can be converted into cash, though a substantial penalty may be incurred if one cannot wait for the right buyer to come along. Where does one draw the line between *money* and *nonmoney?*

Because it is difficult to draw the fine dividing line between monies and nonmonies, U.S. financial authorities use different definitions of the U.S. money supply for different purposes.

Table 1 shows the two definitions of the U.S. money supply that are most frequently used by financial authorities: **M1** and **M2**.

M1 is the sum of currency (and coins), demand deposits at commercial banks held by the nonbanking public, travelers' checks, and other checkable deposits like NOW (negotiable order of withdrawal) and ATS (automatic transfer services) accounts.

M2 equals M1 plus savings and small time deposits plus money-market mutual-fund shares plus other highly liquid assets.

M1 amounted to $442 billion in December of 1981. M1 is the most frequently cited measure of

Table 1
The U.S. Money Supply, M1 and M2, December 1981

Component	Amount (billions of dollars)
Currency and coin	123.1
plus	
Demand deposits[a]	236.8
plus	
Travelers' checks	4.5
plus	
Other checkable deposits[b]	77.9
equals	
M1	**441.9**
plus	
Savings deposits at all depository institutions	335.6
plus	
Small time deposits at all depository institutions[c]	848.6
plus	
Money-market mutual-fund shares	184.5
plus	
Other	34.6
equals	
M2	**1841.2**

[a]Demand deposits at all commercial banks other than those due to other banks, the U.S. government, and foreign official institutions.
[b]Other checkable deposits include NOW and ATS accounts, credit union share-draft balances, and demand deposits at mutual savings banks. NOW (negotiated order of withdrawal) accounts pay interest and are otherwise like demand deposits. ATS (automatic transfer services) accounts transfer funds from savings accounts to checking accounts automatically when a check is written.
[c]A small time deposit is one issued in a denomination of less than $100,000.
Source: *The Federal Reserve Bulletin.*

the money supply; it includes the most liquid assets available in the economy. About one half of M1 is held by nonbanking business enterprises, one third by households, and the rest by an assortment of financial institutions, foreigners, and others.

M2 amounted to $1,841 billion in December of 1981. In addition to M1, it includes assets such as savings and time deposits that are less liquid than the items in M1. For example, many of these accounts have penalties for withdrawal before a specified maturity date. The largest component of M2 is small time deposits ($849 billion).[3]

Why is the distinction between the different money supply definitions important? Because the supply of money has an important effect on the economy, the supply of money is controlled by government monetary authorities. Whether monetary authorities control M1 or M2 will affect the extent to which individuals and firms substitute one form of money for another. It is likely, for example, that the development of checkable money-market funds and NOW and ATS accounts have diverted funds from conventional commercial bank demand deposits. Financial innovations have tended to offer people more substitutes for conventional demand deposits.

THE DEMAND FOR MONEY

Although money has a variety of benefits, as just described, there is also an opportunity cost to holding money. The basic opportunity cost of holding ("demanding") money is that one is passing up the opportunity to accumulate other forms of wealth that promise higher returns. If one holds $10,000 in cash or in one's non-interest-bearing checking account, one is sacrificing the opportunity to buy goods now or to put that money into stocks, bonds, or real estate.

The three motives for demanding money are 1) the **transactions motive,** 2) the **precautionary motive,** and 3) the **speculative motive.**

*People motivated by the **transactions motive** hold money in order to carry out transactions.*

*People motivated by the **precautionary motive** hold money in order to protect themselves against unforeseen emergencies.*

*People motivated by the **speculative motive** hold money in order to take advantage of profitable speculative opportunities.*

3. M2 has undergone considerable reinterpretation over the years. The old M2 excluded time and savings deposits outside of commercial banks (such as deposits in savings and loan associations).

The Transactions Motive

Money is required for transactions purposes because money has the most **liquidity** of all assets.

Liquidity is the ease and speed with which an asset can be converted into a medium of exchange without risk of loss.

One can measure the liquidity of an asset by the speed of its conversion to money or the ease of its acceptance as money. The holder of money does not have to go through the time and expense of selling a less liquid asset (like a stock or bond) in order to get money. Assets such as land, apartment buildings, and paintings may serve as good stores of value during inflationary periods, but they are not liquid in the sense that some time or expense is involved in converting them to cash. Because people have to carry out regular transactions, they must hold part of their wealth in the form of money. The inconvenience of converting other assets into cash would be too great to allow individuals to conduct transactions without holding some money.

The Precautionary Motive

People demand money to carry out their normal transactions. They also hold money as a precaution to handle unforeseen emergencies. If a family member becomes ill, a large hospital bill may have to be paid. If a storm destroys the roof of one's home, one may find that this damage is not covered by insurance. Many people keep extra money in their wallets or hidden in their homes just for such emergencies.

The Speculative Motive

People demand money for speculative reasons as well. If a stock-market speculator gets the hunch that stock prices will fall through the floor within two months' time, he or she would likely sell current stock holdings, put the proceeds into a checking account, and wait for the stock market to fall. The speculator would then be in a position to buy stocks cheap with the money accumulated

for speculative reasons. Today, the speculative motive is not important in the demand for M1 but would be important in the demand for M2 because M2 includes money-market mutual funds. Clearly, a speculator would not wish to hold large balances in low-interest-bearing checking accounts.

Factors Affecting the Demand for Money

At this point, some preliminary statements can be made about the factors that cause the demand for money to change.

First, as incomes rise, people participate in more transactions; therefore, *the transactions demand for money should tend to rise with income*.

Second, that which can be earned by holding assets other than money is the opportunity cost of holding money. Interest rates are one measure of the yields on other assets; therefore, *rising interest rates should reduce the demand for money*.

Third, when prices are rising, money ceases to be a good store of value. Although rising prices may require more money for transactions, a higher anticipated rate of inflation causes people to switch their wealth out of money into assets such as real estate, stock, or rare art works that promise to retain their value. Thus, *a higher inflation rate will lower the demand for money*.

Fourth, *a higher price level* with a given level of real GNP *increases the transactions demand for money* because money income increases.

The economy's demand for money depends upon the economy's income, interest rates, inflation, and the price level.

MONEY AND PRICES

Economists are interested in money because of money's effects on prices, employment, and the level of economic activity. Years of rapid inflation have focused attention on the relationship between the money supply and prices. This chapter will describe the classical theory of 19th-century economists, called the *crude quantity theory* and will summarize the evidence used to support this theory.

Theory

The supply-and-demand analysis presented in Chapter 4 sheds light on the relationship between the stock of money and prices. Remember that if the supply of a good rises relative to its demand, its price or value will fall to equate quantity demanded and quantity supplied. This elementary principle of supply and demand should apply to money as well. As noted earlier, money is demanded, just as shoes, clothing, and beer are demanded. People hold money for transactions, precautionary, and speculative motives. If the supply of money rises more rapidly than its demand, the value of money should fall to again equate quantity demanded and quantity supplied. If the demand for money rises relative to its supply, the value of money should rise—again, to equate quantity demanded and quantity supplied.

When the demand for money stays the same while the supply of money is increasing, supply-and-demand analysis predicts that the value of money should fall. When the demand for money is increasing while the supply of money is fixed, the value of money should rise.

The *value* of money is determined by what one can buy with it. The value of money is declining when each unit of money (say, each dollar) buys fewer goods. If the price of a candy bar is $0.25, $1 is worth 4 candy bars. If the price of a candy bar is $0.50, $1 is worth only 2 candy bars. In terms of a candy bar, the value of $1 is 1 divided by the price of a candy bar. Thus, the value of money falls when prices rise, and the value of money rises when prices fall. In other words, *there is an inverse relationship between the price level and the value of money*.

If P represents the general price level (as measured, say, by the GNP deflator), then the value of money is measured by the *inverse* of P, or by $1/P$. If prices rise by 10 percent, the value of money will fall by 10 percent.

The value of money falls in exact inverse proportion to the increase in the overall level of prices.

Supply-and-demand analysis predicts that when the money supply rises more rapidly than money demand, the economy will respond by raising the price level (lowering the value of money). When the money supply rises more slowly than money demand, the economy responds by lowering the price level (raising the value of money).

Since inflation is defined as an increase in the overall level of prices, inflation is associated with increases in money supply. If the money supply increases more rapidly than the demand for money, the price level will rise.

When the demand for money is constant and the supply of money is increased, people have excess cash balances that they do not want to hold. People try to get rid of their excess cash balances by spending them.

However, *it is impossible for the community as a whole to get rid of money*. Individuals can spend excess cash balances, but the whole community cannot. As each person tries to get rid of an excess supply of money, prices are driven up because there are more dollars in the economy chasing the same number of goods. As prices rise, the community as a whole requires more money for its transactions. Thus, rising prices increase the quantity of money demanded until the excess supply of money disappears and prices stop rising.

Evidence

How can economists measure changes in the demand for money? The demand for money should rise with real GNP since a larger volume of goods and services will require more money for transactions. If there are more goods and services, more money is required to purchase them at the same prices.

One could estimate that the demand for money increases at the same rate as real GNP. The rate of increase in the supply of money is given in Figure 1.

What is the long-run relationship between the growth of the supply of money and the demand for money? Between 1915 and 1980, real GNP rose to 8 times its size, while the money supply (M1) increased to nearly 33 times its size. The growth in the supply of money far outstripped the growth in the demand for money. Under these cir-

Figure 1
The U.S. Money Supply and Price Level, 1915–1981

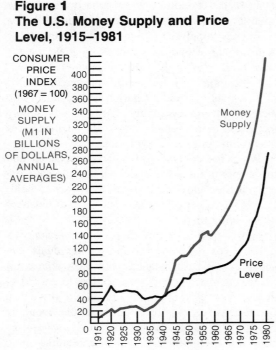

Over the last 65 years, money supply and prices have tended to change together. Notice that over long periods the money supply has grown more than the price level in order to accommodate the growth of real GNP.

Source: *Historical Statistics of the United States, 1980;* U.S. Bureau of the Census; *Federal Reserve Bulletin.*

Table 2
Money and Inflation, United States and Latin American Countries, 1963–1976

Country	Compound Annual Rate of Increase of Money Supply (percent)	Compound Annual Rate of Increase of Consumer Prices (percent)
Chile	67.4	61.1
Argentina	43.4	39.4
Brazil	32.0	26.3
Colombia	17.7	12.2
Mexico	13.4	6.8
United States	4.9	4.4

Source: International Monetary Fund, *International Financial Statistics.*

cumstances where supply exceeds demand, our simple theory predicts that prices should rise—which they did.

Figure 1 plots the U.S. money supply (M1) and prices (the CPI). According to Figure 1, prices rose by more than 8 times while money supply grew almost 33 times. Prices rose because *when money supply grows at a more rapid rate than real GNP, there is an excess supply of money.* People increase their spending in an attempt to get rid of excess cash balances, the price level is bid up, and the value of money falls.

The evidence that money supply and price level are related is not limited to the United States. Table 2 compares the annual rates of growth of money and prices in 5 Latin American

countries and the United States during the period 1963 to 1976. The table shows a remarkable correspondence between the rate of growth in the money supply and the rate of inflation. Those countries that experienced the most rapid growth of money supply also had the highest rates of inflation.

Some countries have experienced dramatic historical episodes of runaway inflations, called **hyperinflations.**

> A **hyperinflation** *is a very rapid and constantly growing rate of inflation, on the order of three digits or more per month.*

Hyperinflations essentially make the money of the country worthless. The economy must resort to barter and must seek out other types of money, often foreign currencies or commodity money.

How well do the historical episodes of hyperinflation support the money supply/money demand interpretation of inflation? The cause of each hyperinflation is well documented: the government printed too much money, often to finance wars or to pay the bills of past wars. Hyperinflations have been caused by excessive growth of money supply. In each hyperinflation, the cure was achieved only when the government slowed down the printing of money.

The German Hyperinflation

The best example of documented hyperinflation is the German inflation following World War 1 (from August 1922 to November 1923). To finance its wartime reparation payments to France and Great Britain, the German government increased the supply of paper money at the rate of 314 percent per month. During this brief span of time, the price level rose astronomically to more than 10 billion times the level of prices in August of 1922! Prices rose 322 percent per month. Hyperinflation destroyed many of the advantages of a monetary economy. Workers, paid in the morning, demanded time off to spend their wages before they became worthless! Firms paid their employees three times a day—after breakfast, lunch, and dinner! Money became like a hot potato: no one wanted to hold it. Wage and price contracts became impossible. Transactions were increasingly conducted in barter. Gold and foreign currencies were the only money people would hold. The German hyperinflation created the civil chaos that helped bring Hitler to power. It also may explain why postwar Germany has had one of the lowest inflation rates in the world. The German fear of inflation remains strong to this day. ◀

THE CRUDE QUANTITY THEORY OF MONEY

Chapter 1 warned against the false-cause fallacy. The fact that money growth and price increases have tended to move together does not prove that increases in money supply have caused increases in the price level. A consistent and logical theory that explains why an increase in money supply will cause an increase in price level must be tested before this conclusion can be drawn. This section will elaborate on a theory of why inflation is caused by excessive growth of the money supply.

That inflation is caused by excessive growth of the money supply is a fairly old notion. The classical economists of the 18th century, such as David Hume and Adam Smith, proposed a theory to explain the relationship between money supply and price level. This theory was taken up by the great American economist, Irving Fisher of Yale University (1867-1947), and by the great English economist, Alfred Marshall (1842-1924), and has come to be called the **crude quantity theory of money,** or simply the **quantity theory.** The quantity theory is the antecedent of important modern macroeconomic theories. It is especially useful because it provides a powerful though simplified view of how the macroeconomy works.

*The basic message of the **crude quantity theory of money** is that the price level is strictly proportional to the money supply.*

In other words, the crude quantity theory taught that an *x* percent increase in money supply will lead to an *x* percent increase in the price level. The proponents of the crude quantity theory did not believe that this relationship would hold exactly in all instances, but they felt it was a reasonably close approximation of the reality of the economy in the late 19th and early 20th centuries.

Velocity of Circulation

The concept of **velocity of circulation** is essential to an understanding of the quantity theory.

*The **velocity of circulation** (V) is the number of times the average dollar is spent on final goods and services in one year's time.*

In 1981, American GNP was $2,926 billion, which means that in 1981, households, government, and businesses spent this sum on final goods and services. The average 1981 supply of money (M1) was $430 billion. In order for the economy to make $2,926 billion worth of purchases in the course of one year with a stock of money of $430 billion, each dollar was spent on average 6.8 times (6.8 = $2,926 ÷ $430). In other words, each dollar financed the purchase of $6.80 worth of final goods and services; the velocity of circulation was equal to 6.8.

The velocity of circulation is the ratio of GNP to the money supply:

$$V \equiv GNP/M$$

The higher the velocity of circulation, the faster people are turning over the available stock of money. In hyperinflations, for example, velocity tends to rise as people try to spend their money as fast as possible before its value declines even further. When prices are stable or falling, people are more inclined to hold on to their money longer. Since nominal GNP equals real GNP (denoted here by Q) multiplied by the price level, P, the velocity of circulation can also be expressed as:

$$V \equiv PQ/M$$

By multiplying both sides of the above equation by M, the equation becomes

$$MV \equiv PQ$$

The Equation of Exchange

The equation giving the definition of velocity can be written as the **equation of exchange.**

*The **equation of exchange** is*

$$MV \equiv PQ$$

The ≡ symbol is used instead of the = symbol because the equation of exchange is a tautology (identity), or an equation that is true by definition. The definition emerges from observed GNP and observed money supply. Velocity is defined in such a way that the equation always works.

In effect, the equation of exchange says that the amount of final purchases in the economy (GNP) must equal the amount of money in circulation times the average number of times each dollar changes hands. Were this not true, then the observed amount of spending would not have been possible.

The equation of exchange can be used to explain the quantity theory. Irving Fisher and Alfred Marshall both believed that the equation of exchange summarized the relevant factors determining the link between the money supply and the price level.

The Relationship Between Money and Prices

The equation of exchange does not guarantee that money supply and the price level will rise at the same rate. The quantity theory assumes that:

1. the velocity of circulation, V, is fixed.
2. real GNP, Q, is fixed in the short run.

These assumptions turn the equation of exchange into a theory. A glance at the equation of exchange shows that if both Q and V are fixed, then P will be proportional to M. The equation of exchange, rewritten to solve for P, is $P = M (V/Q)$. If Q and V are both fixed, V/Q will be a constant. Therefore, an x percent increase in M will cause an x percent increase in P. The quantity theory concludes that P is strictly proportional to M, or, in other words, that inflation is strictly a monetary phenomenon.

Why did the quantity theorists assume that velocity of circulation and real GNP were both fixed in the short run? They felt that velocity is fixed by the monetary habits and institutions of the community. A country with a large number of money substitutes may have a high velocity of circulation; a country with few money substitutes may have a low velocity. A country with frequent pay periods may have a high velocity; a country with few pay periods may have a low velocity. Whatever the case, because habits and institutions change very slowly, for all practical purposes, quantity theorists regarded velocity as constant.

The quantity theorists believed the size of real GNP is fixed in the short run by the size and productivity of the resources (land, labor, and capital) of the country. The real output of the economy is fixed because resources will tend to be fully employed, particularly the most important resource, labor. In this view, the resource pricing system ensures the full employment of resources. If workers are involuntarily unemployed, the wage rate will automatically adjust downwards until all those willing to work at the going wage will be employed. Over time as the labor force expands and technology improves, real output will rise. But in the short run, real output is for all practical purposes fixed by the resource base and technology of the economy.

The Money Sector and the Real Sector

The quantity theorists divided the economy into two sectors: a *real sector* and a *monetary sector*. In the real sector, resources are combined to produce full-employment output. In the monetary sector, the price level is established by the amount of money in the economy. According to the quantity theorists, the two sectors do not overlap. Changes in money supply are not associated with changes in employment or real output, and vice versa.

The *quantity theory, therefore, denies a link between the money supply and unemployment.* According to the quantity theory, employment is determined in the real sector, and changes in money supply will affect only the price level, not real output or employment.

Aggregate Supply and Aggregate Demand

Chapter 5 introduced the concepts of aggregate demand and aggregate supply. The aggregate demand *(AD)* curve shows the amount of real GNP demanded by all agents in the economy at different price levels. The aggregate supply *(AS)* curve shows the amounts of real GNP supplied at different price levels. Chapter 5 gave *AD* a negative slope and *AS* a positive slope.

What types of aggregate demand and aggregate supply curves are suggested by the quantity theory? To obtain the quantity theory aggregate demand curve, the quantity equation $MV = PQ$ can be rearranged as $Q = MV/P$. Like microeconomic demand curves, the aggregate demand curve gives the relationship between output and price level when all other factors that affect output are held constant. According to the quantity theorists,

Figure 2
The Crude Quantity Theory

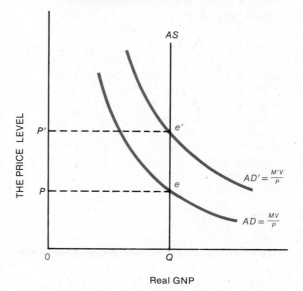

The aggregate demand curve for goods and services, according to the crude quantity theory, is simply MV/P, where V is a constant and M is held constant. Since real GNP is fixed, the aggregate supply curve *(AS)* is vertical. If the money supply increases from M to M', AD shifts to the right, and the equilibrium price level increases proportionately from P to P'.

velocity is already fixed, so the aggregate demand curve only holds money supply constant.

With money supply and velocity fixed, the quantity equation says that the aggregate demand for real GNP will vary inversely with the price level. The higher the price level, the lower the quantity of real goods and services demanded. When money supply increases, aggregate demand increases (*AD* shifts to the right).

Figure 2 shows the aggregate demand and supply curves according to the crude quantity theory. The aggregate demand curve is negatively sloped, and the aggregate supply curve is a vertical line. *AS* is vertical because, according to the crude quantity theory, real GNP is fixed at full employment. Real GNP, therefore, cannot increase as the price level increases; all resources are already fully employed. With real GNP already fixed, the intersection of *AD* and *AS* determines only the price level.

Example 4

Will a Return to the Gold Standard Solve Inflation?

Up to the early 1930s, the United States and most industrialized countries operated on an international gold standard. A gold standard means that the fiat and bank money of the country can be converted into gold at a fixed rate of exchange. Thus the quantity of money is tied strictly to the quantity of gold in the economy. The Great Depression of the 1930s destroyed the international gold standard. When the gold standard was in use, there was long-run price stability but with considerable short-run fluctuations in prices and GNP.

Some economists and government officials are now advocating a return to the gold standard as a means of solving our inflationary problems. Gold-standard advocates believe that making money out of gold will reduce inflationary pressures. They believe that basing money on gold, which is limited in quantity, is the only way to discipline governments to limit the quantity of money. The supply of money would have to depend upon the availability of gold, not upon government printing presses.

Although this proposition is not unreasonable, the supply of money can be limited by less costly means. It is not necessary to go to a gold standard to limit the supply of money.

When the money supply increases, the aggregate demand curve shifts right proportionally, and the equilibrium price level P rises to P'. If M' is twice M, then P' will be twice P.

According to the quantity theory, *the value of money depends on its nominal quantity not on the stuff from which it is made.* Money is valuable because of what it can buy. According to the quantity theory, it makes no difference whether the money is made out of gold, platinum, or just plain old paper on which some engravings of old men have been made. If the quantity of money is limited, the money will have value because it is the generally accepted medium of exchange.

This conclusion has policy implications. Why waste resources using a commodity money like gold or silver? Why not just print the money in a way that is difficult to counterfeit and limit its quantity? Sceptics doubt the ability of governments to resist the lure of printing too much money. For these critics, the cost of resources involved in commodity money is less than the inflationary costs of the excesses of government printing presses.

MODERN QUANTITY THEORY

The crude quantity theory is a direct ancestor of modern monetary economics. Modern monetary economists have relaxed some of the more restrictive assumptions of the crude quantity theory and have turned it into a more sophisticated and realistic theory of the relationship between money, output, and prices. The development of the modern quantity theory is associated with the works of Irving Fisher, Milton Friedman, Allan Meltzer, and Karl Brunner.

The crude quantity theorists left their modern successors with several thorny problems:

1. In the crude quantity theory, money affected only the price level, not real GNP or employment. It did not account for changes in output and employment.

2. The velocity of circulation has not remained constant over the years but has been subject to significant changes, often within a fairly brief period of time. The fact that velocity can change so much is bothersome to those who believe in a close linkage between money supply and economic activity. As the equation of exchange indicates, if velocity is unstable and unpredictable, the linkage between money supply and GNP is also unstable and unpredictable.

Inflation and Velocity

From 1966 to 1981, the velocity of circulation rose from 4.4 to about 6.8—a 50 percent increase in 15 years. Modern monetary economists have sought to explain such movements in velocity. Their work seeks to demonstrate that although velocity is obviously not fixed, it nevertheless moves in a stable and predictable manner.

Modern monetary economists emphasize that inflation is a determinant of velocity. Individuals hold money balances to carry out their transactions, but inflation is like a tax on money balances. People who anticipate inflation try to spend their money balances more quickly. When they do so, velocity increases. People who anticipate inflation will want to be paid more often; they will shop more often; they will make more trips to the bank; they will find ways to limit their holdings of money.

Anticipated inflation tends to increase velocity as people spend their money balances more quickly to limit the "inflation tax."

Velocity changes if people *anticipate a change* in the rate of inflation. If inflation is steady—and people expect it to continue at the same steady rate—there is no reason for velocity to change.

Between 1966 and 1981, the inflation rate was anything but steady. It rose from 3.2 percent in 1966 to 9.1 percent in 1981. Presumably, as people saw the inflation rate rising, they adjusted upward the anticipated rate of inflation and raised their velocity of circulation.

Unanticipated Inflation and Real Economic Activity

Everyone tries to anticipate inflation. Those who correctly anticipate inflation can protect themselves from the inflation tax. Modern economists recognize that people are often surprised by inflation. They may anticipate a 5 percent inflation rate, which turns out to be 10 percent, or vice versa.

According to modern theory, it is entirely possible that unanticipated inflation can affect real output and employment. As noted above, this belief is a major departure from the crude quantity theory.

If product prices rise faster than firms anticipate, business managers in those firms might not realize that rising prices are a general phenome-

non. Instead, they might conclude that their business is profitable because their product prices are rising faster than their costs. Based on this optimistic conclusion, they might expand output and employment. In this case, the unanticipated inflation has fooled them into increasing output and employment. Eventually, however, they will realize that they have been fooled, and they will adjust their output and employment back down. By the same reasoning, an unanticipated deflation can cause firms to reduce their output and employment.

If inflation were correctly anticipated, firms would see their prices rise but would realize that other prices (including their costs) were rising as well. They would correctly see that rising prices were not making the firm any better off, and they would not expand output and employment.

Unanticipated inflation can cause changes in employment and real output over a short-run period; *anticipated* inflation, on the other hand, should have no effect on output and employment.

A Modern Perspective

According to the crude quantity theory, real output and velocity had to be stable in order for the relationship between money supply and price level to be strictly proportional. Modern theorists have demonstrated, however, that unanticipated inflation can affect the amount of real output and that velocity is positively related to anticipated inflation.

When inflation is steady and in excess of the long-run growth of real output, the conditions of the crude quantity theory are most likely to be met. Households and businesses will be able to anticipate correctly the rate of inflation. The greater the departure of the growth rate of the money supply from the growth rate of real output, the more one would expect a close association between percentage changes in money supply and percentage changes in price level. As long as inflation is correctly anticipated, monetary effects on real output will be avoided as well—a second means of disrupting the proportionality of money supply to price level.

Although increases in anticipated inflation raise velocity, massive changes in the institutions of money and banking can also cause substantive changes in velocity and undermine the crude quantity theory. During periods when many new money substitutes are being created, the velocity of old money will increase as people switch from old money to new forms of money.

As the data cited in Figure 1 and Table 2 show, the crude quantity theory holds up fairly well. Money and prices do tend to move together. The data, for example, in Table 2 apply to a 14-year period, and the correspondence between the growth of money supply and the inflation rate is close, especially for the high-inflation countries, such as Chile, Argentina, and Brazil.

This chapter has explained what money is and how to measure the money supply and has introduced the simplest theory of macroeconomics: the quantity theory of money. Before embarking on the task of explaining modern macroeconomics in Chapters 9 through 17, the next chapter will explain how the money supply is actually determined in a modern economy and will describe the role of the banking system.

Summary

1. Money is the medium of exchange ordinarily used in transactions. In addition, money serves as a unit of value, a standard of deferred payment, and a store of value. Inflation complicates the use of money as a standard of deferred payment and as a store of value. When inflation is foreseen, people may be able to protect money's role in these two functions.

2. The money supply consists of commodity money, fiat money, and bank money. Commodity money's value as a commodity is as great as its value as money. Fiat money's value as a commodity is less than its value as money. Bank money consists of checking-account deposits.

3. People demand money for transactions purposes, for precautionary motives, and for speculative motives. Yields on other assets such as interest rates measure the opportunity costs of holding money.

4. Supply-and-demand analysis suggests that when money supply increases more rapidly than money demand, the value of money should fall. The value of money falls when prices rise. A rise in the overall price level is inflation.

5. The crude quantity theory of money suggests that changes in money supply and price level will be strictly proportional. This conclusion follows from the equation of exchange ($MV = PQ$) and from the assumptions that velocity and output are fixed. The velocity of circulation is the number of times the average dollar is spent on goods and services in one year's time. Anticipated inflation raises velocity as people adjust their spending habits to reduce their money balances.

6. Modern theorists argue that unanticipated inflation can affect real output and employment. Thus, changes in the money supply can affect real output. The crude quantity theory holds reasonably well when inflation is relatively stable over long periods. If velocity does not change dramatically, the annual rate of growth of money supply will approximately equal the annual rate of inflation plus the annual rate of growth of real output.

Key Terms

money
commodity money
fiat money
bank money
Gresham's Law
check
demand deposits
time deposits
money supply
stock variables
flow variables
M1
M2
transactions motive
precautionary motive
speculative motive
liquidity

hyperinflation
crude quantity theory of money
velocity of circulation
equation of exchange

Questions and Problems

1. "Anything is money that is legally declared by the government to be money." Evaluate this statement.
2. During hyperinflations money loses its value as a medium of exchange, as a store of value, and as a standard of deferred payment. What would you expect to happen to the overall efficiency of the economy when this happens?
3. "It is foolish to talk about the demand for money. People want all the money they can get their hands on." Evaluate this statement.
4. Explain why the value of fiat money is determined by its relative abundance. What is the lower limit to which the value of fiat money can fall?
5. Discuss the social costs of having a commodity money system. What are its benefits?

How does Gresham's Law enter into into this issue?

6. If prices are rising 5 percent per year, what is happening to the value of money?
7. Assume that the demand for money is increasing at a rate of 20 percent per year and that the supply of money is increasing at a rate of 10 percent per year. What would you expect to happen to the value of money? to prices?
8. Why is the distinction between M1 and M2 important?
9. When answering the following questions, assume $M = \$100$, $Q = 400$, and $P = \$2$.
   a. What is the value of V?
   b. Determine the aggregate demand schedule for a price level of $1, for a price level of $2, and for a price level of $3.
   c. If the money supply is $150, what is the aggregate demand schedule for the three price levels listed in part b?
   d. Use this example to illustrate the basic proposition of the crude quantity theory.
   e. In this example, show that if V is unstable and unpredictable, the basic proposition of the crude quantity theory does not hold.

CHAPTER

8

Commercial Banking and the Federal Reserve

Chapter Preview

The last chapter discussed how the supply of money *(M)* can affect prices, output, and employment. This chapter will explain how and by whom the money supply is determined. Why does money supply increase or decrease? Or, in other words, where does money come from? Where does money go?

The money supply can increase or decrease very rapidly. From 1929 to 1933, money supply fell by a gigantic 25 percent from $26.6 billion to $19.9 billion, yet the amount of currency held by the public actually increased. What happened to the missing $6.7 billion? Those who lived through the Great Depression will argue either that people had it under their mattresses or that Rockefeller had it all.

In order to see how the money supply expands or contracts, one must understand the business of banking and the relationship between banks and the Federal Reserve System.

THE BUSINESS OF BANKING

Most of us have had some experience with banks: a commercial bank cashes our checks; a savings and loan association handles our savings account; the credit union at our place of work will give us a loan for new furniture. What services do these banks perform for us? How do they earn profits?

Financial Intermediaries

A savings and loan association, an insurance company, a commercial bank, a mutual-savings bank, a credit union, a retirement fund, and a mutual fund are all examples of **financial intermediaries,** or financial institutions that mediate between borrowers and lenders.

Financial intermediaries borrow funds from one group of economic agents (people or firms with savings) and lend to other agents.

Financial intermediaries serve a useful purpose in our economy. With financial intermediation, borrowers and lenders do not have to seek each other out. The lender does not have to accept the borrower's IOU, investigate the borrower's credit worthiness, or pass on the wisdom of the borrower's spending plans. The commercial bank, for example, accepts a depositor's deposit with the promise to pay the depositor a specified interest rate and then lends these funds to a borrower at a higher interest rate. Borrowers and lenders thus pay a price for using the services of a financial intermediary. If they had sought each other out, the lender would have received more and the borrower would have paid less.

Is the cost of financial intermediation worth its benefits? Financial intermediation offers at least three benefits: cost minimization, risk pooling, and high liquidity.

Cost Minimization. If a large company wishes to borrow $5 million, it would be very costly to the firm to borrow $5,000 from 1,000 different lenders. An organized market is necessary to bring such a large number of lenders together. The public may not know the corporation, but the bank does. So the bank offers appropriate terms to ultimate lenders, and the bank alone investigates the credit worthiness of the company wanting to borrow $5 million. It would also be costly for 1,000 separate lenders to make their own credit investigations.

Risk Pooling. For a lender, it is better not to put all eggs in one basket. If Jack lends $1,000 to Jill, and Jill cannot pay, Jack loses all his money. But if Jack lends $1 each to 1,000 different Jills, Jack can reduce his risks substantially by *risk pooling*. The financial intermediary pools the savings of smaller individuals and puts them into a number of diversified investments that collectively offer little risk. If one borrower out of 100 defaults, the loss is still relatively small. Financial intermediaries can spread the pooled funds of their depositors over a variety of borrowers, while individual depositors with small sums of money to lend cannot.

High Liquidity. A final benefit of deposit intermediaries, such as commercial banks, savings and loan associations, and mutual savings banks, is that they *borrow short* and *lend long*. Borrowers usually prefer to borrow for a long term (to *borrow long*), because the services of the house, car, or business plant that the borrowed funds pay for last a long time. But lenders prefer to lend funds for a short period of time (to *lend short*) since unexpected needs could always arise. Thus, people in general prefer to lend short and to borrow long. Financial intermediaries fill the gap between borrowers and lenders by being willing to borrow short and lend long. Financial intermediaries offer deposits that are highly liquid. Commercial banks and savings and loan associations borrow money from depositors, who can withdraw their funds at any time. The bank may then turn around and lend to a home buyer on a 30-year mortgage.[1]

The different types of financial intermediaries compete with each other for borrowers and lenders. Savings and loans, mutual-savings banks, and credit unions offer checkable accounts that compete with commercial banks. Financial intermediaries compete among themselves to make loans to qualified borrowers. On the average, profit rates in banking have not been above profit rates elsewhere in the economy.

---

1. During periods of unanticipated inflation, financial intermediaries may become less willing to borrow short and lend long. In the late 1970s and early 1980s, savings and loans were stuck with large volumes of outstanding mortgage loans at 7 to 10 percent when they were borrowing short at 10 to 15 percent. For this reason, financial intermediaries have become cautious about making long-term loan commitments at a fixed rate of interest.

The Magnitude of
Financial Intermediation

In 1981, $353 billion in private domestic funds were advanced for private investment, short-term credits, and the purchase of government securities. These represent funds that were supplied from ultimate lenders to ultimate borrowers. Only $43 billion of the $353 billion (12 percent) were loaned directly from lenders to borrowers. The remaining $310 billion were channeled through commercial banks (supplying 33 percent), insurance and pension funds (22 percent), savings and loans (9 percent), and other assorted financial intermediaries. These figures show that financial intermediaries handle most (about 88 percent) of the flows of private funds from lenders to borrowers.

COMMERCIAL BANKS

In March 1982, there were about 15,214 **commercial banks** in the United States.

Commercial banks are banks that have been chartered either by a state agency or by the U.S. Treasury's Comptroller of the Currency to make loans and receive deposits.

Prior to the mid-1970s, the differences between commercial banks and other financial intermediaries were more clear-cut than they are now. Historically, a commercial bank could be defined as a financial institution that offered its customers checking accounts (as well as savings accounts) and made short-term loans to the general public and to businesses. The feature of commercial banks that distinguished them from *thrift institutions* was that commercial banks offered checking-account deposits.

Thrift institutions, such as savings and loans, mutual-savings banks, and credit unions cater to noncommercial customers and traditionally could not offer checking-account services, but thrift institutions now offer checking accounts like NOW and ATS accounts to families.[2]

In January 1982, America's 15,000 commercial banks held gross assets of about $1.8 trillion.

---

2. Legislation proposed in 1981, but not enacted, would have expanded the powers of thrift institutions to include commercial checking accounts and commercial loans.

The largest 150 banks accounted for 54 percent of commercial bank assets. Savings and loan associations, mutual-savings banks, and credit unions held assets of about $920 billion.

Commercial banks also held virtually all the checkable deposits at the beginning of 1982, though most thrift institutions had been authorized to offer such facilities. Despite radical changes in the banking industry, it is fair to say that commercial banks remain the most important financial intermediaries in today's economy.

The financial system is in a state of flux. Commercial banks continue to dominate other financial intermediaries, but changing laws have modified the margin of competition between commercial banks and thrift institutions. In the early 1980s, a bitter competitive struggle was underway among the different financial intermediaries.

How Commercial Banks Make Profits

Mr. Dooley, the Will Rogers of his day, remarked that a banker is a "man who takes care of your money by lending it out to his friends." Humor and friends aside, this statement captures the essence of modern banking. Bankers ordinarily cannot earn substantial profits by lending only to their friends; to be profitable, a bank must lend funds only to businesses and households that offer the best return on their investment funds. Commercial banks make profits by borrowing from customers in the form of demand deposits and time deposits and then relending these funds in the form of automobile loans, real-estate loans, business loans, and student loans. Commercial banks earn profits by borrowing money at low interest rates and lending money at higher interest rates. The difference between the rate at which banks borrow and the rate at which they lend is called the *interest-rate spread*.

Balance Sheets

The concept of a **balance sheet** is essential to an understanding of how banks operate.

*A **balance sheet** summarizes the current financial position of a firm by comparing the firm's **assets** and **liabilities**.*

Table 1
Consolidated Balance Sheet of All Commercial Banks, January 1982

Assets (billions of dollars)		Liabilities (billions of dollars)	
Vault cash	19.8	Net demand deposits*	216.8
Reserves at Fed	31.3	Savings deposits	223.2
Securities	346.5	Time deposits	693.2
Loans and investments	975.5	Other borrowings	385.5
Other assets	275.2	Net worth	129.6
Total	**1,648.3**	**Total**	**1,648.3**

*Net demand deposits = demand deposits − items in the process of collection − balances with banks.
Source: *Federal Reserve Bulletin,* April 1982, p. A17.

Assets are income-producing property.

The assets of a firm can be buildings, equipment, inventories of goods, money, or even IOUs. A balance sheet lists the claims to these assets.

Liabilities are obligations to nonowners of the firm.

Assets can be claimed by owners or nonowners. Assets claimed by owners of the firm are the firm's *net worth;* assets claimed by nonowners of the firm are the firm's liabilities.

Assets = Liabilities + Net Worth

A bank's assets consist primarily of IOUs of one kind or another—the loans it has made to persons and to firms, the government bonds it has purchased, the deposits it has with other banks. Its liabilities consist principally of the various deposits that its customers have made—demand deposits, savings deposits, and time deposits.

The combined balance sheet of America's commercial banks as of January 1982 is shown in Table 1.

The fact that commercial bank demand-deposit liabilities are less than their savings and time-deposit liabilities is a recent development attributable to the increased use of credit cards, the rise of money-market mutual funds, and new bank overdraft facilities. Historically, demand-deposit liabilities exceeded time deposits. In other words, commercial banks have become more like thrift institutions. The asset side shows how commercial banks serve as financial intermediaries. Commercial bank deposits are loaned to individuals and businesses and are used to purchase securities.[3]

The combined balance sheet in Table 1 reveals a remarkable feature of commercial banking: the demand-deposit liabilities of commercial banks far exceed the sum of commercial bank reserves.

A large fraction of a bank's liabilities are *demand liabilities,* or obligations that can be called in by depositors. Any customer who withdraws a deposit is paid out of the bank's **reserves.**

Reserves are the funds that the bank uses to satisfy the cash demands of its customers.

Bank reserves consist of two components: *vault cash,* which is simply currency and coin in the vaults of the bank, and the *bank's balances with the Federal Reserve System* (explained below).

The combined balance sheet shows that bank reserves are much less than the liabilities of the banking system. In January 1982, bank reserves equaled $51.1 billion, or 24 percent of the net demand-deposit liabilities to the nonbanking public. When savings deposits are included (because in practice banks also pay out their funds on demand), the reserve ratio falls to 12 percent.

3. Further discussion of the bank balance sheet and recent changes can be found in Lloyd B. Thomas, *Money, Banking, and Economic Activity,* 2nd ed. (Englewood Cliffs, N.J.: Prentice-Hall, 1982), pp. 113-21.

The Federal Deposit Insurance Corporation

The best way to prevent a bank scare is to assure people that they can always withdraw their money. The Federal Deposit Insurance Corporation (FDIC) is an independent agency of the U.S. Government that was established by Congress in 1933 to insure bank deposits. An FDIC-insured bank pays FDIC insurance based on the volume of deposits. The deposit-insurance fund insures each depositor's funds up to $100,000. If an FDIC-insured bank should fail, each depositor would be fully reimbursed as long as the deposit did not exceed $100,000.

The FDIC was prompted by the massive bank failures from 1930–1933. Previously, some states had attempted without success to institute their own deposit-insurance schemes. Has the FDIC worked? Since 1934 the FDIC has paid out more than 99 per cent of all deposits in banks that have failed. Today, all but a handful of commercial banks are insured by the FDIC. National banks and members of the Federal Reserve System must belong to the FDIC. Other banks find it advantageous to publicize to their customers that their accounts are insured. Every FDIC-insured bank proudly displays the FDIC emblem.

A good example of the role of the FDIC is provided by the failure of the Franklin National Bank in 1974. The Franklin National Bank was the 20th largest bank in the country; it failed because it made a number of unsound loans and had sizable losses from speculating in foreign currencies (buying and selling, for example, Mexican pesos or British pounds). Even though the bank failed, small depositors did not become alarmed since they knew their deposits were protected (up to $20,000 at the time) by the FDIC. Had the FDIC not been in existence, the failure of the Franklin National Bank may well have triggered a run on many other banks. Financial panics and bank failures are now a rarity.   ✕

Why are depositors and the banks not alarmed by the imbalance between bank reserves and demand or savings-deposit liabilities? On an ordinary business day, some customers deposit money in their checking accounts. Others withdraw money by writing checks on their accounts. If deposits come in at the same pace as withdrawals, bank reserves do not change. Reserves rise when deposits exceed withdrawals; they fall when withdrawals exceed deposits. The normal course of banking is for withdrawals and deposits to proceed at roughly the same rate.

Is it not precarious for bank reserves to be such a small fraction of deposits? What would happen if suddenly there were no deposits—only withdrawals? The reason why people have demand deposits is that checking-account money is safer and more convenient than currency and coin for many transactions. As long as depositors knew that they could get their money from the bank, they would want to leave it on deposit. The moment they felt that they could not get their money, they would want to withdraw it. Thus, people want their money if they can't get it and don't want their money if they can!

This paradox of banking has made commercial banks subject to *bank scares* at times. The history of banking is filled with episodes where large numbers of depositors lose confidence in the banks and demand their cash; when the banks cannot pay, a rash of bank failures occurs. The federal government's Federal Deposit Insurance Corporation was established to deal with this problem (see Example 1).

THE FEDERAL RESERVE SYSTEM

Bankers use the FDIC as their insurance agent and the Federal Reserve System as their banker. The *Federal Reserve System*—or *the Fed*—is the central bank of the United States. The first central bank was the Bank of Sweden. All modern countries have a central bank; the Bank of England, the Banque de France, the Deutsche Bundesbank, and the Bank of Japan are prominent in world financial circles. Even the Soviet Union has its central bank, Gosbank.

The United States did not have a central bank throughout most of the 19th century and into the second decade of the 20th century. During this period the United States became the most important industrial nation in the world without even having a central bank. The Federal Reserve System became a reality in 1913 when President Woodrow Wilson signed the Federal Reserve Act. The financial panic of 1907, in which many banks failed, provided the immediate impetus for the creation of the Fed.

Functions of the Fed

The Fed—like other central banks throughout the world—performs two primary functions:

1. The Fed controls the nation's money supply.
2. The Fed is responsible for the orderly working of the nation's banking system. It supervises private banks; it serves as the bankers' bank; it clears checks; it fills the currency needs of private banks; it acts as a lender of last resort to banks needing to borrow reserves.

The control of the money supply is the Fed's most important function. As already noted, the supply of money is believed to have an important effect on prices, output, and employment. The Fed's control of the money supply, therefore, places it in a position to influence inflation, output, and unemployment.

The Structure of the Federal Reserve System

The 1913 Federal Reserve Act divided the country into 12 districts, each with its own Federal Reserve Bank. These banks are located in Boston, New York, Philadelphia, Cleveland, Richmond, Atlanta, Chicago, St. Louis, Minneapolis, Kansas City, Dallas, and San Francisco. Each Federal Reserve Bank issues currency for its district, administers bank examinations, clears checks, and is the nominal lender of last resort to depository institutions in the district.

The Federal Reserve System is controlled and coordinated by a seven-member *Board of Governors* (formerly known as the Federal Reserve Board) located in Washington, D.C. This powerful group is appointed by the President of the United States. Each member of the Board serves a 14-year term. Terms are staggered so that the appointees of a single U.S. President cannot dominate the Board. The President appoints the chair of the Board, who is the most powerful member and serves for four years. Five of the seven current Board members are economists who have previously worked for the Fed. The Board is an inbred group of men and women.

The Federal Reserve System has much more independence than other governmental agencies. Independence is insured in part by the long terms of the Board members and because the Fed is self-financing. In a legal sense, the Fed is responsible to Congress. Although Fed actions can be taken without congressional approval, the Fed is not free of political pressures. There have been conflicts between the President and the Fed and between Congress and the Fed. There is always the threat that the independence of the Fed could be reduced by congressional action.

Not all commercial banks are member banks of the Federal Reserve System. All national banks must be members, but state-chartered banks may join if they choose. In 1981, 5,472 banks were member banks—only 37 percent of all commercial banks. Yet member banks account for about 75 percent of commercial bank assets. Large banks tend to be member banks.

Reserve Requirements

Private profit-maximizing banks would choose voluntarily to hold a portion of their assets in reserves. A prudent banker knows that sufficient reserves must be on hand to meet the cash demands of customers. In the United Kingdom, the Bank of England does not impose legal reserve requirements on private banks, yet British banks hold prudent levels of reserves, and England has developed an excellent reputation for its banking services. In the United States, however, the Fed imposes uniform **reserve requirements** on all commercial banks, savings and loan associations, mutual savings banks, and credit unions. U.S. banks are required by law to hold reserve levels that meet a standard **required-reserve ratio.**

*A **reserve requirement** is a rule that states the amount of reserves that must be on hand to back bank deposits.*

 **Example 2**

The Monetary Control Act of 1980

The Monetary Control Act of 1980 was designed to increase the Fed's control over all depository institutions. Prior to 1980, the Fed could impose reserve requirements only on its member banks (nationally chartered banks or state banks that elected to join the system). Nonmember state banks were allowed to hold reserves under the rules established by each state. Because state requirements were typically lower than those of the Fed, member state banks often opted to leave the system, and some national banks converted to state charters.

The 1980 Monetary Control Act expanded the power of the Fed to set required-reserve ratios for all depository institutions (not just national banks); all depository institutions were given the right to borrow from the Fed; it phased out interest-rate ceilings on deposits by 1986; and it authorized banks and thrift institutions to offer interest on checking accounts (the NOW and ATS accounts).

The Monetary Control Act of 1980 has been described as the most significant banking legislation since the Federal Reserve Act of 1913. It changed the way in which various types of financial institutions compete with one another. Basically, all depository institutions received the right to issue checking accounts, and the differences between commercial banks and thrift institutions were blurred considerably. The Monetary Control Act sought to unleash competition in the banking industry and to reduce government controls on the banking industry. Where this competition will eventually lead cannot be predicted at this point.

---

*A **required-reserve ratio** is the amount of reserves required for each dollar of deposits.*

A required-reserve ratio of 0.1 (10 percent) means that the bank must hold $0.10 in reserves for each dollar of deposits. The current prevailing reserve requirements are as follows: Transaction accounts such as checking accounts have reserve ratios ranging from 3 to 12 percent, depending on the size of the bank. The reserve requirements on time and savings accounts range from 0 to 3 percent depending on the size of the account and its maturity. The Fed has the power to raise or lower these required-reserve ratios and to impose supplemental requirements.

Borrowing from the Fed

Any depository institution holding reserves with the Fed is entitled to borrow funds from the Fed. Prior to the Monetary Control Act of 1980, only member banks had such borrowing privileges. A bank that is allowed to borrow from the Fed, in the technical banking language, has access to the *discount window*.

Banks do not have unlimited access to the discount window. They must have exhausted all reasonable alternate sources of funds before coming to the Fed. The discount window is available for temporary and immediate cash needs of the banks.

The rate of interest the Fed charges banks at the discount window is called the *discount rate*. The Fed sets the discount rate and can encourage or discourage bank borrowing by raising or lowering the discount rate. If the spread between the rate at which the banks themselves borrow (the discount rate) and the rates at which they lend is small, the bank's incentive to use the discount window is reduced.

The Federal Open Market Committee

The control of the money supply is the responsibility of the Federal Open Market Committee (FOMC). The FOMC meets once a month and holds telephone conferences between meetings. The FOMC consists of the seven members of the Board of Governors and presidents of five of the regional Federal Reserve Banks. The president of the New York Federal Reserve Bank is always one of these five; the presidents of the other regional Federal Reserve banks rotate in the four remaining slots.

The official function of the Federal Open Market Committee is to direct the buying and selling

Table 2
Sample T-Accounts for the First National Bank of Clear Lake

	Assets	Liabilities
(a) Jane's deposit of the Fed's $5,000 check:	Reserves at the Fed + $5,000	Demand deposits due Jane + $5,000
(b) The conversion of $5,000 Fed reserves into $5,000 vault cash:	Vault cash + $5,000 Reserves at the Fed − $5,000	No change
(c) Jane's cash withdrawal of $5,000:	Vault cash − $5,000	Demand deposits due Jane − $5,000

of government securities on the Federal Reserve's account. Since *government securities* are simply the IOUs of the federal government that are continuously traded on the open market, FOMC purchases or sales of government securities are called **open-market operations.**

Open-market operations are purchases and sales of federal government securities by the Fed (as directed by the Federal Open Market Committee).

The Monetary Base

The Fed can do something that other institutions cannot do: it can put money into the economy. Because the Fed can print money, whenever the Fed buys something, it puts money into the economy; whenever the Fed sells something it takes money out of the economy. Imagine, for the moment, that you could print money: whenever you bought something with the money you printed, everyone else (taken together) would have more money; whenever you sold something, you would get some of your money back and everyone else (taken together) would have less money. Similarly, Fed purchases inject money into the economy; Fed sales withdraw money from the economy.

For example, suppose the Fed hires a computer programmer, Jane, and pays her with a check for $5,000. Jane deposits the check in her commercial bank—the First National Bank of Clear Lake. The Fed's check is different from other checks.

When the First National Bank of Clear Lake sends the check in for collection to the Fed, its balance sheet changes in two ways. On the asset side, the Bank of Clear Lake's "reserves with the Fed" have increased by $5,000; on the liability side, the Bank of Clear Lake's "demand deposits due Jane" have increased by $5,000, as shown in part (a) of Table 2. The charts in Table 2 are called **T-accounts.**

T-accounts show bank assets and liabilities.

The T-accounts in this table show only the change in bank assets and liabilities that result from the transaction under discussion.

At this point the money supply has increased by $5,000. Jane's bank account has increased by $5,000. Everyone else's bank account has remained the same, and the currency in circulation (outside banks) is still the same. (Remember the *money supply* is the quantity of checkable deposits plus the currency in circulation held by the nonbanking public.)

Had anyone but the Fed purchased Jane's computer expertise for $5,000, the money supply would have remained the same. Jane's bank account would have increased by $5,000, and the purchaser's account would have fallen by $5,000. The two transactions would cancel each other.

Suppose the Bank of Clear Lake does not wish to hold its new reserves as deposits at the Fed. Instead, the bank feels that it needs $5,000 more in vault cash. So the bank wires the Fed to send the $5,000 in cash. The Fed prints $5,000 in Federal Reserve Notes and issues this $5,000 to the Bank of Clear Lake. At this point, the Fed lowers the Bank of Clear Lake's deposit balance by $5,000. This conversion of reserve balances with the Fed into vault cash, shown in part (b) of Table 2, has no impact on the money supply because neither total demand deposits nor the currency outside of banks has changed.

Finally, suppose that Jane goes to the bank and cashes a $5,000 check. Again, nothing happens to the money supply. Her demand deposit account with the Bank of Clear Lake has fallen by $5,000, and the Bank of Clear Lake's vault cash has fallen by $5,000. Because there is $5,000 more in currency in circulation and $5,000 less in checkable deposits, the money supply is unchanged, as shown in part (c) of Table 2.

Of these three transactions, the only one that changes the money supply is the one where Jane deposited the check for $5,000 that she received from the Fed. The Fed could have simply printed $5,000 and issued the $5,000 to Jane in cash.

Purchases by the Fed 1) raise reserves at the Fed, 2) increase vault cash, or 3) increase currency in circulation. Sales by the Fed 1) reduce reserves at the Fed, 2) reduce vault cash, or 3) reduce currency in circulation.

Our simple example shows that the Fed can inject money into the economy by purchasing something; it can withdraw money from the economy by selling something. Fed purchases and sales alter the **monetary base.**

*The **monetary base** is the sum of reserves on deposit at the Fed, all vault cash, and the currency in circulation.*

The monetary base = reserves with Fed + vault cash + currency in circulation.

We have shown that Fed purchases raise the monetary base; Fed sales lower the monetary base. The Fed can control the monetary base by varying the amounts of things it buys (whether those things are goods and services or government bonds).

Figure 1 compares the monetary base with the money supply (M1). The money supply is greater

Figure 1
The Monetary Base and the Money Supply, January 1982

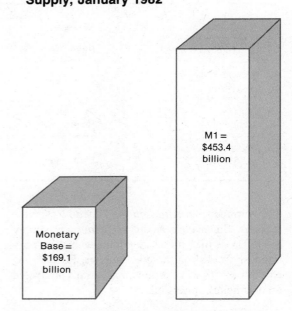

M1 = $453.4 billion

Monetary Base = $169.1 billion

This diagram illustrates the relative size of the monetary base in relation to the money supply as of January 1982.

Source: *The Federal Reserve Bulletin,* April 1982, pp. A13 and A14.

than the monetary base. In January 1982, for example, the money supply M1 was $453.4 billion, and the monetary base was $169.1 billion ($123.3 billion in circulating currency, and the rest in reserves at the Fed and vault cash). Where did the $284.3 billion difference between M1 and the monetary base come from? To answer this question, one must consider how banks create money.

HOW BANKS CREATE MONEY

Banks can create bank demand deposits (money) by lending out the money that people and firms have deposited. Each bank is simply trying to make a profit from financial intermediation. By examining how banks create money, one can understand why the money supply exceeds the monetary base and how the Fed controls the money supply.

Monetization of Debt

Borrowers (business borrowers, home builders, car purchasers) come to the bank to borrow money. If the bank agrees to loan them money, an exchange takes place: the bank sets up a checking account equal to the sum of the loan, and the borrower gives an IOU to the bank spelling out the terms of repayment. In the process of this exchange, money has been created. Demand-deposit liabilities of the bank (remember, demand deposits are the main component of the money supply) have increased by the amount of the loan. Banks create money through the **monetization of debt.**

> The **monetization of debt** is the creation of demand-deposit liabilities in the process of making bank loans.

Monetization of debt can be illustrated by considering how banking first got started. Imagine an ancient goldsmith in the business of shaping gold into fine products used by kings, lords, princes, and wealthy merchants. The goldsmith must keep inventories of gold on hand and, therefore, must have safe storage facilities to prevent theft. Because the goldsmith has such facilities, people find it useful to store gold with the goldsmith. In return, the goldsmith might charge a fee to defray storage costs. When people deposit their gold with the goldsmith, they would want a receipt, and the goldsmith would return the gold only when a receipt is presented.

Assume that the gold is in the form of uniform bars. People would not care whether the goldsmith returns precisely the gold bars they deposited. By not having to keep track of who owns which bar, the goldsmith could hold down storage costs.

The goldsmith would soon discover that only a small amount of gold was needed to accommodate the gold withdrawals on any given day. Each day customers would bring in more gold to exchange for storage receipts; each day customers would bring in storage receipts to exchange for their gold. The goldsmith could keep most of the gold in the back room under strict lock and key, collecting dust, and maintain only a small inventory to service his customers. As long as they re-ceive their gold upon presentation of a storage receipt, they are content.

As the custom of storing gold with the goldsmith becomes more and more widespread, people would find it convenient to use the storage receipts themselves for transactions rather than the bulky gold. Although storage receipts are mere pieces of paper, because they are accepted as a medium of exchange, they are money just like circulating gold. As long as the goldsmith simply kept the gold in the back room, the money supply in such a world would be the gold in circulation (outside the goldsmith's back room) plus the storage receipts issued by the goldsmith. But the storage receipts would only add up to the amount of gold stored in the back room.

Now imagine one fine day the goldsmith discovers a method—presumably illegal—of making additional profit. A friend of the goldsmith might say, "Since all the gold is just sitting in the back room collecting dust, why not lend me some of it?" The goldsmith might at first object that this gold is somebody else's, but a high enough interest rate convinces the goldsmith to lend out some of the gold that is left to him for safekeeping. The friend gives the goldsmith an IOU; the goldsmith gives the friend some gold. The moment this transaction occurs, the money supply increases by the amount of the loan. The money supply now consists of the storage receipts, the gold previously in circulation, and the gold loaned out by the goldsmith. The goldsmith has *monetized* the debt by giving out gold in exchange for an IOU.

To make a long story short, the friend would even take a storage receipt instead of gold. Why? The storage receipt circulates as money. Indeed, what is to prevent the goldsmith from issuing many times his gold reserve in storage receipts as long as he knows very few storage receipts are going to be presented for gold? The goldsmith bank can create money provided that 1) the storage receipts circulate as money and 2) the goldsmith makes loans. If either condition is not satisfied, it is impossible for the goldsmith to create money.

Modern Banking and Money Creation

Modern banks do not issue storage receipts for gold; they accept demand deposits and allow cus-

Table 3
The Effects of a $100 Cash Deposit and $90 Loan

	Assets		Liabilities
Bank A			
(a) After $100 cash deposit:	Cash in vault	+$100	Demand deposits +$100
(b) After $90 loan but before loan funds are spent:	Reserves Loans	+$100 +$ 90	Demand deposits +$190
(c) After $90 loan proceeds are deposited in Bank B:	Reserves Loans	+$ 10 +$ 90	Demand deposits +$100
Bank B			
(d) After the $90 deposit but before new loans are made:	Reserves	+$ 90	Liabilities +$ 90

The cash deposit in part (a) does not create money, since cash in the vault is not part of the money supply. The $90 loan and corresponding $90 demand deposit in (b) creates $90 worth of new money, since demand deposits have increased and currency in circulation has remained the same. When the $90 loan is deposited in Bank B in parts (c) and (d), no new money is created until Bank B makes a loan.

tomers to write checks on those deposits. Checking-account money does not circulate like the storage receipts of the goldsmith. Indeed, the only time checking-account money has any real existence is when a check is being written. Most checking-account money is simply an entry on the books of some bank.

Reserves.   Modern banks are prohibited from printing their own money like the goldsmith's storage receipts.[4] They can only make loans and accept deposits. How do modern commercial banks create money?

Consider what happens when someone makes a deposit of currency in a bank. Assume that $100 in currency is deposited in Bank A. Suppose the depositor has been keeping the cash in an old shoe. Prior to the deposit, the bank was in equilibrium—it was neither making new loans or call-

ing in old loans. The moment the $100 cash deposit is made, Bank A's balance sheet changes as shown in part (a) of Table 3.

Nothing happens to the money supply as long as Bank A remains in this position. Currency in circulation has fallen by the amount that demand deposits have increased; the total money supply outside banks remains the same.

It is likely that Bank A will not be content to stay in this position. Banks have learned through experience that only a small fraction of deposits must be kept as reserves—the rest can be loaned out. The bank is not making any profit from the $100 cash in its vault. Since the bank is interested in making profits, the $100 deposit will allow Bank A to expand its loans. What fraction of the new deposit will Bank A keep? In the United States, banks must maintain the required-reserve ratio of reserves to demand deposits imposed by the Fed. If the Fed requires a reserve ratio of 10 percent, banks will keep $10 as reserves for each $100 of demand deposits.

The Fed's reserve requirements have typically been more conservative than the reserve ratio a profit-minded banker would consider safe and prudent. Hence, reserves above required reserves

---

4.   At one time, state and national banks in the United States operated something like the goldsmith—they issued paper currency. Private bank notes circulated for more than a century. Eventually so many banks tried to get into the profitable business of money creation that it became impossible to determine the legitimacy of the bank notes issued by some of these wildcat banks. Eventually, the United States banned private note issue by banks.

would likely be considered **excess reserves.** Excess reserves will usually be loaned out.

> *Excess reserves are reserves in excess of required reserves. Excess reserves = total reserves − required reserves.*

Banks that have no excess reserves are said to be "loaned up."

Suppose that prior to the $100 cash deposit, the required reserves of Bank A equaled actual reserves (Bank A was loaned up), and suppose the Fed's required-reserve ratio is 10 percent. Because the new $100 deposit would require a $10 increase in required reserves, the bank would have $90 in excess reserves after the deposit. The bank, therefore, makes $90 worth of new loans to eliminate the $90 of excess reserves. The moment the $90 loan is made, the borrower's demand deposit account is credited with $90. Before the borrower spends this $90, Bank A's balance sheet changes as shown in part (b) of Table 3.

Notice that in part (b) the money supply has increased by exactly $90. Bank A has created money! The bank exchanged the borrower's IOU for a demand deposit. The borrower's IOU *is not* money. The bank's IOU—the $90 demand deposit—*is* money. The bank has created money by monetizing debt. If demand deposits were not used as money or if the banks made no loans, banks could not create money.

> *Banks can create money when: 1) demand deposits are used as money, and 2) banks make loans out of such deposits.*

Part (c) of Table 3 takes this process a step further. When the loan recipient spends the $90, Bank A loses $90 of its reserves. The department store, grocery store, or plumber who is paid the borrowed $90 will either cash the $90 check or deposit the $90 check in some other bank.

Whether the $90 ends up in cash that remains in circulation or in a checking account in another bank, the money supply has still increased by $90. If the check is cashed, the amount of cash in circulation goes up by $90 and Bank A's deposit liabilities go down by $90. If the check is deposited in another bank, the increase in the depositor's account equals the decrease in the check

writer's account. Most transactions (in terms of dollar value) are in checks, and the $90 will likely end up as a checking-account deposit in another bank.

Multiple Deposit Creation. The expansion of the money supply does not end with the $90 increase in the money supply as long as transactions continue to be in the form of checks (as long as people do not cash their checks). In our example, we assume that when Bank A loses the $90 in reserves, some other bank—Bank B—gains the entire amount in new deposits. Our example assumes that there is no **cash leakage** from the banking system to the public.

> *A **cash leakage** occurs when a recipient of a check converts it into cash rather than depositing it in a checking account. This cash remains in circulation outside of the banking system.*

In this example, people are paid in checks, and they deposit these checks in their checking accounts.

Since Bank B receives $90 in new deposits, its balance sheet changes as shown in part (d) of Table 3. The transfer of $90 from Bank A to Bank B has no immediate impact on the money supply. The amount of demand deposit liabilities remains the same, and no additional money is created.

If Bank B were originally in equilibrium with no excess reserves, it would now have excess reserves of $81. Since deposits increased by $90, required reserves increased by $9 with a 10 percent reserve requirement. Like Bank A before it, Bank B will loan out its excess reserves of $81. When the recipient of Bank B's loan spends this $81 (with zero leakages of cash), Bank C will receive a new deposit of $81.

The moment Bank B made the loan of $81, the money supply increased by that amount. Bank C will keep 10 percent of the $81 deposit as reserves and lend out the rest—$72.90—which again increases the money supply. When the borrower of $72.90 spends the funds, Bank D receives a new deposit of that amount (again assuming zero leakages of cash).

The $100 increase in reserves has set into motion a pattern of multiple expansion of the money

Table 4
The Multiple Expansion of Bank Deposits

Bank	New Deposits	New Loans or Investments	Additional Reserves
Bank A	$ 100.00	$ 90.00	$ 10.00
Bank B	$ 90.00	$ 81.00	$ 9.00
Bank C	$ 81.00	$ 72.90	$ 8.10
Bank D	$ 72.90	$ 65.61	$ 7.29
Bank E	$ 65.61	$ 59.05	$ 6.56
Sum A-E	$ 409.51	$368.56	$ 40.95
Sum of remaining banks	$ 590.49	$531.44	$ 59.05
Total for whole banking system	$1,000.00	$900.00	$100.00

The banking system as a whole can create a multiple expansion of bank deposits; a single bank can only create money equal to its excess reserves. If the reserve requirement is 0.10 (10 percent), a fresh deposit of $100 will lead to $1,000 in total deposits and $900 in new money provided there are no cash leakages and no bank keeps excess reserves. Thus $10 is created out of $1, or $9 is manufactured by the multiple expansion of bank deposits.

supply. If there are no leakages of cash out of the banking system, the original $100 cash deposit in Bank A leads to demand deposits of $90, $81, and $72.90, with each succeeding figure being 90 percent of the previous deposit. If one sums $100 + $90 + $81 + $72.90 and so on down to the smallest amount, one obtains the total of $1,000.

Table 4 shows what happens to each bank as a consequence of a $100 cash deposit in Bank A. The original $100 cash deposit has led to the creation of $900 in additional deposits or money, or a **multiple deposit expansion.**

Multiple deposit expansion occurs when an increase in reserves causes an expansion of the money supply that is greater than the reserve increase.

Notice that one bank out of many cannot create a multiple expansion of bank deposits. Each single bank can only lend out a fraction of its new deposits. In the above example, each bank can only create new money at a rate equal to 90 percent of any fresh deposit; that is, each bank can only loan out its excess reserves. But when there is no leakage of cash out of the system, an original cash deposit of $100 will lead to a multiple expansion of deposits: as long as the extra cash reserves are in the banking system, they provide the required reserves against deposits. If the reserve requirement is 10 percent, a $100 reserve will support $1,000 worth of deposits. When each bank lends out its excess reserves, it loses those reserves to other banks; these reserves then become the basis for further expansion of the money supply by other banks. The $100 initial cash deposit continues to be passed through the banking system until $900 in new money is created for a total of $1,000 in deposits.

One bank can only lend out its excess reserves. However, the banking system as a whole can lend out a multiple of any excess reserves. What is true of all banks is not true of any single bank (an example of the fallacy of composition).

The Deposit Multiplier. Table 4 showed how the banking system was able to turn a $100 increase in reserves into $900 of new money for a total increase in demand deposits of $1,000. The factor by which demand deposits expand is the **deposit multiplier.**

The deposit multiplier is the ratio of the change in total deposits to the change in reserves.

A deposit multiplier of 10 indicates that for every $1 increase in reserves, demand deposits will increase by $10. We have already calculated the deposit multiplier when the required-reserve ratio is 10 percent (and when there are no cash leakages). With a 10 percent required-reserve ratio, banks will always lend out 90 percent of their excess reserves. Each dollar of new reserves adds $1 to deposits in Bank A, $0.90 to deposits in Bank B, $0.81 to deposits in Bank C, and so on.

When all these deposits are added together, the result is a $10 increase in deposits for each $1 increase in reserves.

If the required-reserve ratio had been 20 percent in our example, the $1 increase in reserves would still add $1 to deposits in Bank A, but would now add $0.80 in Bank B, $0.64 in Bank C, and so on for a total increase of $5 in deposits. With a required-reserve ratio of 20 percent, the deposit multiplier is 5. These two examples suggest a formula for the deposit multiplier.

The deposit multiplier is the reciprocal of the reserve ratio (r) maintained by the banking system.

$$Deposit\ multiplier = \frac{1}{r}.$$

When the reserve ratio is 10 percent, $r = 0.10$, and the deposit multiplier is 10. If the reserve ratio is 20 percent, $r = 0.20$, and the deposit multiplier is 5.

Cash Leakages and Excess Reserves

Our discussion of the multiple expansion of bank deposits assumed that no cash ever leaked out of the banking system and that banks keep excess reserves at zero. Both assumptions are not strictly true.

Cash Leakages.   The public does not hold all of its money balances in demand deposits. When banks begin to create new demand deposits, it is likely that the public will also want to hold more currency. Thus, there will be leakages of cash into hand-to-hand circulation as the multiple creation of bank deposits takes place.

Cash leakages reduce the deposit multiplier. Returning to our numerical example, when $100 was initially deposited in Bank A and $90 was lent out, the next generation of banks—Bank B—might only receive $80 in new deposits rather than $90. Thus Bank B could create only $72 in new deposits rather than $81. This erosion would occur all along the line in Table 4 and would reduce the deposit multiplier accordingly.

If one knows the total cash leakage that will take place, one can apply the deposit multiplier (1/r) to the amount of the new reserves that are left with the banking system. Suppose that out of the $100 originally deposited with Bank A, $20 would eventually leak into hand-to-hand circulation. Since $80 of new reserves would remain in the banking system, then $800 of deposits must result from the $100 deposit. Thus, the 10-to-1 multiplier applies to the quantity of reserves permanently left with the banking system.

The effect of cash leakages on the total money supply explains the mysterious disappearance of $6.7 billion during the Great Depression noted at the beginning of this chapter. As already noted, the Fed controls the monetary base through its purchases and sales. From 1929 to 1933 the Fed did not attempt to pump reserves into the banking system, but the public did draw cash out of the banking system—partially in response to a loss of confidence in banks. These cash withdrawals lowered bank reserves and led to a multiple *contraction* of bank deposits. The $6.7 billion disappeared into thin air. Thus, the deposit multiplier works both in forward and reverse. If reserves contract, demand deposits will fall by a multiple of the fall in reserves.

Excess Reserves.   The deposit multiplier applies when banks lend out all excess reserves. If they do not, the process of multiple expansion will be stopped or slowed. For example, if Bank B in our example did not make any new loans when its reserves increased by $90, there would have been no further multiple deposit expansion.

In recent years most banks have kept very small excess reserves. Indeed, at the beginning of 1982 excess reserves averaged about 1 percent of total reserves. Excess reserves are small for two reasons. First, banks can usually borrow from the Federal Reserve System at the official discount rate to meet any reserve deficiency. Second, banks can always borrow reserves from other banks. The Federal Funds Market is a market in which any bank with excess reserves can lend its reserves to banks with deficient reserves at the Federal Funds rate. This rate varies substantially throughout the day, as banks are borrowing for very short periods of time (often just overnight).

The Money Multiplier

The process of multiple expansion of reserves explains why the money supply can exceed the

Monopoly Banking and Multiple Expansion

The banking system of the United States consists of many banks. The largest bank accounts for only a small fraction of bank assets. If, however, the entire banking system consisted of one bank—a giant monopoly bank—then that bank could create a multiple expansion of bank deposits all by itself. A monopoly bank that has excess reserves can lend out a multiple of those excess reserves because it knows that when those funds are spent they will be redeposited in the monopoly bank. A single bank out of many cannot be so bold. If a single bank loaned out more than its excess reserves, it would in all probability have to pay out those funds to other banks and would find itself with insufficient reserves.

If the banking system consisted of a few large banks, as in Canada or Great Britain, then each bank may be able to count on receiving some portion of its loans back as deposits. If this is the case, a sufficiently large bank can itself create a multiple expansion of deposits. The Bank of America, the largest bank in the United States, consti-

tutes only 6 percent of the banking system. It would be imprudent even for the Bank of America to lend out much more than its excess reserves. But in England there is a "Big Five" that dominates the banking business, so that one of these banks could well create a small multiple expansion of bank deposits.

Does the number of banks affect the speed of multiple expansion of bank deposits? Although one could argue that the multiple expansion of bank deposits occurs much more quickly in England as compared to the United States, the multiple expansion of deposits takes place very quickly in the United States. One study found that most of the multiple expansion of deposits in the United States probably takes place within one month. ⤭

Source: Roy J. Ruffin, "An Econometric Model of Impact of Open Market Operations on Various Bank Classes," *Journal of Finance* (September, 1968), pp. 625–637.

---

monetary base (currency in circulation plus bank reserves). We have shown that the banking system as a whole—by lending out excess reserves—can create deposits that are a multiple of banking system reserves. The size of this multiple depends upon required-reserve ratios, cash leakages, and banks' willingness to hold excess reserves.

Figure 1 illustrated the relationship between the money supply and the monetary base: the money supply (currency in circulation plus checkable deposits) was 2.68 times the monetary base in January 1982. This *money multiplier* is smaller than the deposit multiplier.

Assume banks wish to hold the ratio r of Fed and vault reserves (R) to deposits (D). Thus, $R = rD$. Assume the public wishes to hold the ratio k of currency (C) to deposits (D). Thus, $C = kD$. The monetary base $(H) = R + C$. Since $R = rD$ and $C = kD$,

$$H = rD + kD$$
$$= (r + k)D$$

Dividing by $(r + k)$ yields

$$D = H/(r + k) \qquad (1)$$

The money supply $(M) = C + D$. Since $C = kD$,

$$M = kD + D = (1 + k)D \qquad (2)$$

Substituting equation (1) into equation (2) yields

$$M = \frac{(1 + k)H}{(r + k)}. \qquad (3)$$

This equation shows how the monetary base H is related to the money supply M.[5] If $r = 0.2$ and $k = 0.3$, $M = (1.3)H/0.5 = 2.6H$. In this case, the money multiplier is 2.6, while the deposit multiplier is $D = 1/0.2 = 5$.

5. For a fuller development of the money multiplier see Thomas Mayer, James S. Dusenberry, and Robert Z. Aliber, *Money, Banking, and the Economy* (New York: W. W. Norton, 1981), pp. 217–29.

Table 5
Effects of an Open Market Sale of $10,000 in Government Securities

	Assets		Liabilities	
(a) Individuals and households	Securities Demand deposits	+$10,000 −$10,000	No change	
(b) Commercial banks	Reserves at Fed	−$10,000	Demand deposits	−$10,000
(c) The Fed	Government securities	−$10,000	Reserve balances of banks	−$10,000

FEDERAL RESERVE POLICY

The most important function of the Fed is to control the quantity of money. The quantity of money can affect prices, output, and employment; therefore, the Fed controls—to some degree—the pulse rate of the economy. By expanding the money supply, the Fed can speed up the pulse rate; by contracting the money supply (or by slowing down its rate of growth), the Fed can slow the pulse rate down.

The Fed controls money and credit by:

1. controlling the monetary base through open-market operations.
2. controlling reserve requirements.
3. setting the discount rate.
4. applying moral suasion.
5. imposing selective credit controls.
6. setting margin requirements.

Open-Market Operations

As already mentioned, the Fed can inject or withdraw money from the economy by buying or selling. An injection of money leads to a multiple expansion of deposits; a withdrawal of money leads to a multiple contraction of bank deposits.

The Fed controls bank reserves by buying and selling federal government securities on the open market as directed by the Federal Open Market Committee. The Fed already owns a large sum of government securities. In 1981, the Fed acquired $9.2 billion in government securities to bring its total holdings to about $127 billion at the beginning of 1982.

A substantial portion of the Fed's open-market operations are purely defensive. The Fed responds to changes in the currency-holding habits of the public. For example, a large seasonal influx of cash from the public into the banking system tends to automatically increase bank reserves. Without countering Fed action, banks would begin to loan out excess reserves. Likewise, spontaneous cash drains from the banking system cause a contraction of the supply of money in the absence of offsetting Fed actions.

The mechanics of Fed open-market transactions are the same whether the Fed is simply offsetting actions in the private economy to hold money supply steady or embarking on a course of monetary expansion or contraction.

Open Market Sales. Suppose the Fed sells $10,000 worth of government securities to an individual (by means of some intermediary). The individual sends a personal check written on a commercial bank to the Fed. What happens to the balance sheets of the individual, the commercial bank, and the Fed? The individual's assets stay the same. The individual's bonds increase by $10,000 and demand deposits decrease by $10,000. The commercial bank finds that its demand deposit liabilities have fallen by $10,000, and its reserves with the Fed fall by $10,000. When the Fed receives the check drawn on the commercial bank, it reduces the bank's account by that amount. The Fed's stock of government securities falls by $10,000, and its reserve balance liability to the commercial bank falls by $10,000. These changes are shown in Table 5.

As a consequence of the Fed sale, the money supply falls by $10,000 because demand deposits fall by that amount. In addition, the monetary base also falls by $10,000. By selling $10,000 in securities, the Fed extinguishes $10,000 in reserves. Writing a check to the Fed, unlike writing one to someone else, destroys money instead of transfering it.

The extinction of $10,000 in reserves will cause a multiple contraction of deposits. With a deposit multiplier of 10, the deposits will fall by $100,000.

Open-Market Purchases.   Now suppose the Fed purchases $10,000 worth of securities from a person (by means of some intermediary). That person receives a check from the Fed and deposits it in his or her bank. What happens to the balance sheets of the person, the commercial bank, and the Fed? The individual's assets remain the same: demand deposits increase by $10,000, and government bonds decrease by $10,000. The commercial bank finds that its demand deposits have risen by $10,000, and its reserves with the Fed rise by $10,000. Finally, the Fed's government securities and reserve balances of commercial banks both rise by $10,000. This expansion of bank reserves will set into motion a multiple expansion of deposits.

These changes can be illustrated in Table 5 by changing all the minuses to pluses and the pluses to minuses. Open-market purchases have the exact opposite effects as open-market sales.

Open-market sales destroy reserves, and open-market purchases create reserve balances. The Fed uses these operations to control the size of the money supply by controlling the size of the monetary base. Open-market operations are the most potent weapon of Fed policy because the Fed can buy or sell small or large quantities of government securities and can do so quickly.

Open-market purchases increase the monetary base; open-market sales lower the monetary base. Open-market operations are flexible because they can be transacted quickly and in almost any desired amount. Open-market operations are powerful because they have a magnified impact on the money supply as new reserves are added or subtracted from the banking system.

Changes in Reserve Requirements

The Fed has the power to change reserve requirements within broad limits. This power is po-

tentially a very effective tool of monetary policy. For example, increasing reserve requirements from 10 percent to 12.5 percent would force banks to contract demand deposits by 20 percent. Recall that the deposit multiplier is $1/r$. When $r = 0.10$, $40,000 in reserves would support $400,000 in demand deposits. If reserve requirements were raised to $r = 0.125$, $40,000 in reserves would support only $320,000 in demand deposits; demand deposits would have to contract by $80,000. Conversely, lowering reserve requirements can have a massive impact on increasing the money supply.

Traditionally, the Fed has been reluctant to use this tool of monetary policy. From December 1976 until the Monetary Control Act of 1980 became effective in November 1980, the Fed never used this tool of monetary policy. One argument against reserve-requirement changes is that they are too blunt an instrument. An open-market operation, for example, can be carried out to offset a seasonal currency drain without any fanfare or comment from the press. But a reduction in reserve requirements that is used to simply offset a seasonal currency drain might be interpreted by the financial press as a fundamental change in monetary policy.

Increases in reserve requirements reduce the money supply; reductions in reserve requirements increase the money supply. Changes in reserve requirements, however, are a seldom-used instrument of monetary policy.

Changes in the Discount Rate

The discount rate is the interest rate the Fed charges depository institutions who wish to borrow reserves to meet reserve requirements. As indicated earlier, before 1980 only member banks had access to the discount window. Now all depository institutions with balances at the Fed can borrow from the Fed.

The basic function of the discount window is to perform the lender-of-last-resort function of the central bank. Unanticipated withdrawals from a bank can lead to a deficiency in reserves. The bank can make up this deficiency by borrowing from the Fed. The higher the discount rate relative to other interest rates that the bank can earn on its loans and investments, the more costly it is for the bank to keep a small margin of excess reserves. Thus, a lowering of the discount rate may encourage banks to follow a more lenient credit policy and may expand the money supply—but the effects are small.

Generally speaking, the Fed raises or lowers the discount rate in line with market interest rates on government securities. If market interest rates are rising on Treasury bills (government securities with a maturity of less than one year), banks will be tempted to invest all excess funds in such securities up to the loan limits imposed by reserve requirements. Raising the discount rate will reduce the temptation of banks to follow a more lenient loan and investment policy when interest rates are rising. Thus, raising the discount rate does not necessarily mean the Fed is trying to lower the money supply; the Fed may only be trying to control money supply by restricting Fed borrowing.

Other Instruments of Control

In addition to the three major instruments just mentioned, the Fed has three minor tools for controlling money supply: moral suasion, selective credit controls, and margin credit.

Moral Suasion. The Chairperson of the Fed has been known at times to urge banks to expand their loans or to adopt more restrictive credit policies. *Moral suasion* is the process by which the Fed tries to persuade banks to voluntarily follow a particular policy.

Selective Credit Controls. The Fed can use *selective credit controls* to affect the *distribution* of loans rather than the *overall volume* of loans. The Fed can control terms and conditions of installment credit and requirements for consumer credit cards. Until 1986, the Fed can set interest-rate ceilings on deposits at commercial banks, which can affect bank deposits.

Margin Credit. When investors buy stocks, they are permitted to buy a portion on credit (this practice is called *buying on margin*). This credit, supplied by stock brokers, is called *margin credit*. The Fed sets margin requirements. Current margin requirements allow purchasers of stock to finance 35 percent of the purchase with margin credit. In the speculative stock market boom of the 1920s, speculators could purchase stocks with as little as 10 percent down; the rest was financed with margin loans.

Problems of Monetary Control

From this discussion, one might gain the impression that cash leakages are the main problem faced by the Fed as long as banks hold negligible excess reserves. Controlling Ml is made more difficult by the problem of different reserve requirements for different bank liabilities.

When different bank liabilities have differing reserve requirements, a switch from savings deposits to demand deposits can increase required reserves while a switch from demand to savings deposits can reduce required reserves. Thus, required reserves can change without any change in total bank reserves. Random changes in the ratio of savings deposits to demand deposits can, therefore, cause fluctuations in bank credit and the money supply.

Even if the Fed controlled Ml perfectly, however, as demonstrated in Chapter 7, there is still the problem of competing concepts of money supply. When the Fed controls Ml, individuals and banks can switch to the money substitutes in M2. In early 1982, money-market mutual funds, on which people can write checks, were about 40 percent of the size of Ml. If the Fed controls M2, people may find other forms of money substitutes that are not subject to Fed control.

This chapter explained the relationship between the Federal Reserve System and the money supply. The money supply is important because it affects total expenditures for goods and services. The next chapter will examine a simple income/expenditure model of GNP that will provide the basis for our understanding of aggregate demand in later chapters.

Summary

1. Banks are financial intermediaries. Financial intermediaries borrow money from ultimate lenders and lend this money to ultimate bor-

rowers. Most lending in the United States is done by financial intermediaries. Financial intermediaries offer three advantages: they minimize costs of lending and borrowing, they pool risks, and they offer liquidity to lenders by borrowing short and lending long.

2. Commercial banks are chartered by state banking authorities or by the U.S. Treasury. Commercial banks offer their customers checking account services and savings accounts. They earn money by loaning out funds they have borrowed or investing these funds in government securities. Banks make profits by borrowing at a lower rate of interest than that at which they lend or invest. Bank balance sheets summarize the claims on the assets of a bank. Banks must maintain reserves to meet the cash needs of their depositors. Reserves are held in two forms: cash in the vault and reserve balances at the Fed. Reserves are typically much less than the demand-deposit liabilities of the bank. The FDIC insures deposits and gives depositors the necessary sense of security.

3. The Federal Reserve System is the central bank of the United States and was established in 1913. The Fed consists of 12 district banks, a Board of Governors, and a Federal Open Market Committee in charge of buying and selling government securities for the Fed. Not all commercial banks are members of the Fed system, but the largest banks are. Since 1980, the Fed has the authority to exercise control over nonmember banks. The Fed imposes reserve requirements on banks and thrift institutions. A reserve requirement is a rule that the bank must hold a prescribed portion of their outstanding deposits as reserves. Depository institutions can borrow from the Fed to meet their temporary cash needs, and the interest rate at which they borrow is called the *discount rate*. By buying and selling things, the Fed injects money into the banking system and takes money out of the banking system. When the Fed buys anything, the sum of reserves on deposit with the Fed, vault cash in banks, and currency in circulation increases by the amount of the purchase. The monetary base equals reserve balances with the Fed, vault cash, and currency

in circulation. The monetary base is smaller than the money supply.

4. Banks create money by monetizing debt. Banks can use reserves to make loans, and in the process of making loans, they create money. Private banks can create money because demand deposits are money and because banks make loans out of deposits. An increase in reserves leads to a multiple expansion of deposits. Although any one bank can only lend out its excess reserves, the banking system as a whole can lend out a multiple of the increase in reserves. The deposit multiplier is the ratio of the change in deposits to the change in reserves. If there are no cash leakages and banks lend out excess reserves, the deposit multiplier is the inverse of the required reserve ratio.

5. The Fed has an arsenal of weapons to control the money supply: open-market operations, control of the discount rate, control of the required reserve ratio, and selective credit controls. By buying government securities, the Fed injects reserves into the system and expands the money supply. By selling government securities, the Fed withdraws reserves, and the money supply contracts. Changing reserve requirements can have a large impact on the money supply because it creates excess reserves (when the rate is lowered) and it creates reserve deficiencies when the rate is raised. It is a seldom used policy. Changes in the discount rate have a modest effect on bank reserves. Cash leakages, nonuniform reserve requirements, and the existence of substitutes for M1 present problems for effective monetary control.

Key Terms

financial intermediaries
commercial banks
balance sheet
assets
liabilities
reserves
reserve requirement
required-reserve ratio

open-market operations
T-accounts
monetary base
monetization of debt
excess reserves
cash leakage
multiple deposit expansion
deposit multiplier

Questions and Problems

1. ''Banks get away with murder. They pay you no interest on your checking accounts and then they turn around and lend your money to some poor fellow at 18 percent.'' Evaluate this statement.

2. Table 1 shows that commercial banks in January 1982 had only $20 billion vault cash but had outstanding net demand-deposit liabilities of $217 billion. Explain how banks can get by with so little cash.

3. Explain why even without required reserve ratios bankers would maintain reserves.

4. Assume the Fed sells all its old office furniture to XYZ corporation for $10 million. What effect will this have on the money supply? What will happen if the Fed sells XYZ corporation $10 million worth of its holdings of government securities?

5. Explain why banks can only create money if bank deposits are accepted as money and if banks are willing to make loans. Explain what is meant by *monetization of the debt*.

6. Assume the required reserve ratio is 0.4 (40 percent) and there are no cash leakages. The Fed buys a government security from Jones for $1,000. Explain, using T-accounts, what will happen to the money supply. Answer the same question assuming only that Jones (and only Jones) takes payment from the Fed as follows: $500 cash (which he puts under his mattress) and a $500 check.

7. Rework Table 4 on the assumption that $r = 0.2$. In this case, the deposit multiplier is 5, so that the $100 fresh deposit in Bank A will ultimately lead to $500 in total deposits, or $400 in new money.

CHAPTER

9

Keynesian Economics

Chapter Preview

Chapter 6 explained how GNP is measured. This chapter will examine how real GNP is determined in an economy that has unemployed resources. The focus of this chapter is on the relationship between consumption expenditures and income.

Prior to the 1930s, economists tended to believe that real GNP was determined by the quantity and productivity of the resources available to the economy. To the quantity theorists, the determination of real GNP was no mystery because they believed that the economy operated at or near full employment (on the economy's production-possibilities frontier). The Great Depression of the 1930s was a watershed in macroeconomic thought because it showed that world economies

could operate for extended periods of time well below their potential output. The British economist, John Maynard Keynes, offered an explanation of why economies could operate below their production potential for long periods of time.

Keynes shifted the focus of economics from the supply side to the demand side. On the supply side are those factors that determine the location of an economy's production-possibilities frontier. Keynes agreed with the classical economists that in the long run, the supply side would dominate the determination of real GNP, but in a famous quote declared that "in the long run, we are all dead." To Keynes, the interesting action is in the short run where the demand side dominates. Keynes felt, contrary to the teaching of his day, that an increase in demand for goods and services would increase real GNP because idle or unemployed resources would be available for producing the new, higher level of real GNP. Since any level of real GNP can be produced up to the full employment level, the Keynesian question is: what determines the level of real GNP at any given time?

THE CLASSICAL MODEL

The classical model (discussed in an earlier chapter) can be credited to David Hume (1711–1766), David Ricardo (1772–1823), and Jean Baptiste Say (1767–1832). These classical quantity theorists taught that real GNP was determined by the supply side of the economy, while the price level was determined by the interaction of the supply and demand for money. Up until the work of Keynes, most economists believed that excessive unemployment was a short-lived affair that would quickly disappear if wages and prices are flexible.

According to the classical economists, whatever GNP can be produced will be demanded (Say's Law), and unemployment can only be the short-term consequence of money wages being temporarily too high.

Say's Law

Chapter 6 explained that national income is the other side of the coin from national product. When an economy produces $3 trillion worth of final goods and services $(C + I + G + X - M)$, it also produces the income with which these goods can be purchased. It is always and everywhere true that *actual* aggregate income equals *actual* aggregate expenditures, but classical economists went one step further. They argued that *aggregate supply creates its own demand*. This assertion is called **Say's Law.**

> *According to Say's Law,* desired *aggregate expenditures can never depart from* actual *aggregate expenditures. Whatever output is produced will be demanded.*

How could the classical economists believe that however much aggregate output is produced, consumers and firms will want to buy exactly that amount? Consider a hypothetical economy with no government that produces $600 billion worth of final goods and services, creating a total of $600 billion worth of income paid to land, labor, capital, and entrepreneurship. If households want to spend $500 billion on consumer goods and save $100 billion, the $100 billion saved is a withdrawal from the spending stream. According to Say, the desired saving of $100 billion will be exactly matched by desired investment of $100 billion. In this way, out of the $600 billion of income, households desire to spend $500 billion, and business firms desire to spend $100 billion. The investment injects the saving of households back into the spending stream.

How does the $100 billion of desired saving become $100 billion of desired investment? In Figure 1, the rate of interest is on the vertical axis, and desired saving and investment are on the horizontal axis. The saving curve shows how saving responds to the interest rate: generally speaking, the higher the interest rate, the higher the desired saving. The higher the interest rate, the greater the incentive to save more and spend less on personal consumption. The investment curve shows how desired investment responds to the interest rate: generally speaking, the higher the interest rate the less business managers and others want to invest in buildings, trucks, inventories, and equipment.

As Figure 1 shows, the market interest rate will be set at that rate at which *desired* saving equals *desired* investment. In the classical model, the interest rate coordinates saving and investment decisions. In Figure 1, the interest rate that equates desired saving and desired investment is 5 percent. At any interest rate above 5 percent, desired saving would exceed desired investment, and the interest rate would fall. At any rate below 5 percent, desired investment would exceed desired saving, and the interest rate would be driven up.

The interest rate equates desired saving and desired investment. If, for example, at any given level of income saving increases, consumption will fall. Interest rates will adjust downward sufficiently to insure that desired investment will increase by enough to offset the fall in consumption. Hence, desired aggregate expenditures would always equal aggregate income. Supply creates its own demand.

Figure 1
The Interest Rate Equates Desired Saving and Desired Investment in the Classical Model

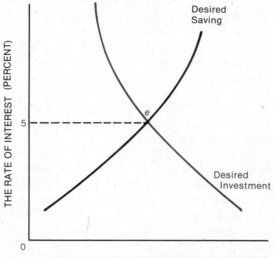

This figure shows the interest rate on the vertical axis and the amount of desired saving and desired investment on the horizontal axis. The saving curve shows the amount of desired saving at different interest rates. The higher the interest rate, the greater the amount of desired saving. The investment curve shows the amount of desired investment at different interest rates. The higher the interest rate, the lower the amount of desired investment. The interest rate equates the amount of desired investment and the amount of desired saving. In this example, the interest rate that equates desired saving and desired investment is 5 percent. At any interest rate above 5 percent, desired saving would exceed desired investment, and the interest rate would fall. At any rate below 5 percent, desired investment would exceed desired saving, and the interest rate would be driven up.

Unemployment

How did classical economists account for the cases where people are unemployed and the economy is operating below its production-possibilities frontier? To the classical quantity theorists all unemployment was voluntary. Unemployment, in their opinion, could be looked upon as an excess supply of labor, and an excess supply of labor, wheat, or any other product results when the price is too high. In the case of labor, the price is the wage rate. If people com-

plained that there was too much unemployment, the classical economist had a ready answer: if unemployed workers would accept a lower wage they would quickly be put back to work by eager employers. Unemployment was considered a problem that the unemployed themselves could correct by accepting lower wages.

Laissez Faire Policy

The classical model supported a *laissez faire* approach to macroeconomic policy, or a hands-off role for government. Classical economists believed the economy was capable of healing itself by allowing wages and prices to adjust to eliminate unemployment. No one needed to worry about an insufficiency of aggregate demand because Say's Law insured that supply creates its own demand. Government actions to regulate employment and real GNP could not be effective.

The classical model taught that the economy's real output would grow over time as its resources (labor and capital) expanded. This growth might not be steady insofar as resources might not grow at a uniform rate, but extended departures from long-term growth in the form of large downturns in output and employment would not be expected.

THE GREAT DEPRESSION

The Great Depression of the 1930s shook economists' belief in the classical quantity theory. Between 1929 and 1933, real GNP in the United States declined by 30 percent. The 1929 output level was not regained until 1939. Unemployment rose from 3.2 percent of the labor force in 1929 to 24.9 percent in 1933 and was still 17.2 percent in 1939. Investment spending suffered much more than consumption spending. Between 1929 and 1933, real investment dropped by 75 percent, while real consumption fell by a more modest 20 percent. The change in net investment (after deducting depreciation) was even more dramatic: it fell from 18.6 billion dollars to −6.0 billion dollars.

Such a substantial downturn in real output and employment did not appear to contemporary observers as the temporary departure from equilibrium described by the classical model. There had been economic recessions and depressions before but none this severe and sustained. The Great

Depression's impact on economic thinking and on public attitudes cannot be overestimated. A generation of Americans grew up during the Depression; for many it remains a frightening experience. The political influence of the Great Depression was enormous. A *laissez faire* economic philosophy that instructed the government to do nothing while one out of four was unemployed became a political liability. The question of the times became: "Why can't the government do something to help us?"

The Great Depression set the stage for what has come to be called the *Keynesian revolution*. The Keynesian revolution was sparked by the publication in 1936 of *The General Theory of Employment, Interest, and Money*. In this landmark book, Keynes argued that economies can reach a fairly stable equilibrium—from which they will budge only slowly—at much less than full employment. Keynes believed that the cyclical instability of investment spending, while not a dominant portion of total spending, tended to have a magnified effect on the rest of the economy.

Keynes's empirical evidence for these propositions was the Great Depression itself, which demonstrated that substantial sustained declines in economic activity were possible. The Keynesian revolution opened up a new approach to macroeconomic policy: it argued that it is the responsibility of government to insure that the economy operates at an acceptable rate of output and employment. Keynes felt that the classical mechanism of letting wage and price adjustments raise output and employment was too slow, unreliable, and unnecessary. Government economic action could be used to restore the economy to full employment more quickly and at much lower social costs.

Keynes's explanation of how an economy determines how much real output to produce and how much employment to provide is known as the *income/expenditure approach*.

THE INCOME/EXPENDITURE APPROACH

A full understanding of macroeconomics requires study of both the demand side and the supply side of the economy. Our study will begin by looking only at the demand side. The income/expenditure approach pioneered by Keynes can also be called *depression economics* because it deals with conditions in which an increase in desired aggregate expenditures calls forth a greater quantity of real GNP without an increase in prices. In the classical world, real expenditures cannot increase without an increase in total resources because the economy is at full employment. This chapter and the next provide an extensive study of the demand side of the economy.

In an economy in a depression it is possible to coax more production out of existing resources without raising wages and prices. A large number of people are out of work and are willing and anxious to work at going wage rates. People are, as it were, sitting around on the courthouse steps waiting for some business firm to give them a job. The firm need not raise wages to get more workers; it simply puts the unemployed worker back on the job. The worker is—according to Keynes—involuntarily unemployed.

This picture is not unreasonable for England at the time Keynes was writing. From 1921 to 1936, the unemployment rate in Great Britain varied between 9.7 and 22.1 percent. In the period 1921 to 1929, the British unemployment rate averaged 12 percent; from 1930 to 1936, it averaged 17.8 percent. Throughout this entire period, prices declined very slowly, and money wages remained more or less at the same level.

If real GNP is less than the full-employment level, what determines the level of real GNP at any given time? Why can it settle at less than full employment? In Keynes's view there were two major flaws in the classical model. The first is that money wages did not have the necessary downward flexibility to eliminate unemployment. The second flaw Keynes saw in the classical model was Say's Law, which he rejected. Keynes believed that desired saving depended in only a minor way on interest rates. Instead, Keynes believed that desired saving depended primarily on disposable income. Thus, the interest rate could not be counted upon to equate desired saving and desired investment. Keynes did not believe that supply creates its own demand in the classical sense.

The chapter on national income accounting identified the major components of GNP as personal consumption expenditures *(C)*, private investment *(I)*, government expenditures for goods and services *(G)*, and net exports *(X-M)*. Since

Figure 2
U.S. Family Income and Expenditures, 1982

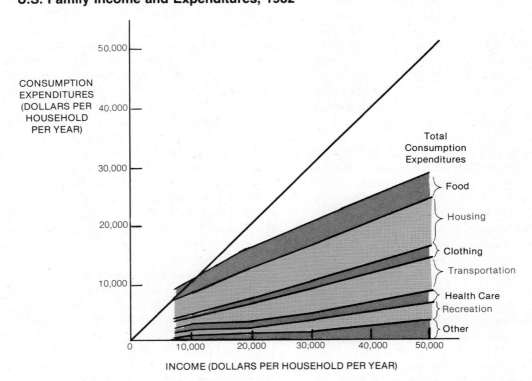

Total consumption expenditures vary positively with family income. The *pattern* of consumption also changes with income. Family saving is read as the difference between the 45-degree reference line and total consumption expenditures.

Source: U.S. Department of Labor, *Handbook of Labor Statistics*, December 1980. These are 1972–1973 data updated to 1982 by the authors.

net exports make up only a small percentage of GNP, they will be ignored in this chapter. (Exports and imports will be discussed in Chapters 20 through 22.) Keynes's income expenditure approach examined how the desired level of these expenditures (and thus, the desired level of GNP) is determined.

The Consumption/Income Schedule

Of every dollar spent in our economy, an average of $0.63 is spent on private consumption—on purchases of food, clothing, shelter, services, and durables such as cars, TV sets, and refrigerators. If one examines how poor, middle-income, and rich families spend their income, three prominent patterns emerge (as shown in Figure 2).

As a general rule, the higher the family's disposable income, the higher the dollar amount of is consumption spending.

Families with higher incomes tend to have higher consumption expenditures. Of course, there are exceptions to this rule; consumption spending does not depend on family income alone but will depend as well on the age and size of the family, expectations, the price level, taxation, and thriftiness—all of which will be examined shortly.

The second pattern is that higher-income families spend a smaller percentage of their disposable income than do lower-income families. Figure 2 shows that the average family earning an income of $50,000 spent about $30,000, or about

60 percent, of its disposable income on consumer goods and services. The average family earning about $10,000, on the other hand, spent all of its income on consumption. When a family spends more than its disposable income, the family is either increasing its indebtedness (borrowing money for consumption) or financing consumption by drawing down its savings. The ones who spend less than their disposable income are saving and adding to their wealth.

Higher-income families tend to save a larger portion of their disposable income than do lower-income families.

A third regularity that emerges from Figure 2 is that higher-income families have a different pattern of consumption spending: higher-income families tend to spend a smaller portion of their disposable income on food than do lower-income families. Figure 2 shows that the $50,000 family spends about 15 percent of its income on food, while the $10,000 family spends 25 percent of its disposable income on food.[1]

Higher-income families spend a smaller portion of disposable income on food than do lower-income families.

The spending habits of entire nations follow the spending patterns of individual families. In Figure 3, real personal consumption expenditures of the United States are plotted against U.S. real personal disposable income for the period 1950 to 1981. As with the household data, the economy's total consumption spending tends to rise as disposable income rises. A line connecting the economy's consumption/income points would obviously be positively sloped. The composition of consumption expenditures also follows the pattern of households: the share of food expenditures of disposable income declines steadily as income rises (from 30 percent in 1950 to 20.5 percent in 1981).

---

1. This pattern holds over time and across countries. The Prussian statistician, Ernst Engel, writing in the mid-19th century noted the universal tendency for the percentage of family income devoted to food to decline as income rises. Thus, the falling share of food expenditures with rising income has come to be called "Engel's Law."

Figure 3
U.S. Consumption Spending and Disposable Income, 1950–1981

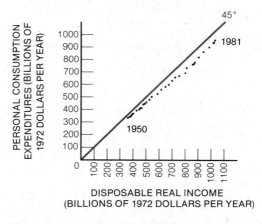

The spending habits of the U.S. economy as a whole are similar to those of average American families shown in Figure 2. U.S. total consumer spending tends to rise as disposable income rises.

Source: *Economic Report of the President,* January 1982, p. 261.

Notably, the national pattern of saving does not follow the household pattern with equal clarity: the percentage of disposable income saved does not exhibit a distinctive upward trend with rising income. In 1950, the economy saved 7.2 percent (spent 92.8 percent of its disposable income on consumption). In 1981, it saved 7.8 percent (spent 92.2 percent)—a slight and scarcely noticeable change.

The most important fact about consumer-spending patterns is the positive relationship between consumption and income. The more income one earns, the more one is likely to spend on personal consumption. What is true for the individual and family should be true for the economy as a whole in this case, and the facts appear to support a positive consumption/income relationship.

Table 1 provides hypothetical data on real consumption spending *(C),* real saving *(S),* and real GNP *(Y)* for an economy with no taxes. Because there are no taxes, every dollar earned is available as disposable income for either consumption or saving. In this special case, GNP equals disposable income. When income is $100 billion, then

Table 1
The Aggregate Expenditure Schedule with No Government Spending and No Government Taxes (billions of dollars)

Output = Income, Y (1)	Consumption, C (2)	Saving, S (3)	Investment, I (4)	Desired Aggregate Expenditures (5) = (2) + (4)	Unintended Investment, S–I (6) = (3) – (4)
100	125	−25	50	175	−75
200	200	0	50	250	−50
300	275	25	50	325	−25
400	350	50	50	400	0
500	425	75	50	475	25
600	500	100	50	550	50

Columns (1) and (2) show the consumption/income schedule for our hypothetical economy. There are no taxes, so income and disposable income are the same. The marginal propensity to consume (MPC) in this example is 0.75 because for every $100 billion increase in income, consumption increases by $75 billion. The marginal propensity to save (MPS) is 0.25 because for every $100 billion increase in income, saving increases by $25 billion. The data in the first three columns are graphed in Figure 4. Panel (a) graphs the consumption/income schedule of columns (1) and (2); panel (b) graphs the saving/income schedule of columns (1) and (3).

Aggregate expenditures equal the sum of desired consumption and desired investment at each income level. Desired investment is assumed to be constant at $50 billion. Unintended investment is the difference between desired saving and desired investment at each income level. Only at an income of $400 billion does desired saving equal desired investment or does the desired aggregate expenditure level equal aggregate output. The equilibrium income is, therefore, at $400 billion.

consumption is $125 billion, and saving is −$25 billion. At this level of income, households are borrowing or drawing down their financial assets (savings accounts, stocks, bonds). As Table 1 shows, when income rises from $100 billion to $200 billion, consumption rises by $75 billion to $200 billion. At this income level, households are now just breaking even. A further increase in income from $200 billion to $300 billion raises consumption spending to $275 billion. Households are now more than breaking even; they have unspent income left over for saving. At $300 billion, saving is a positive $25 billion. The schedules in the first three columns of Table 1 are the **consumption/income schedule** and the **saving/income schedule**.

The consumption/income schedule shows the amount of desired consumption at different levels of national income or output.

The saving/income schedule shows the desired amount of saving at different levels of national income or output.

The Marginal Propensity to Consume. In the consumption/income schedule in columns (1) and (2) of Table 1, whenever income increases by $100 billion, consumption increases by $75 billion. Hence, in our hypothetical economy, every additional $1 of income increases desired consumption by $0.75. This relationship is very important to the income/expenditure model. Keynes called the fraction of additional income that is spent on consumption the **marginal propensity to consume,** or **MPC,** because it refers to extra consumption induced by another dollar of disposable income.

The marginal propensity to consume (MPC) is the change in desired consumption (C) brought about by a change in income (Y) of $1.

$$MPC = \frac{\Delta C}{\Delta Y}$$

The symbol Δ placed before a variable is simply shorthand for "the change in" that variable.

The Marginal Propensity to Save. In our hypothetical economy, every time income increases, saving increases as well. In Table 1, the saving/income schedule in columns (1) and (3) shows that saving increases by $25 billion for every $100 billion increase in income. Every extra $1 of income increases desired saving by $0.25. Keynes called the fraction of the increase in income that is saved the **marginal propensity to save,** or *MPS*.

*The **marginal propensity to save** (MPS) is the change in desired saving (S) that is brought about by a change in income (Y) of $1.*

$$MPS = \frac{\Delta S}{\Delta Y}$$

When there are no taxes in the economy (as in this hypothetical example), an additional dollar of income is either consumed or saved.[2] Hence,

$$MPC + MPS = 1.$$

When some income is spent in taxes, income and disposable income are no longer one and the same. It is, therefore, useful to refer to the marginal propensity to consume and the marginal propensity to save *out of disposable income*. If *MPC* and *MPS* are defined in relation to disposable income, then it is true that *MPC* + *MPS* = 1.

Figure 3 graphs data on real consumption expenditures against real disposable income for the period 1950 to 1981. Although other factors that affect consumption were likely changing during this period along with income, the data in Figure 3 provide a preliminary idea of the values of *MPS* and *MPC* for this period. The *MPC* estimated from the 1950 to 1981 data is 0.91; the *MPS* equals 0.09. On average, out of every extra dollar of disposable income, $0.91 is spent on extra consumption and $0.09 is spent on extra saving.

2.   Keynes was also interested in the average relationships between desired consumption and income and between desired saving and income, which he called the average propensity to consume, *APC,* and the average propensity to save, *APS,* respectively.
   The average propensity to consume is defined as the ratio of desired consumption to income *(APC = C/Y)*. The average propensity to save is defined as the ratio of desired saving to income *(APS = S/Y)*.

Figure 4
The Consumption/Income Curve

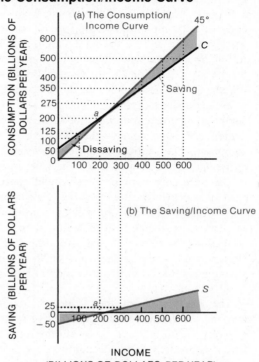

The *C* curve is the consumption/income curve graphed from the data in Table 1 and shows the amount of desired consumption at different levels of income. It is positively sloped because increases in income cause increases in consumption. The slope of *C* is the marginal propensity to consume, *MPC,* which in our example equals 0.75.
   At any income measured on the horizontal axis, the vertical distance to the 45-degree line equals that income. The vertical distance to the *C* line equals consumption; the vertical distance between the 45-degree line and the *C* line equals saving. At the intersection of the 45-degree line and the *C* line (at point a), saving is zero. To the right of *a*, saving is positive; to the left of *a*, saving is negative (the economy is dissaving).
   The saving/income curve (labeled *S*) shows the amount of real saving at each level of income. Saving is positive to the right of *a'*, where income is $200 billion, and it is negative to the left of *a'*. By comparing panels (a) and (b), one can see that saving can be read from the consumption/income curve or from the saving/income curve.

The consumption/income and saving/income schedules of Table 1 are shown graphically in Figure 4. Consider first the consumption/income schedule in panel (a) of Figure 4. The 45-degree line from the origin has the property that any point on it is the same distance from the two axes. For example, the vertical line drawn from an income of $600 billion on the horizontal axis to the 45-degree line will be the same length as a horizontal line drawn from a consumption-spending level of $600 billion on the vertical axis to the 45-degree line. Each point on the 45-degree line is an equal distance from both axes. If the consumption/income curve were identical to the 45-degree line, all income would be spent on consumption. The vertical distance between the *C* curve and the 45-degree line is a visual measure of the difference between income and consumption, or a visual measure of saving. By comparing the 45-degree reference line with the consumption/income curve, the amount of saving at each level of income can be read directly from the diagram. For example, at an income level of $600 billion, saving equals $600 billion minus $500 billion, or $100 billion.

The intersection of the 45-degree reference line and the consumption/income curve (point *a*) is a very useful reference point: to the right of *a*, saving is positive since consumption is below income. For example, when income is $400 billion, consumption is $350 billion, and saving is $50 billion. To the left of *a* the economy is **dissaving** (saving is negative) because the economy's income is less than the amount of consumption spending. For example, when income is $100 billion, consumption is $125 billion and saving is −$25 billion.

*The economy is **dissaving**—total saving is negative—when consumption spending exceeds disposable income. The economy is either increasing its indebtedness or financing consumption by drawing down its savings.*

At point *a*, the economy is neither saving nor dissaving. Total saving equals zero. In our example, the intersection occurs at an income level of $200 billion. At this income, the vertical distance to the 45-degree line is the same height as the vertical line to the consumption/income curve. At this point, income and consumption are the same; no income is left over for saving.

The corresponding relationship between saving and income is graphed in panel (b), which is di-

rectly below panel (a) in Figure 4. The saving/income curve shows the amount of saving at different levels of income. Whether saving is read from the 45-degree reference line of the consumption/income curve or directly from the saving/income curve, zero saving occurs on the saving/income curve at the same income ($200 billion). For income greater than $200 billion, saving is positive; for income below $200 billion, saving is negative (there is dissaving). Like the consumption/income curve, the saving/income curve is positively sloped.

Nonincome Factors That Affect Consumption

Income is not the only determinant of consumption. A number of other nonincome factors can also affect consumption. If any of these other consumption-affecting factors changes, the entire consumption/income curve will shift. It is important to distinguish between *movements along* the consumption/income curve and *shifts in* the consumption/income curve:

A movement along *the consumption/income curve occurs when income changes—with all other factors that affect consumption held constant. A* shift in *the consumption/income function occurs when a consumption-affecting factor other than income changes.*

In Figure 5, a change in income from y_1 to y_2 will cause a movement along the consumption income curve from *a* to *b*. A change in a nonincome consumption-affecting factor could shift the entire curve from *C* to *C'*. A few of the many nonincome factors that affect consumption are: expectations, stocks of assets, the price level, taxation, age, income distribution, and attitudes toward thrift.

Expectations. Consumption expenditures are often responsive to changes in consumer expectations about the future. People form expectations about how rapidly prices will rise, about the likelihood of becoming unemployed, or about whether a war will cause shortages of goods. Those who believe their jobs will remain secure

Figure 5
Shifts in the Consumption/Income Curve

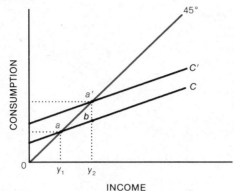

The original consumption/income curve, C, is drawn holding certain consumption-affecting factors other than income constant. Upward shifts in C are caused by increases in financial assets, reductions in the price level, reductions in taxes, a lowering of the average age of the population, a change in the distribution of income in favor of the poor, or the development of a more negative attitude toward thrift.

may consume more than others earning the same income who believe they may lose their jobs sometime in the future. People who believe that inflation will be rapid may spend more than those who believe that inflation will be moderate. If people suddenly become convinced that inflation will speed up, they may accelerate their consumption spending—to buy before the price is too high.

Accordingly, the entire consumption/income curve can shift upward or downward when expectations change. As a general rule, it shifts upward when inflationary expectations increase or when there is a growing sense of job security and shifts downward when the reverse conditions hold.

Stocks of Assets.   Changes in the wealth of consumers can also cause shifts in the consumption/income curve. The money wealth of individuals is the net money value of the assets they own (stocks, cash balances, real estate). As the money value of these assets rises, people feel that they are better off and, if prices are not increasing, they are likely to increase their consumption expenditures. The stock market may rise, and individuals who have seen the value of their assets

rise respond by increasing their consumption—even though their annual income has not changed. For example, if wealth rises, one need not save as much out of current income to meet future retirement or vacation needs.

The Price Level.   Assets can change real consumption even if their money value does not change. For example, the U.S. money supply M1 rose from $391 billion to $442 billion from the end of 1979 to the end of 1981—a rise of 13 percent. But prices rose by 21 percent over the same period. Thus, the actual purchasing power of M1 fell by about 7 percent. As prices rise, the purchasing power of assets falls. People can buy fewer real goods and services with their money wealth. Because they feel worse off, they may cut back on their purchases. As prices fall, the purchasing power of financial assets rises, and people are prone to increase their real consumption spending.

Taxation.   As income taxes rise, disposable income falls, *ceteris paribus*. As taxes increase, one would expect less consumption spending for the same amount of earned income. As income taxes are cut, disposable income rises; thus, one would expect more consumption spending from the same level of earned income.

Age, Income Distribution, and Attitudes toward Thrift.   A number of other nonincome factors can cause the consumption/income curve to shift. For example, the younger the population, typically the higher the percentage of income consumed. Younger families must acquire the durable goods to set up households. They must buy washing machines, cars, and other consumer durables. They must devote their incomes to raising and educating their children. On the other hand, families that have reached middle age have already accumulated a stock of durable goods; their children may have set out on their own. Therefore, middle-age families tend to spend a smaller portion of their income on consumption. To prepare for their retirement years they build up a nest egg by saving.

The *distribution of income* is also expected to affect the consumption/income curve: the rich tend to have a higher propensity to save than poor and middle-income families (as was shown by Figure 2). If the distribution of income is changed (say, by means of a tax reform) to raise the disposable income of the rich proportionally more than that of the poor, this change in distribution could shift down the consumption/income curve. If the distribution of income is changed in favor of the poor, the consumption/income curve should shift up.

Attitudes towards thrift also affect the consumption/income curve. If public attitudes toward saving and thrift change, the consumption/income curve will shift.

THE DETERMINATION OF GNP

The Keynesian income/expenditure approach can be used to explain how real output, Y, is determined in the simple model described in this chapter. The basic ingredient of this explanation is the consumption/income schedule in the first three columns of Table 1, which assumed no government spending or taxes. We now add the assumption that the amount of desired investment is fixed. These assumptions simplify the explanation of income determination. In subsequent chapters, such unrealistic assumptions will be dropped. But this very simple hypothetical model sheds a great deal of light on the process by which income is determined.

The Aggregate Expenditure Schedule

The consumption/income schedule in Table 1 relates the amount of consumption spending at each income (or output) level. The consumption/income schedule shows how much consumption would be *desired* at each income level. This desired amount of consumption will only be *realized* if the economy produces that amount of income. But consumption (C) is only one component of total spending; two other major components of total spending—investment (I) and government spending (G)—must be incorporated into an **aggregate expenditure schedule.** In our example, the business sector desires to spend a fixed amount on real investment—$50 billion dollars—at each level of income (and output) produced by the economy. In our simple economy, the government collects no taxes and purchases no goods or services.

Figure 6
Equilibrium Output

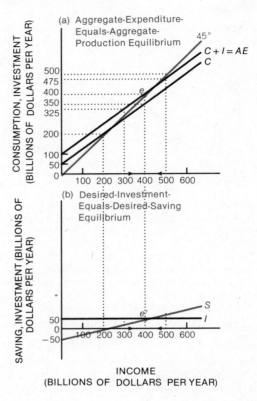

This figure is drawn from the data in Table 1. In panel (a), the intersection of the *AE* curve with the 45-degree line occurs at an income of $400 billion (point e). If the economy were to attempt to produce an income greater than $400 billion (to the right of *e*), aggregate output would exceed desired aggregate expenditures, and income would fall. If the economy were to attempt to produce an income less than $400 billion (to the left of *e*), desired aggregate expenditures would exceed aggregate production, and income would rise. Panel (b) shows how the economy reaches equilibrium by contrasting desired investment and desired saving. At levels of income above $400 billion (*e'*), desired saving exceeds desired investment. Unintended inventory investment (the difference between desired saving and desired investment) signals firms to slow down their rate of output. At levels of income below $400 billion, desired investment exceeds desired saving. Unintended inventory disinvestment signals firms to increase their rate of production.

Equilibrium income is reached at $400 billion where aggregate production equals aggregate expenditures, or where desired saving equals desired investment.

*The **aggregate expenditure (AE)** schedule summarizes the relationship between the desired amount of total spending (C + I + G) and income.*

Our example has eliminated government spending. Because investment is the same for each income level, desired aggregate expenditures at each income level are simply desired consumption plus desired investment, or the sum of columns (2) and (4) in Table 1.

In panel (a) of Figure 6, the consumption/income *(C)* curve is plotted from columns (1) and (2) of Table 1. The aggregate expenditure *(AE)* curve is plotted from columns (1) and (5) but is simply the *C* curve shifted up by the amount of investment.

To understand income/expenditure analysis it is important to understand that *desired* decisions are not necessarily *realized*. Whether they are indeed realized depends upon the relationship between desired aggregate expenditures and aggregate output.

Let us consider what would happen if our economy moved to an output of $500 billion. This decision is made by the hundreds of thousands of producers in the economy acting independently of one another. As the chapter on national income accounting mentioned, the act of producing $500 billion worth of output will create an income of $500 billion. If the economy were to continue to produce output at this rate, at the end of a year's time, it will have created $500 billion worth of income. At an annual income level of $500 billion, the economy would desire to spend $475 billion on consumption and investment, as shown in column (5) of Table 1. Desired aggregate expenditures would fall short of aggregate output by $25 billion, as shown in column (6) of Table 1.

The output rate of $500 billion worth of goods and services per year is, therefore, not an equilibrium output because the economy is producing output at a rate faster than purchasers in the economy are buying. Producers will know that too much output is being produced because unsold goods will accumulate in inventories higher than producers want to hold; excessive inventories of unsold cars, TV sets, sewing machines, and the like will build up. The accumulation of unwanted or excessive inventories will signal to business firms that their current production rates are excessive compared to what the market is prepared to purchase. Producers will have to slow down the rate of output production. (There might also be a tendency for prices to fall, but we are holding the price level constant in this chapter and the next.)

If business firms reduce their rate of production from $500 billion to $300 billion worth of output, desired aggregate expenditures will now exceed the rate of output by $25 billion. Producers will know that there is too little output because purchasers will be buying at too fast a rate. Inventories of goods—such as cars or TV sets—will fall below normal levels. Normal inventories can be replenished only by speeding up the rate of production.

Whenever aggregate production exceeds desired aggregate expenditures, the rate of production (and the rate of income creation) slows down. Whenever production falls short of desired aggregate expenditures, the rate of production (and income creation) speeds up. By adjusting the rate of output in response to total spending, the economy moves towards **Keynesian equilibrium**.

***Keynesian equilibrium** occurs when the economy produces an output that equals desired aggregate expenditures.*

Panel (a) of Figure 6 shows how the equilibrium output is determined. The *AE* curve and the 45-degree reference line show the relationship between aggregate output (or income) and *desired* aggregate expenditures at each output level. Aggregate income (or output) can be measured along the horizontal axis or by the corresponding vertical distance to the 45-degree reference line at that level of income (or output). Point *e*, which is the intersection of the aggregate expenditure curve with the 45-degree line, is the point where desired aggregate expenditures equal aggregate output. To the right of *e*, more output is being produced than the economy wishes to purchase: desired spending falls short of output at every income level. To the left of *e*, less output is being produced than the economy wishes to purchase. The economy adjusts to such disproportions by changing output until it equals $400 billion (at *e*).

Saving and Investment

Investors and savers are typically different individuals. The most important savers in the economy are individual households who consume less than their disposable income. The typical investor is the business firm that invests in plant, equipment, and inventory expansion. Without a coordinating mechanism, there is no reason why desired saving *(S)* should equal desired investment *(I)* in the economy at any time. The classical economists had supposed that desired saving would be quickly translated into desired investment by changing the rate of interest (Say's Law). To Keynes, on the other hand, the main mechanism that coordinated desired investment and desired saving was change in the level of output.

Returning to our numerical example, the movement toward equilibrium output can be seen in the contrast of intended saving and investment decisions. In our example, the business community desires to invest $50 billion at all levels of income (or output). The amount of desired saving depends upon the amount of income.

If firms in the economy are producing an output of $500 billion, Table 1 shows that desired saving equals $75 billion because consumption equals $425 billion. Desired saving exceeds desired investment by $25 billion at this output. At an output of $500 billion, there is too much saving; $25 billion of output is unsold and accumulates as unintended inventory investment. (*Inventory investment* is the addition to the inventories of goods and materials held by business firms.) When goods are unsold (because aggregate expenditures are insufficient), actual investment exceeds planned investment by the sum of unplanned inventory investment. This unintended accumulation of inventories raises actual investment to $75 billion (the sum of desired and unintended investment) to equal desired saving. **Unintended investment** is shown in column (6) of Table 2.

Unintended investment is the difference between desired saving and desired investment at each level of income.[3]

3. The terms *ex ante* (before) and *ex post* (after) are sometimes used to describe desired *(ex ante)* and actual *(ex post)*.

Whenever there is unintended investment in unwanted inventories (caused by too little aggregate expenditures) or unintended reductions in inventories (caused by too much aggregate expenditure), producers change their rate of production and income changes. As income changes, so does desired saving (which depends upon income).

When unintended investment is taking place, output begins to fall. With prices fixed (as Keynes assumed), businesses have only one way to cut back on the amount of unsold goods piling up in unwanted inventories: they cut back on the rate of production. Since desired saving depends upon the amount of income, as output falls so does saving. As this adjustment continues, the disparity between desired investment and desired saving diminishes until income (or output) is $400 billion.

When desired saving is less than desired investment, there is too little saving. The withdrawal from the spending stream is smaller than the injection back into the spending stream by investment. Businesses will see their inventories being drawn down to low levels, and there will be unintended *disinvestment* in inventories. Again with prices fixed, firms have only one way to build their inventories back up to normal levels: they increase the rate of production. As the amount of income increases, the amount of desired saving increases along with income. As desired saving increases, the gap between desired saving and desired investment disappears. This analysis suggests a second definition of **Keynesian equilibrium**:

Keynesian equilibrium is attained at that output at which desired investment equals desired saving.

In panel (b) of Figure 6, the movement to equilibrium output is shown in terms of the relationship between desired saving and desired investment. Point *e'* is the intersection of the horizontal investment curve with the saving/income curve (at an output of $400 billion). At levels of income to the right of *e'*, the withdrawal of saving from the spending stream exceeds the injection of investment back into the spending stream. Aggregate production exceeds desired aggregate expenditures; unsold goods accumulate in unintended inventories, and this unwanted inventory accumulation signals to producers that they are producing too much. At levels of income to the left of e', the injection of investment exceeds the withdrawal of saving. Desired aggregate expenditures exceed aggregate production; unwanted inventory disinvestment takes place, and firms are signaled to increase output. The level of income (or output) adjusts until desired investment equals desired saving.

Two Definitions of Equilibrium Are One

In the simple Keynesian model, the economy will adjust its rate of output until:

1. aggregate output equals desired aggregate expenditures $(Y = AE)$.
2. desired investment equals desired saving $(I = S)$.

As this chapter demonstrated, these two conditions are really different ways of looking at the same thing. When desired investment equals desired saving, output equals desired aggregate expenditures. Saving is the withdrawal households make from the spending stream, and investment is the injection firms put back. Whenever desired saving exceeds desired investment, more is withdrawn from spending than is put back in (desired aggregate expenditure is less than output). When desired saving is less than desired investment, less is withdrawn by savers than is put back in by business investment, or desired aggregate expenditure exceeds output.

THE PARADOX OF THRIFT

The aggregate output the economy tends to produce is the equilibrium output just discussed. The income/expenditure model explains how this equilibrium output is determined.

What will happen to output if thrift increases? An increase in *thrift* is a decrease in the amount of desired consumption at each level of income and an increase in the amount of desired saving at each level of income. An increase in thrift shifts the AE curve down and shifts the saving/income curve up.

Figure 7 shows the effect of an increase in thrift on equilibrium income. As the saving/

Figure 7
The Paradox of Thrift

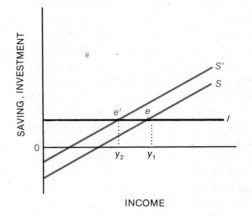

An increase in thrift is shown by an upward shift in the saving/income curve (from S to S'). At the initial equilibrium income, desired saving now exceeds desired investment. Saving withdraws more from the spending stream than investment injects back in. Desired aggregate expenditures are less than aggregate production, and unintended inventory investment causes firms to move to a lower rate of output. Equilibrium is restored at a lower income where desired saving and desired investment are again equal at point e'.

income curve shifts up, desired saving at the equilibrium income level, y_1, exceeds desired investment. Withdrawals from the spending stream exceed injections back in through investment. The economy's aggregate production exceeds desired aggregate expenditures, and unintended inventory investment takes place. This unintended inventory investment signals to firms that they are producing too much. The level of output, therefore, adjusts downward until a new equilibrium income is established (at e') where desired saving equals desired investment.

Notice that at the new equilibrium, actual saving is still the same as before, even though people have tried to save more.

The increase in thrift has caused a reduction in aggregate income; as aggregate income falls, so does desired aggregate saving. Since desired investment is assumed fixed, the economy ends up with the same saving.

Although individuals can save more if they increase their thrift, economies as a whole cannot increase their saving if there is a general increase in thrift. This paradox is a classic example of the fallacy of composition: what is true for each one considered separately need not be true for all together. A general increase in thrift means that less is being spent on consumption at each level of income. More saving is being withdrawn from the economy for each level of income. But investment decisions govern what is being injected back into the economy. Greater thriftiness means that more is being withdrawn than is being injected, and the economy must respond by a reduction in aggregate production and income. When aggregate income falls sufficiently to equate the withdrawals of saving with the injections of investment, the savers in the economy can end up with as much or less saving as before, but with lower incomes (y_2 is less than y_1).

This chapter showed how the equilibrium level of output is determined when the price level is fixed, as explained by the income/expenditure model or the simple Keynesian model. The next chapter will study the workings of the simple Keynesian model. It will consider the impact of changing investment, government spending, and taxation on equilibrium output under conditions where the price level is fixed.

Summary

1. Keynes studied economies operating with unemployed resources. Increases in aggregate expenditures could cause increases in real output and employment. Because of the emphasis on aggregate demand, Keynesian economics has been called *demand-side economics*. Keynes rejected the classical full-employment model. He rejected Say's Law that supply creates its own demand and believed that money wages were not sufficiently flexible to eliminate involuntary unemployment. According to Keynes, desired saving and desired investment would be equated not through the interest rate but through changes in income.

2. The Great Depression of the 1930s created the appropriate climate for the Keynesian notion that the government should ensure full employment.

3. The Keynesian income/expenditure model explains how economies determine their real output. The consumption/income schedule shows the amount of desired consumption at each income level. The saving/income schedule shows the amount of desired saving at each income level. The marginal propensity to consume *(MPC)* is the fraction of an extra dollar of income that is consumed. The *MPS* is the fraction of an extra dollar of income that is saved. In a world without taxes, *MPC* + *MPS* = 1. Factors that cause the consumption/ income (and saving/income) curves to shift are expectations, the real value of assets, taxation, income distribution, age, and attitudes towards thrift.

4. The aggregate expenditure *(AE)* curve shows the amount of desired aggregate expenditures, $C + I + G$, at each income level. The economy will produce that income at which a) aggregate production equals desired aggregate expenditures and b) desired investment equals desired saving. These two equilibrium conditions are two ways of looking at the same thing.

5. The paradox of thrift is that if all individuals attempt to increase their saving at a given level of income, the economy will end up with less income, and aggregate saving will not increase.

Key Terms

Say's Law
consumption/income schedule
saving/income schedule
marginal propensity to consume *(MPC)*
marginal propensity to save *(MPS)*
dissaving
aggregate expenditures *(AE)*
macroeconomic equilibrium
unintended investment

Questions and Problems

1. ''Savers and investors are different people. There is no way desired saving will equal desired investment.'' Describe how quantity theorists and Keynesian economists might respond to this statement.

2. Explain why the classical economists felt that there would be no long-term involuntary unemployment.

3. Using the consumption/income schedule in the table below,

   a. calculate the saving/income schedule.

   b. determine the *MPC* and the *MPS*.

   c. determine at what level of income the break-even point of zero saving is reached.

   d. determine the aggregate expenditure *(AE)* schedule if investment is a constant $50.

   e. find equilibrium output and demonstrate that at this equilibrium, desired investment and desired saving are equal.

   f. determine what happens to equilibrium output if investment falls to zero. What happens to the savings/investment equality?

   g. answer **d** if an increase in thrift occurs and people now desire to consume $50 less at each income (save $50 more at each income); determine equilibrium income and compare income and saving both before and after the increase in thrift.

Income, Y (billions of dollars)	Consumption, C (billions of dollars)
0	50
100	100
200	150
300	200
400	250

4. Explain what is meant by unintended investment. How will businesses respond to unintended investment in the simple Keynesian model? If prices were flexible, would the response of businesses to unintended inventory investment perhaps be different?

CHAPTER

10

Output Fluctuations: The Multiplier and the Accelerator

Chapter Preview

This chapter will examine how government spending and taxes enter the Keynesian model of income determination. It will explain that GNP is unstable in a Keynesian world because of the instability of investment itself and because of the magnified effect of changes in investment on national income.

Chapter 9 showed that the equilibrium level of national income is achieved when desired aggregate expenditures equal national income or, equivalently, when desired investment equals desired saving.

This chapter will study how and why changes in demand affect the equilibrium level of national income. The discussion that follows assumes the economy has stable prices, substantial unemployed resources, and unemployed workers willing and able to work at prevailing wages as it did when Keynes developed his theories. The economy, therefore, has the capacity to raise its real output without driving up prices.

GOVERNMENT SPENDING AND TAXES

The preceding chapter described the determination of equilibrium output in an economy. To simplify this description, Chapter 9 left government spending, G, and taxes, T, out of the picture by setting them equal to zero in our hypothetical economy. This chapter will bring government spending and direct (income) taxes back into the picture.

Figure 1
Macroeconomic Equilibrium with Government Spending and Taxes

(a) Consumption/Income Curve   (b) Aggregate Expenditure Curve

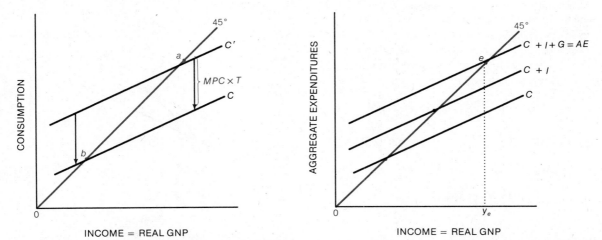

INCOME = REAL GNP   INCOME = REAL GNP

In panel (a) the introduction of taxes lowers disposable income by the amount of the tax. At each income level, consumption is lowered by *MPC* times the level of taxes. The introduction of taxes causes the consumption/income curve to shift down from *C'* to *C*. Panel (b) shows how desired aggregate expenditures *(AE)* are obtained at each income level. Government expenditures *(G)* and investment *(I)* are added to the *C* curve, shifting it up by those amounts. Panel (b) shows that the equilibrium level of output *(y$_e$)* is determined where the *AE* curve (which includes taxes, government spending, and investment) intersects the 45-degree reference line at point *e*.

The introduction of government spending and taxes affects desired aggregate expenditures, *AE,* in two ways, as shown in Figure 1. First, the collection of direct taxes decreases aggregate expenditures at each level of income because the higher are the taxes, the lower is disposable income. Disposable income *(DY)* is the difference between income and tax payments: $DY = Y - T$. Because consumption is a function of disposable income, taxes have an indirect effect on aggregate expenditures: as taxes increase, disposable income falls; as disposable income falls, consumption falls. The amount of this decrease in consumption depends on the marginal propensity to consume *(MPC)*. When disposable income falls, consumption will fall by *MPC* times the decline in disposable income, and the *C'* curve in panel (a) will shift down by this amount.

Second, government expenditures are a component of aggregate expenditures, along with consumption and investment spending. With positive government spending, the desired aggregate expenditure schedule is the sum of the three types

of spending desired at each income level: $AE = C + I + G$. To obtain the *AE* curve, investment and government spending are added to the consumption/income curve (that has been adjusted for taxes) at each income level. This chapter will simplify the discussion considerably by letting both investment and government spending be fixed sums that do not vary with income. The *AE* curve with government spending is shown in panel (b) of Figure 1.

As panel (b) shows, the macroeconomic equilibrium with government spending and taxes is similar to that with no government. Equilibrium income occurs where desired aggregate expenditures (which now include government spending) equal aggregate production (at the intersection of *AE* with the the 45-degree reference line).

With government spending and taxes in the picture, the equality of saving and investment is still an equilibrium condition, but now saving includes both private saving *(S)* and government saving *(T − G)*. Chapter 6 showed that government saving is the difference between government income—taxes—and government spending. Thus, equilibrium occurs when $I = S + (T - G)$.

With government spending, desired aggregate expenditures $(C + I + G)$ equal aggregate production (Y). With taxes, aggregate income (Y) is used for consumption, taxes, or spending and, therefore, equals consumption, saving, and taxes $(C + S + T)$. Because aggregate production (Y) and aggregate income (Y) are the same,

$$C + I + G = C + S + T,$$

or, to simplify,

$$I + G = S + T$$

Therefore,

$$I = S + (T - G)$$

FACTORS THAT CHANGE EQUILIBRIUM INCOME

As long as desired aggregate expenditures do not change, the equilibrium level of output will remain the same. Figure 2 shows that any change that shifts the aggregate expenditure curve *(AE)* will cause equilibrium income to change. If the *AE* curve shifts upward, desired aggregate expenditures $(C + I + G)$ will exceed the old equilibrium output, y. In Figure 2, an increase in government spending shifts the *AE* curve from *AE* to *AE'*. The economy is now purchasing output at a rate faster than output is being produced; inventories are drawn down to subnormal levels; firms respond by increasing their production. Upward shifts in *AE,* therefore, shift equilibrium from e to e' and cause output to increase from y to y' (if there are unemployed resources).

Had *AE* shifted down instead of up, desired aggregate expenditures would have been below the original equilibrium output, $y;$ unwanted inventories would have built up; the economy's producers would be forced to move to a lower output.

When the desired aggregate expenditure curve shifts, equilibrium output changes. The factors that cause increases or decreases in aggregate spending can be divided into direct factors and indirect factors.

Figure 2
A Shift in Aggregate Expenditures Changes Equilibrium Output

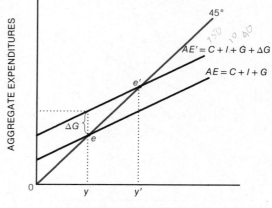

An increase in government spending *(ΔG)* causes the aggregate expenditure curve to shift from *AE* to *AE'*. At the old equilibrium income, y, desired aggregate expenditure exceeds output, and producers are signaled to increase production. The new equilibrium income is reached at y', where output and desired aggregate expenditures are again equal.

Direct Factors:
Autonomous Expenditures

A change in investment or government spending will directly change desired aggregate expenditures. If one or both of these factors increase, there will be more desired aggregate expenditures at each level of income. Graphically, a change in investment or government spending will cause a vertical shift in the *AE* curve by the amount of the change in I or G. Expenditures that shift the level of desired aggregate expenditures are called **autonomous expenditures** if they are independent of the level of national income.

Autonomous expenditures are determined independently of income changes.

Increases or decreases in government spending result when federal, state, and local governments change their level of expenditures for goods and services. Changes in investment occur when the business community decides to either increase or decrease its investment spending.

Table 1
Macroeconomic Equilibrium with Government Spending but No Taxes (billions of dollars)

Output = Income (Y)	Consumption Spending (C)	Investment Spending (I)	Government Spending (G)	Aggregate Expenditure (AE = C + I + G)
(a) With I at $20 billion; equilibrium Y = $400 billion				
100	125	20	30	175
200	200	20	30	250
300	275	20	30	325
400	**350**	**20**	**30**	**400**
500	425	20	30	475
600	500	20	30	550
(b) With I at $70 billion; equilibrium Y = $600 billion				
100	125	70	30	225
200	200	70	30	300
300	275	70	30	375
400	350	70	30	450
500	425	70	30	525
600	**500**	**70**	**30**	**600**

Autonomous changes in consumption are caused by changes in attitudes toward thrift, expectations, age structure, or the distribution of income. Changes in consumption that result from changes in income are induced rather than autonomous.

Indirect Factors: Taxes

Shifts in the aggregate expenditure curve can also result from changes in indirect factors like taxes. Consumers base their consumption decisions on disposable income, not on total income. As taxes are raised, disposable income *(DY)* is reduced. As disposable income declines, so does consumption spending at each level of national income.

When a tax is increased, *consumption will decline by less than the increase in the tax*. For example, if taxes are raised by $50 billion, for each level of national income, disposable income, *DY*, will fall by the amount of the tax increase. But *consumption* will fall by less than the decline in disposable income because households consume only a portion of extra income. If the marginal propensity to consume *(MPC)* is 0.75, a $50 billion decline in disposable income would cause consumption to fall by 75 percent of the decline in disposable income, or by $37.5 billion in this

case. Since the *MPS* (marginal propensity to save) is 0.25 when the *MPC* is 0.75, a $50 billion increase in taxes would also depress savings by $12.5 billion at each level of income. The $50 billion increase in taxes comes out of saving and consumption in proportion to the *MPS* and *MPC*.

> *Because the economy's MPC is less than unity, tax changes will cause shifts in the consumption/income curve that are less than the change in taxes. Accordingly, changes in taxes will cause shifts in desired aggregate expenditures that are less than the change in taxes.*

TYPES OF MULTIPLIERS

Autonomous-Expenditure Multipliers

Table 1 explores the effects of autonomous changes in investment on equilibrium output. In part (a), the first two columns show the consumption/income schedule of the previous chapter. The marginal propensity to consume *(MPC)* is 0.75 (every $1 increase in income results in a $0.75 increase in consumption), investment is constant at $20 billion, and government spending is constant at $30 billion. There are still no taxes; they

Figure 3
The Impact of a $50 Billion Autonomous Increase in Investment on Equilibrium Output

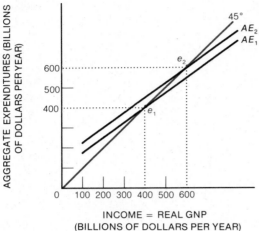

INCOME = REAL GNP
(BILLIONS OF DOLLARS PER YEAR)

The $50 billion increase in investment causes the aggregate expenditure curve *(AE)* to shift up vertically by $50 billion from AE_1 to AE_2. At the original equilibrium, output is $400 billion; desired aggregate expenditures now exceed aggregate production, and desired saving exceeds desired investment. The previous chapter demonstrated that the economy's producers will, therefore, increase their output. Equilibrium is restored at an output of $600 billion. The $50 billion increase in investment has caused a $200 billion increase in output.

will be added to the picture shortly. As part (a) shows, equilibrium output is $400 billion, because desired aggregate expenditures equal total output at $400 billion. The original aggregate expenditure curve is labeled AE_1 in Figure 3.

Part (b) of Table 1 shows what happens when there is an autonomous increase in investment spending of $50 billion (from $20 billion to $70 billion). A $50 billion increase in government spending or in a combination of investment and government spending would have the same effect on desired aggregate expenditures, shifting AE_1 to AE_2 in Figure 3, as an increase in investment spending. Because autonomous investment is a direct demand for goods and services, AE_1 shifts up by the vertical distance of the change in investment.

The position of the AE_2 curve shows that the economy's desired aggregate expenditures are now greater at each income level than at AE_1. Point e_1 represents the original equilibrium for curve AE_1. When increased investment shifts AE_1 to AE_2, the old equilibrium output of $400 billion is less than the desired expenditure level of $450 billion for that level of income. Now the economy wishes to purchase $450 billion worth of goods and services, but the economy is only producing $400 billion worth. Inventories throughout the economy are being drawn down below desired levels, signaling to producers that they should increase their rate of output. The economy raises output until it arrives at its new equilibrium at e_2, where it produces $600 billion worth of output. The output of $600 billion is the new equilibrium output because at that output, desired aggregate expenditures are also $600 billion.

Notice that the $50 billion increase in investment spending causes a $200 billion increase in output (from $400 billion to $600 billion). The increase in output is 4 times the increase in investment. The tendency for an increase in investment or government spending to cause magnified increases in output is called the *expenditure multiplier effect*. **Expenditure multipliers** can be either **investment multipliers** or **government-expenditure multipliers.**

*The **expenditure multiplier** is the ratio of the change in output to the change in autonomous expenditures. The two expenditure multipliers are the **investment multiplier** ($\Delta Y/\Delta I$) and the **government-expenditure multiplier** ($\Delta Y/\Delta G$).*

Why should an autonomous change in investment cause a much larger change in output? When investment expenditures are increased by $100 billion, the immediate effect is for incomes in the economy to increase by $100 billion. These expenditures, after all, end up in the pockets and purses of the suppliers of the factors of production that produced the $100 billion worth of investment goods. If this immediate effect were the only effect, then the increase in investment would cause an equivalent increase in output. But the process does not stop here. *Those households whose incomes have gone up by a total of $100 billion will increase their consumption spending.* When income increases, consumption increases

Table 2
The Multiplier Principle Illustrated

Round	Amount of Increase in Income (ΔY)	Amount of Increase in Consumption (ΔC)	Leakages (increase in saving) (ΔS)
1	**100.00**	75.00	25.00
2	75.00	56.25	18.75
3	56.25	42.19	14.06
4	42.19	31.64	10.55
5	31.64	23.73	7.91
6	23.73	17.80	5.93
All other	71.19	53.39	17.80
Totals	400.00	300.00	**100.00**

A $100 billion increase in investment sets the multiplier process off (marginal propensity to consume = 0.75). The $100 billion increase in investment creates $100 billion in additional income, 75 percent of which is spent in round 1. In round 2, the $75 billion extra consumption enters as a $75 billion increase in income, and 75 percent of this increase is spent on additional consumption ($56.25 billion). This $56.25 billion enters as additional income in round 3, and 75 percent of this income is spent on additional consumption. This process continues through a large number of rounds until income has increased by $400 billion and consumption has increased by $300 billion. The process continues until the sum of leakages into saving equals the initial increase in investment. The investment multiplier equals 4 because a $100 billion increase in investment has caused a $400 billion increase in income.

according to the economy's marginal propensity to consume, or by *MPC* times the increase in income. Aggregate incomes again increase by the amount of the injection of more consumption, and the recipients of this extra income again increase their consumption by *MPC* times the amount of the income increase. This process continues until the successive increases in spending dwindle to zero.

Table 2 shows how an increase in investment leads to a magnified increase in output. A $100 billion increase in investment immediately creates $100 billion worth of additional income. With a marginal propensity to consume of 0.75, this increase in income causes an increase in consumption of $75 billion. This $75 billion increase in consumption creates another $75 billion in income. Of this $75 billion, 75 percent ($56.25 bil-

lion) is spent on additional consumption, creating $56.25 billion of additional income. This $56.25 billion worth of new income stimulates a consumption increase of another $42.19 billion, and so the multiplier process continues until the full effect of the multiplier is felt. In our example, the investment multiplier is 4 because the $100 billion increase in investment eventually causes a $400 billion increase in income.

At each stage, income is leaking out of the economy in the form of saving. As Table 2 shows, of the initial $100 billion increase in income, when $75 billion is consumed, $25 billion is saved. At the next stage, when $56.25 billion is consumed $18.75 billion of the newly generated $75 billion in income is saved, and so on. These leakages in the form of saving limit the ultimate increase in income in response to an increase in investment (or government spending). The increase in income stops when the total leakages equal the initial $100 billion increase. The same result would have been obtained if the original increase in spending had been in government spending rather than in investment. The government-spending multiplier would also have equaled 4. The investment and government-expenditure multipliers have the same numerical value. The simple Keynesian model assumes that only taxes—not government spending—detract from private spending. In other words, government spending is assumed not to be a substitute for private spending. (The next chapter will discuss this assumption in more detail.)

One can see in our numerical example that the *MPC* has a great deal to do with the value of the multiplier. If the *MPC* had been 0.9 rather than 0.75, the initial increase in consumption would have been larger in the first and in subsequent rounds. The smaller the leakages (or the larger *MPC*) the greater is the amount of additional income created at each stage, and the larger is the multiplier. The larger the leakages (or the smaller *MPC*) the smaller is the amount of income generated at each stage, and the smaller is the multiplier.

The formula for determining the investment-expenditure multiplier ($\Delta Y/\Delta I$) is:

$$\Delta Y/\Delta I = \frac{1}{1 - MPC} = \frac{1}{MPS},$$

where there are no taxes ($MPC + MPS = 1$ in the absence of taxes). If investment increases by $1, in the new equilibrium, saving must also increase by $1 since $S = I$. If MPC equals 0.75, however, $MPS = 0.25$, and $4 of extra income is necessary to increase saving by the necessary $1. Thus, income must increase by $4 to generate the extra saving to match the $1 increase in investment.

The relationship between MPC and the expenditure multiplier can also be demonstrated with some simple algebra.[1]

The investment expenditure multiplier is the ratio of the increase in Y to the increase in I. The increase in Y (ΔY) equals the increase in I (ΔI) plus the change in C (ΔC), or

$$\Delta Y = \Delta C + \Delta I \qquad (1)$$

But ΔC will equal MPC times ΔY:

$$\Delta C = MPC \times \Delta Y \qquad (2)$$

Substituting equation (2) into equation (1) yields:

$$\Delta Y = MPC \times \Delta Y + \Delta I \qquad (3)$$

or,

$$\Delta Y (1 - MPC) = \Delta I \qquad (4)$$

---

1. There is a second way to derive the expenditure multiplier. We know that aggregate income must equal aggregate expenditures, $C + I + G$:
$$Y = C + I + G$$
but C is a function of Y:
$$C = a + MPC \times Y$$
When the consumption/income equation is substituted in the first equation, we get:
$$Y = a + MPC \times Y + I + G$$
which reduces to:
$$Y = (a + I + G)/(1 - MPC)$$
The algebraic expression $1/(1 - MPC)$ is the expenditure multiplier. This expression also shows by what factor Y increases if there is a one-unit autonomous increase in a, I, or G, or some combination. The a represents the intercept of the consumption/income curve. If it increases by one unit, the consumption/income curve shifts up by one unit.

Dividing both sides by $(1 - MPC)$ yields:

$$\Delta Y = \frac{\Delta I}{1 - MPC} \qquad (5)$$

Equation (5) is the expenditure multiplier formula when both sides are divided by ΔI:

$$\frac{\Delta Y}{\Delta I} = \frac{1}{(1 - MPC)} = \frac{1}{MPS}$$

The higher is the MPC, the higher is the multiplier. An MPC of 0.75 yields a multiplier of 4; an MPC of 0.9 yields a multiplier of 10. The economy's response to autonomous expenditures, therefore, depends on the MPC (or MPS). The higher is the MPC, the higher is the induced expenditures from any given rise in income. In other words, the higher is the MPC, and the lower is the MPS, the more income must change in order to get the saving leakages to match the injection of new investment.

The higher is the **MPC**, *the higher is the multiplier. The lower is the* **MPC**, *the lower is the multiplier.*

The Tax Multiplier

The effect of changes in taxes can be different from the effect of changes in investment or government spending. Because taxes affect aggregate expenditures only indirectly through their effect on consumption expenditures, taxes do not lower consumption expenditures dollar for dollar. Therefore, the tax multiplier will be smaller than the expenditure multiplier.

Figure 3 retained the assumption of zero taxes in demonstrating the effect of a $50 billion increase in investment. Figure 4 illustrates the effect of a $33.33 billion increase in taxes (from $0 to $33.33 billion).

The $33.33 billion increase in taxes (with an MPC of 0.75) will cause consumption to drop by $25 billion at each income level. At each level of income, the tax increase causes disposable income to fall by $33.33 billion. Consumption will, therefore, fall by 0.75 (the MPC) times the fall in disposable income ($33.33 billion), or by $25 billion. A $25 billion decrease in consumption is

Figure 4
The Effect of a $33.33 Billion Increase in Taxes on Output

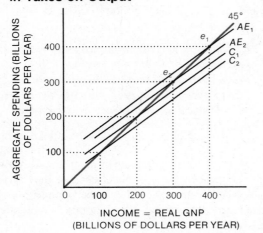

In this example, taxes rise from $0 to $33.33 billion. The original consumption/income curve, C_1, shifts down to C_2, but the vertical downward shift in the consumption/income curve is less than the $33.33 billion increase in taxes. The tax increase of $33.33 billion causes disposable income to fall by the amount of the tax increase, but with an *MPC* of 0.75, *C* falls by only $25 billion. *AE* shifts downward (from AE_1 to AE_2) by $25 billion, not by the amount of the full tax increase. Equilibrium output will be restored at $300 billion. Output has fallen by $100 billion as a consequence of the $33.33 billion increase in taxes; the equilibrium point has shifted from e_1 to e_2.

less than the increase in taxes. When consumption decreases from C_1 to C_2, aggregate expenditures also decrease by $25 billion, from AE_1 to AE_2 in Figure 4.

Point e_1 shows the original equilibrium where output equals desired expenditures at $400 billion. When aggregate expenditures decline by $25 billion to $375 billion, while output is still $400 billion, the economy is buying at a rate slower than the economy is producing; excessive inventories build up; firms cut back on production. The new equilibrium is established at point e_2, where output equals desired expenditures at $300 billion.

The impacts of changes in taxes will be different from changes in investment or government spending. If investment or government spending were to decline by $33.33 billion (with an *MPC*

of 0.75), output would decline by 4 times this amount, or by $133.33 billion. A $33.33 billion increase in taxes, however, causes output to drop by only $100 billion. The **tax multiplier** is smaller than the government expenditure or investment multiplier for the same size change.

*The **tax multiplier** is the change in output divided by the change in the tax, or $\Delta Y / \Delta T$*

In the above example, the tax multiplier equals -3. The $33.33 billion increase in taxes caused output to drop by $100 billion. The tax multiplier is a negative number because *increases* in taxes cause *reductions* in output. The investment and government-spending multipliers are positive because *increases* in investment or government spending cause *increases* in output.

The tax multiplier is the expenditure multiplier applied to the shift in the *AE* curve due to the increase in taxes. A $1 tax shifts the *AE* curve by $-MPC$. In other words, expenditures fall by $$MPC$. Thus, the tax multiplier is:

$$\frac{\Delta Y}{\Delta T} = \frac{-MPC}{1 - MPC}$$

The absolute value of the tax multiplier subtracted from the expenditure multiplier is 1.[2]

$$\frac{1}{1 - MPC} - \frac{MPC}{1 - MPC} = \frac{1 - MPC}{1 - MPC} = 1$$

The Balanced-Budget Multiplier

If the expenditure multiplier is one greater than the tax multiplier in absolute value, then, surprisingly, *equal changes in government spending and*

2. Some algebra shows why the tax multiplier is one less (in absolute value) than the expenditure multiplier. With taxes, the consumption/disposable income function is:

$$C = a + MPC (Y - T)$$

When this expression is substituted in $Y = C + I + G$, we get:

$$Y = (a + I + G) / (1 - MPC) - MPC \times T/(1 - MPC)$$

The tax multiplier is $-MPC/(1-MPC)$ while the expenditure multipliers are $1/(1-MPC)$. The difference between the expenditure multiplier and the tax multiplier always equals 1.

taxes will change income by the amount of the change in government spending. For example, if the government-spending multiplier is 4, the tax multiplier is −3. If government spending and taxes both rise by $10 billion, the effect of the rise in government spending would be to *raise* output by $40 billion; the rise in taxes would *lower* output by $30 billion. The net effect of the simultaneous equal increases in government spending and taxes is, therefore, to raise output by $10 billion—the amount of the increase in government spending.

The multiplier effect of equal changes in government spending and taxes is called the **balanced-budget multiplier.**

The **balanced-budget multiplier** *for changes in government spending is the effect on income of a change in government spending that is covered by an equal change in taxes and equals 1. Equal increases (or decreases) in government spending and taxes will cause income to increase (or decrease) by the amount of the change in government spending.*

THE MULTIPLIER IN KEYNESIAN MACROECONOMIC POLICY

The expenditure and tax multipliers must play an important role in devising Keynesian macroeconomic policy. If society is not satisfied with the current equilibrium output (say, it is well below full employment), it must know by how much to change autonomous expenditures or taxes; it is not sufficient to know simply whether expenditures or taxes should be raised or lowered.

Suppose, for example, that society determines that output should be increased by $200 billion. If one knows that the expenditure multiplier equals 4 and the tax multiplier equals −3, one could devise a macroeconomic policy to raise output by the desired amount. One possible program would be to lower taxes by $20 billion (to yield an increase in output of $60 billion); to raise government spending by $20 billion (to yield an increase in output of $80 billion); and to raise investment by $15 billion (to yield an increase in

output of $60 billion). All these policies combined would raise output by the desired $200 billion. Many other macroeconomic programs would yield the desired $200 billion increase in output.

Expenditure and tax multipliers are essential instruments of Keynesian policy. If expenditure and tax multipliers are known, expenditure and tax programs can be devised to yield the desired increase or decrease in real GNP.

Multipliers are very important to the Keynesian income/expenditure model because they serve as critical instruments of macroeconomic policy making. But a number of limitations of multiplier analysis should be noted:

1. The multiplier theory requires that the economy be able to increase real GNP without limit. In other words, it applies to an economy operating with idle, unemployed, or underemployed resources. Another crucial assumption is that prices remain stable in spite of unemployed resources. If, however, the economy is utilizing all its resources fully, increases in autonomous expenditures will not raise real GNP but will instead raise the price level. Resource constraints or tightness can, in principle, reduce the value of the multiplier. In the full-employment world of the classical economist, the multiplier effect on real GNP is zero. The economy is already producing as much real output as it can. Increases in investment or government spending or a reduction in taxes cannot raise real output.

2. The simple Keynesian model assumes that changes in government expenditures do not influence other private spending decisions, but increases in government spending may lead to reductions in other types of spending—called the *crowding out effect.* Increases in government spending can raise the costs of financing private investment (by pushing up interest rates) and, hence, reduce private investment. Moreover, increased government spending (say, on recreation or public schooling) may cause households to reduce their private spending on close substitutes. A free park or better public schools may cause consumers to spend less on recreation and private schools.

Econometric Models and Multipliers

The branch of economics that deals with estimating actual expenditure and tax multipliers is called *econometric modeling*. Econometric modeling of the U.S. economy was pioneered by Nobel laureate Lawrence Klein of the University of Pennsylvania. Currently, econometric modeling of the U.S. and other world economies has become a major activity of academic, business, and government economists. There are a large number of competing econometric models of the U.S. economy from which to choose. Perhaps the best known are the Wharton Econometric Model, the Data Resources Inc. (DRI) model, and the econometric models of major private banks and regional Federal Reserve banks that are used by many corporations, investment firms, and government agencies.

These econometric models are estimated from historical U.S. data on consumption, investment, and government spending. Unlike the simple hypothetical multiplier models discussed in this chapter, econometric models often consist of hundreds of equations that are designed to describe the behavior of the U.S. economy.

Econometric models are used to simulate the effects of economic policies: What will happen to output and to unemployment if taxes are cut 10 percent across the board? What will happen if the money supply is allowed to expand at a more rapid rate? Such simulations attempt to give policy makers (and businesses whose profits depend on these answers) advance information on the effects of contemplated policies on the economy.

Econometric models can be constructed differently. They more often than not yield different predictions. Some econometricians believe that the economy can be modeled simply, that maybe a few equations (such as the demand and supply of money) will suffice. Others believe that hundreds of equations are required to capture economic activities properly.

Despite their shortcomings, econometric models perform a valuable function: they allow participants in the economy to look into the future, albeit imperfectly, and attach probabilities to different economic outcomes. The fact that American business spends large sums on econometric forecasting suggests that econometrics is performing a positive function. The main reason for forecasting errors is that econometrics must predict the future on the basis of what has happened in the past. Although past behavior is often a good guide, it is far from foolproof. ⚡

---

3. The exact change in output resulting from a change in autonomous expenditures or taxes cannot be predicted in advance. Economic outcomes are based upon the actions of millions of participants in the economy; human beings and businesses face uncertainty and information costs. Thus, there is a random component that the policy maker cannot know. The future need not necessarily conform to what has happened in the past. The crowding-out effect may vary from expenditure to expenditure and from time to time. In reality, the economy is a very complex animal, much different from simple hypothetical models. The consumption/income curve can shift unpredictably; public anticipations may change—perhaps in part because of forecasts economists themselves made; any number of other unpredictable events may occur. Thus, knowledge of the multiplier is inexact (see Example 1).

THE ACCELERATOR

Multiplier analysis attempts to explain why changes in income occur. Fluctuations in autonomous expenditures such as investment spending and government spending exert a magnified effect on income through the multiplier. Real GNP fluctuates because expectations change, because attitudes toward thrift change, or because government changes taxes or government spending. The effect of each of these changes may be magnified through the multiplier.

Keynes felt that the fundamental source of output instability was the instability of investment spending. If investment is highly unstable—increasing rapidly in one year and falling sharply in the next—the multiplier would magnify this instability, causing substantial fluctuations in output.

Figure 5 shows that over the years, real invest-

Figure 5
The Instability of Investment Compared to GNP

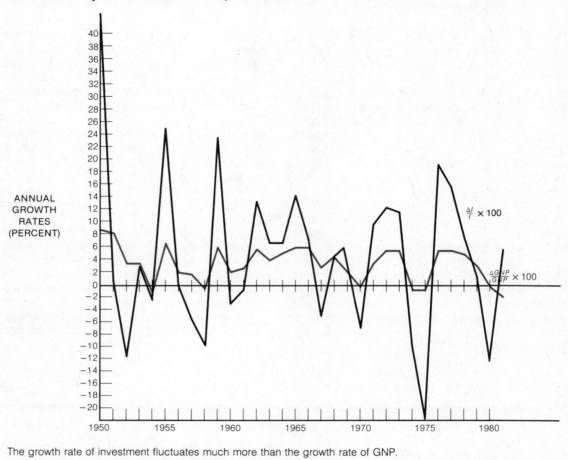

The growth rate of investment fluctuates much more than the growth rate of GNP.
Source: *Economic Report of the President,* January 1982, pp. 234–35

ment spending has fluctuated much more erratically than real GNP, as Keynes predicted.

The Accelerator Principle

In producing output (whether shoes or cars or whatever), firms seek to use that stock of capital (machines, inventories, plants) that allows the most profitable operation of the firm. A grocery store that sells $1 million per year of goods may need an average inventory of $100,000; a manufacturer of steel plates may need $2 million worth of capital to manufacture $1 million worth of output per year.

Net investment is the addition to the stock of capital, but the stock of capital needs to grow

only if the level of sales increases. For example, if the steel manufacturer can sell another $2 million of output per year, it may need additional investments in plants and equipment. At the economy-wide level, final business sales approximate national income. Since the stock of capital needs to grow only if income (and output) grows, net investment requires growth in income or business sales. If business sales are not growing, investment falls off rapidly.

Growth in income and output is the justification for continued investment. If output fails to grow (or its growth even slows down), investment will be seriously affected.

Table 3
The Accelerator Principle Illustrated
(billions of dollars)

Year (1)	Output (2)	Growth of Output over Previous Year (3)	Investment (4)
Increasing growth			
0	600	—	—
1	1,000	$400	$600
2	1,600	$600	$900
Declining growth			
3	1,900	$300	$450
4	2,000	$100	$150
Zero growth			
5	2,000	$ 0	$ 0
Constant growth			
6	2,200	$200	$350
7	2,400	$200	$350

The capital output ratio in this example is 1.5. Investment will, therefore, equal 1.5 times the increase (or decrease) in income. This example shows that investment will grow only if the output growth increases. If the output growth remains constant, there will be no net investment.

Figure 6
The Accelerator Principle

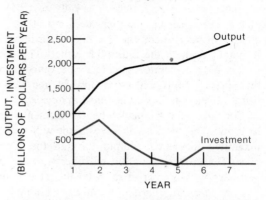

These two curves are plotted from data in Table 3. Output in the first year equals $1,000. Output in each year is, therefore, the previous year's output plus the growth of output. This figure illustrates that the accelerator principle causes investment to fluctuate more than output.

The relationship between capital and output illustrates this point. For example, if for every $1 of output, the economy requires $1.50 worth of capital, the **capital/output ratio** would be 1.5.

*The **capital/output ratio** is the value of capital (K) needed to produce a given level of output divided by the value of that output (Y), or K/Y.*

If the capital/output ratio remains steady, capital must increase for the economy to produce more output. With a capital/output ratio of 1.5, for example, a $10 billion increase in output would require a $15 billion increase in capital. Because investment is the increase in capital ($I = \Delta K$) investment must also depend upon the rate of increase in output. With a fixed capital/output ratio of 1.5, the relationship between investment and output is:

$$I = 1.5\Delta Y,$$

or

$$I = \frac{K}{Y} \times \Delta Y$$

This equation illustrates the **accelerator principle** of investment. It shows that investment will increase only if the growth of output increases. If output fails to increase, investment will fall to zero. If output declines, there will be net disinvestment as business firms allow their capital stock to depreciate without replacement. Thus, investment in an economy depends not on the level of income but on how fast income—or the level of business sales—is rising or falling. To get investment to rise, income not only has to grow; it has to grow *at an increasing rate*.

*The **accelerator principle** of investment is that investment depends upon the growth of output and implies that investment will be unstable. Investment will fall simply because output grows at a slower rate. For investment just to remain stable, output growth must be constant.*

The investment accelerator can explain why investment spending is so unstable. Table 3 shows the behavior of investment when output is experiencing rising, stable, and declining growth. The real GNP and investment figures of Table 3 are plotted in Figure 6. Investment fluctuates much more than output when investment depends on the growth of output.

Multiplier/Accelerator Interaction

The investment accelerator is only part of the picture because, as earlier demonstrated, increases in investment cause a magnified increase in output through the multiplier effect. The multiplier and accelerator interact. The outcome of this interaction is explosive upward and downward movements in output *(business cycles)*.

Consider what happens when investment starts to grow. The increase in investment will have a magnified impact on output through the multiplier. The growth of output will increase, and investment will accelerate as a result. This *multiplier/accelerator interaction* causes a boom with output and investment growing at ever-faster rates. The increasing rate of growth of output causes increasing growth of investment, which pushes up output growth even more. When the boom ends, however, the growth of output slows down, and investment starts to fall. As investment falls, the multiplier will cause output to decline. The accelerator causes investment to become negative, and output falls even further. The boom is, therefore, followed by a bust with falling output and negative net investment.

Limitations of the Accelerator

The accelerator and accelerator/multiplier interaction suggest serious cyclical problems. Investment will fluctuate wildly, and interactions with the multiplier will cause boom-and-bust business cycles. In the real world, cyclical fluctuations are nowhere as large as suggested in our hypothetical examples. The accelerator is based upon the notion that more capital is required to produce more output—which is true when all resources are fully utilized, but an economy operating well below full employment can increase output by other means. As a result, the link between the growth of output and investment is not strong when the economy is operating well below full employment.

The fact that the relationship between increases in output and investment is not rigid for technological reasons does not rule out accelerator-like effects. Businesses will indeed base capital expansion plans on anticipated growth in sales. The accelerator principle likely provides a fairly

strong explanation for the great instability of inventory investment. The amount of inventories business firms hold is strongly linked to the amount of output. As output increases, so must business inventories. As output falls, businesses cut back on inventory holdings.

Determinants of Investment

Unlike government spending and taxation, investment is determined by the private sector. The government can indeed exert some influence on investment through investment tax incentives and the like, but basically the amount of investment is determined by profit-oriented businesses.

The Investment Demand Curve. How does an individual firm decide how much to invest over a certain period of time? The firm will add to its capital stock (invest) using the same rules it uses to buy materials, to rent land, or to hire labor. It compares the marginal costs and benefits of acquiring more or less of the resource in question—in this case, capital.

The firm's cost of acquiring additional capital is, basically, the prevailing cost of borrowing loanable funds—*the interest rate.*[3]

How much investment a typical firm will want to carry out at different interest rates will depend upon the *rates of return* that the firm believes it can earn on the various investment projects that its engineers and managers suggest.

For example, an investment project that promises to add each year an additional $1 million to the profits of the firm for a very long (almost infinite) period costs $10 million. The *rate of return* on this $10 million investment, in this special

---

3.   There is a large literature in macroeconomics on the cost of acquiring capital to the firm. Corporations can purchase capital not only by borrowing funds (selling bonds) but also by issuing new shares of stock and by reinvesting profits in the corporation. The cost of borrowing funds is the interest rate. The cost of plowing back profits is what these funds could have earned in other pursuits (their opportunity cost). One cost of issuing new shares is that the number of owners of the corporation has increased and there is a dilution of the stock of existing owners. Because of these three options, there has been some discussion as to whether the interest rate is the most appropriate cost of capital and as to whether the cost of capital changes as more capital is acquired. This introductory text uses the market interest rate as the cost of capital.

case, is 10 percent—the annual addition to profit divided by the cost of the project.[4] Investment projects are typically more complicated than this one, but the principle remains: investment decisions are based upon the relationship between the rate of return and cost.

In any year, a firm would have a number of potential investment projects. Some would offer higher rates of return; others would offer lower rates of return. In making its investment decisions, the firm would rank its investment projects by rate of return. As long as a project promised a rate of return higher than the rate at which capital funds had to be borrowed (the interest rate), the firm would want to carry out the project. The profit-maximizing firm would, therefore, carry out all those projects that promised returns greater than the interest rate. The last project financed would have a rate of return just equal to the market interest rate.

Firms carry out additional investments as long as their rate of return (R) exceeds the market rate of interest, r. Therefore, the last (marginal) investment project should yield a rate of return equal to the market interest rate (R = r).

The investment demand curve of an individual firm should be negatively sloped just like other demand curves. At high rates of interest, there are fewer projects that offer rates of return equal to or greater than the interest rate. The lower the interest rate, the greater the number of investments that will be undertaken. In this case, what holds for individual firms also holds for the economy as a whole: at low interest rates, there is a greater quantity demanded of investments than at higher interest rates.

Figure 7 shows a representative investment demand curve. Like any other demand curve, it shows the quantity of real investment demanded at different prices, where the price in this case is the market rate of interest. How much investment will this economy carry out? It will invest as long

Figure 7
The Investment Demand Curve for an Entire Economy

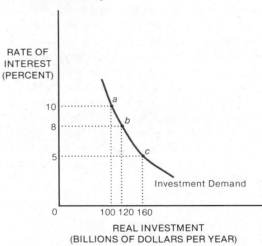

Firms in the economy will be prepared to carry out investment projects as long as the rate of return promised by the project equals or exceeds the interest rate. Insofar as there are fewer investment projects that offer rates of return of 10 percent and above than those that offer 5 percent and above, the investment demand at an interest rate of 5 percent is greater than the investment demand at a 10 percent rate.

as it has projects that offer higher rates of return than the interest rate. It will cease investing when the rate of return on the last investment project equals the interest rate. In our example, at an interest rate of 10 percent the economy will invest $100 billion.

The negative slope of the investment demand curve illustrates that *the amount of investment increases as the interest rate is lowered.* In our example, an interest rate of 10 percent yields an investment of $100 billion. An interest rate of 8 percent yields an investment of $120 billion.

The investment demand curve reveals that desired investment spending increases as the interest rate falls.

Other Factors Influencing Investment Demand. The interest rate is only one of the factors that cause investment to change. Our above discussion demonstrated that the investment demand curve may be sensitive to changes in output

---

4. The rate of return is the rate that equates the present discounted value of the additions to profits to the cost of the project. In this case, a 10 percent rate equates the present value of the perpetual $1 million profit stream to the cost.

(the accelerator principle). The investment demand curve can also be shifted by a number of other factors. Business taxes and investment tax incentives can shift investment demand. When tax laws are changed in such a manner as to lower the after-tax costs of investment projects, more investment will tend to be undertaken at each interest rate. Changing expectations concerning the future on the part of businesses can also alter desired investment. Insofar as rate-of-return calculations depend upon perceptions of prices, costs, and profits in the often-distant future, a shift in expectations towards a more pessimistic outlook can cause desired investment at each interest rate to fall.

ACTIVIST POLICIES AND BUSINESS CYCLES

Two of the factors responsible for the instability of and fluctuations in output are the multiplier and the accelerator. Multipliers show how disturbances can be magnified into fluctuations in output. They also suggest a means to combat the business cycle. By engineering relatively small changes in autonomous expenditures, policy makers may be in a position to counteract business cycles. If a drop in investment spending threatens to move the economy well below full employment, deliberate increases in government spending or deliberate reductions in taxes may neutralize this threat. The multipliers even indicate to policy makers how large these changes should be to neutralize unfavorable movements in the business cycle.

Keynes was an ardent supporter of *activist economic policy:* the deliberate manipulation of autonomous expenditures and taxes to counteract the business cycle. The debate over the use of activist macroeconomic policy is probably the most important unresolved policy issue in all of economics. This debate will be discussed in later chapters.

The next chapter studies the use of activist policy in the setting of a simple Keynesian model and assembles all the ingredients for the theory of aggregate demand.

Summary

1. This chapter examined how and why real output changes in an economy with unemployed resources. When government spending is introduced into the income-expenditure model, the same two equilibrium conditions still determine output: aggregate production equals desired aggregate expenditures, and desired investment equals desired saving. Saving, however, now includes both public $(T - G)$ and private (S) saving.

2. Changes in income (and output) can be caused by either direct factors or indirect factors.

3. Changes in autonomous expenditures—those that are determined independently of income changes—change desired expenditures dollar for dollar. The expenditure multiplier indicates by how much output will change for each change in government spending or investment. The value of the multiplier depends upon the MPC; the higher is the MPC, the higher is the multiplier. The expenditure multiplier formula is $1/(1 - MPC)$ or $1/MPS$. The tax multiplier indicates by how much output will fall for each $1 increase in taxes. The tax multiplier is $-MPC/(1 - MPC)$. The tax multiplier equals (in absolute value) the expenditure multiplier minus 1. For this reason, the balanced-budget multiplier equals unity.

4. The multiplier is important in the income-expenditure model because it predicts the impact on output of changes in autonomous expenditures and taxes. There are three main limitations of the multiplier in the simple income-expenditure model: a) multipliers apply to an economy with unemployed resources and fixed prices, b) multipliers assume there will be no offsetting (crowding out) effects, and c) multipliers are difficult to predict even in an economy with unemployed resources.

5. The accelerator principle explains why investment expenditures tend to be unstable. It postulates that investment depends upon the rate of increase of output. Investment remains constant only if output grows at a con-

stant rate. If the rate of output growth falls, investment will suffer a decline. When the accelerator interacts with the multiplier, booms and busts may result. Increases in investment cause output to grow, and as output growth increases, investment increases further. Desired investment depends upon the interest rate, government tax policy, and expectations concerning the future.

6. Because output tends to be cyclically unstable, the Keynesian income/expenditure model favors activist policy to counteract cycles.

Key Terms

autonomous expenditures
expenditure multiplier
investment multiplier
government-expenditure multiplier
tax multiplier
balanced-budget multiplier
capital/output ratio
accelerator principle

Questions and Problems

1. Will a cut in personal income taxes of $100 billion raise or lower equilibrium real output? Does the answer depend upon whether there are unemployed resources in the economy? Will the effect on equilibrium output be larger if the *MPS* is 0.2 or 0.1? Explain.

2. If there were no government spending, even though the government collected taxes, what would the saving/investment equality look like?

3. "Changes in attitudes towards thrift and personal income taxes both affect the consumption/income curve. Therefore, a $100 billion increase in taxes will have the same effect as a $100 billion decrease in desired consumption expenditures caused by an increase in thrift." Evaluate this statement.

4. The economy has substantial unemployed resources. The *MPS* out of disposable income is 0.25. Government spending increases by $100 billion and taxes are lowered by $100 billion. Using the Keynesian multiplier analysis, by how much would one expect equilibrium output to change?

5. If households spend all their extra income on consumption, what effect will an investment spending increase have on equilibrium income?

6. Explain why multipliers are so important in the conduct of discretionary monetary and fiscal policy.

7. The *MPC* is 0.9; there are substantial unemployed resources. If government spending is increased by $100 million, how can credit markets moderate the multiplier?

8. The most volatile component of investment is inventory investment—the change in inventories held by businesses. According to the accelerator principle, why will inventory investment be more volatile than other forms of investment?

9. Explain why changes in expectations concerning the future can shift the investment demand curve.

11

Keynesian Monetary and Fiscal Policy

Chapter Preview

If output and employment are unstable, government action in the form of discretionary monetary and fiscal policy may be required to combat unemployment and inflation. This chapter develops the basic tools of monetary and fiscal policy in the framework of the Keynesian income/expenditure model.

Keynes's income/expenditure model showed how output is affected by government spending, taxes, and investment when the economy is operating with unemployed resources and with stable prices. The previous chapter showed how autonomous changes in investment, government spending, and taxes can have a magnified effect on the economy's output through the multiplier. Rela-

tively small changes in business investment or government expenditures or taxes can set into motion relatively large changes in output.

The multiplier analysis of Keynes carried both a negative and a positive message. On the negative side, it said that relatively small disturbances in autonomous spending can cause relatively large cyclical disturbances. On the positive side, Keynes's multiplier analysis suggested a possible way to correct these disturbances. By effecting relatively small changes in investment, government spending, and taxes, governments could counteract the disruptive forces of the business cycle.

The policy message of Keynesian economics is: government can actively counteract the inherent instability of the economy that is caused principally by fluctuations in investment expenditures. If output is dropping too low, activist policy should stimulate output and employment. *Expansionary tools* include cutting taxes, increasing government spending, and increasing the money supply.

If output is pushing against full employment or if inflation is getting too high, activist policy should be used to reduce output and to dampen inflationary pressures. *Contractionary tools* include raising taxes and lowering the money supply or government spending.

> *Activist macroeconomic policy uses the tools of government spending, tax policy, and control of the money supply to induce the economy to produce the desired level of output.*

This chapter will explore the tools of activist policy. Although the income/expenditure model argues that automatic adjustments will be slow and weak without activist policy, there is much debate between supporters of activist and hands-off policies. (Chapter 15 will address this debate over activist versus hands-off macroeconomic policy.)

THE LABOR MARKET

The Keynesian income/expenditure approach was formulated to deal with an economy operating with unemployed resources (a depression economy). It draws a picture of labor markets that is much different from the flexible labor market of the classical quantity theorists. According to Keynes, the labor market in modern capitalist economies is very inflexible because of a variety of factors, including union contracts (that often run for two or three years), limited competition, and monopoly elements. Money wages are, thus, said to be *sticky* in a downward direction. In other words, if the demand for labor falls, money wages simply do not fall. Instead, they remain sticky at the prevailing rate. This stickiness means that money wages cannot adjust downward to reduce unemployment.

If the economy is producing at less than full employment, money wages and prices will be sticky; because wages will not fall, the price level will not fall. Because unemployed workers are willing to work at the going money wage, it is possible to expand aggregate expenditures without raising the price level. *At less than full employment, real GNP can increase without an increase in the price level.*

The picture changes when the economy reaches full employment. At full employment, an increase in aggregate expenditures will raise money wages. There is no involuntary unemployment, and it is not possible for the economy to increase its real output any further because resources are already fully employed. Instead, employers bid among themselves for labor and drive up wages; prices rise at the same rate as wages. Because wages and prices rise at the same rate, *real wages* remain the same. Despite the rising price level, the economy is producing the maximum possible output because all labor is employed.

AGGREGATE SUPPLY

Remember that an aggregate supply curve shows the levels of real output (real GNP) that are supplied by businesses at different price levels. The wage behavior described above results in the Keynesian aggregate supply curve.

Figure 1 shows the Keynesian aggregate supply curve. At levels of output less than full employment, wages and prices are sticky; workers willing to work at prevailing wages are unemployed. Therefore, aggregate real output can be increased without an increase in prices. For this reason, the Keynesian aggregate supply curve is horizontal below full-employment output.

The Keynesian supply curve is vertical at full-employment output. All those willing to work at the prevailing wage are employed; the economy cannot produce more real output. Instead, any effort to increase employment and output will drive up money wages and the price level without any increase in real output.

This aggregate supply curve is a gross oversimplification of the way real-world economies behave. Obviously, there are limits to the downward stickiness of wages. At very high rates of unemployment, money wages (and prices) would eventually fall, and the aggregate supply curve would slope upward. Also, the full-employment threshold is not one single level of output. Economies do not reach a unique full-employment real

Figure 1
The Keynesian Aggregate Supply Curve

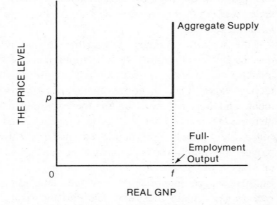

The Keynesian aggregate supply curve is horizontal at less than full-employment output—*f*—because money wages are "sticky" in a downward direction. Money wages do not fall in response to rising unemployment; therefore, different rates of aggregate supply (at less than full employment) are consistent with the same price level. Once the economy is at full employment output *(f)*, money wages rise, but prices are driven up at the same rate, and employment does not increase. At full-employment output, the supply curve becomes vertical. Thus the Keynesian supply curve is a right-angled curve.

output beyond which they cannot produce one more dollar of real output. Money wages may begin to rise at less than full employment as bottlenecks in particular labor markets develop. The dividing line between voluntary and involuntary employment is often poorly defined; there will be some frictional unemployment at full employment.

Like the rigid assumptions of the crude quantity theory, the simple Keynesian model offers the *L*-shaped aggregate supply curve as an approximation of reality. Modern economists have substituted a more flexible version of full employment that will be examined in Chapter 12.

The *L*-shaped aggregate supply curve of Figure 1 plays a vital role in the Keynesian model by defining full-employment real output *(f)*. Full-employment real output is the amount of real output the economy must produce in order to have full employment. If the economy produces below *f*, labor will be unemployed, and the economy has passed up the opportunity to produce a larger volume of output.

Attaining full-employment output is the goal of activist policy in the Keynesian model.

With an *L*-shaped aggregate supply curve, moving from an output less than full employment to *f* brings important benefits but no inflationary costs. As output moves up toward but not yet touching *f*, there is more real income, less unemployment, and no increase in prices! On the horizontal portion of the Keynesian aggregate supply curve, real and nominal output are the same because prices are constant; output can be increased without affecting prices.

INFLATIONARY AND DEFLATIONARY GAPS

Figure 2 returns to the macroeconomic equilibrium described in the preceding two chapters. Macroeconomic equilibrium occurs at the intersection of the aggregate expenditure curve *(AE)* and the 45-degree line. Equilibrium output in panel (a) occurs at an output of *y*, but *y* is greater than full-employment output *(f)*. The relationship between *y* and *f* is crucial to the income/expenditure model. Differences between *y* and *f* signal the existence of an **inflationary gap** or a **deflationary gap**.

*A **deflationary gap** exists if equilibrium output (y) falls short of full-employment output (f).*

*An **inflationary gap** exists if equilibrium output (y) exceeds full-employment output (f).*

Figure 2 shows an inflationary gap in panel (a) and a deflationary gap in panel (b). In panel (a), aggregate expenditures *(ae)* at the full-employment level of output exceed *f*. Activist policy should aim at reducing desired aggregate expenditures because prices are being pushed up without any increase in real output. If the aggregate expenditure curve could be shifted down by exactly the right amount (from *AE* to *AE'*), the inflationary gap would be eliminated and the equilibrium level of output *(y)* would equal *f*.

Panel (b) shows a deflationary gap in which aggregate expenditures *(ae)* at full-employment output fall short of *f*. In this case, if the aggregate expenditure curve could be increased by exactly the right amount (from *AE* to *AE'*), the deflation-

Figure 2
Activist Policy with Inflationary and Deflationary Gaps

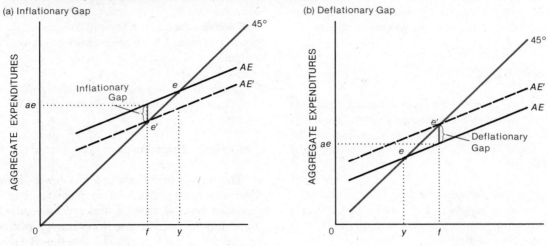

(a) Inflationary Gap

(b) Deflationary Gap

Panel (a) shows how to use activist policy to react to an inflationary gap. Full-employment output is *f;* equilibrium output is *y.* In panel (a), *y* is above *f.* The inflationary gap is the vertical distance between the current aggregate expenditure curve, *AE,* and the aggregate expenditure curve, *AE',* that would yield an equilibrium at *f.* Activist policy should, therefore, seek to reduce desired aggregate expenditures by the vertical distance between *AE* and *AE'.*

Panel (b) shows how to use activist policy to react to a deflationary gap. In (b), *y* is less than *f.* The deflationary gap is the vertical distance between *AE* and *AE'*—the aggregate expenditure curve that would yield an equilibrium at *f.* Activist policy should raise *y* to *f* by raising desired aggregate expenditures by the vertical distance between *AE* and *AE'.*

---

ary gap would disappear and the economy would be at full employment.

Figure 2 suggests an exact measure of the magnitude of the inflationary or deflationary gap:

> *The inflationary gap is the amount by which autonomous expenditures must **fall** for the economy to operate at full employment. The deflationary gap is the amount by which autonomous expenditures must **rise** for the economy to operate at full employment.*

In the Keynesian model, there is an asymmetry between upward and downward movements in prices. If there is an inflationary gap, there will be inflation; however, there will *not* be deflation (falling prices) with a deflationary gap. What does inflation do to the inflationary gap? Ensuing chapters will discuss this question in more detail, but a brief answer can be given now.

If contractionary activist policies are not followed, the process of inflation will automatically

shift the *AE* curve downward toward *AE'* in panel (a) to eliminate the inflationary gap. Inflation reduces the purchasing power of the money supply. When the price level increases by 10 percent, for example, a given nominal money supply suffers a 10 percent decline in its real purchasing power. As people see the purchasing power of their money balances falling, they spend less. Investment falls and the consumption/income curve shifts down (and, hence, the *AE* curve shifts down) as a result of inflation.

If prices would fall in response to a deflationary gap, there would be a tendency for the economy to move by itself towards full employment. Falling prices would raise the purchasing power of the money supply and this increase in purchasing power would encourage more consumption and investment spending.

The flexibility of prices is a crucial issue to macroeconomic policy. If prices are highly flexible in response to both inflationary and deflationary gaps, the economy may cure itself of inflation and unemployment. If, however, prices are inflexible, or if adjustments are slow in coming about, activist policy may be required to eliminate inflationary and deflationary gaps. Keynes adhered to the second view.

MONETARY POLICY

As already mentioned, the general instruments of activist policy are taxes, government spending, and the money supply. Activist policy can be classified as either **monetary policy** or **fiscal policy**.

Monetary policy is the deliberate control of the money supply and, in some cases, credit conditions for the purpose of achieving macroeconomic goals.

Fiscal policy is the deliberate control of federal government spending and taxes for the purpose of achieving macroeconomic goals.

The income/expenditure model pioneered by Keynes viewed the role of money much differently from the classical quantity theorists, whose views were summarized in Chapter 7. The classical economists believed that the supply of money affected the level of money expenditures directly. With velocity *(V)* constant and the economy tending to operate automatically at full employment, the equation of exchange *(MV = PQ)* showed that aggregate expenditures rise at the same rate as the money supply *(M)*. However, classical theorists did not believe that the quantity of money had any effect on real GNP or employment because of the natural tendency for economies to operate at full employment. Increases in money supply would translate into proportionate increases in the price level.

Keynes viewed the link between the money supply and desired aggregate expenditures in a different light. He rejected the two classical notions of fixed velocity and full employment. Keynes felt that velocity could fluctuate unpredictably, as could real GNP; therefore, the direct link between money *(M)* and aggregate expenditures *(PQ)* he believed to be weak and unstable.

Instead, Keynes proposed an indirect link between the money supply *(M)* and real GNP *(Y)*.

This indirect relationship would operate through the effect of money supply on interest rates *(r)*. By affecting real investment and perhaps even real consumption expenditures, changes in the interest rate would have an indirect effect on real output.

In the Keynesian model, monetary policy affects output indirectly through interest rates.

Liquidity Preferences

The last chapter explained that lower interest rates can cause investment to increase. The investment demand curve is negatively sloped with respect to the interest rate; lower interest rates increase the amount of desired investment spending. But what determines interest rates? The Keynesian model espoused a rather simple view of interest-rate determination, called the **liquidity-preference theory**.

According to the liquidity-preference theory, the opportunity cost of holding money—a completely liquid asset—is the interest sacrificed, and the interest rate is determined by the supply of and demand for money.

Cash in one's pocket earns no interest. Money in a checking account earns little or no interest. As defined in Chapter 7, the money supply, M1, is the sum of currency in circulation and checking accounts held by the nonbanking public. The higher the opportunity cost of holding money, the lower the quantity demanded. Therefore, the demand curve for money (the demand curve for liquidity) will have a negative slope relative to the interest rate. At high interest rates, the opportunity cost of holding money is high, and the quantity of money demanded will be low. At low interest rates, the opportunity cost is low, so the quantity of money demanded will be greater.

The Demand for Money. Figure 3 shows a representative money demand curve. The money demand curve is also called a *liquidity preference (LP) curve* because people are demanding liquidity when they demand money. The liquidity pref-

Figure 3
The Demand and Supply of Money and the Interest Rate

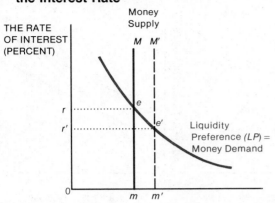

QUANTITY OF MONEY

The money demand curve, or *liquidity preference curve,* has a negative slope. The amount of money demanded by the economy is greater at low rates of interest than at high rates of interest because the interest rate is the opportunity cost of holding money. The supply of money is determined by the monetary authorities (the Federal Reserve Board). The market interest rate *(r)* will be the equilibrium rate at which the demand for money equals the supply of money *(m)*. There will be an excess supply of money as the interest rate exceeds the equilibrium rate or an excess demand for money as the interest rate falls short of the equilibrium rate. As monetary authorities increase the supply of money from *m* to *m',* the interest rate falls from *r* to *r',* *ceteris paribus.*

Figure 4
The Effect of Interest-Rate Changes on Investment

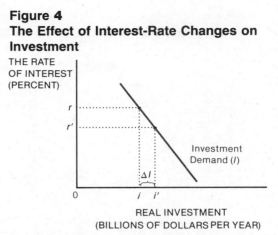

REAL INVESTMENT
(BILLIONS OF DOLLARS PER YEAR)

More loanable funds are demanded for capital investment at lower rates of interest than at higher rates of interest, *ceteris paribus.* Any monetary policy that lowered the interest rate would stimulate investment, *ceteris paribus.*

---

erence curve shows that the amount of money demanded by the economy increases as the interest rate falls. It is like any other demand curve in that the quantity demanded (money) is inversely related to the commodity's price (the interest rate). Like other demand curves, there are a number of demand factors that are held constant, which will be discussed later.

The Supply of Money.   As demonstrated in Chapter 8, the monetary authorities (the Fed) control the supply of money by means of open-market operations, discount rates, and required-reserve ratios. The market rate of interest is established at that rate at which the demand for money equals the supply of money. In Figure 3, the initial money supply is represented by the vertical line, *M.*

At interest rates above the equilibrium rate *(r),* the quantity of money supplied will exceed the quantity demanded. When there is an excess supply of money, people and firms will find credit easier to obtain; as more credit is supplied, interest rates will be driven down. If the interest rate is less than the equilibrium rate *(r),* there will be an excess demand for money, and the interest rate will rise.

Controlling the Interest Rate

According to the simple liquidity-preference theory, monetary authorities can control interest rates by means of their control of the supply of money. By increasing the money supply, monetary authorities can drive down the rate of interest. By reducing the supply of money, monetary authorities can raise the rate of interest.

In Figure 3, the interest rate falls from *r* to *r'* when the money supply increases from *M* to *M',* *ceteris paribus.* A higher quantity of money induces lending institutions (banks, savings and loans, insurance companies) to make more loans, which drives down the market rate of interest.

Money, Investment, and Output

Figure 4 shows that at higher interest rates, less investment is demanded and that at lower in-

Figure 5
How Monetary Policy Works in the Income/Expenditure Model

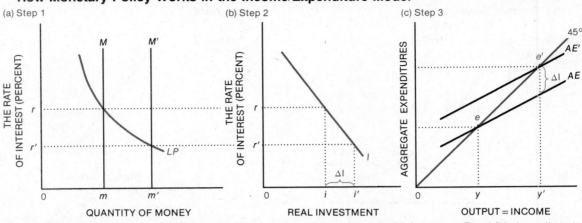

(a) Step 1 (b) Step 2 (c) Step 3

In panel (a), the interest rate, r, initially equates the demand *(LP)* and supply *(M)* for money. Panel (b) shows that at this rate of interest, the amount of investment is *i*. Aggregate expenditures at *i* are shown in panel (c). With investment equal to *i*, equilibrium income is *y*.

If the monetary authorities wish to increase output, they increase the supply of money (from *M* to *M'*). This action drives the interest rate down from *r* to *r'*, and the amount of investment rises from *i* to *i'*. This increase in investment *(ΔI)* shifts *AE* to *AE'* and causes equilibrium output to rise from *y* to *y'*. Notice that the increase in output is greater than the increase in investment by the factor of the multiplier.

---

terest rates, more investment is demanded. Figure 5 shows how the interaction of the money and investment markets depicted in Figures 3 and 4 can affect the economy's level of output.

Assume that the economy is operating well below full-employment output and that monetary authorities want to raise output. Assume also that the price level is fixed (because the economy is operating on the horizontal portion of the Keynesian aggregate supply curve).

The monetary authorities would begin the process of increasing output by increasing the supply of money (to *M'*). The increase in money supply would drive down the market rate of interest (to *r'*). The decrease in the interest rate would cause a movement down the investment demand curve and would increase investment (to *i'*). The increase in investment would (through the multiplier) cause a magnified increase in output (from *y* to *y'*).

Credit Rationing

In the Keynesian model, monetary policy works primarily through interest rates. When the Fed reduces the money supply, interest rates rise

to choke off some investment. **Credit rationing** can, however, be used as a subsidiary instrument of monetary policy.

Credit rationing occurs when interest rates are not allowed to rise to the rate at which the demand for loans equals the supply of loans. In this situation, the demand for investment funds at the prevailing interest rate exceeds the supply. Credit rationing limits investment by making investment funds unavailable to some firms that are prepared to invest at prevailing interest rates.

Although credit rationing and a decrease in the money supply work generally in the same direction, there is an important difference. A decrease in the money supply raises the interest rate, and as the interest rate rises, less investment is demanded. Credit rationing works differently: when the supply of money is reduced, controls on interest rates prevent interest rates from rising to a new equilibrium. Firms are discouraged from investing not because of a reduced demand for investment but because of the reduced availability of loans. Moreover, credit rationing typically

Example 1

The Credit Crunch of 1980

In March of 1980, the Federal Reserve Board was authorized by the President to implement credit controls under the provisions of the Credit Control Act passed by Congress in 1969. Some thought that high interest rates had not been effective in reducing business investment and consumer purchases of durable goods, and an additional anti-inflationary weapon was required. Certain hard-hit sectors—like farming, home builders, and auto dealers—were supposed to be exempted from these selective credit controls.

The credit controls of 1980 were designed to restrain the growth of consumer credit and the credit supplied by large banks to business firms. Banks were supposed to limit voluntarily the growth of total loans to U.S. customers to 6 to 9 percent from the end of 1979 to the end of 1980. Banks were penalized for increases in consumer credit and business loans above certain percentages.

The impact of the imposition of credit controls—combined with interest rates nearing 20 percent—was dramatic. Credit-card sales and applications dropped, and consumer credit declined for the first time in 5 years. Commercial-bank lending to businesses either failed to increase or dropped for the next three months. Although new home sales were supposed to be exempted from selective credit rationing, new home sales plunged in March.

The credit controls program ended in July of 1980 six months after it was initiated. During this period, there is strong evidence that the aggregate expenditure curve shifted down as a consequence of reductions in consumer spending, business investment, and home buying. Real GNP in the second quarter of 1980 plunged 2.5 percent from the first quarter (an annual rate of 10 percent), and the credit crunch is thought to be one cause of this drop.

---

tends to be less even-handed. Often rules are set by the Fed or by the lending institutions themselves as to which customers will be granted credit.

Credit rationing requires the existence of government controls over interest rates. Left uncontrolled, interest rates would adjust to equate the supply and demand for loans. The Fed does have the tools for credit rationing: the Fed can set interest-rate ceilings; it can enact rules for making loans; it can penalize lending institutions that fail to follow its rules. Through credit rationing, the monetary authorities can affect investment in a more direct fashion by regulating the availability of investment funds.

The Limitations of Monetary Policy

The old saying: "You can take a horse to water but you can't make him drink" has been applied to monetary policy. Basically, all the Fed can do is to make additional monetary reserves available to the banking system if it wishes to expand the money supply. It cannot force banks to lend out these reserves and expand the money supply. Nor can it force businesses to increase their investment borrowing when interest rates drop. The use of monetary policy to induce the economy to increase investment can be like pushing on a string. If banks do not loan out additional reserves and if business firms do not invest more when interest rates drop, the monetary authorities are pushing on a string. Many economists dispute the pushing-on-a-string analogy. They argue that lower interest rates provide adequate incentives for businesses and consumers to alter their behavior.

Most economists agree that monetary authorities are more effective when they *pull* on the string. When they wish to contract the money supply, authorities can withdraw reserves and force a contraction of the money supply. If firms do not respond to higher interest rates by investing less, the monetary authorities can always use credit rationing to restrict investment.

The simple income/expenditure model describes an indirect but not an insignificant role for money in the management of the economy. As Figure 5 showed, in the income/expenditure model, increases in money supply lower interest rates; lowering interest rates raises investment; increasing investment raises output. Credit rationing can be employed as a supplemental weapon to restrict aggregate demand.

The link between the money supply and desired aggregate expenditures in the income/expenditure model is very fragile. The link could be broken at any point in the chain. If increases in money supply fail to lower interest rates, or if changes in interest rates fail to elicit changes in investment, money supply would exert no effect on desired aggregate expenditures. Moreover, even if the chain is not broken, the effects may be very weak. Interest rates may respond only weakly to changes in money supply; investment demand may be very insensitive to changes in interest rates.

For these reasons, Keynes felt that monetary policy would be less effective than fiscal policy in combating severe unemployment.

Control Interest Rates or Control Money Supply?

In the income/expenditure model, monetary policy works through interest rates. Should monetary policy aim at setting interest rates and not worry about how much money supply must rise or fall to achieve the desired interest rate? Or should monetary authorities set a target money supply and not worry about the effect of this money supply on interest rates?

Monetary economists generally favor controlling the money supply without excessive worry about interest rates. They argue that the pursuit of interest-rate targets destabilizes the economy.

Assume that the economy is in a boom period and the monetary authorities (following an interest-rate policy) decide to hold interest rates constant. But economic expansion increases the demand for credit, and this increased demand starts to drive up interest rates. To hold interest rates down, therefore, the Fed must create even more money. The increase in money supply will further feed the boom. Likewise, when the economy is depressed, the demand for credit will contract and threaten to push down interest rates. For monetary authorities to hold the interest rate constant, they must reduce the supply of money, thereby depressing economic conditions even further.

Monetary experts warn that the pursuit of rigid interest-rate targets exaggerates the business cycle.

Prior to October 1979, the Fed's monetary policy was directed toward setting interest-rate targets—although these targets were flexible. This policy meant that the growth of the money supply was dictated by the interest-rate targets of the monetary authorities. If very rapid growth of the money supply was required to achieve a target rate of interest, so be it.

In October 1979, in a historic decision, the Fed decided to base monetary policy on targets for the growth of the money supply and to let interest rates settle at the level dictated by that money supply. The Fed now sets specific target growth rates of the money supply. In mid-1982, the Fed's money supply targets were sharply criticized. Evaluation of the Fed's money supply policy may be dependent upon how well the U.S. economy recovers from the 1981–1982 recession.

FISCAL POLICY

Fiscal policy was defined as the deliberate use of government spending and taxes to achieve macroeconomic goals. Although the federal government accounts for 44 percent of total (federal, state, and local) government revenues and for only 39 percent of total government expenditures, fiscal policy is conducted through the federal budget. The taxes and expenditures of state and local governments are decided at the state and local level on an uncoordinated basis.

The two major sources of federal revenues are the personal income tax and contributions for social insurance. The two major types of federal government expenditures are purchases of goods and services and transfer payments.

The federal deficit is defined as federal government revenues from all sources minus federal government expenditures to all sources. Table 1 provides some summary statistics on the 1983 federal budget that was projected in 1982.

In the basic Keynesian model, the link between increases in government spending and aggregate expenditures is very direct. The last chapter showed how an increase in government spending raises desired aggregate expenditures

Table 1
The Projected 1983 Federal Budget

Category	Amount (billions of dollars)
Total receipts	**$686**
Personal tax and nontax receipts	$308
Corporate-profit taxes	$78
Indirect business taxes	$58
Social-insurance contributions	$242
Total expenditures	**$788**
Purchases of goods and services	$273
Transfer payments	$331
Grants in aid to state and local governments	$77
Net interest	$96
Other	$11
Deficit (total revenues minus total expenditures)	**−$102**

Source: *Economic Report of the President,* January 1982, p. 321.

and establishes a higher equilibrium output. Recall that this result assumes there are unemployed resources and that government spending does not displace private spending. The link between lower taxes and higher real GNP was shown to be less direct than the link between spending and output, but as long as the marginal propensity to consume out of current disposable income does not fluctuate too much, reductions in taxes cause the consumption/income curve to shift upward and cause output to increase.

Governments spend money and collect taxes on a continuous basis. Whether intended or not, their spending and taxing actions affect aggregate expenditures.

Many fiscal-policy actions take place automatically and require no policy decisions on the part of government. For example, many federal government expenditures are *entitlements* such as social-security or unemployment-compensation payments. To receive such entitlement payments, recipients need only demonstrate that they qualify under established rules. Once the rules are set, the government does not determine the magnitude of such entitlement-program payments. Instead, the payment totals tend to depend on general economic conditions. Treasury officials maintain that

currently 75 percent of all federal outlays are for "relatively uncontrollable" items like entitlements and interest on the national debt.[1] Federal tax revenues come in on much the same basis. Once income-tax rates are set and rules concerning depreciation, personal exemptions, and the like are set, government tax revenues depend upon general economic conditions.

Other government revenues and expenditures are determined by deliberate discretionary decision making on the part of government. For example, rules concerning entitlement programs can be changed; income-tax rates can be altered; major new defense-expenditure or public-works programs can be started.

Economists distinguish between two types of fiscal policy: **automatic stabilizer** and **discretionary fiscal policies.**

> *Automatic stabilizers are government spending or taxation actions that take place without any deliberate government control and that tend to dampen the business cycle.*

> *Discretionary fiscal policies are government spending and taxation actions that have been deliberately taken to achieve specified macroeconomic goals.*

Automatic Stabilizers

Consider an economy that is operating at full employment but is subjected to a disruptive cyclical disturbance caused by fluctuating investment. If investment declines, output falls below full-employment output (*f*), and a deflationary gap is created. If investment rises, output rises above *f,* and an inflationary gap is created. Will automatic fiscal stabilizers quickly and spontaneously eliminate these inflationary or deflationary gaps?

Two automatic stabilizers are built into most modern economies: 1) the tax system and 2) unemployment-compensation and welfare payments.

The Tax System. In most modern economies, income taxes typically rise and fall with income. If output is falling, taxes will fall as well.

1. *Budget of the U.S. Government,* Fiscal Year 1983, Table 17.

If, on average, 25 percent of personal income is taxed and personal income declines by $100 billion, personal taxes will decline by $25 billion. When the tax rate is 25 percent, a $100 billion fall in income, therefore, lowers disposable income by $75 billion, not by the full $100 billion. If the marginal propensity to consume out of disposable income is 0.75, consumption will fall by $56.25 billion (0.75 × $75 billion), not by $75 billion (0.75 × $100 billion). If income is rising, rising tax collections—in the same fashion—cut back on the increase in consumption spending.[2]

Unemployment Compensation and Other Welfare Payments.   If investment declined substantially, and the economy dropped well below full employment, more people would be unemployed and would apply for unemployment entitlement benefits. Moreover, families whose incomes have declined due to fewer hours of work or unemployment would become eligible for welfare assistance. Unemployment-compensation and increased welfare payments soften the fluctuation of the cycle by preventing consumption expenditures from falling as much as they would have if these programs had not been in effect. Unemployment-compensation and welfare programs also soften the business cycle on the upswing. Welfare recipients are taken off the welfare and unemployment-compensation rolls as they find jobs, and increased deductions from payrolls (to state and local programs and union unemployment funds) reduce the amount of disposable income going to employed workers.

There are two problems with relying exclusively on automatic stabilizers: 1) they don't eliminate fluctuations, and 2) they are counteracted by *automatic destabilizers*.

First, automatic stabilizers cannot fully neutralize the business cycle. If the economy is operating at full employment and investment falls by 20 percent, the automatic stabilizers will neutralize only a part of the decline in output. The effect of taxes will be to reduce the multiplier effect of the reduced investment. Unemployment compensation and other welfare payments will restore only a portion of lost disposable income. Second, not all automatic aspects of federal spending and taxation are stabilizing (cause the economy to soften the fluctuations of the business cycle). An important case in point is the **fiscal drag** of the U.S. progressive tax system, which, during periods of rapid inflation, pushes individuals into higher tax brackets. When prices are rising at the same rate as money income, real income is constant; yet the share of income being paid in federal income taxes is increasing due to the progressive tax rates because inflation pushes people into higher tax brackets. If real income is constant, yet the proportion of disposable income left over after taxes is falling, real disposable income is falling. Therefore, real consumption should fall. Thus, inflation is like an increase in tax rates when taxes are progressive and tax schedules aren't indexed for inflation.

Fiscal drag is the tendency for progressive taxes to act as an automatic destabilizer. If inflation accompanies excessive unemployment, progressive taxes lead to automatic destabilizing increases in taxes.[3]

Discretionary Fiscal Policy

Because automatic stabilizers can only ameliorate cyclical instability—not eliminate it—the

---

2.   When taxes are a fixed proportion of income, the expenditure multiplier formula changes from the previous chapter's formulation. Now:

$$C = a + MPC \times (1 - t) \times Y,$$

where t denotes the proportion of income that is paid in taxes, and tY equals the tax collected.

Substituting this consumption function into $Y = C + I + G$ yields an expenditure multiplier of:

$$\text{expenditure multiplier} = 1/[1 - MPC \times (1 - t)]$$

With an MPC of 0.75 and a t of 0.2, the inclusion of t causes the expenditure multiplier to drop from 4 to 2.5. Thus, taxes act as automatic stabilizers to reduce the effect on output of autonomous changes in aggregate expenditures.

3.   An earlier version of fiscal drag formulated in the late 1950s expressed the concern that a proportional tax system would act as a *drag* on the economy—keeping it at less than full employment. Taxes would rise automatically with income, but there was no similar automatic force causing government spending to rise at the same rate. With taxes rising faster than government spending, drag would be placed upon aggregate expenditures.

Today there is less concern that government spending will fail to keep up with government tax collection.

Unemployment Compensation and Welfare Payments as Automatic Stabilizers

One of the most important automatic stabilizers is the system of unemployment compensation and welfare payments. The accompanying table relates the magnitude of unemployment to the amounts of transfer payments (in 1981 dollars) made by federal, state, and local government. The table shows that these payments tend to rise with the unemployment rate.

These numbers suggest the importance of unemployment compensation and general transfer payments as automatic stabilizers in our economy. Between 1970 and 1975, for example, the unemployment rate rose from 4.9 percent to 8.5 percent while transfer payments nearly doubled in constant dollars. Notice particularly how unemployment compensation varies substantially as the unemployment rate changes.   ✕

Source: *Economic Report of the President,* January 1982, pp. 236, 271, 274, 321, 322.

Year	Unemployment Rate (percent)	Transfer Payments (billions of 1981 dollars)		
		Federal Transfer Payments	State and Local Transfer Payments	Unemployment Compensation
1960	5.5	63.3	16.6	9.2
1965	4.5	74.7	19.2	6.3
1970	4.9	158.5	42.4	12.1
1975	8.5	295.1	55.2	37.7
1980	7.1	259.0	42.9	19.1

proponents of activist macroeconomic policies believe discretionary fiscal policy must play an important role. The aim of discretionary fiscal policy is to eliminate inflationary and deflationary gaps. The direction of activist discretionary fiscal policy is fairly obvious: *discretionary fiscal policy should change government spending and government taxes to close inflationary or deflationary gaps.* If an inflationary gap is present (after the automatic stabilizers have had their effect), government should cut government spending or raise taxes. If a deflationary gap is present, the government should raise spending or cut taxes to raise output.

The two main tools of discretionary fiscal policy are: 1) changes in tax rates and 2) discretionary changes in the level of government expenditures.

If there are no changes in tax rates, tax collections will act as automatic stabilizers. They will fall as income falls; they will rise as income rises. But automatic tax stabilizers (as demonstrated above) cannot completely wipe out the effects of changing income. Government tax authorities can, however, raise or lower tax rates (the percentage of income paid as taxes) to further soften the fluctuation of the cycle. If output is falling below full-employment output, automatic tax stabilizers will only reduce the magnitude of the decline in output. But if the government lowers the tax rate, the decline in disposable income can be *fully* counteracted. As the tax rate is lowered, the *AE* curve shifts upward, and output starts to rise.

As output falls in response to cyclical pressures, the government could raise its expenditures above and beyond the increases called for by the automatic stabilizers (such as unemployment compensation and welfare programs). The government could spend money on relatively controllable programs like dams, public parks, increased police protection, and the like and thereby create more jobs and more disposable income. The government could liberalize unemployment compensation rules and change eligibility requirements for the receipt of welfare checks, thereby raising the incomes of the unemployed and the poor. Discretionary increases in government spending act through the expenditure multiplier explained in the previous chapter.

Because many government taxes and expenditures respond automatically to changes in GNP, the direction of discretionary fiscal policy cannot be gauged simply by looking at government spending, taxes, and the government surplus or deficit. During periods of declining GNP, the government surplus tends to narrow automatically (or the government deficit tends to become even more negative). As income falls, so do tax collections. But government obligations in the form of unemployment-compensation payments and welfare transfers rise as income falls. Therefore, the automatic stabilizers automatically push the government budget in the direction of deficits. For example, budget projections made by the Reagan administration in the 1982 budget message predict a 1986 deficit of $131 billion if economic growth is slow and inflation is high and a balanced budget if growth is rapid and inflation is low.[4] To measure discretionary fiscal policy, the effects of automatic stabilizers must be removed from government revenues and expenditures. The device economists use to measure discretionary fiscal policy is called the **full-employment surplus (deficit).**

*The **full-employment surplus (deficit)** is what the government budget surplus or deficit would have been had the economy been operating at full employment.*

To illustrate, assume that the full-employment unemployment rate is 5 percent and that the economy is operating at 8 percent unemployment. Because the economy is 3 percentage points below full employment, the government must make substantial payments for welfare and unemployment compensation and it will collect fewer taxes. The actual budget deficit (actual revenues minus actual expenditures) is $40 billion, but at full employment revenues would have been $15 billion more and expenditures would have been $10 billion

4. *Budget of the U.S. Government,* Fiscal Year 1983, p. 2–11.

less. The full-employment deficit, therefore, is $15 billion ($40 − $15 − $10)—a deficit much smaller than the actual deficit.

Full-employment budget figures do not have an exact meaning for a single year, but when compared with the full-employment budget for other years, they should indicate the direction of government discretionary fiscal policy. Figure 6 supplies data on the actual government budget and the full-employment budget from 1950 to 1980. Since there are difficulties associated with defining full-employment output, these figures must be regarded as somewhat arbitrary. Many economists and government officials regard them as quite useful despite their arbitrary element, however.

Discretionary fiscal policy was highly touted by the Keynesian model as a weapon for dealing with inflationary and especially deflationary gaps. Keynes feared that monetary policy would not be effective with vast unemployed resources. Automatic built-in stabilizers would ameliorate business cycles but would not eliminate them. In Keynes' view, discretionary fiscal policy would have to carry the heaviest load in the conduct of activist policies. But discretionary fiscal policy is complicated by a number of factors that threaten its effectiveness.

Lags in Fiscal Policy.   Changes in taxation and government spending must be approved by Congress and supported by the President. Changes in tax policies and revisions in tax codes often take several years or more between their inception and enactment. Public-works programs must be approved by Congress, and they are often handled on a case-by-case basis. Often logrolling overrides considerations of macroeconomic stabilization policy. There are actually two fiscal-policy lags: a *recognition lag* and an *implementation lag.* Congress and the President may be slow in recognizing that a change in fiscal policy is necessary. Reliable statistics on real output become available only six months after the fact. No one knows for sure whether a downturn is temporary or the start of a serious downtrend. It is difficult to recognize when a change in fiscal policy is required. After this recognition lag comes the implementation lag—by the time the program goes through Congress and becomes implemented, the

Figure 6
**The Actual Budget versus the Full-Employment Budget of the United States,
1950–1980**

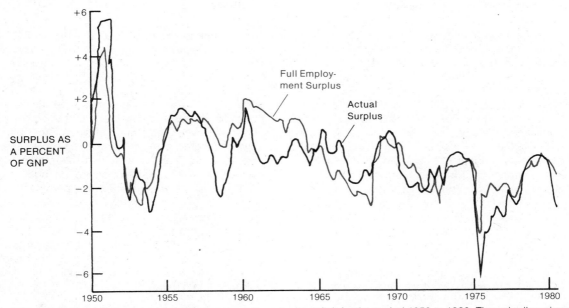

The black line shows the actual federal government surplus or deficit for the period 1950 to 1980. The color line gives the full-employment surplus or deficit for the same years. The full-employment budget should reveal changes in discretionary fiscal policy over this period.

Source: Robert J. Gordon, *Macroeconomics,* 2nd ed. (Boston: Little, Brown & Co., 1981), Appendix B; *Economic Report of the President,* January 1981, p. 157.

policy may no longer be the correct one. Critics of activist fiscal policy ask whether a country can carry out effective discretionary fiscal policy when such enormous time lags and political delays are involved.

Crowding Out. The effects of discretionary increases in government spending are also complicated by *crowding-out* effects. Increases in government spending on schools, public transportation, public hospitals, and universities may cause private spending to decline. If increased government services substitute for private services that the public previously purchased out of its own pockets, reduced private spending will blunt the intended effect of increased government spending. Such a phenomenon is called **direct crowding out.** If the reduction in private spending equals the increase in public spending, *complete crowding out* is said to occur.

Direct crowding out occurs when increased government spending substitutes for privately purchased goods and services and causes a compensating reduction in private spending.

Increased government spending raises incomes and increases the demand for money. If the supply of money is unchanged, interest rates can rise to choke off some private investment spending. The Fed is in a position to limit this **indirect crowding out** by raising the money supply to prevent a tightening of credit from raising interest rates. Thus, the amount of indirect crowding out depends upon whether the monetary authorities hold the money supply constant or pursue an accommodating monetary policy.

Indirect crowding out occurs when increased government spending raises interest rates and causes autonomous spending elsewhere in the economy to decrease.

Example 3

The 1968 Tax Increase and the 1975 Tax Cut

Since the 1964 tax cut (to be discussed in a later chapter), there have been three major discretionary tax changes. In 1968, a one-year 10 percent tax surcharge was imposed in an attempt to slow down the inflationary pressures brought on by the Vietnam conflict. In 1975, the Tax Reduction Act (passed during the deep recession of 1975) gave a one-time rebate on 1974 taxes of about $8 billion and a further one-year reduction in personal income taxes of about $12 billion. In addition, a one-time payment of $50 was paid to each social-security recipient. The tax cut passed in 1981 to go into effect in 1982 and thereafter is the third major use of discretionary tax policy.

Most economists who have studied the 1968 and 1975 tax changes (such as Robert Eisner and Alan Blinder) have concluded that the impacts of these tax changes on the economy were relatively small. In both instances, it was made explicit that the tax change was to be limited to a one-year tax increase (1968) and one-year tax reduction (1975). As a consequence, even though personal disposable income was changed by the tax change, the amount of response of consumer spending was minimal. The most convincing explanation for the failure of the 1968 tax surcharge and the 1975 tax reduction to have a larger effect on the economy is that their impacts on permanent income were likely very small. The public was aware that these were one-shot changes that would have virtually no effect on permanent income. Secure in this knowledge, consumer spending failed to respond as anticipated.

The effect of the tax cut passed in 1981 to go into effect in 1982 and later years remains to be seen and will depend upon whether or not people view this tax cut as changing significantly their permanent income.

Permanent Income. Discretionary tax policy is also complicated by *permanent-income effects*. Tax cuts affect aggregate demand only if lower tax payments cause the consumption/income curve to shift up. As long as the marginal propensity to consume *(MPC)* remains stable, tax-induced changes in disposable income should elicit predictable changes in consumption. But how stable is the consumption/income relationship? Keynes felt it would be one of the most stable relationships in the whole economy, but economists after Keynes have come to question this proposition.

Some modern economists argue that people tend to base their consumption decisions on life-cycle or **permanent income,** not on transitory changes in current income.

Permanent income is an average of the income that an individual anticipates earning over the long run.

If there is a transitory change in this year's income—say, due to a tax increase that is generally regarded as a one-shot affair—the effect on current consumption will be minimal. The impact of the tax on long-run income is so small that few people change their current consumption.

If people do indeed base their spending upon permanent income, the relationship between this year's income and this year's consumption can be quite unstable. This instability means the *MPC* and, hence, the tax multiplier cannot be known in advance. Discretionary tax policy is difficult to pursue if its effects on private spending are unknown.

THE PUBLIC DEBT

The proponents of activist fiscal policy maintain that government expenditures and taxes should be set in order to induce the economy to produce at full employment. If budget deficits (or surpluses) are required to raise output to full employment, then these budget deficits (or surpluses) are a small price to pay for full employment. The actual size of the government surplus or deficit is not crucial. The budget surplus or deficit should not be allowed to stand in the way of important macroeconomic goals.

According to this budgetary philosophy, it would be very unwise to adopt the goal of a balanced federal budget. If the economy is experiencing a cyclical disturbance (say, a reduction in private investment) that causes output to fall below full employment, as output declines, so do tax revenues. Therefore, to balance the budget, government expenditures must be reduced by the amount of the reduction in tax collections. But because of the balanced-budget multiplier (Chapter 10), equivalent reductions in taxes and government spending will cause a reduction of income by the amount of the reduction in government spending. To pursue a balanced budget during a cyclical downturn will only make the downturn more pronounced. A balanced-budget policy will also intensify inflationary cyclical upturns. A balanced budget requires that government expenditures rise with the increase in taxes; therefore, income will increase by the amount of the increase in government spending (the balanced-budget multiplier again).

The Keynesian philosophy can lead to budget deficits and, therefore, to growing public debt. Whenever there is a budget deficit, the government must borrow money by selling its IOUs (federal government bonds and bills). The outstanding amount owed by the federal government is the *national debt,* or the public debt.

The Classical Case for Balanced Budgets

The Keynesian argument against a strict balanced-budget rule was a substantial departure from the philosophy of the classical school. If, as the classical economists maintained, economies tend to operate at full employment, increases in government expenditures cannot raise real GNP. Rather, increased government spending pushes up interest rates and will be perfectly offset by an equivalent reduction in investment. This result is the extreme case of complete crowding out. Every extra dollar of government spending is matched by a dollar reduction in private investment.

In the classical view, government deficits, therefore, tend to increase government spending at the expense of investment. But economic growth in the long run will suffer if government spending crowds out investment. Lower rates of capital accumulation translate into lower rates of growth of real GNP in the long run. In the long run, growing government deficits can mean lower standards of living.

The crowding-out problem remains in the case of incomplete crowding out, in which government deficits choke off some private investment and reduce the capital stock available to the economy for long-run growth.

The Growth of Public Debt

In the early 1960s, economists and public officials almost unanimously embraced the income/expenditure budgetary philosophy. Balanced budgets were no longer regarded as desirable *per se;* instead, budgets were to be constructed to meet macroeconomic goals. The decline in popularity of the balanced-budget philosophy signaled an important triumph for the Keynesian revolution. In 1964, taxes were cut, and the deficit was deliberately increased to reduce unemployment.

It must be emphasized that the Keynesian income/expenditure budgetary approach does not necessarily support sustained deficits or surpluses. During periods of excessive unemployment, budget deficits would be called for, but budget surpluses would be required during inflationary upswings. Therefore, although there was no rule that the budget should be balanced each year, it was expected that budget surpluses and deficits would even out in the long run—especially if cyclical downturns would be of equal duration and magnitude as cyclical upturns.

As Figure 6 shows, the early expectation of a long-run balanced budget has not materialized. Since 1960, the federal budget has had only 2 years of surpluses and 20 years of deficits. In recent years public alarm over the growing size of the federal deficit has grown, setting off bitter political struggles. Annual deficits of more than $100 billion are being forecast for the near future. Deficits are still with us and are growing despite the campaign promises of the last two presidents to balance the budget.

The Burden of the Debt

Why are people so worried about the federal deficit? Are these concerns justified? There are

Figure 7
Public Debt as a Percent of GNP

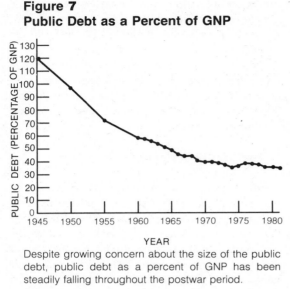

Despite growing concern about the size of the public debt, public debt as a percent of GNP has been steadily falling throughout the postwar period.

Source: *Statistical Abstract of the United States,* 1981, p. 245.

two main reasons for public concern: First, there is the growing belief that federal deficits are the prime cause of inflation. Second, there is the widely held belief that rising deficits will eventually bankrupt the country by building up a public debt that the country simply cannot afford. Even if bankruptcy is avoided, a heavy burden is placed on future generations who must eventually pay off this debt.

Chapter 13 will examine the link between inflation and budget deficits.

Figure 7 provides some facts on the public debt that shed light on the second concern. Whether the debt of the federal government is unreasonably large should be determined just like private debt. The person who goes to a bank to borrow money will be asked immediately what he or she earns and about existing liabilities. The borrower who reports an annual income of $100,000 and no outstanding debts will be able to borrow much more than the borrower reporting a $15,000 annual income with annual debt payments of $5,000. Debt must be judged relative to the ability of the debtor to pay the interest and principal on the debt.

What determines the U.S. government's ability to carry debt? Insofar as tax collections (the government's income) are closely tied to GNP, ulti-

mately the federal government's income depends upon the amount of GNP produced. Government tax receipts since 1960 have averaged around 20 percent of GNP; a GNP of $4 trillion in 1985 would give the federal government a 1985 income of $800 billion. A 1985 GNP of $3 trillion would give the government a smaller annual income of $600 billion. The amount of GNP produced now and in the future is a crucial determinant of the reasonableness of the national debt.

As Figure 7 indicates, public debt as a percentage of GNP has been declining since the end of World War II. In 1945, public debt was 1.2 times GNP. By 1981, the ratio of debt to GNP had fallen to 34.9 percent. If one compares these figures with the indebtedness of individuals, one can see that in 1980 the private debt of families (consumer installment credit plus mortgages) equaled about 80 percent of personal disposable income. On average, the American family has an accumulated personal debt equal to 80 percent of one year's income after taxes.

The burden of the public debt can also be measured by the proportion of current income that is devoted to paying interest and principal on the debt. In 1981, 10.9 percent of federal government revenues were devoted to interest payments on the national debt. For the average American family, approximately 6 percent of personal disposable income was devoted to interest payments on mortgages and consumer debt in the same year. In general, the burden of private debt appears to be less than that of national debt, but there are important reasons (discussed below) why the federal government can safely carry more debt relative to income than can private individuals.

In accumulating public debt, will the United States ever run the risk of bankruptcy? As long as GNP continues to grow at a rate as rapid or more rapid than the public debt, the burden of the debt will remain the same or decline. Therefore, a growing economy is the best protection against an increasing burden of the national debt.

Unlike private individuals, the federal government has a guarantee in addition to earning sufficient income that it will be able to handle the public debt. If the Fed is willing to cooperate, the federal government can finance the national debt by creating money! If the federal government runs a $50 billion deficit in a particular year, the U.S.

Treasury can either sell $50 billion of bonds to the public or can ask the Fed to buy $50 billion worth of bonds. The Fed does not have to finance the federal deficit by buying federal government securities, but if it does, the Fed will have pumped $50 billion worth of additional reserves into the economy. In other words, the federal government has financed its deficit by printing money. Individuals and corporations do not have this option for financing their debt; they are not able to create money. Only the federal government can do so.

Owners of Public Debt

In the early 1950s, only 5 percent of the national debt was owned by foreigners. By 1981, the proportion had risen to 14 percent. Whether debt is held internally or externally makes a difference. If the debt is *internal,* then the United States basically owes it to itself. When interest payments are made on the national debt or when a government bond matures, income is transferred from one U.S. citizen to another. The taxpayers' dollars are used to pay interest and principal to the owner of the government bond. Insofar as the recipient of interest and principal payments is typically a taxpayer as well, the net transfer of income may be small. In the case of an internal debt, servicing the debt does not alter the amount of income in the country; it affects only the distribution of that income between public-debt owners and nonowners.

An *external* debt works differently: interest and principal payments represent transfers of income from U.S. taxpayers to residents of other countries. The amount of income left in the country is affected by this type of transaction. Foreign ownership of the national debt has increased so much over the years for many reasons: The United States has come to be regarded as a safe haven by foreign investors. In recent years, U.S. interest rates have been higher than elsewhere. Moreover, most of the world's trade is conducted in dollars, making investments in U.S. bonds a normal business activity.

Problems with Public Debt

The fact that the U.S. government is not about to be bankrupted by rising public debt does not mean that there are no negative consequences of public debt.

Economists generally worry that a large public debt could lead a myopic population to save less and, hence, in the long run, would lead to less capital accumulation. Chapter 9 argued that an increase in assets held by the public could increase consumption and reduce saving. People who have already accumulated wealth do not have to save as much. The public debt is an asset to those who hold the IOUs, but it is a liability to future generations. If the present generation does not fully recognize the taxes that they must ultimately pay to carry this debt, the public could spend more and save less than otherwise. In other words, the public debt might be treated as net wealth—even though it is not. In a long-run full-employment setting, a smaller capital stock is available for future generations. Empirical evidence on this effect is not decisive.

The way the national debt is financed can have an important effect on the money supply. By selling federal government bonds to the Fed, the supply of money increases. If the money supply is increased at too rapid a rate in order to finance the national debt, inflation will be exacerbated.

The last three chapters have explained Keynesian macroeconomics. Modern macroeconomics uses the Keynesian income/expenditure model as the demand side of a more complete story that explains both prices and output. The next chapter brings together aggregate demand and aggregate supply from a modern perspective.

Summary

1. At less than full employment, Keynes believed real GNP can increase without an increase in the price level.
2. The Keynesian aggregate supply curve is horizontal up to full-employment output and vertical at full-employment output.
3. Keynes advocated activist policy to eliminate deflationary and inflationary gaps. An inflationary gap exists when actual output exceeds full-employment output. A deflationary gap exists when actual output is below full-em-

ployment output. Rising prices will eventually eliminate inflationary gaps.

4. Monetary policy is the control of the money supply to achieve macroeconomic goals. The income/expenditure model suggests an indirect link between the money supply and output. Changes in money supply affect interest rates; changes in interest rates affect investment; changes in investment affect desired aggregate expenditures. If the link is broken at any point in this chain, monetary policy will be ineffective. Rigid interest-rate targets tend to destabilize the economy since monetary aggregates then become the slave of the interest-rate target. In 1979, the Fed decided to pay primary attention to monetary aggregates in its conduct of monetary policy. Credit rationing is another tool of monetary policy; it works by restricting the volume of loans rather than through interest rates.

5. Fiscal policy is the use of government spending and tax policy to achieve macroeconomic goals. Keynes felt that monetary policy would be ineffective in pulling economies out of depressions and deep recessions. He, therefore, argued that primary reliance would have to be placed upon fiscal policy. Many government spending and taxation actions are automatic and require no discretionary decisions. Such automatic built-in stabilizers are the progressive tax system, unemployment compensation, and welfare payments. Automatic stabilizers can reduce the effects of business cycles but cannot eliminate cycles. Some automatic fiscal policies—like progressive taxation—can actually be destabilizing. Discretionary fiscal policy is measured by the full-employment surplus. Problems with discretionary fiscal policy include recognition and implementation lags, crowding-out effects, and permanent-income effects. The income/expenditure model does not require a balanced budget. Government spending and taxation actions should be geared to combating the business cycle. In the long run, surpluses and deficits may cancel each other. The classical school argued in favor of balanced budgets because they believed budget deficits would crowd out private investment and, thus, reduce long-term economic growth.

6. The federal government is in little danger of bankruptcy. Over the past 25 years, the burden of the national debt has fallen—as measured by the ratio of debt to GNP. The true burden of the national debt is that it could lead to less capital accumulation and to more inflation if the debt is purchased by the Fed.

Key Terms

inflationary gap
deflationary gap
monetary policy
fiscal policy
liquidity-preference theory
credit rationing
automatic stabilizers
discretionary fiscal policies
fiscal drag
full-employment surplus (deficit)
direct crowding out
indirect crowding out
permanent income

Questions and Problems

1. Contrast the Keynesian view of how money affects output and employment with that of the monetarists. Does this difference in opinion have any effect on the conduct of macroeconomic policy?
2. In the simple Keynesian model, when the Fed increases the money supply interest rates are expected to drop. Explain why this drop may not occur in the real world.
3. Explain the difference between the way money supply control and credit rationing affect output and employment.
4. This chapter emphasized the Fed's decision in October 1979 to control money aggregates rather than interest rates. Why was the earlier policy of controlling interest rates destabilizing?
5. ''If wages and prices are flexible in both inflationary and deflationary gaps, there is no

need for activist macroeconomic policy.''
Evaluate this statement.

6. What is the difference between automatic
stabilizers and discretionary fiscal policy?
Are they not the same because they both
work through government spending and
taxes?

7. If actual government expenditures are $200
billion and actual government revenues are
$100 billion, and if the economy is at less
than full employment, would the full employment budget show a larger or smaller
deficit than the actual budget? Explain.

8. Explain the distinction between direct
crowding out and indirect crowding out.
Why is crowding out important to the debate over activist policy?

9. Contrast the Keynesian position on balanced
budgets with that of the classical school.

10. Explain why the U.S. government can afford to carry a heavier debt burden than private individuals.

CHAPTER

12

Aggregate Demand and Aggregate Supply

Chapter Preview

This chapter brings together the demand side and the supply side of macroeconomics to study the relationships between real output, the price level, and unemployment.

Keynes studied a depression economy—an economy operating with a stable price level and large quantities of underutilized resources. In such an economy, Keynes concluded that policymakers should focus on the demand side of the economy: if aggregate expenditures could be increased, idle resources could be brought into use, and real GNP and employment could be increased without prices being driven up. Aggregate supply

was of little concern to the depression economy; the existence of idle resources meant that increases in aggregate expenditures would bring about increases in real output. For this reason, Keynesian economics has come to be called *demand-side economics*.

This chapter analyzes aggregate supply under more general conditions than those assumed by Keynes. This chapter assumes that prices could rise before the economy reaches full employment, that in general prices are more flexible than they would be in a depression economy. This chapter examines the relationship between real output, unemployment, and the price level in a world of flexible prices—a key issue of modern macroeconomics.

THE AGGREGATE DEMAND CURVE

The concept of an **aggregate demand schedule** was introduced briefly in Chapter 5. Its shape was derived from the crude quantity theory described in Chapter 7. Knowledge of how equilibrium output is determined can be used to define the aggregate demand schedule in a more exact fashion.

*The **aggregate demand schedule** shows the equilibrium aggregate expenditures at different price levels, holding the nominal money supply, tax rates, and real government expenditures constant. In other words, for any given price level, the aggregate demand schedule shows the level of income where desired expenditures and actual income are equal.*

The income/expenditure model of Keynes can be used to determine what the economy's aggregate demand curve looks like.

Although the aggregate demand curve follows from the Keynesian model of equilibrium output determination, there is a clear distinction between the aggregate demand curve and the aggregate expenditure curve.

*The **aggregate expenditure** (AE) **curve shows** desired aggregate expenditures **at each level of income**. The aggregate demand (AD) curve shows equilibrium aggregate expenditures **at each price level**.*

As noted in Chapter 5, one cannot argue by analogy to single markets that aggregate demand will fall as the price level rises due to the law of demand because the law of demand depends upon relative prices, not price-level changes. The income/expenditure model identifies two major factors that cause equilibrium output to decline as the actual (not expected) price level changes: the real-balance effect and the interest-rate effect.

The Real-Balance Effect

As the price level rises, the purchasing power of a constant nominal money supply falls. When prices fall, the purchasing power of a constant money supply rises. The effect of this change in purchasing power is called the **real-balance effect**.

*The **real-balance effect** occurs when desired real consumption at each income level declines as price increases cut the purchasing power of a given money supply. Similarly, price-level reductions stimulate consumption.*

The real-balance effect shifts the AE curve. As the price level rises, consumers desire to spend less on real consumption at each level of income. As the price level falls, the AE curve shifts up.

The Interest-Rate Effect

As the price level rises, the demand for credit increases. When the cost of goods and services financed by credit—cars, plants, equipment, inventories—rises, businesses and households must borrow more. The increased demand for credit causes interest rates to rise, and the higher interest rates discourage business investment. The **interest-rate effect** shifts the AE curve. As prices rise, interest rates rise, and real investment declines. The aggregate expenditure curve shifts down as investment declines.

*The **interest-rate effect** occurs when rising interest rates discourage investment expenditures as rising prices increase the demand for credit, given the money supply.*

Because of the real-balance effect and the interest-rate effect, the aggregate demand for real goods and services will decline as the price level rises. When monetary and fiscal policy are constant, a once-and-for-all increase in the price level reduces aggregate expenditures because of reductions in desired consumption and desired investment. As the AE curve shifts down, equilibrium output falls. Because *higher* prices mean a *smaller* aggregate demand for goods and services, the aggregate demand curve has a negative slope.

Figure 1 shows how the aggregate demand curve is related to the AE curve. As the price level changes, AE shifts, and a new equilibrium output is established. The aggregate demand

Figure 1
Aggregate Expenditures and Aggregate Demand

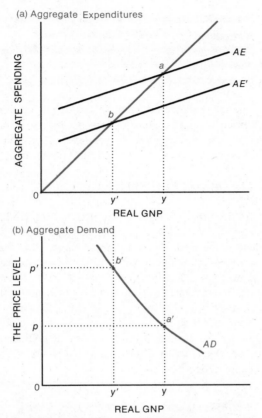

(a) Aggregate Expenditures

(b) Aggregate Demand

At the fixed price level, *p*, the aggregate expenditure curve is *AE*, and the level of equilibrium output is *y*. When the price level increases to *p'*, people reduce real consumption spending, and higher interest rates reduce the amount of real investment. Thus, at *p'*, desired aggregate expenditures shift down to *AE'*, and a new lower real GNP is established at *y'*.

In panel (b), the price level is plotted on the vertical axis, and equilibrium real GNP is plotted on the horizontal axis. Points *y* and *y'* correspond to two points on the aggregate demand curve, which is negatively sloped. Other points can also be found by determining the equilibrium output at various price levels.

curve graphs all the combinations of price levels and equilibrium output levels.

Monetary and Fiscal Policy

Chapter 11 showed how monetary policy affects the level of aggregate expenditures through

Figure 2
Shifts in Aggregate Demand

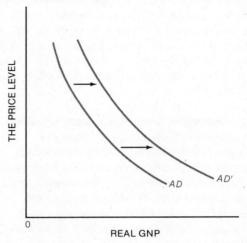

If real government expenditures are raised, if tax rates are lowered, or if the nominal money supply is increased, the desired expenditure curve will shift up, and the aggregate demand curve will shift to the right (from *AD* to *AD'*). Aggregate demand will also increase when people become less thrifty, or when foreign demand for domestic products increases.

interest rates and credit rationing and how government spending and tax policy are determined through fiscal policy.

Monetary and fiscal policy are factors that change the level of aggregate spending. If either monetary or fiscal policy changes, the aggregate demand curve will shift.

A given aggregate demand curve is drawn with both fiscal policy and monetary policy held constant (see Figure 2). Along this aggregate demand curve, real government expenditures, tax rates, and the nominal supply of money are held constant. If there is a change in fiscal or monetary policy, the *AD* curve will shift. For example, if real government expenditures are increased or tax rates are lowered, the *AE* curve will shift up, establishing a new and higher equilibrium aggregate expenditure. Expansionary monetary policy will also shift up the *AE* curve and raise equilibrium aggregate expenditures. An upward shift in the aggregate expenditure curve, in the absence of a change in the price level, will shift the *AD* curve to the right (to *AD'* in Figure 2). When expansionary monetary and fiscal policy cause increases in aggregate demand, the *AD* curve shifts to the right because more real output is demanded at the same price level as before. Contractionary monetary and fiscal policy shift the *AD* curve to the left.

Monetary and fiscal policy are the two main discretionary factors that cause aggregate demand to increase or decrease, but private behavior can also shift the *AD* curve. Changes in attitudes towards thrift, changes in expectations, increases in foreign demand for goods produced in this country, and other kinds of private behavior can alter private consumption, investment, or net exports, and thereby affect aggregate demand and equilibrium output.

THE AGGREGATE SUPPLY CURVE

The **aggregate supply schedule** and the aggregate demand schedule determine the equilibrium real GNP/price level combination, or **macroeconomic equilibrium**.

*An **aggregate supply schedule** shows the quantities of real output the economy is prepared to supply at different price levels,* ceteris paribus.

Macroeconomic equilibrium occurs at that price level at which aggregate demand and aggregate supply are equal.

If the economy were to attempt to settle at a macroeconomic equilibrium at which the aggregate quantity demanded exceeded the aggregate quantity supplied, output would increase. If the economy tried to settle at a macroeconomic equilibrium at which the aggregate quantity demanded fell short of the aggregate quantity supplied, output would fall. Such adjustments would take place until the economy settled at a macroeconomic equilibrium where aggregate quantity demanded equaled aggregate quantity supplied.

The Keynesian Equilibrium

Figure 3 combines the aggregate demand curve of Figure 1 with the Keynesian *L*-shaped aggre-

Figure 3
Equilibrium of Keynesian Aggregate Supply and Aggregate Demand

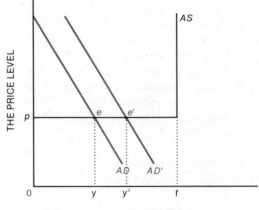

This graph brings together the aggregate demand curve of Figure 1 and the L-shaped Keynesian aggregate supply curve. Equilibrium occurs at point *e*. Point *e* represents an equilibrium at less than full employment and illustrates the Keynesian case of an economy in a depression. If aggregate demand were to increase (shift from *AD* to *AD'*), real GNP and employment could be increased without an increase in prices. This example illustrates why Keynes concentrated on aggregate demand. Under these circumstances, the full multiplier effect holds.

gate supply curve introduced in the preceding chapter. The Keynesian aggregate supply curve is *L*-shaped because prices do not fall when output is below full employment; only when aggregate expenditures exceed full-employment output *(f)* will prices rise. Real GNP *(Y)* and the price level *(P)* are established at the intersection of the aggregate demand and aggregate supply curves.

In Figure 3, macroeconomic equilibrium occurs at point *e*. At any other price level/real GNP combination, aggregate demand would not equal aggregate supply. In Figure 3, equilibrium output *(y)* is less than full-employment output *(f)*, as would be true of an economy with unemployed resources.

Activist Policy with Unemployment

In a situation like the one depicted in Figure 3, the classical quantity theorists felt that automatic forces (falling wages and prices) would restore full employment and that the government should do nothing. Keynes concluded from the experience of the Great Depression that such faith in market forces was misguided. He felt that the government should be responsible for moving the economy to full employment by increasing aggregate demand.

Because the aggregate supply curve in Figure 3 is horizontal at output levels below full-employment output, an increase in aggregate demand (from *AD* to *AD'*) will increase real GNP without increasing the price level. As real output expands, so will employment.

MODERN VIEWS OF AGGREGATE SUPPLY

The simple Keynesian model is based upon an *L*-shaped aggregate supply curve—one that is horizontal until a unique full-employment output is reached and vertical thereafter. In the Keynesian view, as aggregate demand increases, prices should remain stable until full employment is reached. Beyond this point, further increases in aggregate demand would not yield more real output—only higher prices.

Contemporary economists agree that modern economies are not limited to a unique maximum rate of output. Individuals have freedom of choice of employment and of hours worked; some people have a stronger attachment to the labor force than others. More people can be attracted into the labor force or into working longer hours if appropriate incentives are offered. Economies can usually choose to produce more output. There really is not a unique upper limit beyond which the economy cannot expand due to the full employment of the labor force.

Money Illusion

Economists have tended to believe that rational consumers and firms are not subject to **money illusion**.

*Economic decision makers are subject to the **money illusion** when a proportionate change in all money prices and money wages tricks them into thinking real wages or relative prices have changed.*

If economic actors are not subject to the money illusion, changes in the price level that leave relative prices unchanged should not affect output or employment decisions. For example, suppose a worker's *money* wage is rising by 10 percent while consumer prices are also rising by 10 percent. The worker's *real* wage has not been altered by the 10 percent increase in the money wage. If this worker is not subject to the money illusion, this worker's real behavior—purchases of goods and services, offerings of labor services to employers—will not change as a consequence of the money wage increase. The worker will not increase total purchases or work longer hours. The worker will know that real purchasing power has not changed and that real wages have not risen.

Business firms that are not fooled by the money illusion will not change their behavior if money prices rise, either. Suppose shoe prices are rising 10 percent per year, while the shoe-manufacturing firm's input prices—leather, electricity, money wages—are also rising 10 percent per year. If the manufacturer is not subject to the money illusion, its real behavior—number of shoes produced, number of workers hired—should not change.

When Chapter 5 first introduced the aggregate supply curve, it was drawn with an upward slope on the assumption that business firms supply more goods and services at higher price levels. In the discussion of the classical quantity theory in Chapter 7, the aggregate supply curve was drawn as a vertical line on the assumption that money prices should not affect real economic activity because economic actors are not subject to the money illusion. As long as money prices, input prices, and money wages all rise at the same rate with a rising price level, higher money prices should not call forth more real output.

The vertical classical supply curve, in effect, assumes that inflation (a rising price level) has no real effects on the economy. Modern economists, however, have come to recognize that inflation can change the output decisions of business firms and the employment decisions of individuals. The next section will explore modern views of the effects of the price level on the aggregate supply of real goods and services in an attempt to answer the question: How can a higher price level bring about more real output if people are generally not subject to the money illusion?

The Natural Rate of Unemployment

Macroeconomics groups together many sectors of the economy, but the composition of the economy is in a constant state of flux. Some industries are expanding; others are contracting. The labor force is being shuffled from industry to industry and from job to job. In a fully static economy, the full-employment level of output would be that level of employment at which each and every worker would be allocated to his or her best job; unemployment would be essentially zero. Zero unemployment, however, is a fiction in a complicated dynamic economic system. Within the aggregates of consumption, investment, government spending, exports and imports, there is constant change. As a result, there will always be some frictional unemployment (job changing) and some structurally unemployed workers (moving from contracting to expanding industries). There is a constant search for new workers and new jobs.

One can determine the **natural rate of unemployment** by comparing at any given time the number of unfilled jobs (vacancies) with the number of unemployed workers.

*The **natural rate of unemployment** is that rate at which the number of unfilled jobs or vacancies equals the number of unemployed workers in the economy.*

''Natural'' unemployment arises from the inevitable frictions that characterize complicated labor markets in which people are constantly looking for jobs and firms are constantly looking for workers.

In the labor market, wages will behave differently at different rates of unemployment. When the unemployment rate exceeds the natural rate of unemployment—when the number of people looking for work exceeds the number of unfilled jobs—the current rate of wage increase or inflation (on average) will tend to fall. When the unemployment rate falls short of the natural rate—when the number of unfilled jobs exceeds the number of people looking for work—the current rate of wage increase or inflation (on the average) will tend to rise.

The behavior of wages depends on the momentum of wages and prices. First, suppose there is zero wage or price inflation and that the economy is at the natural unemployment rate. Wages and prices have been steady for some time, and everyone expects them to remain stable in the future. For purposes of illustration, assume the unemployment rate of 5 percent is the natural rate. If the unemployment rate were to rise above 5 percent, wages would begin to fall; if the rate of unemployment were to fall below 5 percent, wages would begin to rise. Only at 5 percent would wages remain stable. Next, suppose wages have been rising steadily at 10 percent per annum for a number of years. The natural rate of 5 percent would be that rate at which this rate of wage inflation would continue. If unemployment rose above 5 percent, the rate of wage inflation would decelerate below 10 percent. If unemployment fell below 5 percent, inflation would accelerate above 10 percent.

Natural Real GNP

Corresponding to the natural rate of unemployment is a **natural level of real GNP (y_n).**

*The **natural level of real GNP** (y_n) is the output produced when the economy is operating at the natural rate of unemployment.*

At output levels above the natural rate y_n, the unemployment rate will be below the natural rate of unemployment; wage inflation will accelerate and price increases will accelerate. If output is below natural output, the unemployment rate will be above the natural rate; wage and price inflation will decelerate.

Consider an economy where prices have been holding steady for a number of years, where the economy is at the natural rate of unemployment, and where the real output corresponding to the natural rate is $3 trillion. If output rose above $3 trillion, prices would rise. If output fell below $3 trillion, prices would fall. Only at the natural output level would prices remain stable.[1]

---

1. There is no assurance of symmetrical behavior of prices for outputs above or below y_n. If output rises above natural output, prices may rise rapidly. If output falls below natural output by the same amount, the fall in prices may be small.

Aggregate Supply in the Short Run

The aggregate supply curve *(AS)* shows the real GNP that business firms supply at different price levels, holding constant the expected price level, the resources available to the economy, and the efficiency with which the resources are used. In the short run, the most important condition that the aggregate supply curve holds constant is the expected price level. If inflation is expected to be 10 percent, a worker may be satisfied with a one-year wage of $31,500. If the worker expected no inflation, he or she might agree to a $30,000 wage over the next year. Expected prices, thus, condition the wage bargains between employers and employees. The higher are expected prices, the higher are business costs. In the **natural-rate hypothesis,** modern macroeconomists make the assumption that the relationship between expected and actual prices determines whether output exceeds or equals the natural level of real GNP.

> The **natural-rate hypothesis** *is that prices must be higher than expected for output to exceed the natural output level and that prices must be lower than expected for output to be below the natural output level.*

Figure 4 shows the aggregate supply curve, AS_{100}, drawn holding the expected price level constant at 100. According to the natural-rate hypothesis, the AS_{100} curve must intersect the vertical line denoting the natural level of output, y_n, at the price level 100.

Whether or not firms increase their output as the price level rises unexpectedly from 100 to 105 depends upon their *perception* of the relationship between their selling prices and their costs. If selling prices rise more rapidly than costs (or even if firms only think this is happening), firms will increase production. If selling prices and costs rise at the same rate, firms will have no incentive to produce more.

Actual output can rise above y_n (by definition) only if the actual unemployment rate falls below the natural unemployment rate. When unanticipated inflation occurs, some workers are on contracts that stipulate fixed money wages. Other contracts may have been written with a lower in-

Figure 4
The Short-Run Aggregate Supply Curve

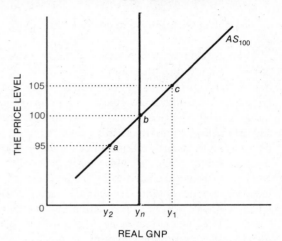

The aggregate supply curve AS_{100} is based on the expected price level of 100. The natural-rate hypothesis requires that when the actual price level is the same as the one expected, output equals the natural level, y_n. Hence, AS_{100} intersects the vertical line denoting y_n at the price level of 100. If inflation rises to a level higher than anticipated—say, to a price level of 105—output rises to y_1. Unanticipated inflation stimulates output because prices of products rise faster than producing firms' costs. When prices fall more than anticipated—say, from 100 to 95—output falls to y_2. Unanticipated deflation discourages output because prices of products fall slower than producing firms' costs.

flation rate in mind. Firms may have negotiated to purchase material inputs at prices that do not escalate as fast as their selling prices. As long as some fixity in input costs is present, selling prices rise faster than costs, and production is raised as business profitability improves.

Individuals and businesses may be fooled by the unanticipated inflation. People who are out of work and looking for jobs will find that wages are rising beyond their expectations and will be tempted to accept the next job offer. Firms may begin to overestimate the tightness of the labor market and become more hesitant to fire or lay off workers. Firms may lower their requirements on worker quality and step up their hiring. The rise in employment is the other side of the coin of increasing output. Unemployment falls below the natural rate when output rises above the natural level. Thus, the aggregate supply curve to the

Example 1

Variable Mortgages: A Protection Against Unanticipated Inflation

Lending institutions that make long-term home-mortgage loans can be hard hit by unanticipated inflation. If a savings and loan makes a 25-year mortgage at 10 percent interest—anticipating a 5 percent rate of inflation—and inflation unexpectedly and permanently accelerates to 10 percent, it has in effect transferred its wealth to its borrowers.

In the 1950s and 1960s when inflation rates were fairly steady (and low by today's standards), lending institutions were reasonably confident that long-term inflation would stay steady. Mortgage companies were willing to make long-term loans at fixed rates of interest. After the roller-coaster inflation rates of the 1970s and 1980s, mortgage companies were left with a large volume of long-term, fixed, low-interest loans outstanding. As a consequence of this bitter lesson, they came up with a new way to protect themselves from unanticipated inflation: the variable-interest mortgage. The variable interest mortgage has an interest rate that rises and falls with the general level of interest rates in the economy. During periods of rising inflation, interest rates tend to rise. Thus, the mortgage interest rate rises with other interest rates (within certain limits). During periods of falling inflation, interest rates tend to decline. The variable-interest-mortgage interest rate will, therefore, decline with generally declining interest rates (within certain limits). In this way, mortgage lenders have learned to protect themselves from unanticipated inflation. ✕

---

right of the natural level of output is upward-sloping.

If the price level unexpectedly falls—say, from 100 to 95 in Figure 4—the firms perceive that their profitability is falling. Their workers may be on contracts calling for fixed or rising wages; they have negotiated the purchase of materials at fixed prices. Their selling prices are falling more rapidly than their costs, and they respond by producing less. When unemployed workers see wages starting to fall, they are less inclined to accept job offers. Firms become more willing to fire unsatisfactory workers and to lay off workers not currently needed. In sum, unanticipated deflation should cause less real output to be produced. To the left of the natural level of output, the short-run supply curve is positively sloped.

Shifts in Short-Run Aggregate Supply

The short-run aggregate supply curve shows what happens to output as the price level rises and falls. It suggests that real output tends to rise and fall with the price level in the short run. Like the aggregate demand curve, factors other than the price level can affect aggregate supply. When these factors change, the aggregate supply curve will shift. Any event that changes the price level at which the business sector will be willing to supply a given volume of real output will change aggregate supply (cause a leftward or rightward shift in *AS*). Events that change aggregate supply include supply shocks, the expectation of inflation, changes in productivity, and changes in labor-market conditions.

Supply shocks such as the creation of a monopoly over a natural resource (like OPEC's acquisition of control over crude-oil exports in the early 1970s), poor harvests, or natural disasters reduce aggregate supply. When supply shocks raise the input costs of businesses, they raise the price level at which businesses are willing to supply a given volume of real output.

If households and businesses raise their *inflationary expectations,* businesses will be less willing to supply output at the prevailing price level, and aggregate supply will decline.

When *increases in productivity* due to technological innovations or improved management techniques lower the unit costs of producing output, firms are prepared to supply more output at the same price as before.

Changing labor-market conditions—such as a change in the willingness of workers to supply labor at different wage rates or an influx of foreign labor—can cause aggregate supply shifts as well.

CHANGES IN AGGREGATE SUPPLY OR AGGREGATE DEMAND

As this chapter has demonstrated, the aggregate demand curve is negatively sloped relative to the price level, and the aggregate supply curve—*in the short run*—is positively sloped with respect to the price level. The aggregate demand curve shifts when there are changes in monetary and fiscal policy or changes in private spending behavior. Shifts in the aggregate supply curve are caused by supply shocks and changes in inflationary expectations, labor-market conditions, or productivity. In the long run, economic agents are given sufficient time to adjust to unanticipated inflation or deflation; therefore, the following discussion of aggregate supply refers only to the short run.

A Supply Shock

Figure 5 shows the effect of a supply shock on prices and real output in the short run. The economy is initially operating at point *e,* where the natural level of output is y_n and price level is p. People expect this situation to continue into the future. Suddenly, unexpectedly bad harvests occur on a worldwide basis. The prices of foods, fibers, and feed rise. Because these price increases represent cost increases to producers, the aggregate supply curve shifts to the left (from *AS* to *AS'*). With the reduction in aggregate supply, aggregate demand exceeds aggregate supply at the original price level, and the price level rises (from p to p'). As the price level rises towards p', the economy moves along the established aggregate demand curve (from *e* to *e'*) as the real-balance effect and the interest-rate effect take hold.

The end result of the supply shock is that the price level has risen (inflation has occurred); the economy ends up producing less real output (actual output is less than the natural level of output), and unemployment has increased.

Supply shocks tend to cause inflation and unemployment in the short run.

An Increase in Aggregate Demand

Figure 6 illustrates the effects of an increase in aggregate demand due to, say, expansionary fiscal

Figure 5
The Effect of a Supply Shock on Prices and Real Output in the Short Run

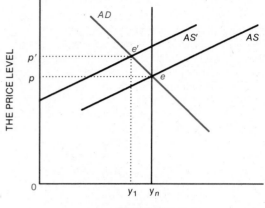

REAL GNP

The economy is initially operating at point *e*. This equilibrium has persisted long enough so that households and business firms expect it to continue into the future. Aggregate supply is reduced (from *AS* to *AS'*) by disasterous harvests. At the original price level, *p,* aggregate demand exceeds aggregate supply, and prices begin to rise. As prices rise, the economy moves along *AD* (from *e* to *e'*) until a new equilibrium is established at *e'*. Supply shocks can cause the economy to operate below y_n (can create unemployment and less real output) and can raise prices in the short run.

policy. The economy is initially producing below the natural level of output, at point *e*. An increase in government spending shifts the aggregate demand curve from *AD* to *AD'*. At the initial price level, *p,* aggregate demand exceeds aggregate supply, so the price level begins to rise. As the price level rises, there is a movement up the short-run supply curve, *AS,* from *e* to *e'*. The new equilibrium is established at *e',* where the economy is producing output y_n at price level p'.

The effect of the increase in aggregate demand in the short run is that real output has risen to the natural level, unemployment has fallen to the natural rate, and prices have risen.

Notice the difference between this outcome and that of the simple Keynesian model in Figure 3. Both Figure 3 and Figure 6 analyze the effect of increasing aggregate demand on employment, output, and prices starting from below full employment. In the simple Keynesian model, the in-

Figure 6
The Effect of an Increase in Aggregate Demand on Real Output and Prices in the Short Run

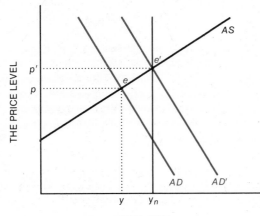

REAL GNP

The economy is initially producing y at the price level p. Government expenditures increase and aggregate demand shifts from AD to AD'. As prices begin to rise, the economy moves along its aggregate supply curve until a new equilibrium is established at e'. The increase in aggregate demand raises output and prices and lowers the unemployment rate to the natural rate, in this particular case.

crease in aggregate demand raises output but does not raise prices. In the current model, the increase in aggregate demand still raises output but also raises prices.

Fiscal and monetary policy can be used to reduce unemployment to the natural rate at the cost of accepting a higher price level.

THE LONG RUN: THE SELF-CORRECTING MECHANISM

Up to this point, this chapter has discussed short-run effects of shifts in aggregate supply or aggregate demand. Such shifts can cause the economy to increase or decrease its real output and its rate of unemployment. Shifts in aggregate supply and aggregate demand can cause the economy to produce a level of output different from the natural level of output.

The *short run* is simply a period of time so short that households and businesses cannot adjust their expectations to the change in the inflation rate. The short-run supply curve is upward-sloping simply because economic agents have not fully anticipated the change in prices. In our examples, economic agents initially expected the prevailing price level to continue into the future. Shifts in either aggregate demand or supply caused unanticipated inflation to occur. Workers were caught off guard with wage contracts that failed to protect them from the unanticipated inflation. Business firms had contracts for the purchase of inputs at prices that were rising less rapidly than selling prices. Moreover, some people were simply fooled by the unanticipated inflation. Firms were fooled into thinking that prices were rising more rapidly than costs. Unemployed workers were fooled into thinking that their real wage offers were improving. Other workers were fooled into working longer hours. Thus, *in the short run, people are subject to a certain amount of money illusion.*

Chapter 5 showed that there is a big difference between reactions to anticipated and unanticipated inflation. Once the inflation comes to be anticipated, people are able to protect themselves from the inflation "tax": workers are no longer willing to accept money wage contracts that do not protect them from the anticipated inflation tax; business firms refuse to supply goods on fixed long-term contracts. Long-term building leases have become a thing of the past; instead, they are renegotiated at short intervals.

Basically, the short-run supply response to rising prices only occurs when economic agents do not correctly anticipate the inflation rate and do not take appropriate precautions to protect themselves from the inflation tax. Abraham Lincoln once noted that you can fool all the people some of the time, and some of the people all of the time but that you can't fool all of the people all the time. Once people are able to anticipate inflation, the short-run supply effects studied above tend to disappear. In the long run, there is no money illusion.

The adjustment to long-run equilibrium is illustrated in Figure 7. The economy is initially at point e, where the output level, y, is less than the natural level, y_n. In other words, the unemployment rate exceeds the natural rate of unemployment. Monetary and fiscal policies are not chang-

Figure 7
The Self-Correcting Mechanism in the Long Run

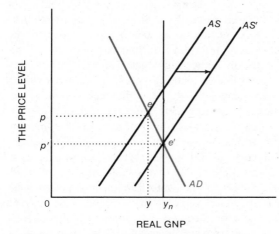

REAL GNP

Initially, the economy's aggregate supply *(AS)* curve intersects aggregate demand *(AD)* at e. At this point, y is less than y_n, and the unemployment rate exceeds the natural rate. Wages fall and prices fall. As prices fall, the economy moves down *AD* toward e' even though there have been no changes in monetary and fiscal policy. The aggregate supply curve's move to the right causes this movement along *AD*. As the inflation rate drops, individuals and businesses adjust downward their inflationary expectations and become willing to supply more at the same price level as before. The long-run equilibrium occurs at the intersection of *AD* and *AS'* where the natural level of output y_n is produced. At this point (e'), there is no longer any tendency for prices to fall further. It is the fall in the price level from p to p' that brings about this automatic adjustment.

ing, so aggregate demand does not change. When money wages start dropping, business firms will begin to cut prices. Falling prices will cause the economy to move up along the established negatively sloped aggregate demand curve, *AD*. Falling prices raise the real value of financial assets (stimulating consumption) and falling interest rates stimulate investment. As prices fall, people begin to expect lower prices. Thus, the curve begins to shift to the right and eventually shifts to *AS'*. The economy moves from point e toward point e'. As long as the economy's output is less than y_n, prices will continue to fall and move the economy closer and closer to y_n. This process stops when the economy is producing y_n at price level p'.

This self-regulating long-run adjustment to the natural level of output takes place only when monetary and fiscal policies do not change. The economy adjusts by moving down a fixed aggregate demand curve, not by altering monetary or fiscal policy to shift the aggregate demand curve.

As long as the unemployment rate remains below the natural rate, falling wages and prices will in the long run move the economy to the natural rate of unemployment. This adjustment is self-correcting; it takes place without the need of changes in monetary or fiscal policy.

The self-correcting mechanism works because the aggregate demand curve is negatively sloped and eventually intersects the vertical y_n line.

Where AD intersects y_n, the price level and the level of output are in long-run equilibrium.

For the economy to move down the aggregate demand curve, the short-run aggregate supply curve must be shifting to the right. As people and firms experience declining prices and wages, they adjust their inflationary expectations downward. Firms are willing to supply more output at the same price level as before when they expect less inflation. In long-run equilibrium, the aggregate supply curve is *AS'*, which intersects *AD* at the natural level of output.[2] Shifts in aggregate supply and aggregate demand may cause the economy to produce more or less than y_n in the short run, but in the long run, the economy should gravitate towards producing y_n.

In the long run, the economy should produce a level of output equal to the natural level of output and have an unemployment rate equal to the natural rate of unemployment.

2. Our examples are of a noninflationary economy that begins to experience inflation. The self-correcting mechanism then restores this economy back to its noninflationary equilibrium. We could just as well have dealt with an economy experiencing a constant rate of inflation. Demand or supply shifts then cause the rate of inflation to accelerate, and the self-correcting mechanism restores the economy back to its original constant rate of inflation.

According to the natural-rate hypothesis, in the long run, the level of real output or the rate of unemployment cannot be controlled by monetary or fiscal policy. There is a surprising degree of consensus among modern economists about the natural-rate hypothesis. What divides economists is how quickly and with what social costs the self-correcting mechanism operates. If inflationary expectations adjust slowly, if wages and prices tend to be sticky, if the real-balance and interest-rate effects are weak, progress from a rate of unemployment above the natural rate may be slow and painful.

The next several chapters provide the basis for understanding the conflicts within modern economics, beginning with inflation.

Summary

1. Keynesian economics applied to economies with unemployed resources. If aggregate demand increased in such an economy, increases in real GNP would be forthcoming. To study the interrelationships among real GNP, unemployment, and the price level, aggregate supply must be brought into the picture. The aggregate demand schedule shows equilibrium aggregate expenditures at different price levels. The aggregate demand curve is drawn holding the nominal money supply, tax rates, and real government expenditures constant. It is downward-sloping because of real-balance effects and interest-rate effects. The aggregate demand curve shifts when monetary and fiscal policy change, when there are autonomous changes in investment, changes in attitudes towards thrift, or changes in inflation expectations.

2. The aggregate supply schedule shows the quantities of real GNP the economy desires to supply at different price levels. The aggregate supply curve holds labor market conditions, productivity, and inflation expectations constant. Macroeconomic equilibrium occurs at that real GNP and price level at which aggregate supply and aggregate demand are equal. With the Keynesian aggregate supply curve, if the equilibrium is at less than full

employment, an increase in aggregate demand will increase real GNP without any increase in the price level.

3. Modern economists use the natural rate of unemployment for full employment. The natural rate of unemployment prevails when unemployment equals the number of unfilled jobs. The natural level of real GNP is the real GNP that is produced when the economy is at the natural rate of unemployment. Aggregate supply in the short-run depends upon whether inflation is unanticipated or anticipated. If there is an unanticipated increase in aggregate demand, both output and the price level will rise.

4. Supply shocks can cause the aggregate supply curve to shift. An adverse supply shock causes the unemployment rate to rise and the price level to rise.

5. In the long run, there is a self-correcting mechanism that causes the economy to return to the natural rate. The economy responds to supply and demand shifts by changes in the price level. The self-correcting mechanism operates with constant monetary and fiscal policy.

Key Terms

aggregate demand schedule
real-balance effect
interest-rate effect
aggregate supply schedule
macroeconomic equilibrium
money illusion
natural rate of unemployment
natural level of real GNP (y_n)
natural-rate hypothesis

Questions and Problems

1. Explain the difference between the aggregate demand curve and the desired aggregate expenditure curve. What is being held constant behind each of these curves?
2. An individual has accumulated stocks worth $500,000. There is an unexpected decline in

prices. What prediction would you make concerning the consumption spending of this person? What would happen if the value of these stock holdings rose while prices held steady?

3. Describe what will happen to real GNP and the price level if government spending increases, and there is a substantial reduction in labor productivity. Use aggregate supply and demand curves to illustrate your answer. Also explain why crowding out effects may be important.

4. What conditions are required in order for the original Keynesian supply curve to hold? Why did this supply curve cause Keynes to emphasize demand-side economics?

5. Contrast the natural-rate view of full employment with that view expressed in the original Keynesian model.

6. The natural rate of unemployment is 6 percent and the inflation rate over the past five years has been steady at 7 percent. The actual unemployment rate falls to 4 percent. What should happen to the inflation rate?

7. The short-run aggregate supply curve appears to depend upon whether price increases are anticipated or not. Explain why the degree to which inflation is anticipated affects aggregate supply.

8. Both workers and businesses anticipate a 20 percent inflation rate. The actual inflation rate turns out to be 5 percent. How would this surprise affect their productive behavior?

9. Explain why supply shocks can be countered in the Keynesian model. What are the costs of acting against supply shocks?

10. Explain how the self-correcting mechanism uses changing prices and wage rates to return the economy to the natural rate. Under what conditions would the self-correcting mechanism not work?

CHAPTER

13

Inflation

Chapter Preview

This chapter will analyze the causes of inflation and possible cures. Inflation has been a serious problem in the United States and the world for more than a decade. In 1981, the U.S. inflation rate was 6 times that of 1964. Why did prices rise at a 1.5 percent rate in 1964 and a 9.1 percent rate in 1981? Inflation's impact on income distribution was discussed in Chapter 5, and *stagflation*—the combination of high unemployment and rapid inflation—is the focus of Chapter 14.

THE FACTS OF INFLATION

Five fundamental facts about inflation that require explanation are:

1. Inflation is not inevitable.
2. High inflation rates are associated with high rates of growth of money supply, especially in the long run.
3. Recent inflation has been more rapid than can be explained by the long-run historical association between money and prices.
4. In the long run, high inflation rates and high interest rates go hand in hand.
5. There has been a clear-cut inflationary bias since the 1930s.

Inflation Is Not Inevitable

Figure 1, which shows the U.S. price level from 1800 to the present, demonstrates that, over the very long run, inflation is not inevitable.

Figure 1
The U.S. Price Level, 1800–1981

The pattern of ever-accelerating price increases has emerged only in the last 30 to 40 years.

Sources: *Historical Statistics of the United States,* 1970, p. 211; *Economic Report of the President,* January 1982, p. 294.

Figure 2
The Growth of U.S. Money Supply and Price Level, 1915–1982

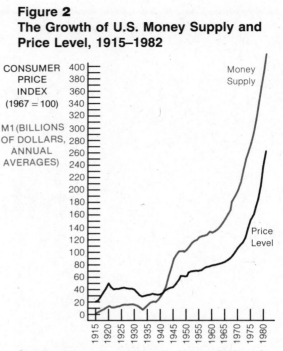

Changes in money supply and changes in the price level have tended to move together, although without exact agreement. Notice that M1 has grown faster than the price level, since the increase in real GNP over time absorbs some of the increase in M1.

Sources: *Historical Statistics of the United States,* 1970, pp. 210–11, 992; *Economic Report of the President,* 1982, pp. 292, 303.

Prices in 1943 were about the same as prices in 1800! Until the Second World War, there was no definitive upward trend in prices. Instead, periods of inflation were followed by periods of deflation; the two tended to cancel each other. Over the entire 19th century, the general price level went up and down over and over again. The clear-cut inflationary bias did not begin until the mid-1930s, when the U.S. economy began its recovery from the Great Depression.

Money and Prices Are Positively Associated

In the long run, Figure 2 shows a positive empirical association between the growth of money and the growth of prices. Money and prices have not grown at the same rate in the long run, however. The money supply (M1) rose nearly 33 times while the price level rose by more than 8 times over this period. One reason why the money supply has grown more rapidly than the price level is that real GNP has been growing along with prices, and more money is required to accommodate the larger quantity of real GNP. Between 1915 and 1981, real GNP increased nearly 8 times.[1]

The relationship between monetary growth and inflation from 1966 to 1981 is shown in Figure 3. Figure 3 is a *scatter diagram* that compares the annual percentage change in the money supply with the annual inflation rate in the next year. The vertical height of each dot shows the rate of inflation in a particular year; the horizontal distance of each dot from the vertical axis shows the rate of growth of money in the *previous* year. (Presumably, the effect of monetary growth on inflation would not be immediate. The change in the money stock should affect economic activity with a lag.)

1. The equation of exchange is $MV = PQ$. In the long run, Q rises with advancing technology and labor force growth. So M must rise to accommodate more Q, with V and P constant.

Figure 3
**The Growth of the U.S. Money Supply
and the Price Level, 1966–1981**

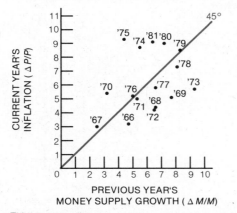

PREVIOUS YEAR'S
MONEY SUPPLY GROWTH (Δ *M/M*)

This scatter diagram compares the annual inflation rate for each year with the rate of change in the previous year's money supply. The 1966–1981 period saw more inflation than can be accounted for by the growth in money supply alone, since money usually grows faster than prices.

Source: *Economic Report of the President,* 1982, pp. 237, 303.

Figure 4
**Inflation Rates and Interest Rates,
1966–1981**

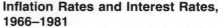
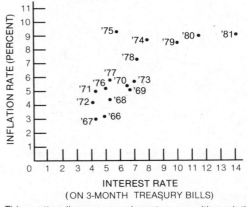

INTEREST RATE
(ON 3-MONTH TREASURY BILLS)

This scatter diagram reveals a strong positive relationship between rapid inflation and high interest rates.

Source: *Economic Report of the President,* 1982, pp. 237, 310.

The 45-degree reference line (not to be confused with the 45-degree line in the income/expenditure model) shows where points would appear if there were equal percentage changes in money supply and the price level. If the price level grows faster than the money supply, the dots lie above the line. Of the 16 dots, 8 are above the line, and 8 are below the line. During the 1966–1981 period, both money and prices grew, on the average, at about the same rate—6 percent per year. This rate is a substantial deviation from the historical record. As demonstrated in Figure 2, money usually grows faster than prices because real GNP grows over time. But the 1966–1981 period saw more inflation than can be accounted for by the growth in the money supply alone.

**Inflation and Interest Rates
Are Positively Associated**

Figure 4 shows the relationship between recent inflation rates and the interest rate for the period 1966 to 1981. If the relationship between inflation and interest rates is positive, the graph should show that interest rates tend to be high when in-

flation is high and low when inflation is low. The scatter diagram reveals a strong positive relationship: periods of rapid inflation tend to be periods of high interest rates, and vice versa.

THE CAUSES OF INFLATION

Any good theory of inflation should account for the five facts of inflation discussed above. The previous chapter used the tools of aggregate supply and aggregate demand to explain how real output, employment, and the price level are determined. Chapter 12 showed how the short-run aggregate supply curve can be positively sloped and why the aggregate demand curve is negatively sloped. It also discussed the tendency of economies to produce the natural level of output in the long run.

Aggregate supply-and-demand analysis suggests two general types of inflation: **demand-pull inflation** and **cost-push inflation.** Figure 5 illustrates both types of inflation using the tools of aggregate supply-and-demand analysis. These diagrams show short-run effects only; they do not show what happens to prices, output, and employment as the automatic-adjustment mechanism does its work.

Figure 5
Demand-Side versus Supply-Side Inflation

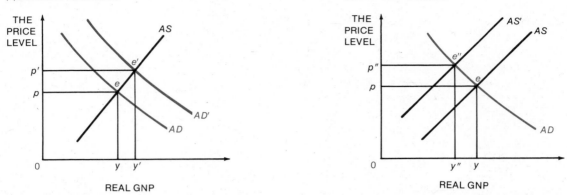

(a) Demand-Pull Inflation

(b) Cost-Push Inflation

Panel (a) shows demand-pull inflation. The economy is initially in equilibrium at e. Aggregate demand increases from AD to AD' and causes the price level to rise from p to p' as the economy moves up along the short-run aggregate supply curve, AS, to e'. In the short run, output increases from y to y'. The increase in aggregate demand has pulled prices up.

Panel (b) shows cost-push or supply-side inflation. The economy is initially in equilibrium at e. A reduction in aggregate supply from AS to AS' causes a movement back along the aggregate demand curve from e to e". Prices rise from p to p"; output declines from y to y"; unemployment increases. The reduction in aggregate supply has pushed prices up.

Demand-Pull Inflation

In panel (a), the economy is initially operating at point e, where output is y and the price level is p. The short-run aggregate supply curve, AS, is positively sloped—which means that the economy will produce more output only at a higher price level. If aggregate demand increases—for example, through an increase in the money supply, a lowering of taxes, an increase in government spending, or an autonomous upward shift in consumption—the aggregate demand curve, AD, shifts to the right. At the new equilibrium, e', more output (y') is produced (and unemployment falls). The increase in demand has caused the equilibrium price level to rise (to p').

Demand-pull inflation (or demand-side inflation) occurs when aggregate demand increases and pulls prices up.

Cost-Push Inflation

In panel (b), the economy is initially operating at point e again, producing output y at price level p. A reduction in aggregate supply—due to a de-

cline in productivity, poor harvests, or autonomous increases in energy prices—shifts the aggregate supply curve to the left from AS to AS'. The drop in aggregate supply disrupts the initial equilibrium of output and prices and shifts the equilibrium to e". At price level p, aggregate demand exceeds aggregate supply, and prices rise (from p to p"). As prices rise, the economy moves back along the aggregate demand curve; output falls to y", and the unemployment rate rises. The reduction in aggregate supply has raised both the price level and unemployment.

Cost-push inflation (or supply-side inflation) occurs when aggregate supply declines and pushes prices up.

Confusing Demand-Pull and Cost-Push Inflation

Demand-pull and cost-push inflation are often confused when inflation is moderate. For example, suppose the quantity of money increases, so that the aggregate demand for goods and services is raised throughout the economy. As each sector seeks to meet the increase in demand, its prices and wages rise. Individual business managers will not see the increase in the money supply; they will only see that their wage costs, material costs, and interest charges are rising, and they will raise prices in response to higher costs (cost-push inflation).

To the microeconomic unit—the individual and the firm—moderate demand-pull inflations look similar to cost-push inflations. To determine whether inflation is demand-pull or cost-push, one must know the source of rising wages and prices.

When inflation is excessive and there is widespread knowledge that the government is printing money at a rapid rate, there is less chance observers will think the demand-pull inflation is really cost-push inflation. In order to decide on the best cure, it is important to know whether inflation is caused by demand-pull or cost-push forces.

THE DEMAND SIDE: MONEY AND INTEREST

Many economists believe that protracted inflation is a monetary phenomenon caused by excessive monetary growth. According to the equation of exchange, $MV = PQ$, where M is money supply, V is velocity, P is price level, and Q is output.

With constant velocity, excessive monetary growth occurs when money supply grows more rapidly than output.

The effects of monetary growth on inflation, output, unemployment, and interest rates can be determined using the tools of aggregate supply-and-demand analysis. Money's effects on prices would be simple to predict if velocity and real output were constant, as the crude quantity theory assumed, but changes in real output and velocity complicate the relationship between money supply and prices.

Unanticipated Inflation

Inflation is not likely to be anticipated if it is caused by a one-shot or once-and-for-all increase in aggregate demand. If prices have been increasing steadily (or even erratically), people will do their best to anticipate inflation to prevent being caught off guard. In the example that follows, the economy has had stable prices for a number of years and is not likely to anticipate inflation.

In Figure 6, a once-and-for-all increase in the money supply causes an increase in aggregate demand. The increase in money supply comes as a surprise to everyone because the money supply had been held constant by monetary authorities.

The Short Run. In panel (a), the economy is initially operating at point *a*, producing the natural level of output y_n at a price level of 100. In panel (b), the increase in money supply (from M to M') adds reserves to the commercial banking system. Banks can use these excess reserves to make loans and other investments. The increase in the supply of credit causes the interest rate to fall along the money demand *(LP)* curve (from 10 percent to 7 percent in our example).

In order for the interest rate to stay this low (at 7 percent), the price level and real output must remain unchanged. But both the price level and output should rise. The short-run aggregate supply curve is upward-sloping, and aggregate demand increases from *AD* to *AD'* (due to the increase in investment spending stimulated by the lower interest rate). Therefore, output rises to y' and the price level rises to 104 as the economy moves from *a* to *b*.

The Long Run. As explained in Chapter 12, increases in aggregate demand can raise output and employment in the short run above the natural rate, but in the long run, both output and employment should return to the natural rate. Is there an equivalent rule for interest rates?

At *b*, output is above the natural level, and the price level begins its long-run ascent towards *e* (where the price level is 110 and output is y_n). But what happens to the liquidity-preference curve as prices rise? At higher prices, people need more money balances to carry out their transactions; the demand for money increases (*LP* shifts towards *LP'*). The interest rate rises as the demand for money increases; it will continue to rise as long as prices are rising. Prices rise until *e* is reached (at a price level of 110), and the interest rate rises as long as prices are rising. When the price level is 110 (at point *e*), prices no longer

Figure 6
The Effects of Increases in Money Supply on Interest Rates, Output, and Prices

(a) Aggregate Supply and Aggregate Demand

(b) The Money Market

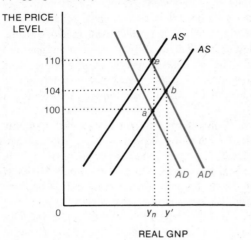
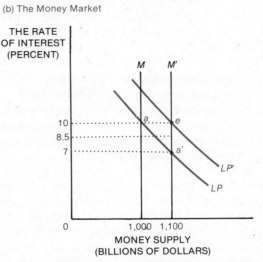

The economy is initially operating at point *a* in both panels, producing an output of y_n with an interest rate of 10 percent. As a result of an unanticipated move by the Fed, money supply increases, and the interest rate drops to 7 percent. At the lower interest rate, aggregate demand increases (due to higher investment spending) from *AD* to *AD'*. Output rises to *y'*, and prices rise from 100 to 104. The diagram ignores the temporary shift in liquidity preference due to the temporary changes in real GNP. The only shift shown is due to the price-level change, which is permanent.

In the long run, at an output greater than y_n, prices will continue to increase until the automatic-adjustment mechanism returns the economy to y_n at a price level of 110. When the price level is expected to be 100, the aggregate-supply curve shifts from *AS* to *AS'*. In the credit market, the rise in price level raises the *LP* curve until the original 10 percent interest rate is restored at *LP'*. The final equilibrium is *e* in both panels.

rise (the inflation rate goes back to being zero, and output is restored to its original level, y_n). The interest rate should be restored to its original rate of 10 percent when the economy reaches *e* in panel (a). At *e,* the economy is operating with the same real income and the same rate of inflation (zero) as before the increase in money supply. The only thing that has changed is that the price level has risen.[2]

There is no money illusion in the long run. If inflation is zero, both the nominal and real interest rate must be equal to 10 percent. In the long run, a once-and-for-all change in the nominal money supply has no impact on real GNP, the real interest rate, or the real money supply. Thus,

in the long run, the interest rate tends to be restored to its original rate. Increases in money supply can drive down interest rates only in the short run. In the long run, rising prices return the interest rate to its original position.

If the economy starts from a long-run equilibrium, an unanticipated one-shot increase in the money supply lowers the rate of interest and raises output above the natural rate in the short run. But in the long run, the economy returns to the natural level of output, and the interest rate will be restored to its original level. Unanticipated increases in money supply will lower interest rates only in the short run.

Adaptive versus Rational Expectations

It is difficult to anticipate inflation in a world where there are one-shot injections of money fol-

2. To simplify the above explanation, we have ignored the shifts in the liquidity-preference curves due to the temporary changes in real GNP. In the long run, real GNP is y_n—the natural level. Thus both *LP* and *LP'* are drawn on the assumption that real GNP equals y_n. *LP* assumes the price level is 100; *LP'* assumes the price level is 110.

lowing long periods of a constant money supply. Instances of one-shot unanticipated inflation like the one just described are rare. Both the money supply and real GNP typically grow. People come to expect a certain rate of inflation or deflation. The economy does not usually bounce back and forth between inflation and deflation or between skyrocketing and moderate inflation. In the real world, people presumably form inflationary expectations using their experiences from immediate and past history.

Adaptive Expectations. How do people form expectations of the future? There is no way to know for sure the mental process by which expectations are formed, but economists have offered two competing hypotheses, viewing expectations as either **adaptive expectations** or **rational expectations.**

Adaptive expectations are expectations of the future that people form from past experience and only gradually modify as experience unfolds.

For example, if the annual inflation rate has been 10 percent year in and year out for the past 10 years, people expect the inflation rate to remain at 10 percent. If the inflation rate jumps to a steady 15 percent, the adaptive-expectations hypothesis argues that people would not immediately adjust their expected inflation up to 15 percent. In the first year, they might raise their expected rate of inflation to 11 or 12 percent. As the rate of inflation continues at 15 percent, people continue to adjust upward their expected rate of inflation each period until finally they reach a 15 percent expected inflation rate.

The main implication of the adaptive-expectations hypothesis is that *it takes time for people to adjust to a new rate of inflation*. If the rate of inflation rises, the anticipated rate of inflation will rise by less. If the rate of inflation falls, the anticipated rate of inflation will fall by less.

Rational Expectations. The adaptive-expectations hypothesis maintains that people change their expectations of inflation slowly in response to changing circumstances. The rational-expectations hypothesis assumes that people change their expectations more quickly and use more information in forming their expectations.

Rational expectations are expectations that people form by using all available information and by relying not only on past experience but also on their predictions about the effects of present and future policy actions.

A major difference between adaptive and rational expectations is the speed of adjustment of expectations. It is conceivable that people could change their rational expectation of the anticipated rate of inflation simply on the basis of a policy pronouncement from monetary or fiscal authorities. If they believe a change in policy will raise a current 10 percent inflation rate to a permanent 15 percent rate, they will immediately raise their inflation projection to 15 percent.

Many people and businesses do indeed study the latest economic projections, money-supply growth statistics, and fiscal policy changes. Banks, investment firms, labor unions, and small investors gather information that they hope will allow them to anticipate the future. It is, therefore, possible that expectations are indeed formed according to the rational-expectations hypothesis. Which hypothesis is correct is an empirical issue that has been the subject of much research and controversy. Do people actually use all the available information on economic policy to form their expectations or do they simply respond slowly to past experience? Chapter 17 will return to the rational-expectations hypothesis in more detail.

Anticipated Inflation

Consider an economy in which inflation has been going on for some time, and people are attempting to anticipate the future rate of inflation. For the time being, we shall assume that they form their expectations adaptively.

Chapter 5 explained that when people begin to anticipate inflation, the nominal interest rate rises. When inflation is anticipated, lenders will be less willing to lend at prevailing interest rates because they know they will be paid back with cheaper dollars. Borrowers will be more anxious to borrow at prevailing interest rates because they can pay back their loans with cheaper dollars.

Figure 7
Velocity and Inflation

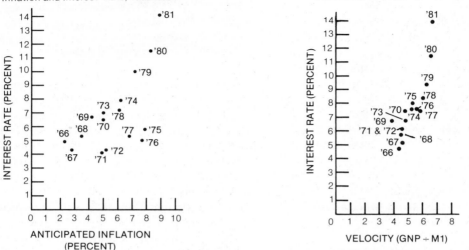

(a) The Relationship Between Anticipated Inflation and Interest Rate, 1966–1981

(b) The Relationship Between the Interest Rate and Velocity, 1966–1981

In panel (a), the anticipated inflation rate is measured as the average inflation rate over the last three years. The interest rate in both panels is the interest rate on 10-year U.S. government bonds. The positive slope of the scatter diagram in panel (a) reveals a positive relationship between anticipated inflation and the interest rate. In panel (b), velocity is the ratio of GNP to M1. This scatter diagrams clearly shows a positive relationship between interest rates and velocity. The results of panels (a) and (b) together show that velocity tends to increase as anticipated inflation rises.

As noted earlier, the interest rate is the opportunity cost of holding money. The higher the opportunity cost of money, the lower the demand for money and the more work each dollar must accomplish for each dollar of GNP. Higher interest rates should, therefore, cause people to turn over their money more often—to raise velocity.

What do the data tell us? Do interest rates rise with the anticipated rate of inflation? Does velocity rise with the interest rate? To answer these two questions requires information on the anticipated rate of inflation. One simple approach (among many) is to say that the anticipated inflation rate is simply the average of the inflation rates of the past few years.[3] This measure of anticipated infla-

tion can then be compared with interest rates, and interest rates can be compared with velocity.

Panel (a) of Figure 7 shows the relationship between our measure of the anticipated rate of inflation and the rate of interest for the period 1966 to 1981. This scatter diagram shows a strong positive relationship between the interest rate and the anticipated rate of inflation. The higher the anticipated rate of inflation, the higher the rate of interest.

Panel (b) of Figure 7 shows the effect of interest rates on velocity. As predicted by theory, there is a strong positive correlation between velocity and interest rates. At high interest rates, velocity is high because the opportunity cost of holding cash balances is high.

Figure 6 showed that when inflation is not anticipated, an increase in money supply lowers the interest rate *in the short run*. (In the long run, prices rise until the economy is restored to the original natural level of output at the original interest rate). If the price increases brought about

3.   For example, the inflation rate in the current year is 10 percent and it was 9 percent last year and 8 percent the year before, people would expect 9 percent (the average of 10, 9, and 8) for the next year. If the inflation rate jumps to 14 percent, the new expected inflation rate is 11 percent, the average of 14, 10, and 9 percent.

Why Interest Rates Remained High in 1982

Interest rates should fall after a period of high inflation when the inflation rate drops. In 1982 the inflation rate began to drop sharply from 9.1 percent in 1981. In March 1982, the inflation rate was even negative. Yet the prime lending rates of commercial banks failed to come down. The prime rate remained in the range of 18 percent.

Why did interest rates not drop with the rate of inflation as they were supposed to? Both the adaptive-expectations and rational-expectations hypotheses provide possible answers. If people adapt their expectations slowly to a declining rate of inflation, the initial drop in the inflation rate would not lower inflationary expectations much.

The rational-expectations hypothesis argues that people look ahead to the effects of current and future policy moves, and in the future they were seeing high rates of inflation. The financial community made known its fear that the decline in inflation would be temporary. In particular, the financial community voiced its concern that the large federal deficits projected for 1983 through 1985 will push inflation into the double-digit range. Because of these high inflationary expectations—formed either adaptively or on the basis of the projected impacts of fiscal policy—interest rates remained high in 1982.   ✂

---

by the increase in money supply are anticipated perfectly, however, the interest rate will not fall at all in response to a higher money supply. Lenders and borrowers will anticipate that prices will increase; lenders will be more reluctant to lend money at prevailing interest rates, and borrowers will be more anxious to borrow at prevailing interest rates. The nominal interest rate will rise to incorporate the anticipated rate of inflation as lenders protect themselves from depreciation in the value of the dollar.

If higher prices are not fully anticipated, there may be some drop in interest rates in response to the increase in money supply, but this drop would depend upon how quickly the public adjusts its expectations of inflation.

Monetary authorities face a dilemma during periods of rapid and anticipated inflation. When inflation is high, interest rates will have to be high enough to incorporate a premium for anticipated inflation. But the response to such high rates will be a public outcry against high interest rates, and pressure will build on the Fed to lower interest rates. In order to lower interest rates when inflationary expectations are high, monetary authorities must lower inflationary expectations.

In the case of adaptive expectations, people will lower their inflationary expectations only slowly as they see inflation actually dropping. In

this situation, the Fed must lower actual inflation to reduce inflationary expectations. In an inflation, both the money supply and the price level are rising; to lower inflation the Fed must reduce the growth of money supply below the growth of prices. The demand for money remains strong because people require more money to carry out their transactions with rising prices. When the supply of money is growing less rapidly than the demand, interest rates rise!

To **lower** *interest rates in an environment of rapid anticipated inflation requires that interest rates be* **raised** *in the short run. When monetary authorities reduce the growth of money supply, interest rates rise further. When the rate of inflation slows, inflationary expectations begin to fall, and only then will interest rates come down.*

Government Deficits

Although it has become increasingly popular to blame inflation on the deficit, the government deficit *per se* may not add to inflation.

The theoretical relationship between government deficits and inflation is ambiguous. On the one hand, deficits produced by deliberate increases in government spending or reductions in

223

Table 1

The Change in the Government Deficit and the Rate of Inflation, 1970–1981

Year	Deficit (billions of dollars)	Change in Deficit* (billions of dollars)	Inflation Rate = GNP Deflator (percent)
1970	−12.4	−34.4	5.4
1971	−22.0	−9.6	5.0
1972	−16.8	+5.2	4.2
1973	−5.6	+11.2	5.7
1974	−11.5	−5.9	8.7
1975	−69.3	−57.8	9.3
1976	−53.1	+16.2	5.2
1977	−46.4	+6.7	5.8
1978	−29.2	+17.2	7.3
1979	−14.8	+14.4	8.5
1980	−61.2	−46.4	9.0
1981	−61.6	−0.4	9.1
1982	−100.4	−38.8	3.9
1983^p	−101.9	−0.5	

*+ denotes a decrease in the deficit
− denotes an increase in the deficit
^{p}denotes "projected"

Source: *Economic Report of the President,* January 1982, pp. 237, 321.

tax rates will raise the rate of inflation as the aggregate demand curve shifts to the right. On the other hand, deficits produced by falling tax revenues induced by a weak economy (aggregate demand shifting to the left due to reductions in private spending) will be associated with a falling rate of inflation.

It would be surprising, therefore, to find a strong empirical association between deficits and inflation. Table 1 gives some facts on the deficit and the U.S. rate of inflation for the years 1970 to 1981—a period of accelerating inflation. These data fail to show a distinct relationship between the growth of the deficit and inflation. In fact, the substantial acceleration of inflation in the late 1970s came during a period of declining deficits. The acceleration of inflation in 1974 and 1975 began with a small deficit change in 1974. When the size of the deficit (say, the projected $100 billion deficit for 1982) is compared to the size of the economy (a projected GNP of almost $3 trillion), what appears to be an enormous increase in the deficit (say, $30 billion) is only 1 percent of

GNP. It would be hard to blame an upsurge in inflation on an increase of this relative magnitude.

The federal deficit can, however, contribute to inflation indirectly through its effect on the money supply. If the newly issued government bonds are sold only to the public, the money supply is not affected, but interest rates may be driven up as government and private borrowers compete for available investment funds. If there is an unwillingness to raise interest rates in the short run, the Fed—although it is not obligated to do so—will purchase the federal debt. When the Fed purchases government bonds, it injects new reserves into the banking system, and the money supply expands. In effect, the government deficit is financed by printing money.

Most macroeconomists believe that a government deficit contributes to inflation indirectly if the money supply is raised by the Fed's purchasing of the government debt. The increase in money supply, not the deficit per se, increases aggregate demand.

SUPPLY-SIDE INFLATION

Supply-side inflation occurs when there is a reduction in aggregate supply—when the *AS* curve shifts to the left, as in panel (b) of Figure 5. The drop in aggregate supply causes the economy to move up the aggregate demand curve to a lower level of output and to a higher price level. Unlike demand-pull inflation—which tends to raise output and employment in the short run—supply-side inflation brings the worst of both worlds: rising prices *and* lower output and employment.

Shifts in aggregate supply can be expected or unexpected. For example, the generally rising trend in technological advances would be expected to cause aggregate supply to increase over time in a fairly predictable manner. Of greater interest to the study of inflation is an unexpected shift in aggregate supply, called a **supply shock.**

*A **supply shock** is an event that unexpectedly causes the aggregate supply curve to shift.*

An adverse supply shock is one that causes a reduction in aggregate supply (the aggregate supply curve shifts up to the left). A favorable supply shock causes an increase in aggregate supply.

Causes of Cost-Push Inflation

There is no single cause of supply-side inflation. Any factor that causes aggregate supply to decrease can initiate cost-push inflation. Changes in labor productivity, autonomous increases in raw material prices, crop failures, and changes in the way labor and product markets work can all cause reductions in aggregate supply.

Supply Shocks. If the costs of production rise spontaneously without being pulled up by increases in demand, the economy will experience a supply shock. Firms, on average, will supply less goods and services than before at prevailing prices, and aggregate supply will fall. As the aggregate supply curve shifts to the left, the general price level is pushed up.

The most dramatic case of cost-push inflation in recent years is the 1475 percent rise in the price of imported oil between 1973 and 1980. When the Organization of Petroleum Exporting Countries (OPEC) discovered the magic of cartel pricing in 1973, the oil-importing countries of the world were hit with an enormous adverse supply shock. OPEC inflicted leftward shifts in the aggregate supply curves of every oil-importing country. The oil-induced reductions of supply pushed up the general price level. Table 2 supplies data on the price of OPEC oil and the average inflation rate in seven major countries.

The upsurge of world inflation rates coincided with the increase in energy prices. Although OPEC was not the only cause of the inflation, the oil shock likely did contribute to the inflation of the 1970s.

Price shocks can also emanate from agriculture. Poor weather and bad harvests throughout the world can raise agricultural prices, and because agricultural goods are a major input for the world economy, this price rise can cause the aggregate supply curve to shift. The year 1973 brought with it not only the beginning of the oil shock, but an increase in the price of wheat from $70 per ton to $140 per ton—due largely to a poor harvest in the United States in 1973 and a crop disaster in the Soviet Union the year before.

Table 2

OPEC Crude Oil Prices and Average Inflation Rates in the Big Seven Countries (U.S., Germany, Japan, France, Canada, Italy, and the U.K.), 1971–1980

Year	Oil Price (dollars per barrel)	Average Inflation Rate
1971–73	2.13	6.4
1974	10.77	14.5
1975	10.72	13.0
1976	11.51	10.0
1977	13.12	10.1
1978	12.93	7.6
1979	18.67	9.7
1980	31.46	9.1*

*preliminary

Source: *Handbook of Economic Statistics,* 1980, pp. 30, 42; James Griffin and Henry Steele, *Energy Economics and Policy* (New York: Academic, 1980), p. 18; *Economic Report of the President,* 1981, p. 189.

Administered Pricing. Some economists argue that another source of supply-side inflation is **administered pricing.**

Administered pricing occurs when prices are not determined by market forces but by large corporations or giant unions that raise prices and wages independently of demand conditions.

Economist John Kenneth Galbraith maintains that supply-side inflation is induced by administered pricing. The agglomeration of monopoly power in the hands of giant corporations and unions has given them the power to set their prices and wages without worrying about the state of demand. Monopolies can raise prices above the levels that would have prevailed under conditions of competition. Powerful unions can demand higher wages independently of any demand pull stimulated by monetary growth or higher productivity. Some claim that the giant corporation does not have to worry about granting these wage increases. It has the market power to pass higher wages on to its customers without worrying about demand.

One problem with the thesis of administered prices is that it blames inflation on *increases* in

Example 2

How to Measure the Deficit

Milton Friedman has pointed out that there is no one measure of the federal deficit. Although most attention is paid to the actual deficit (government revenues minus government expenditures), there are other ways of looking at the deficit.

Macroeconomics concentrates on real economic variables; that is, on monetary variables adjusted to take out the effects of inflation. Why not deal with the federal deficit on the same basis? In fiscal 1981, the federal budget ran a $62 billion deficit—much to the consternation of many. In September of 1980, the federal debt held by the public was $600 billion. With an inflation rate of 10 percent, the debt of the federal government would have had to increase by $60 billion just to stay even with inflation. Since the debt increased by $62 billion, the real public debt for all practical purposes did not change.

There are many other ways to measure the deficit. Should the deficit include the deficits of the postal service, Amtrak, government housing programs, the obligations of social security, and the like? The most inclusive measure of the 1981 federal deficit could yield a deficit of $300 billion.

Friedman's point is that there are many ways to measure the deficit and the deficit's impact on inflation. What is really at stake is whether the country is getting its "money's worth for the vast sums government is spending or obligating us to spend." The government is only one of many deficit units in the economy; households, small businesses, and large corporations add to their debt just as the federal government does. According to Friedman, it is somewhat arbitrary to single out one deficit unit—the federal government—and worry about the ill effects of that particular deficit, however measured.

Source: Milton Friedman, "Which Budget Deficit?" *Newsweek*, November 2, 1981.

---

the monopoly power of business and labor. If inflation is caused by administered pricing, then monopoly power must continue to grow in order for inflation to continue.

It is difficult to measure trends in monopoly power, but the available statistical evidence shows that the degree of monopoly power has likely not changed much over the past 80 years. The most clear-cut case of an increase in monopoly power may have occurred in the 1933–1937 period. In this recovery period from the Great Depression, the Roosevelt administration was operating under the view that a rise in prices would aid recovery. Rising prices, they reasoned, would push up profits and money wages. Accordingly, the administration passed a series of acts (the Wagner Act, the Agricultural Adjustment Act, and the National Recovery Act) that enabled both industry and labor to exercise increasing market power over prices and wages.[4]

4. This example is taken from Milton Friedman, *Dollars and Deficits* (Englewood Cliffs, N.J.: Prentice-Hall, 1968), p. 102.

Ratification of Cost-Push Inflation

As Figure 5 demonstrated, cost-push inflation causes a reduction in output and, hence, more unemployment. Demand-pull inflation, on the other hand, may cause increases in output and employment. The combination of rising prices and rising unemployment characteristic of supply-side inflation puts pressure on government to do something about rising unemployment.

The decline in output and employment that accompanies supply-side inflation can be prevented by raising aggregate demand to offset the reduction in aggregate supply. Since it is difficult (due to recognition and implementation lags) to use fiscal policy to raise aggregate demand, the most common instrument is the use of monetary policy. The use of monetary policy to increase aggregate demand, however, can result in the **ratification** of cost-push inflation.

Ratification of cost-push inflation results if the government increases the money supply to prevent supply-side shocks from raising unemployment.

Figure 8 illustrates the ratification of cost-push inflation. The economy is initially operating at y_1 and p_1 (at point e_1). The economy now suffers a supply shock—aggregate supply shifts to the left (from AS to AS'). If aggregate demand is unchanged, the economy moves to e_2, producing less output but at higher prices (prices rise from p_1 to p_2). As output declines, the unemployment rate rises.

When the government feels pressure to combat the rising unemployment, it raises the money supply and increases aggregate demand (from AD to AD'). The price level rises even further—from p_2 to p_3, and the economy returns to its original level of output and unemployment. As a consequence of the ratification, the supply-shock-induced unemployment has been eliminated, but the price level has been driven up even further.[5]

THE WAGE/PRICE SPIRAL

When inflation has continued for some time, workers and firms will no longer be caught off guard by inflation. They will attempt to anticipate inflation. Contracts between workers and their employers will reflect the anticipated rate of inflation. Workers who anticipate a 10 percent annual inflation rate over the life of a wage contract would negotiate a contract that would protect them from this amount of inflation. Anticipated inflation causes higher wages to be demanded, and firms will be willing to pay. In an inflationary setting, firms can pass these wage increases along in the form of higher prices. Sellers entering into sales contracts will also factor the anticipated rate of inflation into their sales contracts.

In such a situation, the economy gets caught in a **wage/price spiral.** Workers anticipate inflation and demand higher wages. Higher wages raise production costs and shift the aggregate supply curve in Figure 8 to the left. To prevent unemployment from increasing, the monetary authorities ratify the cost-push inflation and drive prices even higher. Workers now anticipate a higher price level; they demand higher wages; aggregate supply falls again; the whole process repeats itself.

5. Our example illustrates a perfectly matched demand response of monetary policy to the supply shock. In practice, this match may be difficult to achieve.

Figure 8
The Ratification of Supply Shocks

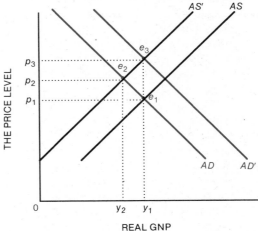

THE PRICE LEVEL

REAL GNP

The economy is initially operating at e_1—producing y_1 at price level p_1. Aggregate supply falls from AS to AS', the price level rises to p_2, and output falls to y_2 (unemployment rises). The government ratifies the cost-push inflation by increasing aggregate demand from AD to AD'. The price level rises to p_3, and output (and unemployment) returns to its original level.

*The **wage/price spiral** is the phenomenon of higher prices pushing wages higher and then higher wages pushing prices higher, or vice versa. This spiral occurs when workers anticipate inflation and demand and get higher wages and when the monetary authorities ratify the cost-push inflation. This process repeats itself.*

As long as monetary authorities continue to ratify the increase in wages, the wage/price spiral can continue indefinitely. A necessary component of the wage/price spiral is the accompanying rise in the money supply.

Is this type of inflation cost-push or demand-pull? The argument is circular: If workers did not demand higher wages, it would not be necessary to ratify this cost-push inflation by increasing money supply. Or if money supply had never increased and the economy were not on an inflationary path, workers would not demand wage increases in excess of productivity advances. In a wage/price spiral, the growth of the money supply is always present but so also is the cost-push element of anticipated inflation forcing up wage contracts. The debate over who has caused the wage/price spiral is also like the argument over which comes first, the chicken or the egg?[6]

One explanation for the existence of wage/price spirals only in recent decades may be the postwar Keynesian policy of attempting to maintain full employment. When aggregate demand falls and threatens unemployment, full-employment policy calls for a stimulation of aggregate demand. If the economy suffers a supply shock, cost-push inflation will be ratified to prevent unemployment, and prices rise more than they would have. In an economy that experiences demand changes and supply shocks, government policy is more likely to prevent price declines than price increases, building an inflationary bias into the economy.

The wage/price spiral cannot be halted painlessly. If the government ceases to ratify cost-push inflation (by refusing to let money supply grow), the wage/price spiral will be broken, but the economy will have to live with the unemployment generated by the supply shock until the long-run self-adjustment mechanism works its course.

Recent inflation rates reveal a shift in the historical relationship between the money supply and the price level. As noted earlier, the percentage increase in money supply usually exceeds the percentage increase in price level. As output rises, it will absorb some of the increase in money supply and hold down the increase in prices.

From 1966 to 1981, however, both the money supply and the price level grew at approximately 6 percent per year even though real GNP grew at an annual rate of 2.5 percent during this period.

---

6. Is the wage/price spiral caused by anticipated inflation that is ratified by monetary authorities or by people asking for a greater share of the economic pie? Abba Lerner has advanced the notion that inflation is caused by sellers of goods and services trying to get more and more rather than trying to protect themselves by correctly anticipating inflation. Remember, the wage/price spiral is initiated by a supply shock that is ratified, after which workers come to anticipate inflation. Seller's inflation could be self-generating. All that is necessary is a little greed.

If inflation is caused by seller's inflation, why has it not always been with us? We can presume that people who lived in the 19th century were as greedy as those of the 20th century; yet we have shown that there was no secular inflation in the 19th century. This discrepancy would suggest that the root of the wage/price spiral must be the expectation of more inflation. These expectations would not be self-generating.

This increase in output did not hold the rate of inflation below the growth of money supply for three reasons:

1. Supply shocks—in the form of OPEC-induced oil-price increases and weather-induced agricultural-price increases—combined to create extraordinary and unexpected price increases in the early 1970s. These supply shocks may also have raised inflationary expectations.

2. Between 1966 and 1981, there were sustained increases in the rate of growth of both the money supply and the price level. The inflation rate was 3 percent in 1966 and 9 percent in 1981. As the inflation rate rose from 3 to 9 percent, there was an increase in inflationary expectations. Increases in the anticipated rate of inflation fuel inflation by increasing velocity, as noted earlier.

3. The increase in velocity was fed not only by rising inflationary expectations but also by changes and innovations in the financial system (described in Chapter 8). People began to use credit cards; brokerage firms began to offer money-market funds with check-writing privileges. NOW accounts were introduced that allowed customers to write checks on savings accounts. Money management by firms was made easier by computerization. With computers, firms could more easily manage their cash balances and thereby lower the demand for money and increase velocity. These innovations increased the number of close substitutes for money (M1). Velocity was 4.4 in 1966 and 6.6 in 1981; hence, velocity increased by 50 percent. In terms of the exchange equation, while the increase in M averaged 6 percent per year, the rise in MV was almost 9 percent per annum due to the increase in V.

SUGGESTED CURES FOR INFLATION

How can inflation be brought under control?

The Keynesian Solution

There is no unique Keynesian solution to the inflation problem because Keynesians do not believe in a single cause of inflation.[7] Most Keynes-

---

7. This section is based largely on Arthur Okun, *Prices and Quantities* (Washington, D.C.: Brookings Institution, 1981), chapter 8.

ians believe that the best approach is active aggregate-demand management combined with some sort of **incomes policy.**

*An **incomes policy** is a set of rules, guidelines, or laws devised by government to influence wage and price increases.*

The basic fear of such well-known Keynesians as Paul Samuelson, Franco Modigliani, James Tobin, and the late Arthur Okun would be that a pure anti-inflation strategy (such as monetarism) would result in excessive unemployment.

Nobel prize laureate James Tobin of Yale University argues, along with many other Keynesians, that moderate inflation is not nearly as bad as unemployment. The basic cost of inflation is that people move away from money. Anticipated inflation causes people to hold smaller money balances per dollar of expenditure. Hence, people will make extra shopping trips and extra trips to the bank.

> . . . . . the ultimate social cost of anticipated inflation is the wasteful use of resources to economize holdings of (money). . . . I suspect the intelligent layman would be utterly astounded if they realized that this is the great evil economists are talking about. They have imagined a much more devastating cataclysm, with Vesuvius vengefully punishing the sinners below. Extra trips between savings banks and commercial banks? What an anti-climax.[8]

When inflation becomes immoderate—near the double-digit rate of the late 1970s and early 1980s—the crawl from money becomes more serious. Runaway inflations can be very dangerous as the economy resorts more and more to barter. Keynesians then suggest restraint in the growth of nominal aggregate demand using a combination of monetary and fiscal policy. This restraint has to be tempered, though, with an eye to the unemployment rate. Countercyclical policy cannot be given up in an inflationary world. If recession threatens, the Keynesian does not hesitate to use expansionary policies. Keynesians hope that in recessions an incomes policy would help keep the inflation rate down.

8. James Tobin, "Inflation and Unemployment," *American Economic Review* 62,1 (March 1972): 15.

Monetarism: Monetary Rules

The major proponent of monetarism, Milton Friedman, argues that "inflation is always and everywhere a monetary phenomenon," that inflation cannot persist unless it is supported by monetary growth. According to Friedman, supply-side inflation is just a temporary phenomenon that is important only in the short run. The major cause of inflation is demand pull, and demand pull is caused by excessive monetary growth.

If inflation is "always and everywhere" caused by excessive monetary growth, it is easy to predict Friedman's solution: strict limitation of the growth of the money supply. Insofar as real GNP over the long run has grown at about 3 percent per year, Friedman would limit the rate of growth of money supply to about 3 percent per year.

Friedman's "3 percent rule" is that the Fed should increase the money supply by 3 percent every year, give or take some small margin of error. Of course, the fixed rate of monetary growth could be any other small number—anywhere from 3 to 5 percent—depending on the output growth rate. Friedman's rule is sometimes called the "*k* percent rule."

Although detailed discussion of monetarism will be postponed until Chapter 15, the general rationale for the 3 percent (or *k* percent) rule follows.

1. Studies of the business cycle reveal that recessions and depressions are always associated with prior sharp reductions in monetary growth. Hence, monetarists argue that it is monetary instability that is largely responsible for the apparent instability of capitalism. Under a 3 percent rule, cyclical ups and downs would still exist, but their magnitude would be smaller.

2. The empirical relationship between changes in the rate of monetary growth and nominal GNP growth is lagged. Milton Friedman argues that the lag between money supply and GNP is long and variable (sometimes 6 months; sometimes 2 years). Since the business cycle cannot be forecasted accurately, attempts to use countercyclical policy can destabilize the economy. A fixed growth of money supply would bring more stability than countercyclical policy.

The U.S. Wage/Price Controls Program

On August 15, 1971, President Richard Nixon announced a 90-day freeze on almost all wages and prices. The control program ran through four phases and was dismantled in late 1973 and early 1974. The first phase was the 90-day freeze from which only taxes, mortgage interest rates, and raw agricultural commodities were exempted. Phase II began in November 1971. A Pay Board was established to enforce Phase II, which set a standard for wage increases of 5.5 percent per year with certain exceptions. A parallel Price Board operated on the rule that firms would be allowed to pass cost increases on in the form of higher prices only on a strict percentage basis. Phase III began in January 1973. The Pay and Price Boards were abolished; the 5.5 percent wage-increase standard was retained, but a more flexible approach was followed in its enforcement; standards for passing on cost increases were loosened. Inflation accelerated alarmingly during Phase III, and a second freeze was announced in June of 1973.

Freeze II froze prices but not wages! Phase IV went into effect in August of 1973, and the standards and regulations of this phase were very much like those of Phases II and III. On April 30, 1974, the President's authority to control wages and prices lapsed, and the experiment with wage/price controls ended.

Why were wage/price controls introduced in 1971? Although the inflation rates of this period appear to us as relatively mild (they averaged 5.1 percent between 1969 and 1971), they were alarming to a country accustomed to much lower inflation rates. The unemployment rate had risen from 3.3 percent in 1969 to 6 percent in January of 1971. Moreover, the value of the dollar abroad was being attacked. How was unemployment to be brought down without a further acceleration of inflation? Wage/price controls were seen as the answer.

The goal was to freeze wages and prices to shock inflationary expectations out of the econ-

---

3. The historical relationship between excessive monetary growth and inflation is impressive and cannot be denied.

Wage/Price Controls

One approach to controlling the inflationary wage/price spiral is to use *wage and price controls,* or government-imposed rules and laws to govern prices and wages. In their mild form, such controls could be an incomes policy of voluntary rules and guidelines concerning wage and price increases. For example, the government may decree that prices can be raised only at the same rate as costs. Or it may say that wages and prices cannot increase by more than x percent in a given year; it may set rules on profit margins. These rules can be anywhere from mandatory to voluntary. The wage/price controls system often requires a substantial bureaucracy to monitor compliance.

In their more extreme form, wage and price controls use rigid wage and price freezes that prohibit raising wages and prices above the level at

which they were on a certain date prior to the freeze. Such freezes are usually not all-inclusive; agricultural commodities and imports, whose prices are set in world markets, are typically exempted.

Arguments For. There are two arguments for wage and price controls. The first is advanced by those economists who believe that inflation is caused by administered prices. If prices and wages are not set by market forces but depend instead upon market power, why doesn't the government simply control wages and prices?

The other argument for wage and price controls is that they might break inflationary expectations. If people form expectations adaptively, these expectations will fall only slowly as inflation rates fall. As long as inflationary expectations remain high, interest rates will remain high, workers will continue to demand wage increases in excess of productivity, and so on. The problem, therefore, is to get people to adjust their inflationary expectations downward in a hurry. A temporary wage/price control system would put

omy. As inflationary expectations subsided, aggregate demand could be increased without pulling up the inflation rate. What happened to the inflation rate during the controls program? During Phase I prices were basically unchanged. During Phase II the inflation rate averaged 3.6 percent. There was an alarming resurgence of inflation during Phase III—inflation rose to a 9.1 percent annual rate.

More important than what happened to prices during the controls program is what happened to inflation after the program: the annual inflation rate was 4.3 percent in 1970 on the eve of the controls. At the end of the controls program (1974), the inflation rate was averaging 9.4 percent. In the two years after controls were lifted (1975 and 1976), inflation averaged 5.9 percent. What happened to unemployment? During the controls program unemployment remained between 5 and 6 percent. After the controls were lifted, the unemployment rate rose to 8.5 percent.

It thus appears that the controls program failed to meet its two objectives: to bring down inflation and unemployment at the same time. There are many possible explanations for this failure, but one of the most important is that nothing was done to prevent a price "catch-up" as the controls were being lifted. The rate of growth of the money supply accelerated from 6.6 percent in 1970, to 7.1 percent in 1971, to 7.5 percent in 1972, and then down to 5.0 percent in 1973. If inflation is everywhere a monetary phenomenon, why should prices not catch up to what they would have been without the controls after the controls are lifted? Economists who have studied the controls program conclude that the controls likely held down the inflation rate somewhat when they were in effect, but they raised the inflation rate in 1974 when the controls were removed.

Source: Alan Blinder, *Economic Policy and the Great Stagflation* (New York: Academic Press, 1979), chapters 3 and 6.

an immediate damper on inflationary expectations.

Arguments Against. The basic argument against rigid wage/price controls is that the productive efficiency of the economy will decline. If relative wages and prices are not allowed to move freely, the economy will be deprived of valuable signals. Higher relative wages can no longer signal to workers which sectors of the economy are rising. Branches experiencing rising demand cannot raise their prices sufficiently to equate supply and demand, and shortages will develop. Economic activity will tend to spill over into industries that are not frozen—such as agriculture and imports and even the underground economy. Supply and demand pressures will encourage evasion of rules.

All economists agree that rigid wage/price controls cannot be used over an extended period because of their effect on efficiency. They can only be used in the short run. If people are aware that these controls are of limited duration, they will attempt to anticipate what will happen to inflation

when the controls are lifted. If people generally expect a price explosion when the program runs out, they will not wind down their inflationary expectations. If the controls program fails to wind down inflationary expectations, it will not have accomplished its goal.

Other Incomes Policies

The difficulty with wage and price controls is that they hamstring the functioning of the price mechanism. To make sure the complicated flow of goods and services through the economy is meeting the least resistance requires numerous adjustments in relative prices and wages. Experience teaches that wage and price controls inflict all sorts of inefficiencies and shortages on the economy. Economists have suggested ways of using incomes policies to control wage and price increases yet still use the market to allocate resources.

Tax-Based Incomes Policy (TIP). Henry Wallich, now a member of the Board of Governors of the Fed, and Sydney Weintraub, of the University of Pennsylvania, have suggested that a *tax-based incomes policy (TIP)* can meet the inefficiency objection to controls. The purpose of a TIP is to use the tax mechanism to accomplish the goals of an incomes policy within the framework of a market economy.

A TIP works as follows: Business corporations are sensitive to the income taxes they pay and will go through considerable effort to reduce their taxes. The TIP imposes a penalty on firms whenever they grant average pay boosts in excess of some norm—say 5 percent per annum. The tax would then vary proportionately to the extent that actual pay increases exceed the percentage norm. Because such a plan would meet substantial opposition from business and labor, Arthur Okun has suggested another version: giving tax *credits* to firms that meet the norm, with the credits being paid to the employees of the firm.

The major difficulty with TIP plans is that a TIP would be an administrative nightmare. The average pay of a firm would reflect the skills and education of the firm's employees, and a TIP would give the firm the incentive to hire lesser skilled employees or to engage in other tax-avoidance schemes. To stay within the norm, firms could simply raise the fringe benefits of employees.

The proponents of TIPs recognize these problems but maintain that the administrative costs are less than the benefits TIP would bring. The other alternative—reducing inflation by raising the unemployment rate—is more costly.

The Market Anti-Inflation Plan.   Abba Lerner and David Colander suggest another market-based incomes policy. The Lerner-Colander *Market Anti-Inflation Plan (MAP)* calls for a market to be established in which the right to inflate (to raise prices) can be freely bought and sold. The government would issue a fixed supply of MAP credits that would be allocated to firms. Firms that wish to raise their prices can use their supply of MAP credits; if they do not have enough, they can buy from other firms. Firms that do not use their MAP credits would be rewarded by selling their MAP credits and raising their revenues. Firms that do raise prices will be penalized by having to buy MAP credits. The MAP system

would, therefore, create an incentive not to raise prices.[9]

Both the TIP and MAP programs seek to find a workable incomes policy that does not disrupt the efficiency of market resource allocation.

The Supply-Side Program

The equation of exchange shows that the rate of inflation will be lower, *ceteris paribus,* the higher the rate of growth of output. Some believe that inflation could be controlled by increasing the growth of real output. The appeal of this proposition is enormous because it obviates the need for pain and suffering (in the form of high unemployment or high interest rates) while curing inflation. If inflation can be cured by the rapid expansion of real goods and services, as real output expands, unemployment will fall along with the inflation rate.

Tax   Incentives.   Supply-side   economists have argued that it is possible to bring about substantial increases in the growth of output. The supply-siders maintain that the progressive tax system discourages people from working and business firms from investing in plants and equipment.

Arthur Laffer uses his "Laffer Curve" to show the relationship between tax rates and tax collections. If tax rates were to rise to 100 percent of income, there would be little or no output since all incentives to produce and work would have been removed. At a 100 percent tax rate, tax revenues would be essentially zero. At the other extreme, if the tax rate were 0 percent of income, incentives to work and produce output would be strong since no taxes are being paid. Although incomes would be high, zero taxes would be collected because of the 0 percent tax rate. Thus, tax collections would be zero at both a 100 percent and a 0 percent tax rate; there must exist some tax rate between these two extremes at which tax revenues are maximized. For example, one might argue that if the tax rate rises above 45 percent, tax revenues would actually fall because people's

9. Abba Lerner and David C. Colander, *MAP: A Market Anti-Inflation Plan (New York: Harcourt, Brace, Jovanovich, 1980).*

work effort and earnings would fall off more rapidly than the tax rate would be increasing.

If an economy has a tax rate above the rate that yields maximum tax revenues, it can attack inflation by reducing the tax rate. If tax rates are reduced, the economy will produce more real output because of improved economic incentives; the government will actually gain tax revenues from the lower tax rate. Both of these effects will reduce inflation. The increase in real output increases the supply of goods and services, and the increase in tax collections reduces the budget deficit. A smaller deficit means a slower rate of growth of money supply because of the tendency for the deficit to be financed by Fed purchases.

The supply-siders propose that cuts in personal and business taxes combined with limited monetary growth would result in smaller increases in aggregate demand. Increases in aggregate output would, therefore, insure that inflation drops in an environment of rising employment.

President Ronald Reagan was much influenced by the ideas of the supply-side school. Indeed, the tax cut passed in 1981 was designed to stimulate work effort by lowering marginal tax rates and offering investment incentives to business firms.

Return to the Gold Standard. Another plank of the supply-side cure of inflation is that the United States should return to the gold standard. As noted in Chapter 8, our money supply is no longer backed by gold. The price of gold is set like that of other raw materials by market forces. It rises and falls relative to the value of the dollar as the market dictates.

The ideal gold standard as proposed by supply-siders would work as follows: The value of the dollar would be fixed in terms of gold—say, one ounce of gold equals $400. The U.S. Treasury would guarantee the value of the dollar in terms of gold. Anyone with $400 could always buy one ounce of gold from the U.S. Treasury. Likewise, the U.S. Treasury would always stand ready to sell one ounce of gold for $400. By buying and selling gold at a fixed price, the relative price of dollars for gold would be fixed.

Under the gold standard, the money supply would be tied to the underlying stock of gold. Monetary authorities would no longer be able to

freely expand or contract the money supply as they have done over the years. The control of the money supply would effectively be taken out of their hands under a gold standard.

Under a gold standard, when inflation threatens, gold production would slack off because the value of gold would fall (a dollar would purchase fewer goods). The supply of gold and, hence, the money supply would no longer grow rapidly, and the rate of inflation would fall. When prices fell, the production of gold would become more profitable because of the increasing value of the dollar. The gold supply would increase more rapidly, and price deflation would disappear. While inflation or deflation would remain under the gold standard, private producers of gold would engage in the appropriate anti-inflationary or anti-deflationary monetary policy. Inflation discourages gold production; deflation encourages gold production (as long as the price of gold remains fixed in terms of the dollar).

Criticisms. Critics of the supply-side approach point out two problems. The first is that most economists are sceptical about the possibility of obtaining sustained increases in real output from tax incentives. Tax reductions are likely to bring about relatively small, one-shot increases in real output, not sustained increases in the rate of growth of real output. Historically, it is very difficult to raise the growth of output; very substantial increases in resources or efficiency are required to raise the annual real growth rate by even 0.5 percent per annum. Note that increasing the output growth rate by a full percentage point will lower the inflation rate by about 1 percentage point. Thus, even under the most favorable of circumstances, supply-side increases will not have much of an effect on inflation.

Critics of the gold-standard plank of the supply-side school argue that a return to the gold standard would make the money supply a hostage of the two leading gold-producing countries (South Africa and the U.S.S.R.). It also seems unwise to dig up gold and then turn around and bury it again in Fort Knox, all for the purpose of restraining the growth rate of the money supply. There must be cheaper ways of limiting monetary growth.

Example 4

A Free Market in Money?

A most ingenious and radical solution to the inflation problem has been advanced by Nobel laureate Friedrich A. von Hayek. Were it not for Hayek's credentials, many would be inclined to write this solution off as a crazy scheme. Hayek proposes that each country of Europe and North America bind themselves to an agreement "not to place any obstacles in the way of the free dealing throughout their territories in one another's currencies or of a similar exercise of the banking business by any institution established in any of their territories." In short, Hayek proposes the denationalization of money and free competition among different types of money. Why should governments have a monopoly on the issue of money?

What Hayek supposes would eventually happen is that large banks would get into the profitable business of issuing currencies. The Bank of America might issue the BAM, the Bank of France the BAF, the First City Bank the FCB, and so on. These banks would then compete with one another for customers for their currency. Banks that succeeded in keeping the value of their currency stable would do well in this competitive struggle.

How would people manage with all these currencies? Within any one city there would be a number of currencies with different rates of exchange. Would money's value as a medium of exchange be hampered by the existence of different currencies? With computers, the checkout clerk at the grocery store need only pass each item over the eye of the computer, which will then announce each price and figure the total amount including change. Computers could easily handle 50 separate currencies simultaneously.

The idea of different currencies competing with one another is not as strange as it sounds. Long before the German hyperinflation had destroyed the value of the mark in the 1920s, foreign currencies had begun to circulate in Germany. Those familiar with American banking history will know of the history of wildcat banking during which American banks issued their own currencies. The system did not work well then, but that was before the age of the computer.

Denationalization of money means the end of monetary policy because the government no longer controls the money supply. Hayek would feel more comfortable if money were taken out of the hands of government where he believes it has been abused for centuries.

One can think of all sorts of criticisms of Hayek's plan. The chances of its adoption are virtually nil, but the idea is a novel one.

Source: Friedrich A. von Hayek, *Denationalization of Money* (Great Britain: Institute of Economic Affairs, 1976).

The basic problem with the gold standard is that the economy is still subject to the random shocks of wars, changes in gold production, crop failures, and so on. Economies on the gold standard went through painful periods of deflation and inflation and depression. As noted earlier, prices were anything but stable during the 19th century. The United States was on the gold standard from 1879 to 1914. During this period, prices fell 47 percent from 1882 to 1896 and then rose 41 percent from 1896 to 1913. Allan Meltzer writes:

> Recessions lasted twice as long, on average, from 1879 to 1913 as in 1945 to 1980 and expansions and recoveries were about one-third shorter.[10]

Both monetarists and Keynesians alike would tend to be suspicious of returning to the gold standard. Monetarists would be opposed because the gold standard could not guarantee a steady and moderate rate of money growth. Keynesians would be opposed because the gold standard disallows the use of monetary policy as a discretionary instrument of economic policy.

This chapter discussed the facts, causes, and possible cures of inflation. The next chapter will turn to the problem of the combination of high unemployment and high inflation.

10. Allan Meltzer, "An Epistle to the Gold Commission," *Wall Street Journal*, September 17, 1981.

Summary

1. The five facts of inflation are the noninevitability of inflation, the positive historical relationship between the money supply and the price level, the correlation between high inflation and high interest rates, the inflationary bias in recent years, and the fact that recent inflation has been higher than can be accounted for by the historical relationship between money supply and prices.
2. Demand-pull (or demand-side) inflation is caused by increases in aggregate demand. Cost-push (or supply-side) inflation is caused by decreases in aggregate supply.
3. If inflation is unanticipated, increases in money supply will cause output and prices to rise. The increase in output beyond the natural level will be only temporary and will be eliminated in the long run by the self-adjustment mechanism. In the short run, an increase in money supply will drive down interest rates, but in the long run, interest rates will tend to return to their original level. Excessive monetary growth occurs when the growth of money supply exceeds the growth of output. The growth of the price level will equal the growth of money supply minus the growth of output with constant velocity. When inflation is persistent, people come to anticipate inflation. Inflationary expectations can be formed either through adaptive expectations or through rational expectations. When inflation is anticipated, monetary authorities can lower interest rates in the long run only by raising interest rates in the short run. The government deficit *per se* does not directly cause inflation unless it is financed by printing money.
4. Supply-side inflation can be caused by supply shocks and by administered pricing. Administered pricing cannot explain rising inflation unless market power is increasing. Ratification of supply shocks is the process of raising aggregate demand to prevent unemployment from rising as a consequence of the supply shock.
5. The wage/price spiral is caused by anticipated inflation and the ratification of cost-push inflation by monetary authorities. Recent inflation experience is explained by the supply shocks of the early 1970s, the increase in velocity, the increase in anticipated inflation, and recent financial innovations.
6. The proposals to cure inflation include the monetarist 3 percent (*k* percent) rule, the complex Keynesian package of demand management, incomes policy, and antirecession policies, wage/price controls, tax-based incentive programs, and supply-side economics.

Key Terms

demand-pull inflation
demand-side inflation
cost-push inflation
supply-side inflation
adaptive expectations
rational expectations
supply shock
administered pricing
ratification of cost-push inflation
wage/price spiral
incomes policy

Questions and Problems

1. The owner of the apartment you are renting complains: "Wages, utilities, and other costs are rising too rapidly. I have no choice but to raise your rent." Is this a case of cost-push inflation?
2. Economists classify inflation as either cost-push or demand-pull. Using aggregate supply-and-demand analysis, explain the differences between these two types of inflation. Is it possible to distinguish between demand-pull and cost-push from observed information on output, employment, and prices?

3. Money supply has been growing at 8 percent per annum, and output has been growing at 3 percent per annum. If velocity is constant, what would the rate of inflation be? If velocity is declining at a rate of 2 percent per year, what would the rate of inflation be?

4. Explain why increases in money supply that are unanticipated are likely to cause the interest rate to drop. Why may the drop in the interest rate be short-lived? If the increase in money supply is fully anticipated, what would happen to interest rates?

5. Using the adaptive-expectations hypothesis, what do you think the expected rate of inflation to be in 1982 if past inflation rates were 10 percent in 1981, 8 percent in 1980, and 6 percent in 1979.

6. What would you expect to happen to velocity as inflationary expectations increase? What is the actual relationship between velocity and anticipated inflation?

7. Many people feel that inflation is caused by large government deficits. Explain why it is unlikely that government deficits *per se* cause accelerating inflation.

8. Using aggregate supply-and-demand analysis, explain why adverse supply shocks combine the worst of two worlds: more inflation and higher unemployment. Also explain why governments tend to ratify cost-push inflation.

9. The wage/price spiral is blamed on unions and management and on expansionary economic policy. Explain why it is difficult to assign the blame for the wage/price spiral.

10. Evaluate the following statement: ''Both the Keynesians and monetarists lay the major blame for inflation on demand-pull inflation. Therefore, there really is not any difference between the two schools' approaches to the inflation problem.''

CHAPTER

14

Inflation
and
Unemployment

Chapter Preview

This chapter will explore one of the great questions of macroeconomics: What is the relationship between inflation and unemployment? The 1970s and 1980s showed that high unemployment and high inflation could occur simultaneously. A new term entered the economist's vocabulary: **stagflation.**

Stagflation is the combination of high unemployment and high inflation in a stagnant economy.

Stagflation presents a serious policy dilemma. As the preceding chapter showed, contractionary monetary and fiscal policies are the traditional remedy for demand-pull inflation, while high unemployment calls for expansionary policies. If an economy has both unemployment and inflation, what should policy makers do? To answer this question, one must understand the relationship between inflation and unemployment.

THE ORIGINAL PHILLIPS CURVE

In 1958, A.W. Phillips of the London School of Economics published a paper that Nobel laureate James Tobin calls "the most influential macroeconomic paper of the last century."[1]

1. A. W. Phillips, "The Relation Between Unemployment and the Rate of Change of Money Wages in the United Kingdom, 1861–1957," *Economica* (November 1958), pp. 283–99.

Figure 1
The Original Phillips Curve: Wage Inflation and Unemployment in the United Kingdom, 1861–1913

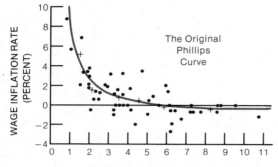

Phillips's research revealed a negative correlation between inflation and unemployment: as wage inflation fell, unemployment increased.

Source: A. W. Phillips, "The Relation Between Unemployment and the Rate of Change of Money Wages in the United Kingdom, 1861–1957," *Economica* 25 (November 1958): 285.

Figure 2
A Hypothetical Phillips Curve: The Inflation/Unemployment Trade-Off

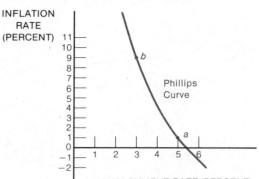

The hypothetical Phillips curve has a negative slope. Point *b* combines high inflation with low unemployment. Point *a* combines high unemployment with low inflation. The Phillips curve reflects the menu of inflation/unemployment choices open to society.

Phillips collected raw data on the relationship between wage inflation and unemployment in the United Kingdom for the years 1861 to 1913. When Phillips fit a curve to the 1861–1913 data, he found that it sketched out a relationship much like the experience of the United Kingdom through 1957. The famous **Phillips curve** suggested a stable and long-lasting trade-off between inflation and unemployment.

*The **Phillips curve** shows the relationship between unemployment and inflation and reveals that a reduction in the rate of unemployment requires an increase in the rate of wage (or price) inflation.*

Figure 1 reproduces the original Phillips curve. It shows a scatter diagram of the rate of change of wage rates and the unemployment rate in the United Kingdom for the years 1861 to 1913. Each dot represents a single year. The vertical height of each dot shows the average rate of change of money wages during the year; the horizontal distance between the vertical axis and the dot shows the average unemployment rate for the year. The

line fitted through these points is the famous Phillips curve. The Phillips curve has a negative slope: low unemployment rates are accompanied by high inflation, and high unemployment is accompanied by low inflation rates.

Phillips's work in England caused economists to examine the relationship between inflation and unemployment in other countries. American economists Paul Samuelson and Robert Solow fit a Phillips curve to the American experience from 1935 to 1959. Instead of looking at wage inflation, as Phillips did, they drew a Phillips curve relating the rate of price inflation and unemployment. Samuelson and Solow discovered that the U.S. data told the same story: to lower inflation, the unemployment rate must rise. In the American case, Samuelson and Solow estimated that an unemployment rate of between 5 and 6 percent was required in order to have an inflation-free economy. The socially acceptable unemployment norm in 1960 was perhaps 3.5 percent (which sounds low today but did not then). The American Phillips curve, therefore, implied a difficult social choice: low unemployment required living with inflation. The policy implication: Inflation could be eliminated only if society was prepared to tolerate an unemployment rate well above full

Figure 3
U.S. Inflation and Unemployment, 1961–1981

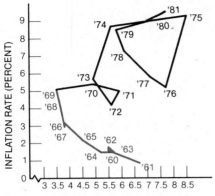

The annual growth rate of the GNP deflator is shown on the vertical axis. Each dot shows the inflation/unemployment combination for that year. The 1960s are connected with a color line, which shows the typical Phillips curve trade-off. The 1970s line in black fails to reveal the expected trade-off between inflation and unemployment.

Source: *Economic Report of the President*, 1982, pp. 237, 271

employment. Inflation was the price of low unemployment![2]

Figure 2 shows a hypothetical Phillips curve—much like the one Samuelson and Solow found for the United States—that illustrates the hard choices that society must make. Point *a* combines low inflation with high unemployment; point *b* combines high inflation with low unemployment. The Phillips curve made economists the bearers of bad news. The dismal science of the Phillips curve condemned society to either perpetual inflation or perpetual unemployment or to some combination of too high unemployment and too high inflation. Despite its gloomy message, however, the Phillips curve at least appeared to give society a choice.

The Phillips curve at least appeared to rule out the combination of high unemployment and high inflation. The stagflation of the 1970s and 1980s burst this bubble. The data on the relationship between U.S. inflation and unemployment from

2. Paul A. Samuelson and Robert M. Solow, "Analytical Aspects of Anti-Inflation Policy," *American Economic Review* (May 1960), pp. 177–94.

1961 to 1981 are graphed in Figure 3. The annual inflation rate in each year is recorded on the vertical axis, and the unemployment rate for that same year is shown on the horizontal axis.

The work of Phillips would lead one to expect a negative relationship between unemployment and inflation: the higher the unemployment rate, the lower the inflation rate. In Figure 3, the dots that represent each year's combination of inflation and unemployment are connected to show the history of inflation and unemployment as it unfolded after 1960.

The 1960s are connected with a color line. The 1960s dots show a classical Phillips curve relationship: unemployment fell from a 5–7 percent level in the early 1960s to a 3–4 percent level in the late 1960s. Inflation rose from 1–2 percent in the early 1960s to 4–5 percent in the late 1960s.

The traditional Phillips curve relationship fell apart in the 1970s. The black line in Figure 3 connects the years 1969 to 1981. The headline story of the 1970s was stagflation. The 1970s failed to yield anything resembling the traditional Phillips curve. For the period as a whole, both unemployment and inflation rose together. According to commentators of the 1970s, the "laws of economics" (namely, the Phillips curve) were no longer working. Economists had been so impressed with the Phillips curve that noneconomists should not be blamed for believing that stagflation violated some basic law of economics.

Indeed, during the 1960s it was difficult to dispute the Phillips curve. The Phillips curve was generally consistent with the teachings of Keynesian economics—which was riding a crest of popular and academic prestige. During the Kennedy-Johnson years, Keynesian economics and the Phillips curve analysis found an eloquent voice in Walter Heller and Arthur Okun, both chairmen of the President's Council of Economic Advisers.

In 1968 two economists, working independently, made a very simple point about the Phillips curve. Milton Friedman and Edmund S. Phelps noted that the Phillips curve makes a crucial assumption: it assumes that the *anticipated* rate of inflation remains constant. Thus, if the anticipated rate of inflation changes, the entire Phillips curve will shift. According to Friedman and Phelps, the inflation/unemployment relationship discussed by Phillips and Samuelson and Solow

Figure 4
The Short-Run Friedman-Phelps Curve

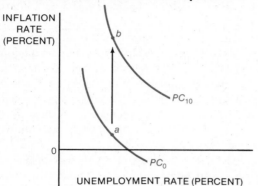

This figure illustrates the Friedman-Phelps analysis of the Phillips curve. PC_0 is the initial Phillips curve when the anticipated inflation rate is 0 percent. PC_{10} is the Phillips curve when the anticipated inflation rate is a higher 10 percent. A higher anticipated inflation rate shifts the entire Phillips curve up.

is stable *only when anticipated inflation is not changing*.

According to Friedman and Phelps, anticipated inflation will not change during periods when there is no distinct trend in inflation. However, if the rate of inflation increases significantly over a number of years, the anticipated inflation rate will increase (recall that according to the adaptive-expectations hypothesis, expectations adapt slowly to current and past experience). As the anticipated rate of inflation increases, the entire Phillips curve will shift upward.

Figure 4 depicts the Friedman-Phelps view of the shifting Phillips curve. PC_0 is the Phillips curve for an anticipated inflation rate of 0 percent, and PC_{10} is the Phillips curve for an anticipated inflation rate of 10 percent. As the anticipated inflation rate rises, so does the entire Phillips curve.

The Friedman-Phelps Phillips curve suggests that stagflation does not violate the laws of economics. If the anticipated rate of inflation is rising, both inflation and unemployment should rise—say, from *a* on PC_0 to *b* on PC_{10}. The stable Phillips curve trade-off between inflation and unemployment holds only when anticipated inflation is not changing.

The Friedman-Phelps analysis has lead to a new Phillips curve that will be discussed later in this chapter. It has altered the way economists view the inflation/unemployment relationship. To understand this new view, one must understand the workings of the labor market and unemployment.

LABOR MARKETS AND UNEMPLOYMENT

The labor market is a vast information-processing network that must match an incredible variety of jobs—from brain surgeons to store clerks—to an equally staggering variety of workers. How are workers to be matched with jobs efficiently? In a world in which everyone possesses complete information, matching jobs to people would be a relatively simple task. Everyone would be aware of all jobs in the economy and employers would know the skills and qualifications of all potential employees. Presumably, in such an economy there would be little or no unemployment.

In our complex economy, some unemployment is an inevitable result of the interplay of supply and demand in constantly changing labor markets. Every day new people enter the labor force; older people retire; new products compete in the market; unprofitable businesses fold; new methods of production are found; people change their attitudes towards working. In a dynamic economy, workers do not stay put. If they did, the economy would be unable to change for the better. The opportunity for people to change jobs is good for society.

Characteristics of the Unemployed

According to the official definition given in Chapter 5, unemployment occurs when someone is available for work, has looked actively for a job in the last four weeks, and is not currently working. As pointed out in Chapter 5, there is no one form of unemployment. Unemployment can be cyclical (associated with downturns in the economy), structural (associated with bad times in a specific industry), or frictional (associated with changing jobs). Some people quit their jobs; others drop out of the labor force because they are discouraged by their job search; others are fired

Table 1
The Duration of Unemployment in the United States (average for 1976–1981)

Percentage of Unemployed	Duration of Unemployment (1976–1981 average)
43	Less than 5 weeks
44	5 to 26 weeks
13	26 weeks or more

Source: *Economic Report of the President,* January 1982, p. 272.

Table 2
Sources of Unemployment, September 1981

Percentage of Unemployed	Source of Unemployment
14	Layoffs
34	Firings
13	Quits
27	Reentrants
12	New entrants

Source: U.S. Department of Labor, *Employment and Earnings* (October 1981), p. 48.

or laid off; still others enter and leave the labor force frequently.

Prevalence of Long-Term Unemployment. When the unemployed are counted at a particular point in time, some will have been out of work a short time; others will have been out of work a long time. *Long-term unemployment* can be defined as being unemployed for more than half a year. Over the business cycle, long-term unemployment defined in this way varies considerably. From 1969 to 1981, the percentage of the unemployed without jobs for a half year or more ranged from a low of 5.7 percent of total unemployment to a high of 18.3 percent. Short-term unemployment (less than 5 weeks) during this period varied somewhat less—from a low of 37 percent to a high of 58 percent of total unemployment.

Table 1 shows the average percentage of long-term and short-term unemployment for the period 1976 to 1981. As the table shows, most unemployment is short-term or medium-term. On average, long-term unemployment constitutes only about 13 percent of the total.[3] Thus, most cases of unemployment are of short duration.

Reasons for Loss of Employment. When one thinks of unemployment, one tends naturally to think of job losses (firings, plant closings, and layoffs). While firings and layoffs are indeed important, there are other ways of becoming unemployed. Table 2 shows the sources of unemployment for those unemployed in the month of September 1981. Of those unemployed, 39 percent had just entered or reentered the labor force after a period of schooling, work in the household, or whatever people do when they are outside the labor force. These people are unemployed not because they have been fired or laid off but because they have not found jobs upon entry (or reentry) into the labor force. The entry and reentry of people into the labor market goes on all the time and is a significant percentage of total unemployment. Table 2 shows that almost 50 percent of those unemployed were fired or were *laid off* (discharged subject to recall to the same job) and that 13 percent quit their jobs.

How did the long-term unemployed become unemployed? In September 1981, 990,000 people were unemployed for 6 months or longer. About 530,000 of these had been fired. A person who is

3. Kim B. Clark and Lawrence K. Summers, in "Labor Market Dynamics and Unemployment: A Reconsideration," *Brookings Papers on Economic Activity* (1979:1), pp. 13–72, argue that long-term unemployment is understated by these figures. For example: If every week 2 people lose their jobs for one week and 1 person loses a job for two weeks, at any time 3 people will be counted as out of work for 1 week plus 1 person for two weeks. According to Clark and Summers, 50 percent of unemployment is accounted for by people out of work for two weeks, although only 25 percent of unemploy-

ment at any given time consists of people out of work for the full two weeks.

Against Clark and Summers, it can be argued that if the people losing their jobs for two weeks were unemployed only one week, the unemployment rate would fall by the 25 percent rather than the 50 percent figure.

Chapter 16 addresses the issue of the *discouraged worker*—the person who drops out of the labor market because suitable jobs do not appear to be available. Should discouraged workers be counted in long-term unemployment?

fired is more likely to end up unemployed for a long term than one who has quit a job or been laid off. Chronic unemployment of this type is both a social and economic problem.

The conclusion that can be drawn from unemployment statistics is that most unemployment can be associated with the complex and changing character of the labor market. Although there is the problem of chronic long-term unemployment that typically begins with a firing, long-term unemployment of this type accounts for a fairly small share of total unemployment. Most unemployment is due to layoffs that may be perceived to be temporary, to difficulties of finding a job upon entry or reentry into the labor force, or to quits.

With the possible exception of the laid-off worker who expects to be recalled to his or her old job or the person who has voluntarily quit a job, the unemployed are involved in a search for jobs. Notice that quits and layoffs account for only 27 percent of unemployment; the remaining 73 percent of the unemployed are involved in the search for jobs.

Search and Contracting

The unemployment associated with firings or plant closings, quits, new entrants, and reentrants can in a broad sense be considered as *searching*. The process of job searching is complicated. The amount of information concerning employment opportunities and work conditions is limited. It is too expensive for employers to determine the exact characteristics of the people they hire; employers use rules of thumb—such as hiring only college graduates. People cannot know about all the jobs that are currently available or may become available in the future. People must make employment decisions under conditions of uncertainty.

How should a rational worker conduct his or her job search?

The rational worker should search in the labor market as long as the expected benefits from more searching exceed the expected costs.

Employed workers must decide whether to devote effort to finding a better job. Unemployed workers must decide how to conduct their search. They must decide whether to look for a new job now or to wait until employment opportunities improve. If they are laid off, what are the chances of being recalled to their old jobs and when?

The firm is in a similar position. Employers have a difficult time staffing their firms—not because people are lazy, but because it is hard to get information about people. Information is costly and sometimes even inaccurate.

Firms will search for new employees as long as the cost of more searching is less than the expected benefits.

What are the costs of searching for employers? Firms must place ads in newspapers and trade journals; they must conduct interviews; they must pay the training costs of new employees. What are the benefits? The firm gains by finding employees whose benefit to the firm exceeds their wage plus all the hiring costs. How much the firm should search for employees can only be determined at the microeconomic level at which the firm is operating, and the firm can obtain information only by searching.

The Friedman-Phelps view of the Phillips curve arises from the differential effects of anticipated and unanticipated inflation on labor markets.

Search with Unanticipated Inflation. Inflation (or deflation) that is *unanticipated* can affect unemployment. If the inflation rate rises above the anticipated rate due, say, to an unanticipated increase in aggregate demand, contracting and search activities can be affected in a number of ways:

1. When prices and wages are rising above expectations, wage offers will start to look more attractive to people looking for jobs. If wages and prices both rise, on average, by 7 percent while people anticipate a 5 percent inflation rate, workers will think they are being offered higher real wages, and job seekers will be more inclined to take jobs sooner. Those receiving unemployment insurance will find that market wages are rising relative to insurance benefits (which respond

slowly to rising living costs) and will be more likely to accept jobs.

2. Firms who were anticipating or contemplating firing marginal workers may now reconsider the costs and benefits of such an action. As wages rise in the marketplace, it may be better for the time being to keep the marginal worker (who is a known quantity) rather than try to replace him or her. If the labor market is tight, the expected benefits from search fall, and it pays to keep the marginal worker. When the firm's expected inflation is less than actual inflation, it overestimates the tightness of the labor market. As firings slow down, the actual tightness of the labor market increases.

3. Firms and employees set wage contracts on the basis of anticipated inflation rates as well as anticipated employee productivity. Employees seek to protect themselves from the inflation tax by factoring the anticipated inflation rate into their money-wage contracts. When the actual inflation rate exceeds the anticipated rate, employees are stuck with contracts that do not protect them fully from inflation. The firm finds that its prices (that are being pulled up by inflation) are rising faster than production costs since wages were set on a lower basis. The firm has an incentive to hire more and to fire less.[4]

When inflation is less than anticipated, the three factors noted above now work in reverse to increase unemployment. Fixed wage contracts factor in a higher rate of inflation than actually occurs and reduce business profitability. The firm increases its firings of marginal workers and reduces its search for new employees. Unemployment insurance looks better to the unemployed, and so on.

When inflation is greater than anticipated, unemployment falls. When inflation is less than anticipated, unemployment rises.

4. These factors explain why firings and entrant and reentrant unemployment fall when the actual inflation rate exceeds the anticipated inflation rate. Quits do not follow the Phillips curve pattern. When unemployment is falling, quit rates tend to increase as workers become more confident about securing a better job. Therefore a higher-than-anticipated inflation rate should cause quits to rise. But as noted above, quits are a small fraction of total unemployment, and most workers who quit already have another job arranged beforehand. Their unemployment—if any—will be of very short duration.

Layoffs and Implicit Contracts. In late 1981 layoffs represented about one seventh of total unemployment. Unlike firings, quits, and new entrants, layoffs cannot be classified as search activity (except in a broad sense). Layoffs are used by firms that require a career labor force. Such firms want a labor force that is attached more-or-less permanently to the firm because the firm requires a quality labor force with a good deal of on-the-job experience. On the other hand, the firm cannot guarantee employment to all its workers all the time. In some years, business may be bad, and fewer workers will be required.[5]

The firm strikes an explicit or implicit contract with its workers. It guarantees them a given wage plus generous fringe benefits and overtime pay but does not guarantee the hours of employment. The best it can do is to promise to use the laid-off workers rather than someone else when business is good. In this way, firms that experience cyclical fluctuations in demand are able to keep an experienced cadre of quality workers who know that they may be laid off from time to time.

Such a firm has an implicit contract with the worker to vary employment (or unemployment) more than the worker's wage rate. When the demand for labor falls, the wage rates of workers on such contracts will not fall sufficiently to prevent layoffs. Instead of wages adjusting, the amount of employment declines; some workers are laid off.

The contracts that such firms make with their workers take into account anticipated inflation rates. Workers will protect themselves from the inflation tax by demanding wage increases sufficient to protect them from inflation. If the actual rate of inflation equals the rate anticipated in the contract, inflation would not lead to fewer layoffs. But if the inflation rate exceeds the anticipated rate, firms will overestimate the tightness of labor markets, and they will lay off fewer workers. Moreover, the wages of current workers will not have kept pace with inflation (the workers have made an expectational mistake), and the firm will want to employ more workers. The amount of employment expands, and the number of layoffs contracts.

5. This discussion is based on Arthur Okun, *Prices and Quantities* (Washington, D.C.: Brookings Institution, 1981). Okun draws on the research of Martin N. Bailey, Donald F. Gordon, and Costas Azariadis on implicit contracts.

If the anticipated rate of inflation is less than the actual rate, firms will find their costs rising faster than their prices; they will step up the pace of layoffs. The workers are prepared to accept this variation in employment in return for a satisfactory long-term employment contract.

THE NATURAL-RATE HYPOTHESIS

The economy is full of dynamic undercurrents of job changing, firings, withdrawal and reentry into the labor force, and layoffs. The individual actors in this drama—the firms and the workers—are making their decisions by weighing the costs and benefits of search. The collectivity of these decisions determines the nation's aggregate unemployment rate at any point in time.

Chapter 12 defined the natural rate of unemployment as the rate at which the number of job vacancies matches the number of unemployed workers. Milton Friedman and Edmund Phelps hypothesized that at the natural rate of unemployment, actual and anticipated inflation are equal. In addition, the natural rate is independent of the inflation rate. The natural rate does not rise or fall with changes in inflation.

The basic justification for the natural-rate hypothesis is that rational individuals are not subject to money illusion. If all wages, prices, and incomes increase by 10 percent, the real behavior of people should not change with regards to employment and unemployment under conditions of perfect information.

The natural rate of unemployment is independent of the rate of inflation. The natural rate of unemployment does not rise or fall with changes in inflation. If an economy is operating at a natural rate of 5 percent unemployment, and the actual and anticipated inflation rates are the same at 8 percent, workers and firms are aware that real variables are not changing, so there is no reason for the amount of unemployment to change. Workers and firms are aware that rising money wages and prices are simply a money phenomenon. The only way for people to fall prey to money illusion is when the rate of inflation is different from the rate that is anticipated.

When inflation is anticipated, unemployment will equal the natural rate—no matter what

the anticipated rate of inflation. When inflation exceeds the anticipated rate, unemployment falls below the natural rate. When inflation is less than the anticipated rate, unemployment rises above the natural rate.

THE NEW PHILLIPS CURVE

The Friedman-Phelps analysis differentiates between two Phillips curves: the short-run Phillips curve and the long-run Phillips curve. The short-run curve will be recognized as the original Phillips curve. The long-run Phillips curve indicates *no* trade-off between inflation and unemployment in the long run.

The **short-run Phillips curve** shows the inflation/unemployment relationship when anticipated inflation remains constant. The **long-run Phillips curve** shows the inflation/unemployment relationship when the anticipated rate of inflation is changing and equals the actual rate of inflation.

The Short-Run Phillips Curve

Suppose that the rate of inflation is 0 percent and people expect no inflation (the anticipated inflation rate is also 0 percent). According to the natural-rate hypothesis, under these conditions, the actual unemployment rate will be the natural rate. If the natural rate of unemployment is 5 percent, this economy is operating at point c in Figure 5. The Phillips curve that prevails when the anticipated inflation rate is 0 percent is PC_0. Now suppose a sudden increase in aggregate demand raises the rate of inflation to 2 percent. People have failed to anticipate the increase in inflation (they still anticipate 0 inflation). The economy will, therefore, move to point a on the same Phillips curve where the unemployment rate is 4 percent.

The economics of search and contracting explains why the economy moves to an unemployment rate below the natural rate. Contracts written with a 0 percent anticipated inflation cause wage increases to fall behind price increases. Firms increase their output and employment. Those unemployed perceive money wages to be rising faster than prices; they accept job offers more readily. Firms can be fooled into thinking their

Figure 5
The New Phillips Curve

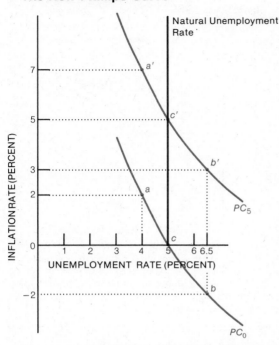

The economy is initially operating at the natural rate (assumed to be 5 percent) at point c on the Phillips curve PC_0. The actual and anticipated inflation rates are 0 percent. An expansionary policy raises the inflation rate, and the unanticipated inflation moves the economy to a, where the unemployment rate is 4 percent. If the economy had been instead at c' with an anticipated inflation rate of 5 percent, the Phillips curve would be PC_5. On PC_5, a 7 percent inflation rate is required to move the economy to a' where the unemployment rate is again 4 percent.

selling prices are rising more rapidly than their costs. They, therefore, expand output and employment.

If aggregate demand had fallen unexpectedly and brought about a 2 percent rate of deflation, the economy would move down to point b where the unemployment rate is 6.5 percent. At b, the unemployment rate exceeds the natural rate because the actual rate of inflation is less than the anticipated rate of inflation (-2 percent is less than 0 percent). Again, the search and contracting behavior of firms and individuals explains why unanticipated deflation causes more unemployment.

*The **short-run Phillips curve**, like the original Phillips curve, shows a negative relationship between inflation and unemployment. Less inflation means more unemployment.*

The Long-Run Phillips Curve

Suppose now that the rate of inflation has risen to 5 percent instead of the original 0 percent and that the anticipated rate of inflation has also risen to 5 percent. According to the natural-rate hypothesis, the Phillips curve has shifted up from PC_0 to PC_5. The economy is now at c' on PC_5. When inflation is anticipated, no one will be fooled by money illusion. The employment decisions of individuals and firms will not be different at a 5 percent anticipated inflation rate than at a 0 percent anticipated inflation rate. Therefore, the shifted Phillips curve PC_5 maintains the same shape as curve PC_0.

The upward shift in the Phillips curve has now disrupted the negative statistical correlation between inflation and unemployment. To have a 4 percent unemployment rate (point a') now requires a 7 percent inflation rate (one that exceeds the anticipated rate). To have a 6.5 percent unemployment rate (point b') requires a 3 percent inflation rate (one that is below the anticipated rate of inflation).

The Phillips curves shift up along the vertical natural unemployment rate line as anticipated inflation increases. Each PC curve passes through the vertical natural-rate line at exactly the point where the anticipated inflation rate equals the actual inflation rate. This result follows from the natural-rate hypothesis; there is an entire family of short-run Phillips curves—one for each anticipated rate of inflation. The **long-run Phillips curve** is the curve that connects each of the short-run curves at the point where actual inflation equals anticipated inflation.

*The **long-run Phillips curve** is a vertical line that shows that in the long run, the unemployment rate is independent of the inflation rate. Unemployment will not decline with more inflation in the long run.*

Inflation greater than the anticipated rate moves the economy up the short-run Phillips curve (from *c* to *a* in Figure 5). Inflation less than anticipated moves the economy down the short-run Phillips curve (from *c* to *b*). When actual inflation is different from anticipated inflation, a trade-off exists between inflation and unemployment. In the long run, the economy comes to anticipate a higher rate of inflation, and the short-run Phillips curve shifts up as anticipated inflation increases to match actual inflation.

EXPLAINING STAGFLATION AND ACCELERATING INFLATION

The new theory of the Phillips curve predicts that there will be a trade-off between inflation and unemployment *only if the anticipated rate of inflation does not change*. It predicts that the Phillips curve will shift up as the anticipated rate of inflation increases. Once the higher rate of inflation is anticipated, the economy will operate at the natural unemployment rate. How well does the available evidence support the Friedman-Phelps theory of the Phillips curve?

Stagflation, 1966–1981

The period 1966 to 1981 was one of sharply accelerating inflation—a period in which there was likely unanticipated inflation. Figure 6 is a scatter diagram showing the unemployment rate on the horizontal axis and a simple measure of the unanticipated rate of inflation on the vertical axis. Each dot represents a single year. The unanticipated inflation rate is measured as the difference between the actual annual percentage change in the GNP price deflator and the anticipated inflation rate for that year. The anticipated rate of inflation is calculated using adaptive expectations as the average rate for the last three years. For example, in 1978, 1979, and 1980 the inflation rates were 7.3, 8.5, and 9.0 percent. The anticipated inflation rate in 1980 is, therefore, taken to be 8.3 percent, the average of the three years. No one knows for sure what the anticipated inflation rate is in any year, but this method likely gives a reasonable approximation.

If the new theory is correct, there should be a negative relationship between unemployment and the *unanticipated* inflation rate. Remember, un-

Figure 6
U.S. Unemployment and Unanticipated Inflation, 1966–1980

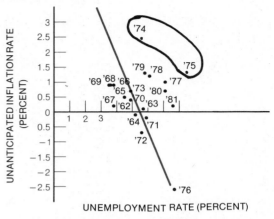

In this graph, the anticipated inflation rate is calculated as the average inflation rate over the past three years. The unanticipated rate is the GNP deflator minus this anticipated rate. The graph shows that the unemployment rate tends to drop when there is unanticipated inflation.

anticipated inflation causes unemployment to decline. If the inflation is *anticipated,* it should have *no effect* on unemployment. The data shows that except for 1974 and 1975, there is indeed a negative relationship between unemployment and unanticipated inflation. The years 1974 and 1975, it might be noted, were exceptional years when the extraordinary effects of the quadrupling of oil prices were most severe. Supply shocks of this type would be expected to disrupt the normal relationship between unanticipated inflation and unemployment.

Except for 1974 and 1975, the dots are generally consistent with the Friedman-Phelps story. For instance, in 1976 people expected a 7.7 percent inflation rate but experienced only a 5.2 percent inflation rate. As the theory predicts, unemployment was quite high in that year. In 1979, the anticipated inflation rate was 7.2 percent, and the actual rate was 8.5 percent. As predicted by the theory, unemployment was a relatively low 5.8 percent. The first quarter of 1982, not shown in the graph, was striking confirmation of the Friedman-Phelps curve. Unemployment reached 10 percent and the actual inflation rate was far below

Figure 7
Accelerating Inflation

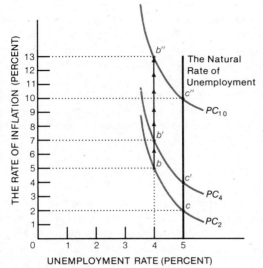

Maintaining a 4 percent unemployment rate causes accelerating inflation. For unemployment rates below the natural rate, actual inflation must exceed anticipated inflation, but this requirement increases the anticipated rate of inflation. Hence, the Phillips curve shifts ever upward.

the anticipated rate (in March 1982, inflation was near zero).

Accelerating Inflation

The new Phillips curve doctrine is consistent with the phenomenon of accelerating inflation. Recall that from the mid 1960s to the late 1970s, inflation rates as measured by the GNP deflator rose from 1.5 percent per annum to near double-digit levels (9.1 percent in 1981). In 1979, the CPI rose by 11.3 percent, and the GNP deflator rose by 8.5 percent. The new Phillips curve offers an explanation for accelerating inflation.

Suppose the economy is operating at point c in Figure 7. The inflation rate is 2 percent, the anticipated inflation rate also equals 2 percent, and unemployment is at the natural rate of 5 percent. The government now decides to lower the unemployment rate to 4 percent and to hold it at that level. By increasing aggregate demand, the inflation rate rises unexpectedly to 5 percent (there is a 3 percent unanticipated inflation), and the un-

anticipated inflation lowers the unemployment rate to 4 percent. The economy has moved along the established short-run Phillips curve, PC_2, from c to b.

At a 5 percent inflation rate, however, people will raise their inflation expectations. People might raise the anticipated rate of inflation initially from 2 to 4 percent. When the anticipated rate of inflation rises, the entire short-run Phillips curve shifts up (from PC_2 to PC_4). With the new and higher short-run Phillips curve, PC_4, a 7 percent inflation rate is required to keep the economy at a 4 percent unemployment rate (point b' on PC_4). A 7 percent inflation rate causes the Phillips curve to shift up again, and an even higher inflation rate is required to keep the economy at a 4 percent unemployment rate.

If monetary and fiscal authorities try to hold the unemployment rate below the natural rate, they must continuously keep the inflation rate above the anticipated inflation rate. Inflation will continue to accelerate as long as the unemployment rate is held below the natural rate. The process of accelerating inflation is shown by the continuous upward shifting of the short-run Phillips curve.

Stop-and-Go Policies

The world does not proceed as smoothly as in Figure 7. As the government sees the inflation rate accelerating, political pressures will build up to stop inflation. Hence, it is likely that the government will respond to these pressures by cutting the growth of money supply. For example, the U.S. economy experienced accelerating inflation from 1964 to 1968. The growth of the money supply trended upward, and by 1968 money was growing at an 8 percent annual rate. In the next year, 1969, money supply growth was cut to 3 percent per year. When money supply growth is cut, the effect on inflation is typically not immediate. Inflation does not immediately fall; instead, the inflation rate will first peak and then eventually slow down.

As the inflation rate falls, the actual inflation rate will fall below the anticipated rate. As already demonstrated, unemployment rises when the actual rate of inflation falls below the antici-

Figure 8
Stop-and-Go Economic Policies

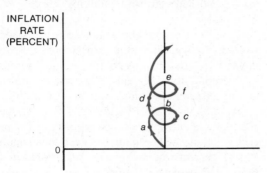

INFLATION
RATE
(PERCENT)

UNEMPLOYMENT RATE (PERCENT)

The economy is initially experiencing unanticipated inflation that drives the unemployment rate below the natural rate (point *a*). Accelerating inflation moves the economy to *b*. Political pressure builds to stop inflation, and the growth of money supply is reduced. Unanticipated deflation causes unemployment, and the economy moves to point *c*. Monetary authorities are now pressured to fight unemployment. The growth of money supply is speeded up, and the economy moves to *d*, where inflation becomes the major political problem once again. This process may repeat itself.

pated rate. Now the problem is rising unemployment, not inflation. Political pressure now builds to combat high unemployment. Monetary authorities may be persuaded to step up the growth of the money supply once again. For example, in the early 1970s, the unemployment rate was around 6 percent—which was considered high for the time. The monetary authorities began speeding up the rate of monetary growth. By 1972, the money supply was growing at an annual rate of 9.2 percent—the highest monetary growth rate since World War II.

Figure 8 shows the effects of such stop-and-go policies. First, the unemployment rate is pushed below the natural rate (at *a*) by expansionary policies that create unanticipated inflation. As the inflation rate accelerates (at *b*), the monetary authorities become concerned about inflation, and they cut back on monetary growth, pushing the economy to point *c*, where unemployment is high but the inflation rate is falling. Monetary authorities respond to high unemployment by stepping up the growth of the money supply and moving the economy to *d*. Accelerating inflation again be-

comes a problem at *e,* and authorities reduce monetary growth, moving the economy to *f*. The cycle may repeat itself.

The spiral movements in Figure 8 look uncannily like the U.S. data in Figure 3 with one important difference. The U.S. data in Figure 3 reveal stop-and-go movements with the unemployment rate trending up—unlike our hypothetical stop-and-go diagram with fluctuations around a stable natural rate of unemployment. Why the unemployment rate has trended upwards is investigated in Chapter 16.

Political Business Cycles

Stop-and-go policies can generate *political business cycles*. The alternating concern of the monetary authorities may represent the Fed's response to political pressures. When inflation is singled out as public enemy number one, the executive branch and the Congress put pressure on monetary authorities to reduce the inflation rate. If the public regards inflation as getting out of hand, the party in power will worry about the next election. When unemployment is regarded as the main villain, political pressure is put on the Fed to lower the unemployment rate. The alternating focus on fighting inflation and fighting unemployment leads to the spiral motions of Figure 8. Insofar as these cycles are caused by responses to political pressures, they have been dubbed political business cycles.

Is it in the interests of democratic governments to induce business cycles? Will not the voters recognize what is going on and "throw the rascals out"? Unfortunately, politics is a short-run business. In good times, the politicians in power are usually rewarded by reelection; in bad times, they are penalized by losing their offices. Voters do not have long memories and are impatient for good times to reappear. A politician who enacts a policy of slowly reducing inflation and unemployment over a 10-year period would stand little chance of reelection—even though the problem of anticipated inflation may have been decades in the making. The politician who wants to get reelected must act now. The price of acting now to achieve a low unemployment rate at election time may be a high rate of anticipated inflation in the future. But the vote-maximizing politician cannot afford to worry about such long-range concerns. The politician's attitude often is to worry about tomorrow when tomorrow comes.

A number of economists and political scientists have studied the political business cycle. Edward Tufte, a political scientist from Yale University, looked at U.S. data on real disposable income from 1947 to 1976. He found that, excluding the Eisenhower years of 1953 to 1960, about 80 percent of the election years showed an increase in the growth of real disposable income and about 80 percent of the nonelection years showed a decrease in the rate of growth of real disposable income. Tufte found that this phenomenon is not unique to the United States and that a similar pattern existed in 27 different democratic countries.[6]

The evidence on the political business cycle is still inconclusive, but if there is indeed a political business cycle, what can be done about it? One proposal is to increase the term of the President from 4 to 6 years and to limit the President to one term in office. The advocates of this proposal maintain that this system would allow the President to pursue more long-term economic goals with less concern about the reelection just a couple of years away.[7]

WHAT TO DO ABOUT STAGFLATION

Stagflation presents policy makers with the serious dilemma of how to fight inflation without worsening unemployment or how to fight unemployment without worsening inflation.

The Unemployment Costs of Reducing Inflation

The new Phillips-curve analysis suggests that there may be substantial unemployment costs to reducing inflation if expectations are slow to adjust. Anti-inflationary monetary policy will raise the unemployment rate if the anticipated rate of inflation does not drop at the same rate as the inflation rate. If the actual inflation rate is below the

6. Edward Tufte, *Political Control of the Economy* (Princeton, N.J.: Princeton University Press, 1978).
7. Politicians are well aware of the power of the political business cycle. In his memoirs, Richard Nixon blames his loss of the close 1960 election on Eisenhower's failure to reduce unemployment prior to election time.

Figure 9
The Unemployment Costs of Reducing Inflation

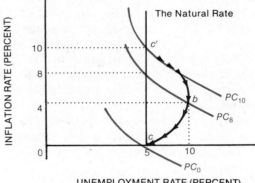

UNEMPLOYMENT RATE (PERCENT)

The economy is initially operating at c'—at the natural rate of 5 percent unemployment with an anticipated inflation rate of 10 percent (which equals the actual inflation rate). Monetary authorities reduce the growth of the money supply and the rate of inflation begins to slow down. The economy begins to move along $c'bc$. Point b is a representative intermediate point: at b, the inflation rate is 4 percent, but the anticipated inflation rate is 8 percent; unemployment is 10 percent. Until the expected rate of inflation falls to 0 percent, the economy will continue to experience unemployment above the natural rate.

anticipated inflation rate, unemployment will rise, according to the new Phillips-curve analysis.

Figure 9 illustrates this problem. The economy is initially operating at the natural rate of unemployment (5 percent) with an inflation rate of 10 percent. Because the economy is operating at the natural rate, actual and anticipated inflation are equal. How can the economy move from a high rate of inflation to a 0 rate of inflation without causing unemployment (how can it move from c' to c)?

According to the new Phillips-curve analysis, getting from c' to c is very difficult because inflationary *expectations* must be beaten down to 0 percent! If expectations are adaptive, a number of years must be endured in which the actual rate of inflation is less than the anticipated rate. But unemployment increases when actual inflation is below anticipated inflation. During this period, a simplified picture of the path of the economy might look something like the loop $c'bc$. The economy starts at c' with inflation at 10 percent, unemployment at 5 percent, and the anticipated inflation rate at 10 percent. When contractionary policies are applied, the economy moves to *b*. At the intermediate point *b,* the unemployment rate has risen to 10 percent and the inflation rate has dropped to 4 percent, but the anticipated inflation rate is 8 percent. Unemployment above the natural rate has been caused by an anticipated rate of inflation higher than actual inflation. The hardships of unemployment at *b* may be considerable. As the inflation rate continues to drop towards 0 percent, inflationary expectations will continue to drop. Once the economy reaches point *c,* the natural rate of unemployment is restored, and the actual and anticipated rates of inflation are both 0 percent.

Suggested Remedies

The price paid for a sudden shift to an anti-inflationary policy is unemployment when inflationary expectations are adjusting downward. Two policies have been suggested for lightening this load: gradualism and indexation.

Gradualism.   To move from *c'* to *c* requires reducing the rate of growth of the money supply drastically. Even if this is done all at once—say, the rate of growth of money supply is cut from 13 percent to a permanent 3 percent—the economy may require 3 to 5 years to move along *c'bc* to *c*. During these years, the economy would have to endure considerable unemployment. A gradualist policy might lessen the impact on unemployment. Instead of reducing the growth of money supply from 13 percent to 3 percent all at once, monetary authorities might do it gradually over a period of, say, 5 years. Moreover, in order to persuade the public to lower its expectations about inflation, the monetary authorities would announce in advance the scheduled reductions in the rate of monetary growth. If expectations are rational, when people believe the government policy announcements they will immediately lower the anticipated rate of inflation. If the people do not believe the government's monetary growth plans (they may have long ago lost faith in such pronouncements), the anticipated inflation rate will drop only when people see the actual inflation rate dropping.

Indexing.   Some economists suggest that **indexing** the income tax, private wage contracts, unemployment insurance, and social security to the actual rate of inflation will reduce the unemployment costs of reducing inflation.

Indexing is the tying of the rate of increase of the thing being indexed (wages, income taxes, social-security benefits) to the actual inflation rate. If social-security payments are indexed to the inflation rate, for example, they would rise by the rate of actual inflation.

One reason an unanticipated decline in the rate of inflation increases unemployment is that wage contracts are fixed in money terms. A three-year wage contract builds in an anticipated rate of inflation. If the actual inflation rate is below the anticipated rate, wage costs will rise more rapidly than product prices, and there will be less employment. If money wages are indexed to the actual inflation rate, the rate of increase of money wages will automatically respond to reductions in the inflation rate. As Friedman has written:

> Here is an employer who has committed himself to paying higher and higher wages at a fixed rate without an escalator clause. When the process of slowing inflation starts, he suddenly discovers that the prices at which he sells his product aren't going up as fast as they were before. What's he going to do? His costs stay up. He can't do anything about costs, so he has to cut down on his output. With indexation, his costs would, after a lag . . . also adjust. Therefore he would not be under anything like as much pressure to reduce his output and employment.[8]

The main objection to indexing is that it may formalize the wage/price spiral. On the way down, indexing might prove beneficial, but on the way up, wages would increase more than they otherwise would have. The fear is that indexation would feed inflation on the way up.

The main difficulty with Friedman's proposal is how to put it into operation. The indexing of

8. The American Enterprise Institute for Public Policy Research, *Indexing and Inflation* (Washington, D.C.: AEI Institute, 1974), p. 21.

income taxes and government benefits would require only legislative action, but what about private wage and price contracts? Friedman opposes passing a law that requires indexing of private contracts, and so would most other economists. The question, therefore, is: why should business firms start indexing on their own?

The last two chapters have been concerned with inflation and unemployment and have suggested possible policies to deal with reducing the rate of inflation with minimum effects on unemployment. If the problem of inflation were solved, the economy would still be subject to ups and downs in unemployment—the business cycle. The next chapter explores how the business cycle can be stabilized.

Summary

1. Stagflation is the combination of high unemployment and high inflation in a stagnant economy. The original Phillips curve showed a stable negative relationship between unemployment and inflation. It predicted that to reduce inflation, a higher unemployment rate had to be accepted and that to reduce unemployment, a higher inflation rate had to be endured. Recent U.S. history shows that the typical Phillips curve relationship held for the 1960s but not for the 1970s, when increasing inflation was accompanied by increasing unemployment.

2. The facts of unemployment show that long-term unemployment accounts for a small percentage of total unemployment. Quits, firings, new entrants, and reentrants account for most of unemployment. Individuals unemployed for these reasons are engaged in searching in the labor market. An actual inflation rate that is greater than the anticipated rate will cause the unemployment rate to fall. An actual inflation rate that is less than the anticipated rate will cause unemployment to rise.

3. Milton Friedman and Edmund Phelps offered

the natural-rate hypothesis to explain the phenomenon of stagflation. They argued that the Phillips curve will shift up with the anticipated rate of inflation.

4. As the anticipated inflation rate rises, the Phillips curve shifts up. Because the economy tends to return to the natural rate in the long run, the different Phillips curves tend to pass through the natural rate. The new Phillips-curve hypothesis is consistent with recent American experience. Unemployment does vary with unanticipated inflation, and the new Phillips curve does explain accelerating inflation. If the government attempts to hold the unemployment rate below the natural rate, inflation will accelerate.

5. Unanticipated reductions in the rate of inflation cause increases in unemployment. Therefore, political pressures will cause the government to use stop-and-go economic policies. Stop-and-go economic policies may lead to the political business cycle.

6. Inflation can be reduced by permanently lowering the rate of growth of the money supply. But until inflationary expectations fall, the unemployment rate will rise. The unemployment costs of fighting inflation can extend over a period of years. Gradualism is one solution to the problem of fighting inflation without creating too much unemployment in the process. Instead of a once-and-for-all reduction in money-supply growth, the government could announce and carry through a policy of gradually reducing money-supply growth. Another solution is indexing private contracts, income taxes, and government benefits programs.

Key Terms

stagflation
Phillips curve
short-run Phillips curve
long-run Phillips curve
indexing

Questions and Problems

1. ''The Friedman-Phelps natural-rate hypothesis unites microeconomics and macroeconomics.'' Evaluate this statement.
2. Explain why inflation will likely not affect real behavior (the job choices of individuals, the production decisions of firms) when it is anticipated. Why would it then affect real behavior when it is unanticipated?
3. If the unemployment rate is above the natural rate, what will happen to prices? When the unemployment rate is below the natural rate, what will happen to prices?
4. Explain why the short-run Phillips curve shows a negative relationship between inflation and unemployment. Explain why the long-run Phillips curve is vertical.
5. If the rate of inflation anticipated by workers is 5 percent, but the actual rate of inflation turns out to be 10 percent, how would this surprise affect employment decisions?
6. What will be the consequences when monetary authorities attempt to hold the unemployment rate permanently below the natural rate? Explain your answer with aggregate supply-and-demand diagrams.
7. Evaluate the ability of different proposals to combat inflation without creating serious unemployment in the process.

15

Stabilization Policy

Chapter Preview

One of the most controversial questions in macroeconomics today is how to stabilize business cycles. Economists are widely agreed about many things, but economists still disagree on how best to keep inflation under control, and how to keep unemployment from getting out of hand. These issues worry the average person on the street who looks to policy makers and economists for answers.

Activists argue that monetary and fiscal policies should be deliberately used to moderate the business cycle. *Nonactivists,* on the other hand, argue that deliberate countercyclical policies should not be followed. They believe that deliberate policy should be replaced by a stable monetary and fiscal framework and that rules should be established in place of activist policies. Activist economists usually follow the tradition of Keynes; nonactivists are usually monetarists or proponents of rational-expectations theory. The monetarist/Keynesian controversy began with arguments over whether monetary or fiscal policy is more important but has spilled over into the broader debate of activism versus nonactivism.

THE POLICY OPTIONS

Fiscal policy actions are changes in government expenditures or tax schedules for the purpose of achieving macroeconomic goals. *Monetary policy* actions are changes in the money supply or the rate of growth of the money supply for the purpose of achieving macroeconomic goals. As noted in earlier chapters, both monetary and fiscal policy work through their effect on aggregate demand. The discussion that follows refers to aggregate demand policies if no distinction between monetary and fiscal policy is needed.

Activism

Policy activism is the deliberate manipulation of fiscal and monetary policy to iron out fluctuations in the business cycle. An activist policy does not include the use of built-in fiscal stabilizers or changes in government spending or taxation carried out for reasons of public finance (for example, raising revenue to support public goods like police protection or national defense). The objective of activist policy is to soften the fluctuation of the business cycle. Activist policies can be carried out either through *feedback rules* or *discretionary policy*.

Feedback Rules.   Activist policy can be rigid in the sense that one can set policy dials to respond in a predetermined manner to changes in the state of the economy through the use of **feedback rules**.

*A **feedback rule** establishes a feedback relationship between activist policy and the state of the economy.*

For example, a simple monetary-policy feedback rule might be to raise monetary growth by 1 percent for every 1 percent increase in the unemployment rate above a specified unemployment-rate target. A fiscal-policy feedback rule might be to increase government expenditures by a certain percentage for every 1 percent increase in the unemployment rate above a target rate. Once the state of the economy changes in a specific manner, feedback rules prescibe the monetary and fiscal policies that respond to the change.

Discretionary Policy.   Feedback rules are fixed rules. Opponents of fixed rules argue that different economic situations may call for subtle policy differences. The optimal feedback rule may be difficult to determine. If policy making is an art rather than a science, it is better to let the

President's Council of Economic Advisers, the Treasury, Congress, and the Fed decide what monetary and fiscal policies are appropriate in each circumstance. Economic policy makers can look at a number of indicators of the state of the economy—inflation, unemployment, interest rates, the balance of payments, and political factors—to determine monetary and fiscal policy. Rather than tying their hands with rigid feedback rules, it may be better to rely on the judgment of those responsible for the economic health of our nation.

How active should activist policies be? Should stabilization policies respond only to major disturbances or to small changes in the business cycle? In the heady days of the 1960s, economists spoke of *fine tuning*—the frequent use of discretionary monetary and fiscal policy to counteract even small movements in business activity. Today few economists argue for fine tuning but believe that the dials should be fiddled with only in response to major movements in real GNP and inflation. Feedback rules could be written in a way that allows for a range of fluctuation in real GNP and unemployment before any policies are activated.

Nonactivism

Milton Friedman has argued for a stable monetary and fiscal framework without activism. In his view, attempts to deliberately manage monetary and fiscal policy should be scrapped as ineffective and even harmful. Friedman's proposal for nonactivism consists of two parts:

1.   There should be a fixed monetary rule that requires constant (or nearly constant) growth of the nominal money supply year after year at a rate equal to the long-run average growth rate of real GNP.
2.   The federal budget should be balanced over the business cycle. Surpluses during the recovery phase should cancel out deficits during the recession stage. Government spending should be dictated by the need for public spending and not by the needs of discretionary fiscal policy.

Friedman argues that such a stable monetary and fiscal framework would provide the ideal setting for economic stability. The self-correcting mechanism would work at its maximum efficiency under a fixed monetary rule and a cyclically balanced budget.

FISCAL VERSUS MONETARY POLICY

Should fiscal or monetary policy or both be used in an activist world? Traditionally Keynesians have argued that fiscal policy is relatively more important than monetary policy, particularly in bringing the economy out of a deep recession or depression. But modern Keynesians believe that both monetary and fiscal policy are important tools of activist policy. Monetarists have argued that fiscal policy is close to being ineffective and that fiscal policy has little or no impact on output and employment.

The Modern Keynesian Position

The original Keynesian argument for the potency of fiscal policy in a world with unemployed resources is that *fiscal policy has a direct impact on aggregate demand.* As government expenditures increase and taxes are reduced, aggregate demand increases. When aggregate demand increases, unemployed resources will be employed and real output will increase.

This simple fiscal multiplier argument is the heart and soul of the Keynesian's basic position that fiscal policy is a potent and powerful stabilization instrument. Monetary policy, on the other hand, has only an indirect impact on aggregate demand. If the money supply is increased, individuals and firms must still decide to spend more before the monetary expansion can lead to greater aggregate demand. But several problems can arise along the way: the increase in money supply may not lower interest rates very much; a reduction in interest rates may not stimulate investment demand very much. Changes in velocity can offset changes in money supply.

Does fiscal policy—deliberately managed—have the effects on the economy that were predicted by the Keynesians? Keynesians cite two types of evidence of the effectiveness of fiscal policy: the 1964 tax cut and the results of econometric models.

The 1964 Tax Cut. Keynesian economic policy was first used in the 1960s in the Kennedy and Johnson administrations. During the 1960s, Keynesian economics was given its first test, and the first major use of discretionary fiscal policy was the Revenue Act of 1964.

The 1950s saw two recessions in which the unemployment rate rose to 5.5 percent (1954) and to 6.8 percent (1958). In the early 1960s, the unemployment rate remained in the 5–7 percent range. According to the Keynesian activists, this period illustrated a classic case of underemployed resources. Keynesians called for activist fiscal policies to lower unemployment and raise the growth of real GNP. The 1964 Revenue Act cut personal taxes by $10 billion—the equivalent of a 20 percent cut—and reduced corporate taxes by $3 billion, for an 8 percent reduction in corporate taxes.

How did Keynesian economics score on its first test? According to the calculations of Arthur Okun—one of the architects of economic policy during the 1960s—the 1964 tax cut caused GNP to increase by $36.2 billion (GNP in 1964 was $638 billion). In 1964, the unemployment rate was 5.2 percent; two years later it had dropped to 3.8 percent. In the four years prior to the tax cut, real GNP increased by a total of 11.3 percent. From 1964 to 1967, real GNP expanded by a total of 15.4 percent. For the decade of the 1950s, real GNP grew by 38 percent; for the decade of the 1960s, real GNP grew by 47 percent. Fiscal policy operating from a starting point of unemployed resources did indeed appear to raise real output and employment.

The apparent success of the 1964 tax cut caused Keynesians to be exuberant about fiscal policy. According to Walter Heller, the Chairman of the Council of Economic Advisers under Presidents Kennedy and Johnson,

> The capstone of postwar policy for putting the U.S. economy more or less into full employment orbit was, of course, the great tax cut of 1964 . . . it ushered in a new era in which the avowed and active use of tax, budget, and monetary instruments would keep the economy operating in the vicinity of full employment, with all the pleasures and pains that the management of prosperity involves.[1]

---

1. Milton Friedman and Walter W. Heller, *Monetary Versus Fiscal Policy* (New York: W. W. Norton, 1969), p. 32.

The experiences of the early and mid-1960s persuaded many economists that activist fiscal policies—if appropriately applied—could effectively eliminate the business cycle. The United States would no longer have to worry about massive unemployment or runaway inflation; these problems would be taken care of by the wise use of fiscal policy. Monetary policy could serve a useful supportive role to fiscal policy, but with unemployed resources, fiscal policy would be the more powerful instrument.

The increases in real GNP growth and the reduction in unemployment following the 1964 tax cut do not by themselves prove the potency of fiscal policy. To obtain a broader picture, it is necessary to look at what was happening to other policy instruments. In the period leading up to the tax cut (1959 to 1964), the money supply (M1) grew at an annual rate of 2.7 percent. From 1964 to 1967, the annual growth of money supply accelerated to 4.6 percent. The declining unemployment and increasing rate of growth of output could either be explained by the tax cut or by the expanding growth of money supply—or by a combination of the two. In Walter Heller's words:

> So far as I know, we have no evidence consisting of a . . . simple correlation between fiscal actions and the level of economic activity.[2]

Econometric Evidence. The effects of fiscal policy cannot be established simply by examining one policy variable, such as a tax cut, in isolation. As just explained, monetary growth accelerated after the 1964 tax cut. To determine whether the tax cut can take credit for the decline in unemployment after 1964, the effects of fiscal policy must be disentangled from those of monetary policy.

Econometric modeling of the U.S. economy—pioneered by Nobel laureate Lawrence Klein of the University of Pennsylvania—was developed with this problem in mind. By estimating statistical models of the economy from actual historical data with equations to describe consumption, investment, export-import, and government-spending behavior, the impact of fiscal policy theoretically could be isolated. By learning how

2. Friedman and Heller, *Monetary Versus Fiscal Policy*, p. 6.

Table 1
The Impact of Fiscal Policy: Government Expenditure and Tax Multipliers

Model	Government Expenditure Multiplier (real dollars) $\Delta Y/\Delta G$	Tax Multiplier (real dollars) $\Delta Y/\Delta T$
Bureau of Economic Analysis	2.2	−1.4
Brookings	2.7	−1.6
Data Resources Inc.	1.6	−1.3
Wharton	2.0	−1.7

This table shows the effects of fiscal policy eight quarters after the policy was executed. The DRI multipliers, however, are for the effects after one year. The DRI fiscal multipliers show quicker responses to fiscal policy with maximum effects felt in one year's time.

Source: Gary Fromm and Lawrence Klein, "A Comparison of Eleven Econometric Models of the United States," *American Economic Review*, 63, 2 (May 1973): 391–92.

investment, consumption, employment, and real GNP have responded in the past to changes in fiscal policy, econometric models can draw conclusions about the effectiveness of fiscal policy.

By the early 1970s, a number of large econometric models had been estimated from data on the U.S. economy—including the Brookings model, the Wharton model, the Data Resources Inc. model, and the Bureau of Economic Analysis model. These econometric models are Keynesian in structure. They postulate, for example, that disposable income is the principal determinant of consumption spending and that investment spending depends upon interest rates and upon accelerator effects.

Table 1 gives the estimates of various econometric models of the government-expenditure multiplier and tax multiplier effects of a sustained shift in government expenditures or personal taxes two years (8 quarters) after the policy was initiated. These multipliers are not identical, but they would not be expected to be because they were estimated for different time periods; they trace the effects of fiscal policy from different starting points in the U.S. business cycle. These data do indicate, however, that fiscal policy tends to work in the fashion predicted by Keynesian economics.

Econometric models constructed in the Keynesian tradition all show substantial effects of fiscal policy on real GNP and, hence, unemployment. They suggest a government-expenditure multiplier of approximately 1.7 to 2.7 after the policy had been given time to run its course. The government spending multipliers are larger than the tax multipliers, as Keynesian theory predicted, and the multipliers are larger than one.

Modern Keynesians have come to accept the fact that both monetary and fiscal policy are important. In drawing this conclusion, they were influenced by the work of Milton Friedman and other monetarists and by their own econometric models.

Modern Keynesians argue that both monetary and fiscal policy should be used in countercyclical policy. A sound countercyclical policy should not put all of its eggs in one basket. In a world of uncertainty about the effects of policy, diversification pays off both in private financial management and macroeconomic policy.

Moreover, monetary and fiscal policy can complement and soften each other's impact. If Congress acts too strongly on fiscal policy, the Fed can soften the blow by countervailing monetary policy. If the economy is in a deep recession without inflation, both monetary and fiscal expansion may be needed to get the economy moving again. Keynesians, for example, view the 1964 tax cut as being aided by the accompanying monetary growth.[3]

The Monetarist Position

According to Milton Friedman and other monetarists, fiscal policy is much less important than monetary policy. The monetarist position that government spending and taxes are not important does not agree with the Keynesian income/expenditure analysis described in Chapters 9 and 10.

Monetarists regard the Keynesian multiplier analysis of fiscal policy as flawed. The Keynesian model assumes that when government spending increases, private spending does not decrease. This assumption allows the Keynesian model to generate substantial fiscal multipliers. But what if the increase in government spending *crowds out* private spending?[4]

Chapter 10 examined some of the ways in which increased government spending might crowd out private spending. Direct crowding out occurs when government spending directly reduces private spending. When the government spends more on police protection and public schools, the public may then reduce its private spending for private security guards and for private school tuition. Increased government spending can also lead to indirect crowding out: as government spending rises, the bidding up of interest rates can depress private investment and consumption spending.

The Keynesian-inspired econometric models cited in Table 1 show smaller multipliers than would be expected from observed marginal propensities to consume; therefore, some crowding out must have occurred. The extreme monetarist position that fiscal policy does not affect output and employment *at all* requires evidence that there is *complete* crowding out. This question remains a point of active debate among economists.

Monetarists believe that crowding out reduces or eliminates government-expenditure multipliers. What about tax multipliers? According to Friedman, the effects of tax changes will be difficult if not impossible to determine in advance. Chapter 9 explained that *permanent income* is an average of the income that a person expects to earn over his or her lifetime. If people base their spending on permanent income rather than on current income, tax-induced changes in disposable income may have only a limited effect on current consumption spending. Since permanent income has

3. Walter Heller argues that monetary policy alone would not have been enough to move into a high employment economy from the high unemployment rates of 1963–1964: "I don't see how the economy could have climbed to full employment under the incubus of a $12 to $13 billion full employment surplus. Given the . . . constraints of the real world, the idea that monetary policy would have been capable of generating a matching amount of private investment—in order to reach a saving-investment relationship consistent with full employment—is next to inconceivable." Friedman and Heller, *Monetary Versus Fiscal Policy,* p. 67.

4. Friedman writes: "The fascinating thing to me is that the widespread belief in the potency of fiscal policy . . . rests on no evidence whatsoever. It's based on pure assumption. It's based on a priori reasoning." Friedman and Heller, *Monetary Versus Fiscal Policy,* pp. 52–53.

more of an effect than current income on consumer spending, one must be able to determine the effects of tax changes on permanent income, not its effects on current income. Yet the effects of tax policy on permanent income are difficult to predict because they depend upon whether people think the tax-policy changes will be permanent or transitory.

Monetarists rely on evidence from their own econometric models and from economic history to support their position that fiscal policy is not effective as a stabilization tool.

The St. Louis Model.

A famous econometric study by the Federal Reserve Bank of St. Louis in the late 1960s—an early bastion of monetarism—has been cited by monetarists as proof that monetary policy is more effective than fiscal policy.[5]

The St. Louis model was developed about the time the large Keynesian econometric models were being formulated. Its authors argued that the correct test of the effectiveness of monetary and fiscal policy is simply to correlate changes of monetary and fiscal policy with changes in real GNP. The St. Louis model used the full-employment surplus as its measure of fiscal policy and the money supply and the monetary base as alternate measures of monetary policy. The St. Louis model found no significant correlation between real GNP and fiscal-policy variables, while it did find highly significant correlations between monetary policy variables and real GNP. In effect, the St. Louis model suggests that the government-spending multiplier is zero.

Historical Evidence.

Milton Friedman and Anna Schwartz studied the monetary history of the United States over nearly a century's time. Friedman and Schwartz were particularly interested in the historical relationship between monetary growth, GNP, and inflation. According to Friedman,

We have studied the relation between monetary magnitudes and economic magnitudes over the course of a hundred years, roughly a century. During that period, fiscal policy changed enormously. At the beginning of that period, the government budget was negligible. In the period since World War II, the government budget has been mammoth. And yet we found roughly the same kind of relationship between monetary and economic magnitudes over the whole of that one-hundred-year period.[6]

According to Friedman and Schwartz, therefore, if fiscal policy matters, it should have disrupted the steady relationship between money, GNP, and prices. Friedman's evidence against fiscal policy is not limited to this long-run study. Friedman has examined the behavior of prices in three wars: the Civil War, World War I, and World War II. He found that monetary magnitudes explain the behavior of prices in wartime in a clear and satisfactory way and that fiscal variables have no explanatory value.

THE CASE FOR ACTIVISM

The debate over whether fiscal or monetary policy is more important is really a sideshow to the main debate between the policy activists represented by modern Keynesians and the policy nonactivists represented by the monetarist/rational-expectations school.

The crucial conflict between the modern Keynesians and the monetarist/rational-expectations school is over whether deliberate monetary and fiscal policy should be used to stabilize the economy. The modern Keynesians support an activist policy. The monetarists believe that activist policy is ineffective at best and destabilizes the economy at worst. Rational-expectations economists believe that activist policy cannot stabilize the economy in the long run and will, at best, have only a short-run effect when the activist policy is not anticipated.

The Keynesian Case

Keynesian economists believe that self-correcting mechanisms operate in a stable monetary and

5. The St. Louis model was developed by Leonall C. Andersen and Jerry L. Jordan, then of the St. Louis Federal Reserve Bank in "Monetary and Fiscal Actions: A Test of their Relative Importance in Economic Stabilization," *Federal Reserve Bank of St. Louis Review* 50, 11 (November 1968): 11–23.

6. Friedman and Heller, *Monetary Versus Fiscal Policy,* p. 59; Milton Friedman and Anna Schwartz, *A Monetary History of the United States,* 1867–1960 (Princeton, N.J.: Princeton University Press, 1963).

fiscal framework. The private economy can generate enough steam on its own power to reach the natural (full) rate of unemployment in the long run. No change in monetary or fiscal policy is required; the adjustment to the natural rate is automatic. Even Keynes felt that in the long run, the economy would tend toward full employment. Some early Keynesians doubted even that; according to their doctrine of *secular stagnation,* as the economy grew the gap between full employment saving and investment would widen, and a growing government sector would be required to achieve full employment. Modern evidence on the consumption function has demonstrated that secular stagnation is not a threat.

In spite of the operation of the self-correcting mechanism, Keynesian economists asserted that sharp fluctuations in real GNP and employment would occur if monetary and fiscal policy were held constant. The economy is subject to all kinds of shocks. Investment is naturally unstable because of the accelerator; supply shocks can disrupt the economy; unpredictable shifts in consumer demand take place. Changes in autonomous spending induce magnified changes in real GNP and unemployment through the multiplier. If the economy is beset by adverse supply shocks, both unemployment and prices can be pushed up.

The basic Keynesian rationale for activist stabilization policy is that *waiting for the economy to cure itself by wage and price adjustments (the self-correcting mechanism) is too costly.*

When the economy is subjected to an adverse demand or supply shock, the economy will not be operating at full employment. In addition to the private anguish of unemployment, society must bear a social cost—the cost of lost GNP. If the economy had been at full employment, a larger real GNP would have been produced. The **GNP gap** measures this loss of output.

> The **GNP gap** *is the difference between current GNP and potential GNP (the output the economy would conceivably have produced at full employment) and is a measure of the social costs of unemployed resources.*

No one knows for sure the exact size of the GNP gap. First, full employment is difficult to

Table 2
The GNP Gap (billions of 1981 dollars)

Year	Potential GNP	Actual GNP	GNP Loss
1975	2536	2369	− 167
1976	2620	2497	− 123
1977	2710	2634	− 76
1978	2802	2759	− 43
1979	2889	2847	− 41
1980	2973	2843	− 130
Total loss			**−580**

Source: *Economic Report of the President,* 1980, p. 181. The GNP deflator is used to update to 1981 prices from the *Economic Report* of 1980.

define exactly. How much unemployment is quasi voluntary? Are discouraged workers unemployed? Second, it is difficult to estimate what unemployed resources would have produced had they been employed. Table 2 supplies estimates of the GNP gap for the period 1975 to 1980 prepared by the President's Council of Economic Advisers (under President Carter). These figures (updated to 1981 prices to avoid inflation distortions) reveal that the economy lost $580 billion worth of output between 1975 and 1980 by operating at less than full employment.

According to the Keynesian position, the GNP gap is the price society must pay while waiting for the self-correcting mechanism to operate. In the Keynesian view, it is better to use activist policies to speed up the movement toward full employment.

> *The objective of activist policy is to limit the private and social costs of unemployed resources by speeding up the economy's adjustment toward full employment.*

The Effectiveness of Activism

The period 1964 to 1980 was one in which Keynesian activist policies were used. Discretionary monetary and fiscal policies were used to soften the fluctuations of unemployment and inflation. Yet even activist economists agree that the last 20 years have seen considerable unemployment, recessions, inflation, and even stagflation.

The fact that the business cycle remains despite the use of activist policy does suggest that

Figure 1
The Annual Rate of Growth of Real GNP, 1890–1981

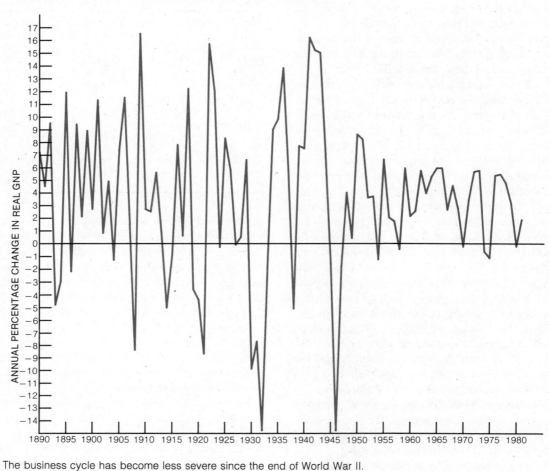

The business cycle has become less severe since the end of World War II.

Sources: *Historical Statistics of the United States,* p. 224; *Economic Report of the President,* 1982, p. 235.

discretionary policies have not worked perfectly. In defense of activism, it could be argued that activist policies prevented the business cycle from fluctuating even more. Perhaps activist policies avoided a Great Depression or a hyperinflation. At least two pieces of evidence support the claim that activism has reduced the GNP gap.

1. The history of fluctuations in real output is shown in Figure 1, which plots the annual rates of growth of real GNP from 1890 to 1981. The historical data show that, while the business cycle has not been eliminated, it has become less severe since activist policies first came into use after

World War II. Episodes of negative real growth still occur, but severe depressions have been avoided. According to Keynesians, the experience of the last 30 years provides dramatic evidence that activist policy has reduced the amplitude of economic fluctuations.

2. The experience of roughly constant monetary policy in the mid-1970s has been cited by Keynesians in support of activist policies. Franco Modigliani in his 1976 address to the American Economic Association pointed to this period as an example of how the absence of activism can lead to excess unemployment.

In 1973, 1974, and 1975, the annual rates of growth of money supply were 5.5 percent, 4.3 percent, and 4.8 percent, respectively. These percentages indicate an almost constant rate of growth of the money supply over a three-year period. During this time, the economy went through a great recession. Unemployment was 5.6 percent in 1974, soared to 8.5 percent in 1975, and then declined slightly to 7.7 percent in 1976. According to Modigliani, the constant growth of the money supply cost the economy dearly in unemployment and lost output.

The recession of 1974 to 1976 was in large measure caused by the explosion of oil prices. When an adverse supply shock of this magnitude occurs, Keynesians find it wasteful to let the economy grind back to full employment under the self-correcting mechanism. Policy makers must choose between doing nothing and paying the price of higher unemployment and lost output and following an activist policy of monetary and fiscal expansion that brings a higher rate of inflation. During the severe 1981–82 recession, counter-cyclical policies were not used—and unemployment reached its highest levels since the 1930s.

Activism and Inflation

Activism calls for expansionary policies when unemployment rises. Yet the modern experience with stagflation is that expansionary policies induce accelerating inflation.

To justify activist policy in a world of high inflation, policy makers must find some means of expanding aggregate demand—when deemed necessary for activist policy—without increasing the inflation rate. Modern Keynesians such as James Tobin, Paul Samuelson, Franco Modigliani, and Arthur Okun suggest incomes policies as a solution to this dilemma. The greatest challenge currently facing activist stabilization policies is to design a workable incomes policy.

Activists maintain that efficient market-based incomes policies can allow the use of activist countercyclical policy. As Chapter 13 explained, a tax-based incentive program (TIP) seeks to accomplish the goal of fighting inflation without driving up unemployment. Arthur Okun supports the TIP program:

. . . The U.S. inflation rate will be lowered over the next decade; the serious question is whether that is going to be accomplished by inefficient and inhumane recessions, by stifling wage-price controls, or by some innovative, sensible method like TIP.[7]

In effect, activists argue that the known is better than the unknown. The United States has had 30 years of activism without major economic catastrophes like a great depression or a hyperinflation. Without activist policies, the United States might not be able to respond to some major economic emergency in the future with a suitable policy.

THE CASE FOR RULES OR NONACTIVISM

The case for activist policy is that it is too costly to do nothing. Modern Keynesians, therefore, maintain that activist monetary and fiscal policies must be used to fight the business cycle. Monetarists and rational-expectations economists offer a radically different policy prescription:

The monetarist and rational-expectations view is that it is better to do nothing in the face of demand and supply shocks and to let the self-correcting mechanism work without interference.

The nonactivists have a more difficult task ahead of them to prove their case. They must not only show that the costs of the business cycle cannot be reduced by activist policies but that activist policies actually make the business cycle worse.

The monetarists, led by Milton Friedman, Karl Brunner, and Allan Meltzer, maintain that activist policies either fail to improve the business cycle or actually make the cycle worse. The rational-expectations school, led by Robert Lucas, Thomas Sargent, and Robert Barro, maintains that activist policies affect only inflation, not cyclical unemployment. Activist policies can make inflation better or worse but have no lasting effect on reducing real GNP fluctuations.

7. Arthur Okun, "Implications for Policy: A Symposium," Brookings Economic Papers, *Innovative Policies to Slow Inflation* (1978:2), p. 522.

The case against activism consists of three points: 1) the economy is much more stable than Keynesians contend, 2) it is exceedingly difficult to devise activist policies, and 3) rational expectations may defeat activist policies.

A Relatively Stable Economy

Figure 1 shows that the amplitude of the business cycle has been less in the postwar period—after activist policies came to be used to moderate the business cycle. According to the monetarists, to allege that the cycle has been moderated by countercyclical policy does not fit the facts. Friedman and Schwartz, in their study of the U.S. business cycle over a century's time, conclude that discretionary policy was *destabilizing* the economy, not stabilizing it. In their view, the Great Depression was a business downturn that was turned into a Great Depression because of a series of incredible government blunders and because the natural self-correcting mechanism was not allowed to work.

What were the policy blunders of the 1930s?

1. From 1929 to 1933, the nominal supply of money (M1) fell 25 percent. The price level also fell nearly 25 percent. Therefore, there was no change in the real money supply, but an increase in the real money supply was required to get the economy moving again. If monetary policy had been stable in the early 1930s, falling prices would have caused the real money supply to increase; the economy would not have fallen into the Great Depression.

2. As Nobel prize winners James Tobin and Milton Friedman have pointed out, various government actions taken by Roosevelt's New Deal program caused wages and prices to rise after 1933 even though there was mass unemployment, while the self-correcting mechanism required falling wages and prices. The New Deal increased the power of labor unions, gave more monopoly power to business firms, encouraged them to raise prices. In short, from 1933 to 1936 a cost-push inflation in the middle of a deep depression retarded the move towards full employment.[8]

8.   James Tobin, ''Inflation and Unemployment,'' *American Economic Review* 62 (March 1972): 14; Milton Friedman, *Dollars and Deficits* (Englewood Cliffs, N.J.: Prentice-Hall, 1968).

3. In 1937, in perhaps the most incredible act of self-destruction in American economic history, the Federal Reserve System doubled reserve requirements. The banking system did have large excess reserves at the time, but excess reserves were being held by banks because of the prevailing economic situation. Accordingly, the increase in the reserve requirement brought the needed money growth to a halt and sent the economy into another recession within the Great Depression.

4. Large tax increases were passed in 1932 and 1937 during periods of massive unemployment.

Keynesians maintain that activist countercyclical policy is responsible for the reduced fluctuations in real GNP after the Second World War. Monetarists counter that the reduced amplitude of the business cycle is a consequence *not* of countercyclical policies but of a reduction in the amplitude of money supply growth. The major episode of cyclical instability prior to the Second World War—the Great Depression—was itself caused by improper monetary policy, not by natural cyclical forces.

The monetarist evidence is presented in Figure 2, which shows the annual growth rate of the money supply since 1890. Comparison of money growth (in Figure 2) and output growth (in Figure 1) reveals that the reduction in the amplitude of GNP fluctuations coincides with the sharp reduction in the amplitude of money supply growth. From this evidence, the monetarists conclude that the greater relative stability over the past 35 years is not the result of activist policy but of the increased stability of the rate of growth of the money supply.

In most cases, reductions in the rate of growth of money supply lead to recessions. Consider again the case of the Great Depression. Figure 2 shows that, beginning in 1926, the growth *rate* of money supply was reduced almost every year until 1933. This pattern holds up in the postwar period as well; postwar recessions were preceded by reductions in the *rate* of growth of money supply.

If the business cycle is caused by fluctuations in the rate of growth of money supply, monetarists believe that cyclical instability can be reduced or eliminated by eliminating the unstable growth pattern of the money supply. This belief is the rationale for Milton Friedman's 3 percent rule.

Figure 2
The Annual Growth Rate of Money Supply, 1890–1981

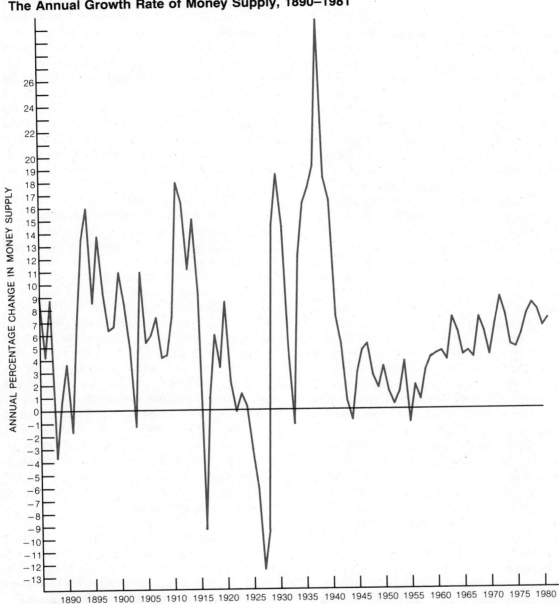

A comparison of this figure with Figure 1 shows that the reduction in the amplitude of GNP fluctuations coincides with the reduction in fluctuations in the growth rate of money supply in the past 30 years.

Source: *Historical Statistics of the United States*, p. 892, *Economic Report of the President*, 1982, p. 303; *Survey of Current Business*, March 1982. The percentage growth rate in money supply is based on M1 for the years 1915 to 1981 and includes time deposits (formerly M2) for the years 1890–1915.

Monetarists argue that monetary authorities should be ordered to expand the money supply at a constant annual rate year in and year out. If the growth of money supply is held constant at a rate equal to the long-run growth of real GNP, cyclical instability and inflation could be reduced at the same time.

The Difficulty of Devising Activist Policy

The monetarist attack against countercyclical policy rests upon the proposition that countercyclical policy historically has destabilized the economy. Monetarists conclude from the policy blunders of the 1930s that a constant growth rate of money supply is preferable to activist policy. Although the proponents of activism could defend activist policy by saying the biggest policy blunders were made when economists did not understand how the economy works, there are four reasons why countercyclical policy—even in this modern age—will still be destabilizing.

1. *There are long and variable lags in the effect of money on the economy.* If monetary authorities decide to combat a rising unemployment rate by increasing the growth of money supply, this monetary expansion will not have an immediate effect on real output and unemployment. Friedman's own research suggests that there is a lag of from 6 months to 2 years before changes in money supply affect GNP. Thus, monetary authorities can never be sure when the change in money supply will begin to affect real output and employment. If the lag is short, the chances are less that the monetary policy will be inappropriate, but if the lag is long (say, 2 years), it may be that the policy will take effect when contraction rather than expansion is called for.

2. *The effects of fiscal policy are uncertain.* Because of permanent-income and crowding-out effects, it is virtually impossible to predict in advance the impact of fiscal policy. An accurate estimate would require knowledge in advance of the amount of crowding out and the effects of tax changes on consumption expenditures. Moreover, just like monetary policy, fiscal policy—if the fiscal multiplier is not zero—affects the economy after a lag. Not only is fiscal policy difficult to implement because of recognition lags and implementation lags, fiscal planners must also be able to determine when the change in fiscal policy will affect economic activity.

3. *It is difficult for activist policy makers to know if the economy is approaching a recession.* Because of the lagged effects of monetary and fiscal policy, it is very important to be able to anticipate changes in the business cycle. If policy makers knew 6 months in advance, for example, that a recession was coming, it would be much easier to devise countercyclical policy. But recessions vary in length and in predictability. Through econometric models and indexes of leading indicators, policy makers attempt to anticipate recessions. But these models and indexes are far from accurate guides to the future (see Example 1).

Monetary and fiscal authorities who attempt to carry out activist countercyclical policies at the wrong time run the risk of actually destabilizing the economy. Monetarists believe policy makers do not possess sufficient information to diagnose and cure the disease before it spontaneously corrects itself. By acting without adequate information, they may actually use the wrong medicine and make the patient even worse.

4. *Activist policies can aim for the wrong target.* Most modern economists agree that the appropriate target of activist policy is the natural rate of unemployment. If the economy is operating with an unemployment rate above the natural rate, expansionary policies can lower unemployment without accelerating inflation. But policy makers may not always know what the natural rate is at any point in time. The natural rate itself changes from year to year. Changes in the composition of the labor force cause the natural rate to change. Substantial raw-material price changes may permanently affect the natural rate. Since the natural rate itself fluctuates, it is difficult to chase it with deliberate policy actions. As Chapter 14 showed, aiming for a natural rate target that is too low (a rate that is below the natural rate) leads to accelerating inflation.

Rational Expectations

Even if countercyclical policy is not destabilizing as the monetarists claim, the logical case that activism should be used still has potential flaws. Some members of the rational-expectations school argue that countercyclical policies—*if predictable*—will have no impact on the business cycle. If both monetary and fiscal policies lead to predictable shifts in aggregate demand, as the Keynesians assume, shifts in aggregate demand that are correctly anticipated will be offset by rising prices and wages.

If monetary and fiscal authorities want to reduce unemployment, they might use monetary and fiscal expansion to stimulate aggregate demand. In order to persuade people to work more

How Reliable is the Index of Leading Indicators?

The Department of Commerce compiles an index of leading indicators, whose job it is to predict recessions. This index is used by monetary and fiscal authorities to prepare countercyclical policy.

How reliable is the index of leading indicators? While most recessions have been preceded by a downturn in the leading indicators, 3 out of 11 downturns in the leading indicators have turned out to be false signals. Even if the index of leading indicators correctly predicts an oncoming recession, it cannot predict how deep it will be or how long it will last.

Note that the leading indicators peaked 23 months before the 1957–58 recession and only 5 months before the Great Recession of 1974–75. The leading indicators signaled three false recessions in this period. ✕

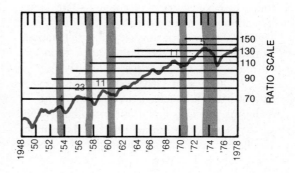

Source: U.S. Department of Commerce, *Business Conditions Digest,* October 1981.

---

hours and firms to produce more real output, workers would have to perceive that their real wages were rising, and firms would have to perceive that their prices were rising more rapidly than their costs. If people correctly anticipate the effects of expansionary policies on wages and prices, they will realize that real wages are not rising and that prices are not rising more rapidly than costs. Unless people are fooled by the expansionary policies, their real behavior will not change. Workers and firms will raise prices right along with the expansion of aggregate demand. At the economywide level, real GNP will not change and unemployment will not change. The expansionary policies will cause nominal GNP to rise as a consequence of rising prices, but real GNP will remain unchanged.

The full implications of the rational-expectations approach and the evidence for it are presented in Chapter 17.

THE DEBATE CONTINUES

The Activist Response to the Case for Nonactivism

The monetarists claim that legislated rules for monetary growth would prevent substantial policy blunders and would put the economy on the path to steady long-run growth without inflation. The Keynesian response to the case for nonactivism consists of four general points: 1) rigid rules are dangerous, 2) money supply growth is difficult to control, 3) it is difficult to determine which money supply to control, and 4) increases in real GNP may be causing money supply to grow, not vice versa.

If the economy were to encounter a real economic emergency—war, a supply shock of unprecedented proportions, or a collapse in investment demand—a rigid rule would not allow authorities to respond appropriately to the current economic situation. They would have to sit back and wait for the slow and painful adjustment process to work.

Money-supply growth is more difficult to control than the monetarists admit. As proof, actual money-growth rates often diverge from the targeted growth rate in countries that have money-growth-rate policies. The demand for credit moves up and down during the business cycle; the currency needs of the public are in flux; many banks are not subject to regulations of the Fed; international banks have the means of circumventing Fed controls.[9]

9. This point has been made in reference to the English experiment with monetary rules in the late 1970s and early 1980s where the English money supply growth has consistently exceeded the targets set by monetary authorities.

There are a number of different money concepts. When the monetarists speak of controlling money supply, which money supply do they mean? The concept of a money supply is changing in a modern economy that is constantly inventing close substitutes for money—like credit cards and money market funds.

Figure 2 shows conclusively that fluctuations in money supply and GNP go together. Monetarists believe that the changes in money supply cause the changes in GNP, but modern Keynesians argue that the increase in GNP could be increasing the money supply. When nominal GNP rises, the demand for money rises. If the Fed accommodates this demand, the supply of money should increase. In addition, when the demand for money increases, interest rates rise, and banks have a greater incentive to lend out their excess reserves. Through such mechanisms, Keynesians believe that the money supply is in part determined by the level of economic activity. Economists are intensively studying the issue of causality between money and economic activity.[10]

The Nonactivist Response to the Activist Response

To these criticisms, the monetarists respond that fluctuations in money supply have been the destabilizing factor historically. Thus, it is highly unlikely for the economy to slide into a deep depression or a hyperinflation in a world of steady monetary growth. Monetarists admit that at times monetary authorities do not hit their monetary growth targets on the nose over short periods of time, but they argue that in the long run, the monetary authorities can indeed control the growth of money supply. The monetarists argue that the actual choice of which money supply to control is not that important. The Fed simply needs to select one measure of the money supply and control that.

As one can see from this series of arguments and counter arguments, this debate is likely to remain unresolved for some time.

10. Christopher Sims, ''Comparison of Interwar and Postwar Business Cycles: Monetarism Reconsidered,'' *American Economic Review* 70 (May 1980): 251–57.

IS THERE A MIDDLE GROUND?

The disagreement between activist Keynesians and nonactivist monetarists and rational expectationists appears profound. One side believes in activist policy; the other side says that countercyclical policies either do not matter or make matters worse.

If one examines the postwar development of macroeconomics, faint signs of agreement are beginning to emerge. First, the Keynesian position has come much closer to the monetarist position in the last 20 years. Remember, the Keynesians began with the notion that money scarcely matters at all; now Keynesians hold a more balanced view that both monetary and fiscal policy matter. Because of the greater flexibility of monetary policy, even Keynesians probably regard monetary policy as the major tool of countercyclical policy. Modern Keynesians have also largely abandoned the notion of fine tuning, the constant fiddling with the dials of discretionary policy. Instead, it is agreed that activist policy should respond only to major cyclical disturbances.

The fundamental monetarist critique of activist policy is that it is more likely to do harm than good. Keynesians also realize that policy makers have committed costly errors in the past. It is unlikely that policy blunders as large as those committed in the 1930s will ever be repeated. Presumably, the ability to forecast the business cycle improves over time; economists learn more from experience about the effects of past policies. Yet economists are far from reaching the point where monetarists would be satisfied that they know enough to devise error-free activist policy.

Monetarists have done the Keynesians a favor by pointing out how complex our economy actually is. They have shown that the multiplier analysis of Keynes paints too simple a picture. Crowding out, permanent-income effects, accelerating inflation, and expectations all markedly affect the way economic policy works. As a result, Keynesian economists will be more cautious in their conduct of economic policy.

Both monetarists and Keynesians are concerned about policy effects on unemployment. The next chapter will take a closer look at trends in unemployment.

Summary

1. The two main macroeconomic policy options are activist monetary and fiscal policy or non-activism. Activist policies aim to stabilize the business cycle; activist policies can be either discretionary or use feedback rules. Nonactivist policy uses fixed rules. The two rules suggested by Friedman for nonactivism are: a) let the money supply grow at a constant rate and b) have a cyclically balanced budget.

2. The original Keynesian position was that fiscal policy would be more powerful than monetary policy. Keynesians use the 1964 tax cut and the evidence of macroeconometric models to support their case for fiscal policy. The modern Keynesian position is that both money and fiscal policy matter. The monetarists claim that only money matters, and that fiscal policy does not affect cyclical real GNP. Fiscal policy crowds out private spending. As evidence for their position, the monetarists use long-term historical evidence and the St. Louis model to show that money matters and fiscal variables do not. The basic debate between Keynesians and monetarists/rational-expectations economists is over the issue of activism. Keynesians argue that activism is necessary; monetarists and rational-expectations economists maintain that activist policies do not work and often make matters worse.

3. The case for activism is that the self-correcting mechanism is too slow. The main evidence in favor of activism is the long-term reduction in GNP fluctuations since the Second World War. The negative experience with constant money growth between 1973 and 1976 is cited by some Keynesians in support of activism. Activists must solve the problem of how to use discretionary policy without increasing inflation. Innovative incomes policies are seen by some Keynesians as the answer.

4. The case against activism rests on the following points: The economy is not as unstable as the activists believe; instability has been caused by policy blunders; the reduced GNP fluctuations since the Second World War are due to smaller fluctuations in monetary growth. Activist policy tends to be destabilizing because monetary lags make it difficult to devise discretionary policy, the effects of fiscal policy are uncertain, it is difficult to know when a recession is coming and how severe it will be, and activist policy can aim for the wrong employment target (the natural rate is not known with certainty). Rational-expectations theory teaches that activist stabilization policy will not stabilize the economy if policy is anticipated.

5. The activist critique of rules is that there is danger in rigid rules, the money supply is difficult to control, and the change in GNP may be causing the change in money supply instead of vice versa.

6. Modern Keynesians now take into account many of the monetarist points, such as crowding out, permanent income, accelerating inflation, and the role of expectations.

Key Terms

feedback rules
GNP gap

Questions and Problems

1. Distinguish between feedback rules and discretionary policy. What is meant by ''fine tuning?''

2. Explain how crowding out affects the Keynesian analysis of fiscal multipliers.

3. Summarize the evidence that supports the claim that ''only money matters.''

4. Most economists believe that there is a self-correcting mechanism that automatically moves the economy towards full employment. If this is the case, how can anyone advocate discretionary policy? Will the economy not take care of itself?

5. It was pointed out in this chapter that the advocates of nonactivism must demonstrate that activist policies tend to worsen the business cycle. What arguments are there that activism actually makes matters worse?

6. How could we have had the Great Depression of the 1930s if there is a self-correcting mechanism at work in the economy?

7. The rational-expectations argument is that expectations can defeat activist policy. Assume Congress decides to pass a tax cut to stimulate the economy. How could rational expectations defeat the purpose of the tax cut?

CHAPTER

16

Unemployment Trends

Chapter Preview

This chapter will take a closer look at unemployment in an attempt to determine the costs and benefits of unemployment and to explain why unemployment has been increasing over the past 20 years. The problems of unemployment and inflation have occupied center stage in our discussion of macroeconomics. The preceding chapters have surveyed various explanations of the causes of inflation and unemployment in modern economies. The income/expenditure theory pioneered by Keynes maintains that inflation and unemployment problems can be traced to imbalances between aggregate demand and full-employment GNP. The classical economists believed that inflation and unemployment were unrelated phe-

nomena, that inflation is caused by excessive growth of money and that employment is determined independently in the real sector. The natural-rate hypothesis and rational-expectations theory teach that inflation can bring only short-run reductions in unemployment, and then only if inflation is unanticipated. Different schools of economics debate the causes of unemployment and disagree about its cure.

Since the 1960s, the American unemployment rate has trended upward. In the mid-1950s, the average unemployment rate was 4.2 percent. In the late 1970s and early 1980s, it averaged close to 7 percent. The unemployment rate of the early 1980s was 60 percent higher than the unemployment rate of the 1950s. As the unemployment rate has risen, economists' estimate of what consti-

269

tutes *full employment* has also risen. In the early 1960s, government officials regarded a 3 percent unemployment rate as full employment. Now, officials aim at a full employment rate of 5 percent or slightly higher.

One important point that is frequently overlooked is that a dramatic *increase in employment* has accompanied the rising trend in unemployment. Since 1960, the number employed has expanded by 51 percent (from 64.6 million to 100.4 million). The U.S. economy has succeeded in creating an additional 35 million jobs over the last 20 years. The rising unemployment rate is explained by the fact that unemployment has been rising at a more rapid rate than employment.

THE PROBLEM OF DEFINING UNEMPLOYMENT

The official U.S. government definition of unemployment is:

*A person is **unemployed** if he or she is not currently working, has actively looked for work during the previous four weeks, and is currently available for work.*

This statistical definition of unemployment raises a number of questions, the answers to which affect the measured unemployment rate. Four of the most important problems with the current system of measuring unemployment are: the discouraged-worker effect, involuntary part-time employment, differing intensities of job search, and the unsuitability of available jobs.

Discouraged Workers

One controversy surrounding the statistical definition of unemployment is the effect of the **discouraged worker.**

*A **discouraged worker** is an unemployed worker who becomes convinced that no job is or will be available in his or her field and stops looking for work, at which point that worker is no longer classified as unemployed.*

Discouraged workers are counted as "not in the labor force" because they fail to meet the sec-

Table 1
Discouraged Workers, 1970 and 1982

Category	1970	1982
Total	**638,000**	**1,103,000**
Males	221,000	399,000
Females	415,000	704,000
Whites	494,000	751,000
Black and other	145,000	353,000

Source: *Statistical Abstract of the United States,* 1982, p. 399.

ond unemployment condition of actively looking for work. According to government statistics, the number of discouraged workers is substantial—more than 1 million in 1981 (see Table 1).

How discouraged workers are treated by government statistics and by economic theory is quite important. If they are counted as unemployed, then the unemployment rate increases from 8.2 percent to 9.4 percent of the labor force. Table 1 shows that the incidence of discouraged workers is much higher for women and blacks and other minorities than it is for males and whites. Women account for 63 percent of all discouraged workers, and blacks and other minorities (who account for only 12 percent of the labor force) account for 28 percent of discouraged workers.

Part-Time Work

Critics of the existing system of measuring unemployment claim that unemployment statistics fail to delineate those involuntarily working part time. A person is "employed" as long as that person is working, either full time or part time, even if the person has had to settle for a part-time job in place of a full-time job. With the current system, it is difficult to determine the number of persons who wish to work full time but are settling for part-time jobs.

Intensity of Job Search

Another problem with measuring unemployment is that it is virtually impossible to measure the intensity and seriousness with which the unemployed search for jobs. Is the person unemployed because the job search is perfunctory and

Example   1

Are Discouraged Workers the Uncounted Jobless?

The Congress of the United States established the National Commission of Employment and Unemployment Statistics to consider changes in the current system of unemployment statistics. One proposal placed before the commission was to include discouraged workers in the ranks of the unemployed. Critics of the official statistics argued that it is unfair not to count discouraged workers as unemployed because they have dropped out of the labor force due to the lack of suitable jobs.

The commission decided to continue not to count discouraged workers as unemployed. The commission's rationale: The concept of a discouraged worker is too soft. The commission ruled that "discouragement is a state of mind." How can one tell the strength of attachment of discouraged workers to the labor force? Are they only casually looking for jobs, or have they made a long and exhaustive search for a job, concluding reluctantly that a further search would be futile? Until it is possible to distinguish between these two types of discouraged workers, the commission decided it would be better to leave them out of the labor force.

casual, or is the unemployed person carrying out a serious and conscientious search for open positions? As in the case of discouraged workers, it is not possible to distinguish between the two types of job searches.

Job Suitability

The unemployed are searching for jobs that suit their skills and qualifications. If their expectations are not met, they typically remain unemployed. Jobs may be available for unemployed workers that are not taken because they do not meet the job expectations of the job searcher.

CHARACTERISTICS OF THE UNEMPLOYED

Not every person in the American labor force has an equal chance of being unemployed. Some individuals work in occupations that suffer considerable ups and downs (automobile manufacturing, aerospace engineering, and construction). Others work in jobs that offer steady and stable employment (the civil service, public utilities, tenured college professors). Members of some socioeconomic groups or age groups typically experience higher unemployment than other groups. Some individuals live in sections of the country in which job opportunities are few; others live in expanding regions where jobs are plentiful.

An Unemployment Profile

Who are the unemployed? Table 2 lists average unemployment rates for persons of different age, education, marital-status, race, and sex characteristics. The differences in unemployment rates are striking. Unemployment rates range from 2 percent for white married men to more than 40 percent for female black teenagers. Married men, workers in prime working ages (35-44), whites, persons with college degrees, professionals, and workers in finance and real estate tend to have low rates of unemployment. Blacks and other minorities, teenagers, construction workers, nonfarm laborers, and separated women with preschool children suffer high unemployment rates. These groups are not mutually exclusive: professionals tend to be college graduates; teenagers have low levels of education and few skills; blacks tend to be concentrated in the nonfarm-labor categories.

As Table 2 shows, there is no single factor that determines the likelihood of unemployment. The choice of occupation affects the probability of unemployment. Persons implicitly choose their rate of lifetime unemployment when they choose their occupation and profession. The amount of education and training influences the probability of unemployment. Generally, the higher the level of education and training, the lower the rate of lifetime unemployment.

Table 2
Unemployment Rates of Different Population Groups, 1981

Population Category	Unemployment Rate
Low unemployment rates:	
Married men	4.0
Professional and technical workers	4.0
Workers in finance, insurance, real estate	3.4
White males, 25–54 years	4.9
Persons with 5 or more years of college	1.9
High unemployment:	
Persons with incomplete high-school education	14.1
Wives with unemployed husbands	17.6
Women who maintain families	10.4
Teenagers	19.6
Blacks and other minorities	14.2
Nonfarm laborers	14.7
Male construction workers	16.0

Source: *Statistical Abstract of the United States,* 1981, p. 385; *Employment and Earnings,* March 1982, pp. 132, 133, 162.

Table 3
Unemployment Rates in Seven Industrialized Countries

Country	1970	1975	1981
United States	4.9	8.5	7.6
Canada	5.7	6.9	7.6
France	2.6	4.3	7.6
West Germany	0.8	4.1	4.3
Great Britain	3.1	4.1	5.8
Italy	3.1	3.2	4.2
Japan	1.2	1.9	2.2

Source: *Economic Report of the President,* January 1982, p. 357.

International Perspectives

Rising unemployment rates are not merely a U.S. phenomenon. Other countries share the U.S. experience of rising postwar unemployment. Different countries have different unemployment rates (Table 3). Some of these differences are probably due to the different composition of the labor force in each country. Female and teenage employment is less prevalent in some countries, and unemployment statistics are gathered differently in different countries.

Nevertheless, the unemployment statistics for the industrialized countries show an unmistakable rise in unemployment rates over the past decade. Most countries have seen their unemployment rates slide up in the 1970s at a more rapid rate than in the United States.

Voluntary versus Involuntary Unemployment

Earlier chapters emphasized that unemployment is a complex phenomenon. Some workers quit their jobs. Other workers are fired or tempo-

rarily laid off. In still other cases, new entrants to the job market (or persons reentering the labor force) are unable to find jobs.

Chapter 5 described three general types of unemployment: cyclical, structural, and frictional unemployment. Cyclical unemployment is the unemployment associated with general downturns in the economy. Frictional unemployment is the unemployment associated with the normal changing of jobs in a dynamic economy. Structural unemployment is the unemployment associated with the long-term decline of specific industries.

The Keynesian revolution blamed cyclical unemployment on deficient aggregate demand. In the Keynesian depression model, cyclical unemployment was strictly involuntary because people were ready and willing to work at going wages; the jobs simply were not there. Structural unemployment was also typically associated with involuntary unemployment because of the long-term evaporation of jobs in specific industries. In the Keynesian view, only frictional unemployment had a strong voluntary element in that it was associated with the changing of jobs required by a changing economy.

Modern economists have come to recognize that distinctions between voluntary and involuntary unemployment are not black and white. The dividing line between voluntary and involuntary unemployment is often difficult to draw. There is more voluntarism in unemployment than had previously been imagined.

Most unemployment is partly voluntary and partly involuntary. To mention an extreme case, the person who is holding out for the job of President of the United States has a strong voluntary element to his or her unemployment. The unemployment is also somewhat involuntary in the sense that there is no demand for the person's services as President. At the other extreme, the person who is willing to accept any job offered irrespective of salary and conditions of work, yet is still unable to find a job, has an overriding involuntary element to his or her unemployment. Most cases of unemployment fall between these two extremes.

How can there be a voluntary element to unemployment? The unemployed skilled craftsworker may turn down employment as an unskilled worker. The unionized automobile worker who is laid off may decide to wait to be recalled to the old job rather than search for a new job. People who believe that wages are currently depressed may wait for wages to rise before accepting jobs. The middle-income homemaker may decide to search casually for a job, to wait for just the right job to come along.[1]

UNEMPLOYMENT PATTERNS

Modern economists believe that employment decisions—like other economic decisions—are based upon evaluations of costs and benefits of alternate actions. If the costs of remaining unemployed are low relative to the benefits of other options, then the result is unemployment.

The cost/benefit analysis of unemployment is valid only if people do have options from which to choose. If they are like the extreme case of the unemployed person willing to accept any job offer, the economy in effect offers them no options. The extent to which the unemployed exercise options is reflected in statistics on job mobility, quits, firings, and long-term unemployment.

In general terms, high mobility, voluntary quits, and limited duration of unemployment are evident when unemployment results from frictional causes. Unemployment that rises during downturns in the economy is cyclical unemployment, and unemployment that occurs when partic-

ular industries or regions experience declines is structural unemployment.

Mobility and Turnover

The American labor market is constantly changing. Each year the economy must provide jobs for hundreds of thousands of graduates and other new job entrants. Established workers move from one job to another. Some workers are fired; new workers are hired in their place. Some workers are laid off for an indefinite period; others are recalled to their old jobs. Labor turnover serves an important function in a dynamic economy. It allows the labor force to respond to employment opportunities. It reallocates labor from jobs in declining industries and unprofitable companies to jobs in rising industries and profitable companies. Job turnover gives workers the opportunity to improve their economic position. Unemployment *per se* is not all bad.

Two startling statistics demonstrate the striking amount of mobility in our economy:

1. One half of all workers have been employed in their current job for three years or less; 30 percent have held their job for one year or less.
2. Almost one half of the U.S. population over the age of 5 years moves within a five-year period.

The Business Cycle

The American labor force is in a state of motion. This motion changes with the ebb and tide of the business cycle. The character of unemployment changes perceptibly during expansions and contractions. During expansions unemployment due to people quitting their jobs increases; during contractions people losing their jobs due to firing or **layoff** increases.

*A **layoff** is a suspension without pay and without prejudice that lasts (or is expected to last) seven days or more. The laid-off worker is not fired but is expected to return to his or her old job if economic conditions improve.*

The distinctive pattern of quits and layoffs during the business cycle is shown in Figure 1. Recessions cause sharp drops in the quit rate as

1. Economist Edmund S. Phelps, in *Inflation Policy and Unemployment Theory* (New York: W. W. Norton, 1972), distinguishes among three types of voluntary employment: wait unemployment, speculative unemployment, and search unemployment.

Figure 1
Quit Rates and Layoff Rates, 1950–1981

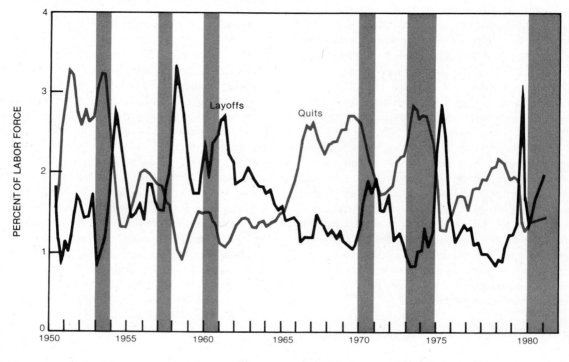

Quit rates tend to drop and layoff rates tend to rise during periods of recession.

Source: U.S. Department of Labor; *Economic Report of the President,* 1982, p. 273; *Survey of Current Business* (July 1981), p. 3.

people become wary about job changing. The layoff rate rises sharply during recessions as employers lay off workers. The expansion period sees sharp rises in quits and sharp declines in layoffs.

During recessions and downturns in business activity, labor-market conditions deteriorate. Companies lay off more workers, and those with jobs are reluctant to quit. On the other hand, during expansions, the demand for labor grows; companies are reluctant to let workers go; workers finding that job opportunities are plentiful quit their jobs to move to better jobs. When the layoff rate is rising, the quit rate typically is falling; when the layoff rate is falling, the quit rate is typically rising.

The years 1982 (a recession year) and 1969 (a peak year) are typical: In 1969, 36 percent of the unemployed were job losers (laid off or fired) and 15 percent quit. In 1982, 59 percent were job losers and only 9 percent were quits.

Duration of Unemployment

Not all unemployment is a consequence of the dynamic nature of the economy. If unemployment is largely associated with job moves and is of short duration, then the phenomenon of unemployment appears less threatening. If unemployment is associated with job changes that involve moving up the ladder, unemployment can even be benign. On the other hand, if unemployment tends to be long-term and concentrated on particular population groups, it is a severe social and economic problem.

The data on the duration of unemployment in Table 4 show that some people remain unemployed for long periods of time (6 months or more). The duration of unemployment is strongly influenced by the business cycle. During the expansion phase of the cycle, long-term unemployment (27 weeks or more) falls to 10 percent of

Table 4
Proportion of Unemployment by Duration During Contractions and Expansions

| Year | Cycle | Percent of Unemployed Out of Work for: | |
		Less than 5 Weeks	27 Weeks or More
1959	Expansion	44.4	15.3
1961	Contraction	38.3	17.1
1965	Expansion	48.4	10.4
1975	Contraction	37.0	15.2
1978	Expansion	46.2	10.4
1981	Contraction	41.7	14.0

Source: *Economic Report of the President,* January 1982, p. 272.

total unemployment or below. During the contraction phase, long-term unemployment rises to 15 percent or above. The statistics reveal a consistent cadre of hard-core unemployed.

Even in the worst of times—during recessions—long-term unemployment accounts for a relatively small proportion of total unemployment. Even during recessions, roughly 40 percent of the unemployed are unemployed for 5 weeks or less. During expansions, about one half of the unemployed are unemployed 5 weeks or less.[2]

CAUSES OF RISING UNEMPLOYMENT

The national unemployment rate in the United States and in other countries has been rising over the last 20 years because of 1) changes in the composition of the labor force and 2) changes in the private costs and benefits of unemployment.

The Changing Composition of the Labor Force

The fact that different workers have different rates of unemployment accounts for part of the long-term increase in the unemployment rate. The composition of the American labor force has changed dramatically since the end of World War

2. Some economists have argued that these figures understate the amount of long-term unemployment for two reasons: First, the discouraged worker should be counted in long-term unemployment. Second, it has been argued that these statistics understate the proportion of the long-term unemployed.

II. In 1950, women accounted for 30 percent of the labor force; in 1981 they accounted for 43 percent. In 1950, only 1.4 million women with children under 6 years of age were in the labor force; by 1981, their number had increased to almost 5 million.

Figure 2 shows that different groups of workers have experienced different rates of unemployment since 1947 (see Figure 2). The unemployment rate of married men, while varying from year to year, has not increased over the long run. The unemployment rates of males and females 20 years and older have been rising slightly in the long run. The unemployment rates of young people 16-19 years of age reveal a distinct upward trend, as do the unemployment rates of women who maintain families. The unemployment rates of experienced wage and salary workers have risen less than those of blue-collar workers.

To what extent can the rise in the American unemployment rate be explained by the rising labor-force shares of those groups that have higher-than-average unemployment rates? Although the labor-force shares of women with children and of teenagers have increased, so have the shares of professional workers and employees in low-unemployment sectors, like the service industries.

The effect of the changing composition of the labor force on the national unemployment rate can be determined by calculating what current unemployment rates would have been if today's labor force composition were the same as in the 1950s. Economists calculate that approximately one third of the 60 percent increase in the unemployment rate between the late 1950s and the present is accounted for by changes in the composition of the labor force.[3]

The rising U.S. unemployment rate is not just the result of more women, minorities, and teenagers in the labor force. The changing composition of the U.S. labor force accounts for approximately one third of the long-term increase in unemployment.

3. For example, N. J. Simler has calculated what the 1976 unemployment rate would have been had the labor-force composition not changed over the preceding 20 years. Simler finds that the 1976 unemployment rate would have been only one-third lower. See Simler, "Employment and Unemployment," *Federal Reserve Bank of Minneapolis Review,* April 1978, p. 13.

Figure 2
Selected Unemployment Rates, 1948–1981

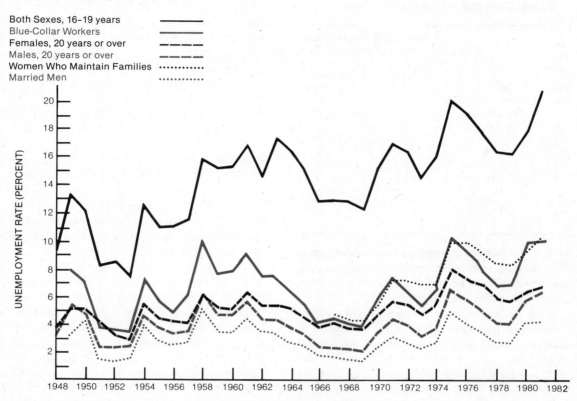

Both Sexes, 16–19 years ────────
Blue-Collar Workers ────────
Females, 20 years or over ─── ─── ───
Males, 20 years or over ── ── ── ──
Women Who Maintain Families ············
Married Men ············

Unemployment rates vary for different segments of the labor force. Women who maintain families and teenagers have experienced rising unemployment rates in recent decades.

Source: *Economic Report of the President,* January 1982, p. 271.

Changing Private Costs and Private Benefits

Modern economists maintain that much unemployment can be explained in cost/benefit terms: if the costs of being unemployed are reduced, the unemployment rate should rise. The costs of unemployment are affected by a number of institutional arrangements, including unemployment insurance, taxes, and minimum-wage laws.

Multiple Earners. In 1960, about 23 percent of the U.S. female population over the age of 16 was employed. By 1982, this figure was approaching 50 percent. The trend toward two or more working members in a household has changed the costs of unemployment. Before 1960, the unemployment of a household head meant an almost total loss of family income in the majority of cases. In the 1980s, the earnings losses to a household of one unemployed member are cushioned by the earnings of other employed members. In the recession year of 1982, for example, only 28 percent of families with an unemployed member had no employed person in the family. Only in single-parent families with children is the percent of families with unemployment and no employed member high (47 percent for single-parent families headed by females and 37.5 percent for single-parent families headed by males).

Unemployment Insurance. Martin Feldstein and other economists have argued that rising cov-

Example 2

Voluntary Unemployment and Unemployment Benefits

Detroit Michigan has one of the highest unemployment rates in the country. Yet even in Detroit many jobs go unfilled. Burger Chef restaurants report 40 unfilled jobs for cooks and counter jobs paying $3.50 per hour. Why are jobs unfilled in cities like Detroit with soaring unemployment? The answer is that the available jobs are mismatched with those who are unemployed. Out-of-work auto workers are accustomed to earning $10.75 per hour. They prefer to wait for economic conditions to improve. Moreover, unemployed auto workers are entitled to collect 90 percent of their former pay for one year from state unemployment insurance and employer-financed benefits. Some of these benefits are not taxed; therefore, their after-tax income may actually be higher when they are unemployed. Such workers, as one might imagine, would not be attracted to jobs earning $3.50 per hour. The benefits from unemployment exceed the benefits from working.

Unemployed auto workers are an exceptional case, but they shed light on the behavior of other unemployed workers who receive less generous unemployment benefits. Out-of-work loggers in California, who do not receive good unemployment benefits, are unwilling to work at available jobs offering $3.25 per hour digging lily bulbs. Employers note that workers accustomed to working with heavy machinery have a prejudice against manual field labor. Moreover, employers know that workers accustomed to higher wages will soon quit.

Are these automobile workers and California loggers involuntarily unemployed?

Source: "The Unemployed Shun Much Mundane Work, at Least for a While," *Wall Street Journal,* December 5, 1980.

erage and rising benefits offered by unemployment insurance have markedly altered the costs of unemployment. According to Feldstein, the substantial decline in the personal costs of unemployment over the past 20 years can explain much of the rise in the unemployment rate.[4]

Unemployment benefits affect the behavior of an unemployed worker in a predictable manner. If unemployment benefits are generous and can be drawn upon for a long period of time, it may not be worthwhile for the worker to search for a new job, especially if that worker places a high value on leisure. The benefits of unemployment may exceed the costs in the case of the laid-off worker who has good prospects of being recalled to a former job where the worker has built up seniority rights and a pension. In fact, laid-off workers usually do not search for new jobs unless it becomes apparent that there is no chance of recall. Instead, they wait to be recalled to their old job. In addition, most unemployment benefits are not taxed. A worker who pays 30 percent of his or her income in income taxes and who receives 70 percent of former income in unemployment benefits receives the same after-tax income unemployed or employed.

Over the past 20 years, the proportion of *covered employment* (workers and employees covered by state and federal unemployment insurance) has risen dramatically. In 1950, 58 percent of the labor force was covered. By 1981, 95 percent of the labor force was covered. In 1950, the average weekly unemployment benefit represented 39 percent of average weekly earnings when working. In 1981, it accounted for 43 percent. State and federal unemployment benefits average about 50 percent as much as after-tax wage incomes.[5]

The average unemployed worker in the United States can, therefore, count on state and federal programs to cover roughly one half of after-tax wage income. This figure does not include em-

4. Martin Feldstein, "The Economics of the New Unemployment," *Public Interest* 33 (Fall 1973).

5. These figures are from *The Economic Report of the President,* January 1982, p. 272 and from Rudiger Dornbusch and Stanley Fischer, *Macroeconomics,* 2nd ed. (New York: McGraw-Hill, 1981), p. 523.

ployer-provided benefits and union unemployment funds that in certain instances (such as the auto workers in Example 2) raise benefits well above 50 percent of former wage income. Moreover, the duration of unemployment is typically short enough so that unemployment benefits are not exhausted. At the end of 1981, only 1.4 percent of unemployment-benefit recipients had exhausted their benefits.

Minimum-Wage Laws. Statistics show that teenage unemployment is high because teenagers enter and exit from jobs with greater frequency than adults. Also, once out of work, teenagers require more time to find a new job.

Many economists argue that the minimum wage has contributed to rising teenage unemployment. The minimum wage is too high to encourage employers to spend money on training teenage employees for skilled positions. As a consequence, teenagers occupy menial positions, receive little on-the-job training, see little opportunity for eventual advancement, and leave unappealing jobs at high rates.

Government statistics show that the minimum wage as a percentage of average wages has actually declined (from 54 percent in 1950 to 47 percent in 1980). This fact suggests that minimum-wage laws should not necessarily have priced more teenagers out of the market. However, as the relative minimum wage declined, the percentage of those covered by minimum-wage legislation increased. It is, therefore, difficult to determine the overall effect of minimum-wage legislation on the relative wage of teenagers.

Progressive Taxation. Some economists argue that the combination of a progressive tax system with rapid inflation has pushed up the unemployment rate. First, highly progressive tax rates push middle- and upper-income households into higher and higher tax brackets. Thus as the after-tax rewards to employment are reduced by progressive taxes during inflations, the costs of being unemployed are reduced. The benefits of non-taxed unemployment benefits increase as the costs of unemployment decline. Moreover, the combination of inflation and progressive taxes pushes people into the underground economy where, although they are actually working, they will not be counted as employed.

It is easy to document changing institutions like unemployment benefits and minimum-wage laws that potentially could account for rising unemployment. It remains difficult to document their exact impact on unemployment over the years.

Other factors that may have raised the unemployment rate over the years are more difficult to quantify. The organization of the labor market can affect the unemployment rate. How rapidly and effectively information on job availabilities and job specifications is disseminated and how big a role labor unions play in the market can also affect unemployment. If jobs are expanding more rapidly in industries that have higher than average rates of unemployment, the unemployment rate should rise.

SOCIAL COSTS AND SOCIAL BENEFITS

A consistent warning of the activist Keynesians is that the business cycle imposes high social costs. As already noted, layoffs rise and quits fall during the contraction phase of the business cycle. If cyclically unemployed resources had been productively employed, more output could have been produced, and society could have had a higher standard of living, *ceteris paribus*. Keynesians regard the aggregate loss of income and output due to cyclical unemployment as the social cost of cyclically unemployed resources.

Social Costs

Economist Arthur Okun measures the social cost of unemployment by measuring real GNP at different unemployment rates.

Okun's Law is that for every 1 percentage point increase in the unemployment rate there is a 3 percent drop in real GNP.[6]

---

6. Arthur Okun, "Upward Mobility in a High Pressure Economy," Brookings Papers in Economic Activity (1973:2). More recent estimates place the ratio at 2.5. On this, see Jeffrey Perloff and Michael Wachter, "A Production Function Non-Accelerating Inflation Approach to Potential Output," eds. Karl Brunner and Allan Meltzer, *Carnegie-Rochester Conference Series*, North Holland.

Thus, if the unemployment rate rises from 6 to 7 percent, **Okun's Law** predicts a 3 percent drop in real GNP. At present levels of GNP, every 1 percentage point increase in the unemployment rate costs American society approximately $79 billion or $355 for every person in the United States.

Okun's Law measures the short-run losses of output due to a cyclical increase in the unemployment rate. Okun's Law assumes that cyclical increases in employment are accompanied by rising employment, rising hours worked per person, and increased productivity. Thus, in the short run, there are substantial output gains when people return to productive employment. Idle capital will be utilized more efficiently, and people doing part-time work will return to full-time jobs.[7]

The private costs of unemployment are not evenly distributed across society. The long-term unemployed with minimal unemployment-insurance protection bear a substantial burden of the private unemployment cost, especially if they place a low value on their leisure. The unemployed with generous unemployment benefits suffer less. Employees of declining industries who must pull up stakes to find employment in rising industries must also pay a personal cost. The worker in a cyclically depressed industry must bear the anxiety of waiting to be recalled and the belt tightening associated with layoffs. It is obviously not pleasant to be unemployed, except when it is a short interruption due to moving up the job ladder.

Social Benefits

As already noted, the effects of unemployment are not all negative. Job turnover allows workers to seek out better jobs. As workers move into jobs in which they are more productive, real GNP increases. If unemployed workers were to accept the first job that came along—even if it were below the salary and skill level to which they were accustomed—short-run incomes would increase, but long-run incomes would suffer. From the standpoint of society, it is sometimes better for individuals to opt for unemployment to wait for better jobs. In the long run, society and the individuals involved benefit more from the efficient allocation of people into jobs than from the automatic acceptance of the first job that comes along.

Although there is a rational case to be made that some unemployment is essential and beneficial—even to the unemployed—our society's attitude is that all unemployment is bad and that social policy should be geared to minimizing all types of unemployment, even the socially beneficial kind.

REDUCING UNEMPLOYMENT

Can the government do anything to control long-term unemployment? If the government can enact programs that improve the efficiency of labor markets and provide job skills to those with limited training and experience, the long-term unemployment rate should decline.

The Employment Act of 1946 gave the federal government responsibility for fighting excessive unemployment. Cyclical unemployment was to be attacked using monetary and fiscal policy, but monetary and fiscal policy cannot affect the structural unemployment that results from a declining industry or a severe lack of employable skills. For this reason, the federal government—in conjunction with state governments—instituted a series of job programs designed to combat structural unemployment.

The most ambitious programs of the federal government in the area of labor-force training were enacted during the Johnson administration's drive for the "Great Society." Programs such as the Job Corps, Manpower Training and Development, and Neighborhood Youth Programs were enacted in the 1960s. The first full-scale government training program was established in 1962 under the Manpower Development and Training Act. The programs provided under this act were designed to provide vocational and remedial training for those with low skills and high unemployment rate (particularly disadvantaged youths). The intent of such programs is to train workers to do jobs that are in high demand. In 1971, the

---

7. Okun's Law applies only to cyclical fluctuations in the unemployment rate. It overstates the effects of a permanent increase in the natural rate of unemployment. In the long run, the sole effect of the increase in the unemployment rate is the decrease in numbers employed; long-run effects on productivity and hours worked are not expected. In the long run, a 1 percentage point increase in the natural rate of unemployment is calculated to yield about a 1 percent reduction in real GNP.

Public Employment Program was passed, and in 1973 the Comprehensive Employment and Training Act (CETA) was enacted.

In 1978, almost 1 million workers—mainly under age 20—were enrolled in federally funded classroom or on-the-job training programs at a cost of around $2,000 per person. How successful have these programs been? As noted above, the unemployment rates of those whom the training programs were designed to help—particularly teenagers—have *increased* over a period of time when massive government outlays were being devoted to training. These statistics do not demonstrate the failure of such programs—the rise in unemployment could have been much worse without them—but they do not indicate outstanding successes either.

Modern economists no longer accept the proposition that unemployment is caused entirely by demand deficiencies. Modern economists believe there is more voluntarism to unemployment today than economists believed existed 30 years ago and that the employment/unemployment decision involves cost/benefit calculations, like most other economic decisions. The dividing line between voluntary and involuntary unemployment is becoming increasingly difficult to draw.

The next chapter will take an in-depth look at the rational-expectations explanation of the stagflation of recent years. Rational-expectations theory questions many of the tenets of macroeconomics presented in earlier chapters of this book.

Summary

1. Since the 1960s, the unemployment rate has been rising in the United States as well as in other industrialized countries. The statistical definition of unemployment does not account for discouraged workers, for job suitability, for intensity of job search, or for involuntary part-time employment.
2. Unemployment rates differ substantially by age, education, occupation, sex, marital status, and race.
3. The dividing line between voluntary and involuntary unemployment is often difficult to

draw. Some unemployment is voluntary because employees choose to quit their jobs. Quits fall during recessions and rise during periods of prosperity. Layoffs do just the opposite. The duration of unemployment rises during recessions, but most unemployment is of short duration.
4. Only about one third of the rise in the unemployment rate is explained by the changing composition of the labor force. The rise in the long-term unemployment rate has likely been affected by changing unemployment benefits, families with more than one income-earner, minimum-wage laws, and progressive taxation. The unemployment rate is affected by both the costs and benefits to workers of being unemployed.
5. The principal social cost of unemployment is the loss of output that unemployed labor would have produced. Okun's Law states that in the short run, every 1 percentage point increase in the unemployment rate causes output to fall by 3 percent. Unemployment does yield benefits to society. Society benefits when workers move to better jobs and when the overall allocation of labor improves.
6. Government programs that improve the efficiency of labor markets and provide job skills to those with limited training and experience should reduce unemployment.

Key Terms

discouraged worker
layoff
Okun's law

Questions and Problems

1. To what extent can the different types of unemployment—cyclical, structural, and frictional—be considered voluntary or involuntary?
2. I am prepared to take a job that pays $25,000 per year with a two-week paid vacation in the

first year, but I cannot find such a job. Would I be classified as unemployed?

3. Explain why it is unlikely for cyclical unemployment to account for the long-run rise in unemployment in the United States.

4. "Economists are on the wrong track when they say that unemployment decisions are based upon cost/benefit analysis. Cost/benefit analysis applies to most economic decision making, but not to unemployment. Able-bodied people want to work." Evaluate this statement.

5. Using cost/benefit analysis, explain why rising coverage for unemployment benefits may affect the unemployment rate.

6. Assume that prices start falling at a rate of 10 percent per year with a highly progressive tax system. In what ways would you expect the measured unemployment rate to react?

7. Okun's law underlines the high costs of unemployment. Yet this chapter stated that unemployment has a positive side as well. Are these two views of unemployment inconsistent?

CHAPTER

17

Rational Expectations: The New Classical Macroeconomics

The agonizing truth is that the public can be better off in the short run if it believes a lie.

Arthur Okun

Chapter Preview

This chapter will introduce a new theory of macroeconomics, called the *new classical macroeconomics* or *rational-expectations theory*. This new theory provides an alternative to the Keynesian model. Its proponents believe that it accounts for the basic facts of the business cycle but still explains why countercyclical policy appears not to work.

Just as the Great Depression of the 1930s brought forth the Keynesian Revolution, so the apparent inability of the Keynesian model to resolve the stagflation problems of the 1970s and 1980s has spawned a new alternative theory of macroeconomics.

The dissatisfaction with the Keynesian prescription is reflected in a remarkable speech by former Primer Minister of Great Britian, James Callaghan, in 1976:

> We used to think you could just spend your way out of a recession and increase employment by cutting taxes and boosting government spending. I can tell you, in all candour, that option no longer exists, and that, insofar as it ever did exist, it only worked by injecting bigger doses of inflation into the economy followed by higher levels of unemployment as the next step. This is the history of the past 20 years.

In the United States, government officials and economists, confronted with both rising unemployment and accelerating inflation, complained that "things don't work the way they used to" and that traditional economic remedies were no longer effective.

Economists Robert Lucas and Thomas Sargent, contributors to this new theory, summarize their dissatisfaction with Keynesian economics:

> . . . the inflationary bias *on average* of monetary and fiscal policy during this period (the 1970's) should, according to (Keynesian economics) . . ., have produced the lowest average unemployment rates for any decade since the 1940's. In fact, as we know, they produced the highest unemployment since the 1930's. This was . . . failure on a grand scale.

THE NEW CLASSICAL MACROECONOMICS

Keynes rejected the old classical macroeconomics—the crude quantity theory—as unrealistic. The facts of the business cycle (studied in Chapter 5) clearly supported Keynes's criticism. The level of real GNP has fluctuated substantially over time, and some explanation of this fact was needed. The perceived need for a theory to explain large fluctuations in real GNP originally accounted for the extraordinary success of Keynesian economics.

The new classical macroeconomics was developed by Robert Lucas of the University of Chicago by essentially combining the Friedman-Phelps analysis of the Phillips curve with the innovative rational-expectations hypothesis of John F. Muth.[1] Muth himself applied the rational-expectations hypothesis only to commodity markets at the microeconomic level. But Lucas went much further; he applied the rational-expectations idea to the entire macroeconomy. Thomas Sargent and Robert Barro also contributed important em-

1. This discussion is based on: Robert E. Lucas, Jr., "Some International Evidence on the Output-Inflation Trade-Off," *American Economic Review* 63 (June 1973); Robert Lucas and Thomas Sargent, "After Keynesian Macroeconomics," Thomas J. Sargent and Neil Wallace, "'Rational' Expectations, the Optimal Monetary Instrument, and the Optimal Money Supply Rule," *Journal of Political Economy* 83 (April 1975) and "Rational Expectations and the Theory of Economic Policy," *Journal of Monetary Economics* 2 (April 1976).

pirical work supporting the new classical economics and have helped develop the theory.

The central idea of rational expectations is that consumers and business managers are more than just passive observers of the economic scenery. People are active observers; they *think*. A person will, in making economic decisions, not only take objective economic data into account but will also form **rational expectations** about the future course of economic activity and governmental policy. People will not only make use of current and past history to form expectations but will also apply their best available information about what the government (or other people) are going to do in the future. People combine the limited information they have about how the economy works to form expectations about the future. For example, if the government is expected to increase the money supply by 10 percent, people who believe in the crude quantity theory would expect a 10 percent inflation rate.

> *Rational expectations are expectations that people form about macroeconomic variables, such as the inflation rate and the unemployment rate, using public knowledge about future monetary and fiscal policy, business and consumer spending plans, and current macroeconomic models.*

The basic notion of rational expectations is simply that people pursue their self-interest as far as possible. Households and business firms who maximize satisfaction try to anticipate what is going to happen using the best available information. Employers and employees negotiate wage contracts not only on the basis of current prices and costs but also on the basis of wages and prices rationally expected to prevail in the future. Individuals base decisions to purchase homes not only on current housing prices, interest rates, and personal income but also on their perceptions of the *future* home prices, interest rates, and income that are rationally expected to prevail.

Do People Anticipate Policy?

Do consumers and producers form expectations concerning government monetary and fiscal policy from which they rationally forecast expected wages and prices? The average person likely does not keep up with the latest moves of the Fed or analyze changes in the federal budget. Most people do not understand enough economics to use an economic model for forming rational expectations. Many individuals and businesses, however, do subscribe to newsletters and commercial reports or use the services of macroeconomic forecasting firms, such as Data Resources, Inc. or Wharton Econometrics, that in effect perform the needed calculations. The President's Economic Report, published yearly, also contains predictions for real GNP, the inflation rate, and the unemployment rate for the next five years. The Department of Commerce's Index of Leading Indicators is widely followed by business, the press, and the public as a guide to the future of the business cycle. Business firms and labor unions hire their own economists to make predictions about the variables that are of greatest concern to them. When prominent economists predict the future inflation rate, that prediction often makes the newspapers or evening television news. Thus, even though most people do not make elaborate economic predictions, they can use data provided by economists to form rational expectations about future prices and wages.

Generating information and projections about government monetary and fiscal policy has become a substantial industry in the United States. Business and organized labor do form expectations about monetary and fiscal policy. What about the average person on the street? It might be argued that the average person is scarcely aware of current monetary and fiscal policies, let alone surprised by them. Yet most people are reasonably well informed about the taxes they pay and form expectations of changes in tax policy. When individuals decide whether to invest in real estate (buy a home), in the stock market, or in money-market certificates, they must make some guesses about future monetary policy. Even average citizens, whether they are aware of it or not, form some expectations or guesses concerning government economic policies. They, like the large corporation or the labor union, can guess correctly, or they can be surprised. To say that people do not attempt to anticipate government economic policy is almost like saying that they

are not interested in maximizing their own personal well-being.

The World Is Uncertain

The next crucial hypothesis of the new classical macroeconomics is that even though people form rational expectations, no single person has perfect information. Individuals do not and, indeed, cannot be expected to know everything, especially when it comes to predicting the future.

This mundane observation has profound implications when combined with another observation: *people are more specialized in their selling activities than in their buying activities*. The line of products a business manager sells is much smaller than the myriad of products that manager needs to purchase in order to produce and market the product. The wheat farmer sells wheat but buys fertilizers, rents land, hires workers, and purchases tractors and equipment. Workers sell only the services of their labor, but they buy a vast array of consumer goods. Thus, virtually every economic agent—whether a firm or a worker—sells fewer things than it buys.

The typical producer (worker, business firm, farm) knows the prices of the things it sells better than the prices of the things it buys.

Price-Level Surprises

Almost everyone has had the experience of discovering that prices are higher or lower than expected. Some examples are more dramatic than others. The national news media have described how engineers attracted by high-paying jobs to Southern California experience unpleasant price surprises in the form of housing prices higher than anticipated. These engineers were specialized in the prices of the thing they sold (their engineering skills) and not in the prices of the things they bought (homes in Southern California). There are numerous examples of businesses ruined by agreeing to supply their product at a price that leads to losses when production costs rise more rapidly than expected.

A *price surprise* occurs when the actual price is different from the price expected to prevail. Just as individuals experience price surprises, so the economy as a whole can experience a **price-level surprise**. The price level *(P)* is a weighted average of the prices (a price index such as the CPI or wholesale price index) of all the individual goods and services the consumer or firm purchases. When prices are higher than consumers expect (on the average), the actual price level is higher than the price level that people expect. The price level that people expect to prevail is called the *expected price level (P_e)*.

*A **price-level surprise** occurs when the actual price level, P, is not equal to the expected price level, P_e.*

A convenient way to measure the extent to which people are surprised is to take the ratio of P to P_e; that is, P/P_e. If $P/P_e = 1$, people (on the average) are not surprised by the prices they encounter in the market place; if $P/P_e > 1$, prices are higher than expected; if $P/P_e < 1$, prices are lower than people expected. For example, if P/P_e is 1.05, prices are 5 percent higher than expected.

Demand and Supply Shocks

Price-level surprises are caused either by **demand shocks** or **supply shocks**.

Demand shocks are unanticipated shifts in aggregate demand due to unanticipated changes in monetary or fiscal policy or sudden changes in private consumption or investment behavior.

For example, the unanticipated increase in Soviet purchases of U.S. wheat in 1972 was a demand shock that caused price-level surprises throughout the economy. Since 1979, the Fed has announced its monetary-growth targets. If the actual growth of the money supply exceeds the target range, a demand shock results from a **policy surprise**.

*A **policy surprise** is a demand shock that results from an unanticipated monetary or fiscal policy.*

Supply shocks are unanticipated shifts in the aggregate supply curve.

Figure 1
Rational Expectations: Aggregate Supply and Demand

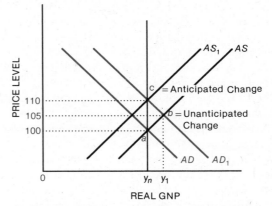

The initial equilibrium is at point *a*, where *AD* intersects *AS*. *AD* shifts upward to AD_1 as a result of monetary or demand-side fiscal policy. If the policy is anticipated, the rational-expectations hypothesis implies that the aggregate supply curve will shift up at the same time to AS_1. The new equilibrium is then *c*, with the same GNP but a higher price level. The Keynesian equilibrium would be at point *b*.

For example, the unanticipated 4-fold increase in the OPEC oil prices in 1974 was a supply shock that caused extensive price-level surprises. The decline in OPEC oil prices in 1982 may have set into motion price-level surprises in the opposite direction: prices rising less rapidly than anticipated.

Aggregate Demand and Supply

A tranquil economy would be one without demand or supply shocks of any kind. All monetary or fiscal policies would be fully anticipated; any shifts in aggregate demand or aggregate supply would be perfectly anticipated.

Figure 1 shows what would happen to such a tranquil economy if an *anticipated* change in monetary policy occurred. Before the change in policy, the aggregate demand and supply curves would be *AD* and *AS*, which intersect at point *a*, where the economy is producing the natural level of output at a price level of 100. If the money supply increases, the *AD* curve will shift to AD_1, where it intersects the original aggregate supply curve at point *b*. Keynesian economists would argue that point *b* is the new short-run equilibrium. At point *b*, both output and the price level have risen compared to point *a*.

Rational expectations economists do not agree that *b* would be the new short-run equilibrium. Since the policy change is anticipated, people will generally recognize that prices and wages will rise. Indeed, this expectation of a higher price level causes aggregate supply to decrease. Chapter 13 showed that the aggregate supply curve shifts upward to the left as the anticipated price level rises because rational firms will not be subject to money illusion. They realize that at the higher price level, they are no better off in real terms than before because costs have also risen. Since expectations are rational, the new aggregate supply curve will be AS_1, and the new equilibrium will be point *c*. At *c*, the price level is 110, and the level of output remains at the natural level because firms realize that at a price level of 110 they are no better off in real terms than they were at a price level of 100. Thus, the anticipated change in policy simply raises the price level from 100 to 110 without any stimulus to real GNP. No price-level surprises are unleashed because the shift in *AD* is anticipated.

> *When expectations are rational, there can be no price-level surprises without a demand or supply shock. Fiscal and monetary policies will be anticipated and will simply raise (or lower) the price level without any change in real GNP. Without price surprises, real GNP stays at the natural level of output.*

When expectations are rational, *the automatic adjustment mechanism works instantaneously.* The supply curve does not adjust slowly to rising prices. Firms and workers anticipate the full magnitude of the price increase, and aggregate supply shifts immediately from *AS* to AS_1.

The above analysis applies to fiscal policy if the primary effects of the fiscal actions are on aggregate demand. A fully anticipated increase in government spending would be one that was accompanied by a shift in aggregate supply that reflected the higher expected price level. However, a fully anticipated fiscal policy can affect real GNP if the policy involves direct supply-side factors, as in the case of a tax cut that increased work incentives.

PRICE SURPRISES

The rational-expectations economist knows as well as the Keynesian economist that an economy is unlikely to remain tranquil in the real world for any length of time. The new classical macroeconomist assumes that demand and supply shocks are an inevitable feature of economic life. Had the policy change in Figure 1 been *unanticipated,* the new equilibrium position would have been point *b* with prices higher than anticipated. When a *price surprise* occurs, the economy moves up its aggregate supply curve to a *higher output* and a higher price level.

Since the distinction between anticipated and unanticipated demand or supply shifts is so crucial in the new classical macroeconomics, it is useful to be able to represent the degree of surprise graphically. The Lucas demand and supply curves described below can illustrate better than aggregate demand and supply curves the effect of demand and supply shocks on output.

The Lucas Supply Curve

The **Lucas supply curve**, named for Robert Lucas of the University of Chicago, shows the relationship between output and the degree to which a change in aggregate demand was anticipated.

*The **Lucas supply curve** shows the quantity of real aggregate output supplied for every level of price surprise* (P/P_e).

The derivation of the Lucas supply curve is shown in Figure 2. The economy is initially in equilibrium at point *a*, where *AD* equals *AS* at the natural level of output. An unanticipated increase in aggregate demand (a demand shock) causes a price surprise. Actual prices are higher than expected prices, and firms supply more output. The price surprise has caused more real output to be produced. The curve in panel (b) shows the real outputs that are supplied at different levels of price surprises. At the initial equilibrium *a'*, there is no price surprise $(P/P_e = 1)$, and the economy supplies the natural level of output. When there is a positive price surprise $(P/P_e > 1)$, the economy supplies an output greater than the natural level. The curve associating each level of price surprise with the corresponding supply of real output is the Lucas supply *(LS)* curve.

Figure 2
Derivation of the Lucas Supply Curve

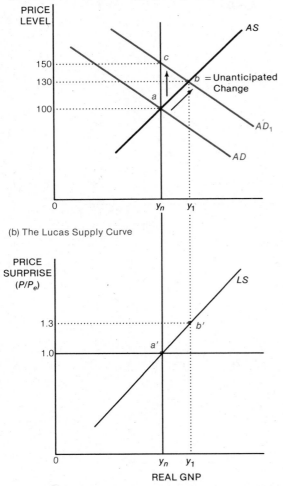

(a) Aggregate Supply and Aggregate Demand

(b) The Lucas Supply Curve

REAL GNP

Panel (a) shows that the economy is initially at *a*, producing the natural level of output *(y_n)* with a price level of 100. A demand shock increases aggregate demand unexpectedly from *AD* to *AD_1*. Because economic agents have not anticipated the demand shock, the resulting inflation (prices rise from a level of 100 to a level of 130) catches people off guard. The economy is fooled into producing more real output and moves from *a* to *b*.

Panel (b) relates the increase in the supply of aggregate output to the price surprise itself rather than to the price level. The price level of 130 in panel (a) translates into a price-level surprise of 1.3 in panel (b).

If the increase in demand had been anticipated, the aggregate supply curve would shift immediately to the left, until it intersected y_n, so that the

economy would continue to supply the same real output as at *a'*. In this case, there is no price surprise $(P/P_e = 1)$, and the economy continues to supply the same real output, as again shown by point *a'*.

If there had been an unanticipated *reduction* in aggregate demand (not shown in Figure 2), there would have been a *negative* price surprise $(P/P_e < 1)$, and the economy would have supplied less real output. When the price surprise is less than one, a real output below the natural level will be supplied.

Because the economy supplies more real output when prices are higher than expected, the Lucas supply curve is upward-sloping. Recall that people know the prices of the things they sell better than the things they buy. If prices are higher than people have anticipated, the sellers of products (firms) or of labor (workers) will think that the prices of the goods they sell have risen *relative* to the things they buy. This mistaken belief will induce producers (in the aggregate) to supply more real GNP. Sellers will think they are being offered a good deal in the marketplace and will try to take advantage of it by increasing their output (for example, labor will work harder). With positive price surprises people will try to "make hay while the sun shines." If prices are lower than people have anticipated, real output will shrink because sellers will mistakenly assume that selling prices have fallen relative to buying prices.

An example can demonstrate how the Lucas supply schedule works. Suppose increases in aggregate demand are pushing up wages and prices throughout the country. Machinists in Topeka, Kansas have just received a 14 percent wage increase—of which they are well aware. Collectively, they anticipate a 10 percent increase in the prices they pay. It is more difficult for them to judge what is happening to the prices of the things they buy, but they believe that their *real wage* has risen by 4 percent (their wage has increased more than the prices of the things they buy). They, therefore, increase the quantity of the labor they supply in order to increase their income before prices catch up with wages. Their labor-supply actions are based upon their *expectation* of prices. Even if prices rise at the same rate as their wage (14 percent), they have been fooled (by incorrectly anticipating price increases) into working more even though their real wage may be unchanged.

The Lucas supply curve passes through the natural level of real GNP, y_n, when there are no price surprises because when inflation is perfectly anticipated, the economy will automatically operate at the natural level of unemployment, by definition.

To the new classical macroeconomist, there is a different level of full employment for each level of price surprise. Prices higher than expected lead to higher employment and more output; prices lower than expected lead to lower employment and less output. Here they part company with the old classical economists, who where unable to explain fluctuations in real GNP. When the level of prices is the same as expected ($P/P_e = 1$), or, in other words, when price inflation and deflation are perfectly anticipated, the resulting natural level of real GNP, y_n, can be maintained indefinitely (in principle). As in the old classical system, y_n will rise slowly over time with rising productivity and growth in the labor force. However, price surprises can cause fluctuations around the natural level.

The Lucas Demand Curve

A **Lucas demand curve** shows the relationship between the output level and the degree to which a change in aggregate supply is anticipated.

*The **Lucas demand curve** shows the quantity of real aggregate output demanded at each level of price surprise (P/P_e).*

The Lucas demand curve holds the level of demand shocks constant. In other words, it shows the reaction of the demand for real GNP to price-level surprises when there are no demand shocks (or when the level of demand shocks is not changing). Demand shocks cause the Lucas demand curve to shift, as shown below.

Figure 3 shows the relationship between aggregate supply-and-demand analysis and the Lucas demand curve. In panel (a), the economy is initially in equilibrium at point *a*, where the economy is producing the natural level of output with no price surprises. A temporary unexpected supply shock shifts the aggregate supply curve to the

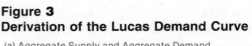

Figure 3
Derivation of the Lucas Demand Curve

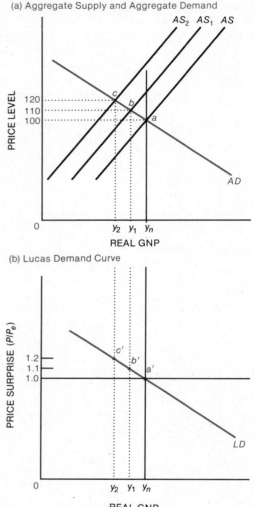

Panel (a) shows the effect of a temporary and unanticipated reduction in aggregate supply (an adverse supply shock). When the normal aggregate supply curve, *AS*, shifts to AS_1, the economy moves along *AD* from *a* to *b*. At *b*, the economy produces less than the natural level of output. If there is a further unanticipated supply shock (to AS_2) the economy moves to *c* at a still higher price level and a still lower real output.

Panel (b) shows the same sequence of events on the Lucas demand curve—which plots the aggregate demand for real GNP at different levels of price surprise. The economy is initially at the natural level of output with no price surprise ($P/P_e = 1$). At *b'*, the price surprise is 1.1 and y_1 is demanded. At *c'*, the price surprise is 1.2 and y_2 is demanded.

left. The supply shock sets off unanticipated inflation. When people who anticipate a lower price level see the higher prices as reducing real money balances (they perceive prices to be rising faster than their nominal money balances), they cut back on their demand for real output. The adverse supply shock thus causes the economy to move along the aggregate demand curve from a to b, where less real output is produced at a higher price level. If there had been an even larger temporary adverse supply shock, the economy would move further up the AD curve to c, where real GNP is even lower.

In panel (b), the Lucas demand curve plots the level of real GNP demanded at each level of price surprise. It shows the equilibrium levels of output (y_n, y_1, y_2) at each level of supply shock (1.0, 1.1, 1.2).

Temporary and fairly permanent shifts in aggregate supply have different effects on the level of price surprise. An example of a random transitory shift in aggregate supply would be fluctuating agricultural harvests that follow no distinctive pattern. In this case, people would recognize that the shift in supply is random and transitory. Such a supply shift would have no effect on the natural level of output because the amount of resources and their productivity would not have changed. The transitory supply reduction would, therefore, have no impact on the expected price level because the aggregate supply curve would be expected to return to its original position. The expected price level would remain at 100 in Figure 3.

A permanent supply shift, on the other hand, would change the natural level of output. For example, the reduction in world oil supply engineered by the OPEC cartel in the early 1970s raised world oil prices and reduced the effective resource base of oil-importing economies. Such a fundamental change lowers the natural rate of output. People would come to expect a permanently higher price level (once they realized OPEC was not a temporary phenomenon), and the natural rate would shift to the left (say, to output y_1 in Figure 3).

As another example, to the extent that a reduced tax rate may induce more work effort or reduce the incentive to remain on untaxed unemployment insurance, a reduced tax rate could increase the natural level of real GNP.

Figure 4
A Tranquil Economy

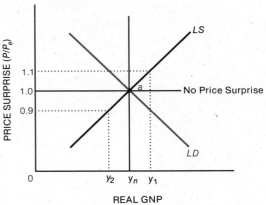

The Lucas supply (LS) curve and the Lucas demand (LD) curve both pass through point a when there are no supply or demand shocks. At point a, the economy is producing at the natural or full-employment level with no price surprises. Price surprises are measured by the ratio of actual prices (P) to the expected price level (P_e). The LS curve shows that the supply of real output increases when P/P_e increases; the LD curve shows that the demand for real output decreases when P/P_e increases.

Lucas Equilibrium

Equilibrium with No Shocks. Figure 4 shows a Lucas equilibrium in a tranquil economy in which there are no supply or demand shocks. Equilibrium occurs at that output and level of price surprise where LD and LS intersect. All fiscal and monetary policies are fully and completely anticipated. There are no supply shocks. Suppliers and demanders (on average) correctly anticipate the price level. Therefore, the natural level of real GNP is produced (y_n), and there is no price surprise at the macro level $(P/P_e = 1)$.

Equilibrium with a Supply Shock. In Figure 5, the Lucas demand curve, LD, passes through point a, where there are no demand-shock-induced price surprises and where the demand for real GNP equals the natural level. The Lucas supply curve, LS, shifts left to LS_1 as the result of an adverse supply shock. An adverse supply shock causes the original LS curve to shift to the left to LS_1. The economy is in equilibrium where LD crosses LS_1 at point e. At this equilib-

Figure 5
An Adverse Supply Shock

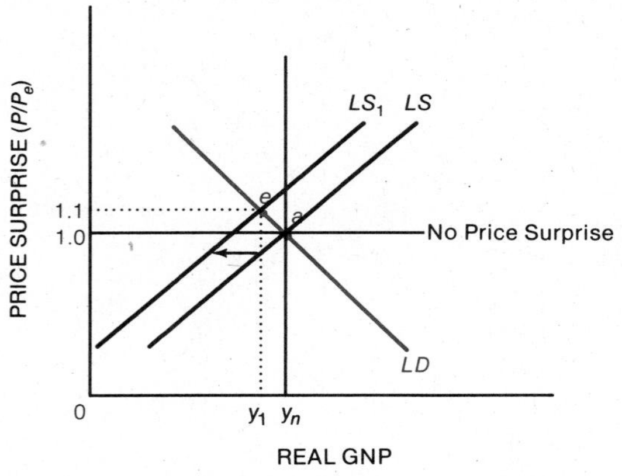

Because there is no demand shock, *LD* passes through point *a*. An adverse supply shock, however, shifts *LS* to the left of point *a*. The new equilibrium occurs at point *e*, where output is less than the natural level and prices are higher than expected.

Figure 6
An Adverse Demand Shock with No Supply Shocks

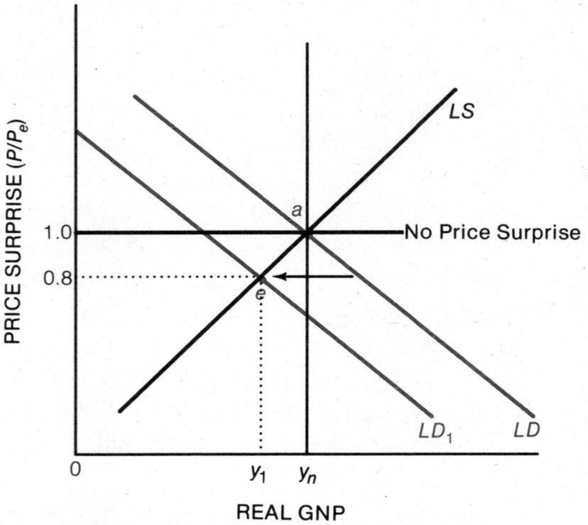

Since there are no supply shocks, the *LS* curve passes through point *a*. An adverse demand shock—such as an unexpected reduction in government spending or in the rate of monetary growth—shifts the *LD* curve to the left of point *a* and shifts the intersection to point *e*. Real GNP falls below the natural level, and prices are lower than expected.

rium, prices are higher than anticipated ($P/P_e > 1$), and output is less than the natural level. A supply shock in the next period might shift the Lucas supply curve to the right or even further to the left. If the supply shock is only temporary and there is no supply shock in the next period, the Lucas supply curve will shift back to the right and again pass through point *a*. A temporary supply shock is random and reversible—due to the weather or a strike, for example.

Equilibrium with a Demand Shock. Figure 6 shows an adverse demand shock, due either to an unanticipated reduction in the growth of the money supply or a contractionary fiscal policy that catches people by surprise. The adverse demand shock could also arise from unexpected changes in private behavior—sudden reductions in exports or sudden increases in imports, an unanticipated reduction in business investment, or a change in consumer preferences. An adverse demand shock shifts *LD* to the left to LD_1. At the equilibrium of LD_1 and *LS* at point *e*, people experience lower prices than they anticipate. Output has decreased and unemployment has increased.

Equilibrium with Supply and Demand Shocks. Finally, Figure 7 shows an adverse supply shock combined with an expansionary demand shock. If the supply shock is larger than the demand shock, as shown, real GNP falls below the natural level, and prices rise more than anticipated. If the expansionary demand shock had been larger than the adverse supply shock, prices would still be higher than expected, but real GNP would be above the natural level.

ANTICIPATED VERSUS UNANTICIPATED POLICY

Can the economy be made to produce more (or less) real GNP through the use of monetary and fiscal policy? If there is significant measured unemployment, can policy makers increase real output to create more jobs using expansionary monetary and (demand-side) fiscal policies? According to the new classical macroeconomics, the desired result will be achieved only if people are surprised or fooled. For the effect to be long lasting, people must be continuously fooled. If the countercyclical policy is anticipated, it will have

Figure 7
An Adverse Supply Shock and a
Positive Demand Shock

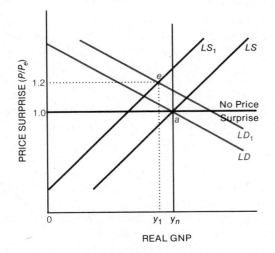

This graph illustrates a simultaneous adverse supply shock and a positive demand shock. Because the demand shock is less than the supply shock, real output falls, but the price surprise rises (prices are higher than expected).

no effect on output and employment. Of course, supply-side fiscal policies can affect output and employment.

Policy Surprises

Consumers, workers, unions, small producers, and giant corporations all form expectations concerning government monetary and fiscal policy. Participants in the economy will seek to anticipate changes in the money supply and in government spending and taxation. A policy surprise can be either a **money surprise** or a **fiscal surprise**.

*A **money surprise** occurs if the actual money supply is different from that generally expected.*

*A **fiscal surprise** occurs if government spending or taxation turns out different than people anticipated.*

As already mentioned, labor unions, corporations, and individuals expend a great deal of ef-

fort to predict (or anticipate) future government monetary and fiscal policies. Unions must anticipate government economic policy to avoid price surprises. If a major union were to incorrectly anticipate a slowing in the inflation rate and then settle for a smaller wage package, it would be in deep trouble with its members. If a major bank were to guess wrong on monetary policy, its profits could be damaged. Corporations must anticipate changes in corporate taxation if they are to make rational economic decisions.

Anticipated Policy

According to the new classical macroeconomics, if the government embarks on a fully anticipated countercyclical monetary or demand-side fiscal policy real GNP and, hence, unemployment will not change. Only the rate of inflation or price level will be affected by an anticipated policy change, as shown in Figure 1. The expansionary policy shifts up the original aggregate demand curve, *AD,* but since the policy is anticipated the familiar aggregate supply curve, *AS,* shifts up to offset the impact on real GNP. *The Lucas demand and supply equilibrium does not change when policy is anticipated.* The *LS* and *LD* curves remain in exactly the same position because there are no surprises.

Figure 5 described an economy where an adverse supply shock had lowered real GNP and raised unemployment above the natural rate. If the standard policy of the government in such a situation is to counter supply shocks with expansionary monetary and fiscal policy, the public will anticipate the policy, and, hence, there will be no demand shock. Only if the government fools the public will there be an increase in *LD* to offset the adverse supply shock. *A policy change can only cause a demand shock when people fail to anticipate the policy.* The aggregate demand curve shifts whenever monetary or fiscal policy is changed; the Lucas demand curve shifts only when there is an *unanticipated* demand shock or policy surprise.

Anticipated Monetary Policy. A monetary policy is anticipated when the public anticipates the rate of growth in the nominal money supply. An anticipated monetary policy causes no change in the Lucas demand curve, *LD*. As the money supply increases, rational agents (consumers and producers) anticipate that prices and wages will increase at the same rate as the money supply. Even though the supply of monetary assets in the hands of the public is increasing, it is generally recognized that prices will increase at the same rate as the money supply. Because the public realizes it is no better off in real terms than before the monetary expansion, there is no reason for aggregate demand to increase in real terms.

The effect of a policy change on interest rates depends on whether the *rate* of monetary expansion is increased or not. If the *rate* of money growth has been increased, and the public anticipates it, the expected rate of inflation will increase. Hence, an increase in the rate of monetary growth will increase interest rates as lenders require a premium for higher anticipated inflation. Nominal interest rates will rise by precisely the increase in the anticipated rate of inflation. The *real interest rate,* defined as the nominal rate minus the anticipated inflation rate, does not change; real business investment stays the same. Since people on average anticipate a higher rate of inflation, the corporations that borrow for real investment are willing to pay the higher interest rate; lenders demand a higher interest rate—an inflation premium—in order to insulate themselves from the inflation tax.

The new classical macroeconomics argues that an anticipated increase in the rate of growth in the money supply will leave real GNP unchanged (because participants will act to neutralize the monetary policy) but will raise the rate of inflation and the nominal rate of interest.

Anticipated Fiscal Policy. Expectations can defeat the demand-side effects of fiscal policy as well as monetary policy. The Lucas supply and demand curves remain the same in the case of a fully anticipated fiscal policy. Consider, once again, the aggregate demand and supply curves in Figure 1. The initial equilibrium is point *a*, where the prevailing aggregate demand curve, *AD,* intersects the prevailing aggregate supply curve, *AS.* The equilibrium price level is 100. If real government expenditures increase, the aggregate demand curve shifts to the right to AD_1. Because there is no change in monetary policy, the nominal money supply will not change as aggregate demand increases.

When aggregate demand increases to AD_1, aggregate supply decreases to AS_1 because producers anticipate the change. At the new price level of 110, total GNP doesn't change, but desired consumption and desired investment decline just as much as government expenditures rise, and the real money supply falls. In other words, the price level of 110 *crowds out* a quantity of private expenditures equal to the increase in government expenditures. When policy is fully anticipated, the aggregate supply curve shifts to AS_1 as workers and firms perceive that prices and wages will rise due to the expansionary fiscal policy.

Does it make any difference whether government expenditures are financed out of taxes or by selling public debt (assuming that deficit financing does not lead to increases in the money supply)? According to the rational-expectations hypothesis, when fiscal policy is fully anticipated so-called deficit financing is an unimportant detail because rational taxpayers will consider the long-term implications of financing the increased government spending. If government spending increases by $20 billion and is financed by selling $20 billion worth of government bonds, the rational taxpayer will realize that the obligation to pay the interest income and the principal on this debt will call for higher taxes in the future. Although current tax obligations are not being increased, the taxpayer might cut back on current consumption to save for the increased tax burden in future years.

Rational-expectations theorists see little difference in the fiscal stimulus provided by balanced budgets and deficit financing when the latter is not accompanied by an expansionary monetary policy. Neither one, if fully anticipated, will have any effect on real GNP. The composition of output will change in favor of government; real interest rates will also rise if government takes a larger share of GNP.

To the extent that deficits lead to further monetary expansion, however, the two types of fiscal stimulus will be quite different, as explained later.

Unanticipated Monetary and Fiscal Policies

If the public is fooled by monetary and fiscal policy, rational-expectations theory predicts results similar in some respects to those predicted by the Keynesian model. Obviously, the public cannot always anticipate government policy. The future is uncertain, and the government may, without warning, change the monetary and fiscal rules under which it operates. For example, the Federal Reserve System in October 1979 without warning changed its goals from maintaining interest-rate objectives to maintaining specified monetary-growth targets.

If the Fed surprises the public with an *unanticipated increase* in the money supply, the public sees its money balances increasing but fails to recognize that price increases will soon wipe out any real gains. Real spending, therefore, increases. The increase in the money supply starts to drive down interest rates, and savers (who fail to anticipate the impending increase in inflation) do not require an added inflation premium on interest rates. The interest rate falls, and real business investment increases.

This process is shown in Figure 8. The unanticipated increase in the money supply shifts the Lucas demand curve to the right from LD to LD_1. Real GNP increases from y_n to y_1, and there is a price surprise of 1.05 (prices are 5 percent above the expected level). As wage rates rise (in response to the increase in aggregate demand), the supply of labor rises as workers fail to anticipate that inflation will ultimately wipe out the gains from rising money wages. Thus, the economy moves up the Lucas supply schedule from point a to point e.

A similar effect would result from unanticipated fiscal policy. If the public had had no prior experience with deficit financing and the government added $20 billion worth of government spending to its budget without raising taxes, the unanticipated fiscal policy would raise real aggregate demand. This increase in demand is also illustrated in Figure 8 by a shift in the demand curve from LD to LD_1. The unanticipated fiscal stimulus increases aggregate demand and raises prices to more than otherwise expected, just as in the case of unanticipated monetary policy.

Figure 8
Unanticipated Fiscal or Monetary Expansion

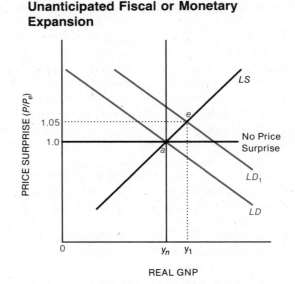

An unanticipated expansionary monetary policy or demand-side fiscal policy will shift the LD curve to the right from LD to LD_1. The equilibrium will occur at point e if there are no supply shocks. Output rises from y_n to y_1, and prices are higher than expected.

When unanticipated monetary or fiscal expansions increase Lucas demand (shift it to the right), both real GNP and prices increase.

Learning from the Past

The public, however, learns from these experiences. As Abraham Lincoln said, "you can't fool all the people all the time." The shift in demand from LD to LD_1 occurs because the public is surprised by a particular policy of the government. As the public learns about the new policy (that the rate of monetary growth was higher than expected or that deficit financing raises future taxes) they will make adjustments, and the Lucas demand curve will shift back towards its original position. The LD curve can be sustained only by further demand shocks or policy surprises. *Anticipated* shifts in aggregate demand *do not* shift the LD curve because such shifts will be deflated by offsetting shifts in aggregate supply. Over time, the economy will tend to return to the original natural level of real GNP.

How does the public adjust over time to policy surprises? Unions that have underestimated the degree of inflation will renegotiate contracts to catch up with inflation. Lenders, initially caught unawares by unanticipated inflation, will require inflation premiums from borrowers. Thus, it is unlikely that policy by surprise can be applied successfully in the long run. If the public is no longer surprised by monetary and fiscal policy, countercyclical policies will have no impact on real GNP and employment.

> *Countercyclical policy cannot be used to stabilize fluctuations in real GNP unless the public fails to learn from past experience.*

Supply Shocks: The Bad News

Price surprises can be caused either by policy surprises or by supply and demand shocks. Rather than trying to examine in depth the various supply and demand shocks (fluctuations in exports and imports, crop failures, changes in export prices) consider a specific example: the generally unanticipated quadrupling of crude oil prices in 1973 and 1974. The new classical macroeconomic model paints the following picture.

Unanticipated increases in the cost of production will shift the Lucas supply schedule to the left. An unanticipated increase in the price of crude oil, therefore, would cause a shift in aggregate supply from LS to LS_1 in Figure 9. This supply shock would create a major price surprise; that is, prices would rise to well above the anticipated level, and the economy would move along the demand schedule, LD, to a new equilibrium at e (at a lower real GNP and a higher price level). This equilibrium, however, would only be a temporary one, insofar as consumers and producers would have the opportunity to adjust to the oil price surprise as time passes.

Consumers and businesses would realize that the purchasing power of their money assets had declined more than anticipated and would reduce their real consumer and investment spending. The Lucas demand curve would decrease (shift down from LD to LD_1). Gradually, the economy would adjust to a *new* equilibrium (at a'), where the economy would produce a new natural level of real GNP (y'_n) with a lower level of real output.

Figure 9
A Supply Shock: The Unanticipated Increase in OPEC Prices

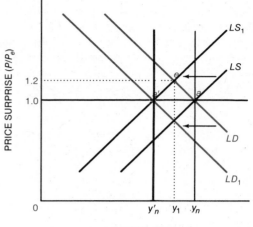

The economy is initially at equilibrium at a with no price surprises and with production at the natural level of real GNP, y_n. The unanticipated increase in OPEC prices shifts the LS curve to LS_1, and a new equilibrium is achieved at a' at a lower real GNP and higher price level and price surprise. As the public adjusts to this price surprise, aggregate demand will shift from LD to LD_1, and a new and lower natural level of real GNP, y'_n, will be established.

According to rational-expectations theory, countercyclical monetary and demand-side fiscal policies cannot return the economy to the original higher natural level of real GNP if the public could be surprised, and it is unlikely that the public could be surprised permanently. According to the rational-expectations approach, real GNP declines caused by supply shocks must simply be accepted. They cannot be bought off with higher prices. In contrast, the Keynesian approach is that the original level of real GNP could be restored if one were willing to accept a higher price level or accelerating inflation.

Inflation: The Good News

This new theory of macroeconomics gives a very optimistic report about inflation: like the new Phillips curve, it says that there is no long-run trade-off between inflation and unemployment; rational-expectations theory even claims that there need be no short-run trade-off either.

An earlier chapter emphasized that the cost of curing inflation is likely to be a substantial rise in unemployment in the short run. People will respond slowly to a decline in inflation brought about by tightening money. In the mean time, unemployment must be borne until inflationary expectations are slowly beaten down.

Rational-expectations theorists recommend that the government tell the public what fiscal and monetary policy will be—say, a stable growth policy of 4 percent monetary growth per year. There will be no price and policy surprises; as the inflation rate drops, inflationary expectations will adjust downward instantly, and the economy will settle down to the natural level of real GNP and employment with a low rate of inflation.

However, if government officials announced in an inflationary period that henceforth the rate of monetary growth would equal 5 percent a year, the public simply would not believe them. In terms of the rational-expectations model, the result would be an actual price level *below* the anticipated level ($P/P_e < 1$). The sharp recession in late 1981 and 1982 can be interpreted as the unbelieving response of the public to Reagan's restrictive monetary and fiscal policies. When the actual price level fell below that expected, the public experienced a price surprise ($P/P_e < 1$) and moved down the Lucas supply schedule to a lower real GNP. The high levels of unemployment in late 1981 and early 1982 suggest that preannounced policies will not work if people don't believe the government. In the first quarter of 1982 the inflation rate was running at 3.5 percent per year when people were expecting inflation between 7 percent and 10 percent, judging by the high interest rates.

As long as policy is discretionary, the public's disbelief of government promises is entirely rational. Therefore, many rational-expectations theorists believe in fixed constitutional rules of the game that bind the government's actions.

EVALUATING THE NEW MACROECONOMICS

Conflicts with Keynesian Economics

The most substantial differences between the Keynesian school and the new classical macroeconomics are:

1. The Keynesians believe that activist monetary and fiscal policy will change real GNP and employment in the desired direction. The new classical macroeconomists believe that activist aggregate-demand policies will work only if the policy is unanticipated and, even then, the effect will be temporary.
2. Keynesians doubt that policy can be fully anticipated, since in many markets (like labor and product markets) prices may be fixed over the short term. The rational-expectations economist responds that fixed money contracts are themselves a response to past policies. Inflationary policies shorten such contracts.
3. The Keynesians believe that monetary and fiscal policy can be used to achieve a trade-off between increased prices and reduced employment based on the belief that expansionary monetary and fiscal policies can be used to increase real GNP and employment through the short-run Phillips curve. The new classical macroeconomists believe that a trade-off between increased prices and lower unemployment exists only in the short run in the case of unanticipated policy. If policy is anticipated, there will be no trade-off between higher prices and lower unemployment.
4. Rational-expectations economists view the business cycle as something to be explained rather than controlled. By reducing the random fluttering of fiscal and monetary policy, the business cycle may be somewhat moderated.

Supporting Evidence

The evidence in support of the Keynesian approach was presented in the chapter on stabilization policy. What evidence is there to support the new classical macroeconomics?

The best direct evidence that people can forecast the effects of future policies rather than form simple adaptive expectations is the rather dramatic endings to the hyperinflations that have plagued the world. Following World War I, Austria, Germany, Hungary, and Poland experienced enormous inflation rates (in Germany they were more than 300 percent per month). Each hyperinflation was suddenly stopped without plunging these economies into deep recessions. In each case, the governments took concrete and widely announced steps to end government deficits and runaway monetary growth. By changing the name of the monetary unit and by radically reconstructing the monetary and fiscal rules of the game, inflation was brought to an abrupt halt.

Perhaps the reason the Reagan administration's tight monetary and fiscal policies apparently led to such high unemployment rates without much reduction in interest rates is that the projected deficit (in early 1982) was so large (more than $100 billion) that people simply did not believe that the government could end the inflation. Hence, expectations of inflation persisted, and the reduced rate of inflation simply raised unemployment while interest rates remained high.

Evidence that only unanticipated monetary policy affects real GNP and employment has been compiled by Robert Barro, who compared unanticipated increases in the rate of growth of the money supply with the rate of unemployment. Panel (a) of Figure 10 shows Barro's measure of the unanticipated growth in the money supply (a negative number indicates that monetary growth was lower than anticipated, a positive number indicates that it was higher than expected). Panel (b) plots the unemployment rate. As Barro's work shows, when money growth was higher than anticipated, the unemployment rate was low. This evidence is consistent with the rational-expectations view that only unanticipated monetary policy will affect real GNP and employment.

Third, experience with postwar fiscal policy appears to be consistent with the rational-expectations hypothesis. The 1964 tax cut is commonly credited with having a larger effect on real output and unemployment than subsequent tax cuts. The 1964 tax cut was the first use of discretionary tax policy. People would have had great difficulty anticipating its effect on aggregate demand. The impacts of subsequent tax changes would be easier to predict and, hence, offset.

Fourth, the evidence concerning the new Phillips curve (presented in Chapter 14 on inflation and unemployment) is consistent with the new classical macroeconomics. The widely accepted Friedman-Phelps analysis of the Phillips curve is part of the rational-expectations story. Indeed, the Lucas supply curve is just a simple representation of the "new" Phillips curve. The additional ingredient added by the new classical macroeconomics is that expectations are formed rationally rather than adaptively. The rational-expectations model allows for more rapid (in some cases even

Figure 10
The Relationship Between Unanticipated Money Supply Growth and Unemployment

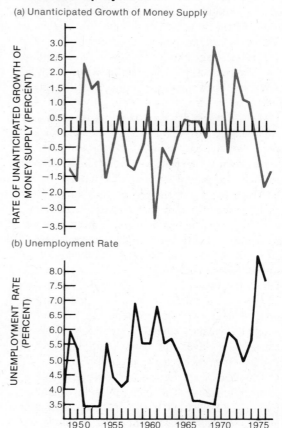

(a) Unanticipated Growth of Money Supply

(b) Unemployment Rate

Panel (a) shows Robert Barro's estimates of the unanticipated rate of growth of the money supply (measured as the actual money growth rate minus the anticipated money growth rate). These estimates assume that people believe the rate of growth of the money supply depends on past rates of growth, the unemployment rate, and the federal fiscal deficit. Panel (b) shows that the unemployment rate for different years tends to fall when there is unanticipated growth of the money supply.

Source: Based on Robert Barro, "Unanticipated Money, Output, and the Price Level in Its Natural State," *Journal of Political Economy* 86 (August 1978).

instantaneous) shifts in the short-run Phillips curve.

How would one expect rational labor to behave during periods of rapid inflation? First, there would be a tendency for more workers to insist on cost-of-living escalator clauses during periods of high inflation, which has been the case. Second, one would expect shorter contracts to be negotiated during periods of high inflation because workers would want to avoid getting locked in to long-term contracts. The move towards shorter wage contracts during episodes of high inflation can also be documented.

Naturally, Keynesian economists do not accept the rational-expectations revolution just as the new classical macroeconomists do not accept the Keynesian revolution. For the moment, the rational-expectations hypothesis is too new for the opponents of the hypothesis to have marshalled all their evidence. In time, a synthesis will probably emerge that combines elements of both theories. It remains to determine the extent to which expectations are formed rationally. The extent to which supply-side fiscal policy (such as tax cuts) can be used to stabilize GNP is still controversial, even in a rational-expectations framework. The interplay of fixed contracts, ignorance, and expectations is not fully understood.

For the present, however, both theories have merit. The Keynesian theory explains the Great Depression as the result of a massive reduction in aggregate demand and the emergence of involuntary employment on a large scale. The new classical macroeconomics explains the Great Depression as a period of massive price surprises causing enormous increases in unemployment. Indeed, under the circumstances of the Great Depression, where policies could not be anticipated, both schools may have advocated the same aggregate-demand policies.

This chapter completes our analysis of the basic workings of the macroeconomy. The next five chapters will turn to broader aspects of the world economy: economic growth, development, and international trade.

Summary

1. Rational expectations offers an explanation for why countercyclical policy appears not to have worked well in recent years. The central idea of rational expectations is that people use all the information available to them to attempt to anticipate the future. People combine their knowledge of the macroeconomy with forecasts of government policy to form their expectations about future prices. The typical producer knows the prices of the things it sells better than the prices of the things it buys. General inflation or deflation can, therefore, cause errors of judgment. A price surprise occurs when the actual price level is different from the expected price level.

2. Price-level surprises are caused by supply and demand shocks. A supply shock is an unexpected shift in aggregate supply. A demand shock is an unexpected shift in aggregate demand. Unanticipated changes in policy are an important source of demand shocks. The Lucas demand curve shows the aggregate demand for real GNP at each level of price surprise. The Lucas supply curve shows the aggregate supply of real GNP at each level of price surprise. The Lucas demand curve is downward-sloping; the Lucas supply curve is positively sloped.

3. When a shift in aggregate demand is anticipated, it will have no effect on output or employment. It will affect only the price level. Because the resulting change in the price level is anticipated, the economy will move immediately to the higher price level but will remain at the same level of real GNP. When there are no supply or demand shocks, equilibrium occurs at the natural level of real GNP. A temporary supply shock changes output and the price level but does not change the natural level of GNP. A permanent supply shock will change the natural level of GNP. Demand shocks change temporarily real output. In the long run, people will no longer be surprised and the economy will return to the natural level of GNP. Only if people fail to learn from past experience will they be continuously surprised by policy. Anticipated monetary and demand-side fiscal policy should have no effect on real output and employment.

4. Rational expectations teaches that adverse supply shocks can be countered only if policy is unexpected. Rational expectations also teaches that there is no long run trade-off between unemployment and inflation. The evidence on the rational-expectations hypothesis

is still being gathered. Evidence in favor of rational expectations is found in the quick ends to historical episodes of hyperinflation and the fact that unanticipated monetary growth appears to affect real output and employment.

Key Terms

rational expectations
price-level surprise
demand shocks
supply shocks
policy surprise
Lucas supply curve
Lucas demand curve
money surprise
fiscal surprise

Questions and Problems

1. "I do not know much about economics. In fact, before this course I did not even know that the Fed controls the money supply, and I am not much different from other people. How can the rational-expectations theory claim that people in general attempt to anticipate the effects of monetary and fiscal policy?" Evaluate this statement.

2. Consider a very simple economy that consists of four people. One anticipates that prices will rise 10 percent; another thinks prices will not rise at all; the other two expect prices to rise 5 percent. The actual price increase turns out to be 7 percent. What is the expected price increase? What is the price-level surprise?

3. "How can there be price-level surprises in the economy? After all, all we have to do is to turn on the radio or television to learn how rapidly prices are rising." Evaluate this statement.

4. In a secret session of Congress, the President and Congress agree on a 20 percent tax cut. Would this tax cut affect real output and employment?

5. Explain why the long-run response to the tax cut described in question 4 may be different from the short-run response.

6. *Optional:* Using the conventional aggregate supply and demand curves and the Lucas supply and demand curves, demonstrate the effect of an anticipated reduction in aggregate demand on the Lucas supply/demand equilibrium. Then demonstrate the effect of an unanticipated reduction in aggregate demand on the Lucas supply/demand equilibrium.

18

Economic Growth

Chapter Preview

The material well-being provided by an economy is measured by the material goods and services that it produces. *Growth economics* is the study of how the capacity of economies to produce goods and services changes over time. Why are some economies rich in material goods while others are poor? Why does the output of goods and services expand rapidly in some countries, while expanding slowly or even contracting in others? This chapter will examine why economies grow and will try to determine the sources of growth.

WHAT IS ECONOMIC GROWTH?

The definition of economic growth uses the measure of the total output of the economy devel-

oped by national income accounting. Because the value of the total output of goods and services can rise because of increases in prices, the measure of material well-being must be corrected for price changes to reflect only the real goods and services produced. Economic growth is, therefore, defined in terms of changes in real GNP. **Economic growth** is defined in two ways:

Economic growth is an increase from one period to the next in real GNP.

Economic growth is an increase from one period to the next in real GNP per capita, which is real GNP divided by the country's population.

Typically, economic growth is calculated in terms of annual percentage rates of growth. If real

Table 1
Average Annual Growth Rates of GNP and GNP per Capita, 1978

Country	Annual Growth Rate of GNP	Annual Growth Rate of GNP per Capita
United States	4.0	3.2
Japan	5.8	4.9
West Germany	3.4	3.6
Italy	2.0	1.5
U.S.S.R.	3.1	2.2
China	11.7	10.2
Kuwait	6.0	0.1
Venezuela	5.5	2.2
Iran	0.2	− 2.8
Kenya	4.7	1.2
Hong Kong	11.8	10.2
India	3.9	1.8
Chile	6.0	4.5

Source: National Foreign Assessment Center, *Handbook of Economic Statistics* (Washington, D.C.: U.S. Government Printing Office, 1979), pp. 10–12.

GNP in 1982 is $500 billion and was $450 billion in 1981, then the annual growth rate of GNP is 11.1 percent, or ($500 − $450)/$450.

Each of the two measures of economic growth provides different information about the change in the real output of an economy. The rate of increase in GNP is a measure of how much the total output of goods and services has increased and is a valuable indicator of the change in the economic power of an economy. Economies that produce large volumes of goods and services—such as the United States, Japan, the Soviet Union, West Germany, China, and India—tend to have more military power, greater influence on the world economy, and more political influence. The rate of increase of GNP per capita indicates the rate at which the amount of goods and services available, on average, to each person in the economy is increasing. Per capita GNP is a measure of average living standards. Materially speaking, people who live in economies that produce large GNPs per capita are better off, on average, than those who live in economies that produce small GNPs per capita.

The two rates of economic growth can be quite different for any given country. Some countries with rapid GNP growth also have rapid population growth; such a country may have a smaller increase in living standards than a country in which GNP growth is more modest but in which there is little or no population growth. Table 1 shows the differences between the rate of growth of GNP and of GNP per capita for 13 countries.

The difference between the two measures of economic growth are most prominent in international comparisons of countries at the same point in time. The total output of The Peoples Republic of China in 1979 was $577 billion, that of India was $120 billion, while the GNP of the Netherlands was $152 billion. China and India are large countries; the Netherlands has a fairly small population. On a per capita basis, the output of China was $510, that of India was $180, while that of Netherlands was $10,860. Although the total output of Netherlands was below that of China and India, Dutch living standards were 21 times China's and 60 times India's.

Economists typically pay more attention to the growth of per capita GNP than to the growth of GNP because standards of living are considered to be a better measure of economic well-being. Nevertheless, there is no universal agreement on which objective is more important: the growth of GNP or the growth of GNP per capita. In the Soviet Union and many less developed countries, the growth of the absolute size of the economy is considered of great importance. In other countries, absolute size is less important than the growth of living standards.

DOES GROWTH MATTER?

Economic growth is affected by changes in the output of material goods and services. Economic growth is not directly related to changes in happiness or contentment; philosophers and psychologists are better able to delve into the determinants of happiness than economists. Yet changes in material well-being or in total output are extremely important. The economic rise of the Soviet Union has definitely changed the social politics of the 20th century. Japan's phenomenal growth after the Second World War has materially altered Japan's position in the world economic order. Declining living standards in countries that are accustomed to improving living

U.S. Affluence and Growth Rates

The accompanying table shows the changing position of the United States in the rankings of gross domestic product (GDP) per capita between 1960 and 1980. (GDP is the total value of goods and services excluding transactions with foreign countries.) Measures like this are inaccurate because they depend heavily on the exchange rates used to convert the gross domestic product of other countries into U.S. dollars, but they do illustrate what can happen when countries grow at different rates of per capita growth. The most notable ex-

ample is the changing position of Japan. In 1960, Japan's per capita GNP was only 16 percent that of the United States. By 1980, per capita GNP in Japan had risen to 78 percent of that in the United States. If Japan's rapid growth of per capita GNP were to continue at this rate, the Japanese would eventually enjoy the highest standards of living in the world.   🔀

Source: Organization for Economic Cooperation and Development.

1960			1970			1980		
1. **United States**		**2,805**	1. **United States**		**4,789**	1. Switzerland		15,922
2. Canada		2,230	2. Sweden		4,094	2. Sweden		14,761
3. Sweden		1,867	3. Canada		3,883	3. West Germany		13,305
4. Luxembourg		1,656	4. Switzerland		3,356	4. Denmark		12,952
5. Switzerland		1,614	5. Denmark		3,221	5. Luxembourg		12,570
6. Britain		1,362	6. Luxembourg		3,172	6. Iceland		12,469
7. Iceland		1,333	7. West Germany		3,069	7. France		12,136
8. France		1,323	8. France		2,788	8. Netherlands		11,851
9. West Germany		1,310	9. Belgium		2,676	9. Belgium		11,816
10. Denmark		1,296	10. Netherlands		2,431	10. **United States**		**11,364**
11. Belgium		1,236	11. Iceland		2,418	11. Canada		10,582
12. Finland		1,140	12. Finland		2,318	12. Finland		10,440
13. Netherlands		996	13. Britain		2,193	13. Britain		9,335
14. Japan		463	14. Japan		1,989	14. Japan		8,905

conditions can be a national trauma. One need only consider the dramatic decline in living standards in Poland or Iran in the years 1980 and 1981 and its effect on everyday living to understand the importance of trends in material well-being. A less dramatic case is the gradual decline in England's living standard relative to England's European neighbors, which has had a profound impact on life and politics in the United Kingdom. The severe recessions of the 1970s and early 1980s caused people to question for the first time in a long time whether their material well-being would continue to increase.

THE CLASSICAL GROWTH MODEL

Economists first became interested in economic growth in the late 18th and early 19th centuries. The classical economists—most specifically David Ricardo and Thomas Malthus—devoted much of their attention to explaining the factors that cause economies to grow.

Ricardo and Malthus were interested in explaining why predominantly agricultural economies reach an upper limit to economic growth, which they called a *stationary state*. Modern economists have addressed another issue: why economies continue to grow over long periods of time.

From the perspective of the classical economists, writing at the very beginning of the industrial revolution, the stationary state of zero growth seemed the normal state of affairs. The classical economists were interested in explaining the stationary state because there was very little growth of output or of population prior to 1750, the approximate starting point of modern economic growth in Great Britain.

Diminishing Returns

Ricardo and Malthus were interested in explaining the growth of a traditional agrarian economy. In such an economy, modern science and technology had yet to be applied to agriculture, and capital equipment (such as hoes or plows) was a relatively minor input. Output was produced primarily by combining land and labor, and agricultural land was essentially fixed in supply.

The *law of diminishing returns* applies to situations where more and more units of a variable factor (labor) are being added to a fixed factor of production (land). According to this law, at low levels of population and labor force, increases in labor initially yield fairly substantial increases in output, but eventually additional inputs of labor bring in smaller and smaller additions to output as more and more labor is combined with the fixed factor of production. The average product of labor, after first rising, will fall as diminishing returns set in.

Panel (a) of Figure 1 shows the behavior of the aggregate output of such an economy as more and more units of the variable input (labor) are combined with the fixed input. Initially, output rises at an increasing rate, but the rise in output tapers off and eventually output could even decline as more units of labor are added. Panel (b) of Figure 1 shows how the average product of labor first rises but then declines.

The law of diminishing returns suggests that an agricultural economy with a fixed amount of land, primitive technology, and rudimentary capital resources should avoid excessively large inputs of labor insofar as these labor injections would drive down the average product of labor. Labor productivity determines real wages; therefore, an economy that had too large a population and labor force should expect to experience falling real wages and falling living standards for laborers.

Malthusian Population Laws

Because of the writings of Thomas R. Malthus, whose *Essay on the Principle of Population* was published in 1798, classical economics came

Figure 1
An Agricultural Economy with Diminishing Returns

(a) Total Output

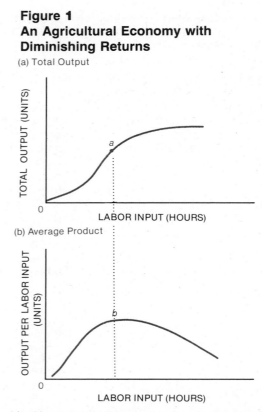

(b) Average Product

In this economy, the amount of agricultural land is fixed. As the variable factor, labor, is combined with the fixed factor, output initially rises at an increasing rate. Panel (a) shows that as more and more units of the variable factor are added, output increases at a decreasing rate. Panel (b) shows that the average product of labor first increases and then decreases.

to be called the "dismal science." Malthus believed that there would be a long-term disproportion between the rate of growth of population and the rate of growth of food production. Population, Malthus argued, tends to increase at *geometric* rates (the *ratio* between each rate and its predecessor is constant) because the "passion between the sexes" and factors such as disease and war remain constant throughout human history. On the other hand, food production tends to increase at *arithmetic* rates (the *difference* between each rate and its predecessor is constant) due to the law of diminishing returns. Because a geometric series, such as 1, 2, 4, 8, 16, . . . , grows at a faster rate and will inevitably overtake an arithmetic series such as 10, 11, 12, 13, . . . , Malthus felt that humanity would eventually find itself on the verge of starvation, living at subsistence wages.

Basically, the root of the Malthusian population problem is that because people tend to reproduce whenever their wages rise above subsistence, wages can never rise above subsistence for long periods of time. Once wages rise above subsistence level, the population and labor force will expand geometrically, and the increase in the supply of labor will drive wages back down to subsistence. If wages fall below subsistence, famine and higher mortality will reduce the population and allow wages to rise back to subsistence.

The Classical Dynamics

The classical economists came to the pessimistic conclusion that there were distinct limits to growth. In the long run, economies would end up in a stationary state characterized by 1) a zero growth rate of output, population, and per capita output and 2) subsistence wages.

In Figure 2, the quantity of labor is given on the horizontal axis, and the real wage rate is shown on the vertical axis. The downward-sloping labor demand curve shows the economy's demand for labor at different wage rates, and the upward-sloping labor supply curve shows the amounts of labor supplied at different wage rates. The subsistence wage (w_s) is drawn as a horizontal line.

In the short run, the supply of labor is determined by the size of the population, which changes slowly over time. In the short run, wages can be above subsistence; they are determined by the forces of supply and demand. If the wage rate is above subsistence, as in Figure 2, the birth rate will rise, and death rates will fall due to better nutrition and health. The increase in population will cause the labor supply to increase (the curve will shift to the right), thereby driving down the equilibrium wage rate. Not until population growth shifts the labor supply curve to S' will population growth cease. At this point, wages are driven down to subsistence, population growth ceases, and wages stabilize at the subsistence level.

According to the classical model, in the long run, economies will find themselves in a station-

Figure 2
The Classical Stationary State

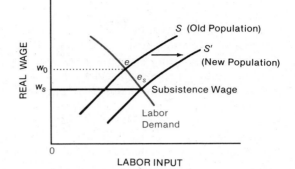

In the short run, the market wage rate will be at w_0— the equilibrium wage rate. The horizontal line shows the subsistence wage rate, w_s. If the market wage is above subsistence, as it is in this case, population will expand, and the labor supply curve will shift to the right (supply will increase). As long as the market wage remains above subsistence, population will continue to expand, thereby driving wages down even further. Population growth will cease when the market wage is driven down to subsistence. At this point, the economy is in a stationary state. The growth of output ceases, and wages are stuck at the subsistence level.

ary state where there is no expansion of population, no growth of output, and subsistence wages.

If a severe famine or war reduces the number of workers, wages will temporarily rise above subsistence, the population will begin to reproduce, and wages will be driven back to subsistence. During the Black Death plague of the Middle Ages, which destroyed one third of Europe's population, studies show that real wages rose substantially but declined thereafter as population growth accelerated.

MODERN ECONOMIC GROWTH

Modern economic growth has contradicted the pessimistic conclusions of the classical economists, at least as far as the industrialized countries are concerned. The classical model appears to have greater value for poor countries, as the next chapter will show. The historical record of economic growth of the industrialized countries indicates that these countries managed to escape the stationary state of diminishing returns and overpopulation.

The Historical Record

The dismal predictions of the classical growth model were far off the mark for the countries of Europe, North America, and Japan. Beginning in the mid-18th century—first in the United Kingdom and then spreading to the European continent and to the areas of European settlement in North America and Australia—"industrial revolutions" occurred. The result of these industrial revolutions in all these economies was the acceleration of the growth rates of real GNP and of population. The growth of output exceeded the growth of population, however, and per capita GNP began to grow at a sustained or increasing rate. In the past, there had been isolated episodes of economic growth at the rise of the Egyptian, Greek, and Roman empires. Each of these episodes of past growth was followed by a reversal, however, so that living standards always reverted more or less back to what they had been.

The principal feature of modern economic growth has been its sustained nature. There is no simple explanation for why the industrialized world was able to sustain economic growth for the first time in human history. The industrial revolution was accompanied by a scientific/engineering revolution. Productivity-increasing inventions produced by 18th- and 19th-century science, including the steam engine, the mechanized cotton spindle, and the blast furnace, help explain modern economic growth.

Modern economic growth brought about substantial changes in lifestyles. In all countries that experienced industrial revolutions, the share of economic activity devoted to industry and services rose; the share devoted to agriculture declined. The declining share of agriculture was accompanied by rising urbanization; the typical worker was no longer a farmer but an industrial worker. Rising per capita income translated into rising real wages, and items that had previously been available only to the rich—quality textiles, long-distance transportation, phonographs, automobiles—became items of mass consumption. With rising living standards, birth rates began to fall—contrary to the Malthusian proposition that prosperity would bring rising fertility. After the initial acceleration of population growth, the rate

Figure 3
The Effects of Technological Progress and Capital Deepening

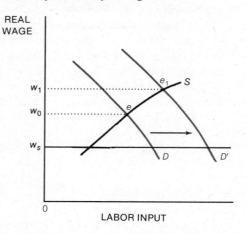

The market wage is initially above subsistence. Technological advances and capital deepening raise labor productivity and increase the demand for labor (from D to D'). Even if population were to grow, the increased demand for labor would prevent the wage rate from falling to subsistence. Furthermore, if population fails to respond to rising prosperity by expanding, productivity increases will raise wage rates even more.

of population growth began to decline in industrialized countries.

The Limitations of the Classical Model

The classical growth model failed to anticipate three forces that would indefinitely avoid diminishing returns and prevent a stationary state in the industrialized world: 1) sustained technological advances, 2) rising capital per worker, and 3) declining fertility.

Technological advances allowed the existing work force to become more productive with the same quantity of land and capital. As the amount of capital per worker increased, the productivity of the existing work force was raised as well. A slowly growing population (and labor force) meant that diminishing returns could be avoided.

Figure 3 illustrates why the classical model's dire predictions failed to materialize. In the industrialized countries, advances in technology caused

Table 2
Long-Term Growth of Real GNP and Real GNP per Capita for Selected Countries (average annual growth rates)

Country	1929–1950 GNP	1929–1950 GNP per Capita	1950–1960 GNP	1950–1960 GNP per Capita	1960–1978 GNP	1960–1978 GNP per Capita
United States	2.9	1.8	3.2	1.4	3.6	2.5
Canada	3.2	1.8	4.6	1.9	4.9	3.4
France	0.0	−0.1	4.6	3.6	4.8	3.9
West Germany	1.9	0.7	8.0	6.4	3.8	3.2
Italy	1.0	0.3	5.5	4.8	4.4	3.7
Japan	0.6	NA	8.0	6.9	8.6	7.3
United Kingdom	1.6	1.2	2.8	2.4	2.6	2.2
U.S.S.R.	5.4*	3.5*	6.0	4.2	4.5	3.3

*1928–1940

Sources: *Statistical Abstract of the United States,* 1980, p. 439; Paul Gregory and Robert Stuart, *Soviet Economic Structure and Performance,* 2nd ed. (New York: Harper and Row, 1981), p. 332.

the productivity of labor to increase. As workers became more productive, the demand for labor increased, thereby raising market wages. In the industrialized countries, capital was accumulated at a rate higher than the growth rate of labor. Capital per worker rose, and the amount of output produced by a given quantity of labor increased as the added equipment made existing workers more productive. Rising capital per worker—called *capital deepening*—also caused labor demand to increase.

The process of economic growth is a race between diminishing returns and those forces (such as technological advances and capital deepening) that cause labor productivity to increase. In Figure 3, without technological progress or capital deepening, labor productivity would remain constant, and the labor demand curve would not shift. If, on the other hand, technological progress and capital deepening increase the demand for labor, wages can be kept above subsistence as long as labor productivity continues to rise.

The increase in real wages is reinforced if population fails to respond to rising prosperity by increasing in size. Real wages are not bid down by an increasing labor force, and the economy is not pushed in the direction of diminishing returns.

SOURCES OF ECONOMIC GROWTH

Since the beginning of modern economic growth, industrialized economies have experienced sustained growth of GNP and of GNP per capita. Although there have been cyclical episodes of zero or negative growth—the most serious such episode was the Great Depression of the 1930s—the industrialized economies have continued to grow with surprising strength over the long run (see Table 2).

Economies grow when:

1. the total amount of land, labor, and capital inputs expands.
2. available inputs are used more effectively.

The more effective use of inputs shows up as increases in output per unit of input; that is, as increases in factor productivity. Economists therefore distinguish between **extensive growth** and **intensive growth.**

Extensive growth is economic growth that results from the expansion of factor inputs.

Intensive growth is growth that results from increases in output per unit of factor input.

Table 3
Annual Growth Rates of U.S. Inputs and GNP, 1800–1973

Category	Annual Growth Rates (percent)				
	1800–1855	1855–1898	1899–1919	1919–1948	1948–1973
Real GNP	4.2	4.0	3.9	3.0	3.8
Labor inputs, hours	3.7	2.8	1.8	0.6	0.7
Capital inputs	4.3	4.6	3.1	1.2	2.5
Combined inputs	3.9	3.6	2.2	0.8	1.4
Output per unit of labor	0.5	1.1	2.0	2.4	3.1
Output per unit of capital	−0.1	−0.6	0.7	1.6	1.3
Output per unit of combined inputs	0.3	0.3	1.7	2.2	2.4
Proportion of growth explained by inputs	93%	90%	46%	20%	37%
Unexplained residual	7%	10%	54%	80%	63%

Source: John W. Kendrick, "Survey of the Factors Contributing to the Decline in U.S. Productivity Growth," Federal Reserve Bank of Boston, *The Decline in Productivity Growth,* Conference Series No. 22, June 1980, p. 2.

To expand labor inputs, people must sacrifice leisure or household production to produce more market output. To expand capital inputs, people must sacrifice current consumption for future consumption. Compared to these costs of extensive growth, the costs of intensive growth are smaller. More output can be produced without the sacrifices just described.

The Growth of Inputs

Factor inputs can grow in two dimensions: they can grow quantitatively and qualitatively. Inputs grow quantitatively when more hours are worked in the economy, when more machines are placed in service, or when more factories are built. As workers acquire additional education or industrial skills and become physically healthier and stronger, the labor input grows qualitatively. As the quality of the labor force increases, one hour's work produces more output than before.

Economists disagree about whether increases in output brought about by increases in input quality should be classified as intensive or extensive growth. This chapter treats quality improvements—particularly improvements in labor quality—as intensive growth.

The Growth of Productivity

The second source of economic growth is advances in productivity. A productivity improvement has occurred when more output is produced from the same volume of factor inputs. A major source of productivity improvements is technological change. Scientists and engineers may discover new and improved technologies for combining industrial inputs. Agronomists may develop new drought-resistant grains or new types of chemical fertilizers or insecticides. New modes of transportation—the railroad, the jet aircraft, the space shuttle—may make it possible for manufacturers to deliver their financial products at lower costs. All such efficiency improvements can be attributed to advances in the state of technological knowledge.

Improvements in the way resources are combined can also lead to efficiency improvements. Managers may develop new business techniques that allow them to combine resources in a more effective manner. The assembly line may replace handicraft production. New management techniques may make possible the efficient management of huge enterprises. Government restrictions and rules that prevent the private sector from utilizing available resources in the most cost-effective manner may be withdrawn.

The Sources of GNP Growth

Has economic growth been caused by the growth inputs or by improvements in efficiency? American economists such as Edward Denison, John Kendrick, and Robert Solow have all studied the empirical record of American and European growth to find the answer to this question.

Table 3 supplies long-term data for American economic growth. The first row gives the growth rates of real GNP for different periods from 1800 to 1973. The next two rows give the corresponding growth rates of labor inputs (measured in hours) and of capital inputs. To obtain the growth rates of labor and capital inputs combined, the two input growth rates are averaged using labor's share and capital's share of national income as weights. During this period, labor earned from 60 to 75 percent of all income; therefore, the growth of labor inputs is the prime determinant of the growth of combined labor and capital inputs.

If labor earns 60 percent of income and capital the remaining 40 percent, then the growth rate of both factors combined is 0.6 times labor growth rate plus 0.4 times capital growth rate.

From 1948 to 1973 in the United States, the labor input grew by a 0.7 percent annual rate and capital grew at a 2.5 percent annual rate. Applying the above formula, we find that the combined growth rate of capital and labor was 0.6 (0.7) + 0.4 (2.5) = 1.4.

To determine what proportion of growth is accounted for by the growth of inputs and what proportion is explained by the growth of input productivity (output per unit of input), the growth of inputs is subtracted from growth of output. During the period 1948-1973, combined inputs grew at 1.4 percent per year. If there had been no improvements in productivity, GNP would have grown at the same rate as inputs (also at 1.4 percent per year). But GNP actually grew much faster than inputs, at 3.8 percent per year. The difference between the growth of output and the growth of inputs (3.8-1.4) is productivity growth, or the *residual*. The term *residual* is used because economists can only guess what factors are in the

Table 4

Sources of Growth of Real GNP in the United States, 1948–1978

Sources	Annual Growth Rate	
	1948–1966	1966–1978
Real GNP	3.9	3.0
Labor, hours	0.4	1.4
Capital	2.8	2.9
Combined inputs	1.1	1.8
Total factor productivity	2.8	1.2
Sources of factor productivity growth		
Advances in knowledge	1.4	1.0
Changes in labor quality	0.6	0.5
Changes in land quality	0.0	−0.2
Resource reallocations	0.8	0.5
Other factors	0.4	−0.8
Sum	2.8	1.2

Source: John W. Kendrick, "Survey of the Factors Contributing to the Decline in U.S. Productivity Growth," Federal Reserve Bank of Boston, *The Decline in Productivity Growth*, Conference Series No. 22, June 1980, p. 2. The data to 1969 are based upon Edward Denison, *Accounting for U.S. Economic Growth*, 1948–1969 (Washington, D.C.: Brookings, 1974).

residual. For the 1948–1973 period, the residual explains 63 percent of GNP growth, while the growth of factor inputs explains the remaining 37 percent of growth.

As Table 3 demonstrates, over the last 50 years, the major portion of American—or western European or Japanese—economic growth is explained by the growth of productivity. The exact causes of productivity growth will never be known. Some economists—such as Edward Denison and John Kendrick—have attempted to break down the residual into different sources: advances in knowledge, changes in the quality of labor and land inputs, resource reallocations, and other factors. The results of Denison's and Kendrick's research are given in Table 4. They find that the major source of productivity growth is advances in knowledge obtained through formal investment in research and development and through informal advances in knowledge. The second major factor in productivity advances is improvements in the

Table 5

Sources of Growth of Real GNP per Capita in the United States, 1948–1973

Category	Annual Growth Rate
GNP per capita	2.3
Labor inputs per capita	−0.8
Capital inputs per capita	1.0
Combined inputs per capita	−0.1
Proportion of GNP per capita growth explained by productivity increases	more than 100%

Source: John W. Kendrick "Survey of the Factors Contributing to the Decline in U.S. Productivity Growth," Federal Reserve Bank of Boston, *The Decline in Productivity Growth,* Conference Series No. 22, June 1980, p. 2.

quality of labor, primarily the consequence of improvements in education and training.

The Sources of Per Capita GNP Growth

Table 5 assembles data on the sources of growth of per capita GNP. In order for input growth to account for per capita increases in GNP, factor inputs would have to rise more rapidly than population growth. Hours worked per capita would have to increase, and the capital stock would have to expand more rapidly than population. In fact, combined factor inputs have grown more slowly than population; therefore, increases in per capita GNP cannot be explained by the increase in factor inputs. The entire explanation for rising per capita GNP is found in productivity improvements. In effect, the growth of inputs has only been sufficient to prevent per capita GNP from declining. Improvements in factor productivity account for the positive growth of per capita GNP. Thus, productivity advances are responsible for increases in our standard of living. Labor and capital inputs have been increased only at a rate sufficient to keep our standards of living constant.

RECENT DECLINES IN LABOR PRODUCTIVITY

Figure 4 shows the annual rate of growth of labor productivity in the U.S. business sector from 1958 to the present. Labor productivity

growth—as measured by the rate of growth of real GNP per hour of labor—fluctuates a great deal from year to year. The annual fluctuations in labor productivity tend to distract attention from long-run trends in productivity. Since the mid-1960s, there has been a gradual decline in the growth of labor productivity. From 1950 to 1957, labor productivity grew at an average of 2.9 percent per year; from 1958 to 1965, it grew at 3.2 percent per year; however, from 1966 to 1981, it grew at only 1.6 percent per annum. Looking only at the 8 years from 1973–1981, labor productivity growth was only 0.9 percent per annum with half of the years showing negative productivity growth.

A slowdown in labor productivity growth means that increases in money wage rates are not being offset by increased output per worker. Average costs of production should, therefore, rise. Because, as already demonstrated, productivity growth is the major source of economic growth, if the growth of productivity of a major factor like labor declines, the growth of output should decline, *ceteris paribus*.

Much attention has been devoted to explaining the long-term decline in American labor productivity. Labor productivity, as measured by output per hour of labor, rises 1) because other factors that cooperate with labor in the production process grow (qualitatively or quantitatively) more rapidly than labor hours, 2) because the quality of the labor input rises, or 3) because technological advances or better ways of combining resources (so that labor productivity rises without an increase in cooperating factors) are made available.

Cooperating Factors

The available data show that the decline in labor productivity has been caused by a deterioration in the relationship between the number of machines and the number of workers. Prior to 1966, capital grew 7 times faster than labor. From 1966 to 1973, capital grew 2.4 times as fast as labor, and from 1973 to 1981, capital grew 1.4 times as fast as labor.[1] One reason why the

1. John Kendrick, "Survey of the Factors Contributing to the Decline in U.S. Productivity Growth," Federal Reserve Bank of Boston, *The Decline in Productivity Growth,* Conference Series No. 22, June 1980, p. 3.

Figure 4
Annual Growth Rates of U.S. Labor Productivity

Although the growth rate of labor productivity tends to fluctuate from year to year, there has been a general decline in labor productivity growth since the mid-1960s.

Source: *Economic Report of the President,* January 1982, p. 276.

growth of labor productivity has slowed is the significant decline in the growth of capital per worker.

There has also been a decline in a particular type of investment spending—*research and development* (R&D)—relative to gross national product. In the early 1960s, over 2 percent of GNP was devoted to R&D spending. Since the mid-1960s, this percentage has fallen to slightly less than 1.6 percent of GNP.

Composition of the Labor Force

A second potential cause of the labor productivity slowdown is a decline in the quality of the labor force. The productivity decline began approximately at that time when those people born during the "baby boom" of the 1950s entered the labor force in large numbers. As young, relatively inexperienced workers replaced older experienced workers, the overall quality of the labor force declined. In addition to the baby-boom effect, more women entered the labor force after having forgone experience and on-the-job training in order to carry out homemaking activities.

Did these labor-force composition changes have a major effect on labor productivity? Studies show that the labor productivity of experienced adult workers continued to increase at about historical rates throughout the productivity slowdown. The major drops in productivity growth were exhibited by young and inexperienced workers.[2]

2. Jeffrey Perloff and Michael Wachter, "The Decline in Labor Productivity: A Labor Problem?" in Federal Reserve Bank of Boston, *Conference Series No. 22,* June 1980, p. 125.

Example 2

An Economist's Critique of Doomsday Forecasts

Economist Julian Simon has conducted a careful investigation of charges that our globe is running out of resources and that there is a growing disproportion between our resources and the growing world population.

Simon finds that these charges are based upon very flimsy evidence:

1. Contrary to doomsday claims that economic growth is robbing the world of arable land, the quantity of arable land has actually increased markedly in recent years. In fact, the amount of land taken out of cultivation by the much-publicized urban sprawl has been more than offset by the amount of arable land added by swamp drainage and land improvement.
2. Contrary to doomsday forecasts, Simon finds that the incidence of famine is actually decreasing rather than increasing. In reality, per capita food production has been increasing at nearly 1 percent per annum—25 percent over the last 25 years—and even countries like India

are becoming increasingly self-sufficient in grains.
3. Contrary to doomsday warnings against overpopulation, Simon finds no negative statistical correlation between population growth and percapita-income growth.
4. Contrary to doomsday warnings that we are running out of natural resources and raw materials, Simon finds that the most direct measure of rising scarcity—rising relative prices—does not support the thesis of growing shortages of natural resources and raw materials. Relative to other prices paid by consumers, raw materials and natural resources are growing cheaper, not more expensive. Although petroleum prices have been rising in relative terms, Simon notes that the production costs per barrel of oil have probably fallen in relative terms.

Source: Julian Simon, "Resources, Population, Environment: An Oversupply of False Bad News," *Science* 208, 4451 (June 27, 1980).

The Residual

The changing relationship between capital and labor and the changing composition of the labor force explain only a portion of the decline in the growth of labor productivity. Economist William Nordhaus, for example, estimates that only 20 percent of the decline results from these two factors.[3]

The major portion of the labor productivity slowdown can be attributed to other factors not associated with the qualitative or quantitative growth of the factors of production.

One factor that is frequently cited is government regulation. During the period of the productivity slowdown, there was an increase in government environmental and safety regulations that required businesses to invest in pollution-reduction and safety equipment rather than in plant and

equipment. Another factor is the stagflation of this period. Stagflation hurt business confidence in the future, pushed businesses into higher tax brackets, reduced business profits adjusted for inflation, and caused stock prices to fall. In general, stagflation created a negative atmosphere for business investment that is reflected by the changing relationship between capital and labor growth rates noted above.

No matter how carefully economists attempt to explain the labor productivity slowdown of recent years, a large unexplained element remains.

DOOMSDAY FORECASTS

The sustained growth of GNP per capita over a long period of time has provided Americans with a high standard of living. The average citizen of the United States has the ability to acquire enough goods and services to enjoy a comfortable standard of living. In recent years, some social critics have come to question the wisdom of further economic growth. They argue that economic

3. William Nordhaus, "Policy Responses to the Productivity Slowdown," Federal Reserve Bank of Boston, *Conference Series No. 22*, June 1980, p. 153.

growth increases environmental problems (more factories create more pollution) and that economic growth threatens to exhaust the globe's scarce natural resources. Insofar as there are only finite supplies of natural resources, clean air, and pure water, economic growth may some day in the future threaten our very existence.

Modern doomsday forecasts are reminiscent of the predictions of the classical stationary state; instead of seeing agricultural land as the limiting factor of production, doomsday forecasters see natural resources (arable land, minerals, air, and water) in this role. The most famous doomsday model is that published by the Club of Rome, using the computer models developed at MIT by Dennis L. Meadows and Jay Forrester.[4]

The 1972 Club of Rome computer model—like the stationary state models of the 19th century—predicted that continued economic growth will put such a severe strain on our natural resources and on our environment that shortly after the turn of the 21st century, GNP per capita will begin to decline. The basic conclusion of this doomsday model is that our planet cannot sustain further economic growth and that humanity should adopt social policies to stop the growth of GNP and of population in order to avoid catastrophe.

Since the appearance of its doomsday model in 1972, the Club of Rome has decided that our planet can continue to grow without catastrophe if growth is well managed.

How much credence should one attach to the dire predictions of the doomsday philosophers? Economists can raise certain legitimate questions about the assumptions of their models. First, such doomsday models are based upon the assumption that the world economy will continue to use resources at the same rates as they have been used in the past. If, in the past, petroleum usage grew at the same rate as real GNP, the doomsday prophets assume that this relationship will continue in the future. Economists—using the elementary laws of supply and demand—argue that when a natural resource becomes short in supply, its relative price will rise, and the higher relative price will reduce its quantity demanded. Econo-

mists, therefore, maintain that a freely functioning price system will retard the depletion of scarce natural resources. Second, the doomsday models—like the models of Malthus and Ricardo—assume static technology.

The world economy in the 21st century may very well develop new energy-saving technologies or may discover good substitutes for natural resources that are rising in relative price. If the world supply of petroleum and natural gas threatens to run out, for example, scientists may discover new energy sources that will be economically feasible.

Only the future will show whether the gloomy predictions of the doomsday philosophers will prove true or whether technological progress will continue to save the day, as it did in the case of the classical stationary state. Economists tend to be sceptical of doomsday models because they believe that a correctly functioning price system will cause people and firms to economize on the use of scarce resources and create incentives to develop new technologies to replace depleting resources. Our experience with rising energy prices suggests how market economies will deal with future shortages of natural resources. Rising relative prices have forced our economies to combine economic growth with declining usage of petroleum inputs. In this case, economic growth has proven to be compatible with declining usage of a scarce natural resource.

The industrialized countries of the world have enjoyed sustained economic growth for more than a century, thanks largely to technological advances. The next chapter will turn to an examination of less developed countries.

4. Dennis Meadows et al., *The Limits to Growth* (Washington, D.C.: Potomac Associates, 1972).

Summary

1. Economic growth is defined either as an increase in real GNP or as an increase in real GNP per capita. The latter measure tells more about the growth of living standards.

2. Economic growth is important because a country's position in the world economic or-

der is determined by the size of the economy and by its relative affluence.

3. The classical economists David Ricardo and Thomas Malthus predicted that economies would reach a stationary state of zero growth and subsistence living standards. The stationary state would be caused by the law of diminishing returns and by the tendency of the population to expand whenever wages rose above subsistence. Because of its teachings on the stationary state, classical economics was called the "dismal science."

4. The industrialized countries have grown at a sustained rate since the mid-19th century. Modern economic growth is characterized by sustained growth of per capita GNP and by structural changes in the economy. The stationary state has been avoided by rapid technological progress, capital deepening, and by slow population growth.

5. Economies grow for two reasons: because the total amount of factor inputs increases and because output per unit of input (or productivity) increases. Research shows that the major factor causing economic growth is the growth of productivity.

6. Labor productivity has declined in recent' years because of the change in the relationship between capital and labor and because of the change in the composition of the labor force.

7. Doomsday forecasts predict that economic growth cannot be sustained because the exhaustion of scarce natural resources and pollution will cause a new stationary state to be reached. Doomsday predictions, however, are based upon the assumption that scarce resources will continue to be used at the same rates as in the past.

Key Terms

economic growth
extensive growth
intensive growth

Questions and Problems

1. Explain why the two measures of economic growth can yield different results.

2. The amount of land in the world is fixed. The law of diminishing returns indicates that, with a fixed input, the marginal productivity of variable inputs will ultimately decline. Will we not ultimately reach Ricardo's stationary state? Explain your answer.

3. Malthus maintained that whenever wages rise above the subsistence level, the population will grow. Has this proven to be true in the industrialized countries? Why not?

4. Explain why intensive growth is less costly than extensive growth.

5. Over a 10-year period, real output grew at 5 percent per annum, combined inputs at 2 percent per annum, and population at 1 percent per annum. What is the annual growth rate of factor productivity? What proportion of the 5 percent growth rate is explained by productivity growth (the residual)? What proportion of the per capita output growth rate is explained by rising inputs per capita?

6. Economists criticize the doomsday models on the grounds that they don't take the effects of relative prices into account. Why should prices matter if the supply of natural resources is fixed?

19

Problems
of Population and
Economic Development

Chapter Preview

The industrialized countries first experienced modern economic growth in the 18th and 19th centuries. Since then, they have continued to grow steadily. For these fortunate countries, a century's growth of per capita GNP has brought higher living standards and, for the average citizen, has made problems of malnutrition and inadequate shelter and clothing less common.

Affluence is, however, still a relatively rare phenomenon, even in the 1980s. Affluence is the product of sustained growth of per capita GNP, but relatively few countries have experienced steady long-term growth of living standards. Affluence, as we know it, is still limited to a relatively small circle of countries—to the countries

of Europe and to the areas of European settlement in North America and Australia. The list of newcomers to this circle is short. In Asia, only Japan has been able to make the transition from poverty to relative affluence. Although living standards in the Soviet Union remain well below those of Europe and North America, the U.S.S.R. has also succeeded in making the transition from backwardness to industrialization. The most recent newcomers to affluence have achieved this status not through a century of patient growth of living standards but through enormous windfalls brought about by the ownership of mineral resources.

This chapter will examine why the fruits of industrialization have been denied to so many and why affluence is still a relatively rare phenomenon in today's world.

313

Development economics is the study of why most countries are poor. It seeks to explain the causes of poverty and to determine how poor countries can make the transition from poverty to relative affluence.

THE CHARACTERISTICS OF NATIONAL POVERTY

Economists and international organizations (such as the United Nations or the World Bank) group the countries of the globe according to their level of economic development. At the very top are the industrialized or affluent capitalist countries. At the very bottom come those unfortunate countries that are still living on the margin of physical subsistence. Most of the world's population lives in countries that lie between these two extremes of poverty and wealth.

The Level of Economic Development

There is no single measure of economic development because economic development is a multidimensional phenomenon. The most frequently used measure is per capita income. Under most circumstances, the higher the per capita income, the higher the country's level of development. Yet per capita income does not tell the whole story. The level of industrialization or modernization of a country is another indicator of the level of economic development. Some countries—such as the oil-rich nations—may earn substantial per capita incomes but have yet to develop a domestic industry. Such countries may retain the features of a traditional premodern society. Although wealthy in terms of per capita income, they may lack certain characteristics of modern life—urbanization, jobs in offices or factories, social mobility, universal education—that are available in less wealthy countries. Income is highly concentrated in the hands of a very few who were born into this wealth. Other countries with more modest per capita GNPs may be highly urbanized, educated, and industrialized societies. Alternatively, the level of economic development may be measured in terms of the health and education of its population. Some countries provide their residents with good educational and public-health facilities

that raise life expectancy, lower infant mortality, allow families the choice of limiting family size, and provide a wide range of cultural facilities.

The level of economic development of a country cannot be fully captured by any one statistical measure. But in most cases, the various indicators of economic development move together, except in the case of high-income countries that are not industrialized, urbanized, or well educated. Table 1 ranks countries according to per capita income, life expectancy, urbanization, and agriculture's share of GNP. Although the correlation among these different measures of economic development is not perfect, especially for the oil-rich countries, it is nevertheless a close one.

Less Developed Countries

In contrast to **less developed countries (LDCs),** countries that have attained a high level of economic development are called *developed countries* or *industrialized countries*.

Less developed countries (LDCs) are countries that have yet to reach a high level of economic development.

Optimists like to refer to such countries as *developing countries*.

Where does one draw the line between an LDC and a developed country? Is a less developed country one that is unable to meet certain subsistence requirements, or should an LDC be defined in relation to a developed country? This issue of how to define an LDC is very much like the problem of defining who is poor in a given country. Poverty definitions can be either *absolute* or *relative*. An absolute definition of an LDC might be a country in which per capita income is less than that required to purchase the basic essentials of food, clothing, shelter, and education. However, national poverty exists just as strongly in a relative sense. If the citizens of one country know that their standard of living is only a small fraction of that of other countries, they will likely conclude that they are poor even if they can afford the basic necessities of life. According to this relative definition of poverty, an LDC can become developed only if it can narrow the gap between it and the more affluent countries.

Table 1
Indicators of Economic Development

	GNP per Capita, 1977 (dollars)	Agriculture's Share of GNP (percent)	Percent of Urban Population	Life Expectancy (years)
United Arab Emirates	14,800	0.9	65.3	48.0
Luxembourg	9,638	3.4	73.7	70.8
Sweden	9,343	4.3	84.6	75.0
United States	8,750	3.2	70.4	73.0
West Germany	8,619	3.0	83.1	72.0
Australia	7,287	6.4	87.2	72.4
Libya	6,516	2.0	44.0	55.0
Japan	6,511	5.4	75.1	76.0
United Kingdom	4,543	2.5	89.8	73.0
Israel	3,764	6.8	87.0	72.0
Spain	3,255	10.4	70.5	73.0
Greece	2,946	18.6	57.4	73.0
Singapore	2,820	1.9	100.0	69.5
Venezuela	2,625	5.7	80.0	66.4
Hong Kong	2,622	1.7	89.9	72.0
Uruguay	1,449	12.4	83.0	71.0
Brazil	1,411	11.3	60.7	62.0
Mexico	1,164	10.1	63.2	64.7
South Korea	977	25.4	49.0	63.0
Tunisia	837	20.7	48.0	57.0
Ecuador	819	21.9	41.9	59.6
Paraguay	747	35.3	37.9	63.0
Nigeria	513	30.8	18.1	48.0
Philippines	458	28.5	34.0	60.0
Senegal	377	27.3	24.2	42.0
Egypt	342	30.9	43.9	54.0
Pakistan	201	33.6	26.4	51.0
India	158	43.3	20.7	51.0
Chad	132	51.8	14.4	43.0
Ethiopia	108	50.3	12.0	39.0
Bangladesh	80	60.2	9.3	47.0

Source: World Bank, *World Tables,* 1980.

Economists and international organizations typically use the relative standard of poverty to distinguish LDCs from developed countries.

An exact dividing line between developed and less developed countries cannot be drawn. Instead, the international organizations charged with classifying countries as developed or less developed call all those countries that have yet to attain a high level of economic development *developing countries*. Within the developing-country group, a distinction is made between those LDCs that operate at the margin of subsistence (called *low-income LDCs*) and those that have per capita incomes well above subsistence (called *middle-income LDCs*). The low-income countries are sometimes called "fourth-world nations" because they show few signs of progress toward overcoming their development gap.

What proportion of the world's population, according to this classification, resides in LDCs? As Figure 1 shows, approximately 3 out of every 4 persons lives in an LDC if the U.S.S.R. and Eastern Europe are classified as belonging to the developed countries. Only 15 percent of the world's population lives in the developed capitalist countries of the United States, Canada, Australia, Ja-

Figure 1
World Population, 1978

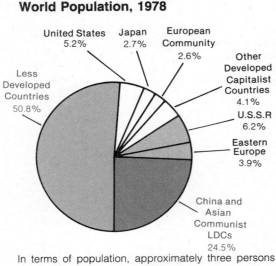

In terms of population, approximately three persons live in less developed countries for every one person who lives in a developed country.

Source: National Foreign Assessment Center, *Handbook of Economic Statistics,* 1979, Table 30.

Figure 2
World Gross National Product, 1978

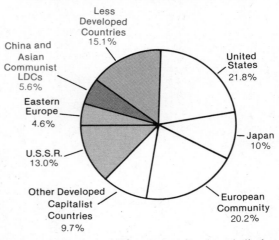

While noncommunist LDCs account for about half of the world's population (see Figure 1), they produce only about 15 percent of world GNP.

Source: National Foreign Assessment Center, *Handbook of Economic Statistics,* 1979, p. 1.

pan, and Western Europe, and 10 percent of the world's population lives in the European communist countries of the U.S.S.R. and Eastern Europe. Of the 75 percent of the world's population that lives in LDCs, 50.8 percent resides in countries outside the communist blocs, and 24.5 percent lives in Asian communist countries.

The Haves and the Have-Nots

A comparison of the distribution of world population with the distribution of world income dramatizes how unequally income is distributed among the different countries of the globe. As Figure 2 shows, the developed capitalist countries, which account for only 14.6 percent of the world's population, account for 61.7 percent of the world's GNP. The noncommunist LDCs, while accounting for 50.8 percent of the world's population, account for only 15.1 percent of world GNP. In other words, per capita GNP in the developed countries is, on average, about 15 times that in the LDCs. The unequal distribution of income among countries also leads to an unequal distribution of the consumption of natural resources between the rich and poor countries.

The industrialized capitalist countries, for example, consume 70.5 percent of the world's oil production. After allowing for consumption by the U.S.S.R. and Eastern Europe, only 9 percent of the world's oil production is available for the LDCs.

Life in an LDC is very different from life in the United States. Only one of 6 people in a low-income LDC lives in an urban area (as opposed to 70 percent in the United States). One out of every 5 children dies before the age of four (as compared with one out of every 140 in the United States). In a community of 13,000 people, there is one physician (as opposed to 22 in the United States). Only one out of every 3 adults can read or write, and only 6 out of 10 school-age children attend primary school. There is a better than 50/50 chance that a girl will never attend school. Only 2 out of every 100 persons own their own radio receiver, and a private automobile is a virtually unheard-of luxury. LDC residents come from large families and plan on having a large number of children, many of whom will not survive their infancy.[1]

1.   World Bank, *World Tables,* 1980, series III.

Table 2

A Comparison of Developed Countries and Less Developed Countries (LDCs)

	1950–1960	1960–1970	1970–1977
1. Rate of population growth			
in developed countries	1.2	1.0	0.8
in middle-income LDCs	2.4	2.5	2.5
in low-income LDCs	2.0	2.4	2.2
2. Rate of per capita GNP growth			
in developed countries	2.5	4.0	2.4
in middle-income LDCs	2.8	3.7	3.4
in low-income LDCs	1.8	2.1	1.7
	1960	**1970**	**1977**
3. Life expectancy (years)			
in developed countries	68.9	71.8	72.9
in middle-income LDCs	50.6	54.9	58.1
in low-income LDCs	40.8	45.3	47.9
4. Adult literacy (per 100)			
in developed countries	96.9	98.3	98.7
in middle-income LDCs	44.0	56.2	63.2
in low-income LDCs	22.6	31.0	36.7

Source: World Bank, *World Tables* 1980, series III; World Bank, *World Development Report,* published for the World Bank by Oxford University Press, 1981, p. 5.

IS WORLD POVERTY A PROBLEM?

The picture of life in a low-income LDC is not a very pretty one. Is material life in LDCs getting better? Have there been significant improvements in living conditions that might suggest that third-world poverty is a temporary inconvenience to be suffered only by the current generation?

Table 2 gives data on average rates of growth of population and per capita GNP and on changes in two social indicators from 1950 to the late 1970s. On the whole, there is little evidence that the LDCs are catching up with per capita incomes in the developed countries. The evidence suggests that low-income LDCs have fallen even further behind since 1950, while the middle-income LDCs have just about held their own. The LDCs have clearly experienced more rapid population growth than the developed countries. Both the low- and middle-income LDCs have experienced GNP growth as rapid or more rapid than that of the developed countries, but more rapid population growth has meant equivalent or slower per capita GNP growth.

In terms of life expectancy and literacy, the LDCs have indeed been catching up with the developed countries. The developed countries are approaching natural upper limits (one cannot raise the literacy rate above 100 percent, and human beings are mortal), and the LDCs have succeeded in improving the health and education of their populations.

On the basis of absolute poverty standards, LDCs have made significant progress. If the low-income LDC per capita GNP were to continue to grow at an annual rate of 2 percent, today's per capita income of $350 will be $525 20 years from now. Such a rate of growth, while not earthshaking, would slowly take the populations of the LDCs away from the edge of physical subsistence. The 3 percent growth rate of the middle-income LDCs would mean a doubling of per capita income within 25 years.

Significant improvements in agricultural output per capita have been achieved over the last decade even in some very poor LDCs. Countries like India are nearing self-sufficiency in food production according to the statistical studies of international organizations. As a group, the LDCs have significantly lessened their dependence upon grain imports from the developed countries. These important improvements in agricultural production are called the "Green Revolution" and are the consequence of the application of new developments in seed technology in the LDCs.

If a relative poverty standard is used, then the progress of the LDCs has not been satisfactory. There is no significant trend toward reducing the income gap between the rich and the poor countries. Per capita incomes in the rich and poor countries appear to be growing at roughly the same rate.

As already demonstrated, most of the world's population lives in material conditions that would be intolerable to those accustomed to the affluence of the developed countries. Just as poverty at home amid conditions of general affluence can create moral pressure to redistribute income to the poor, so the existence of international poverty can motivate the more fortunate countries to assist the poor countries. The poor countries are an economic problem because international poverty may violate individual notions of justice and fair play. Many individuals have ethical objections to the poverty that exists in the very poor LDCs.

International poverty is also a political problem for the capitalist West. The noncommunist third- and fourth-world countries (with capitalist and communist countries making up the first two "worlds") represent more than 50 percent of the world's population, and, in most instances, they remain ideologically and politically uncommitted. Will they ultimately decide that Soviet or Chinese communism offers them the best opportunity to overcome their relative poverty, or will they decide that ideological and political commitment to capitalism and participatory democracy offers them the best prospects for progress? Or will they develop some other ideology?

Soviet ideologists have long argued that the ideological struggle between capitalism and socialism will be decided in the third and fourth worlds. Would the LDCs be willing to embrace capitalism and democracy if the western world fails to assist the LDCs and if they continue to fall farther and farther behind the affluent West? There is no way of knowing for sure. As individuals accumulate private wealth, they have more

to lose under a communist regime; the chances of a country choosing communism are diminished by the existence of private wealth.

Resentment and envy can also play a role in the LDCs' choice of capitalism or communism. Modern telecommunications have made everyone, even in the poor countries, aware of their relative standard of living. Even in some remote villages in the LDCs, villagers watch American and European television programs, which make them painfully aware of their relative poverty. This information means that the residents of the LDCs are unlikely to be satisfied with absolute improvements in their standard of living but may judge their own economic progress and form their expectations of the future on the basis of living standards in the more affluent countries.

WHY ARE THE LDCS POOR?

Although economic development means more than a high per capita income, a rising per capita income is indeed a necessary condition for economic development. If per capita income is to grow, real GNP must grow more rapidly than population.

The classical stationary state of Ricardo and Malthus described in the preceding chapter provides one explanation of why the LDCs are poor. LDCs are typically economies that rely primarily on agricultural output for their income, where arable land is limited in supply, where population is growing at a rapid rate, and where technological improvements are practically nonexistent. Thus, LDCs contain all the basic ingredients of the stationary state. Population pressure forces such an economy to operate with diminishing returns as technological progress fails to offset declining labor productivity. Wages are kept near subsistence, and population growth is regulated by rising and falling mortality. Good harvests cause lower mortality but more population pressure. Poor harvests cause higher mortality and less population pressure.

The classical model supplies a first approximation of why the LDCs are poor. It is especially appropriate for the low-income LDCs, which appear to be caught in something approaching a stationary state. The classical model also suggests what could be done to release the LDCs from the confines of the stationary state:

1. If the rate of population growth were to decline, the pressures of diminishing returns would be abated.
2. If technological progress could be achieved, diminishing returns could be avoided.
3. If capital formation could be accelerated, labor productivity could be raised.

Why are most countries still underdeveloped if these solutions to national poverty are available? The answer is that serious obstacles make it difficult to slow population growth, to achieve technological progress, or to accelerate capital formation.

Population Pressures

The rate of growth of per capita GNP equals the rate of growth of GNP minus the rate of growth of population. Per capita growth can, therefore, be accelerated either by increasing the growth of GNP or by decreasing the growth of population. This simple exercise in arithmetic explains why many analysts of LDCs tend to regard rapid population growth as an enemy of economic development. As already noted, if population growth had been less rapid in the LDCs (and if GNP growth had remained the same), the per capita income of the LDCs would have done some catching up with that of the developed countries.

The Demographic Transition. Why is population growth more rapid in the LDCs than in the developed countries? Demographers have long studied a "law" of population growth called the **demographic transition.**

*The **demographic transition** is the process by which countries change from rapid population growth to slow population growth as they modernize.*

To understand why the demographic transition tends to accompany the process of modernization, one must first understand the fundamental equation of population growth. The **rate of natural increase** is the net addition to the population.

*The **rate of natural increase** equals the **crude birth rate** minus the **crude death rate.***

*The **crude birth rate** is the number of births per 1,000 population.*

*The **crude death rate** is the number of deaths per 1,000 population.*

In a country's premodern era, there is little or no population growth because the birth rate and death rate are roughly equal, and there are no net additions to the population. However, as the process of modernization begins, there is an acceleration of population growth. Modernization brings with it better health care and nutrition, and the death rate declines. In addition, rising incomes may cause birth rates to rise in the early phases of modernization. The first phases of modernization are, therefore, characterized by an acceleration in the rate of population growth.

As modernization proceeds, further reductions in the death rate become harder to achieve. Mortality due to infectious diseases has already become rare, and medical science is left with harder-to-combat chronic diseases, such as heart disease and cancer. On the other side of the population equation, modernization eventually causes the birth rate to decline. As married couples become more educated, they regulate more effectively the number of births through the practice of contraception. The desired number of children decreases. In modern societies, a large number of children is no longer the ticket to old-age security. Infant mortality has been reduced, so it is no longer necessary to have many children to insure that some will survive to adulthood. Employment opportunities for women improve, and the opportunity costs of having children increase. All of these factors combine to reduce the birth rate.

As the death rate stabilizes and the birth rate declines, a demographic transition from high rates of population growth to low rates takes place. The Malthusian spectre of overpopulation is removed, and some advanced societies must even start to worry about underpopulation—about negative population growth.

The LDCs as a group have failed to participate in the demographic transition for a number of reasons.

1. Unlike the industrialized countries, declines in death rates in the LDCs were not coordinated with rising modernization and prosperity. Instead, public-health improvements (such as typhoid and cholera immunizations) were introduced by the colonial powers prior to significant economic development. Improved health care and sanitation in the LDCs caused significant declines in mortality *prior* to modernization.

2. In many LDCs—which remain rural societies without government old-age security programs—children are still the only guarantee that one will be looked after in one's old age. Parents that have many children stand a better chance of health and income security in their old age.

3. In many LDCs, there are century-old traditions that favor large families. The proof of manhood may be the number of children fathered. Immortality is considered assured by having many children, grandchildren, and great grandchildren.

4. As long as the country remains underdeveloped and employment opportunities are primarily in agriculture, the opportunity costs to women of having additional children are low. In many LDCs, having a baby means the loss of only a few days or weeks in the fields. At an early age, the child becomes productive in the fields and helps his or her parents.

5. As long as education—particularly the education of women—remains unavailable, the ability to practice birth control remains limited.

For these reasons, the LDCs are caught in a vicious circle: rapid population growth inhibits increases in per capita income; without substantial increases in per capita income (and the modernization that accompanies rising incomes) it is difficult to bring about substantial reductions in birth rates.

Optimal Population Growth. Many development economists and public officials have concluded that the LDCs would be better off with zero population growth. The advantages of zero population growth are that there would be less pressure on land resources, larger per capita growth per percentage increase of GNP, and a lower ratio of dependent children to working adults. But there are also disadvantages to zero population growth. If there were no population growth, the population would begin to age. An aged population is less productive than a young population. Zero population growth means that the domestic economy would grow less rapidly, but growing markets encourage investment and risk taking. Growing populations also mean more minds, and more minds increase the opportunity for more scientific knowledge and technological progress.[2]

Public officials who follow simple rules like zero population growth could do more harm than good. But even if the optimal rate of population growth could be determined, the difficult task of achieving this rate through appropriate public policies—perhaps in the face of considerable public opposition—remains. Governments in LDCs such as India have been toppled by public opposition to government population policies.

Capital-Formation Problems

The LDCs encounter another vicious circle in the area of capital formation. The major portion of a nation's saving is carried out by the affluent; the poor save little or nothing. Therefore, if a whole country is poor—with most of its population living near subsistence—its saving rate should be low. Moreover, the wealthy in the LDCs tend to invest their savings into nonproductive areas, such as land, precious metals, and foreign bank accounts. The wealthy are simply reacting to the realities of LDC life: the political uncertainties and the apparently poor development prospects of their own countries.

The Saving Rate. The English economist Sir Roy Harrod and Evsey Domar studied in the 1950s the relationship between a nation's rate of saving and its economic growth. Their work is summarized in the *Harrod-Domar growth model*.

The Harrod-Domar growth equation is based upon two definitions and an identity. The identity is the macroeconomic equality of investment and saving ($I = S$). The first definition is that investment (I) is the addition to the stock of capital, or $I = \Delta K$, where ΔK denotes the change in the

---

2. Julian Simon, *The Economics of Population Growth* (Princeton: Princeton University Press, 1977).

stock of capital. The second definition is the **marginal output/capital ratio** *(MOCR)*.

*The **marginal output/capital ratio** (MOCR) is the change in output divided by the change in capital.*

$$MOCR = \Delta Q / \Delta K$$

where ΔQ is the change in output. From the definition of the *MOCR,* one can see that the increase in output equals the *MOCR* times the increase in capital:

$$\Delta Q = MOCR \times \Delta K$$

Dividing both sides of the equation by Q yields an equation for the growth rate of output $(\Delta Q/Q)$:

The growth rate of output $(\Delta Q/Q) = $ MOCR $\times$ $\Delta K/Q$

Because investment *(I)* is simply the change in the capital stock (ΔK), and saving *(S)* identically equals investment *(I),* the term $\Delta K/Q$ equals the percentage of output saved—the saving rate.

The growth rate of output equals the MOCR times the saving rate.

If, for example, the *MOCR* equals 0.5 and the saving rate equals 0.1 (10 percent), the growth rate of output is 0.05 (5 percent) per year (0.5 × 0.1). The growth rate can be increased by raising the saving rate: if the saving rate had been 0.2 (20 percent), the growth rate would be 0.1 (10 percent) per year if the *MOCR* does not change. By doubling the saving rate, the growth rate of output is doubled.

The Harrod-Domar growth model implies that the LDCs could solve many of their problems by raising national saving rates. As long as the *MOCR* remains stable, every 1 percentage point increase in the saving rate would mean a 1 percentage point increase in the growth rate.

Contemporary growth theory (described in the preceding chapter) teaches that economic growth depends as much or more on the growth of labor inputs (in both quantity and quality) and on technological progress as on capital accumulation. The Harrod-Domar growth equation does not contradict this more modern approach. Growth depends not only on the saving rate but also on the behavior of *MOCR*. Because technological improvements raise the productivity of existing factors, they raise the *MOCR*. If increases in the saving rate cause the *MOCR* to fall, the growth rate will rise more slowly than the percentage increase in the saving rate. Modern growth theory teaches that the relationship between the saving rate of a country and its growth rate is very complex. It does not deny that increases in capital formation have a beneficial effect on economic growth; however, it does demonstrate that limited capital formation is only part of the problem.

Social Overhead Capital. Modern economic growth began in the developed countries after centuries of preparation. Canals, schools, roads, and cathedrals had been built in the centuries that preceded the industrial revolution. By the time of the industrial revolution, the developed countries had accumulated an impressive stock of **social overhead capital** goods.

Social overhead capital such as roads, canals, schools, and hospitals benefits society more than it benefits specific individuals.

Some development economists argue that the LDCs have not had the luxury of centuries of slow accumulation of social overhead capital. In effect, an infrastructure of social overhead capital is required before real economic development can take place. Yet it may take years or decades to accumulate sufficient social overhead capital to sustain economic development.

Technological Backwardness

On the surface, it would appear that the industrialized countries have already developed modern technology that need simply be borrowed by the LDCs. The technology of the industrialized countries represents a response to the factor endowments that are present in these countries. Relative to the LDCs, capital is abundant in the developed countries; the quantity of labor is scarce, but the quality of each worker (in training, health, and education) is quite high. Because of these factor endowments, the industrialized countries have developed over the years technologies that emphasize labor saving and require large inputs of highly skilled labor and capital.

The modern production techniques of the developed countries are, therefore, not well suited for application in the LDCs. The LDCs require technologies that take advantage of their abundant supplies of unskilled labor and do not place heavy burdens on their more limited resources—skilled labor and capital. Although a wealth of sophisticated technology is on hand in the industrialized countries, the LDCs remain in the ironic position of having to develop their own technologies. Although there is evidence that Japan was successful in adapting modern technology to its particular needs, most LDCs have been less successful.

Not only must production techniques suited to LDC factor endowments be developed, but these new techniques must be put into productive use. They must be accepted by farms and factories in the LDCs. In the developed countries, particularly the United States, Canada, and Australia, new agricultural technology—such as new seed types, chemical fertilizers, or automated farm equipment—were put into practice by farmers with few delays because profit-motivated farmers realized these new technologies were good for business.

In the LDCs, where peasant farming dominates and traditional forms of agriculture still prevail, there is a great reluctance to adopt new ways of doing things. There is also the unanswered question of the economic motivation of peasant families. Are they, like western farmers, profit maximizers or has diminishing returns and surplus labor forced them to use other criteria for allocating resources?[3]

---

3. Economists and social scientists have studied the rationality of peasant behavior. The most famous analysis is that by Nobel laureate, Sir W. Arthur Lewis, who concludes that peasants in traditional labor-surplus economies cannot employ profit-maximization rules because the opportunity cost of additional workers is zero in a labor surplus economy. Paying workers their opportunity costs would suggest widescale starvation. Therefore, traditional methods of allocating resources are used instead.

SOLUTIONS TO WORLD POVERTY

The LDCs are poor because they have fewer economic resources—labor, entrepreneurs, capital, and technology—than the developed countries. Moreover, obstacles in the form of tradition, religious tabus, and bureaucratic restrictions have prevented them from utilizing their limited resources as effectively as the industrialized countries. The LDCs are caught in a vicious circle: low income prevents them from accumulating new resources, and the failure to accumulate new resources leaves them poor.

Preconditions versus Substitutions

Economic historian W. W. Rostow, in *The Stages of Economic Growth,* formulated the notion that economies must pass through a series of stages or phases on their way to economic development. Rostow wrote that economies, in preparation for industrialization—or the "take-off" as he called it—must first establish the preconditions for economic development. As a precondition to take-off, a country must first develop a middle class to assume entrepreneurial responsibilities; it must accumulate social overhead capital; it must create a literate population; it must establish a legal system compatible with economic development. The length of time required to establish these preconditions may be substantial; countries that lack these preconditions must establish them before the take-off can occur.

Rostow's view of preconditions is basically a pessimistic one as far as the contemporary LDCs are concerned. Most of them lack the necessary social overhead capital or a strong middle class, for example. Must they patiently wait for all the preconditions to be met before they can hope for sustained economic development?

Prominent economic historian Alexander Gerschenkron offers a markedly different vision of the process of economic development. Gerschenkron maintained that countries can substitute for missing preconditions and in this way speed up economic development. Relying primarily on the historical experiences of Japan and czarist Russia, Gerschenkron described how these economies found suitable substitutes for missing preconditions. Foreign capital and foreign entrepreneurs were substituted for inadequate domestic savings and for missing entrepreneurial skills. Government bureaucracies took the place of the missing middle class. Capital-intensive techniques were substituted for scarce trained industrial workers.

The views of both Rostow and Gerschenkron have been disputed, and many exceptions to their general rules have been found. Must LDCs go through the laborious process of establishing preconditions or can they skip over the most hard-to-create preconditions by making innovative substitutions?

Bootstrap Solutions

The most optimistic analysts of economic development believe that the LDCs, by following the appropriate policies, can generate economic development without outside assistance. In other words, the LDCs can "pull themselves up by their own bootstraps."

The Labor Surplus Economy. One bootstrap approach to economic development has been offered by Nobel laureate Sir W. Arthur Lewis. Lewis maintains that many LDCs suffer from a surplus of labor in agriculture. Agricultural overpopulation is so severe in many instances that labor could be shifted from agriculture to industry without a loss of output in agriculture. If a method could be found for shifting some of the redundant labor into alternative employment in industry, an *agricultural surplus* could be created to finance overall economic development.

When redundant workers are shifted from agriculture to industry, the economy is able to produce more output. Agricultural output has not declined, but industrial output has increased. To motivate workers to move voluntarily from agriculture to industry, it is only necessary for industry to pay a slight premium over agricultural wages. As long as there is redundant labor in agriculture, agricultural wages will not rise; shifting surplus workers to industry will not raise the total wage bill of the economy (wages in industry and agriculture) even though more output is being produced.

If income from this surplus output is channeled into industrial investment, more jobs are created in industry, more redundant workers are drawn from agriculture, and more surplus is earned to be plowed back into industry. This process of reinvestment continues until all surplus labor has been drawn out of agriculture and the agricultural surplus has been exhausted. By this time, the economy will be well on the way to economic development.

The utilization of a hidden agricultural surplus to pull an economy up by its own bootstraps is an appealing notion, especially to independent-minded LDCs. Development economists have pointed out two problems with the Lewis approach. The first is that there is little evidence to support the view that large numbers can indeed be drawn out of agriculture without a loss of agricultural output. Most studies of LDC agriculture show that the amount of rural overpopulation has been overestimated and that most agricultural workers make a positive contribution to agricultural output. The second problem is the mechanism whereby redundant labor, if it indeed exists, is to be withdrawn from agriculture. One option would be a Soviet-type forced collectivization, but this approach would likely meet with fierce peasant opposition. Other approaches—the use of rapid inflation or government taxation—remain untested.

Unbalanced Growth. Balanced growth is a broad-based simultaneous advance of all branches of the economy. Ragnar Nurkse and Paul Rosenstein-Rodan—early proponents of balanced growth—point out that without balanced growth, the national market in an LDC would be too small to support isolated modern industrial branches. Economic branches are interdependent; one sector cannot prosper in isolation from other branches upon which it depends for its inputs and sales. The basic problem with balanced growth is that it requires more resources than are available to the LDCs. If an LDC had the resources to support a broad simultaneous expansion of all branches, it would not be underdeveloped. The only way balanced growth appears feasible is with enormous sums of foreign assistance.

Albert Hirschman of Yale University has argued that LDCs can pull themselves up by their own bootstraps by pursuing an *unbalanced-growth strategy*. The unbalanced-growth approach requires that the LDCs determine which of their economic branches require substantial inputs from other industries (the steel industry, for example, relies on inputs from the coal and ore industries) and which industries are significant suppliers of other industries (again, the steel industry is an important supplier for automobile-production, machinery, and bridge-building industries).

According to Hirschman, LDCs should one-sidedly push the development of industries that require inputs from other industries or supply inputs to other industries. Entrepreneurial talent is a very scarce resource in the poor countries; the domestic price system may be distorted. Consequently, there are risks that incorrect economic decisions will be made. Unbalanced growth will force correct resource-allocation decisions. The growth of the steel industry will create an excess demand for coal and ore that will signal that resources should be devoted to developing these industries. The greater availability of steel will also signal to steel-using industries that they should expand. By deliberately pursuing unbalanced growth, economic decision making is simplified. The economy will move spontaneously from one shortage to another, and, in the process, one branch of the economy will develop after another.

The Soviet Union in the 1930s, for example, pursued a deliberate policy of unbalanced growth in favor of heavy industry, while starving agriculture and light industry of resources. As a consequence of this unbalanced-growth policy, the Soviet economy was transformed in less than one decade from a fairly backward agricultural economy to a self-sufficient industry-oriented economy that was capable of producing its own machinery and weapons.

The unbalanced-growth model assumes that the pattern of sectoral expansion must be planned. A deliberate plan that specifies which industries are to be favored must be established, and the state must have the authority to enforce the plan. It is unlikely that spontaneous market forces would result in unbalanced growth. Therefore, unbalanced growth and economic planning are deeply intertwined.

Trade Policies. The examples of Great Britain in the 19th century and Hong Kong today show how extensive international trade can bring many benefits to a country. Trade harnesses the power of specialization to raise national income beyond what is possible in isolation. Some LDCs have tried to grow by denying the benefits of specialization and have attempted to copy the industrialized countries. They want their own automobile and steel industries even though it is cheaper to buy cars and steel indirectly by producing goods for which the economy's resource base is suited (textiles, natural resources). Countries such as Argentina and India have attempted to follow the inward-looking policy of **import substitution.**

Import substitution occurs when a country substitutes domestic production for imports by subsidizing domestic production through tariffs, quotas, and other devices.

Cases of successful import substitution are rare, primarily because the products manufactured with the assistance of tariffs and other forms of protection are not as competitive in the long run at home as abroad.

An alternative course followed by countries such as Hong Kong, South Korea, Taiwan, Brazil, and Singapore has been the outward-looking policy of **export promotion**—encouraging exports through various types of incentive schemes.

Export promotion occurs when a country encourages exports by subsidizing the production of goods for export.

In general, those LDCs that have followed export-promotion policies have done better as a group than those that followed import-substitution policies.

External Assistance

Can the LDCs realistically expect to develop on their own, or must they have outside assistance? The issue of assistance from the industrialized countries is an explosive one in the third world because many LDCs blame their poverty on exploitation by the developed countries. Because many LDCs believe the developed countries are responsible for the low income of the LDCs, they believe it is their obligation to help.[4]

For both humanitarian and political reasons, the industrialized capitalist countries have concluded that they should assist the LDC.

Foreign Aid. If the industrialized countries give foreign aid to the LDCs, will this aid stimulate economic growth or make the LDCs more dependent on the developed countries?

Foreign economic assistance adds a new source of saving to an LDC economy. With foreign aid, total savings equals domestic saving plus foreign assistance. Using the Harrod-Domar growth equation, with foreign assistance, the rate of economic growth is:

$$\Delta Q/Q = MOCR \times (s + f)$$

where s is the domestic saving rate and f is foreign aid as a percentage of GNP. If the *MOCR* is 0.5 and s equals 0.1 (10 percent), the growth rate is 0.05 (5 percent). If f equals 0.1 (10 percent), then the growth rate is raised to 0.1 (10 percent). Foreign assistance increases a low domestic saving rate.

Hollis Chenery, a former vice-president of the World Bank, and Allen Strout conclude that if the LDCs use their foreign assistance wisely they will eventually be able to stand on their own feet without assistance.[5]

A New International Economic Order. Direct foreign assistance is one means by which the industrialized countries assist the LDCs. In the view of the LDCs, the current level of foreign assistance (approximately $20 billion annually), while welcome, is grossly inadequate. The LDCs

call for a doubling of foreign assistance, suggesting that the industrialized countries should donate approximately 1 percent of their GNP to the LDCs. Few industrialized nations, including the United States, contribute anything close to the 1 percent figure.

According to the LDCs, the industrialized countries could (and should) provide forms of assistance other than direct foreign aid.

Most LDCs trade raw materials for the machinery and equipment required for economic development. The LDCs complain that their dependence upon raw-material exports places them at a disadvantage in the world economy. Their earnings from raw materials—coffee, rubber, flax, sugar, ores—fluctuate more dramatically than the prices of manufactured goods. The LDCs believe as well that the long-run tendency is for the prices of raw materials to fall relative to manufactured goods. Such a decline would cause the incomes of the LDCs to continue to fall in the long run relative to the developed countries, but studies show no clear-cut trends. Representatives of the LDCs allege that they are in a boom-or-bust environment and that they are unable to develop in a steady and predictable manner.

In the United Nations, a coalition of the poor countries has argued that the developed countries should set up commodity-stabilization funds to control the fluctuations of raw material prices. This fund would operate under the auspices of the United Nations and would be funded by contributions from the rich countries. Dialogues between the LDCs and the industrialized countries—called "North-South dialogues" by the press—could yield long-term raw-materials pricing agreements that earn a fair and predictable return for the LDCs. If the world price threatens to fall below a specific price, then the commodity-stabilization fund would buy the commodity to prevent the price decline.

The commodity-price-stabilization program is the centerpiece of the New Order, but a number of economic studies indicate that export instability may promote economic development for two reasons. First, export instability will be correlated with international trade policies that promote international specialization and, thus, enable the LDCs to capture the gains from specialization.

4. The belief that the developed countries are responsible for the plight of the LDCs is widely held in the LDCs. This conclusion has been supported by the Marxist-Leninist theories of colonialism that maintain that the wealth of the industrialized countries was created by exploiting the labor and natural resources of the poor countries.
5. Hollis Chenery and Allen Strout, "Foreign Assistance and Economic Development," *American Economic Review* 56, 4 (September 1966): 679–733.

Second, export instability will tend to decrease the average propensity to consume, since individuals faced with greater variation in income tend to consume less. Thus, export instability can raise saving rates and capital formation. A substantial amount of empirical research supports the conclusion that export instability actually promotes economic development.[6] Paradoxically, commodity-price-stabilization funds might backfire and hurt the LDCs.

In addition to more foreign aid and commodity stabilization, the LDCs have called for improved access to the markets and technology of the industrialized countries and reforms of the international monetary system.[7]

CAPITALISM OR SOCIALISM FOR THE LDCS?

The LDCs must decide which economic system offers them better prospects for economic development. Studies of comparative economic systems reveal that, as a group, the LDCs have a greater tendency to substitute administrative resource allocation for market resource allocation, but the rigid authoritarian control required to carry through a regimented economic plan is typically not present in the LDCs.

Some western economists argue that one reason why the LDCs remain poor is the very fact that they have allowed too little market resource allocation. The LDCs have numerous barriers to market decision making—commodity price controls, tariffs, franchises and monopolies, and social barriers—that prevent the LDCs from efficiently utilizing their resources. Moreover, the lack of market resource allocation and the weak protection of private-property rights discourage investments by the wealthy and by foreign capitalists. Advocates of a greater role for capitalist market forces cite the success stories of Hong Kong, South Korea, Taiwan, and Singapore as proof of their position.[8]

Economic growth has been different in the industrialized countries and in the third world. The next three chapters will examine international economics.

Summary

1. Affluence is still a rare phenomenon in the world today. About 75 percent of the world's population lives in poor countries. Less developed countries, or LDCs, are those countries that have a low level of economic development relative to the developed countries. National poverty can be defined in absolute terms (countries that live close to subsistence) or in relative terms (low income relative to more affluent countries). LDCs are characterized by low per capita income, high mortality, low life expectancies, low rates of urbanization, and high illiteracy. The LDCs are poor because they have fewer economic resources than the rich countries, and they use their resources less efficiently than the developed countries.

2. While poor countries have made considerable progress to reduce their *absolute* poverty, the LDCs have failed to overcome their backwardness *relative* to the rich countries. International poverty is a political as well as an economic problem.

3. The classical stationary state model provides a first explanation of LDC poverty. The combination of rapid population growth and limited technological progress has caused diminishing returns to be a serious problem in LDCs. Possible solutions to the diminishing returns problem are reduced population growth, increased capital formation, and more rapid technological progress. The demographic transition is the process by which countries change from rapid to slow population growth during the course of moderniza-

6. See Odin Knudsen and Andrew Parnes, *Trade Instability and Economic Development* (Lexington, Mass.: D. C. Heath, 1975), chap. 6. This study confirms the pioneering study of Alastair MacBean, *Export Instability and Economic Development* (Cambridge, Mass.: Harvard University Press, 1966), chap. 4.

7. Mordecai E. Kreinin and J. M. Finger, "A Critical Survey of the New International Economic Order," *Journal of World Trade Law* (November/December 1976).

8. For a serious case study of the free enterprise Hong Kong experiment, see Steven Chow and Gustav Papanek, "Laissez Faire, Growth, and Equity—Hong Kong," *Economic Journal* 91, 362 (June 1981): 466–85.

tion. The LDCs have yet to experience as a group the demographic transition. The LDCs suffer from inadequate capital formation. The growth rate equals the marginal capital/output ratio times the saving rate. An increase in the saving rate will cause an increase in growth, *ceteris paribus*. LDCs also lack adequate social overhead capital to support economic growth. Although it appears that the LDCs could borrow the advanced technology of the developed countries, this technology is generally not well suited to the factor endowments of the LDCs.

4. One approach to the poverty problem of the LDCs is to pull the economy up by its own bootstraps without significant outside assistance. The labor-surplus model and the unbalanced-growth model have been suggested as possible bootstrap approaches to economic development. The LDCs must also choose between import-substitution and export-promotion policies of economic development. A second general approach to economic development is to use outside assistance. Foreign aid raises the saving rate and thus raises economic growth. The LDCs have asked for a New International Economic Order, the cornerstone of which is an international commodity-stabilization program funded by the developed countries. Its benefits have been questioned by some western economists.

5. The LDCs must decide whether planned or market allocation systems offer them a better chance for economic development.

Key Terms

less developed countries (LDCs)
demographic transition
rate of natural increase
crude birth rate
crude death rate
marginal output/capital ratio *(MOCR)*
social overhead capital
import substitution
export promotion

Questions and Problems

1. Explain why GNP or GNP per capita can be an imperfect guide to the level of economic development.

2. "The stationary state of Ricardo and Malthus is not an accurate description of the industrialized countries. On the other hand, it does appear to describe accurately the LDCs." Evaluate this position.

3. Describe the demographic transition. Why has the demographic transition not occurred in many of the LDCs?

4. Using the Harrod-Domar model, calculate the growth of output if the marginal output/capital ratio is 0.4 and the national saving rate is 0.2 (20 percent). What happens to the growth rate if the *MOCR* rises to 0.5? What happens if the saving rate rises to 0.3? According to this model, what role could foreign aid play in raising the growth rate?

5. Explain how the existence of an agricultural surplus could lead to bootstrap economic development.

6. Contrast the different trade policies that an LDC might pursue in trying to promote its economic development.

7. Describe the New International Order that the LDCs want from the industrialized countries.

PART

III

International Economics

CHAPTER

20

International Trade and Comparative Advantage

Chapter Preview

International economics is divided into two branches: 1) the study of international trade in physical goods and services and 2) the study of the monetary consequences of international payments between countries. This chapter studies the reasons for and consequences of international trade; Chapter 21 will study the effects of tariffs and quotas on trade; Chapter 22 will study foreign exchange rates, the balance of payments, and the evolution of the international monetary system. International economics is the oldest branch of economics: David Hume laid out the basic monetary mechanism of international trade in 1752; David Ricardo established the famous law of

comparative advantage in 1817. This chapter will describe the workings of the law of comparative advantage and the comparative advantages of the U.S. economy.

THE REASONS FOR INTERNATIONAL TRADE

This book has emphasized that people benefit from specialization. People find that their incomes are increased by specializing in those tasks for which they are particularly suited. Different jobs have different intellectual, physical, and personality requirements. Since people are all different and since each person has the capacity to learn, it pays to specialize. As Adam Smith stated:

"It is the maxim of every prudent master of a family never to attempt to make at home what it will cost him more to make than to buy."

Trade among persons takes place because each individual is endowed with a mix of traits that are different from most other people. Some of these traits are an inherent part of the individual that cannot be shared with other individuals.

Trade between individuals has much in common with international trade between countries. Each country is endowed with certain traits: a particular climate, so much fertile farm land, so much desert, so many lakes and rivers, and the kinds of people that comprise its population. Over the years, some countries have accumulated a lot of physical and human capital while other countries are poor in capital. In short, each country is defined in part by the endowments of productive factors (land, labor, and capital) inside its borders. Just as a person cannot transfer intelligence, strength, personality, or health to another, a country's land and other natural-resource deposits cannot be transferred to another country. Similarly, the labor force that resides within a country is not easily moved; people have friends and family ties in their native land and share a common language and culture with their fellows. Even if they wish to leave, immigration laws may render the labor force internationally immobile. Thus, each country will have different (to some degree) proportions of the supplies of land, labor, and capital. A country like Australia has very little labor compared to land and, hence, will devote itself to land-intensive products like sheep farming or wheat production. A country like Great Britain will tend to produce goods that use comparatively little land but more of the other factors of labor and capital. Sweden's Nobel-prize-winning economist Bertil Ohlin pointed out that when each country specializes in those goods for which its factor proportions are most suited, international trade in goods and services acts as a substitute for movements of the various productive factors.

The fundamental fact upon which international trade rests is that goods and services are much more mobile internationally than the resources used in their production. Each country will tend to export those goods and services for which its resource base is most suited.

It is easier to transfer the goods and services produced by land, labor, and capital to another country than to transfer the land, labor, and capital itself. As Adam Smith noted,

What is prudence in the conduct of every private family can scarce be folly in that of a great kingdom. If a foreign country can supply us with a commodity cheaper than we ourselves can make it, better buy it with some part of the produce of our industry employed in a way in which we have some advantage.

International trade allows a country to specialize in the goods and services that it can produce at a relatively low cost and export those goods in return for imports whose domestic production is relatively costly. As a consequence, international trade enables a country—and the world—to consume and produce more than would be possible without trade.

We shall later show that a country can even benefit from trade when it is more efficient (uses fewer resources) in the production of *all* goods than any other country.

Aside from the tangible benefit of providing the potential for greater totals of all the goods and services the world consumes, trade has intangible benefits as well. The major intangible benefit is the diversity trade offers to the way people live and work. The advantages of particular climates and lands are shared by the rest of the world. The United States imports oil from the hot desert of Saudi Arabia to drive cars in cool comfort. Americans can enjoy coffee, bananas, and spices without living in the tropics. The economy and durability of Japanese cars can be enjoyed without driving in hectic Tokyo. Thus, international (and interregional) trade enables us to enjoy a more diverse menu of goods and services than would be possible without trade. World trade also encourages the diffusion of knowledge and culture because trade serves as a point of contact between people of different lands.

Table 1
Size of Exports in Seven Major Countries, 1979

Country	Exports as Percent of GNP	Total Exports (billions of dollars)
United States	8	221
West Germany	23	192
Japan	13	130
United Kingdom	22	115
France	17	111
Italy	20	78
Canada	26	65
Belgium (Luxembourg)	53	65

Source: *Statistical Abstract of the United States*, 1981, p. 879.

Table 2
Principal Commodities of U.S. Merchandise Trade, 1981

Commodities	Quantity (billions of dollars)	Percentage of Total
Exports		
Agricultural	43.8	19
Chemical	18.0	8
Business machines, computers	19.4	8
Civilian aircraft	13.5	6
Construction machinery	11.6	5
Other exports	127.4	54
Total	**233.7**	**100**
Imports		
Petroleum	77.1	30
Consumer goods (nonauto)	38.7	15
Automotive vehicles	29.7	11
Iron and steel	11.3	4
Coffee, cocoa, sugar	5.2	2
Other imports	99.3	38
Total	**261.3**	**100**

Source: U.S. Department of Commerce, *Survey of Current Business*, March 1982, pp. 51–52.

THE UNITED STATES IN WORLD TRADE

The Volume of U.S. Trade

The U.S. share of world exports was about 15 percent in 1960. Although the U.S. *share* of world trade dropped to 11 percent by 1980, the *volume* of U.S. trade increased astonishingly. In real terms, the volume of merchandise exports from the United States has almost quadrupled over the past two decades, while the rest of the world has been running even faster. For example, Japan's merchandise exports rose between 1960 and 1979 by about 7 times in real terms.

Currently, the United States is still the world's largest exporting country but may not be for long. The United States exported $221 billion in 1980, while the second-largest exporting nation, West Germany, trailed at $192 billion. Table 1 shows the merchandise exports of the United States, Japan, France, Italy, the United Kingdom, West Germany, and Belgium/Luxembourg. These countries account for about half of world trade. Because of its size and diversity, the United States is less dependent on trade than any of these 6 countries, as the lower U.S. ratio of exports to GNP demonstrates.

U.S. Exports and Imports

Table 2 shows the principal commodity exports and imports of the United States in 1981. About 19 percent of American exports consist of agricultural goods, such as wheat, soybeans, corn, cotton, and tobacco. Chemicals, business machines and computers, and aircraft make up about 22 percent of total merchandise exports. Petroleum products dominate American imports. The American propensity to drive foreign cars, wear clothes made in Taiwan or shoes made in Italy or Brazil, and watch Japanese TV sets shows up in the heavy imports of consumer goods and automotive vehicles. These aggregate statistics hide the fact that the United States is almost entirely dependent on foreign suppliers for bananas, cocoa, coffee, diamonds, manganese, cobalt, nickel, natural rubber, tea, tin, natural silk, and spices.

The major trade partner of the United States is Canada, which bought 19 percent of U.S. exports

Figure 1
U.S. Merchandise Exports and Imports

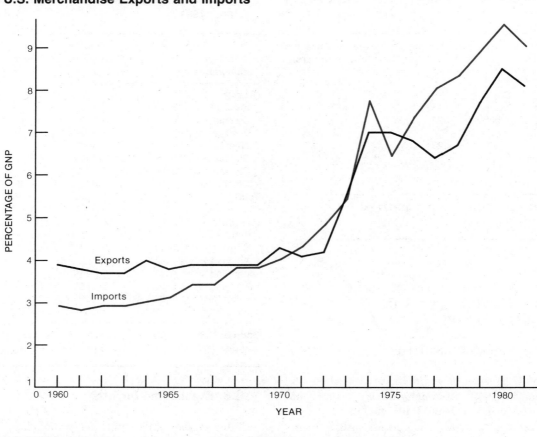

U.S. trade (exports and imports) as a percentage of GNP has increased since 1960.

Source: *Economic Report of the President, 1982; Survey of Current Business,* March 1982.

and supplied 18 percent of U.S. imports in 1981. Japan supplied 18 percent of U.S. imports and bought 9 percent of U.S. exports. Over one fourth of U.S. exports go to Western Europe; about one fifth of U.S. imports come from Western Europe.

Figure 1 shows how the U.S. involvement in foreign trade has increased from 1960 to 1981. In 1960, the United States exported about 4 percent of GNP, and imports were only 3 percent of GNP. In 1981, imports had grown to about 9 percent of GNP, and exports had risen to about 8 percent of GNP.

These increases are only partly due to America's growing dependence on foreign oil since the spectacular increases in oil prices beginning in the

early 1970s. The acceleration of imports as a percentage of GNP had already begun to rise in the late 1960s and early 1970s before the oil cartel was established. In 1981 nonpetroleum imports constituted more than 6 percent of GNP, which is double the rate of total merchandise imports in 1960. Thus, the benefits the U.S. enjoys from international trade have been increasing.

THE LAW OF COMPARATIVE ADVANTAGE

Chapter 3 showed how the **law of comparative advantage** could be used to explain the benefits people enjoy from specialization. Individuals are made better off by specializing and engaging in trade with other people. The law of comparative advantage can also help explain the gains from international specialization. Interpersonal trade and international trade are very similar because many of the individual traits of persons and nations cannot be transferred to other persons and nations. David Ricardo proved in 1817 that international specialization pays if each country devotes its resources to those activities in which it has a comparative advantage.

*The **law of comparative advantage** is that people or countries specialize in those activities in which they have the greatest advantage or the least disadvantage compared to other people or countries.*

Profound truths are sometimes difficult to discover; the real world is so complex it can hide their working. Ricardo's genius, aside from being a self-made millionaire, was that he was able to provide a simplified model of trade without the thousands of irrelevant details that cloud our vision. He considered a hypothetical world with only two countries and only two goods. The two ''countries'' could be America and Europe; the two goods could be food and clothing. For the sake of simplicity, assume also that:

1. labor is the only productive factor, and there is only one type of labor. (The assumption that labor is the only factor does not compromise the fact that resources are used to produce goods and services.)
2. labor cannot move between the two countries. This assumption reflects the relative international immobility of productive factors compared to goods.
3. the (labor) costs of production are constant. (*Constant costs* are present if the cost of producing each unit stays the same no matter how many units are produced.)
4. Laborers are indifferent between working in the food or clothing industries, provided only that wages are the same.
5. there is no unemployment. Each worker can produce food or clothing on his or her own without being attached to a firm that has capital.

Table 3

Hypothetical Labor Requirements for Producing One Unit of Food and Clothing

Country	Labor Required for 1 Unit of Food (worker hours)	Labor Required for 1 Unit of Clothing (worker hours)
America	1	3
Europe	6	6

Trade patterns depend on comparative and not absolute advantages. In our hypothetical example, America is 6 times more efficient than Europe in food production and twice as efficient in clothing production. America has an absolute advantage in both food and clothing but has only a comparative advantage in food production. Europe has an absolute disadvantage in both goods but has a comparative advantage in clothing production. Europe will export clothing to America in return for food, and both will gain by this pattern of trade. Each country exports the good in which it has the greatest efficiency advantage (in the case of America) or the smallest inefficiency disadvantage (in the case of Europe). America's opportunity cost of clothing production is 3 units of food; Europe's opportunity cost of clothing production is only 1 unit of food. Equivalently, each country exports the good for which it has the lowest opportunity cost of production compared to the rest of the world.

An immediate objection to all of these simplifications is that the assumptions remove a reason for protecting domestic industry from foreign competition. In the real world, foreign competition can throw people out of work in a particular domestic industry and idle fixed plant and equipment. This objection is well taken and will be addressed in Chapter 21 on protection and free trade.

Table 3 shows the hypothetical labor requirements for producing one unit each of food or clothing in each of the two hypothetical countries. America can produce a unit of food with 1 hour of labor and can produce a unit of clothing with 3 hours of labor. Europe can produce either a unit of food or a unit of clothing with 6 hours of labor. America is 6 times more efficient than Europe in food production (it requires only one sixth the labor to produce the same output); America is only twice as efficient in clothing production (it requires only one half the labor).

We have deliberately constructed a case where America has an **absolute advantage** over Europe in all lines of production.

> *A country has an **absolute advantage** in the production of a good if it uses fewer resources to produce a unit of the good than the rest of the world.*

Even under these circumstances, however, both countries stand to benefit from specialization and trade according to comparative advantage, as demonstrated below.

The Case of Self-Sufficiency

Assume that each country is initially self-sufficient and must consume only what it produced at home.

America. A self-sufficient America must produce both food and clothing. American workers must work 3 hours to obtain 1 unit of clothing or work 3 hours to obtain 3 units of food (see Table 3). Three units of food *(F)* will have the same value as 1 unit of clothing *(C)*, since these quantities use the same amount of labor. In other words, to acquire 1 unit of clothing, a worker must sacrifice 3 units of food.

America's opportunity cost of 1 unit of clothing is 3 units of food.

$$3F = 1C.$$

Under conditions of self-sufficiency the American price of a unit of clothing will be 3 times the price of a unit of food.

These same facts are shown in panel (a) of Figure 2. Panel (a) shows America's production-possibilities frontier. Labor is the only factor of production, and a total of 90 units of labor are assumed to be available to the American economy. America's production-possibilities frontier is a straight line because costs are constant in our example. If everyone worked in clothing production, 30 units of clothing could be produced. If everyone worked in food production 90 units of food could be produced. The economy would likely produce a mix of food and clothing to meet

domestic consumption. Such a combination could be point *x* where 45 units of food and 15 units of clothing are produced and consumed in America. Without trade, America consumes 45F and 15C, the combination of which reflects America's preferences.

Europe. In a self-sufficient Europe, workers must work 6 hours to produce 1 unit of food or 1 unit of clothing. A unit of clothing and food have the same labor costs and, hence, the same price. In other words, Europeans must give up 1 unit of food to get 1 unit of clothing.

Europe's opportunity cost of a unit of clothing is a unit of food:

$$1F = 1C$$

Panel (b) of Figure 2 shows Europe's production-possibilities frontier. In our example, Europe is more populous than the United States; it has 300 units of labor available. Europe has a straight-line production-possibilities frontier as well and can produce either 50 units of food, 50 units of clothing, or some combination of the two. A likely situation would be for Europe to produce and consume at a point such as *z*, where 30 units of food and 20 units of clothing are produced. Without trade, Europe can consume 30F and 20C.

Without trade, each country must consume on its production-possibilities frontier. To produce (and consume) more requires either a larger labor force or an increase in the efficiency of labor.

The World. If both Europe and America were self-sufficient the total amount of food and clothing produced would be the amount produced by America (45F and 15C) plus the amount produced by Europe (30F and 20C). Thus, the total amount of food produced would be 75 units (45F + 30F), and the total amount of clothing produced would be 35 units (15C + 20C).

The Case of International Trade

If trade opened up between Europe and America, an American trader would find that 1 unit of clothing sells for 1 unit of food in Europe but

Figure 2
American and European Production-Possibilities Frontiers

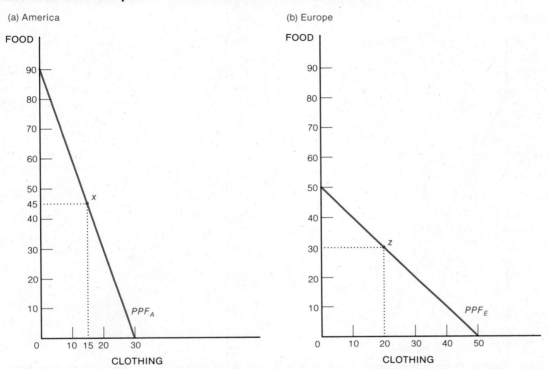

(a) America

(b) Europe

Panel (a) shows a hypothetical production-possibilities frontier for America. If 90 units of labor are available and labor is the only factor of production, America could either produce 30 units of clothing, 90 units of food, or some mixture of the two—such as point *x* where 45 units of food and 15 units of clothing are produced. Panel (b) shows a hypothetical *PPF* for Europe, where 300 units of labor are available. Europe could produce 50 units of clothing, 50 units of food, or a combination, such as *z*, where 30 units of food and 20 units of clothing are produced.

sells for 3 units of food in America. If the trader works only 1 hour in America and ships the resulting unit of food to Europe, he or she can obtain 1 unit of cloth more cheaply than by producing it at home! It makes no difference that clothing requires 6 hours of labor in Europe. What matters is that in Europe food requires 6 hours of labor as well and so food and clothing sell for the same price in Europe.

Americans would soon discover that clothing could be bought more cheaply in Europe than at home. Soon the law of supply and demand would do its work. Americans would stop producing clothing, to concentrate on food production and would begin to demand European clothing. This increased demand would drive up the price of European clothing. Europe would presumably shift from food production to clothing; eventually the

pressure of American demand would lead Europe to specialize completely in clothing production.

The end result would be that Americans would get clothing more cheaply (at less than 3*F* for 1*C*) than before trade; Europeans would receive a higher price for their clothing (at more than 1*F* for 1*C*).

In making decisions about trading, each country needs to know how much clothing is worth in terms of food, or the **terms of trade:**

*The **terms of trade** is the rate at which two products can be exchanged for each other between countries.*

The terms of trade between Europe and America will settle some place between America's and Europe's opportunity costs:

Figure 3
The Effects of Trade

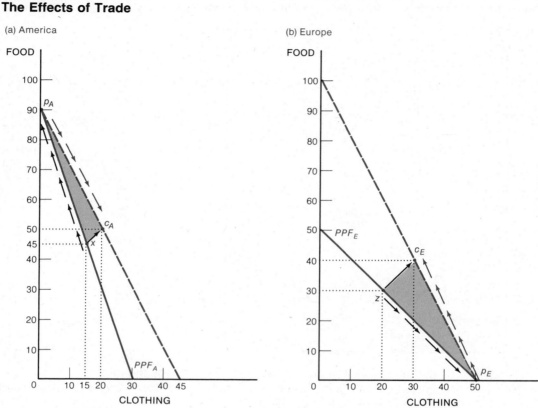

(a) America

(b) Europe

As shown in panel (a), before trade America produces and consumes at point x. When trade opens up at the terms of 2F = 1C (where F = units of food and C = units of clothing), America produces at p_A, specializing in food production, and trades 40 units of food for 20 units of clothing. America, therefore, consumes at point c_A, where it consumes 50 units of food and 20 units of clothing. Trade shifts American consumption from x to c_A. As shown in panel (b), before trade Europe produces and consumes at point z. When trade opens up, Europe shifts production to p_E, specializing in clothing production, and trades 20 units of clothing for 40 units of food. Europe, therefore, shifts consumption from z to point c_E, where 30 units of clothing and 40 units of food are consumed. In both panels, the black arrows show the effects of trade on domestic production, and the color arrows show the effects of trade on domestic consumption. Both countries consume somewhere on the dashed line above their original production-possibilities frontiers.

If America's opportunity cost of 1 unit of cloth is 3 units of food, and Europe's opportunity cost of 1 unit of cloth is 1 unit of food, the terms of trade will settle between 1C = 3F and 1C = 1F. Europe is willing to sell 1 unit of cloth for at least 1 unit of food; America is willing to pay no more than 3 units of food for 1 unit of cloth.

The cheap imports of clothing from Europe will drive down the price of clothing in America. When Europe exports clothing to America, the European price of clothing will rise.

Although the final equilibrium terms of trade cannnot be determined without knowing each

country's preferences, one can determine the range in which the terms of trade will settle. If the world terms of trade at which both Europe and America can trade are set by the market at 2F = 1C, Americans no longer have to work 3 hours for a unit of cloth (an American could work only 2 hours, obtain 2 units of food, and trade that food away for 1 unit of clothing), and Europeans no longer have to work 6 hours to acquire a unit of food (a European could work for 6 hours producing cloth and trade the resulting unit of cloth for two units of food).

When the terms of trade in the world are 2F

Table 4
The Effects of International Trade (F = unit of food; C = unit of clothing)

Country	Consumption and Production Before Trade (a)	Production After Trade (2)	Exports (3)	Imports (4)	Consumption After Trade (5)	Gains (6)
(a) America	45F	90F	40F	0F	50F	5F
	15C	0C	0C	20C	20C	5C
(b) Europe	30F	0F	0F	40F	40F	10F
	20C	50C	20C	0C	30C	10C
(c) World	75F	90F	—	—	90F	15F
	35C	50C	—	—	50C	15C

= $1C$, Americans will devote all their labor to food production, and Europeans will devote all their labor to clothing production. (If increasing rather than constant opportunity costs had been assumed, the two countries need not have been driven to such complete specialization.)

THE GAINS FROM TRADE

When American workers are specialized in food, and European workers are specialized in clothing, the gains to each may be measured by the labor saved. Americans before trade spent 1 hour on a unit of food and 3 hours on a unit of clothing. Now after trade, Americans still spend 1 hour on a unit of food but only 2 hours on a unit of clothing (with terms of trade $2F = 1C$). Europeans before trade spend 6 hours on a unit of food or clothing. After trade Europeans still spend 6 hours on a unit of clothing but only 3 hours on a unit of food (since only half of a unit of clothing trades for a unit of food).

The gains from trade are shown more dramatically in Figure 3. Before trade, America is at point x in panel (a), and Europe is at point z in panel (b). When trade opens up at the terms of trade $2F = 1C$, America moves its production to point p_A (specialization in food production), as the arrows show. Thus America increases its food production from 45 units to 90 units. America can now trade each unit of food for half of a unit of cloth. America trades 40 units of food for 20 units of clothing. Now America consumes at point c_A, with consumption at 50 units of food and 20 units of clothing. Trade enables America to consume

above its production-possibilities frontier. In this example, trade shifts consumption from x to c_A.

As column (1) of Table 4 shows, America produces $45F$ and $15C$ before trade. The opening of trade causes America to shift labor entirely out of C production. As column (2) shows, America produces only F ($90F$) after trade opens. Columns (3) and (4) describe America's trade: America keeps $50F$ for domestic consumption and sells $40F$ for $20C$. Column (5) shows consumption after trade and column (6) shows America's benefits from trade. As a result of trade, America can consume more of both products (5 more of each) than before trade.

Europe's story is told in panel (b) of Figure 3. Europe shifts production from z, where $30F$ and $20C$ are produced, to point p_E, where 50 units of clothing are produced. The terms of trade are $2F = 1C$; when Europe trades 20 units of clothing for 40 units of food, Europe's consumption shifts from z to c_E—which is above the original production-possibilities frontier. Europe is also better off. Row (b) of Table 4 tells the same story in simple arithmetic. Columns (3) and (4) show that Europe's trade is consistent with America's. For example, America exports $40F$ and Europe imports $40F$.

In this simple world, the benefits of trade are dramatic. America consumes 5 units more of both food and clothing; Europe consumes 10 units more of both food and clothing. Row (c) of Table 4 shows that the world increases its production of food by 15 units, or 20 percent (from 75 to 90 units), and increases its production of clothing by 15 units, or 43 percent (from 35 to 50 units). Everybody is made better off; nobody is hurt by trade in this case. In effect, trade has the same effect on consumption as an increase in national resources or an improvement in efficiency of resource use. As a consequence of trade, countries are able to consume beyond their original production-possibilities frontiers.

In the real world, imports of goods from abroad displace domestic production of competing goods, and in the process some people may find that their income falls. Since the Ricardian model assumes only one factor of production, the model simply cannot account for changes in the distribution of income. The model does demonstrate that in a world with many factors and shifts in distribution of income, trade increases average real income. Although trade makes the average person better off, some people are made even better off than the average while others are made worse off.

Small and Large Countries

If America began to grow due to some shift of population from Europe to America, America would want to buy more European clothing, and the supply of European clothing would tend to fall. To maintain equilibrium between the demand and supply for clothing in the world, the price of clothing would rise above the original $2F = 1C$ terms of trade. If America became so large that Europe could not satisfy its enormous demands for clothing, the terms of trade for Europe would have to rise all the way to $3F = 1C$—which is the exchange ratio America has under self-sufficiency. America gains from trade only when it can buy clothing at less than $3F = 1C$. When $3F = 1C$, a large enough America gains nothing from trade. The remaining Europeans, however, now find that exporting 1 unit of clothing brings them 3 food instead of only 2 food; Europeans are better off. When the small country trades at the large country's opportunity costs, it receives all the gains from trade. Thus, small countries tend to gain more from trade than large countries.

Some people argue that small countries cannot gain as much as the large countries from trade because they have less power. There is a germ of truth in this argument. Theoretically, it is possible for large countries to use trade restrictions, such as tariffs and quotas, to gobble up the trade gains of the small countries. But the facts speak otherwise. Small countries tend to restrict trade more than large countries. Both Mexico and Canada, America's smaller neighbors, restrict imports from the United States more than the United States restricts imports from them. The poor, uninformed resident of the small country loses. Ignorance of economics can be costly.

Low-Wage and High-Wage Countries

U.S. hourly wages are more than 3 times hourly Mexican wages. Hourly Japanese wages are about 4 times higher than hourly Korean wages. Yet the United States traditionally exports more to Mexico than it imports; Japan traditionally exports more to Korea than it imports. The law of comparative advantage explains how high-wage countries can compete with low-wage countries.

Table 3 showed that America is 6 times as productive in food and 2 times as productive in clothing production as Europe. Therefore, American wages should be between 6 and 2 times as high as European wages. When the world terms of trade are $2F = 1C$, the price of clothing is twice that of food. If the price of food is $3, and since 1 hour of labor produces 1 unit of food in America, wages in America must be $3 per hour.

If the price of clothing is $6, in Europe, and if 6 hours of labor are needed to produce 1 unit of clothing, the European wage rate must be $1 per hour. (Prices are measured in dollars to avoid currency differences.)

Reports that high-wage countries like the United States cannot possibly compete with low-wage countries like Taiwan or Korea are nonsense. Wages are higher in the United States because productivity is higher. Reports that people who live in low-wage countries cannot compete with high-productivity countries like the United States are also nonsense. When comparative advantage directs the allocation of resources, both high-wage and low-wage countries will share in the benefits of trade. The high-productivity country's wage rate will not be high enough to wipe out all the productivity advantage or low enough to undercut the low-productivity country's comparative advantage. Likewise, the low-productivity country's wage will not be high enough to make it impossible to sell goods to the rich country nor low enough to undercut the rich country's comparative advantage. Given the labor-cost data in Table 3, both countries will be able to show their comparative advantage to the world if American wages are no more than 6 times higher than European wages nor lower than twice as high as European wages.

American wages will be somewhere between 6 and 2 times as high as European wages. If American money wages were 7 times higher than European money wages, American money prices would be higher than European money prices for both food and clothing, since America's labor productivity advantage could not offset such a high wage disadvantage. This situation could not persist. The demand for American labor would dry up while the demand for European labor would rise. With American wages 7 times European wages, forces would be set into operation to reduce American wages and raise European wages until the ratio of American to European wages returned to a level between 6 and 2.

Differences in comparative costs are one reason for international trade. Two other reasons for trade are 1) decreasing costs, or economies of scale, and 2) differences in consumer preferences.

Economies of Scale

The discussion thus far assumed that food and clothing were produced under constant returns to scale. If America and Europe could produce food and clothing with the same labor costs but with **decreasing costs** as production increases (economies of scale), advantages of large-scale specialization would be gained if each product were produced by only one country.

Decreasing costs are present when each unit costs less to produce the more units are produced.

Good illustrations are the Japanese shipbuilding industry and the American commercial aircraft industry. Both of these industries are char-

acterized by economies of large-scale production. America's early start in the aircraft industry and Japan's in shipbuilding explain in part the current competitive advantage of each country. America is the dominant world exporter of commercial aircraft. Japan is the dominant world exporter of large cargo ships. Without economies of scale, the competitive advantage of each country would be smaller.

Preference Differences

If our two countries had identical labor costs but were subject to **increasing costs** of production, there would be no trade *unless consumer preferences in the two countries were different.*

Increasing costs are present when each unit costs more to produce the more units are produced.

If America's preference for clothing increased relative to Europe's preference for clothing in the absence of international trade, the relative price of clothing would increase in America compared to Europe. When trade is opened up, America will import clothing and export food!

For example, some Asian countries can produce rice easily because they have the necessary rainfall, but some of these countries actually import rice because of the enormous importance of rice in their diets. For example, Indonesia is a traditional rice importer and yet devotes about one third of its resources to agricultural output. The United States, which devotes less than 3 percent of its resources to agriculture, is a rice exporter. This rice trade is explained in part by preference differences.

U.S. COMPARATIVE ADVANTAGE

According to Swedish economist Bertil Ohlin, countries tend to export those goods that intensively use the abundant productive factors they are blessed with. The Ohlin theory is based on the relative abundance of different productive factors. For instance, if a country has a lot of labor relative to land or capital, its wages will tend to be lower than countries with abundant land or capi-

The Multinational Corporation

The multinational corporation has been the focus of more debate than most economic institutions. Some have considered its development to be a major event in economic history, on a par with the development of the steam engine or the automobile. Others consider it an engine of monopoly capital and a sinister agent of capitalistic imperialism. Thus the analysis of the multinational corporation is clouded by the polarization in the positions taken by different experts.

The multinational corporation (MNC) is an enterprise that has subsidiaries or branches in more than one country. The crucial element is that the MNC controls the decision-making processes of a business enterprise in a foreign country. More simply, it is a corporation that controls income-generating assets in more than one country. Thus the MNC engages in international production of goods and services, rather than simple exporting or importing.

Who are the MNCs? The largest 10 are Exxon, General Motors, Royal Dutch/Shell, Ford, Texaco, Mobil, Standard Oil, British Petroleum, Gulf Oil, and IBM. Of the 260 largest MNCs (in 1973), 126 were U.S. companies, 49 were British companies, 21 were West German companies, and 19 were French companies.

The Exxon Corporation—a multinational for 80 years—has 400 corporate entities operating in 100 countries. It is the world's largest industrial company. The name *Exxon* (chosen in 1972) even had to be selected by a computer in order to guarantee that the new name would not have an adverse connotation in one of the many languages of the world (to select the name itself cost $100 million!). That's big business.

The MNCs have been criticized on a broad front. Some think that a country whose economic structure is dominated by MNCs (e.g. Canada) loses some of its national sovereignty. MNCs, for example, might be able to escape domestic taxation (for valuable social programs) by simply shifting taxable profits from high-tax countries to low-tax countries *(tax havens)* by using creative ac-

tal. Even if technical know-how were the same across countries, labor-cheap countries would have a comparative advantage in the production of labor-intensive goods. While the Ricardian theory assumes only one factor and takes cost differences as given, the Ohlin theory explains comparative advantage as the consequence of differences in the relative abundance of different factors.

The United States has an abundance of two factors: fertile farm land and highly skilled, technical labor. The United States tends to export farm goods and goods that use highly skilled labor. The United States has a comparative advantage in manufactured goods that require intensive investment in research and development (R&D); industries with relatively high R&D expenditures contribute most to American export sales. Chemicals, nonelectrical or electrical machinery, aircraft, and professional and scientific instruments are the major R&D-intensive industries. In 1977, these industries generated a surplus of exports over imports of $28 billion. The manufacturing industries that were not in this category—like textiles or paper products, or food manufactures—generated a trade deficit (a surplus of imports over exports) of about $24 billion.

The products of R&D industries tend to be new products, which are nonstandardized and not well suited to simple, repetitive mass-production techniques. The older these products become, such as hand-held calculators, the more standardized the production process can become. The longer a given product has been on the market the easier it is for the good to become standardized and the smaller the need for highly trained workers. When new goods become old goods, other countries can gain a comparative advantage over the United States in these goods. The United States then moves on to the next new product generated with its giant research establishment

counting. Moreover, MNCs may even be able to neutralize domestic monetary policies by shifting funds abroad when home credit is easy and borrowing abroad when home credit is tight. Another basic criticism is that the MNCs exercise too much market power—exploiting consumers, workers, and the valuable natural resources of some small country.

Many also favor the rise in the MNC. The rise in the MNC in the last several decades has been accompanied by enormous increases in worldwide competition. But the most fundamental argument in favor of the MNC has been that it is an instrument of progress: it serves to diffuse technical and managerial know-how from rich countries to poor countries.

Do MNCs encourage trade along lines of comparative advantage and so promote world efficiency? No one really knows the answer to this question. On the one hand, it can be argued that since the MNCs operate on a worldwide basis they can—better than anyone else—produce out-

put in the least-cost locations, clearly enhancing world efficiency. On the other hand, it has been charged that sometimes MNCs use the wrong technology in the less developed countries. Moreover, trade may be distorted away from true comparative advantage by the creative accounting techniques employed by MNCs. These techniques involve pricing goods at less than cost in some locations and more than cost in other locations; this practice may distort trade.

It is difficult to evaluate the MNCs. People tend to line up on one side if they are sympathetic to big business and on the other side if they instinctively dislike big business, but the hard evidence is not clear-cut. ✄

Source: Neil Hood and Stephen Young, *The Economics of Multinational Enterprise* (New York: Longman, 1979).

and abundant supply of engineers, scientists, and skilled labor in order to fulfill its comparative advantage. It is the nature of U.S. comparative advantage in manufacturing to be in new products and processes.

This chapter studied the law of comparative advantage, the gains from trade, and the pattern of U.S. trade. The next chapter will examine the arguments for and against protection of American industries and the arguments for and against free trade.

Summary

1. Just as trade and specialization can increase the economic well-being of individuals, so

specialization and trade between countries can increase the economic well-being of the residents of the trading countries. The basic reason for trade is that countries cannot readily transfer their endowments of productive factors to other countries. Trade in goods and services acts as a substitute for the transfer of productive resources among countries. The Swedish economist, Bertil Ohlin, has demonstrated that countries specialize in those goods for which its factor proportions are most suited. In 1817, David Ricardo formulated the law of comparative advantage, which demonstrates that countries export according to comparative not absolute advantage. Countries export those goods in which they are most efficient, or least inefficient, compared to the rest of the world.

2. The United States is the world's largest exporting country, but trade as a percentage of

GNP is less in the United States than in most other countries.

3. In a simple two-country two-good world, even if one country has an absolute advantage in both goods, both countries can still gain by specialization and trade. If the two countries were denied the opportunity to trade, they would have to use domestic production to meet domestic consumption. With trade, specialization allows them to consume beyond their domestic production-possibilities frontiers by producing at home the product in which the country has comparative advantage and trading it. Countries will specialize in those products whose domestic opportunity costs are low relative to their opportunity costs in the other countries. Through trade, countries are able to exchange goods at more favorable terms than dictated by domestic opportunity costs.

4. Unless large countries use trade restrictions, small countries gain more from trade than do large countries. Money wages are set to reflect the average productivity of labor in each country. Higher average labor productivity will be reflected in higher wages. Money wages are not set in such a manner as to undercut each country's comparative advantage. Economies of scale and preference differences are also reasons for trade among countries.

5. The United States has an abundance of two factors: fertile farm land and highly skilled, technical labor. America's exports of agricultural products and high-technology research-and-development products are determined by the relative abundance of these two factors.

Key Terms

law of comparative advantage
absolute advantage

terms of trade
decreasing costs
increasing costs

Questions and Problems

1. The text quoted, with approval, Adam Smith's statement that "What is prudence in the conduct of every private family can scarce be folly in that of a great kingdom." Strictly speaking, a fallacy of composition is involved in Smith's famous remark. But when applied to international trade, what is true of the family is also true of the kingdom. Why does not the fallacy of composition apply?

2. Suppose that 4 units of labor are required to produce 1 unit of food in Asia and 8 units of labor are required to produce 1 unit of clothing in Asia. Also suppose that 10 units of labor are required to produce 1 unit of food in South America, while 40 units of labor are required to produce 1 unit of clothing in South America.
   a. Which country has an absolute advantage in food? In clothing?
   b. What is the relative cost of producing food in Asia? In South America?
   c. Which country will export food? Clothing?
   d. Draw the production-possibilities frontier for each country if Asia has 400 workers and South America has 800 workers.
   e. What is the range for the final terms of trade between the two countries?
   f. If the final terms of trade is 3 clothing for 1 food, compute the wage in Asia and the wage in South America on the assumption that a unit of food costs $40 and a unit of clothing $120.

3. What happens to the answers to parts a, b, and c of question 2 when the South American

labor figures are changed to 1 unit of labor for 1 unit of food and 4 units of labor for 1 unit of clothing?

4. In Congressional hearings, American producers of such goods as gloves and motorcycles claim they are the most efficient in the world but have been injured by domestic wages being too high compared to foreign wages. Without disputing the facts of their case, how would you evaluate their plight?

CHAPTER

21

Protection and Free Trade

Chapter Preview

This chapter examines the economics of trade barriers. When each country specializes and trades according to comparative advantage, each country can consume more than would be possible if it had to produce at home everything that it consumed. With **free trade,** a country can consume above its production-possibilities frontier.

> *Free trade is international trade unimpeded by artificial barriers such as tariffs (import taxes) or import quotas.*

Is it to a country's advantage to adopt complete free trade or is it to a country's advantage

to interpose some trade barriers between it and the rest of the world? This chapter discusses the nature of trade barriers, the case against protection, the arguments for trade barriers, and American trade policies.

TRADE BARRIERS

Tariffs

An import **tariff** raises the price paid by domestic consumers as well as the price received by domestic producers of similar or identical products.

> *A **tariff** is a tax levied on imports.*

A tariff on clothing from Taiwan will raise the prices paid by American consumers of clothing imports and the prices charged by American clothing producers.

Suppose a country levies a $1 tariff on imported shoes that cost $10 in the foreign market. If domestic and foreign shoes are the same, both imported and domestically produced shoes will sell for $11 in the home market. Because consumers will pay more for shoes than otherwise, the tariff discourages shoe consumption. Because the domestic producer of shoes will be able to charge more for shoes, the tariff encourages domestic production. The $1 tariff discourages shoe imports and foreign shoe production.

The same result (of discouraging shoe consumption and encouraging domestic production) could also be accomplished by taxing domestic consumption of shoes by $1 and giving every domestic firm a $1 subsidy per pair of shoes produced.

An import tariff has the same effect as a consumption tax plus a production subsidy.

Import Quotas

An **import quota** sets the number of units of a particular product that can be imported into the country during a specified period of time. U.S. import quotas on imported steel, for example, might specify the number of tons of steel of a specified grade that can be imported into the United States in a particular year.

*An **import quota** is a quantitative limitation on the amount of imports of a specific product during a given period.*

Generally speaking, importers of products that fall under quota restrictions must obtain an import license to import the good. By limiting the number of licenses issued to the number specified by the quota, the quantity of imports cannot exceed the maximum quota limit.

Import licenses can be distributed in a variety of ways. One option is for import licenses to be auctioned off by the government in a free and fair market. If import licenses are scarce (more importers want licenses than are available), they will sell for a price that reflects their scarcity. In such a case, an import license is similar to a tariff: it restricts imports and raises revenue for the government.

Import licenses may also be handed out on a first-come-first-served basis, on the basis of favoritism, or according to the amount of past imports by the importer. When import quotas are not auctioned off, the potential revenue that the government could collect goes to the lucky few importers who get the scarce import licenses. For this reason, some importers, especially those who are likely to obtain import licenses, prefer import quotas to tariffs. Instead of the government collecting the revenue, the importers can cash in on the scarcity value of the import licenses. The license permits them to buy a product cheaply in the world market and then to sell it at a handsome profit in the home market. For example, in May 1982, world sugar prices were about $0.08 a pound. The Reagan administration proposed a quota that would keep domestic sugar prices at about $0.20 a pound. The importers collect the difference! American consumers pay higher prices, and the government gains no revenues.

The scarcity value of import licenses accrues to the government if the licenses are auctioned in a free market but accrues to importers if licenses are allocated by a nonprice scheme.

Voluntary Export Quotas

A **voluntary export quota** is a popular trade barrier in use by the United States.

*A **voluntary export quota** is effected when the home government bargains with the foreign government to impose export quotas that will limit their exports over a specified period of time.*

Voluntary export quotas (or *orderly marketing arrangements*) are especially popular in the United States. The U.S. government has negotiated a number of voluntary export quotas with foreign governments that limit their volume of commodity exports to the U.S. market. Unlike tariffs or import quotas, voluntary export quotas do not generate any revenue for the importing country or its government. Instead, foreign exporters or the foreign government collect the scarcity value of the right to export to the huge American market.

Voluntary export restrictions are particularly widespread in textiles. An agreement among 29 countries restricts trade in textiles. The importing country induces the exporting country to impose export quotas under the threat of imposing tariff or import quotas. Under these quota agreements, not all those who wish to export textiles to the United States can do so. First, they must acquire scarce export licenses. The privilege to export textiles to the United States is a property right that can be bought and sold in several Asian countries. The voluntary export quotas imposed by Japan on automobile exports to the United States is another example. Under the U.S. threat of imposing an import quota, the Japanese government ordered its auto companies to voluntarily limit exports to the United States to 1.7 million units from April 1, 1981 to March 31, 1982. This figure is down 5 percent from the 1.8 million units the United States imported from Japan in 1980.

Over the last decade, animal feeds, brooms, color TV sets, cattle, cotton, crude petroleum, dairy products, fish, meat, peanuts, potatoes, sugar, candy, textiles, stainless steel flatware, steel, wheat and wheat flour, and automobiles have been subjected to import quotas or voluntary export quotas. According to C. Fred Bergsten, a Washington-based trade expert, "The U.S. now has an array of quotas and 'voluntary' export restraints that have an even greater price effect than tariffs."[1]

Like import tariffs, import quotas and voluntary export quotas limit the quantity of foreign goods available in the domestic market. Such nontariff barriers raise the price paid by domestic consumers and the price that can be charged by domestic producers on their import-competing products. Domestic producers benefit from quotas by being able to charge higher prices. The importer who receives a license to buy cheap imports gains, or, if licenses are auctioned, the government gains some revenues. The big loser from quotas is the consumer who must pay higher prices.

Other Nontariff Barriers

Import and voluntary export quotas are not the only nontariff barriers. Two other major impediments to trade are government procurement practices and technical standards. Governments tend to give preferential treatment to domestic producers when they purchase goods and services. Further, the free flow of products can be impeded by technical standards that imported products must meet. For example, imported cars must pass American pollution-control and safety standards; imported foods and drugs must meet U.S. food and drug standards. Recent agreements among the major trading nations indicate a desire to limit such nontariff barriers, but no agreements have been forthcoming on limiting import quotas or voluntary export quotas.

Tariffs and nontariff barriers raise costs to consumers and protect the domestic producers of import-competing products. The following discussion of the economics of protection will refer to tariffs, but tariff and nontariff barriers have similar effects.

THE CASE AGAINST PROTECTION

According to a recent study, 97 percent of economists agree that tariffs and quotas lower real income. Probably no other issue in economics commands so much support among economists.[2] Economists' enthusiasm for free trade has remained steadfast for more than 210 years.

The Costs of Protection

According to the law of comparative advantage, specialization benefits the country as a whole, while tariffs or quotas eliminate or reduce

1. C. Fred Bergsten, *The Cost of Import Restrictions to American Consumers* (New York: American Importers Association, 1972).

2. J. R. Kearl, et al., "A Confusion of Economists?" *American Economic Review* 69 (May 1979): 28–37.

Figure 1
Consumer Benefits from Lower Prices

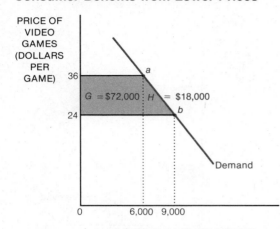

When the price falls from $36 to $24 per video game, consumers benefit by the area G + H. Those who would buy 6,000 units at $36 each (point a) benefit by area G because they save $12 per unit. Those new customers who buy the 3,000 additional units when the price is $24 (point b) benefit by area H.

Figure 2
Producer Benefits from Higher Prices

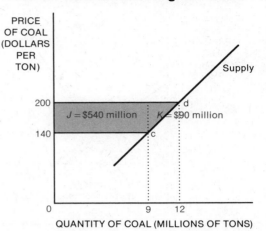

When the price rises from $140 to $200, producers benefit by the area J + K. Those who would sell 9 million tons at $140 per ton (point c) benefit by area J. Those new suppliers who sell 3 million additional tons when the price is $200 per ton (point d) benefit by area K.

those gains from specialization. The argument for free trade presented thus far has rested on the rather simple Ricardian model of the last chapter, which, for simplicity, ruled out the existence of different types of land, labor, and capital. In the real world, when trade opens, some people are hurt. The import of Japanese cars keeps domestic car prices lower than otherwise, which keeps car buyers happy but certainly hurts domestic auto producers. The export of American wheat keeps domestic prices of bread higher than otherwise but makes wheat farmers happy. The law of comparative advantage, however, guarantees that the *net* advantages are on the side of trade rather than protection.

Figure 1 shows why consumers benefit from lower prices. If the price of a Pac Man video game is $36, the demand curve in Figure 1 shows that 6,000 games are demanded. If the price of the game were to fall to $24, 9,000 games would be demanded. The gain to consumers of the lower price is the area G + H. The people who would have bought 6,000 units at $36 only have to pay $24 and, therefore, save $12 per unit. Their gain is $12 × 6,000 or $72,000 (area G). When the

price is $24, new customers come into the market who buy 3,000 additional video games. The average new customer would have been willing to pay $30 (the average of $36 and $24). Since new customers are paying only $24 per game, their gain is $6 × 3,000 or $18,000 (area H). Thus, if the price falls from $36 to $24 per game, consumers gain G + H. Conversely, if the price rises from $24 to $36, consumers lose G + H.

The demand curve in Figure 1 showed how consumers benefit from lower prices. Similarly, the supply curve in Figure 2 can show how producers benefit from higher prices. If the price of a ton of coal is $140, Figure 2 shows that at that price 9 million tons of coal would be supplied. If the price of coal were $200, 12 million tons would be supplied. The gain to producers from raising the price from $140 to $200 is the area J + K. Coal producers who would have supplied 9 million tons at a price of $140 receive $200 per ton (a $60 gain on each of the 9 million tons). Their gain is $60 × 9 million or $540 million (area J). When the price rises to $200 per ton, 3 million additional tons are produced. The average producer of this new coal would have been willing to receive $170 (the average of $200 and

Figure 3
The Costs of a Prohibitive Tariff

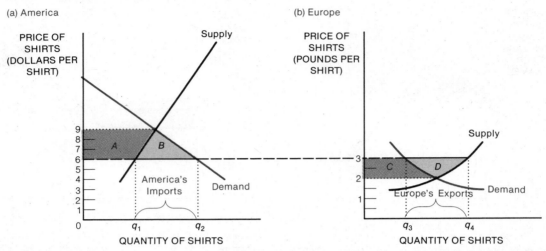

With a prohibitive tariff, the prices paid in each country are determined by the supply and demand curves in each country. To compare prices, we assume that $2 = £1. If there were no tariff, prices would be the same in the two countries. The prohibitive tariff in America raises the price in America from $6 to $9. Consumers lose area $A + B$, but producers gain area A. The net loss to America is area B. In Europe, prices fall from £3 to £2, and producers lose area $C + D$, while consumers gain C. The gain to consumers is less than the loss of producers. The net loss to Europe is area D.

$140) for a ton of coal. Since the new suppliers are in fact receiving $200, their gain is $30 × 3· million or $90 million (area K). Thus, if the price of a ton of coal rises from $140 to $200, producers gain $J + K$. Conversely, if the price falls from $200 to $140, producers lose $J + K$.

A Prohibitive Tariff. The costs of protection are easiest to understand by examining the effects of a **prohibitive tariff** (as opposed to a **nonprohibitive tariff**).

*A **prohibitive tariff** is a tariff that is high enough to cut off all imports of the product. A **nonprohibitive tariff** does not wipe out all imports of the product.*

Panel (a) of Figure 3 shows the hypothetical demand-and-supply situation in America for shirts; and panel (b) shows the hypothetical demand-and-supply situation in Europe for shirts. For each "country," the supply curve shows the quantity of shirts supplied by domestic producers at each price. The demand curve shows the quan-

tity demanded by domestic consumers at each price. For simplicity, we will assume that American and European shirts are the same and that the European currency is the pound, where $2 equals £1. For simplicity, we will also assume that Europe and America are the only countries in the world economy.

Using these simple assumptions, one can determine the gains to trade in shirts. With free trade, the price of shirts would be the same in America and Europe. If prices were different, importers would buy in the cheap market and sell in the dear market until prices were equalized. In our example, the price in America would be $6 (in Europe £3). America is importing shirts from Europe. America's excess of consumption over production (imports) is just matched by Europe's excess of production over consumption (exports).

Suppose America imposed a prohibitive tariff on shirt imports high enough to cut off all shirt imports. Without any trade, the prices in the two countries would diverge; they would be determined exclusively by domestic supply and demand conditions. Europe's price of shirts would be £2 (or the equivalent of $4) and America's price would be $9 (or the equivalent of £4.5).

Without trade, the difference between American and European shirt prices is $5. Thus, if America imposed a tariff exceeding $5, the incentive to trade would be wiped out because imported shirts would cost more than the domestic price ($4 plus the tariff of more than $5).

As demonstrated earlier, the increase in price from $6 (with trade) to $9 (with a prohibitive tariff) would result in consumers losing the shaded areas $A + B$. America's shirt consumers lose, but American producers gain, as a consequence of higher prices. The producers of shirts in America would gain area A. In panel (a) of Figure 3, the cost of tariff protection to consumers $(A + B)$ exceeds the gains to producers (A). The net cost of tariff protection to the whole American economy is area B.

Europe also loses from a prohibitive tariff, as shown in panel (b). With free trade, Europe's price of shirts is £3 (or $6). A prohibitive tariff eliminates exports, and the European price must equate domestic supply with domestic demand. If Europe cannot export shirts, the price of its shirts must be £2. The prohibitive American tariff hurts European shirt producers by the area $C + D$ but benefits European shirt consumers by area C. The gain to consumers (C) is less than the loss to producers $(C + D)$. Thus, Europe suffers a net loss of area D.

A Nonprohibitive Tariff. As just demonstrated, a prohibitive tariff causes losses in both the exporting and importing countries. Nonprohibitive tariffs, however, do not eliminate imports entirely. Figure 4 shows the supply and demand conditions in a country whose imports of a particular good are so small relative to the world supply that the world price (p_w) is taken as given. The amount imported by this country will not affect the world price.[3]

With a zero tariff, consumers can purchase all they want at the prevailing world price, p_w. According to Figure 4, the quantity represented by

---

3.   Note that this assumption is not satisfied in Figure 3: there are only two countries, and the amount of shirts imported by America affects the world price of shirts.

Figure 4
The Effects of a Nonprohibitive Tariff

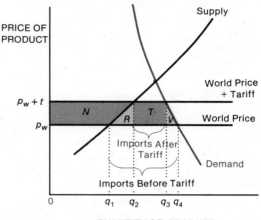

Before the nonprohibitive tariff, the price of the product is p_w. The tariff raises the price to $p_w + t$; that is, the world price plus the amount of the duty. Consumers lose area $N + R + T + V$. Producers gain N. The government gains the tariff revenue T, which equals the tariff per unit times the quantity of imports. The net loss is $R + V$. The tariff lowers imports from $(q_4 - q_1)$ to $(q_3 - q_2)$

---

the distance between q_1 and q_4 would be imported because this quantity is the difference between the quantity demanded at p_w and the quantity supplied by domestic producers.

When a tariff (t) is imposed, the price rises to $p_w + t$; the new domestic price equals the world price plus the tariff rate. The country now imports only that quantity represented by the distance between q_2 and q_3.

The tariff benefits domestic producers by the area N. The government (or public) benefits by area T—which equals the revenue from the tariff (the tariff rate times the quantity of imports). The loss to consumers from the increase in price is the sum of areas $N + R + T + V$. If the gains (area $N + T$) are subtracted from the losses (area $N + R + T + V$), the nonprohibitive tariff imposes a net loss to the country of area $R + V$.

This net loss is an underestimate, according to economists Gordon Tullock and Anne Krueger. Tullock and Krueger argue that because producers have an incentive to expend resources to get the tariff passed, the import-competing industry may form a committee, lobby Congress, or advertise the plight of its industry. When the color-TV industry was hurt by imports, the industry formed COMPACT (the Committee to Preserve American Color Television). Such expenditures reduce gains to protected producers and, thus, increase the costs of protection.

Exports Pay for Imports

Exports subtract from domestic consumption; imports add to domestic consumption. The gains from trade consist of imported goods that can be gained cheaper by importing them than by producing them at home.

From 1970 to 1981 the United States exported goods and services worth $2,209.2 billion and imported $2,140.4 billion worth of goods and services. Over the past decade, the United States exported a scant 3 percent more than it imported in goods and services. The close correspondance is no accident. In the long run, exports must pay for imports. Chapter 20 described a simple world where America trades only with Europe and simply ships food in return for clothing. In this case, American exports of food are paying for clothing imports from Europe. The more America exports food the more clothing imports are brought in, and vice versa. The reason exports of goods and services must pay for imports of goods and services is that, in the long run, countries want each other's goods, not each other's money.

If the United States, or any country, restricts imports it necessarily restricts exports. In other words, subsidizing import-competing industries by means of tariff or nontariff barriers penalizes a whole host of unseen export industries. Imports can be more visible than exports.[4]

If tariffs impose a cost on the community, why do they exist? Why would a representative democracy, which is supposed to represent consumer interests, establish trade barriers that impose greater costs than benefits on the community?

The explanation for tariffs is that the costs imposed by a tariff are highly diffused among millions of people, while the (smaller) benefits are concentrated among specific sectors of the economy associated with the protected industry. The costs imposed on the community are large in total but so small per person that it is not worth the trouble to any one person to join a committee to fight tariffs on each and every imported good, while the benefits to protected sectors are well worth the costs of lobbying. For example, assume people devote about 0.5 percent of all consumption to sugar (in all its various forms). A trade barrier that raises the price of sugar by 50 percent helps domestic sugar producers enormously, but it raises the cost of living to consumers by only 0.25 percent (50 percent of 0.5 percent). To the consumer, this cost is just too small to worry about. The costs of fighting against each request for protection are prohibitive.

The people who would have an incentive to lobby Congress heavily would be the foreign competitors of the domestic import-competing industry seeking protection. But these foreign competitors have comparatively little political clout in the United States.

PROTECTIONIST ARGUMENTS

Unfair Foreign Competition

The economy gains from foreign trade because it can obtain imports cheaper from abroad than by making them at home. The domestic producers of goods that are close or perfect substitutes for these imports try to convince their governments, and others, that such competition is unfair. This argument takes many forms and is probably the most widely used protectionist argument.

Low Foreign Wages. According to the theory of comparative advantage, high-wage countries will be able to export to or compete effectively against low-wage countries in those industries in which their productivity advantage more than offsets their wage disadvantage. Like-

---

4. One of the authors was once on a flight to Europe to sell his services to a foreign university for a short time (exporting). Sitting next to him was an engineer off to Europe to sell his engineering talents. Even the Boeing 747 was an export to the foreign airline. The engineer fretted that the United States "can't export anything and imports too much." The author decided it was better to have a pleasant trip than win a debating point!

wise, low-wage countries will be able to export to or compete effectively against high-productivity countries in those industries in which their wage advantage more than offsets their productivity disadvantage (see Chapter 20). The industries in the high-wage country that can export are the industries in which the country has a comparative advantage. The industries in the high-wage country that cannot compete, due to their low productivity advantage, are the industries in which the high-wage country has a comparative disadvantage. Moreover, every country will have industries in which it has a comparative advantage and industries in which it has a comparative disadvantage. If one country could undercut every other country in every good, its wages (relative to the rest of the world) would be bid up until the country would begin to import.

The industries in the advanced countries that cannot compete complain that they are subjected to unfair competition because of the low wages abroad. Some years ago during a House Committee hearing, Representative Noah Mason observed:

> We have just listened to the American Knit Handwear Association and the America Seafood Association and the Harley-Davidson Motorcycle Co. representative, and all three state that they represent an industry that is most efficient in the world, as compared to the industries abroad. But they all three stated that they are being injured because of imports from abroad . . . because . . . of low wages there, high wages here.
>
> If our people are to compete against the people of the other countries then we have got to cut our wages in half.

To some business managers and politicians, it seems unfair to be more efficient on a productivity basis and yet be unable to compete because wages are too high. If the above view were sound, it would be necessary to erect trade barriers so that all of the industries in which the United States had a comparative disadvantage could supply the home market. The erection of such barriers, however, would destroy U.S. export trade and would severely lower the real income of the American people. One could argue that it is unfair to erect trade barriers that would raise the incomes of those hurt by import compe-

tition but would lower the incomes of the rest of the community even more. This trade-off is illustrated by the theory of comparative advantage.

Dumping. Another version of the complaint that foreign competition is unfair alleges that foreign goods are "dumped" on the home market at a cost less than the foreign cost.

The **dumping** complaint is even enshrined in law. The U.S. Tariff Act of 1930, as amended by the Trade Agreements Act of 1979, provides for special antidumping duties to be imposed when foreign goods are sold in the home market for less than the price they would fetch in the foreign market. The original Anti-Dumping Law was passed in 1921.

Dumping occurs when a country sells a good in another country at a price less than the price of the home country.

Public attitudes towards dumping are peculiar. As Charles P. Kindleberger has pointed out, most people appear to have a subconscious producer's bias, which leads them to applaud antidumping actions. When dumping occurs, however, domestic consumers are buying goods more cheaply than foreign consumers. The beneficiaries are the domestic consumers, and the losers are the domestic firms competing with the dumped products. The theory of comparative advantage points out that the advantage of foreign trade is that a country (as a whole) is made better off if it can obtain goods more cheaply abroad than at home; the cheaper the foreign goods the greater the consumer benefit.

International trade economists are suspicious of antidumping laws. The case against them has been made by Charles Kindleberger:

> Countervailing measures against alleged dumping are obnoxious because they reduce the flexibility and elasticity of international markets and reduce the potential gain from trade. From 1846 to 1913, when Britain followed a free-trade policy, distress goods in any part of the world could be disposed of in London . . . to the benefit of the British consumer and the overseas producer. With anitdumping tariffs everywhere, adjustment after miscalculations

Example 1

The U.S. Countervailing-Duty Statute and the Law of Comparative Advantage

The U.S. has had a *countervailing-duty statute* since the late 1890s. Such a statute requires a countervailing duty if a foreign government subsidizes its exports to the United States. The current countervailing-duty code passed in 1979 is an example of how an understanding of the law of comparative advantage helped to frame a better statute.

For many years the United States had a countervailing-duty code that caused two basic conflicts with the code approved by European countries and GATT (the General Agreement on Tariffs and Trade). The first conflict was that the United States did not have an "injury test" included in its code. Hence, even if a foreign export subsidy did not do serious harm to a domestic industry, the United States was still bound to impose a counter-

vailing duty. This provision, of course, conflicts seriously with the law of comparative advantage. When the foreign government subsidizes exports to the United States, the United States benefits. The next best thing to no countervailing duties is to have an injury test, which reduces the range of application of the countervailing-duty statute. The Trade Agreements Act of 1979 included an injury test in the new code. Now significant injury to domestic industry must be demonstrated before a countervailing duty can be imposed.

The second conflict in the old U.S. code was its failure to distinguish between pure export subsidies and rebates of sales or value-added taxes levied on foreign exporters. A typical European firm pays a *value-added tax (VAT)* on the value of the labor, land, and capital used in the business.

---

which result in overproduction is much less readily effected.[5]

The only time antidumping duties might be appropriate is in the case of predatory dumping, where the foreign firm monopolizes the domestic market by temporarily lowering prices and then raising them to an even higher level after the domestic competitors have been driven out of business. Whether such cases have been documented or not is beside the point. What is important is that such activities are already prohibited by the U.S. Tariff Act of 1930 (section 337). The Anti-Dumping Code need not be invoked in such cases.[6]

Foreign Export Subsidies. One of the most important arguments for protection in today's

5. Charles P. Kindleberger, *International Economics,* 5th ed. (Homewood: Richard D. Irwin, 1973), p. 156.

6. The U.S. Tariff Act appears to provide protection against this type of dumping practice. In 1979, the International Trade Commission completed 19 investigations of cases involving complex patent infringement and antitrust issues under section 337. The commission found violations in eight of these cases. For accounts of these cases, see the *Annual Report of United States International Trade Commission,* 1979 (Washington, D.C.: Superintendent of Documents).

world is similar to the dumping complaint, but the "dumping" is caused by the actions of a foreign government rather than the actions of a foreign firm. Business managers who must compete against foreign imports argue that if a foreign government provides export subsidies to their exporters, then they face unfair competition. This argument, like the dumping argument, is supported by the U.S. countervailing-duty statute.

When a foreign government subsidizes exports to, say, the United States, the ultimate beneficiaries are the American people. The losers are the residents of the foreign country and the special interests in the United States that produce domestic import substitutes. Textiles from Argentina, radial tires from Canada, sugar from the European Economic Community, molasses from France, tomato products from Greece, refrigerators from Italy, and chains from Spain are all actual examples of goods exported to the United States that have received governmental subsidies. Even the United States, which has a solid comparative advantage in commercial aircraft, subsidizes the export of aircraft through below-market loans to the Boeing and McDonnell-Douglas corporations.

Those who desire protection from subsidized foreign exports have a powerful political argu-

If the firm exports goods to another country, the value-added tax is rebated. Many argued, incorrectly, that American firms were handicapped in world trade because the corporate income tax was not rebated to American exporters.

This argument conflicts with the theory of international trade because exports pay for imports. Import restrictions ultimately restrict exports. Export encouragements ultimately encourage imports. Restricting imports by a 10 percent tax can be offset by encouraging exports by a 10 percent subsidy. The European VAT tax applies to Europe's imports. Thus, a European country imposes extra duties on imports that correspond to the VAT on that category of goods. The extra import duties restrict trade away from the European comparative advantage. To offset the VAT on imports, the European countries use an export subsidy equal to the VAT on the category of goods being exported. This export subsidy encourages trade. As the outstanding economists who advised the European Common Market countries had perceived, a general export subsidy of x percent merely offsets a general import duty of x percent. Except for the short-term impact on exchange rates, the European export subsidies and added import duties (called *border tax adjustments*) have little influence on Europe's trade with the rest of the world.

The new U.S. code distinguishes between price export subsidies and rebates of sales or VAT taxes—an important improvement over the old law.

ment, but there is no economic argument for countervailing duties. The benefit of foreign trade is imports; the opportunity cost of foreign trade is exports. Protectionists reason that exports are good and imports are bad. This reasoning is true for the businesses that must compete with foreign imports but not for the economy as a whole. Foreign export subsidies are a gift to the American people. To offset this gift by imposing countervailing duties is a perverse policy—like the dog biting the hand that feeds it.

The Infant-Industry Argument

Alexander Hamilton, the first U.S. Secretary of the Treasury, argued that the ''infant'' or new industries of newly developing economies need protection in their initial stages. This Hamiltonian argument is repeated today by many economists and politicians interested in accelerating the economic development of nonindustrialized countries. There are two versions of the infant-industry argument. One version is difficult to defend in terms of economic theory; the other makes more sense.

The most frequently encountered infant-industry argument amounts to a disguised brand of simple protectionism. It is argued that in many industries economies of scale are present and that an initial stage of learning by doing is necessary to make the plant competitive on an international basis. A small, new plant must face higher costs than its foreign rivals because the rivals are larger and have been in the business a long time. Hence, some argue that it is necessary to protect new industries until they can stand on their own feet.

This argument ignores the fact that in virtually every business enterprise the first few years of activity are characterized by losses. Until businesses become known externally, until a competent staff is acquired, and until early production difficulties are overcome, it is difficult to make a profit. Most successful businesses are characterized by losses in the first few years and profits thereafter. To wait five or ten years or even more for a business venture to pay off is not unusual in business. Capital markets allow business firms to borrow the funds from lenders or venture capitalists to finance their investments. If these investments paid profits from the beginning, it would not be necessary to borrow.

To argue that the government must protect an industry from foreign competition implies that the private market has failed to see the profit oppor-

Example 2

Japan's Automobile Industry: A Successful Infant Industry?

Japan's automobile industry illustrates that a government can be involved in the development of an export industry. In 1979 Japan produced more than 6 million automobiles and exported more than half of them (1.5 million cars went to the United States). Japan imported only 65,000 autos. The industry grew from zero after World War II to its present lofty position in the world automobile industry.

When Japan started producing automobiles after World War II, the Governor of the Bank of Japan felt that Japanese cars were uncomfortable and that Japan should specialize in truck production. Hence, the early development of the Japanese passenger car industry had to begin without government assistance. The highly creative Japanese automotive entrepreneurs and engineers did not have the initial backing of the government. By 1951, however, there were signs that Japan could produce a competitive automobile without long-run government assistance. The Ministry of International Trade and Industry (MITI) met with the four Japanese motor vehicle manufacturers (Toyota, Nissan, Isuzu, and Prince) to make arrangements for encouraging the fledging infant industry. The Japanese government granted temporary quota and tariff protection to the automobile industry. Japanese automobile manufacturers were protected in the domestic market from foreign competition. The industry received small but direct financial assistance in the form of government loans financing about 9 percent of the industry's investments during 1951–1955. By the 1960s, the Japanese automobile industry had demonstrated its ability to stand on its own feet. Protection was no longer required. Quotas were lifted in 1965; Japan lowered its tariffs unilaterally to 10 percent in 1971 and abolished all duties in 1978. In addition, the government guaranteed the licensing agreements between Japanese producers and foreign

---

tunities in the infant industry. Given the way information is distributed in this world the argument is highly improbable. Information is costly to acquire. Those who are most likely to have information are those who would benefit the most from it. Thus, it is very unlikely that a government bureaucracy or a House committee would have more valuable information about the future course of profits in an industry than potential investors.

Economists Leland Yeager and David Tuerck have found that historically new industries do not need protection:

> Manufacture of iron, hats, and other goods got a foothold in Colonial America despite British attempts at suppression. Manufacture of textiles, shoes, steel, machine tools, airplanes, and countless other goods has arisen and flourished in the American West and South despite competition under internal free trade with the established industries of the Northeast.[7]

7. Leland B. Yeager and David G. Tuerck, *Trade Policy and the Price System* (Scranton, Pa.: International Textbook Company, 1966). This excellent book contains almost all the arguments pro and con for free trade but is strongly opposed to protection.

Another version of the infant-industry argument is that a particular industry may yield external benefits to the rest of the community for a certain period of time. These external benefits cannot be captured by the initial investors and, thus, will not be included in private profitability calculations. A new firm might have to adapt from foreign to local conditions. The knowledge it acquires about new technology would not be patentable and later users could take full advantage of their experience. The knowledge acquired by the one firm could be used by all; hence, public action in the form of protection may be called for to promote this activity.

Robert Baldwin of the University of Wisconsin has pointed out that even this reason for supporting an infant industry does not justify import duties. Baldwin argues that even if external benefits are present, a tariff does not guarantee that the most desirable type of knowledge-acquisition expenditures will be made. It may be better to subsidize firms who make the initial contacts or first acquire the knowledge to use new technology.

Another reason why tariffs are a poor device for subsidizing an industry is that tariffs raise

producers on the use of foreign or imported technology.

Three remaining nontariff barriers discourage the export of U.S.-made cars to Japan:

1. Japan imposes a 15 percent commodity tax on small (Japanese style) cars and a higher 20 percent tax on large cars (such as most U.S. cars). This tax is used to finance road construction in Japan. A 5 percent extra tax on large cars is hardly protective, since the way the tax is imposed raises the price of large cars by only 2.5 percent.

2. The modification of U.S. automobiles that is necessary in order to meet Japanese pollution and safety standards is a second nontariff barrier. These costs add 4 or 5 percent to the price of a car. The modifications include exhaust temperature alarms, overspeed warning devices, and head restraints.

3. The most important nontariff barrier is the cost of distributing a car in Japan. It is estimated that these costs are 20 percent higher than the distribution costs in the United States for a subcompact and about 40 percent higher for a compact. A compact U.S. car that retailed in the United States for $6,600 would sell in Japan for $12,000, with distribution costs accounting for $3,300 of the difference! Why distribution costs are higher in Japan is not known. Whether they result from the absence of competition, the necessity of providing better service, or some combination is not known with certainty.

It should finally be remembered that U.S. cars sold in Japan are usually purchased by the rich. U.S. auto manufacturers have not produced a car that the average Japanese person wants. Indeed, the United States ships cars to Japan with standard left-hand drive while all Japanese cars are equipped with right-hand drive. Japan, of course, adapts its cars to U.S. standards *before* shipping them to this country. ⌧

---

costs to consumers. Hence, if it is desirable to stimulate some industries, a direct subsidy that can be easily measured and does not lead to higher costs to consumers would be the preferred option.

Economists, however, do not adamantly oppose protection of infant industries if it is temporary and carried out in selected circumstances where it is apparent that a country has a long-run comparative advantage (see Example 2).

Keeping Money in the Country

Some protectionist arguments are grossly false. The first is one attributed (perhaps falsely) to Abraham Lincoln: "I don't know much about the tariff. But I do know that when I buy a coat from England, I have the coat and England has the money. But when I buy a coat in America, I have the coat and America has the money."

While this argument is appealing at first glance, it contains an error in logic. It supposes that money is somehow more valuable than goods. This *mercantilist fallacy* was committed by the mercantilist writers of the 17th and 18th centuries who feared that unrestricted trade would lead to the loss of gold. Writers such as David Hume and Adam Smith pointed out that this argument confuses ends with means. The end of economic activity is consumption; money is only a means to that end. When England sells an American a coat, the money is eventually used to buy, say, American wheat. The cost is the wheat, not the money.[8]

Saving Domestic Jobs

Another false protectionist argument is that imports deprive Americans of jobs: "The American

---

8. Under the existing international monetary system, trade imbalances do not even lead to the loss of money (currency) to other countries. The "prices" of foreign currencies are set in foreign-exchange markets, where the supply and demand for each currency is equated. A foreign currency is demanded to pay for goods purchased from the foreign country. No actual money crosses foreign borders. Transactions in each country must be carried out in that country's currency, not in the currency of another country. When one hears of the "loss of money abroad," the reference usually is to foreign loans, which are a different matter entirely.

market is the greatest in the world, and necessarily it should be reserved for American producers . . .," we hear from a 1952 Senate speech. An American Senator once explained the mysterious mechanism by which foreign imports cause unemployment:

> The importation of . . . foreign beef is not a stimulant to our economy. For foreign producers do not employ American labor; they do not buy our feed grain and fertilizers; they do not use our slaughterhouses; they do not use our truckers; they do not invest in or borrow from our banks; they do not buy our insurance; they do very little to stimulate the national economy.[9]

As already demonstrated, if each country specializes according to its comparative advantage, every country has more real GNP. The presumption the above senators make is that when a job is lost through import competition, a job is lost forever to the economy—which is simply untrue.

In the long run, a country must export in order to import. Jobs destroyed by competition from imports are eventually restored by increased exports. Foreign trade increases economic efficiency. In the long run, import barriers simply make it costlier to purchase the goods and services. The enormous efficiency changes over the last century did not result in permanent unemployment but rather in a higher standard of living for all. Trade according to comparative advantage raises economic efficiency. A country would not benefit by forgoing long-term efficiency gains for short-term reductions in unemployment.

NONPROTECTIONIST ARGUMENTS FOR TARIFFS

Protectionists argue that tariffs should be used to benefit certain special interests (at the public expense). Four arguments for tariffs are not protectionist in nature.

The National-Defense Argument

An industry that is essential to the national defense presumably should be subsidized to encour-

---

9. The quotes in this section come from Yeager and Tuerck, *Trade Policy and the Price System.*

age it to produce at a prudent level for the public safety. Although this argument does make some sense, it is not entirely applicable to the United States. A look at the comparative advantage of the United States reveals that the manufacturing industries in which the United States excells—chemicals, machinery, transportation equipment, aircraft—are the same ones that would be important in times of war. Significant exceptions to this, perhaps, are shipbuilding, which the United States does subsidize, and steel. The industries that for the most part would gain from protection—such as handbags, pottery, flatware, fish, nuts, cheese, cherries, hats, furs, pianos, toys, TV sets, and so forth—are not essential to a defense effort.

In some cases, protection even appears contrary to defense interests. Consider oil imports. The United States protected domestic oil by a tariff from the 1950s to the early 1970s. One could argue that it would be better to import foreign oil, save domestic oil reserves, and follow a policy of stockpiling imported oil in the case of war. The U.S. policy instead used up American oil.

Many industries that have little to do with national defense have used the national-defense argument as a rationale for protection. These industries are, to name but a few, gloves, pens, pottery, peanuts, paper, candles, thumbtacks, pencils, lacemaking, tuna fishing, and even clothespins.

If an industry is deemed essential for the national defense, a better way of obtaining more peacetime production by that industry is the domestic-production subsidy. Such subsidies could be handed out by the Department of Defense, where the experts on defense presumably reside. As noted, a tariff has the same effect as the combination of a production subsidy and a consumption tax. A direct subsidy is almost always better than a tariff since the tariff also raises the cost of living of consumers.

The Terms-of-Trade Argument

International economists have long recognized that it is logically possible for a country to raise tariffs and, so, shift the terms of trade to raise the country's real income. If a country imports widgets under free trade at a price of $10 a widget and this country is a major importer of widgets, the less the country imports, the lower the world price. In the extreme case, a $1 tariff might drive down the world price of widgets from $10 to $9. The country's consumers would still pay a $10 price for widgets, but the country could then import them for $9 and fill the national treasury with the tariff revenues, benefiting the entire country.

A famous turn-of-the-century British economist, Francis Edgeworth, warned that the terms-of-trade argument is like a bottle of poison: one should always label it *DANGER*. The argument presupposes that the rest of the world cannot retaliate. Very special circumstances would have to be present for one country to be able to beat down everybody else's terms of trade by tariffs while the rest of the world could not respond. Once the possibility of retailiation is present, countries that try to use this policy might simply start a tariff war that would result in everybody being made worse off.

The Diversification Argument

An argument closely related to the infant-industry argument is that free trade may lead an economy to specialize too much and expose it to the risks of putting all of its eggs in one basket. When an economy is highly dependent on only one export good—such as Ghana on cocoa, Bolivia on tin, and Colombia on coffee—the fortunes of the country wax and wane with the price of the main export good. Such cyclical fluctuations in raw material prices allegedly impose hardships on the specialized economy.

Dr. Raul Prebisch, a well-known Latin American economist, has argued that if such countries impose tariffs to protect their domestic industry, this protection would permit them to diversify their industrial base. The greater the range of goods produced, the less risk imposed on the economy by price changes.

One seldom hears this argument in fair weather, only in foul. No one questioned the wisdom of the oil-exporting countries' specialization in oil. Kuwait is heavily dependent on oil exports and is the richest country in the world (on a per capita basis) because of this specialization. When prices are going up, the diversification theorists remain strangely quiet. Private investors find it

profitable to invest in the goods that promise to bring the highest return. In nondiversified economies, investors have concluded that only a few goods are worthy of their attention. To conclude that diversification should be forced by government policy is sound only if the policy maker has more information about the future of an economy than private investors. It is difficult to determine which industries will be profitable in the future. If one industry is risky and another is not so risky, private investors will demand a risk premium in the risky industry—such as copper in Chile, cocoa in Ghana. Only if governments can make better decisions than investors about future comparative advantage can a case be made for deliberate diversification.

The Tariffs-for-Revenue Argument

Tariffs provide protection and raise government revenue. The two goals are partly in conflict. A perfect protectionist tariff would eliminate trade entirely and, so, would eliminate tariff revenue!

A nonprohibitive tariff does raise government revenue. Tariffs are not an important source of revenue in the United States (slightly more than 1 percent of the Federal government's revenue), but in some countries tariff revenue is significant. Indeed, 19th-century America relied heavily on tariff revenues.

A revenue tariff has special justification if it is difficult for a country to raise revenues in other ways. In a poor country where tax avoidance and nonmarket transactions restrict the amount of revenue yielded by income taxes, the government may be forced to collect its revenues by imposing taxes on traded goods. Customs officers located in airports and ports may be able to collect tax revenue to pay for roads, education, and other public goods. Under these circumstances, a tariff probably has greater justification than in any other case.

U.S. TRADE POLICIES

The tariff history of the United States is shown in Figure 5, which shows that tariffs have fluctuated up and down with the ebb and flow of protectionism in the U.S. Congress. In modern

Figure 5
Average Import Duties, 1821–1980

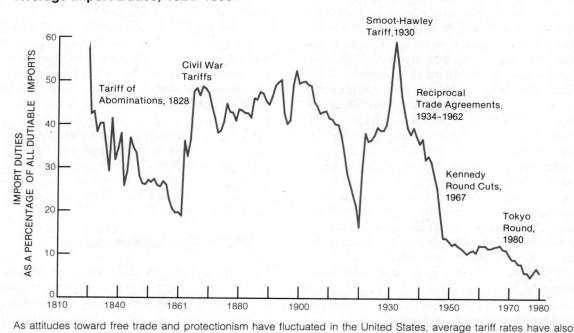

As attitudes toward free trade and protectionism have fluctuated in the United States, average tariff rates have also fluctuated but have shown a distinct downward trend.

Source: *Historical Statistics of the United States; Statistical Abstract of the United States,* 1981.

times, tariffs hit their peak with the infamous Smoot-Hawley Tariff of 1930. Economists were so appalled by the prospect of this tariff bill that in a rare show of agreement 1,028 of them signed a petition asking President Hoover to veto the bill. Since politics tends to override economics in tariff legislation, the bill was signed.

The Trade Agreements Program and GATT

The Smoot-Hawley tariff, like most of the preceding 18 tariff acts stretching back to 1779, was the result of political *logrolling* in the U.S. Congress. Logrolling occurs when some politicians trade their own votes on issues of minor concern to their constituents in return for other politicians' votes on issues of greater concern to their constituents. Tariffs, historically, are the best example of the sacrifice of general interests for special interests.

Having established the highest tariff rates in U.S. history, the Smoot-Hawley Act triggered angry reactions overseas, as predicted by economists. As one nation after another erected trade barriers, the volume of world trade declined more than it would have due to the Great Depression. The export markets of the United States shrank at a time of a very deep domestic depression.

In order to secure a larger market for U.S. exports, Congress amended the Tariff Act of 1930 with the Reciprocal Trade Agreements Act of 1934. The President was authorized to negotiate reciprocal agreements that promised to lower U.S. trade barriers or tariffs in return for similar concessions abroad. The fact that Congress did not have to approve the tariff cuts marked a significant change in the power of special interests to influence U.S. tariff policy.

The Trade Agreements Program has been broadened under successive extensions and modifications. The Trade Expansion Act of 1962 gave the President the power to reduce tariffs by up to 50 percent and to remove duties of less than 5 percent. Under the authority of this Act, the United States engaged in multilateral negotiations, known as the Kennedy Round, which resulted in an average reduction of 35 percent on industrial tariff rates. The Trade Reform Act of 1974 allowed the President to reduce tariffs by up to 60 percent and to eliminate duties less than 5 percent. This act resulted in the Tokyo Round (1980) of multilateral reductions, in which the United States agreed to cut tariffs on industrial goods by 31 percent, the European Community agreed to cut tariffs by 27 percent, and Japan agreed to cut tariffs by 28 percent.

Clearly, the Trade Agreement Program has been an enormous success. In 1932, the average tariff rate was about 59 percent; today the average tariff rate is less than 7 percent. The trade-agreement obligations of the United States and other countries are carried out under the General Agreement on Tariffs and Trade (GATT), established in 1948. GATT is an agreement that spells out rules on the conduct of trade and procedures to settle trade disputes. GATT is also the forum in which international tariff negotiations now take place. As of January 1, 1980, 85 countries belonged to GATT, and several other countries conform to its codes without being formal members.

Escape Clauses

The President's authority to reduce tariffs in reciprocal trade agreements can only be used if the anticipated increases in imports are considered unlikely to threaten or cause serious injury to a domestic industry. Protectionists can now use this "escape clause" to avoid competition from cheaper foreign imports. But an escape clause (Section 201 of the Trade Act of 1974) can only be invoked if three conditions are met: 1) imports must be increasing, 2) the domestic import-competing industry must be (or potentially be) seriously injured, and 3) the increased imports must be a substantial cause of the serious injury or threat to the domestic import-competing industry. Escape-clause cases are initiated by petition from the industry to the U.S. International Trade Commission (formerly the U.S. Tariff Commission).

The escape clause cannot be invoked simply because the increased imports affect a domestic industry adversely or because the domestic industry is seriously depressed. At the beginning of 1979, the United States had in effect escape-clause relief on specialty steel, nonrubber footwear, color television receivers, CB radios, high carbon ferrochromium, and industrial nuts, bolts, and screws. During 1979, only two other industries received escape-clause relief: clothespins and porcelain-and-steel cookware.

The Trade Commission did not grant the U.S. automobile industry escape-clause protection because the major difficulties in the auto industry have been caused by the reduced demand for automobiles. Even if imports had not increased their penetration, the U.S. auto industry would have been depressed in the early 1980s.

Economists tend to be critical of escape clauses because the greater the net social gains that can be expected from tariff cuts, the larger will be the reallocation of resources away from the import-competing industries into export industries and other industries. Thus, escape clauses are invoked presumably in those industries where trade gains may be the greatest.

Trade-Adjustment Assistance

When tariffs are lowered and, say, textile or auto workers are thrown out of jobs, hardships are imposed on them. If escape-clause action is inefficient, an alternative is to assist workers and firms to adjust to the changed conditions by supplementing unemployment insurance, job counseling and training, and grants for moving expenses.

The Trade Expansion Act of 1962 provided for modest trade-adjustment assistance, but the Trade Act of 1974 substantially added to the worker-assistance program. Table 1 shows how the trade-related layoff benefits are distributed. The cost of the program was about $2.7 billion up to 1981 as imports hurt shoes, textiles, and most importantly, the automobile industry. Table 1 shows that most of the trade-adjustment assistance went to the automobile worker.

President Ronald Reagan's 1982 budget cutting may bring an end to the 1975–1981 period

Table 1
Distribution of Trade-Related Benefits, April 1975 to May 1981

Industry	Number of Workers	Amount of Trade-Related Benefits (millions of dollars) Paid Out
Auto	685,066	$2,155
Steel	136,176	348
Apparel	144,923	184
Footwear	75,565	91
Electronics	58,373	87
Fabricated metals	29,105	69
Textiles	25,827	43
Coal	4,605	18

Source: U.S. Department of Labor.

of liberal trade-adjustment benefits. To satisfy the requirements for trade-adjustment assistance during this liberal period, it was necessary only to show that imports "contributed importantly" to the worker's unemployment. Reagan proposes that imports be a "substantial cause" of the worker's unemployment. Trade-adjustment assistance may be coming to an end.

The big problem with trade-adjustment assistance under the Trade Act of 1974 was that the benefits were so liberal that the worker could afford to wait until recall to the original job! In other words, the 685,000 or so workers in the auto industry that received such assistance did not all leave the auto industry; many of them stayed on—defeating the purpose of the legislation.

A case can still be made that government trade-adjustment assistance is necessary because a government policy (tariff reductions) brought about the short-term unemployment of the workers. The question is how to provide this assistance without discouraging the transfer of resources out of declining protected sectors into the exporting sectors of the economy.[10]

10. For a further discussion of Trade Adjustment Assistance, see J. David Richardson, *Understanding International Economics: Theory and Practice* (Boston: Little Brown, 1980), pp. 340–50.

A Drift Towards Protectionism?

The fall in average tariff levels for the United States recorded in Figure 5 indicates a move toward free trade. Similar changes have occurred abroad. But tariff rates do not adequately measure protection in today's world. When the Trade Agreement Program took the power of tariff making away from Congress, the United States began to lower tariff rates and raise nontariff barriers, such as import quotas and voluntary export restrictions. The main method for industries to obtain protection today seems to be by lobbying Congress. When Congress threatens to impose import quotas, the Executive Branch, to keep the peace, arranges for a voluntary export quota with the foreign exporter.

During the late 1970s and early 1980s, stagflation in the United States, Britian, France, Italy, and elsewhere led democratic governments to make compromises with the special interests seeking protection. The protectionist argument that imports cause unemployment becomes *politically* effective in periods of high unemployment, even though rising protectionism in the West will only serve to add to the stagflation problem. The Ottawa summit meeting in July 1981 between the Western leaders recognized the existence of this problem; whether it will be avoided in practice is another question.

This chapter examined the nature and consequences of trade barriers. Imports are bought with money; exports are sold for money. The next chapter will examine how monetary relationships fit into the international exchange of goods and services.

Summary

1. The major trade barriers are tariffs, import quotas, voluntary export quotas, and other nontariff barriers. A *tariff* is a tax levied on imports. It raises the price paid by the domestic consumer and the price received by the domestic producer of the import-competing product. *Import quotas* limit the amount

of imports of specified products. They raise the prices paid by domestic consumers and the prices received by domestic producers of import-competing products. Quotas are normally regulated by import licenses. If import licenses are sold to importers, the government receives their scarcity value. If they are not sold, private importers benefit from their scarcity value. *Voluntary export quotas* direct governments to restrict their exports to another country. Voluntary export quotas create scarcity values for the right to export to the U.S. market, but these scarcity values do not accrue to the United States. Other nontariff barriers are government procurement practices and the setting of technical standards.

2. The basic argument against protection is that the costs of protection outweigh the benefits of protection. The loss to consumers from a tariff is greater than the gain to producers. Additional losses from tariffs are caused by the necessity to expend money to lobby for and obtain tariff or quota protection.

3. The politics of tariffs explains why tariffs are passed. Although the costs of tariffs are large in total, these costs are small per person. Special-interest groups, therefore, lobby and spend funds to obtain tariff protection. The major economic arguments for protection are to avoid unfair foreign competition (low foreign wages, dumping, foreign export subsidies), to protect infant industries, to keep money in the country, and to save domestic jobs.

4. The nonprotectionist arguments for tariffs are the national defense argument, the terms-of-trade argument, the diversification argument, and the tariffs-for-revenue argument. The national defense argument is potentially valid but tends to be misused and applied to industries of little importance to national defense. The terms-of-trade argument works only if the nation's trading partners fail to retaliate against protective tariffs. The diversification argument fails to take into account the fact that private investors prefer to specialize their investments in specific domestic industries. The tariff-revenue argument may have a special justification in poor countries that have

difficulty raising revenues through other means.

5. U.S. trade policies have changed over the years. The Smoot-Hawley Tariff of 1930 caused a further restriction of trade during the Great Depression by setting very high tariff rates. Since then, legislation has been passed that allows the U.S. President to negotiate tariff reductions. As a consequence of this legislation, the average tariff rate declined from 59 percent in 1932 to 7 percent in 1982. Existing legislation does contain escape clauses that can reverse the trend towards free trade. Prior to 1974, tariff reductions could be prevented if the tariff reduction threatened to harm domestic industry. The Trade Act of 1974 required proof that increasing imports would seriously injure the domestic industry and that increasing imports were a substantial cause of the serious injury. Trade-adjustment assistance is given to workers in industries that are materially harmed by the lowering of tariffs. Currently trade-adjustment assistance is concentrated in the automobile industry and the steel industry.

Key Terms

free trade
tariff
import quota
voluntary export quota
prohibitive tariff
nonprohibitive tariff
dumping

Questions and Problems

1. What are the differences and similarities between an import duty and an import quota?
2. What is the difference between an import quota and a voluntary export quota?
3. Economists agree that tariffs hurt the countries that impose them. Yet nearly all countries impose tariffs. Is something wrong with the economists' argument?

4. Assume a country can export all the wheat it wants at the world price of $5 per bushel. Using an analysis parallel to the discussion of Figure 4 in the text, show the impact of imposing a $1 per bushel export tariff on every bushel exported. Does the benefit to consumers and government exceed the cost to producers of wheat? (*Hint:* an export tariff means that if a foreigner purchases wheat he or she must pay the domestic price plus the $1 export duty).

5. What are the best arguments that can be made for tariffs? What are the worst arguments that can be made for tariffs?

6. Frederic Bastiat, a 19th-century French economist/journalist, called tariffs "negative railroads." In what respects are tariffs negative railroads? In what respects is the analogy faulty?

7. Why have import and voluntary export quotas grown in popularity in the United States in recent years?

8. "Ignoring political considerations, importing from the Soviet Union may not benefit the United States because under communism prices need not correspond to the true Soviet comparative advantage." Evaluate this statement.

CHAPTER

22

The International Monetary System

Chapter Preview

This chapter will examine the monetary mechanism behind the international exchange of goods and services. How does the foreign exchange market work? What happens when a currency depreciates? Why are exchange rates between the currencies of different countries allowed to fluctuate? What are the advantages and disadvantages of the present international monetary system?

These questions and others will be answered as this chapter discusses the U.S. balance of payments, international capital movements, fixed versus floating exchange rates, the gold standard, the European currency unit, special drawing rights, the International Monetary Fund (IMF), interna-

tional monetary speculation, and the recycling of OPEC oil revenues.

INTERNATIONAL MONETARY MECHANISMS

The Foreign Exchange Market

Money is the medium of exchange for domestic transactions because it is accepted by all sellers in exchange for their goods and services. Each seller generally wants the national currency of his or her own country. Thus, Americans want U.S. dollars, the English want pounds sterling, the Japanese want yen, Germans want marks, and the French want francs.

When an international transaction takes place, buyers and sellers reside in different countries. An American farmer sells wheat to a British miller or a British firm sells a bicycle to an American cyclist. To make the purchase, the buyer needs the currency of the seller's place of residence. The currency of another country that is needed for international transactions is called **foreign exchange.**

Foreign exchange is the national currency of another country that is needed to carry out international transactions. Normally, foreign exchange consists of bank deposits denominated in the foreign currency but may sometimes consist of foreign paper money when foreign travel is involved.

The buyer of international goods and services obtains his or her currency requirements from the foreign-exchange market. This market is highly dispersed around the world. Exchange between different currencies takes place between large banks and brokers. For example, an American importer of a British bicycle priced in pounds sterling pays in sterling that is deposited in a British bank. The money is transfered by a check or draft or cable that is purchased with dollars from the importer's American bank that holds a sterling deposit in a British bank. Where does the American bank get these sterling deposits? They come from British importers of American goods who want dollars and supply pounds.[1]

America's demand for foreign exchange comes from its demand for the things that residents of the United States want to buy abroad; America's supply of foreign exchange comes from the demand by foreign residents for the things that they want to buy in the United States.

The price of one currency in terms of another is the *foreign-exchange rate*. These exchange rates change from day to day and from hour to hour. In the first week of May 1982, the British pound cost about $1.80, the German mark about $0.43, the French franc about $0.17; $1 was worth about 235 Japanese yen and about 47 Mexican pesos.

Foreign exchange rates are needed to convert foreign prices into American prices. When the exchange rate is expressed in terms of dollars per unit of foreign currency, the rate can be multiplied by the foreign price to obtain the American price. For example, if a British bicycle costs 60 pounds (£), the American importer pays $108 when the pound is worth $1.80 ($108 = $1.80 × 60). When the exchange rate is expressed in terms of foreign currency per dollar, the foreign price can be divided by the rate to obtain the American price. For example, a Japanese car costing 1,410,000 yen costs $6000, when 235 yen equal $1.

Floating or Flexible Exchange Rates

How the exchange rate is determined depends upon whether the rate is a **fixed exchange rate** or a **floating exchange rate.**

*A **floating** or **flexible exchange rate** is an exchange rate that is freely determined by the interaction of supply and demand.*

*A **fixed exchange rate** is an exchange rate that is set by government decree or intervention.*

The real world is a blend of these two polar cases.

The floating system is easier to understand and roughly corresponds to the present regime adopted by the United States as well as the major industrial nations (about 45 countries in total). Many small countries maintain fixed exchange rates against the dollar, the English pound, the French franc, or some basket of currencies. But even the floating systems of today's world have some of the characteristics of the fixed-exchange-rate system.

Americans demand foreign exchange to buy

---

1. For a further discussion of the foreign exchange market, see Peter H. Lindert and Charles P. Kindleberger, *International Economics*, 7th ed. (Homewood, Ill.: Richard D. Irwin, 1982), pp. 243–62.

Figure 1
The Foreign Exchange Market

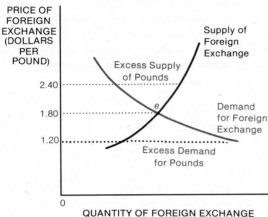

PRICE OF
FOREIGN
EXCHANGE
(DOLLARS
PER
POUND)

Supply of
Foreign
Exchange

Excess Supply
of Pounds

2.40

1.80   *e*

Demand
for Foreign
Exchange

1.20

Excess Demand
for Pounds

0

QUANTITY OF FOREIGN EXCHANGE
(BRITISH POUNDS)

The dollar price of pounds is measured on the vertical axis; the flow of pounds on the foreign exchange market per unit of time is measured on the horizontal axis. The equilibrium exchange rate is $1.80 = £1. If the exchange rate were $2.40 = £1, the excess supply of pounds on the market would drive down the price. At $1.20, there would be an excess demand for pounds on the market, bidding the price up.

imported commodities, to use foreign transportation services and insurance, to travel abroad, to make payments to U.S. troops stationed abroad, to remit dividends, interest, and profits to the foreign owners of American stocks, bonds, and business firms, to grant foreign aid, and to make short-term and long-term investments in foreign assets.

America's supply of foreign exchange is generated by foreigners' demand for American dollars to buy American exports, to travel in America, to pay American owners of stocks, bonds, and businesses, and to invest in American assets.

To simplify the explanation of the foreign exchange market, imagine again that the world consists of two countries: America and England. The American demand for foreign exchange is, thus, a demand for British pounds sterling. Also assume that exports and imports of goods and services are the only things traded internationally.

Figure 1 shows the demand curve for foreign exchange by Americans. On the vertical axis is measured the dollar price of pounds; on the horizontal axis is measured the flow of pounds coming into the foreign-exchange market during the relevant period of time. The demand curve is downward-sloping because the higher the price of pounds in dollars, *ceteris paribus,* the higher the cost of British goods to American importers. For example, if a British bicycle costs 60 pounds and the pound price rises from $1.80 to $2.40, the bike rises from $108 to $144 to the American importer. This price increase will induce Americans to buy fewer bikes or switch to an American-made brand. Thus, the higher the price of pounds, the lower the quantity of foreign exchange demanded by Americans.

The American supply curve of foreign exchange depends on British importers of American goods. When the English buy American wheat, they supply pounds to the foreign exchange market (because pounds must be exchanged to buy U.S. goods). The supply curve is upward-sloping because when the dollar price of pounds rises—or when the dollar falls in value—American goods appear cheaper to foreigners. As a result, they will buy more American goods, thereby increasing the supply of pounds available to Americans in the foreign-exchange market. For example, a bushel of U.S. wheat costs $5.40, a fall in the value of the dollar from £1 = $1.80 to £1 = $2.40 will lower the cost of a bushel of wheat to foreigners from £3 to £2.25. The English will then shift their demand for wheat from British to American wheat and increase wheat consumption, stimulating American exports.

When the price of pounds is $2.40, Figure 1 shows that there is an excess supply of pounds on the foreign exchange market. At the $2.40 exchange rate, desired U.S. exports exceed U.S. imports. With a floating exchange rate, the dollar price of a pound could not be high enough to cause an excess supply. An excess supply of pounds bids the price of pounds down, as in any competitive market. Similarly, at a price of $1.20, there would be an excess demand for pounds and the price of pounds would be bid up. The market-clearing price of $1.80 in Figure 1

Figure 2
The Effect of an Increase in American Investment in England

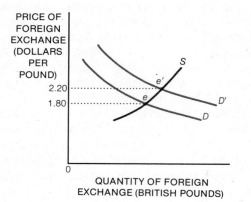

If Americans decided to invest more in England, the demand curve for foreign exchange would shift from *D* to *D'*. The equilibrium price of pounds would rise to $2.20 and would allow a surplus of exports over imports to pay for the increased foreign investment abroad.

not only equates the supply and demand for foreign exchange but also maintains an equilibrium between U.S. exports and imports. Equilibrium between imports and exports is achieved because they are the mirror image of the demand and supply for foreign exchange.

Exports and imports will be equal only if there are no other factors besides exports or imports (tourism, paying dividends, foreign investments) entering the foreign-exchange market. Suppose in addition to exporting and importing, some Americans wish to invest in foreign securities. The demand curve *(D)* in Figure 2 reflects America's foreign-exchange requirements for imports of goods. The desire for making new foreign investments shifts the demand curve for foreign exchange outward to *D'*. The dollar price of pounds rises, or the dollar gets cheaper. This depreciation in the dollar, or appreciation in the pound, makes American goods cheaper and brings about the required excess of exports over imports needed to

accommodate the outflow of American capital to a foreign country.[2]

A currency is said to depreciate if it falls in value on the foreign-exchange market (if it buys less foreign exchange) and to appreciate if it rises in value on the foreign-exchange market (if it buys more foreign exchange).

In our example, the depreciation of the dollar is the same thing as the appreciation of the pound because the dollar/pound exchange rate reflects the relative values of the two currencies: when one goes up the other must go down. In the actual world, of course, the dollar can rise in terms of the pound while falling in terms of the franc or the mark. For this reason, the value of the dollar on the foreign-exchange market as a whole is best expressed in terms of a **currency basket:**

A currency basket is simply a bundle of currencies such as 2 French francs, 1 German mark, 400 Japanese yen, and so on. The dollar, on the average, depreciates if this currency basket becomes more expensive and appreciates if this currency basket becomes less expensive.

Inflation rates in different countries play an important role in determining floating exchange rates. Countries that have enormous rates of inflation can still trade with the rest of the world because the exchange rate reflects the relative purchasing power of the two currencies in their respective countries.

---

2. The foreign exchange market is explained here in terms of the flows of exports, imports, investment, and so forth entering the channels of international exchange. An alternate approach to explaining the foreign-exchange market is the *monetary approach to the balance of payments.* This approach focuses on the demand and supply for different national monies. At any given time, the array of exchange rates that prevails must induce people around the world to be willing to hold the various money supplies (as stocks) that each country has chosen to produce. An excellent introduction to the monetary approach can be found in Lindert and Kindleberger, *International Economics,* pp. 319–35.

This theory, popularized by Sweden's Gustav Cassel around 1917, works well when the inflation rates between two countries are quite different. When inflation rate differentials are small, exchange rate movements will be dominated by other developments, such as fluctuations in the business cycle, capital movements, and changes in comparative advantage.

Suppose England and America were in equilibrium with an exchange rate of $1.80 = £1. If England doubles its supply of money while America maintains a constant money supply, there will be a tendency for the price of all English goods to double. If the price of the pound falls to a mere $0.90 (it falls to one half its previous exchange value), English prices appear exactly the same to Americans. The British bike that used to cost £60 rises to £120; but since the pound falls from $1.80 to $0.90, the bike still costs Americans $108. The exchange rate has maintained its *purchasing power parity*. A dollar still buys the same goods in England as before the inflation.

Fixed Exchange Rates and the Gold Standard

The gold standard is the prototype of the fixed exchange rate system. The classical gold standard was in its heyday before World War I, from about the 1870s to 1914. The United Kingdom was on the gold standard as far back as the 1820s and used both gold and silver during the 18th century—the century in which David Hume and Adam Smith lived.

A fixed-exchange-rate system does not have to use gold, silver, or any commodity, but *each country must adopt monetary rules that correspond to those of the classical gold standard.*

When Spain conquered the New World, it brought back enormous quantities of gold. As the quantity theory predicts, a major consequence of the inflow of gold into Spain was inflation of wages and production costs. This inflation made it more difficult for Spain to compete with other European countries in world markets. Thus, Spain developed an excess of imports over exports and shipped gold to pay for the difference. Eventually, this gold caused inflation elsewhere, and

Spain's exports and imports were brought into approximate balance.

The blueprint for an international gold standard, brilliantly outlined by David Hume in 1752, showed how a fixed-exchange-rate system can work to maintain equilibrium in the balance of payments with the rest of the world.

The gold-flow mechanism can be explained using our hypothetical two-country world. If America defined the dollar as equal to $\frac{1}{20}$ of an ounce of gold and England defined the pound as equal to $\frac{1}{4}$ of an ounce of gold, an English pound would contain 5 times as much gold as a U.S. dollar. England will convert gold into pounds (and vice versa) at the established rate of £1 = $\frac{1}{4}$th of an ounce of gold; America will convert gold into dollars at the rate of $1 = $\frac{1}{20}$th of an ounce of gold. Under these circumstances, the exchange rate would be $5 = £1. No rational person would pay more than $5 for an English pound, because $5 would buy $\frac{1}{4}$ of an ounce of gold from the U.S. Treasury and that amount of gold would buy one £1 note from the British Treasury.[3] The next key ingredient of the gold standard is that England and America let their money supplies depend on how much gold is in their national treasuries.

If America had a surplus of exports over imports in our hypothetical world, gold would be shipped from England to America to pay for the surplus of exports over imports. This gold shipment would raise the money supply in America and reduce the money supply in England. As a result, inflation of costs and prices would occur in America, and a deflation of costs and prices would occur in England. Thus, America's exports would become less competitive and England's exports would become more competitive. As America's exports decreased and England's exports increased, America's surplus of exports over

---

3. Since shipping gold back and forth between American and England is costly (transportation and insurance), the dollar price of pounds might range between $5.02 and $4.98, if it costs 2 cents to ship $\frac{1}{4}$ ounce of gold between the countries. These upper and lower limits of exchange rate are called the *gold points.*

Figure 3
American Balance of Payments

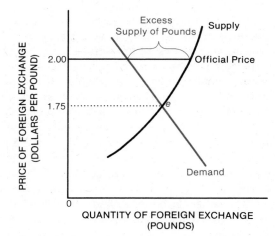

If the exchange rate were $1.75 = £1, America's balance of payments would be in equilibrium. If the dollar price of pounds is fixed at $2.00 = £1, however, the dollar will be undervalued (the pound will be overvalued), and America's balance of payments will be in surplus by the excess supply of pounds on the foreign exchange market. These pounds will have to be purchased by the central banks of either America or England.

imports would disappear—as long as the rules of the gold standard game were followed. The equilibrating mechanism of the international gold standard is the *relationship between the domestic money supplies and the state of the balance of payments*. It is not actually necessary for gold or silver to be involved. If the country with a payments deficit allows its money supply to fall, while the country with a payments surplus allows its money supply to rise, automatic adjustment mechanisms will tend to restore equilibrium. In the country with a payments surplus, the expansion of the money supply will 1) lower exports because of higher prices and costs, 2) raise imports because prices and costs are now cheaper abroad, and 3) raise imports because real GNP may be increased due to expansion in the money

supply. In the deficit country, the contraction of the money supply will 1) raise exports because prices and costs are lower, 2) lower imports because prices and costs are now higher abroad, and 3) lower imports because real GNP may be lower due to the contraction of the money supply.

The central objection to the equilibrating mechanism of a fixed-exchange-rate system is that balance of payments surpluses and deficits may produce unwanted inflationary or deflationary pressures. During the Great Depression, with its enormous unemployment, countries could no longer afford to allow a deficit to produce further deflation and unemployment. Hence, country after country left the gold standard during the 1930s.

Gold is not necessary to establish a fixed-exchange-rate system that works like the gold standard. Fixed exchange rates can be established by official decree reinforced by central bank intervention in the foreign exchange market. For example, in Figure 3, America is assumed to maintain its currency at a $2 exchange rate against the English pound, but the equilibrium exchange rate is $1.75. Thus, at the official rate there is an excess supply of foreign exchange, because the pound is overvalued (or the dollar is undervalued). To maintain the $2 price of pounds, America's central bank must purchase the excess supply of pounds coming onto the foreign exchange market. While America is experiencing this balance-of-payments surplus, the American central bank is adding to its inventory of pounds. This inventory of pounds can later be used as international reserves to defend the value of the dollar when a deficit appears—when the supply and demand curves intersect above the $2 official price.

The surplus of exports over imports in the above example will not persist if America and England follow the rules of the gold standard game. If America lets its money supply rise and England allows its money supply to fall, mechanisms will be set in motion that will shift the demand curve to the right and the supply curve to the left. When America suffers inflation relative to England, America exports less (decreasing supply) and imports more (increasing demand).

In a floating-exchange-rate system, if the dollar/pound exchange rate changes from $1.80 to $1.90, the dollar *depreciates* and the pound *appreciates*.

The term *devaluation* refers to official changes in the exchange rate in a fixed-exchange-rate system. Under the old gold standard, a devaluation of the dollar occurred when the price of gold rose. Today, a country with a fixed exchange rate devalues its currency simply by lowering the official price of its currency. The country announces that it will no longer defend the old price and sets a new price to maintain by official intervention.

In Figure 3, America has a surplus and England has a deficit at the official price of $2 per pound. This price can be maintained if the American central bank buys pounds or if the English central bank sells dollars (or if both actions take place). To avoid this inflation in America and deflation in England, England might, with America's agreement, decide to simply devalue its currency! In Figure 3, lowering the price of pounds to $1.75 will (temporarily at least) solve England's deficit and America's surplus. When the official value of a currency is raised, a *revaluation* is said to occur. Thus, in this case, England *devalues* its currency and America *revalues* its currency.

THE BALANCE OF PAYMENTS AND INTERNATIONAL CAPITAL MOVEMENTS

The Balance of Payments

A country's **balance of payments** is a source of much information about the country's exports, imports, earnings by domestic residents on assets located abroad, earnings on domestic assets owned by foreign residents, international capital movements between countries, and official transactions by central banks and governments.

*A country's **balance of payments** is a summary record of its economic transactions with foreign residents over a year or any other period.*

The balance of payments is a two-sided summary of international transactions. Each transaction is recorded by standard double-entry bookkeeping. In other words, every transaction is entered on two sides of the balance-of-payments accounts. For example, when America exports wheat, the foreign importer might simply give an IOU in exchange for the wheat. The wheat sale is recorded on the minus (debit) side and the IOU is recorded on the plus (credit) side. Because each amount recorded on the minus side is recorded on the plus side, the balance of payments record will always be *in balance*.

Although the balance of payments always balances if all transactions are considered, specific *accounts* of the balance of payments need not balance. U.S. merchandise exports need not equal U.S. merchandise imports, for example. Thus, a specific account of the balance of payments may have a surplus or deficit, but all the surpluses in the balance of payments as a whole will cancel out the deficits.

Since the balance of payments as a whole must balance, a deficit on one account implies a surplus on some other account.

These observations should serve as a warning that a deficit in a particular account should not be treated as unfavorable or a surplus as favorable to a country. Mercantilists, those seventeenth and eighteenth century writers whom Adam Smith and David Hume criticized, treated a surplus of exports over imports as a good thing and even called it a "favorable trade balance." That such a surplus benefits a country more than an "unfavorable" trade balance is a fallacy. A trade deficit may be a good thing. If a country is importing more than it is exporting, more goods are being brought in than are being sent out. Mercantilists committed the fallacy of treating exports as business sales and imports as business expenses. The mercantilist fallacy still lingers on in many press reports and in the minds of many people.

As noted above, the balance of payments records each transaction on two sides: the credit side and the debit side. In the plus or credit column is placed the part of the transaction that increases the *supply* of foreign exchange: the payments for exports of merchandise or the income earned by

Table 1
The U.S. Balance of Payments, 1981

Item	Amount (billions of dollars)	
1. **Exports of goods and services**		+376.0
a. Exports of merchandise	236.3	
b. Military sales	9.3	
c. Services	40.3	
d. Income from U.S. investments abroad	90.1	
2. **Imports of goods and services**		−362.7
a. Imports of merchandise	−264.1	
b. Military purchases	−11.3	
c. Services	−34	
d. Income on foreign investments in U.S.	−53.3	
3. **Net unilateral transfers abroad**		−6.8
a. U.S. government grants and pensions	−5.9	
b. Private remittances	−.9	
4. **Balance on current account**		+6.5
5. **Net capital movements**		−32.3
a. U.S. capital outflow	−101.4	
b. Foreign capital inflow	+69.1	
6. **Allocations of new SDRs to U.S. by IMF**		+1.1
7. **Statistical discrepancy**		+24.7
8. **Increase (−) in U.S. official reserve assets**		−5.2
9. **Increase (+) in foreign official assets in the U.S.**		+5.2
a. OPEC members	+13.4	
b. Other	−8.2	
10. **Total**		0

Source: *Survey of Current Business,* March 1982. (Categories may not add to totals because of rounding errors.)

providing services like transportation, insurance, and even capital to foreigners. In the minus or debit column is placed the part of a transaction that increases the demand for foreign exchange: payments for imports of merchandise and the income earned by foreigners when they provide domestic residents with transportation, insurance, or capital.

Exports and Imports. Table 1 shows the U.S. balance of payments for 1981. The most important categories are found under items 1 and 2. U.S. merchandise imports (item 2a) exceeded U.S. merchandise exports (item 1a) by $27.8 billion.

*The **merchandise trade balance** = exports of merchandise − imports of merchandise. If positive, it is the (merchandise) trade surplus. If negative, it is the (merchandise) trade deficit.*

The **merchandise trade balance** is sometimes called the *visible trade balance,* because it is easy to see physical movements of goods, such as wheat, cars, airplanes, computers, and steel. Yet the visible trade balance does not give an accurate picture of what the U.S. exports and imports from abroad. There are also many invisible items in the balance of payments. The United States furnishes transportation, insurance, and capital to foreigners. Payments are received in exchange for these services. When these less visible items are taken into account, the United States exports more goods and services than it imports by $6.5 billion (item 4).

Net Unilateral Transfers Abroad. If an American sends money to a relative in a foreign country, if the government gives money to a foreign country as a gift or grant, or if an American decides to retire in a foreign country and receives a pension check there, such transactions enter the balance of payments as *unilateral transfers.* Nothing concrete is exchanged for these payments, but these transactions do give rise to a demand for foreign exchange. In 1981, the United States made $6.8 billion worth of such transfers, two thirds of which consisted of government grants in one form or another. The net difference between exports of goods and services and imports of goods and services minus net unilateral transfers is the *current account balance.*

*The **current account balance** equals exports of goods (merchandise) and services minus imports of goods (merchandise) and services minus net unilateral transfers abroad.*

The United States had a surplus on the current account because the income from U.S. investments abroad (item 1d) exceeded the income on foreign investments in the United States by $36.8 billion, which more than offset the deficit on the merchandise trade balance and gave the U.S. an overall current account surplus. From 1960 to 1981 the United States had only 4 current account deficits and 18 current account surpluses. The United States can typically import more merchandise from foreign countries than it sells in return because income is earned on capital located abroad. The United States exchanges the goods and services its capital could produce at home for the goods and services that its capital could produce abroad. Such a situation usually results in a trade deficit on the merchandise account.

Net Capital Movements. When Americans buy foreign bonds, stocks, and invest in foreign factories, capital that would otherwise be available for investment at home becomes invested abroad. This capital outflow was a staggering $101.4 billion in 1981 (item 5a). When foreigners invest in U.S. stocks, bonds, and factories, there is a capital inflow. In 1981, the capital inflow into the United States was estimated to be $69.1 billion. Capital outflows—sometimes called *capital exports*—are a debit item, since they give rise to a demand for foreign exchange and, like imports, represent an increase in a domestically held asset (the foreigner's IOU). Capital inflows—sometimes called *capital imports*—are a credit item, since they give rise to an increase in the supply of foreign exchange and represent an increase in U.S. liabilities to foreigners.

The excess of capital exports over capital imports of $32.3 billion (item 5) is typical. As noted in the discussion of items 1d and 2d, the United States earns more from investments it makes abroad than from the investments foreigners make in the United States. U.S. net income from foreign investment—about $37 billion in 1981—is

simply a reflection of exporting more capital than was imported over a long period of time.

Item 7 in Table 1 is "statistical discrepancy." In 1981, the statistical discrepancy was a whopping $24.7 billion credit item. From 1975 to 1980, the statistical discrepancy was an average $12.7 billion credit item. This statistical discrepancy arose from the fact that when all the observable credits and debits were recorded, the debits outweighed the credit items by this amount. Thus, unobserved credits, such as spending by foreign tourists here, hidden exports, or unnoticed capital inflows, must have occurred. It is generally believed by international finance experts that these substantial credits represent unrecorded capital inflows.

Official Reserve Assets. A country's *official reserve assets* are that country's gold, special drawing rights (SDRs), its reserve position in the International Monetary Fund (discussed later), foreign exchange, or any financial assets held in official agencies, such as the central bank or treasury.

Item 9, *the increase in foreign official assets in the U.S.,* records the investments of official agencies of foreign countries in the U.S. In 1981, official foreign agencies invested a net $5.2 billion in the United States. OPEC countries invested $13.4 billion, and other countries reduced their official assets by $8.2 billion, for a net total of $5.2 billion. Governments of the OPEC countries receive so much in oil revenues that they need an investment outlet. Had these oil revenues gone into private hands, they probably would have found their way into U.S. investments as well.[4]

Government agencies engage in buying and

---

4. In this case, item 9a could be added to item 5b. Together with the statistical discrepancy, which may be a capital inflow, the total capital inflow into the United States in 1981 may well have been around $107 billion. Compared to the capital outflow of $101.4 billion, the United States was a net capital importer of about $5.6 billion in 1981, when properly measured!

selling assets and foreign exchange. When official agencies like the central bank or the treasury do this, there is a presumption that the agency is demanding or supplying foreign exchange for the purpose of stabilizing the exchange rate. This presumption does not hold in the case of the OPEC countries. The $5.2 billion increase in foreign official assets in the United States (item 9) was not undertaken to support the dollar, or to supply foreign exchange. Indeed, item 9b indicates that foreign official assets (excluding OPEC) fell by $8.2 billion. Item 8, the increase in U.S. official reserve assets, consists for the most part of foreign currencies. It is a debit item, since it is a demand for foreign exchange and represents an increase in an asset, as when a good is imported on private account.

The entire $5.2 billion in item 8 (coincidentally the same as item 9) cannot be considered a true demand for foreign exchange by the U.S. monetary authorities. The allocations of new special drawing rights by the International Monetary Fund (IMF) are included in item 6 and item 8. These new allocations can be used as an official reserve asset of the United States—namely, to buy foreign exchange. SDRs were allocated to every member of the IMF in 1970, 1971, 1972, 1979, 1980, and 1981.

If the SDR allocation is excluded from line 8, the increase in U.S. official reserve assets that corresponds roughly to the increase in the official U.S. holdings of foreign exchange amounted to about $4.1 billion in 1981. Item 9b indicates that foreign official agencies reduced their holdings of dollars by $8.2 billion. Thus, the official supply of dollars by foreign and U.S. central banks and treasuries in 1981 was $12.3 billion ($8.2 billion + $4.1 billion). Since these actions increased the supply of dollars on the foreign exchange market, the exchange value of the dollar was kept lower.

This analysis of the U.S. balance of payments in 1981 shows that the dollar was "strong" on international foreign exchange markets. If an overall measure of surplus or deficit had to be used, a careful analyst would have to say that the U.S. payments position was in surplus. This conclusion is reinforced by the rise in the exchange value of the dollar during 1981. Using an average

of 10 European currencies, the dollar rose by almost 16 percent. Had official government agencies not sold dollars for other foreign currencies, the dollar would have risen even more.

International Capital Movements

International capital movements considerably complicate what is happening to a country's balance of payments. Without such capital movements, exports would more closely approximate imports, and there would be fewer measures of deficit or surplus in the balance of payments.

Capital movements enable capital-importing nations to raise their physical capital stocks—dams, buildings, roads—above what such stocks would be in the absence of international capital flows. When a country exports capital, it is furnishing residents of another country with funds for financing investments in plant and equipment. Thus, capital exports divert one country's saving into investments in another country. Saving still equals investments in the world as a whole, but when international trade is involved, this equality need not hold for any individual country.

Recall from Chapter 6 that GNP = consumption (C) + government spending (G) + investment (I) + exports (X) − Imports (M). Because GNP equals income, GNP = consumption (C) + saving (S). If government spending and taxes are assumed to be zero (for simplicity),

$$C + S = C + I + X - M,$$

or

$$S = I + X - M$$

or

$$S - I = X - M$$

This equation shows that the excess of saving over investment in a country is reflected in the excess of exports over imports. The excess of saving over investment is the net export of capital to other countries. Thus, the export of capital is

Figure 4
U.S. and Foreign Interest Rates

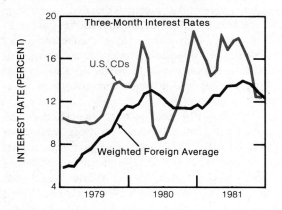

The black curve shows the foreign average interest rate for a group of 10 countries plus Switzerland weighted by average total trade shares in 1972–76. The color curve shows the interest rate on certificates of deposit (CDs) in the United States. Throughout most of 1981, interest rates were higher in the United States.

Source: *Survey of Current Business.*

transferred into physical goods through the current account surplus.

Capital movements take place for two reasons: investors wish to take advantage of earning a higher interest rate on their capital, or investors wish to gain some measure of security. Capital seeks higher returns and lower risks.

The capital account of any country's balance of payments contains both capital inflows and outflows because investors are seeking to diversify their portfolios of investments and securities. A fundamental principle of sound investment strategy is not to put all of one's eggs in one basket. By holding a portfolio of international securities—for example, investments in German companies, Japanese companies, and American companies—an investor can reduce the risk of achieving a given expected rate of return.

Net capital movement is governed by the desire for higher interest rates. For example, in a simple world with no risks, investors would place their capital in the country that paid the highest

interest rate (the highest rate of return on investments). This process of capital exportation would raise interest rates in low-interest-rate regions and lower interest rates in high-interest-rate regions. This allocation of capital gives rise to greater production everywhere in the world and, thus, a more efficient utilization of the world's scarce stock of capital.

Figure 4 shows that during 1981 the United States was a high-interest-rate region. Since U.S. inflation rates were also falling relative to other countries in 1981, U.S. real interest rates were high in 1981. That the dollar rose substantially in 1981 is not surprising. When newspaper reports emphasize the merchandise trade deficit without describing capital movements, they give the public the illusion that the dollar is weak on world markets. In 1981 (and 1980), the dollar was strong.

Stages of the Balance of Payments. When a country first begins to export capital, the country's earnings on previous foreign investments are small or zero. To finance this export of capital, it is essential to generate a surplus of merchandise exports over merchandise imports. The trade balance surplus of such an immature creditor country enables the world to use the scarce capital stock efficiently. As time goes on the country begins to collect on its investments. As it becomes a mature creditor country, it is able to import more than it was exporting. The United States was an immature creditor country in the 1920s; partly because it is a mature creditor country today it has a merchandise trade deficit year in and year out.

Foreign Investment and Nationalism. When capital is exported from the United States, labor complains that the United States is giving employment to foreigners and depressing home wages. When capital is imported, capitalists complain that their rate of return is depressed. When a foreign country takes over a particular business firm, many people will regard this takeover as a bad thing. In recent years, for example, the Japanese have bought up some American banks, trading companies, and hotels and office buildings. Is it somehow to the disadvantage of the

United States to allow foreigners to take over American businesses?

When foreign investment takes the form of actual control of a domestic firm, another issue is at stake: trade in entrepreneurial services.[5] Like trade in all goods and services, if the Japanese can operate American business more efficiently than the former management, the American people will benefit—just as they benefit from buying cheaper foreign imports of TV sets or cars.

THE EVOLUTION OF THE INTERNATIONAL MONETARY SYSTEM

In 1870, the world was not on an international gold standard; in 1900 the world was on an international gold standard. The gold standard was dead in 1945 and was replaced by a system of fixed but adjustable exchange rates. The post-war system was dead by 1973, and today the world is on a system of floating exchange rates with active exchange-rate-stabilization policies by the major central banks. To understand the current system, it is useful to take a backward look at this evolution.

The Breakdown of the Gold Standard

An international gold standard requires that 1) each country set a price of its currency in terms of gold, 2) each country allow anyone to convert gold into its currency and vice versa at the set price, and 3) the domestic money supply be tied to the domestic stock of monetary gold so that deficits reduce the money supply and surpluses increase the money supply. Under a gold standard, balance-of-payments deficits are defined as the reduction in the supply of monetary gold used for financing an excess of debits over credits by ordinary market participants; a surplus means the supply of monetary gold rises.

5. Indeed, there is no reason why the taking over of a domestic firm by a foreign firm should be associated with foreign investment because a Japanese firm can take over an American firm by borrowing in the American capital market.

If these rules are followed, each country is giving up its own monetary autonomy because the money supply takes a course dictated by the state of the balance of payments. Indeed, the gold standard may be considered a rather cumbersome way of setting up a world currency. A more straightforward method would be to set up a world currency directly with a single central bank or monetary authority.

The pre-1914 gold standard, centered in the United Kingdom, appeared to work well from 1870 to 1914. The balance-of-payments adjustment mechanism worked smoothly to eliminate surpluses and deficits. After World War I, the gold standard broke down. While a "new" gold standard was established in the 1920s, the turbulent 1930s brought it to an end. The gold standard broke down for three main reasons:

1. After World War I, many countries, especially the United States, began to depart significantly from the rules of the gold-standard game. To abide by the gold standard, a country must let its money supply rise and fall with inflows and outflows of gold. The United States, an important country after the war, abandoned this principle.

2. When Britain and France tried to restore the old gold standard in the 1920s, they set inappropriate exchange rates. The United Kingdom overvalued the pound sterling; France undervalued the French franc. Since Winston Churchill was the Chancellor of the Exchequer in Britain, John Maynard Keynes wrote an essay entitled, "The Economic Consequences of Mr. Churchill," in which he spelled out the consequences of an overvalued exchange rate. With Britain on an overvalued rate and France with an undervalued rate, large deficits in Britain and surpluses in France were inevitable. To make the system work along the lines of Hume's gold-flow mechanism, Britain would have had to deflate substantially and France would have had to inflate substantially. It is safe to say that in the 1920s countries were not that interested in sacrificing themselves to the discipline of the gold standard.

3. The Great Depression of the 1930s put the final nail in the coffin of the gold standard. With widespread unemployment, deficit countries would

would never accept the discipline of further un-anticipated deflation and more unemployment. Indeed, countries tried to do precisely the opposite; that is, they tried to export their unemployment to other countries. The opposite of the gold standard is to engage in so-called competitive devaluations. If Country A can unexpectedly devalue its currency, its exports will become more competitive, and it will find importing more expensive. With widespread unemployment, an unanticipated competitive devaluation (without retaliation from other countries) might increase employment at home at the expense of employment abroad. While such policies were not as widespread as sometimes alleged, the 1930s were characterized by exchange rate gyrations and numerous currency devaluations.

In retrospect, it is easy to see that the 1930s were not a laboratory for studying a flexible-exchange-rate system. Throughout the 1930s governments were controlling changes in exchange rates or, after letting exchange rates find their own level, setting new exchange rates. With the world economy grinding through one of the worst depressions in history, it would be foolish to associate the gyrating exchange rates with a floating-exchange-rate system.[6]

The Bretton Woods System

The International Monetary Fund (IMF) was established in 1947 after a 1944 conference in Bretton Woods, New Hampshire. The international monetary arrangements set up at this conference are now called either the "old IMF" system or the "Bretton Woods" system.

Each member of the IMF was assigned a quota that was determined by its trade and national income. A country contributed 25 percent of its quota in gold or U.S. dollars and 75 percent in its own currency. Thus the IMF consisted of a pool

---

6. A good review of the 1930s will be found in Leland B. Yeager, *International Monetary Relations: Theory, History, and Policy*, 2nd ed. (New York: Harper & Row, 1976), chap. 18.

---

of gold, dollars, and all other major currencies that could be used to lend assistance to any member country having balance-of-payments difficulties.

A country's international reserves under the old IMF consisted of gold, dollars, its drawing or borrowing rights from the IMF, and foreign exchange.

The Bretton Woods system was set up on the theory that balance-of-payments *deficits* and *surpluses*—reductions or increases in international reserves—were usually temporary in a fixed-exchange-rate system. Thus, the discipline of the Hume reserve-flow mechanism—deflation for deficit countries and inflation for surplus countries—could in many cases be avoided. Thus, each country pledged to maintain a par value for its currency in gold or in dollars that were worth $\frac{1}{35}$ of an ounce of gold and to maintain the exchange rate of its currency within 1 percent of this par value. Should a deficit develop, the country could rely on its international reserves to help it weather the storm until a surplus on the balance of payments developed. In the meantime, the country would not have to go through the adjustment of a domestic deflation.

If the deficit did not reverse itself, the country was considered to be facing a "fundamental disequilibrium" and was then allowed to adjust its exchange rate. A country in fundamental deficit could devalue its currency; a country in fundamental surplus could revalue its currency.

The Fall of Bretton Woods

The United States was the center of the Bretton Woods system. Under the old IMF system, countries tied their currencies to the U.S. dollar. The United States, in turn, tied the dollar to gold. Until 1971, the United States allowed foreign monetary authorities to convert dollars into gold at the rate of $35 an ounce. The dollar became a crucial source of international reserves. Countries obtained dollars by accepting dollar payments in exchange for their goods and services. With other countries needing international reserves, the United

The European Monetary System

The present international monetary system has a rich menu of possibilities. Countries can float, tie their exchange rate to another country, or engage in joint floating. In 1979, the countries of the European Community established a joint float, which is believed to be a step in the direction of European monetary unification. The European system is characterized by the following two features:

1. The exchange rates of the participating European countries are supposed to be maintained within a range of 2.25 percent from the various par values. The entire group of currencies can fluctuate against the dollar or other currencies. Since each currency must maintain a fixed distance from the others, the movements of the various currencies look like a "snake in a tunnel" when each is plotted against, say, the dollar.
2. Each member country pools one fifth of its monetary reserves in return for a new monetary unit, called the European Currency Unit (ECU).

This ECU is currently a European version of an SDR; that is, it is used only by central monetary authorities, but some hope that it may someday become a true transactions currency.

The basic problem of the European Monetary System is that to successfully maintain a fixed exchange rate relative to any subset of countries, the individual countries must follow the rules of the gold-standard game. In particular, the European Monetary System requires each country to give up its own monetary autonomy—which, of course, has not happened. Pressures will develop for some currencies in the joint float to revalue and for others to devalue. Since it is obvious which currencies will devalue, the same speculation that plagued the currency-adjustment feature of Bretton Woods also causes difficulties within the European Monetary System. Wide differences between the inflation rates of different countries make it very difficult to maintain fixed exchange rates. ⨳

States could run an import surplus, or a surplus of capital exports over capital imports, without too much difficulty. In other words, because the United States could buy the goods and factories of the rest of the world with its own dollars, it was in a very enviable position during this period.

The expectation was that when the U.S. import surplus came to an end, the Bretton Woods system would begin to work smoothly. In the 1950s and 1960s the United States had a deficit in its official accounts virtually every year. The expectation of the deficit turning into a surplus or at least equilibrium never materialized.

The fact that the U.S. dollar was the international money of the world also made it very difficult for the United States to adjust the value of its own currency. If the United States devalued the dollar, every country holding dollars as reserves would find itself losing a substantial fraction of its wealth. Thus, the most important member of the IMF could not use its safety valve when its deficit was permanent.

Special Drawing Rights (SDRs). In the late 1960s, it was believed that part of the U.S. deficit problem was caused by inadequate international reserves. Thus, at the IMF's annual meeting in 1967, a new kind of international money was created—the special drawing right (SDR). SDRs are essentially an international money that can be used between monetary authorities. Basically, the IMF simply creates SDRs out of thin air and allocates them to the various member countries in accordance with their quotas. If a deficit country needs international reserves, it can transfer its SDR balance to other countries. The rate of exchange that a country gets for SDRs depends upon the prevailing value. At first, 1SDR = $1. Later the SDR's value was determined by making 1SDR equal to a bundle of currencies. In the early 1980s, for example, an SDR was worth more than $1.

But SDRs were essentially a stopgap measure. While they may eventually become the basis for an international currency, the SDR solution did nothing to solve the fundamental problem of the Bretton Woods system: speculation.

Speculation. In addition to the U.S. official deficit, another problem was that the currency adjustment system itself suffered from incompatibility with relatively free international capital movements. If a country had a fundamental deficit and needed to devalue its currency, speculators would know this fact better than anyone else. The chances of the country revaluing or raising the value of its currency would be virtually zero. The speculators would be in a no-lose situation if they sold weak currencies with a vengeance and bought strong currencies. For example, the British pound was often weak and the German Deutschmark (DM) was often strong. Accordingly, speculators would sell pounds and buy DMs. This exacerbated the deficit in the United Kingdom and the surplus in Germany.

In 1971, speculators began to speculate against the U.S. dollar. President Nixon, in August 1971, changed the fundamental character of the IMF system when he severed the dollar's link with gold. No longer could countries convert dollars into gold at $35 an ounce; the dollar was essentially set free to fluctuate. After a few attempts to fix up the system, by March 1973 all major currencies of the world were on a managed floating system, and the Bretton Woods system was shattered.

The Current International Monetary System

The Jamaica Agreements. At a conference in Kingston, Jamaica in early 1976, the original IMF charter was amended to legalize the widespread managed floating that replaced the Bretton Woods par value system.

According to the new agreements each country can adopt whatever exchange-rate system it prefered (fixed or floating). Countries are asked to "avoid manipulating exchange rates . . . in order to prevent effective balance-of-payments adjustment or to gain an unfair competitive advantage over other members." The IMF is directed to "oversee the compliance of each member with its obligations" in order to "exercise firm surveillance of the exchange-rate policies of its members." Monetary authorities of a country can buy and sell foreign exchange in order to "prevent or moderate sharp and disruptive fluctuations from day to day and from week to week," but it is considered unacceptable to suppress or reverse a long-run exchange-rate movement.

The policy of the Reagan administration is to limit intervention in the foreign-exchange markets. Under a policy announced in 1981, intervention will occur only if there is unusual disorder in foreign-exchange markets. Thus, official U.S. purchases of foreign exchange were more than $3 billion less in 1981 than in 1980.

Advantages. All of the major countries are floating against the dollar. A number of small countries are tied to the dollar, and some others are tied to the French franc and the pound sterling. Thus, the entire system is one of individual floating, joint floating, and intervention in the foreign-exchange markets to keep the exchange rate from appreciating or depreciating too sharply. The advantages of this system are 1) monetary autonomy, 2) ease of balance-of-payments adjustment, 3) recycling of oil revenues, and 4) market efficiency.

When exchange rates are flexible, one country's monetary policy does not have to be dictated by the monetary policies of other countries. If everybody else wants to inflate, a country can maintain stable prices simply by following a long-run monetary policy of tight money (low monetary growth) and allowing its exchange rate to appreciate relative to the countries that choose to follow inflationary policies. Likewise, flexible exchange rates enable a country to follow highly inflationary policies by simply allowing its rate of exchange to depreciate.

Under a fixed-exchange-rate regime, a deficit can be solved by internal deflation or unemployment. If this solution is not in the best interests of the country, a flexible exchange rate allows a country to depreciate its currency rather than undergo the discipline of Hume's reserve-flow mechanism. It is much easier to lower the value of a country's currency than to lower every internal commodity price and wage rate!

The most dramatic achievement of the current system is that when the OPEC countries quadrupled the price of oil in 1973–74, the resulting shock to the world economy was absorbed by floating exchange rates. The enormous deficits that developed in the oil-importing countries and the necessity of the oil-exporting countries to invest their oil revenues meant that the foreign exchange markets had a lot of recycling of oil revenues to process. The previous Bretton Woods system could not have accomplished this recycling. Indeed, the Bretton Woods system could not take much smaller pressures. While exchange rates fluctuated dramatically after the oil shock, the system worked. It did not break down or cause crises like those that the world witnessed in the late 1960s and early 1970s.

Studies of the foreign-exchange market in the 1970s show over and over again that the market, while volatile, was efficient. If a market is efficient, the price of the commodity being traded should reflect all currently available information. For example, on May 12, 1982, the British pound was worth $1.8375. The same day a person could arrange a futures contract to buy a British pound in 90 days for about $1.8455. Thus, on May 12, people expected the pound to be $1.8455 in 3 months. If the market works efficiently such predictions (that are made daily) should not be biased one way or the other. Sometimes the futures price will overestimate the exchange rate and sometimes it will underestimate the exchange rate, but on the average it will turn out to be right. This view appears to be supported by most of the studies of the foreign-exchange market.[7]

7. It was again confirmed in Jacob A. Frenkel, "Flexible Exchange Rates, Prices, and the Role of 'News': Lessons from the 1970s," *Journal of Political Economy* (August 1981): 665–705.

Figure 5
Foreign Currency Price of U.S. Dollar in Selected Currencies

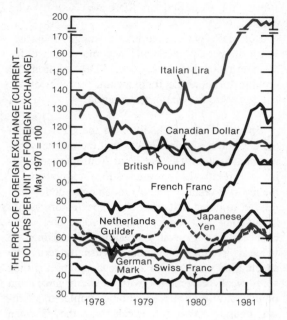

Exchange rates are volatile because they reflect many real and monetary shocks and changing expectations.

Source: *Survey of Current Business,* March 1982, p. 39.

Disadvantages. Critics of the present system of managed floating exchange rates claim that the system 1) is a nonsystem, 2) is characterized by exchange-rate volatility, 3) has increased world inflation, and 4) requires monetary unification.

It is impossible for the monetary authorities to know what the equilibrium exchange rate should be. Hence, any attempt by the monetary authorities to intervene in the foreign-exchange markets will inevitably reflect other goals. When an exchange rate appreciates, for example, exporters may complain that it is harder to sell in foreign markets. By moderating the appreciation of an exchange rate by purchasing foreign currencies, which the Federal Reserve System did quite a bit of in 1980–81, exporters are not hit quite as hard. With each country having all sorts of such domestic objectives, manipulation of exchange rates is inevitable and does not foster the achievement of long-run equilibrium. Because the economics of managing exchange rates is not well understood, it is difficult to evaluate this criticism.

Figure 5 shows the behavior of some selected exchange rates from 1978 to the end of 1981. Some suggest that volatile exchange rates indicate that the system is not working. The world economy is subject to many real shocks (like the oil shock) and monetary shocks. Changes in the exchange rate reflect these shocks and changing expectations. When President Reagan took office in early 1981, it was widely anticipated that the United States would follow a less inflationary policy. This expectation resulted in appreciation of the dollar. In addition, the Federal Reserve System followed a policy that raised interest rates in the short run relative to the rest of the world (see Figure 4). These higher interest rates led to enormous inflows of capital and further appreciation of the U.S. dollar. One criterion for determining whether exchange rates are too volatile is whether or not exchange rate uncertainty contributes to a lower volume of real international trade and, hence, fewer benefits to the world from international specialization. So far there is evidence that floating rates or volatile exchange rates do not have this impact.[8]

The fact that world inflation rates have increased since the adoption of generalized floating has led some to believe that there is a link between floating rates and inflation. Under a fixed exchange rate, a country is constrained from following an inflationary policy because balance-of-payments deficits are produced. A floating exchange rate removes this constraint on domestic monetary policy. Hence, as a practical political matter, one should expect greater inflation with floating rates than with fixed rates. Some economists, such as Arthur Laffer and Robert Mundell, are now suggesting that the United States should return to the gold standard in order to prevent inflation. This suggestion may receive more attention in the next few years if the Reagan administration is not successful in bringing the U.S. inflation rate down to moderate levels.

A final criticism of the present system is that the only way to enjoy the full benefits of a monetary economy is for every country to adopt the same currency. In other words, the current system is just a long detour away from the most efficient monetary arrangement. Presumably, in a world without nationalism and with free trade, the adoption of a truly international currency unit would come almost automatically. An international currency, however, requires the sacrifice of national monetary autonomy and other nationalistic goals. One unified world is a long way off.

Summary

1. Foreign exchange is the national currency of another country that is needed to carry out international transactions. America's demand for foreign exchange increases when U.S. residents demand more foreign goods and services. America's supply of foreign exchange increases when residents of foreign countries demand more U.S. goods and services. The demand curve for foreign exchange is downward-sloping because the higher the dollar price of foreign currency, the higher the cost of foreign goods to American importers. The supply curve of foreign exchange tends to be upward-sloping because as the dollar price of foreign currency rises, American goods appear cheaper to foreigners. Under a floating-exchange-rate system, the exchange rate is allowed to float to the point where the demand for foreign exchange equals the supply. When the exchange rate reflects the relative purchasing power of the currencies of two different countries, purchasing power parity prevails between the two currencies. Under a fixed-exchange-rate system, equilibrium in the demand for and supply of foreign exchange is brought about

8. See Leland Yeager, *International Monetary Relations,* chap. 13; for the opposing view see "International Trade Flows under Flexible Exchange Rates," *Economic Review* 65 (March 1980): 3–10 (Federal Reserve Bank of Kansas City).

by Hume's gold-flow mechanism. The key to this mechanism is that surplus countries (experiencing an inflow of gold) allow their money supplies to rise while the deficit countries (experiencing an outflow of gold) allow their money supplies to fall. The ensuing inflation in the surplus countries and deflations in the deficit countries correct the imbalance in the demand for and supply of foreign exchange.

2. A country's balance of payments provides a summary record of its economic transactions with foreign residents over a period of one year. It is a two-sided (credit/debit) summary that must always be in accounting balance. International capital movements raise the physical capital stocks in the capital-importing countries and lower them in the capital-exporting countries.

3. Today the world is on a system of floating exchange rates with active exchange-rate stabilization by the major central banks. The Bretton Woods system set up after World War II broke down because a currency-adjustment system is fundamentally in conflict with free international capital movements. Speculation destroyed the old Bretton Woods System. The new international monetary system involves a mixture of floating and fixed exchange rates. Since 1973 the U.S. dollar has floated with respect to all the major currencies of the world.

Key Terms

foreign exchange
fixed exchange rate
floating exchange rate
currency basket
balance of payments
merchandise trade balance
current account balance

Questions and Problems

1. In May 1982, the West German mark was worth $0.44 (in U.S. dollars) and $1 was worth about 233 Japanese yen. How much would a Mercedes-Benz cost in U.S. dollars if the German price were 30,000 Deutsch-Marks (DM)? How much would a Toyota cost in U.S. dollars if the Japanese price were 1,165,000 yen?

2. The accompanying table shows part of an actual newspaper report on the foreign exchange market. Did the British pound rise or fall from Tuesday to Wednesday? Did the Japanese yen rise or fall from Tuesday to Wednesday? What happened to the dollar in terms of the pound? What happened to the dollar in terms of the yen?

	Foreign Currency in Dollars		Dollar in Foreign Currency	
	Wed.	Tue.	Wed.	Tue.
British pound	$1.8375	1.8335	0.5442	0.5454
Japanese yen	0.0004284	0.004296	233.40	232.80

3. If there were a floating exchange rate between Japan and the United States, which of the following events would cause the Japanese yen to appreciate? Which would cause the yen to depreciate? Explain your answers.
   a. The government of Japan orders its automobile companies to limit exports to the United States.
   b. The United States places a quota on Japanese automobiles.
   c. The United States increases its money supply relative to Japan's money supply.
   d. Interest rates in the United States rise relative to Japanese interest rates.

e. More Japanese decide to visit America.

f. Japanese productivity growth rises relative to the United States.

4. Indicate whether each of the following transactions represents a debit (a supply of U.S. dollars) or a credit (a demand for U.S. dollars) in the U.S. balance of payments:

a. An American commercial airline buys the European-made Airbus (an airplane competing with the Boeing 747).

b. A European airline buys an American Boeing 747.

c. An American makes a trip around the world.

d. A French company pays dividends to an American owning its stock.

e. An American buys stock in a French company.

f. An American company borrows from a European investor.

g. A Canadian oil company exports oil to Japan on an American tanker.

h. An American banker makes a loan to a European manufacturer.

5. Explain the mechanism under which U.S. restrictions on its imports will lead to fewer U.S. exports under a floating-exchange-rate system.

6. What would happen if Mexico and the United States had a fixed exchange rate but for 20 years Mexico had more inflation than the United States?

Glossary

accelerator principle of investment that investment depends upon the growth of output; implies that investment will be unstable. Investment will fall simply because output grows at a slower rate. For investment to just remain stable, output growth must be constant **(10)**.

adaptive expectations expectations that people form from past experience and modify only gradually as experience unfolds **(13)**.

administered pricing prices are not determined by market forces but by large corporations or giant unions that raise prices and wages independently of demand conditions **(13)**.

*The number of the chapter in which each term is defined appears in parentheses.

aggregate demand *(AD)* the amounts of goods and services that agents in the economy (households, business firms, and government) are prepared to buy at different price levels (5); the equilibrium aggregate expenditure levels (where desired expenditures and actual income are equal) at different price levels, holding the nominal money supply, tax rates, and real government expenditures constant **(12)**.

aggregate expenditures *(AE)* the relationship between the desired amount of total spending $(C + I + G)$ and income **(9)**.

aggregate supply *(AS)* the quantities of real output the economy is prepared to supply at different price levels **(5, 12)**.

allocation the apportionment of resources for a

specific purpose or to particular persons or groups **(2)**.

assets income-producing property **(8)**.

automatic stabilizers government spending or taxation actions that take place without any deliberate government control and that tend to dampen the business cycle **(11)**.

autonomous expenditures expenditures determined independently of income changes **(10)**.

"bad" (see **economic "bad"**)

balanced-budget multiplier the effect on income of a change in government spending that is covered by an equal change in taxes; equals 1. Equal increases (or decreases) in government spending and taxes will cause income to increase (or decrease) by the amount of the change in government spending **(10)**.

balance of payments a summary record of a country's economic transactions with foreign residents over a specified period **(22)**.

balance sheet a summary of the current financial position of a firm that compares the firm's assets and liabilities **(8)**.

bank money money that is on deposit in checking accounts **(7)**.

business cycle the pattern of upward and downward movements in the general level of real business activity **(5)**.

capital the equipment, plants, buildings, and inventories that are available to society **(8)** (see also **human capital**).

capitalism an economic system characterized by private ownership of the factors of production, market allocation of resources, the use of economic incentives, and decentralized decision making **(3)**.

capital/output ratio the value of capital *(K)* needed to produce a given level of output divided by the value of that output *(Y)*, or *K/Y* **(10)**.

cash leakage occurs when a check is converted into cash instead of being deposited in a checking account **(8)**.

ceteris paribus fallacy the false attribution of the effects of changes in one set of variables to changes in another set of variables **(1)**.

check a directive to the check writer's bank to pay lawful money to the bearer of the check **(7)**.

circular-flow diagram summarizes the flows of goods and services from producers to households and the flows of the factors of production from households to business firms **(3)**.

commercial banks banks that have been chartered either by a state agency or by the U.S. Treasury's Comptroller of the Currency to make loans and receive deposits **(8)**.

commodity money money whose value as a commodity is as great as its value as money **(7)**.

comparative advantage (see **law of comparative advantage**)

competing ends the different purposes for which resources can be used **(2)**.

competition (see **perfect competition, monopolistic competition**)

consumption/income schedule shows the amount of desired consumption at different levels of national income or output **(9)**.

cost (see **opportunity cost**)

cost-push inflation (or **supply-side inflation**) occurs when autonomous increases in the prices of the factors of production or disruptions in supplies of factors generally cause firms to reduce their offerings of goods and services to the market at prevailing prices, resulting in the bidding up of their prices **(5)**; occurs when aggregate supply declines and pushes prices up **(13)**.

credit rationing occurs when interest rates are not allowed to rise to the rate at which the demand for loans equals the supply of loans. In this situation, the demand for investment funds at the prevailing interest rate exceeds the supply. Credit rationing limits investment by making investment funds unavailable to some firms that are prepared to invest at prevailing interest rates **(11)**.

crowding out (see **direct crowding out, indirect crowding out**)

crude birth rate the number of births per 1,000 population **(19)**.

crude death rate the number of deaths per 1,000 population **(19)**.

crude quantity theory of money that the price

level is strictly proportional to the money supply (7).

currency basket a bundle of currencies of different countries against which the dollar can be measured. The dollar on the average depreciates if this currency basket becomes more expensive and appreciates if this currency basket becomes less expensive (22).

current account balance equals exports of goods and services minus imports of goods and services minus net unilateral transfers abroad. (22).

cyclical unemployment unemployment associated with general downturns in the economy (5).

decreasing returns to scale are present when each unit costs less to produce the greater is the number of units produced (20) (see also **increasing returns to scale**).

deflationary gap exists if equilibrium output falls short of full-employment output (11).

demand the relationship between the amount of the good or service consumers are prepared to buy at a given price and the price of the good or service (4) (see also **law of demand**).

demand deposit a deposit of funds that can be withdrawn ("demanded") from a depository institution at any time without restrictions. The funds are usually withdrawn by writing a check (7).

demand-pull inflation (or **demand-side inflation**) occurs when aggregate demand increases and pulls prices up (13).

demand shocks are unanticipated shifts in aggregate demand due to unanticipated changes in monetary or fiscal policy or sudden changes in private consumption or investment behavior (17).

demand-side economics focuses on the causes and effects of shifts in the aggregate demand curve (5).

demographic transition the process by which countries change from rapid population growth to slow population growth as they modernize (19).

deposit (see **demand deposit, time deposit**)

deposit multiplier the ratio of the change in total deposits to the change in reserves (8).

depreciation the value of the existing capital stock that has been consumed or used up in the process of producing output; includes not only the physical wear and tear on capital goods but also the loss of value due to the obsolescence of old capital (6).

depression a very severe downturn in economic activity that lasts for several years. Real output declines during this period by a significant amount, and the unemployment rate rises to 15 percent or more (5).

direct crowding out occurs when increased government spending substitutes for privately purchased goods and services and causes a compensating reduction in private spending (11).

discouraged worker an unemployed worker who becomes convinced that no job is or will be available in his or her field and stops looking for work—at which point that worker is no longer classified as unemployed (5, 16).

discretionary fiscal policy a government spending or taxation action that has been deliberately taken to achieve a specified macroeconomic goal (11).

dissaving occurs when the economy's total saving is negative—when consumption spending exceeds disposable income—at which point the economy is either increasing its indebtedness or financing consumption by drawing down its savings (9).

dumping occurs when a country sells a good in another country at a price less than the cost of producing the good (21).

economic "bad" a good or service that does not contribute to society's economic well-being (6).

economic growth an increase from one period to the next in *real GNP per capita* (which is real GNP divided by the country's population); an increase from one period to the next in real GNP (18).

economics the study of how scarce resources are allocated among competing ends (2); the study of how people choose to use their limited resources (land, labor, and capital goods) to produce, exchange, and consume goods and services **(1)**.

economic system the set of organizational arrangements and institutions that are established to solve the economic problem **(2)**.

efficiency results when no resources are unemployed and when no resources are misallocated **(2)**.

entrepreneur one who organizes, manages, and assumes the risks for an enterprise **(2)**.

equation of exchange $MV = PQ$, where M represents money supply, V represents the velocity of money, P represents the price level, and Q represents aggregate output **(7)**.

equilibrium (see **Keynesian equilibrium**)

equilibrium (or *market-clearing*) **price** the price at which the quantity demanded by consumers equals the quantity supplied by producers **(3, 4)**.

excess reserves reserves in excess of required reserves **(8)**.

exchange rate (see **floating exchange rate, fixed exchange rate**)

expectations (see **adaptive expectations, rational expectations**)

expenditure multiplier the ratio of the change in output to the change in autonomous expenditures. The two expenditure multipliers are the *investment multiplier* and the *government-expenditure multiplier* **(10)**.

export promotion occurs when a country encourages exports by subsidizing the production of goods for export **(19)**.

extensive growth economic growth that results from the expansion of factor inputs **(18)**.

factors of production land, labor, capital, and entrepreneurship **(2)**.

fallacy (see **false-cause fallacy, fallacy of composition, ceteris paribus fallacy**)

fallacy of composition the false belief that what is true for each part taken separately is also true for the whole, or that what is true for the whole is true for each part considered separately **(1)**.

false-cause fallacy the false belief that, because

two events occur together, one event has caused the other **(1)**.

feedback rule establishes a feedback relationship between activist policy and the state of the economy **(15)**.

fiat money money whose value or cost as a commodity is less than its value as money **(7)**.

final goods goods that are not used up in the production of any other goods **(6)**.

financial intermediaries borrow funds from one group of economic agents (people or firms with savings) and lend to other agents **(8)**.

fiscal drag the tendency for progressive taxes to act as an automatic destabilizer **(11)**.

fiscal policy the deliberate control of federal government spending and taxes for the purpose of achieving macroeconomic goals **(11)** (see also **discretionary fiscal policy**).

fiscal surprise occurs if government spending or taxation turns out different from what people expected **(17)**.

fixed exchange rate an exchange rate that is set by government decree or intervention and to which supply and demand must conform **(22)**.

fixed investment the addition of new plants, equipment, commercial buildings, and residential structures **(6)**.

floating or **flexible exchange rate** an exchange rate that is freely determined by the interaction of supply and demand **(22)**.

flow variable a variable that can be defined only over a specified period of time **(7)**.

foreign exchange the national currency of another country that is needed to carry out international transactions. Normally, foreign exchange consists of bank deposits denominated in the foreign currency, but may sometimes consist of foreign paper money when foreign travel is involved **(22)**.

free good a good of which the amount available is greater than the amount people want at a zero price **(2)**.

free trade international trade unimpeded by artificial barriers, such as tariffs or import quotas **(20)**.

frictional unemployment the unemployment associated with the changing of jobs in a dynamic economy **(5)**.

full-employment surplus (deficit) what the government budget surplus (or deficit) would be if the economy is operating at full employment (**11**).

GNP (see **gross national product, real GNP, nominal GNP**)

GNP deflator measures the change in the prices of all goods and services produced by the economy (**5**).

GNP gap the difference between current GNP and *potential GNP* (the output the economy would conceivably have produced at full employment); a measure of the social costs of unemployed resources (**15**).

government-expenditure multiplier (see **expenditure multiplier**)

Gresham's Law that bad money drives out good. When depreciated, mutilated, or debased currency is circulated along with money of high value, the good money will disappear from circulation; only the bad money will remain in circulation (**7**).

gross national income (GNI) the sum of all factor incomes (**6**).

gross national product (GNP) the market value of all final goods and services produced by an economy in one year's time (**6**) (see also **GNP deflator, GNP gap**).

growth (see **economic growth, extensive growth, intensive growth**)

human capital the accumulation of past investments in schooling, training, and health care that raises the productive capacity of people (**2**).

hyperinflation a very rapid and constantly growing rate of inflation, on the order of three digits or more per month (**7**).

import quota a quantitative limitation on the amount of a specific product that can be imported during a given period (**21**).

import substitution occurs when a country substitutes domestic production for imports by subsidizing domestic production through tariffs, quotas, and other devices (**19**).

income (see **permanent income, personal disposable income, personal income, national income**)

incomes policy a set of rules, guidelines, or laws devised by government to influence wage and price increases (**13**).

increasing returns to scale are present when each unit costs more to produce the greater is the number of units produced (**20**) (see also **decreasing returns to scale**).

index (see **price index**)

indexing the tying of a variable's rate of increase to the actual inflation rate (**14**).

indirect crowding out occurs when increased government spending raises interest rates and causes autonomous spending elsewhere in the economy to decrease (**11**).

inferior good a good the demand for which will fall as income rises (**4**).

inflation a general increase in prices (**5**) (see also **cost-push inflation, demand-pull inflation, structural inflation**)

inflationary gap exists if equilibrium output exceeds full-employment output (**11**).

intensive growth growth that results from increases in output per unit of factor input (**18**).

interest the price of credit, usually a percentage of the amount of money borrowed (**3**).

interest-rate effect occurs when rising interest rates discourage investment expenditures as rising prices increase the demand for credit (**12**).

intermediate goods goods that are completely used up in the production of another good; the value of intermediate goods is reflected in the price of the final goods (**3, 6**).

investory investment the increase (or decrease) in the value of the stocks of inventories that businesses have on hand (**6**).

investment additions to the stock of capital (**2**).

investment multiplier (see **expenditure multiplier**)

Keynesian equilibrium occurs when the economy produces an output that equals desired aggregate expenditures (**9**).

labor the physical and mental talents that human beings contribute to the production process (**2**).

labor force the number employed plus the number unemployed **(5)**.

land any part of nature's bounty—including minerals, forests, land, water resources, or oxygen **(2)**.

law of comparative advantage people or countries specialize in those activities in which they have the greatest advantage or the least disadvantage compared to other people or countries. Equivalently, people or countries specialize in those activities in which they have the least disadvantage compared to other people or countries **(3, 20)**.

law of demand there is a negative (or inverse) relationship between the price of a good and quantity demanded, holding other factors constant **(4)**.

law of diminishing returns as ever larger quantities of a variable factor are combined with fixed amounts of other factors, the marginal physical product of the variable factor will eventually decline **(2)**.

law of increasing costs as more of a particular commodity is produced, its opportunity cost per unit will eventually increase **(2)**.

layoff a suspension without pay and without prejudice that lasts (or is expected to last) seven days or more; the laid-off worker is expected to return to the job if economic conditions improve **(16)**.

leading indicators measures of specific economic activities that tend to rise or fall prior to the general rise or fall in business activity **(5)**.

less developed countries (LDCs) countries that have yet to reach a high level of economic development **(19)**.

liabilities a firm's obligations to nonowners of the firm **(8)**.

liquidity the ease and speed with which an asset can be converted into a medium of exchange without risk of loss **(7)**.

liquidity-preference theory the opportunity cost of holding money—a completely liquid asset—is the interest sacrificed **(11)**.

long-run Phillips curve a vertical line that shows that in the long run, the unemployment rate is independent of the inflation rate and that unemployment will not decline with more inflation in the long run **(14)**.

Lucas demand curve shows the quantity of real aggregate output demanded at each level of price surprise **(17)**.

Lucas supply curve shows the quantity of real aggregate output supplied for every level of price surprise **(17)**.

M1 the sum of currency (and coins), demand deposits at commercial banks held by the non-banking public, travelers' checks, and other checkable deposits like NOW (negotiable orders of withdrawal) accounts and ATS (automatic transfer services) accounts **(7)**.

M2 M1 plus savings and small time deposits plus money-market mutual-fund shares plus other highly liquid assets **(7)**.

macroeconomics the study of the economy in the large; deals with the economy as a whole rather than with individual markets and individual consumers and producers **(1)**.

marginal analysis a strategy for decision making that examines the consequences of making relatively small changes from the current state of affairs **(1)**.

marginal output/capital ratio *(MOCR)* the change in output divided by the change in capital **(19)**.

marginal propensity to consume *(MPC)* the change in desired consumption brought about by a change in income of $1 **(9)**.

marginal propensity to save *(MPS)* the change in desired saving brought about by a change in income of $1 **(9)**.

market an established arrangement by which buyers and sellers come together to exchange particular goods or services **(2, 4)**.

market demand curve the demand curve of all consumers of a particular product **(4)**.

merchandise trade balance exports of merchandise minus imports of merchandise **(22)**.

microeconomics the study of the economic decision making of firms and individuals in a market setting; the study of the economy in the small **(1)**.

monetary base the sum of reserves on deposit at the Fed, all vault cash, and the currency in circulation, or the sum of the money supply and reserves at the Fed **(8)**.

monetary policy the deliberate control of the money supply and, in some cases, credit conditions for the purpose of achieving macroeconomic goals (11).

monetization of debt the creation of demand-deposit liabilities in the process of making bank loans (8).

money anything that is widely accepted in exchange for goods and services and that can be used for paying debts and taxes (3); the medium of exchange used by an economy; the commodity ordinarily used in transactions that transfer ownership of goods and services from one person to another (7) (see also **bank money, commodity money, fiat money, M1, M2**).

money illusion exists when economic decision makers are tricked by a proportionate change in all money prices and money wages into thinking relative prices have changed (12).

money price a price expressed in monetary units (such as dollars, francs, etc.) (3).

money supply (M) the sum of all commodity moneys, fiat moneys, and bank moneys that are held by the nonbanking public in a given country as of a given date (7).

money surprise occurs if the actual money supply is different from that generally expected (17).

motive (see **precautionary motive, speculative motive, transactions motive**)

multiple deposit expansion occurs when an increase in reserves causes an expansion of the money supply that is greater than the reserve increase (8).

multiplier (see **balanced-budget multiplier, deposit multiplier, expenditure multiplier, tax multiplier**)

national income net national product minus indirect business taxes; the sum of all factor payments made to the factors of production in the economy (6).

national income accounting the science of measuring the aggregate output and income of an economy (6).

natural increase (see **rate of natural increase**)

natural level of real GNP the output produced when the economy is operating at the natural rate of unemployment (12).

natural-rate hypothesis that prices must be higher than expected for output to exceed the natural output level and that prices must be lower than expected for output to be below the natural output level (12).

natural rate of unemployment that rate at which the number of unfilled jobs or vacancies equals the number of unemployed workers in the economy (12).

negative (inverse) relationship exists between two variables if an increase in the value of one variable is associated with a reduction in the value of the other variable (1A).

net national product (*NNP*) GNP minus depreciation (6).

net output (see **value added**)

nominal GNP the value of final goods and services for a given year in that year's prevailing market prices; GNP in current dollars (6).

nominal rate of interest the rate of interest expressed in terms of today's dollars (3).

nonmarketed goods goods and services exchanged through barter arrangements or acquired through do-it-yourself activities that take the place of goods and services that would otherwise have been purchased in organized markets (6).

nonprohibitive tariff a tariff that does not wipe out all imports of the product (21).

normal good a good the demand for which increases as income rises (4).

normative economics the study of what *ought to be* in the economy (1).

Okun's law for every 1 percent increase in the unemployment rate there is a 3 percent drop in real GNP (6).

open-market operations purchases and sales of federal government securities by the Fed (as directed by the Federal Open Market Committee) (8).

opportunity cost the loss of the next best alternative (2).

perfect competition a type of market structure in which 1) there is a large enough number of buyers and sellers that no single buyer or seller has a perceptible influence on the market price, 2) each seller and buyer has perfect information about prices and product quality, 3) the product being sold is homogeneous, 4) there are no barriers to entry into or exit from the market, and 5) all firms are price takers **(4)**.

perfect market (see **perfect competition**)

permanent income an average of the income that an individual anticipates earning over the long run **(11)**.

personal disposable income personal income minus income-tax payments **(6)**.

personal income national income 1) *minus* retained corporate profits, corporate income taxes, and social security contributions 2) *plus* transfer payments **(6)**.

Phillips curve shows the relationship between unemployment and inflation and reveals that a reduction in the rate of unemployment requires an increase in the rate of wage (or price) inflation **(14)** (see also **long-run Phillips curve, short-run Phillips curve**).

policy (see **fiscal policy, monetary policy**)

policy surprise a demand shock that results from an unanticipated monetary or fiscal policy **(17)**.

positive economics the study of *what is* in the economy **(1)**.

positive (or **direct**) **relationship** exists between two variables if an increase in the value of one variable is associated with an increase in the value of the other variable **(1A)**.

precautionary motive the desire to hold money in order to protect oneself against unforeseen emergencies **(7)**.

price (see **money price, relative price**)

price index shows the current year's cost of a particular market basket as a percentage of the cost of the same market basket in some base year **(5)**.

price-level surprise occurs when the actual price level, P, is not equal to the expected price level, P_e **(17)**.

price system the entire set of millions of relative prices that provides information to buyers and sellers **(3)**.

principle of substitution practically no good is irreplaceable in meeting demand because users are able to substitute one product for another to satisfy demand **(3)**.

private saving personal disposable income minus personal-consumption expenditures **(6)**.

production-possibilities frontier *(PPF)* shows the combinations of goods that can be produced when the factors of production are utilized to their full potential; reveals the economic choices open to society **(2)**.

prohibitive tariff a tariff that is high enough to cut off all imports of the product **(21)**.

property rights the right of an owner to use and exchange property **(3)**.

quantity demanded the amount of a good or service consumers are prepared to buy at a given price **(4)**.

quantity supplied the amount of a good or service offered for sale at a given price **(4)**.

quantity theory of money (see **crude quantity theory of money**)

rate of natural increase the crude birth rate minus the crude death rate **(19)**.

ratification of cost-push inflation results if the government increases the money supply to prevent supply-side shock from raising unemployment **(13)**.

rational expectations expectations that people form about macroeconomic variables, such as the inflation rate and the unemployment rate, using public knowledge about future monetary and fiscal policy, business and consumer spending plans, and current macroeconomic models **(17)**; expectations that people form by using all available information and by relying not only on past experience but also on their predictions about the effects of present and future policy actions **(13)**.

real-balance effect occurs when desired real consumption at each income level declines as price increases cut the purchasing power of a given money supply; similarly, price-level reductions stimulate consumption **(12)**.

real GNP or **GNP in constant dollars** measures the volume of real goods and services by removing the effects of rising prices on nominal GNP **(6)**.

real interest rate the nominal interest rate minus the anticipated rate of inflation **(3)**.

recession a decline in real output that lasts for six months or more **(5)**.

relative price a price expressed in terms of other commodities **(3)**.

required-reserve ratio the amount of reserves a bank is required to hold for each dollar of deposits **(8)**.

reserve requirement a rule that states the amount of reserves that must be on hand to back bank deposits **(8)**.

reserves the funds that the bank uses to satisfy the cash demands of its cutomers **(8)** (see also **excess reserves**).

roundabout production the production of goods that do not immediately meet consumption needs; the production of intermediate goods **(3)**.

saving the amount of national income (total factor income) that is not spent on consumption or direct taxes **(6)** (see also **private saving**).

saving/income schedule shows the desired amount of saving at different levels of national income or output **(9)**.

Say's Law "desired aggregate expenditures can never depart from actual aggregate expenditures; whatever output is produced will be demanded" **(9)**.

scarce good a good the amount of which available is less than the amount people would want if it were given away free of charge **(2)**.

scientific method the process of formulating theories, collecting data, testing theories, and revising theories **(1)**.

shortage results if at the current price the quantity demanded exceeds the quantity supplied; the price is too low to equate the quantity demanded with the quantity supplied **(4)**.

short-run Phillips curve shows a negative relationship between inflation and unemployment (like the original Phillips curve) **(14)**.

slope the ratio of the change in x to the run in y **(1A)**.

socialism a society characterized by collective ownership of property and government allocation of resources **(3)**.

social overhead capital capital goods (such as roads, canals, schools, and hospitals) that benefit society more than they benefit specific individuals **(19)**.

speculative motive the desire to hold money in order to take advantage of profitable speculative opportunities **(7)**.

stabilizers (see **automatic stabilizers**)

stagflation the combination of high unemployment and high inflation in a stagnant economy **(14)**.

stock variable a variable that can be defined for a given moment in time **(7)**.

structural inflation occurs when prices in some areas of the economy do not fall as readily as prices rise in a bottleneck sector, resulting in a general upward creep in prices **(5)**.

structural unemployment the unemployment that results from the decline of certain industries because of rising costs, changes in consumer preferences, or technological advances that make the industry's product obsolete **(5)**.

substitution (see **principle of substitution**)

supply the relationship between the amount of a good or service offered for sale at a given price and the price of the good or service **(4)**.

supply shock an event that unexpectedly causes the aggregate supply curve to shift **(13, 17)**.

supply-side economics focuses on the causes and effects of shifts in the aggregate supply curve **(5)**.

supply-side inflation (see **cost-push inflation**)

surplus results if at the current price the quantity supplied exceeds the quantity demanded; the price is too high to equate the quantity demanded with quantity supplied **(4)**.

surprise (see **fiscal surprise, money surprise, policy surprise, price-level surprise**)

T-account a summary of bank assets and liabilities **(8)**.

tangent a straight line that touches the curve at only one point **(1A)**.

tariff a tax levied on imports or exports **(21)** (see **nonprohibitive tariff, prohibitive tariff**).

tax multiplier the change in output divided by the change in the tax **(10)**.

terms of trade the rate at which two products can

be exchanged for each other between countries **(20).**

theory isolates those factors that may be crucial determinants of the phenomenon being explained **(1).**

time deposit a deposit of funds that cannot legally be withdrawn from a depository institution without at least 30 days' notice of withdrawal and on which the financial institution pays the depositor interest **(7).**

transactions motive the desire to hold money in order to carry out transactions **(7).**

transfer payments payments to recipients who have not supplied current goods or services in exchange for these payments **(6).**

unemployment (see **cyclical unemployment, frictional unemployment, structural unemployment**)

unemployment rate the number of unemployed divided by the number in the labor force **(5).**

unintended investment the difference between desired saving and desired investment at each income level **(9).**

value added the value of a firm's (or an industry's) output minus the value of its purchases from other firms (or industries); also called *net output* **(6).**

velocity of circulation *(V)* the number of times the average dollar is spent on final goods and services in one year's time **(7).**

voluntary export quota the result of a bargain between a home government and a foreign government to limit the home government's exports over a specified period of time **(21).**

wage/price spiral the phenomenon of higher prices pushing wages higher and then higher wages pushing prices higher, or vice versa. This spiral occurs when workers anticipate inflation and demand and get higher wages and when the monetary authorities ratify the cost-push inflation. This process repeats itself **(13).**

Suggested Readings

CHAPTER 1

Friedman, Milton. *Essays in Positive Economics*. Chicago: University of Chicago Press, 1953.

Kohler, Heinz. *Scarcity and Freedom*. Lexington, Mass.: D.C. Heath, 1977, part 1.

McCloskey, Donald. *The Applied Theory of Price*. New York: Macmillan, 1982, pp. 1–6.

Mundell, Robert A. *Man and Economics*. New York: McGraw-Hill, 1968, chap. 1.

CHAPTER 2

Franklin, Raymond S., *American Capitalism: Two Visions*. New York: Random House, 1977, chap. 1.

Heilbroner, Robert L., *The Making of Economic Society*. Englewood Cliffs, N.J.: Prentice-Hall, 1962, chap. 1.

Mundell, Robert A. *Man and Economics*. New York: McGraw-Hill, 1968, chap. 1 & 2.

North, Douglass C. and Roger LeRoy Miller. ''The Economics of Clamming and Other 'Free' Goods.'' In *The Economics of Public Issues,* 5th ed., New York: Harper and Row, 1980, pp. 152–56.

CHAPTER 3

Hayek, Frederick A. ''The Price System as a Mechanism for Using Knowledge.'' In *Comparative Economic Systems: Models and Cases,* 4th ed., ed. Morris Bornstein. Homewood, Ill.: Richard D. Irwin, 1974, pp. 49–60.

McKenzie, Richard B. and Gordon Tullock. *Modern Political Economy*. New York: McGraw-Hill, 1978.

Neuberger, Egon. "Comparative Economic System." In *Perspectives in Economics: Economists Look at Their Field of Study*, eds. Alan A. Brown *et al*. New York: McGraw-Hill, 1971, pp. 252–66.

Radford, R. A. "The Economic Organization of a P.O.W. Camp." In *Economica* 12 (November 1945): 189–201.

Smith, Adam. *The Wealth of Nations*. ed. Edwin Cannan. New York: The Modern Library, 1937, book 1.

CHAPTER 4

Kohler, Heinz. *Intermediate Microeconomics: Theory and Applications*. Glenview, Ill.: Scott, Foresman, 1982, pp. 188–192.

Leftwich, Richard H. and Ansel M. Sharp. *Economics of Social Issues*, 3rd ed. Dallas: Business Publications, Inc., 1978, chap. 2.

Manne, Henry G. "The Parable of the Parking Lots." In *The Public Interest* 23 (Spring 1971): 10–15.

North, Douglass C. and Roger LeRoy Miller. *The Economics of Public Issues*, 5th ed. New York: Harper and Row, 1980, chap. 1.

Stigler, George. *The Theory of Price*, rev. ed. New York: Macmillan, 1952, chaps. 1 & 3.

CHAPTER 5

Bresciani-Turroni, Costanino. *The Economics of Inflation*. London: Allen & Unwin, 1937.

Friedman, Milton. *Dollars and Deficits*. Englewood Cliffs, N.J.: Prentice-Hall, 1968.

Gordon, Robert J. "The Consumer Price Index: Measuring Inflation and Causing It." *Public Interest*, (Spring, 1981): 112–34.

Samuelson, Paul A. *Economics*, 11th ed. New York: McGraw-Hill, 1980, chap. 14.

CHAPTER 6

Dornbusch, Rudiger and Stanley Fischer. *Macroeconomics*, 2nd ed. New York: McGraw-Hill, 1981, chap. 2.

Ruggles, Richard and Nancy D. Ruggles. "Integrated Economic Accounts for the United States, 1947–1980." *Survey of Current Business* 62 (May 1982): 1–12.

Tanzi, Vito. "Underground Economy Built on Illicit Pursuits Is Growing Concern of Economic Policymakers." *IMF Survey*, February 4, 1980.

CHAPTER 7

Friedman, Milton. *Dollars and Deficits*. Englewood Cliffs, N.J.: Prentice-Hall, 1968.

Galbraith, John K. *Money*. Boston, Mass.: Houghton Mifflin, 1975.

Solow, Robert. "The Intelligent Citizen's Guide to Inflation." *The Public Interest* (Winter 1975), pp. 30–66.

CHAPTER 8

Burns, Arthur F. "The Independence of the Federal Reserve System." *Challenge* (July/August 1976), pp. 21–24.

Mayer, Martin. *The Bankers*. New York: Ballantine Books, 1974.

Mayer, Thomas *et al*. *Money, Banking, and the Economy*. New York: W. W. Norton, 1981.

Ritter, Lawrence S. and William L. Silber, *Money*, 3rd ed. New York: Basic Books, 1977.

Thompson, Lloyd B. *Money, Banking, and Economic Activity,* 2nd ed. Englewood Cliffs, N.J.: Prentice-Hall, 1982.

CHAPTER 9

Gordon, Robert J. *Macroeconomics.* Boston, Mass.: Little, Brown, 1978.

Keynes, John Maynard. *The General Theory of Employment, Interest, and Money.* New York: Macmillan, 1936, preface, chaps. 1–3.

Samuelson, Paul A. *Economics,* 11th ed. New York: McGraw-Hill, 1980, chaps. 11–12.

CHAPTER 10

Fusfeld, Daniel. *The Age of the Economist.* Glenview, Ill.: Scott, Foresman, 1982.

Stein, Herbert. *The Fiscal Revolution in America.* Chicago, Ill.: University of Chicago Press, 1969.

CHAPTER 11

Pechman, Joseph A. *Federal Tax Policy.* Washington, D.C.: The Brookings Institution, 1966, chaps. 1–3.

Samuelson, Paul A. *Economics,* 11th ed. New York: McGraw-Hill, 1980, chaps. 13 & 18.

Schultz, George P. and Kenneth W. Dam. *Economic Policy Beyond the Headlines.* New York: W. W. Norton, 1977, chaps. 2 & 3.

Thomas Lloyd B., Jr. *Money, Banking, and Economic Activity,* 2nd ed. Englewood Cliffs, N.J.: Prentice-Hall, 1982, chap. 18.

CHAPTER 12

Dornbusch, Rudiger and Stanley Fischer. *Macroeconomics,* 2nd ed. New York: McGraw-Hill, 1981, chap. 11.

Maisel, Sherman. *Macroeconomics.* New York: W. W. Norton, 1982.

CHAPTER 13

Blinder, Alan. *Economic Policy and the Great Stagflation.* New York: Academic Press, 1979.

Lerner, Abba P. "Stagflation—Its Cause and Cure." *Challenge* 20 (September/October 1977): 14–19.

Perry, George L. "Slowing the Wage-Price Spiral: The Macroeconomic View." *Brookings Papers on Economic Activity* 2 (1978): 259–91.

Seidman, Laurence S. "A New Approach to the Control of Inflation." *Challenge* 19 (July/August 1976): 39–43.

CHAPTER 14

Friedman, Milton. *Dollars and Deficits.* Englewood Cliffs, N.J.: Prentice-Hall, 1968.

Okun, Arthur. *Prices and Quantities.* Washington, D.C.: Brookings Institution, 1981.

Phelps, Edmund S. *Inflation Policy and Unemployment Theory.* New York: W. W. Norton, 1972.

Tobin, James. "Inflation and Unemployment." *American Economic Review* 62 (March 1972): 1–18.

CHAPTER 15

Carlson, Keith and Roger Spencer. "Crowding out and Its Critics." Federal Reserve Bank of St. Louis *Review* (December 1975), pp. 2–17.

Friedman, Milton and Walter W. Heller. *Monetary Versus Fiscal Policy.* New York: W. W. Norton, 1969.

Friedman, Milton. *A Program for Monetary Stability.* New York: Fordham University Press, 1960.

Meltzer, Allan H. "Monetarism and the Crisis in Economics." *The Public Interest* (Special Issue, 1980), pp. 35–45.

Modigliani, Franco. "The Monetarist Controversy, or Should We Forsake Stabilization Policies?" *American Economic Review* 67 (March 1977): 1–19.

CHAPTER 16

Benjamin, Daniel K. and Levis A. Kochin. "Searching for an Explanation of Unemployment in Interwar Britain." *Journal of Political Economy* 87 (June 1979): 441–74.

Feldstein, Martin. "The Economics of the New Unemployment." *Public Interest* 33 (Fall, 1973).

Feldstein, Martin. "The Private and Social Costs of Unemployment." *American Economic Review* 68 (May 1978): 155–58.

CHAPTER 17

Forman, Leonard. "Rational Expectations and the Real World." *Challenge* (November/December 1980).

McCallum, Bennett. "The Significance of Rational Expectations Theory." *Challenge* (January/February, 1980).

Willes, Mark H. "'Rational Expectations' as a Counterrevolution." *The Public Interest* (Special Issue, 1980), pp. 81–96.

CHAPTER 18

Federal Reserve Bank of Boston. "The Decline in U.S. Productivity Growth." *Conference Series No. 22,* June 1980.

Meadows, Dennis *et al. The Limits to Growth.* Washington, D.C.: Potomac Associates, 1972.

Phelps, Edmund, ed. *The Goal of Economic Growth.* New York: W. W. Norton, 1969.

Simon, Julian. "Resources, Population, Environment: An Oversupply of False Bad News." *Science,* June 27, 1980.

CHAPTER 19

Hagar, Everett C. *The Economics of Development,* 3rd ed. Homewood, Ill.: Richard D. Irwin, 1980.

Hughes, Jonathan. *American Economic History.* Glenview, Ill.: Scott, Foresman, 1982.

Kreinin, Mordecai E. and J. M. Finger. "A Critical Survey of the New International Economic Order." *Journal of World Trade Law* (November/December 1976).

Maddison, Angus. *Economic Progress and Policy in Developing Countries.* New York: W. W. Norton, 1970.

Simon, Julian. *The Economics of Population Growth.* Princeton, N.J.: Princeton University Press, 1977.

CHAPTER 20

Hood, Neil and Stephen Young. *The Economics of Multinational Enterprise.* New York: Longman, 1979.

Kreinin, Mordecai E. *International Economics,* 3rd ed. New York: Harcourt Brace Jovanovich, 1979, chaps. 11–12.

Lindert, Peter H. and Charles P. Kindleberger, *International Economics,* 7th ed. Homewood, Ill.: Richard D. Irwin, 1982, chaps. 1–4.

CHAPTER 21

Bergsten, C. Fred. *The Cost of Import Restrictions to American Consumers.* New York: American Importers Association, 1972.

George, Henry. *Protection or Free Trade?* New York: Doubleday and Page, 1905.

Richardson, J. David. *Understanding International Economics: Theory and Practice*. Boston: Little, Brown, 1980, chaps. 9–10.

Yeager, Leland B. and David G. Tuerck. *Trade Policy and the Price System*. Scranton, Pa.: International Textbook, 1966.

CHAPTER 22

Adams, John, ed. *The Contemporary International Economy: A Reader*. New York: St. Martins Press, 1979).

Lindert, Peter H. and Charles P. Kindleberger. *International Economics,* 7th ed. Homewood, Ill.: Richard D. Irwin, 1982, pp. 243–62.

Rolfe, Sidney E. and James L. Burtle. *The Great Wheel: The World Monetary System*. New York: McGraw-Hill, 1973.

Yeager, Leland B. *International Monetary Relations,* 2nd ed. New York: Harper & Row, 1976, chaps. 13, 18.

Yeager, Leland B. *The International Monetary Mechanism*. New York: Holt, Rinehart and Winston, 1968.

Index